D1074704

Le Corbusier in America

Le Corbusier in America

Travels in the Land of the Timid

Mardges Bacon

The MIT Press
Cambridge, Massachusetts
London, England

© 2001 Mardges Bacon

All rights reserved. No part of this book may be reproduced in any form by any electronic or mechanical means (including photo-copying, recording, or information storage and retrieval) without permission in writing from the publisher.

Frontispiece: Le Corbusier at railroad station, Detroit, November 21, 1935. (Detroit News Archives.) Copy print © 2001 Artists Rights Society (ARS), New York/ADAGP, Paris/FLC.

For captions to photographs that appear on Contents pages, see figures 1.5, 3.4, 5.15, 8.16, 10.40.

This book was set in Garamond 3 and Futura by Graphic Compo-sition, Inc., Athens, Georgia and was printed and bound in the United States of America.

Library of Congress Cataloging-in-Publication Data

Bacon, Mardges.
    Le Corbusier in America : travels in the land of the timid / Mardges Bacon.
        p. cm.
    Includes bibliographical references and index.
    ISBN 0-262-02479-9 (hc. : alk. paper)
        1. Le Corbusier, 1887–1965—Journeys—United States.
2. Le Corbusier, 1887–1965—Influence. 3. Architecture—United States—Influence.   I. Title.

NA1053.J4 B25 2001
720'.92—dc21
                                    00-032900

To William H. Jordy
who understood the "symbolic essence"
of Le Corbusier's work

Contents

1.5

3.4

5.15

8.16

10.40

Acknowledgments

The idea for a book on Le Corbusier and the United States emerged from a web of events and associations. As a graduate student at Brown University during the mid-1970s I was introduced to William Jordy's brilliant article "The Symbolic Essence of Modern Architecture" (1963). Jordy's formulation of symbolic objectivity, with its oscillation between fact and essence, defined the conceptual framework and the cultural exegesis for European modern architecture. With gratitude and affection this book is dedicated to his memory. Research on transatlantic exchange for my dissertation and subsequent book *Ernest Flagg: Beaux-Arts Architect and Urban Reformer* (1986) led me to Le Corbusier's love-hate encounter with America and his chronicle of it, *When the Cathedrals Were White.* My study of that encounter would have been limited to an orbit of archival research had it not been for the generous contributions of two individuals whom I interviewed in 1984. The first was Marguerite Tjader Harris, American writer and publisher of the leftist cultural journal *Direction.* I set out to visit her on the advice of a New York editor who claimed that she had been an intimate friend of Le Corbusier. There on the threshold of her cottage in Darien, Connecticut, Marguerite Harris extended her hand and announced flatly, "I just want you to know that I was not Le Cor-

busier's mistress, as everyone says. I was Theodore Dreiser's mistress." As her story unfolded and her disclaimer was unmasked, Marguerite's significance came into focus. The second was the architect Robert Allan Jacobs, who served as Le Corbusier's interpreter on the American tour. Interviews with the man whom the lecturer called his "faithful shadow" (see figure 3.9) enriched my study with anecdotes and revealing details that allowed me to build a case study in transatlantic exchange with dense and meaningful patterns.

My study benefited from many other individuals, especially those who read the entire manuscript: Peter Kemble, Mary McLeod, Francesco Passanti, Nancy Stieber, and Adolf Max Vogt. Their criticism and counsel made this a far better book and my debt to them is especially great because they set aside their own work to do so. Juliette Gilman deserves my gratitude for sharing her expertise in French and assisting me with translations. Notwithstanding our efforts, many uncertainties still remain in deciphering Le Corbusier's handwriting. I thank Elizabeth Streicher for her help with German. A number of colleagues provided their abiding support during the long incubation: Sarah Bradford Landau, Peter Serenyi, and Barbara Sicherman. I am much indebted to them. I also thank a number of individuals who generously shared their knowledge and expertise: Stanford Anderson, Joseph L. Arnold, Nancy Austin, Miroslava Beneš, Peter Blake, David Block, Mosette Glaser Broderick, H. Allen Brooks, Jack Cheng, Jean-Louis Cohen, Wanda Corn, Marc Dessauce, Marc-Albert Émery, Thomas Fisher, Isabelle Gournay, Elizabeth Grossman, Samuel Haber, Isabelle Hyman, Peter Johnson, Carol Herselle Krinsky, Lorraine Welling Lanmon, François LeCoeur, Bradford Lee, Eric Mumford, Dietrich Neumann, Joan Ockman, Hyungmin Pai, Danièle Pauly, Linda Phipps, the late Richard Pommer, Sylvie Riszfeld, Joseph Rosa, Miles David Samson, Eduard Sekler, Patricia May Sekler, Jane Thompson, Beeke Sell Tower, Marc Treib, Ellen Weiss, Charlotte Whitney, Gwendolyn Wright, and Ivan Žaknić.

For their willingness to share important recollections I am grateful to Max Abramovitz, William Lake Addkison, the late Lawrence B. Anderson, Edmund N. Bacon, the late William F. R. Ballard, Virginia P. Bardeen, Peter Blake, Melville C. Branch, Jr., the late Joseph Brewer, the late Nell Bunce, the late Gordon Bunshaft, Virginia Chapin, Richard Creadick, Frederick G. Frost, Jr., the late Percival Goodman, the late Genevieve Harlow Goodwin, Ronald Gourlay, Lois Homer Graham, the late Alma Clayburgh Grew, the late Hilary Harris, the late Henry-Russell Hitchcock, Kathryn Hodgman, Margot Jacobs, Philip Johnson, Sarah Spock Jordy, the late G. E. Kidder Smith, Daniel Kiley, Carl Koch, the late Katherine Kuh, Mildred Lynes, the late Agnes Mongan, George Nichols, the late Elizabeth H. Paepcke, Ieoh Ming Pei, Jan Reiner, the late Norman Rice, the late William Shellman, the late Elbridge Sibley, Amelia Thompson Vose, Harry Weese, and Helen Nowell Wood. Their memories of Le Corbusier and events in the 1930s considerably enriched this study.

A number of institutions made resources available and greatly facilitated my research. First and foremost, I thank the Fondation Le Corbusier in Paris and, most especially, Evelyne Tréhin for her generous support. I would also like to express my gratitude to Christian Pattyn, president of the Fondation Le Corbusier, and its superb librarians Martine Lasson, Holy Raveloarisoa, and Valerie Valentin who lent their able assistance to me on so many occasions. It is a pleasure to acknowledge the help of Ralph Emerick and the staff of the Trinity College Library, as well as Alan R. Benefeld and the staff of Northeastern University Library. I am indebted to the staff members of the many museums, libraries, and archives where my research was carried out. I thank Hugh Wilburn, Hinda Sklar, Mary Daniels, and Ann Whiteside (Frances Loeb Library, Harvard Design School); the late Arthur Drexler, Rona Roob, Michelle Elligott, Cara McCartney, Peter Reed, Daniel Starr, and Pierre Adler (Museum of Modern Art); Angela Giral, Adolf Placzek, Janet Parks, and Anne-Sophie Roure (Avery Architectural and Fine Arts Library, Columbia University); Phyllis Lambert (Canadian Centre for Architecture, Montréal); Darwin H. Stapleton and Thomas Rosenbaum (Rockefeller Archive Center); Eugene Gaddis (Wadsworth Atheneum); William L. Joyce, Richard M. Ludwig, Earle Coleman, and Barbara T. Ross (Princeton University); Anselmo (Sam) Carini, Betty Blum, John Zukowsky, Luigi Mumford, and Mary Woolever (Art Institute of Chicago); Richard L. Popp (University of Chicago); Bernard Schermetzler (University of Wisconsin-Madison); Mark Coir and Cathy Price (Cranbrook Academy of Art Museum); Margaret Kulis (Newberry Library); Helen Sheridan (Kalamazoo Institute of Arts); and Arthur Breton (Archives of American Art, Smithsonian Institution).

Research for this study was made possible by the generous support of the John Simon Guggenheim Memorial Foundation. The Center for Advanced Study in the Visual Arts at the National Gallery of Art in Washington, D.C., facilitated my research and offered me an opportunity to share it with colleagues. Trinity College in Hartford, Connecticut, and Northeastern University in Boston provided both individual research grants and sabbatical leave. I wish to convey my appreciation to Vice Provost Coleen Pantalone and Provost David Hall at Northeastern. The Graham Foundation awarded a publication grant for the purchase of photographs. I owe a great debt of gratitude to Joel Conarroe, Henry A. Millon, Therese O'Malley, Richard Solomon, and the anonymous reviewers who recommended funding.

Many individuals assisted me in locating superb photographs, including several who made loans from their personal collections. I am most indebted to Joseph Aronson, Christine Cordazzo, Frank Driggs, the late Jeannette S. Glenn, Henry Sage Goodwin, Jennifer Hegarty, George Krambles, Georgia Kunze, Jean Ferriss Leich, Marian Moffett, Roberta Moudry, Dion Neutra, Stephen Watson, Lawrence Wodehouse, and Roderick H. Wolfson. For their assistance with institutional collections of visual resources, I thank Melanie Harwood and Georgeanna Linthicum (Baltimore Museum of Art), John Dorsey (Boston Public Library), Mattie Kelley (Bowdoin College), Octavio O. Olvera (University of California, Los Angeles), Suzelle Baudouin and Cammie McAtee (Canadian Centre for Architecture, Montréal), Adam Schiesl (Chicago Historical Society), Mark A. Patrick (Detroit Public Library), Robert Dishon (La Guardia and Wagner Archives, La Guardia Community College), Pam Morris (GM Archives), Wim de Wit (Getty Research Institute for the History of Arts and the Humanities), Cathrine Wolcott (Harvard University), Judith Kirsch (Henry Ford Museum), James R. Mosby, Jr. (Kalamazoo Gazette), Catherine Larson (Kalamazoo Public Library), Edye Weissler (Knoedler Art Gallery), Mary Ison (Library of Congress), Daniel B. May (Metropolitan Life Insurance Co.), Kimberly Shilland (MIT Museum), Ann Easterling (Museum of the City of New York), Thomas Grischkowsky and Jeffery Ryan (Museum of Modern Art), Holly Hinman and Nicole Wells (New-York Historical Society), Julia Van Haaften (New York Public Library), Derrick Beckner (Pennsylvania State University), Julia Moore Converse (University of Pennsylvania), Karen Richter (Princeton University), Paul Schlotthauer (Queens Borough Public Library), James V. Reed (Rockefeller Center Archive Center), Carolyn A. Davis (Syracuse University), Esther L. Mes and Melissa Miller (University of Texas at Austin), and Ginny Kilander (University of Wyoming). John F. Cook provided fine copy photographs.

For their friendship and generous hospitality during many research trips to Paris I would like to thank Marie-Pierre Mitterrand Landry and Colette Mitterrand Landry.

Roger Conover of the MIT Press deserves my gratitude for his commitment to this project. I thank Matthew Abbate for his thoughtful and dedicated editing. Yasuyo Iguchi's sensitive design has transformed the manuscript into a vivid book. I also thank Sarah Jeffries, Cristina Sanmartín, Julie Grimaldi, and Margaret Tedeschi for their many contributions.

Finally I am grateful for the support of my family. I extend my warmest thanks to my husband Charles Wood, the late Ruth E. Bacon, Ruth Anne Argento, William Hope Bacon, Susan Bacon, Carolyn Wood, Chauncey Wood, and Lisa Marie Kavanaugh.

Introduction

During the first decades of the twentieth century, transatlantic exchange within the culture of architecture reached its first maturity. Most scholarship exploring that conversation has focused on the impact of Europe on America. In recent years, however, architects and historians have examined ways in which Europeans by the time of World War I began to look increasingly to American culture as a means of renewing and regenerating their own. This search for a new transatlantic culture, and attitudes that emerged from it, came to be known in France as *américanisme,* in Germany as *Amerikanismus,* and in Russia as *Amerikanizm. Le Corbusier in America* is a case study in transatlantic exchange that examines the architect's cultural critique of America, especially those attitudes and issues associated with *américanisme.* This book argues that within the discipline and practice of architecture in America, Le Corbusier was central both to the critical reception of ideas imported from Europe and to the transition to modernism.

In the fall of 1935 Le Corbusier made his first visit to America and wrote a bittersweet book about the country's culture and his experiences, entitled *Quand les cathédrales étaient blanches: Voyage aux pays des timides.* His tour received little critical attention because it produced no immediate commissions and was considered a failure by most architects and historians. When investigators did note the impact of America on Le Corbusier's work, their analyses proceeded from a formalist perspective focused on style. This study seeks to reframe the issues surrounding the architect and the country.

The operating premise is that Le Corbusier came to America with an armature of preconceptions that shaped his encounter. My contention is that his preconceptions and experience were drafted within an already spirited intra-European and interdisciplinary debate on *américanisme.* As a result, a transatlantic misunderstanding was fueled by the disparity between Le Corbusier's personal expectations of securing work in the United States and his disappointing experience there. Yet he emerged from the tour with a new understanding of the country that alone seemed to offer him the best possibility for achieving a mythical second machine age, uniting standardized industrial methods of mass production—the old technocratic means—with a new humanism in which architecture embraced vernacular and regional concerns, as well as planning ideas he thought were responsive to social and spiritual needs.

Two notions were especially associated with the concept of *américanisme* in France and its counterparts: first, celebration of a new age of mechanization and modernity, and second, America as the agent of that new age. Americanization permeated different aspects of European culture—technological, economic, political, social, as well as artistic. This process had evolved from the time of the Enlightenment. In shedding its colonial status, America came to represent a land of democratic promise for the disaffected of Europe. By the early twentieth century the European avant-garde was fascinated with the idea of a new Western culture without ancient traditions, mythologizing this industrialized democracy as a model of modern society.

A fascination with America was projected strongly in the area of popular culture. Europeans appreciated American popular culture, but rarely its high culture. In effect, the United States conveyed the image of a youthful, open society unfettered by intransigent historical roots. Films of Charlie Chaplin, heroic adventure stories of Jack London, and socially conscious novels of Sinclair Lewis and Upton Sinclair found enthusiastic audiences in Europe. Moreover, the European avant-garde valued African-American culture, especially jazz, for its primitivism and promise of modernity. They also appreciated American sports. But in matters of high culture most Europeans, especially the French, considered their own superior.

The idea of a land of promise, coupled with a recognition of the technological and organizational preeminence of American mechanization, created a mythology. Europeans were particularly captivated by such demonstrations of mechanization and consumerism as skyscrapers, infrastructure, plumbing, gadgets, and advertising. The writings of Frederick Winslow Taylor and methods of Henry Ford swept Europe before World War I with the assurance of more efficiency of production and scientific management. Europeans were especially drawn to the social and political implications of Taylorism and Fordism. As Charles Maier noted, more rationalized production and "optimalization" seemed to offer Americans a way out of the dilemma of capitalism and its attending social problems.[1]

The French discourse on *américanisme* informed Le Corbusier's shifting opinions about the New World from the 1920s to the 1930s and helped fix his preconceptions on the eve of his departure. Narratives of European travelers that appeared in popular and professional journals, as well as anecdotal accounts of friends, shaped his view. From at least the early 1920s when he coedited the avant-garde journal *L'Esprit Nouveau*, Le Corbusier developed the habit of saving news clippings and images on American topics. His personal and professional library, maintained today at the Fondation Le Corbusier in Paris, contains many such books and documents. Le Corbusier frequently annotated his copies and appropriated their contents for his own publications. Among the most important for this study are Werner Hegemann's *Der Städtebau* (1911–1913) and *Amerikanische Architektur und Stadtbaukunst* (1925), the *Jahrbuch des deutschen Werkbundes* (1913), Paul Morand's *New York* (1930), Georges Duhamel's *Scènes de la vie future* (1930), André Maurois's *En Amérique* (1933), Robert Aron and Arnaud Dandieu's *Décadence de la nation française* (1931), Jean de Pierrefeu's *Contre la vie chère* (1933), and other tracts, especially in the neosyndicalist journals *Plans* and *Prélude*.[2] Equally significant are travel narratives (oral, published, and unpublished) and novels about America by friends among the European avant-garde, most notably Blaise Cendrars, Louis-Ferdinand Céline, Fernand Léger, Christian Zervos, and Sigfried Giedion.[3]

In addition to their associations with *américanisme*, Le Corbusier's 1935 American tour and *Cathédrales* may now be situated in a series of his own *voyages* and accounts of them, both written and pictorial. The architect's formative travels and travel narratives include his 1907 trip to Tuscany during which he produced a sketchbook; a 1910–1911 trip to Germany that resulted in four sketchbooks and his publication *Etude sur le mouvement d'art décoratif en Allemagne* (1912); his celebrated "Journey to the East" in 1911 recorded in *Le Voyage d'Orient* and six volumes of sketchbooks; three trips to Moscow between 1928 and 1930 in connection with his Centrosoyuz building project during which he produced many drawings of the city; and his South American travels in 1929 that resulted in several sketchbooks and the publication of *Précisions sur un état présent de l'architecture et de l'urbanisme* (1930). Le Corbusier's travels to these and other regions have been the subject of important scholarship including facsimile editions of his *carnets* or sketchbooks.[4] Although he recorded his impressions of the 1935 American tour in at least one sketchbook, none has survived.[5]

Le Corbusier's two trips to the New World in 1929 and 1935 shared a common purpose as lecture tours. In this respect and others they are similar to his trips to Algiers in 1933 and Rome in 1934.[6] But they went beyond mere architectural interests to engage fundamental issues of culture. Aside from his lecture drawings, *Précisions* and *Cathédrales* emerged from these tours as his most important projects. *Précisions* is largely devoted to the texts of his lectures in Argentina and Brazil, with only a brief introductory "American Prologue" affirming the new culture. By contrast, *Cathédrales* offers nearly the reverse organization and intention. Its long narrative critique of North American culture is pitched toward personal diagnosis and remedy. With the exception of his lectures for Baltimore and Chicago, darkly entitled "The Great Waste," no other lecture text appears. Yet both books are vigorously didactic and indulgently polemical.

In many respects *Cathédrales* builds on themes first presented in *Précisions* and reflects an evolution in Le Corbusier's thinking about these new cultures. Both respond to his increasing interest in the vernacular and regional. Both convey a position against the academy as well as support for authority and the power of the state, propose design strategies based on aesthetics and poetry, and advocate mechanization to solve social problems. In doing so the books extend the discussions of the first four meetings of the Congrès Internationaux d'Architecture Moderne (CIAM) from 1928 to 1933. As Mary McLeod has explained, however, *Précisions* was less concerned with social and political issues.[7] Le Corbusier's engagement with regional syndicalism, a small nonconformist political movement with roots in prewar trade unionism, involved him directly in the social, political, and economic concerns that gripped Europe in the years after the American stock market crash. The architect's political commitments during the early 1930s mark a significant interlude. Situated after the crash, therefore, *Cathédrales* reflects Le Corbusier's new awakening. But at

the same time it seems to reach back to technocratic solutions in an effort to perfect the "first machine age" by advocating a reformed "second machine age." Le Corbusier used *Cathédrales* to promote his demolition-based planning proposal for Manhattan as an empirical model for the Radiant City. While employing modern building techniques, it engaged new aesthetic, poetic, and visionary sensibilities that confirm the shift in his design work during the 1930s.

This investigation recasts an important episode of architectural history within the modern movement in architecture and, more broadly, within the discipline of cultural history. A case study in transatlantic exchange, it builds on recent scholarship. In 1985 Jean-Louis Cohen and Hubert Damisch organized the Paris conference "L'Américanisme et la modernité." Among papers that explored the role of America in the European discourse on modernism and made significant contributions to scholarship on Le Corbusier, two should be mentioned here. Francesco Passanti identified the American skyscraper as an influential model in the development of Le Corbusier's Plan Voisin (1925). Mary McLeod examined Le Corbusier's reactions to American culture in terms of his recent trip to South America and his political and social engagement with regional syndicalism. At that time I presented a preliminary investigation of this topic. The conference papers were published in 1993.[8] The European-American dialogue was also the subject of my session "In Search of a Transatlantic Culture: European Travel Accounts of American Buildings and Civic Spaces, 1900–1925" at the 1990 meeting of the Society of Architectural Historians in Boston.

Le Corbusier's engagement with American developments has figured prominently in specialized as well as more broadly conceived studies. In Colin Rowe's seminal essay (1956) on the Chicago frame he suggested that it was such European modernists as Le Corbusier and Mies van der Rohe who treated the skeletal steel frame as a "vehicle of spatial expression," rather than merely the pragmatic tool it had been for the architects of Chicago's commercial skyscrapers.[9] In *A Concrete Atlantis* (1986) Reyner Banham explored the impact of American industrial buildings in the iconographic and functional development of modern European architecture. His study identified the influence of American structures and systems on the architecture of Le Corbusier and other European modernists.[10] McLeod also analyzed Le Corbusier's endorsement of America's efficiency movement as a vehicle for social change in her article "'Architecture or Revolution': Taylorism, Technocracy, and Social Change."[11] The French literature of transatlantic exchange in architecture was the subject of Isabelle Gournay's 1989 dissertation "France Discovers America 1917–1939."[12] Jean-Louis Cohen produced a comprehensive synthesis of the European response to the culture of America in his 1995 exhibition at the Canadian Centre for Architecture in Montreal and the accompanying catalogue, *Scenes of the World to Come: European Architecture and the American Challenge, 1893–1960.*[13] Cohen's work is especially significant because it engaged the wider European debate on *américanisme.* And Le Corbusier's relationship with North America was the theme of the 1996 VIIes Rencontres, jointly sponsored by the Fondation Le Corbusier and Harvard University.[14]

Recent studies have explored the German discourse on American culture and the response of European artists to it. In the domain of architecture *Amerikanismus* has received its most extensive investigation in Miles David Samson's 1989 dissertation "German-American Dialogues and the Modern Movement before the 'Design Migration,' 1910–1933" and his subsequent unpublished study "A World Like a Ford."[15] In 1990 Beeke Sell Tower mounted an exhibition and produced a catalogue for the Busch-Reisinger Museum at Harvard University devoted to the theme "Envisioning America: Prints, Drawings, and Photographs by George Grosz and His Contemporaries, 1915–1933." Concurrently, the Busch-Reisinger and Goethe-Institut Boston sponsored a conference devoted to the German reception of American culture.[16] Other specialists in European modern art have also debated the concept of *américanisme.* Wanda Corn's 1989 College Art Association session, "*Américanisme:* Old World Discovers the New," explored the appropriation by European artists of images associated with American industry and popular culture, their meaning and significance.

Within the discourse on *américanisme* Le Corbusier's enunciations assume a role of new importance. This study casts him as a *revealer* of issues about American culture and society during the 1930s, both large and small. As an outsider by nationality, culture, and intention, he looked at the American scene through an acutely focused lens, and in the process made perceptive observations and even exposed raw truths. These form some of the most powerful themes in his lectures and in *Cathédrales:* a new society marred by capitalism and consumerism with serious consequences for the groups it marginalizes, the effect of decentralization and suburbanization, the sociopsychological state of the American family, and redemptive forces within the new society. Much of his criticism, however, was flawed by cultural stereotyping and other weaknesses associated with the most conservative elements of *américanisme.*

The American writer Marguerite Tjader Harris, Le Corbusier's intimate friend during the American tour, plays an especially significant role in this study. Cautious that his liaison with her might compromise his opportunities for work in America, and that news of her might reach his wife Yvonne in Paris, Le Corbusier concealed the relationship. It is only through the letters Marguerite kept, her unpublished "portrait" of him, and the recollections of her son Hilary that her significance as guide and muse emerges. During the tour Marguerite revealed to Le Corbusier the deeper dimensions of American culture, allowed him to acquire a more diverse experience of it, and encouraged his creativity.

A few words now on my methodology. This study did not begin with a clear-cut set of assumptions to be proved or disproved. Rather, it took shape as an "open work." The complexity of Le Corbusier's relationship with America and, by extension, relations between Europe and America during the 1930s suggested a field of engagement in which the study could develop.[17] My objective was not to propose a new interpretation of the architect. Rather, it was to seek authenticity in the dialogue between Le Corbusier and the Americans, in the dynamics of the exchange between two cultures, and in the observations of the outsider who could see Americans as Americans could not see themselves; a subtext of the book is the search to understand Le Corbusier's development as a modern man as well as a modernist. The timing of his trip turned it into a reality check of sorts. From an American perspective, the demise of the Beaux-Arts system in America meant that for avant-garde practitioners France and French culture were no longer model subjects. From a French perspective, the financial collapse of capitalism resulting from the American stock market crash in 1929 meant that the United States was no longer a country to emulate, even if to Le Corbusier its resources seemed more abundant than those in Europe.

In its examination of such a rich episode this study embraces some of the methods of the "new history."[18] Taking a heroic figure as its subject, this book is not so much a view from above—the great deeds of a great man—as much as a view from below—the small, ordinary events that together construct the view from above. I have attempted a cultural construction based on the convergence of architectural history, biography, and social history. I approach this historical episode in terms of cultural relativism and consider such issues as motivation, stereotypical responses, and preconceptions in relation to experience. If the procedures are detailed, they are also inclusive, admitting a broad range of documents and resources, objective and factual as well as subjective and anecdotal.

Although not a biography, this study uses methods of the biographer. It examines how the personal intersects with larger impersonal forces. It attempts to counter the rigid historicism and abstraction of those forces with richness of detail and concern for subtleties and human expression that reside with the individual. My objective in creating a nuanced portrait is not to debunk as much as to demythologize Le Corbusier so that a more complex yet balanced interpretation may emerge. In my effort to understand the arena of human activity within the culture of architecture during the 1930s, I look at individuals actively making decisions and also functioning in a web of circumstances over which they have little control.

Through the intersection of microhistory and biography I have still sought to clarify traditional patterns of historical development. This study considers, for example, Le Corbusier's initiatives to build a social network of clients in the United States to support his work and ideas. It suggests ways in which his powerful critique of American culture serves as a marker for assessing nationalism and internationalism. It identifies the significance of his tour as a threshold to his late work, one that might validate his concept of a second machine age (uniting modern technology with social and cultural concerns) and shape the direction of his design work toward a more sculptural expression of mass and a use of tensile structures. This investigation also reexamines Le Corbusier's role in the debate on New York City public housing by separating form from policy to show that, notwithstanding some debt to the formal image of Corbusian models, this housing was produced by specialists who relied on their own empirical models and housing policies.

In reaching beyond the biographical to construct a broader cross-cultural context for Le Corbusier's engagement with America, I benefited from analytical tools of recent critical theory focusing on the study of discourse. Methodologies developed by Michel Foucault and Umberto Eco were particularly helpful in examining Le Corbusier's statements about America within the larger arena of discursive thought.[19] They also helped to frame arguments that informed both the concept of *américanisme* and transatlantic exchange.

In the end this study asks to whom and for whom Le Corbusier's lecture tour and his cultural critique were significant. Americans responded in diverse ways. Identifying the various positions of Henry-Russell Hitchcock, Philip Johnson, Joseph Hudnut, A. Lawrence Kocher, Lewis Mumford, Catherine Bauer, Douglas Haskell, George Howe, Elizabeth Mock, and others, this study situates Le Corbusier's theory and design within the historiography of the modern movement in America. At the same time that his tour inspired what Sigfried Giedion called a "cross-fertilization of viewpoints," his confrontation with the reality and dimensions of the United States was a powerful experience that unleashed his own creativity.[20] In examining Le Corbusier's dialogue with America I hope that the reader will achieve greater understanding of the richness and complexity of transatlantic culture during the 1930s.

Prelude

1

Le Corbusier and Transatlantic Exchange

In the fall of 1935 the Swiss-born French architect Charles-Edouard Jeanneret-Gris (1887–1965), called Le Corbusier, made his first visit to the United States, lasting nearly two months.[1] Sponsored by the Museum of Modern Art in New York, the visit was timed to coincide with the opening of an exhibition of his work followed by a lecture tour. With Manhattan as his base, Le Corbusier gave over twenty lectures to architecture schools and to professional and cultural organizations throughout parts of the East and Midwest. After his return home he published an assemblage of ambivalent impressions in *Quand les cathédrales étaient blanches: Voyage au pays des timides* of 1937.[2] But it would be another decade before an English edition, *When the Cathedrals Were White: A Journey to the Country of Timid People,* was published in America.[3]

The trip had been long deferred. Like most of the European avant-garde, Le Corbusier was intrigued with America, seeing it as a place of opportunity and escape. As early as 1909 the young Edouard Jeanneret feigned a trip abroad when he sent a farewell postcard from Le Havre to his cousin Marguerite, announcing his departure on a transatlantic liner bound for America. But the joke did not endear Edouard to his distraught family.[4] During the summer of 1913, lack of work in his home town of La Chaux-de-Fonds, Switzerland, led Edouard to express an interest in working abroad. He complained to Karl Ernst Osthaus, director of the Deutsches Museum in Hagen, Germany: "There is nothing to do there [La Chaux-de-Fonds] and I am trying to leave for America. I need important work where art plays a great role, where my strengths and enthusiasm are used."[5] Again in 1921 and 1922 in his capacity as editor of *L'Esprit Nouveau,* he entertained the idea of a trip to the United States, this time to give lectures and negotiate an American edition of the journal.[6]

During the 1920s and 1930s no European architect wrote more passionately or polemically than Le Corbusier about the American landscape, its skyscrapers and city plans, as well as its icons of machine age modernity. This was ironic as he had yet to visit the country. His notions about its culture and design derived from many sources: American clients, young American architects in his atelier, travel accounts and impressions by the European avant-garde including many of his friends, and a range of professional and popular literature and advertising. Through them he had acquired a wide range of preconceptions that irrevocably shaped his experiences in America.

From the mid-1920s a number of wealthy and influential American clients associated with the Parisian avant-garde engaged Le Corbusier. They gave him three commissions. Le Corbusier designed Les Terrasses in Garches, Vaucresson (1926–1928), for Gabrielle de Monzie, but it was soon acquired by American banker-collector Michael Stein and his wife, Sarah, who jointly financed the project.[7] Films of Les Terrasses in 1928 and 1930 convey the shared intention of architect, clients, and filmmakers to apply purist aesthetics to the suburban villa and thereby portray the Steins in a modern house (figure 1.1).[8] During the late 1920s Michael's sister, Gertrude Stein, also wanted Le Corbusier to design a house. In the end she was not able to acquire land in the French countryside at Belley where she and her companion, Alice B. Toklas, spent their summers, and elected instead to rent a house.[9] American journalist and painter William E. Cook and his French wife, Jeanne, members of the Stein circle, were also Le Corbusier's clients. The Villa Cook in Boulogne-sur-Seine (1926–1927) fused the ideals of classical proportions, purist abstraction, and the symbolic imagery of machine age forms.[10] There Le

Corbusier first demonstrated his wholly formulated "five points of a new architecture," which he later drew upon in his American lectures.[11] In 1927 expatriate American writer Henry Church and his wife, Barbara, commissioned Le Corbusier to remodel an existing property at Ville d'Avray. A music pavilion, involving renovation of the existing main house, formed the centerpiece of the project. The library loft (*bibliothèque en soupente*) was equipped with furniture designed by Le Corbusier, his cousin Pierre Jeanneret, and Charlotte Perriand, a young French designer whose collaboration inspired many interiors.[12] Like the Villa Stein-de Monzie, the Villa Church (1927–1929, demolished) incorporated elements of formal classicism—complex proportional relationships, an axial approach to a formal setting, and terracing—with references to the machine age and to the typology of Le Corbusier's Esprit Nouveau pavilion (1925; see figure 1.11).[13]

In addition to these clients, American-born philanthropist Princess Edmond de Polignac (née Winnaretta Singer) provided Le Corbusier with abiding support. An heir to the Singer Manufacturing Company fortune, she

1.1

Le Corbusier at the Villa Stein, "Les Terrasses," still from Pierre Chenal film *L'Architecture d'aujourd'hui* (1930). (James Ward, "Les Terrasses," *Architectural Review* 177 [March 1985], p. 68, fig. 15.) © 2001 Artists Rights Society (ARS), New York/ADAGP, Paris/FLC.

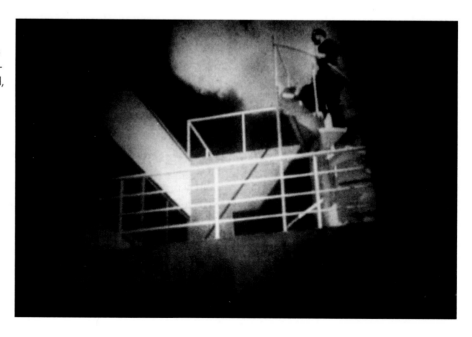

first retained the architect in 1926 to design a house in Neuilly that was never built.[14] The Fondation Singer-Polignac, the charity organization she established in France to promote better housing conditions for the urban poor, subsequently commissioned Le Corbusier to design two buildings for the Salvation Army in Paris. The first was a new dormitory wing for the Palais du Peuple on the rue des Cordeliers (1926–1927).[15] The second was a model hostel, the Cité de Refuge (1929–1933), located on the rue Cantagrel.[16] Although the latter project was aided by the 1928 Loi Loucheur, a French law that increased government funding for housing, both were primarily supported by Singer philanthropy.[17]

Outside Paris Le Corbusier met two American women whom he soon regarded as potential clients. The first was the exotic African-American singer Josephine Baker. His friendship with her began in the fall of 1929 as a chance encounter aboard the *Giulio Cesare* during the course of his travels in South America. Until 1936 Le Corbusier pursued Baker's interest in a project for an orphanage in France, although nothing ever came of it.[18] The second was Marguerite Tjader Harris, a wealthy young American writer whom he met in Vevey, Switzerland, in 1932 and shortly thereafter provided with plans for a house she planned to build there. With both women Le Corbusier commingled the personal and professional, but their greater significance was in the personal sphere. Through them he enriched his understanding of American culture.

Le Corbusier assigned a special significance to these individuals that resonated both during and after his American tour. The Steins, Cooks, Churches, the Princess Edmond de Polignac, Josephine Baker, and Marguerite Harris embraced French culture, which in Le Corbusier's world view made them truly enlightened. Their support predisposed him to assume that he would receive similar commissions from the avant-garde in America, especially from those similarly fortified by French culture.

Although Americans in Paris were interested in his architecture, they were largely indifferent to his painting. For example, Michael and Sarah Stein may have been clients of Les Terrasses, but when it came to collecting they had little taste for Le Corbusier and Amédée Ozenfant's purist paintings.[19] Similarly, Le Corbusier's canvases were not included in the collections of either Gertrude Stein or Claribel and Etta Cone, her close friends from Baltimore. There the works of Matisse and Picasso took center stage.[20] Indeed, before World War II Le Corbusier's paintings were not widely represented in private collections or public museums of modern art in America.[21] By contrast, his Swiss friends, notably banker and art collector Raoul La Roche, were early collectors of his work.[22]

Before his trip, Le Corbusier's knowledge of the United States came in part from direct contacts with Americans, notably from a handful of young architects who were formally trained in the Beaux-Arts tradition but worked in his atelier at 35 rue de Sèvres. The first of these was Norman Rice (1905–1986), a young architect who had come across a copy of *Vers une architecture* in a Paris bookshop in June 1929 and looked up Le Corbusier's office in the telephone directory. Rice worked in the atelier from 1929 to 1930 on a number of projects including the Porte Maillot development, a Salvation Army building, the Villa Savoye at Poissy, the Beistegui apartment in Paris, and the auditorium of the Centrosoyuz in Moscow. Many nationalities were represented in the atelier, especially among younger architects. Rice remembered in particular Ernst Weissmann from Zagreb who immigrated to the United States in 1932; José Luis Sert from Barcelona who later immigrated to the United States; Kunio Maekawa from Tokyo; Nikolaj Kolli, a Russian architect who had come to work on designs for the Centrosoyuz in Moscow; and Albert Frey from Switzerland, who immigrated to the United States in 1930.[23] Among the Americans, Hamilton Beatty, a young midwesterner, also worked on the Centrosoyuz. He spent most of 1930 in the atelier, as did Matthew Ehrlich from Philadelphia.[24] Hugh D. McClellan, a Bostonian who joined the office for three months in 1931, later sought Le Corbusier's assistance in securing work in the Soviet Union.[25] During the winter of 1932 Jane West became the first American woman to join the atelier; she worked on the Pavillon Suisse. After her return to America she married and practiced architecture with German-born architect Alfred (Zeppel) Clauss.[26]

Of all these young Americans, Robert Allan Jacobs (1905–1993) had a direct effect on Le Corbusier's understanding of the United States. For six months during the winter of 1934–1935 Jacobs worked on proposals for the 1937 Exposition Internationale "Arts et Techniques" (see figure 10.9), and also on the competition for the Musées de la Ville et de l'Etat in Paris (see figure 3.12). The next fall he served as Le Corbusier's interpreter, guide, and *copain* on the American lecture tour.[27] Because most American partisans of Le Corbusier did not work in his atelier at the same time and never formed a school or organized group, they did not import their mentor's theory and design in any formal or systematic way. Nonetheless, Le Corbusier's influence on them helped shape American architecture in the years before and after 1935.

The Culture of *américanisme*

Le Corbusier formulated his preconceptions about America within a culture of *américanisme,* a process of Americanization in which Europeans looked abroad for cultural renewal. During the early decades of this century Europeans considered America to be a model culture inextricably linked to their myth of modernity. By World War I they looked increasingly to this industrial democracy as a catalyst for change. European writers of the period, therefore, fixed on the idea that the New World might serve as a model for the Old World. Aldous Huxley summarized the European position in 1926 when he claimed that "the world would be Americanized."[28]

During the teens, twenties, and early thirties, the European avant-garde was drawn to America to learn from its technology, its institutions, and its culture. Many European writers, artists, and architects visited America and some even sought work there. The list of Le Corbusier's friends and associates who made transatlantic tours before him is long but includes Blaise Cendrars, Fernand Léger, Frederick Kiesler, Walter Gropius, Richard Neutra, Albert Frey, A. Lawrence Kocher, Sigfried Giedion, Werner Hegemann, and Christian Zer-

vos. Their letters and postcards from America, as well as their narratives, both published and unpublished, helped inform Le Corbusier's general preconceptions and his writings. He also sought contacts with American friends and colleagues, including architect Paul Nelson, a native of Chicago, and city planner George B. Ford (1879–1930), whom Le Corbusier mistakenly took to be the son of Henry Ford.[29]

The literature of *américanisme,* especially French accounts of Georges Duhamel, Paul Morand, André Maurois, and others, shaped Le Corbusier's preconceptions as well as the polemical view of America that threaded through his writings. Images of America saturated such popular journals as the French *Revue des Deux Mondes* and *L'Illustration* and the Swiss *L'Illustré,* as well as such French newspapers as *L'Intransigeant* from which Le Corbusier frequently took clippings for use in his own publications.[30] French professional journals gave wide coverage to American buildings, construction practices, and city planning, particularly in New York and Chicago.[31]

Le Corbusier punctuated his writings of the 1920s with selective images of American technology. Machine age forms illustrated the pages of *L'Esprit Nouveau,* the French journal of modern culture that he edited with Amédée Ozenfant.[32] His subsequent publications, *Vers une architecture* (1923), *L'Art décoratif d'aujourd'hui* (1925), *Urbanisme* (1925), and *Almanach d'architecture moderne* (1926) continued to celebrate the methods and techniques as well as the visual and symbolic language of American mass production and industrial organization.[33] Collectively, these diverse images and symbols formed a recurring theme in his writings. He adopted the imagery and symbolism of American mechanization, industrial forms, and engineering techniques to promote his view of "the first machine age."

Images of American grain elevators, daylight factories, and skeletal steel skyscrapers were ready for appropriation and manipulation. As scholars have long recognized, Le Corbusier retouched a photograph of a South American silo that first appeared in Walter Gropius's article in the *Jahrbuch des deutschen Werkbundes* of 1913 (figure 1.2). In *L'Esprit Nouveau* and again in his manifesto *Vers une architecture* (*Towards a New Architecture*), Le Corbusier published a photograph in which the structure's pediments were eliminated, thereby conveying the illusion of a flat roof (figure 1.3). This alteration not only emphasized its geometry and purism but also formed an alliance between classicism and mechanization.[34] Yet Le Corbusier countered his admiration of the American engineer with an attack on the American architect. Skyscraper design, he thought, was still dominated by retrogressive academic styles. The famous dialectic between the architect and the engineer in *Vers une architecture* is encapsulated in Le Corbusier's advice: "Let us listen to the counsels of American engineers. But let us beware of American architects." An unidentified photograph of a battered but standing Spreckels Building in San Francisco (1897) illustrated his argument (figure 1.4). This academic, masonry-clad skyscraper by James and Merritt Reid, with its effusive ornament, concealed a state-of-the-art skeletal frame and concrete dome that had enabled it to withstand the devastating earthquake of 1906.[35]

The skeletal steel frame expressed functional clarity to Le Corbusier and was also a means to achieve the effect of spatial volumes. In *Urbanisme* he captioned a photograph of an American skyscraper frame *Un building . . . On met du verre autour* (A building . . . One encloses it in glass; figure 1.5). In *Almanach d'architecture moderne* he reproduced the same photograph to illustrate the use of skeletal steel construction in America which signaled "modern times."[36] In *Urbanisme* he deliberately juxtaposed this image with a view of the central station from his Ville Contemporaine, a project of 1922 (figure 1.6).[37] In so doing he suggested that the horizontal beams of the American frame expressed the discrete identity of the floors on the towers of his Ville Contemporaine. Even the indented envelope of his skyscrapers recalled the bow windows of such Chicago buildings as the Reliance (1891–1894) by D. H. Burnham (Charles Atwood, chief designer) and the Tacoma (1888–1889) by Holabird and Roche.[38]

More than models of technical proficiency, American skyscrapers and projects employing them offered Le Corbusier a new typology and plan for his own visionary

1.2
Silo, Buenos Aires. Photograph from article by Walter Gropius. ("Die Entwicklung moderner Industriebaukunst," in *Jahrbuch des deutschen Werkbundes* [Jena, 1913], opp. p. 16.)

1.3
Silo. Photograph from article by Le Corbusier. ("Trois rappels à MM. les Architectes," *L'Esprit Nouveau* 1 [October 1920], p. 95; reprinted in *Vers une architecture*, p. 17.) © 2001 Artists Rights Society (ARS), New York/ADAGP, Paris/FLC.

Preuve :

1.4
James and Merritt Reid, Spreckels
Building, San Francisco, after
the 1906 earthquake. (*Vers une
architecture*, p. 29.) © 2001
Artists Rights Society (ARS), New
York/ADAGP, Paris/FLC.

1.5
Unidentified American skeletal
steel frame captioned "A building
. . . One encloses it in glass."
(*Urbanisme*, p. 185.) © 2001
Artists Rights Society (ARS), New
York/ADAGP, Paris/FLC.

1.6
Le Corbusier, "Central Station,"
Ville Contemporaine, project of
1922. (*Urbanisme*, pp. 178–179;
reprinted in *Oeuvre complète
1910–1929*, p. 109. Plan FLC
30850.) © 2001 Artists Rights
Society (ARS), New York/ADAGP,
Paris/FLC.

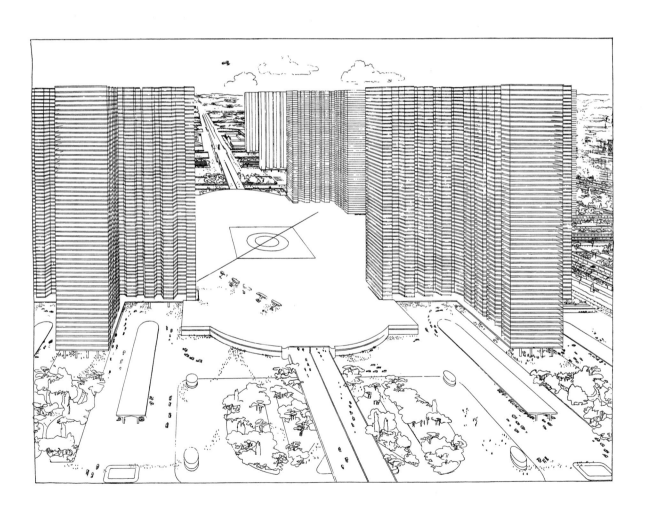

1.7
Le Corbusier, Villes-Tours, 1921.
(*L'Esprit Nouveau 4* [January 1921], p. 466. Plan FLC 31910.)
© 2001 Artists Rights Society (ARS), New York/ADAGP, Paris/FLC.

schemes. He originally intended his Villes-Tours or cities of towers (figure 1.7) as a housing scheme when it was published in *L'Esprit Nouveau* (1921), but later deemed it more appropriate for offices when it appeared in *Vers une architecture*.[39] As Stanislaus von Moos and Francesco Passanti showed, the Villes-Tours project looked first to the vision of Auguste Perret (with whom Le Corbusier worked in Paris from 1908 to 1909) and ultimately to American models. Le Corbusier was aware of Perret's intention in 1915 to concentrate housing into twenty-story towers aligned to a boulevard, a metropolitan infrastructure, and also to a green space like a park. Indeed, reports of Perret's visionary research had circulated in the Parisian press for two decades; but it was not until 1922 that a drawing by Jacques Lambert of a project for skyscraper apartment houses on the periphery of Paris inspired by Perret's sketches appeared in *L'Illustration* (figure 1.8).[40] Notwithstanding Perret's efforts to distance such projects from American skyscrapers, especially those with cruciform plans, he clearly looked to

American models. His towers—laid out on a grid with classically detailed masonry facades, setback massing, and cruciform plans—suggested two Louis Sullivan projects of 1891: a thirty-six-story Fraternity Temple, Chicago (figure 1.9) and a setback skyscraper city.[41] Both Le Corbusier and Perret found inspiration in gridded American cities and cruciform towers.[42] But if the skyscrapers in the Perret-inspired project of 1922 derived their expression of mass from American buildings, those of Le Corbusier's visionary projects of the 1920s derived their expression of volume from American skeletal frames.

The significance of appropriating these building types and construction practices lies in the elevation of industrial and building technology to high art forms, which Gropius, Le Corbusier, and others promoted as icons of modernity. The abstract geometrical forms of American buildings confirmed for them, as they did for Erich Mendelsohn, Wilhelm Worringer's thesis of 1908 linking primitive art and high culture. Such monumental forms were created by modern engineers whose unspoiled rational vision paralleled the artistic will of ancient cultures.[43]

1.9
Louis Sullivan, Fraternity Temple, Chicago, 1891. (*Graphic 5* [December 19, 1891]; The Chicago Historical Society.)

Le Corbusier's endorsement of American technology during the 1920s embraced Taylorism, a system of scientific management developed by Frederick Winslow Taylor and linked to the efficiency movement. Like Fordism, this rationalized system of industrialization and management promised economic benefits and social change through efficiency of production.[44] Le Corbusier revered Henry Ford's methods and models of production (he owned the 1925 French edition of Ford's book *My Life and My Work*) and was particularly influenced by the writings of Hyacinthe Dubreuil that endorsed assembly line production and Taylorism.[45] In effect, the Ville Contemporaine and Plan Voisin featured urban architectural images based on the application of such rationalized systems. Le Corbusier's diorama of the Plan Voisin, a project to rebuild the center of Paris that he exhibited at the 1925 Pavillon de l'Esprit Nouveau, suggested an example of *américanisme* to French journalists. A newspaper clipping with an image of the Plan Voisin interpreted Esprit Nouveau ideals through its accompanying hypothesis: Si Paris s'américanisait . . . (If Paris Americanized Itself; figure 1.10). Le Corbusier, in turn, published the clipping in *Almanach d'architecture moderne*.[46] Ironi-

cally, even though the Plan Voisin relied on the American model of production and management, its futuristic cruciform towers with their glazed envelopes contrasted sharply with American examples of skyscraper design, which in comparison looked old-fashioned.

By the mid-1920s, and especially after the American stock market crash in 1929, European discourse on America assumed a vigilant, even ominous posture. To Le Corbusier and other European observers during the early years of the Great Depression, America had unwittingly transformed itself from a model of production during the teens and twenties into one of consumerism and waste, with destructive consequences for its culture and its cities, particularly New York and Chicago. If the country was admired for its power, mechanization, and modernity, it was also feared for its attending social problems—problems that inevitably found their way to Europe and especially to France. Thus, as the economic and social deficits of the Depression crossed the Atlantic, they threatened to destabilize European culture. During the early 1930s these fears entered more roundly into the French debate on *américanisme*. Writer Georges Duhamel harbored them in 1930 when he declared, "America,

1.10
"If Paris Americanized Itself . . . ," diorama exhibited at the Pavillon de l'Esprit Nouveau, 1925. (*Almanach d'architecture moderne*, p. 188.) © 2001 Artists Rights Society (ARS), New York/ADAGP, Paris/FLC.

then, represents for us the Future."[47] As a result, Le Corbusier repeatedly cast America during this period as a country of paradoxes.

America Discovers Le Corbusier

The American discovery of Le Corbusier's theory and design during the 1920s was gradual and diffuse. Reports focused on three aspects of his work: city planning and early villas, the Esprit Nouveau pavilion for the 1925 Paris fair, and *Vers une architecture,* his seminal publication of 1923 with its English and American editions of 1927 as *Towards a New Architecture.* The years between 1920 and 1925 when Le Corbusier and Ozenfant edited and wrote for *L'Esprit Nouveau* were especially creative ones, but most Americans had little knowledge of or access to the journal because few individuals or institutions subscribed.[48] Wallace K. Harrison was among those Americans introduced to Le Corbusier's writings in the journal during his studies at the Ecole des Beaux-Arts in 1920–1921.[49] Most interest in Le Corbusier came from architects and members of the avant-garde receptive to European modernism.

It is ironic then that the timely presentation of Le Corbusier's work and ideas in America came from the journal sponsored by the profession. When the American architectural press first turned its attention to European modernism, the *Journal of the American Institute of Architects (JAIA)* published Le Corbusier's work. In 1923 and 1924 *JAIA* reproduced illustrations of his Ville Contemporaine (1922), as well as the Ribot house prototype and Villa Ker-Ka-Ré (Villa Besnus) at Vaucresson (1922–1923).[50] The next year its French correspondent G. F. Sebille introduced American readers to Corbusian polemics. Sebille's account of Le Corbusier's speech at a conference during the Paris Salon d'Automne of 1924 underscored the architect's tenacious attack on the academy that he later continued in his American lectures: "In the first ten minutes of it, the speaker said nothing, but had run off on the projection screen a series of the most characteristic amenities of modern life: a steamship, an automobile, a safe, and aeroplane, a business office (in polished oak, which we Frenchmen call

American), a skyscraper, a hospital operating room, and many others. In the midst of these pictures he suddenly flashed upon the screen a hall in the chateau of Fontainebleau and the facade of a nineteenth century house in an ornate style." Sebille endorsed Le Corbusier and his colleagues for their "logical employment, disassociated from all prejudice, of modern construction methods." Cautioning Americans that the new architecture lacked subtlety, Sebille thanked Le Corbusier and his fellow modernists who "wake us from our idle slumbers," even if "a trifle brutally."[51]

Most Americans, however, were introduced to Le Corbusier through accounts of his Pavillon de l'Esprit Nouveau (figure 1.11) at the Exposition Internationale des Arts Décoratifs et Industriels Modernes held in Paris in 1925 and 1926. Although a simplified neoclassicism dominated the fair architecture, there were displays of modernity in exhibit buildings by Tony Garnier, Auguste Perret, Peter Behrens, Otto Wagner, Konstantin Melnikov, and Kay Fisker, as well as Le Corbusier. American visitors, according to Beaux-Arts architect John Harbeson, "saw, for the first time, an art entirely new to them."[52] In response to the fair, American architects became enamored of art deco, a hybrid of forms reflecting influences from cubism, futurism, planar elements of the Wiener Werkstätte, and the pared-down classicism of late Beaux-Arts design.[53] A decade later when Le Corbusier visited America it remained a dominant architectural style.

In 1925 Americans were eager to see the new architecture of modernity but few actually visited Le Corbusier's pavilion, due in part to its obscure location. Because of official hostility to it, the pavilion was sequestered on a back lot of the fairgrounds behind the Grand Palais.[54] Consequently, Henry-Russell Hitchcock and others predisposed to European modernism missed it. As both model house and exhibit, the pavilion encapsulated an ideal purist environment and realized in three-dimensional form the ideas Le Corbusier had written about.[55] Constructed of steel, reinforced concrete, and blocks, it was conceived, in effect, as one unit of Immeuble-villas, an apartment house project of 1922. It contained purist paintings, decorative arts (his *objets-*

1.11
Le Corbusier, Pavillon de
l'Esprit Nouveau, Exposition
Internationale des Arts Déco-
ratifs et Industriels Modernes,
Paris, 1925. (FLC L2(8)1-3.)
© 2001 Artists Rights Society
(ARS), New York/ADAGP,
Paris/FLC.

types), and dioramas of both the Ville Contemporaine and the Plan Voisin.[56]

News of the controversial pavilion and the theory that informed it, however, soon circulated among academic groups and the avant-garde as well as in American press reports. Lewis Mumford, who did manage to see the model house, dismissed it as "fanatically barren."[57] But according to Alfred H. Barr, Jr., first director of the Museum of Modern Art, "I knew nothing of Corbu when I was abroad on my first European trip in the summer of 1924. I think the first time I heard his name was in the fall of 1925 at Princeton [University] where I heard accounts of the Pavillon de l'Esprit Nouveau." At the same time Barr was affected greatly by his reading of *Vers une architecture* and *La Peinture moderne* (1925, with Amédée Ozenfant).[58]

Official reports on the Paris fair attempted to explain its architecture. They came from a Herbert Hoover-appointed commission whose delegates included American Institute of Architects (AIA) president

D. Everett Waid, critic Richardson Wright, and Frank Leslie Baker of the *New York Times*.[59] Other, largely unpublished narratives came from critics as well as a few young architects including George Howe, Wallace K. Harrison, and Raymond Hood.[60] These accounts, as well as those by art critics, conveyed the sense that Le Corbusier's pavilion was a statement of significance. Waid's report is significant because it signaled a softening of the Beaux-Arts position in identifying the fair's principal characteristic as "an effort to solve problems honestly in a new way and to do it attractively." Yet Waid cautioned that the new architecture was "not always as honest as it intends to be." When he cited the example of "a heavy superstructure [that] seems to be supported on glass," he probably had in mind the Esprit Nouveau pavilion. Such honesty smacked of "affectation," he argued, but Melnikov's USSR Pavilion was an "exception" because its design suggested a Russian zeitgeist.[61] In his article on the Paris exposition for *House and Garden* Wright referred obliquely to Le Corbusier's theory of design when he identified "the modernist movement" whose proponents sought to "create styles . . . suitable to the age in which we live," that is, "an age of motor cars."[62]

An anonymous *New York Times* report of March 1926 endorsed Le Corbusier's work and especially his pavilion. Although made of the "simplest and most inexpensive materials," the "model villa" had "light, air and space" with "a balance of form more satisfying than luxury." The reviewer suggested that Le Corbusier's architecture ought to interest Americans because it derived its form partly from "American engineering." Moreover, unlike other critics, the *Times* reporter applauded the architect's social, aesthetic, and functional concerns. Le Corbusier's "modern point of view," his "*l'esprit nouveau,*" illustrate his efforts "to improve the living conditions of a needy class," thereby reflecting his "dual personality of social consciousness and artist." At the same time the report applauded the sympathetic relationship in Le Corbusier's work between "the beautiful" and "the efficient," while alluding directly to the ideals of *Vers une architecture.* Still another account, published in the Anglo-American journal *Creative Art,* concluded that the pavilion was the fair's "only original contribution to architecture."[63]

In February 1926 the Architectural League of New York sponsored an exhibition of 500 photographs and drawings of the architecture and decorative arts of the Paris fair,[64] but the controversial pavilion was conspicuously absent. Either French collaborators barred it or Alfred Bossom, who chaired the League's Foreign Exhibits Committee that arranged the New York show, kept it out.[65]

Many Americans who learned about Le Corbusier through press reports of his Esprit Nouveau pavilion and other work, as well as discussions of his ideas in academic circles, were led to his *Vers une architecture.* Circulated among architects, intellectuals, and the avant-garde at a time when French was the language of architecture and high culture, the book came to the immediate attention of Francophiles in America. In 1924 Mumford had noted it as "an able exposition of the absolutist point of view" (a position that predisposed him, unlike his colleagues, to judge the pavilion harshly).[66] An anonymous review in the *New York Times* was among the first to elucidate Le Corbusier's theory and design for American readers while acknowledging it as the source of "much controversy on the Continent."[67] Even those closely associated with the academy were especially alert to its import. Paul Cret, distinguished French professor of design at the University of Pennsylvania, was open-minded. In 1927 Beaux-Arts-trained Cret endorsed Le Corbusier's theory of design in a lecture presented to the T-Square Club in Philadelphia and subsequent publications. As David Brownlee showed, Cret's sympathy with Le Corbusier's concept of the plan as "generator," alliance of classicism and modernism, and criticism of ornament allowed him to advance a view of modernism as an evolution from Beaux-Arts principles.[68] He also supported the suggestion in *Vers une architecture* that the architect "listen" to the engineer, thereby becoming his "collaborator."[69] Early that same year Samuel Chamberlain applauded Le Corbusier as the "uncompromising voice" of modernism. Chamberlain recommended not only *Vers une architecture* but also *L'Art décoratif d'aujourd'hui* and *Urbanisme* for their "curt, incisive sentences, their strange illustrations and their almost irresistible logic."[70]

At the close of 1927 Le Corbusier's writings acquired a broader American audience through Frederick Etchells's translation *Towards a New Architecture,* published first in London by John Rodker and subsequently in New York by Payson and Clarke from the thirteenth French edition.[71] British professional journals were also reporting on Le Corbusier and these were, of course, read in America.[72] An early review of the American edition in the conservative journal *Architect* called Le Corbusier's manifesto no less than an "awakening." The editor admitted that his name had "heretofore been unknown to us," but hoped that the profession would recognize "the sincerity and truth in this brilliant and arresting book."[73] George Chappell's review in the *New Yorker* called it an "important index of the direction which many acute, thoughtful minds are taking in their progress 'toward a new architecture'."[74] In time, the book evoked as much controversy in America as the original French edition caused in Europe.

Le Corbusier's Theory and Design Shape Three Critical Debates

During the 1920s Le Corbusier's theory and design, well articulated in *Vers une architecture,* became central to three critical debates within the discourse on American architecture. The first distinguished two camps: modernists and traditionalists. This debate pitted progressive architects against the academy and, more specifically, those trained in the Beaux-Arts system then in decline. If the first debate was between the avant-garde and the old guard, the second was within the ranks of the avant-garde. Advocates of European modernism opposed proponents of a native technocratic movement advancing production-based design. The second debate embraced internationalism versus nationalism, intellectual abstractions versus pragmatism, and European modernism versus the organic architecture of Frank Lloyd Wright. The third debate, a corollary of the second, countered rational planning with social concerns.

Modernists and Traditionalists

By the mid-1920s, American architecture was in the throes of an identity crisis between the avant-garde and the old guard. Le Corbusier's writings, especially *Towards a New Architecture,* soon assumed a seminal role in that debate. The 1925 Paris exposition helped to define the split in European architecture between a new approach to design seemingly independent from the past and a conservative academic tradition associated with late Beaux-Arts theory. The example of the fair encouraged American architects to divide into opposing camps of modernism and tradition.[75] Moreover, the League exhibition helped to polarize the architectural community in New York City, launching a similar debate between evolutionists and fundamentalists.[76]

As American proponents of modernism endorsed the new architecture of the French exposition, they distanced themselves from late Beaux-Arts practice and began to appropriate the language of Le Corbusier's theory and design. Raymond Hood declared that, as a result of the Paris fair, "the American architect will no longer have to steal, borrow, copy or adapt inspiration from a prototype." Hood also noted that the exhibition signaled a transformation in architectural practice from "craftsman" to "designer."[77] One anonymous *New York Times* report noted "the possibilities of standardization . . . thus achieving the strictest economy."[78] And Harvey Wiley Corbett applauded the new architecture for demonstrating "the machine age" character of the period.[79]

By contrast, a conservative backlash to the French exposition from traditionalists H. Van Buren Magonigle and Ely J. Kahn dismissed "the new order of architecture" as "only transitory."[80] Their fellow Beaux-Arts architect Ralph Walker and eminent historian and Columbia professor Talbot Faulkner Hamlin joined them. The debate among professionals reflected divisions in architectural discourse both inside and outside the academy during the 1920s.[81] Significantly, traditionalists used *Towards a New Architecture* as the target of their opposition. To Walker its publication in 1927 marked a significant juncture in the history of architecture between the familiar "road of imitation" that had securely guided the past, and the unknown "narrow way of creation" ahead. Walker summarized the position of most traditionalists when he criticized the "austere design of the engineer-architect" that Le Corbusier supported. Such design would satisfy only a "robot" and ignore the "spiritual and intellectual needs of men." In place of Le Corbusier's "primary forms," Walker proposed his own "new architecture" with its "complex forms" evolved rather than severed from the past. Such forms would be evolutionary, not revolutionary. Walker's strident criticism may be viewed as a response to the image of his own recently completed Barclay-Vesey Telephone Building in New York (1923–1926) as frontispiece to Etchells's translation. Walker would have agreed with Hitchcock's explanation that it was "an inappropriate choice doubtless made by the publishers."[82]

Talbot Hamlin's critique of Le Corbusier's architecture, city planning, and interiors aligned him with traditionalists. In his review of *Towards a New Architecture* Hamlin was sympathetic to Le Corbusier's historical analyses but cautioned readers against a troubled side to his theory. Moreover, he rejected the "psychological perversity" of its underlying argument that clarity and beauty should be found in what he interpreted to be "designs of a fantastic and monotonous ugliness, towns of rectangular harshness, and interiors like the inside of an operating room." Beauty in such machine-inspired forms was not achieved by aesthetic determinism, he insisted, but by mere accident. There was also psychological perversity in Le Corbusier's tendency to elevate the world outside art and exploit its impact on art. Such dadaist and surrealist tendencies, of course, contributed to both its argument and its appeal to the avant-garde. Perhaps because of this, Hamlin found it "disturbing" that a book so "completely doctrinaire" should be so "persuasive."[83]

In his landmark series of 1930 for *Pencil Points,* "Design in Modern Architecture," John Harbeson added his voice to this now widespread debate between modernists and traditionalists.[84] Identifying Le Corbusier as the most influential leader of modern architecture, Harbeson endorsed the economical use of new materials and construction techniques in steel and reinforced concrete in such works as the Villa Stein, "designed in much the same spirit as a steamboat or a locomotive."[85] But like Hamlin, he took exception to Le Corbusier's notion of an aesthetic determinism based on the symbolic import of machinelike forms. He also identified a new form of commodification of modern architecture, criticizing Le Corbusier's Nestlé's chocolate pavilion of 1928 as an example of "poster architecture," an advertisement "in three dimensions."[86]

This schism within the discipline and profession of architecture in America claimed an official position at the annual convention of the AIA in 1930.[87] Although organizers wanted to find "common ground" between the camps, their profession was ineluctably divided.[88] George Howe, spokesperson for the modernists, presented a functionalist argument urging the use of "modern construction and modern materials to the full, for architectural expression as well as for practical ends."[89] To Howe, modernism was determined by "a new technique," the modern movement the result of a "common technique."[90] Speaking for the conservatives, C. Howard Walker, MIT professor and Boston architect, criticized modernists for their "cult of elimination of everything that is not strictly utilitarian."[91] Although Dean Everett Meeks of Yale University and Ralph Walker sought to reconcile the factions, they were critical of Le Corbusier's symbolic alliance of architecture and the machine. Meeks was explicit: "Le Corbusier, much admired by many students and critics of architecture, has developed the theory that we should take our architectural forms from the steamship, the motorcar and the aeroplane, as being true expressions of the modern age. The fallacy lies in his failing to recognize the fact that these favorite examples cited by him are true expressions of motion above all, and that the idea of motion is the very antithesis of the idea of architectural structure."[92] Like Hamlin and Harbeson, Meeks's and Walker's criticism of the machine metaphors were shared by some avant-gardists. During the early 1930s the debate continued to resonate in the architectural press.[93]

Factionalism Inside the Avant-Garde: European Modernism versus Technocratic Developments

Within the discourse on modernism in America, discord between two factions of the avant-garde caused a second debate on the role of the machine in architectural design. Once again, Le Corbusier's polemical book helped to define the two sides and shape their positions. The first viewed modernism as a received European tradition. It embraced the notion that modern architecture represented symbolic and idealist concerns, what William Jordy called "symbolic essence."[94] If the machine signified the modern era, then architecture should be expressive of that machine age. Such aphorisms as "the house is a machine for living in" defined Le Corbusier's ideal.[95] The second camp was identified with native technocratic and production-based developments. Emphasizing the real over the ideal, its proponents did not view architecture as a symbol of the machine but as the application of advanced technology. For this group Le Corbusier's theory and design served as an object lesson.

But progressive journals, such as *Architectural Record* and to a lesser extent *Architectural Forum,* supported an inclusive view of modernism devoid of factional politics. They promoted both European modernism and native technocratic developments. Indeed, from the late 1920s the editorial staff of *Record* engaged the two ideological camps within the avant-garde: the formalist concerned with style and the production-based concerned with functional design. Hitchcock represented the formalist position, and Robert L. Davison, Knud Lönberg-Holm, *New Republic* critic Douglas Haskell, and Theodore Larson supported technocratic interests; A. Lawrence Kocher supported both. At the same time that Kocher promoted European modernism, he established new editorial policies favoring rationalization and a new department of technical news and research that endorsed mass production methods, modern technics, and increasing architectural specializations.[96] Only the Philadelphia-based journal *Shelter* (formerly *T-Square*), as Marc Dessauce has shown, was critical of the privileged position of the "International Style."[97]

Avant-gardists on one side were committed to advancing the cause of European modernism in America. Its most ardent promoters were Henry-Russell Hitchcock and Philip Johnson. For them the stylistic and aesthetic elements of European modernism provided the template for American architects. Toward that objective they came to view Le Corbusier's ideas and forms in their various sites as rhetorical tools.

As critic, editor, and curator, Hitchcock was largely responsible for constructing the dominant view of modernism in America, based almost exclusively on his interpretation of the formalist canon of the European modern movement. He came to be identified as Le Corbusier's principal supporter in America. Hitchcock first read *Vers une architecture* before its appearance in translation, while he was working toward a master's degree in fine arts at Harvard University from 1925 to 1927. As graduate students, he recalled, "we had our own copies of one of the Paris issues, soon worn out by repeated reading."[98] In the spring of 1927 Hitchcock gave his first lectures at Wellesley College and "emphasized Corbu."[99] That year he singled out Le Corbusier together with Erich Mendelsohn, as a "modernist" or "aesthetically-conscious-contemporary-architect" in an essay "The Decline of Architecture" that formally launched his own career. He identified a "surrealist [which he later explained meant 'functionalist'] theory of contemporary architecture" to account for the then current "admiration for technical perfection."[100] His enthusiastic and premonitory review of *Towards a New Architecture* deemed it "the one great statement of the potentialities of an architecture of the future and a document of vital historical significance," notwithstanding its "broken style" and "irritating" frequency of "repetitions."[101] The book made Le Corbusier "the leader of contemporary architecture in Europe."[102] When Fiske Kimball attempted to project future developments in his *American Architecture* of 1928, yet omitted any reference to Le Corbusier, Hitchock and Douglas Haskell responded by counseling Kimball to consult *Towards a New Architecture,* which both reviewers considered the seminal book of the new era.[103]

A change in the editorial direction of *Architectural Record* around 1927 made it the most progressive journal of the period. Under the editorship of A. Lawrence Kocher (1885–1969), *Record* promoted European modernism and championed Le Corbusier's work.[104] In 1928, when Hitchcock became a contributing editor, he advanced his narrative of European modernism and his formalist position based on style. In a groundbreaking series of articles for the magazine that year and later in *Modern Architecture: Romanticism and Reintegration,* Hitchcock introduced Le Corbusier as one of the "new pioneers."[105] Thereafter *Record* regularly published Le Corbusier's work and helped popularize his writings. In soliciting the magazine's first article by Le Corbusier, Kocher expressed optimism about its reception. "In this land of standardized products and mass production," he wrote the author, "there should be a universal acceptance of your arguments." Kocher provided the title, "Architecture, the Expression of the Materials and Methods of Our Times."[106] In his reply to Kocher Le Corbusier suggested that he would advocate "the total re-formation of all construction since the founding of our architectural tradition."[107] On a less lofty plane his article would introduce American readers to such recent works as the Centrosoyuz, Plan Voisin, Villa Stein-de Monzie, and the Weissenhof housing.[108] Also writing in *Record,* Norman Rice praised Le Corbusier's efforts in low-cost standardized construction in his project for a Minimal House of 1928–1929 known as the Maison Loucheur.[109] Photographs of the Planeix House in Paris (1924–1928) also appeared in *Record*.[110]

The opposing faction within the avant-garde supporting technologically advanced and production-based design looked to well-established developments in art and architecture that engaged technocracy and mechanization, long acknowledged as powerful themes in American culture.[111] Rejecting the machine as a mere symbol in architecture, they embraced a productivist alliance between art and technology. Their supporters distanced themselves from Le Corbusier's rhetoric. For example, Haskell was cautious about the implications of *Towards a New Architecture*. He may have considered Le Corbusier's "ideas of a 'modern' architecture . . . profound." He may also have admired the theory that "calls men back to sound bases," to first principles. But he found Le Corbusier's "devotion to machine precision" decidedly suspect, counseling instead "a certain austerity."[112] In advancing production over symbolism, the real over the ideal, critics frequently cited Frank Lloyd Wright's work in opposition to Le Corbusier's theory and design. Even Lewis Mumford, who opposed mass production at the expense of social and economic concerns, championed Wright in this way. In *Sticks and Stones* (1924) Mumford mocked the notion of Le Corbusier's and Gropius's machine age metaphors, and applauded Wright's buildings because they "do not resemble either factories of garages or grain elevators."[113]

The year 1927 has been suggested as the high-water mark in the development of modernism in Europe and its importation to America (e.g., the year many European "form givers" produced important early works, including the Weissenhof Siedlung, and Le Corbusier submitted his design for the League of Nations competition).[114] Events during 1927 also suggested a movement toward native technocratic developments and American cultural independence (e.g., the date of Buckminster Fuller's Dymaxion House and publication of Charles and Mary Beard's *The Rise of American Civilization*). The American edition of *Towards a New Architecture* that year brought the issue of cultural independence to a head. Increasingly the technocratic faction of the avant-garde in America wanted to reclaim as their own images of a vernacular mechanization, which Europeans had previously appropriated as signs of modernity. The debate between an imported European modernism and native technocratic developments that embraced art, industry, and modernism was played out in a number of landmark exhibitions in New York City.[115] Many of the Architectural League of New York's exhibits were devoted to the theme of mechanization and modernity. Its popular "Allied Arts Exhibition" of 1927, for example, displayed the latest "expansion bolts" and "pavement-hoists." It attracted an astounding 150,000 visitors.[116]

The production-based assumptions of modernism, as well as those based on style, were first fully synthesized in the "Machine-Age Exposition" of 1927. It was organized by Jane Heap, coeditor with Margaret Anderson of the modernist journal *Little Review,* with European and American artists and architects on the advisory board. Supporting an inclusive view of modernism, the exhibition assembled a diverse collection of over 400 items from Europe and America: photographs and drawings of American skyscrapers, painting and sculpture by European modernists that linked the "machine and art," a Buffalo grain elevator, actual American industrial products—Crane plumbing valves, Curtis airplane parts, a Studebaker crankshaft—and their counterparts abroad. Images of German power plants, a Russian boiler, and a German Air Hansa plane appeared alongside buildings by Josef Hoffmann, Victor Bourgeois, André Lurçat, and Gropius.[117]

Organizers of the "Machine-Age Exposition" intended it to be an American counterpart to various exhibits of the Pavillon de l'Esprit Nouveau.[118] The images in and powerful rhetoric of Le Corbusier's articles in *L'Esprit Nouveau,* to which Jane Heap was an early subscriber, and in *Vers une architecture* helped shape the themes of the exhibit. Yet Le Corbusier's work did not appear because he and Pierre Jeanneret failed to respond to Heap's request for material and to "organize . . . a section for France," possibly because she could not provide remuneration.[119] At the exposition the technological assumptions of modernism met the artistic ones. In the architecture section critic Herbert Lippmann saw a forceful linkage between "mechanical radicalism" and "emotional purism."[120] Although uncredited, allusions to Le Corbusier's theory of design were effective in promoting the exhibition's discourse on modernism. In his catalogue essay, "Architecture Opens up Volume," Polish architect Szymon Syrkus made obvious allusions to Le Corbusier's book.[121] And Jane Heap's essay echoed Le Corbusier when she identified the engineer as "a great new race of men in America."[122] Essays by European architects and artists instructed Americans to follow their lead, ironically by finding inspiration in their own culture of the machine. Louis Lozowick, a Russian-born artist working in America, persuasively argued for "the Americanization of Art." He advised artists to consult the "intriguing novelty, the crude virility, the stupendous magnitude of the new American environment"; like Heap and Le Corbusier, he recognized that America had a history of "gigantic engineering feats and colossal mechanical construction." His art influenced by constructivism and his thought by Corbusian rhetoric, Lozowick found primal geometry beneath the surface chaos in America. The dominant impulse in the country was "towards order and organization," manifested in the "rigid geometry of the American city: in the verticals of its smokestacks, in the parallels of its car tracks, the squares of its streets, the cubes of its factories, the arc of its bridges, the cylinders of its gas tanks."[123]

The significance of Jane Heap's innovative exhibition should not be underestimated. In a narrow sense it influenced the Museum of Modern Art's "Machine Art" exhibition of 1934, curated by Philip Johnson.[124] More important, however, Heap and Lozowick used the 1927 exhibition to explore the sources of modern architecture and design in American mechanization as well as in such artistic movements as cubism, futurism, and constructivism. In so doing, they affirmed the roots of modernism in American industrial forms, and identified both the productivist intentions in the new architecture and design as well as their symbolic use of machine imagery. In these ways the "Machine-Age Exposition" and catalogue advanced the discourse on modernism and *américanisme,* and Le Corbusier's contributions to it.

It was Catherine Bauer, the housing expert and Mumford's kindred spirit, who brought Le Corbusier squarely into the American dialogue on modernism while assuming a critical position sympathetic to European developments. Bauer was among the first American critics to popularize such Le Corbusier aphorisms as "the house is a machine for living in" and to underscore the architect's debt to American technology. Like Heap and Lozowick, she believed that in spite of America's contributions to modernism, its architects were not yet enfranchised participants. She found this ironic. In her *New York Times* article of 1928 "Machine-Age Mansions for Ultra Moderns," Bauer called on Americans to reappropriate their own industrial forms. Under the spell of *Vers une architecture,* she shared Le Corbusier's contempt for their importation of "styles" and their reticence to develop a "twentieth century American style." Adopting Le Corbusier's paternalistic position, she maintained that modern French architects saw more clearly than their counterparts in the United States "the virtues of a brand-new architecture," derived from American engineering, skyscrapers, automobiles, and factories. Moreover, she regarded the aesthetic, rational, and symbolic premise for using steel and concrete in "Machine Age" houses as distinctly American. Notwithstanding the irony that European modernism was indebted to her country, Bauer shared with other Le Corbusier supporters in America the hope that its architects might learn from Europeans about the ways in which its domestic architecture could benefit from the directness and inventiveness of native technologies, building systems, and typologies. She agreed with French architects who maintained that Americans, having "invented and perfected" such technologies in their commercial work, ought now to adapt them in the domestic sphere. Thus, like European modernists, Heap, and Le Corbusier, Bauer may have recognized the significance of American technocratic and productivist developments, but her sympathies with European modernism led her to promote them through importation.[125]

By the early 1930s the Architectural League of New York had become associated as much with technocratic sympathies as with the academy. Consequently, it became the target of a counteroffensive.[126] In the spring of 1931 Philip Johnson, soon to become director of the Museum of Modern Art's Department of Architecture and a cocurator of its 1932 "Modern Architecture" exhibition, organized a group show of early modernists in America. He conceived the outsider exhibition, called "Rejected Architects," in protest to the League's fiftieth anniversary show whose organizers Raymond Hood and Harvey Wiley Corbett had accepted Howe and Lescaze's Philadelphia Saving Fund Society (PSFS; 1931) as well as Kocher and Frey's Aluminaire House, but excluded the models of a number of young modernists.[127] According to the exhibition brochure, the "rejected architects" in this emerging group all worked in the "International Style," a term that according to Terence Riley, "had some currency with Barr, Hitchcock and Johnson from 1928 onward."[128] Most of those "rejected architects" had in common their association with Le Corbusier, some as atelier assistants. Oscar Stonorov (of Stonorov and Morgan) who edited *Ihr gesamtes Werk von 1910–1929,* the 1930 German edition of the first volume of the complete works of Le Corbusier and Pierre Jeanneret, was represented by two recent houses.[129] Canadian Hazen Sise and German-born Elroy Webber, both of whom had worked in Le Corbusier's atelier in 1930, were also among the "rejected architects."[130] Henry-Russell Hitchcock signaled the importance of these associations when he forwarded to Le Corbusier a copy of the exhibition brochure inscribed, "your students and their colleagues attract attention in New York with their Salon des Refusés."[131]

Organizers and critics recognized that of the "four leaders" of modern architecture in Europe—Le Corbusier, J. J. P. Oud, Gropius, and Ludwig Mies van der Rohe—the influence of Le Corbusier dominated the "Rejected Architects" exhibition. Critics regarded the exhibition as prophetic because it launched the polemic that dominated the Museum of Modern Art exhibition the next year. Douglas Haskell's review emphasized nationalism and native technocratic concerns. To Haskell, the work of Clauss and Daub demonstrated that "Le Corbusier has captured these designer's [sic] imaginations," going so far as to suggest that they needed to "burst the bonds of foreign restraint" to "do justice either to

themselves or to science in American architecture."[132] Catherine Bauer found little social meaning there except in "a model of three houses for a housing development" by Alfred Clauss and George Daub that she ranked the "best thing in the show."[133] In effect, Haskell's and Bauer's criticisms sent a didactic message to architects. It counseled them to reject foreign influence and to turn instead to native developments in science, mass production, and rational design, and to social issues. During the 1930s the rising tide of nationalism and technocratic concerns, supported by such influential critics as Haskell, accounted for a resurgent interest in Frank Lloyd Wright and significant consequences for Le Corbusier.

The polemic both within and without the avant-garde gained momentum when Johnson joined forces with Hitchcock and Alfred Barr to produce "Modern Architecture: International Exhibition" for the Museum of Modern Art early in 1932. The exhibition advanced the museum's mission to promote European modernism. As Barr recalled, it "initiate[d] reform in American architecture by bringing before the public the finest European work which was, in 1930, from five to twenty-five years ahead of America."[134] Recognizing the importance of Le Corbusier's contributions, Hitchcock and Johnson exhibited drawings and photographs of his villas, the Weissenhof houses in Stuttgart, and the Swiss Pavilion at the Cité Universitaire in Paris. A model of the Villa Savoye (1928–1930), which the Modern had commissioned, was prominently displayed in the Le Corbusier section and later became an icon of the show (figure 1.12), accompanying the popular and well-publicized traveling exhibition.[135] In their catalogue *Modern Architecture: International Exhibition,* written in 1931 (with a section on housing by Mumford), and related book *The International Style: Architecture since 1922* (1932), Hitchcock and Johnson distinguished Le Corbusier from other practitioners of the "new style."[136]

Barr's foreword to the catalogue identified Le Corbusier as "perhaps the greatest theorist, the most erudite, and the boldest experimenter."[137] Johnson called him "more of an innovator than Oud," "more consistent than Gropius."[138] In their historical account, Hitchcock and Johnson regarded his Maison Citrohan (1920–

1.12
Installation view of the exhibition "Modern Architecture: International Exhibition," Museum of Modern Art, New York, February 10 through March 23, 1932. Photograph © 1999 The Museum of Modern Art, New York. Architectural works © Artists Rights Society (ARS), New York/ADAGP, Paris/FLC.

1922) as groundbreaking, calling it "as radical technically as Gropius' [Fagus] factory and as novel aesthetically as Oud's village." They admired in the Citrohan house model the "enormous window area and the terraces made possible by the use of ferroconcrete." They also endorsed the "asymmetry of the composition" that resulted in "a design more thoroughly infused with a new spirit, more completely freed from the conventions of the past than any thus far projected."[139] By contrast, in his essay on housing, Mumford made no mention of Le Corbusier's architecture, though he would see examples of it during a trip to Paris and a visit to Le Corbusier's atelier with Catherine Bauer later in 1932. In his essay he had eyes only for Oud's work in Rotterdam.[140]

By this time architecture critics had come to think of Le Corbusier in polemical terms. *New York Times* critic Henry Irving Brock called Le Corbusier the "archpropagandist" among "the hierarchs of the movement."[141] Harold Sterner, writing in the avant-garde journal *Hound and Horn,* called him the movement's "Romantic leader," as opposed to Mies van der Rohe, the movement's "classicist."[142] Fiske Kimball's and Catherine Bauer's reviews endorsed the exhibition as a consensus on style, identifying Le Corbusier's contributions to it. Like Mumford, these reviewers were partisans of Frank Lloyd Wright, seeking to establish his paternity to the modern movement. Kimball noted, for example, "the immediate spiritual ancestry" of the European school "in the work of a great pioneer in modernism, the American Frank Lloyd Wright."[143] And Wright used his own review of *Towards a New Architecture* to help secure that position. On the one hand, he agreed with Le Corbusier that effects of "surface" and "mass [volume]" were neglected in "our architecture," pointing to the "aeroplane, the ocean greyhounds, and to certain machinery" that expressed "in the simplest terms the nature of its necessity." On the other hand, Wright accused the "Frenchman" of making a fashion out of a persuasion in the minority in America (ironically, Wright's position in 1928). Using his review to further debate—Le Corbusier versus Wright, international versus national, intellectual abstraction versus pragmatism, and style versus necessity—he staked his own claim to modernism: "all Le Corbusier says or means was at home in architecture in America in the work of Louis Sullivan and myself—more than twenty-five years ago, is fully on record in both building and writing here and abroad."[144] Thus, the efforts of Kimball, Bauer, and Wright himself paralleled those of Heap, Lozowick, and others who regarded the use of industrial forms by Le Corbusier and the European modernists as a received *American* tradition in Europe.

But a more incisive backlash to the International Style came from the technocratic camp and specifically from a group of critics and practitioners who in 1932 employed the journal *Shelter* as their organ of dissent. Buckminster Fuller's criticism is especially noteworthy because it denigrated European modernism for its superficial reliance on style and symbol at the expense of process. At the same time Fuller also emphasized that European functionalism was a received tradition of American origin. The "Quasi Functional Style" of Gropius, Le Corbusier, Behrens, Mies van der Rohe, and Mendelsohn "has been codified in European Schools, such as the Bauhaus," Fuller maintained, "reinfiltrating itself into this country, from which it sprung, as an aesthetic, static, dogma—of its original economic science." "For this reason the International Mode must perish, being eclectic rather than scientific, science being the life blood of function." Fuller, in association with the technocratically inclined Structural Study Associates in New York City, offered instead "'Universal Conditions' of the industrially reproducable [sic] architecture."[145] In open competition with Le Corbusier, he claimed for his 4D house "the world's first tangible embodiment of what one French architect hopefully designated as a 'Machine-for-Living.'"[146] As Reyner Banham noted, Fuller's Dymaxion House of 1927 forcefully demonstrated the deployment of advanced technology, rather than mere metaphorical allusions to the machine that characterized Le Corbusier's villas of the late 1920s.[147]

If a formalist notion of style dominated the 1932 "Modern Architecture: International Exhibition," it did so inconsistently. Hitchcock and Johnson did not account for their inclusion of such Le Corbusier works as the de Mandrot House at Le Pradet near Toulon

(1929–1931; see figure 2.4) whose rubble wall, emphasizing mass rather than volume, did not adhere to a canon of the International Style. In their efforts to promote European modernism, as Johnson later conceded to his biographer Franz Schulze, their concept of an International Style had been "codified too hastily from Le Corbusier's theories as interpreted by Hitchcock."[148] Indeed, there was little evidence in the exhibition literature of more than a superficial understanding of those theories. Although initially receiving only 33,000 visitors during its run at the Modern in New York, the exhibition eventually acquired a vast public audience.[149] For the next twenty months a version of it traveled around the country to over a dozen cities including Chicago (Sears, Roebuck and Company), Los Angeles (Bullock's Wilshire), and Cambridge (Fogg Art Museum), helping popularize the International Style, as did their book by that name.[150]

Rational Planning Opposes Social Concerns

The third debate within the discourse on American architecture opposed rational planning to social concerns, themes encountered in the first two debates. Here Le Corbusier's urbanism and the housing he proposed for it were associated with rational planning (not to be confused with the technocratic position in favor of rationalized methods of building production). The success of the Museum of Modern Art's exhibition that showcased Le Corbusier's work so effectively helped to gain support for his architecture among American critics.[151] Such was not the case with his ideas on city planning, which were far more controversial. Nearly a decade earlier, for example, *JAIA* critic Irving Pond was skeptical of the "mechanistic, cubistic, ultra-modernistic" character of Le Corbusier's Ville Contemporaine, but assured his readers that such cities would "never develop beyond the paper stage."[152]

By 1929 the appearance of *The City of Tomorrow and Its Planning*, the American edition of *Urbanisme*, and the numerous reviews it generated in newspapers and professional journals helped acquaint the public further with the urban vision Le Corbusier had developed in both the Ville Contemporaine and Plan Voisin.[153] Despite

Pond's early skepticism, critics predisposed to Le Corbusier's architecture recognized the intensity of his urbanism. Published at the crest of interest in the machine age and during a time of increasing attention to the visionary schemes of Hugh Ferriss, Harvey Wiley Corbett, and Raymond Hood, Le Corbusier's proposals, in comparison, advanced a comprehensive approach to rational planning. One critic emphasized his thesis to standardize cities, "to Fordize them."[154] In a 1930 article on *The City of Tomorrow* for his series in *Pencil Points*, Harbeson applauded Le Corbusier's residential system of "freehold maisonettes." He cited their rational design and construction, their standardization, their communal services and cooperative financing, all of which distinguished this mass housing as a "modern achievement." But Harbeson was decidedly less certain about the sixty-story cruciform towers of Le Corbusier's business district, which promoted a comfortable if "monotonous" office environment.[155] However, it was still Le Corbusier's call for "order" in the modern city, and particularly the American one, that won Harbeson's general endorsement.[156] Another critic noted Le Corbusier's approach to the centralized city as "a process of redistribution upwards instead of outwards" and as a method for increased circulation of traffic.[157] Hitchcock's review of *The City of Tomorrow* summarized the position of Le Corbusier's supporters that his proposals were not merely Utopian and that, to his credit, he recognized the problem of the city to be a multidimensional one.[158]

By contrast, American housing reformers and social planners criticized the functional, structural, and managerial constituents of Le Corbusier's urban designs. If the Depression gave greater currency to modern over tradition, it made urban reformers exceptionally cautious about Le Corbusier's visionary plans. In 1930 housing expert Henry Wright opposed the Ville Contemporaine because it called for changes in infrastructure and for redistribution of land that required an immediate "revolution of our entire ideas of city building and land ownership."[159] Lawrence Veiller, prominent American urban reformer and editor of *Housing*, took a combative position. With sharp words for Le Corbusier's account of his "City of the Future," published in a London newspaper, he despaired, "If that is the kind of city that we are to live in . . . give us the chloroform now!"[160]

On the eve of the "Modern Architecture: International Exhibition," Le Corbusier launched a direct attack on the chaotic American city. In an article solicited by the *New York Times,* "A Noted Architect Dissects Our Cities," he ridiculed the architecture and planning of New York and Chicago as "mighty storms, tornadoes, cataclysms . . . so utterly devoid of harmony."[161] One reviewer responded to such condemnation, calling the article "a diatribe" and his plans "Utopian."[162] The curators of the exhibition chose to steer clear of Le Corbusier's planning projects, with no illustrations of them in either the exhibition or the catalogue.[163] Even Mumford was uncharacteristically circumspect when he remarked that Le Corbusier's *The City of Tomorrow* was "mainly theoretical," but "full of suggestions" (for he did endorse its functional planning).[164] Mumford deferred his barbed criticism until 1935 when he reviewed Le Corbusier's exhibition at the Modern.

Americans Respond to Le Corbusier's Paintings

By late 1933 the traveling version of the exhibition secured for Le Corbusier a place in architecture as "one of the first . . . one of the most famous, of the 'moderns'."[165] But critics were reluctant to endorse his painting. The two books on painting that he wrote with Amédée Ozenfant, *Après le cubisme* (1918) and *La Peinture moderne,* still had no English or American editions.[166] Le Corbusier did not receive his first solo art exhibition in America until the fall of 1933 when the John Becker Gallery in New York City presented his paintings, watercolors, and drawings. Hitchcock provided a sympathetic catalogue essay.[167] American critics considered his paintings spirited and "decorative" but largely derivative. *New York Times* critic Edward Alden Jewell found his "abstractions" full of "references and cross-references to fellow-artists" Léger, Miró, and Picasso.[168] Le Corbusier's purist painting "may be overwhelmingly 'intellectual'," Jewell advised his readers, "but somehow the impact is softened for people of average intelligence by a sense of humor, a sense of color and a genuine sense of de-

sign."[169] *New York Sun* critic Henry McBride appreciated its "bold" character, noting that Le Corbusier himself was incapable of "being timid in any form of aesthetic expression."[170] (Le Corbusier later turned that judgment to his advantage by declaring Americans "timid.") But McBride called the canvases "unorganized" and "too slavishly enchained to the designs by Léger which inspired them." If critics were cautious or negative, American art collectors, both at home and abroad, showed little immediate interest in purchasing his paintings.[171]

Four Initiatives Launch Le Corbusier's American Lecture Tour

Le Corbusier's fame, the controversy over the Esprit Nouveau pavilion and his entry for the Palace of the League of Nations, the critical attention given his work, the publication of *Towards a New Architecture* and *The City of Tomorrow,* and the appearance of his first article in an American journal, sparked a group of modernists in New York City to invite him to the United States. From 1929 to 1935 these partisans made four initiatives to organize an American lecture tour for him.

In November 1929, only weeks after the American stock market crash, the Architectural League of New York, with Raymond Hood as its president and through its liaison with a French organization sponsoring artistic exchanges, invited Le Corbusier to participate in the annual League show the next March and to give a series of lectures. The League suggested a fee of between $2,000 and $3,000.[172] At the time Le Corbusier was in the midst of a lecture tour to South America. The League's invitation evidently reached him there, for he received generous letters of introduction from Robert Woods Bliss, then United States ambassador to Brazil, announcing the architect's imminent visit to the United States.[173] But Le Corbusier did not respond immediately to the League's offer. Instead, he was preoccupied with his trip to Buenos Aires, Montevideo, São Paulo, and Rio de Janeiro, followed by embarkation for Europe in December aboard the ocean liner *Lutétia.*[174] Returning to Paris in January, he finally accepted the League's invitation to exhibit his work (with no mention of lectures), stipulating the higher figure of $3,000. He expressed his intention "to transact some business there (office buildings or rental property or some elegantly beautiful country house)" and a desire to have his plans and diorama for the Cité Mondiale (World City) for Geneva make an American tour, at least to New York, Washington, and Chicago.[175] He even informed his New York publisher, Joseph Brewer, of the proposed visit and his plans for a "book on American architecture" after his trip.[176] But he sent his letter of acceptance too late for the League to consider it. In conveying his regrets, Hood was full of adulation ("I have always been a great admirer") and expressed "a very great personal interest to try to arrange to meet you."[177]

Obviously encouraged by Le Corbusier's enthusiasm, Hood and Kocher, together with a French organization for artistic exchanges, coordinated a second initiative from January to October 1930. They continued to pursue with their colleagues in other cities the possibilities of organizing a lecture series during the winter of 1930–1931, but actual sponsorship, either by the League or now by Columbia University, was undetermined.[178] In setting conditions for the prospective tour, Le Corbusier wanted his sponsors to match the generous honoraria paid for his 1929 lectures in Brazil. He inflated the terms of the original League offer, proposing not only a fee of $3,000 for the New York City lectures but also a sum of $500 to $600 for each lecture in other cities, plus travel expenses.[179] During these negotiations Le Corbusier looked forward to the prospect of finding work in America. In accepting the League's second invitation in the fall of 1930, he intended to address his lectures to professionals as well as students and "to the general public (in particular on issues of large urban projects)," as he wished his trip to have "a practical echo: the construction of something interesting." Moreover, he directed the League's liaison in France to make "two soundings" about potential work in America.[180] The first was with Irwin S. Chanin, a New York building contractor whom he had met in Paris in 1929.[181] The second was with Melville M. Easterday, who had sought Le Corbusier's services in 1929 for a forty-two-story office building for the Oklahoma State Athletic Club in Oklahoma City.[182] Understandably, given the financial

constraints of the period following the Wall Street crash, the trip proposed for 1931 never materialized because the League, Columbia University, and a committee hoping to sponsor the lectures could not secure the necessary funds. Early that year Kocher conveyed the committee's decision to Le Corbusier, expressing regret that "American architects had not yet understood the importance of your visit," all the more because increasing numbers of them would be sympathetic to his lectures on "the new architecture." Still, Kocher looked forward to an eventual visit.[183]

As the result of greater public interest in modernism through the architecture exhibitions and increasing debate among factions of the avant-garde about his theory and design, Le Corbusier finally made his long-awaited journey to America in the fall of 1935. This trip resulted from efforts on different fronts, including a failed third initiative in the fall of 1933. Joseph Hudnut (1886–1968), who led Columbia's School of Architecture from 1933 to 1935, sought to promote the modern movement in America. His considerable backing proved essential in making Le Corbusier's tour a reality. Publication of Le Corbusier's work in *Record,* through the efforts of Kocher and Hitchcock, and the influence of colleagues from Switzerland also helped. Finally, the Museum of Modern Art, under the direction of Alfred Barr and Philip Goodwin, had a major interest in promoting modern architecture, if not specifically Le Corbusier's career. Notwithstanding its early interest in the architect, however, the AIA had no direct involvement in these efforts. Le Corbusier's tour was not sponsored by the professional community, but rather by avant-garde practitioners, critics, academics, the Modern, and other groups committed to advancing European modernism in America.

Undiscouraged by the unrealistic conditions of Le Corbusier's counteroffers of 1930, Hudnut launched the third attempt in November of 1933 to pursue the possibility of his visit, jointly sponsored by Columbia's School of Architecture and the Museum of Modern Art.[184] For American schools of architecture, the visit was timely. During the early 1930s architectural education was undergoing a dramatic transition from the

Beaux-Arts system to a curriculum based on the theory and design associated with the modern movement. In his capacity as dean, first at Columbia and later at Harvard's Graduate School of Architecture, Hudnut was the prime mover in shaping the curriculum to include courses on "the science of construction," with electives in "economic and intellectual currents," as well as in encouraging foreign architects to accept teaching posts and give guest lectures.[185] Earlier, as acting dean at Columbia, Hudnut offered his counterparts in other institutions a plan for bringing three "distinguished European architects" on an extended lecture tour of America during the fall of 1934. They would choose from a list of six: Oud, Gropius, Mendelsohn, Ivar Tengbom (from Sweden), Le Corbusier, and André Lurçat.[186] Even Hudnut had reservations about his new role as impresario: "I feel very much like Barnum with his collection of curiosities. I have the job of selling tickets and of providing tents throughout the country for their performance," he confided to George Harold Edgell, dean of Harvard's School of Architecture.[187] But in spite of his considerable efforts, including a pilot project in the spring of 1934 to invite Oud (for a modest honorarium of $200 per lecture plus expenses), Hudnut's plan was never realized.[188]

A fourth initiative, independent of the League's earlier endeavors and Hudnut's more recent efforts, involved Le Corbusier's Swiss connections in America. Two friends encouraged Le Corbusier to pursue his proposed visit: Swiss architect Albert Frey (1903–1998) and Swiss-educated American curator of prints and drawings Carl Schniewind (1900–1957). Frey, recipient of a Swiss diploma in architecture, worked in Le Corbusier's atelier in 1928–1929.[189] On immigrating to the United States in 1930, he became an associate of Kocher in New York. Renewing his association with Le Corbusier early in 1931, just after Kocher notified Le Corbusier that funds for the tour were not available, Frey sent words of encouragement. First, he cast Kocher and himself as Le Corbusier's followers in America. Reporting on their plans to construct a house for the annual exhibition of the Architectural League of New York in the spring of 1931, later known as the Aluminaire, "A House for Contemporary Life," Frey proclaimed it based

on "your principles as a foundation for our time."[190] Then he tempted Le Corbusier with the advantages of New York City: magnificent views at the top of skyscrapers, air quality like the Mediterranean, a new bridge [the George Washington] spanning 1,500 meters, and parkways. "America," he concluded, "offers hope."[191] During the summer and fall of 1934 Frey encouraged his friend: "I am convinced that one day the United States will ask for men like you."[192] Thereafter, Le Corbusier continued to pursue with Frey his fervent interest in coming to America, asking for assistance in organizing the trip. Never modest, Le Corbusier pressed his case to Frey: "I truly have things to say in America." But he still haggled over fees, insisting that "as the dollar is no longer worth much, it is necessary to get many more than were formerly offered to me." Because "I have repeatedly played Peter the Hermit [Pierre l'Hermite]," he warned Frey, "I end up having holes in my pockets and at a certain point that becomes unpleasant."[193] Notwithstanding the monetary disorder in France during the post-crash period from 1929 to 1934, the value of the French franc increased as the dollar declined in foreign exchange markets; the declining dollar deflated Le Corbusier's expectations for a profitable American lecture tour.[194]

The second participant in the Swiss connection, Carl Schniewind, was born in America but educated at the universities of Zurich and Bern and later worked in Bern for Le Corbusier's friend, art dealer Auguste Klipstein.[195] In that capacity Schniewind traveled frequently to Paris during the late 1920s and early 1930s where he purchased drawings and watercolors from Le Corbusier. He also traveled intermittently to America. Le Corbusier respected Schniewind's knowledge of prints and drawings, and Schniewind, in turn, appreciated Le Corbusier's art. As a result the two formed a close friendship during the early 1930s, Carl and his Swiss wife, Hedwig (Hedi), visiting Le Corbusier's apartment on the rue Nungesser et Coli (figure 1.13). But toward the end of 1934 Schniewind returned home in search of a museum position.[196] Le Corbusier's American lecture tour began to take its final shape when, out of friendship and even before he had secured work for himself, Schniewind assumed the role of Le Corbusier's "manager," coordinating

1.13
Carl and Hedi (Hedwig)
Schniewind with Pinceau at
Le Corbusier's apartment, rue
Nungesser et Coli, 1934. (FLC
LI(7)1-399.) © 2001 Artists
Rights Society (ARS), New
York/ADAGP, Paris/FLC.

the efforts of Kocher, Hudnut, and representatives of the Museum of Modern Art.[197] Kocher supplied Schniewind with a list of institutions that had invited Gropius (who could not come) that year. Hudnut all but promised a lecture series at Columbia, and James Johnson (John) Sweeney, curator of painting at the Museum of Modern Art, thought that he could guarantee a series of lectures in Chicago where he had been a curator at the Art Institute. Hudnut proposed sympathetic conditions: first-class passage on a luxury liner, travel and living expenses, plus an honorarium of $75 to $100 per lecture or $250 to $300 for a series of three. Wary of the low lecture fees proposed by the schools, Schniewind promised his friend that he would try his best to make these Americans "*cracher de* [sic] *dollars*" (spit dollars), but warned him that such institutions were "very poor now" and advised Le Corbusier to make concessions. On the basis of these negotiations, Schniewind proposed a lecture series.[198] Tentatively scheduled for March and April but later postponed, it originally included such distant cities as San Francisco and New Orleans. During the winter and spring of 1935 Schniewind served as Le Corbusier's liaison with the Modern. On Kocher's advice, he also negotiated directly with institutions requesting lectures. By March seven American universities—Columbia, Cornell, University of Minnesota, Yale, Harvard, MIT, and Princeton—and an unidentified institution in Mexico City were signed on.[199]

But Schniewind's most strategic and vexing task was to negotiate with his friend. Remuneration for the lectures as well as the timing and duration of the tour were thorny issues. Le Corbusier felt "humiliated" by the "minuscule" American offer in relation to sums he claimed were three and four times as large for his lectures in South America and Algeria. He argued that it was "a question of standing and I cannot accept the honoraria of a little man who goes about from city to city on a little tour to speak . . . on Chopin." Rather, he insisted, "I bring constructive ideas that may be useful to your country, especially in city planning and in the industrialization of the building trade. That is worth something."[200] But Schniewind warned of financial restrictions now governing such institutions and added, "they cannot change them even if the Pope were to speak to them."[201] Schniewind had met recently with a group of sponsors, including Columbia professor Jan Ruhtenberg, Leon Solon (new president of the Architectural League of New York), and Kocher, to discuss finances and other aspects of the trip. Consequently, he urged Le Corbusier to consider as his principal objective the useful contacts he would make. Although there were "rich patrons," he cautioned, "the fine days of prosperity are over here."[202] Le Corbusier was won over to Schniewind's point of view, conceding that "for me the essential thing is to see the U.S.A., being paid for the out-of-pocket expenses of the trip, and to leave large honoraria for another occasion."[203] By May, Schniewind had attempted to secure an "important" dealer and gallery for Le Corbusier to exhibit his paintings, and he had begun to publicize the tour, both through James Johnson Sweeney. Indeed, it was Schniewind's understanding of the arrangement that he brokered between the museum and Le Corbusier that was the source of considerable future discord. "You could say," he wrote, "that you are invited by the Museum of Modern Art and by the country's principal universities."[204] Schniewind continued to negotiate directly with the institutions until the Modern officially assumed sponsorship of the lecture tour, assigned a staff assistant to it, and promised a deficit reserve, all through the newly formed Department of Architecture and its chairman, Philip Goodwin (1885–1958; figure 1.14). "With this under our feet," Schniewind wrote jubilantly, "we can proceed to skate!" That month the tour was advanced to the fall to tap university budgets for the new fiscal year.[205]

After a period of delay over uncertainties in scheduling the visit due to his participation in the 1937 Exposition Internationale "Arts et Techniques" in Paris, Le Corbusier definitively committed himself to the American trip, but still thought that he could limit the swelling itinerary.[206] In the hope that the French government might provide free passage or a reduced ticket to America as "propaganda" for the Paris exhibition, Philip Goodwin wrote to Georges Huismans, *directeur général des Beaux-Arts* and a Le Corbusier supporter.[207] Le Corbusier's similar request to Huismans set higher

1.14
Philip Lippincott Goodwin.
(Photograph courtesy of Henry
Sage Goodwin.)

expectations. He suggested that a first-class cabin be upgraded to a "luxury cabin . . . separated from other passengers, and situated on an [outside] deck," similar to his accommodations aboard the *Lutétia* returning from South America in 1929.[208] Yet even these arrangements were thrown into question by a sudden request for a lecture series in Buenos Aires, where Le Corbusier at first planned to go (by zeppelin) before traveling to New York but later postponed in response to opposition from the Modern.[209]

By July Goodwin had taken over from Schniewind most of the tour management. An ever-expanding version of the itinerary indicating the possibility of as many as thirty-six lectures was forwarded to Le Corbusier (appendix A). Goodwin also made arrangements for an autumn exhibition of Le Corbusier's work including plans, models, and photographs.[210] Meanwhile, Robert Jacobs, who had worked in Le Corbusier's atelier the previous winter, enthusiastically agreed to accompany Le Corbusier on the American tour and serve as translator for his lectures.[211]

When Le Corbusier returned from his summer travels to receive from Schniewind a version of the Modern's itinerary that included venues in the Pacific Northwest and extended into the next year (so that the tour would not incur a large deficit), he determined that the organizers had gone too far (see appendix A).[212] In response to such an "unacceptable peregrination," Le Corbusier informed the Modern once again of his decision to curtail the tour at the beginning of December due to his responsibilities for the 1937 Paris exhibition. He insisted that he had "no taste" for countless lectures: "My desire is to be useful for something by speaking to certain circles of authority and I have the intention to limit myself exclusively to New York and its satellites Chicago, San Francisco, Los Angeles, and Mexico"—a somewhat warped perspective of New York City![213] To Schniewind, he stated the motive of his trip more candidly. These cities, he insisted, are "sufficient for the work that I want to do there and the ideas that I have to bring there." He further directed Schniewind to get in touch with Irwin Chanin in the hope that there might be some prospective work for him. Cautious about the indifference of American collectors to his painting, Le Corbusier abandoned the idea of an exhibition with dealer Marie Harriman because he did not wish "to mix ideas of such different character, in which one might bring prejudice to the other." He conceded, "the hour of painting has not yet struck for me."[214]

Why did Le Corbusier agree to come to America during the low ebb of the Depression? Evidence suggests motives linked to professional expectations and personal finances. He was driven to undertake such a tour by his lack of work in Europe. The collapse of capitalism that occurred in the late 1920s and early 1930s in Germany, France, and elsewhere precluded any large buildings, no less the adoption of his ideal cities. Notwithstanding his Centrosoyuz commission, Le Corbusier's encounters with Soviet communism and Italian fascism did not provide him with the stream of important works he sought. Thus his decision was prompted more by the pessimism he encountered in Europe than by any tangible prospects of commissions in America. At the beginning of 1935 he wrote to Schniewind: "I believe that the time would be favorable enough for this far-reaching undertaking. Business conditions at present are gloomy. One is not able to unfreeze capital. As a result I shall soon have some free time."[215] Since 1913 he had set his prospects on America. Again in 1929 and 1930 he hoped that the United States would provide him with clients for an office building or a country house. By 1935, as a result of encouragement from Hitchcock, Kocher, Hood, Hudnut, Frey, and Schniewind, as well as from the Modern and other sponsoring institutions, he experienced rising expectations that he hoped would be met with commissions from "certain circles of authority." At the very least, based on his experiences in Paris, he expected to acquire a number of wealthy and influential clients among the American avant-garde.

Yet, placed in an international context, the trip was mistimed. From 1926 to 1932, as Isabelle Gournay determined, France encouraged engineers to travel to America to learn about its technology.[216] These efforts toward international exchange coincided with America's first initiatives to Le Corbusier. However, after 1932 French engineers responded to American isolationism and stopped coming. Thus when Le Corbusier set out he did so in a climate that discouraged such exchange. Like so many of his enterprises, therefore, his American tour worked against the prevailing order of things.

Departure for America

On October 16 the 48-year-old Le Corbusier set sail from Le Havre aboard the French luxury liner *Normandie.* He traveled first class with a diverse assembly of European royalty, diplomats, industrialists, musicians, and artists.[217] Beaux-Arts architect Whitney Warren, whom the French popular press called "un grand ami de la France," was on board. "The Architect Le Corbusier" appeared on the passenger list of notables, but the only lasting friend he made among his fellow shipmates was André Jaoul, a French steel and chemical company executive.[218] In comparison with his return from South America in 1929 on the *Lutétia* in the company of Josephine Baker (where he appeared at a costume ball masquerading as the American singer, complete with dark make-up and a corset of feathers), this voyage must have been dull and disappointing.[219] Americans in first class were passengers of real social standing, rather than theater people like Baker. Most were not proponents of modernism. Some must have regarded Le Corbusier as an amusing curiosity, others with contempt. It is not surprising, therefore, that he failed to form friendships with these shipmates.

During the crossing Le Corbusier made some efforts to learn strategic English words that might prove useful for both the lecture tour and his personal relations abroad. Although he had studied English for three years in secondary school and made a brief trip to London in 1909, he seems to have known little of the language. Marguerite Harris later insisted that he "spoke not one word of English," although his interpreter Robert Jacobs thought that "he understood plenty."[220] During the leisurely days of the crossing Le Corbusier was taught English probably by American surrealist painter Abraham Rattner, as the lists of English words and expressions with their inept French translations written on S.S. *Normandie* stationery appear to be in Rattner's hand.

These reveal the architect's range of preoccupations with both the serious and the frivolous. Such phrases as "inside street not exposed to rain, snow, or sun," "link or connect," and "100%–per cent," showed his attempts to learn enough English to convey his ideas on city planning. By contrast, his vocabulary lists identify American (or English equivalents to French) colloquialisms of the 1930s, among them "o gee you're swell" and "you're a lousy dope." Le Corbusier's efforts to learn English also demonstrated his preoccupation with social pastimes, leisure, recreation, women, and cocktail chat. The lists include words and expressions that reflect his obsessions of the moment or anticipate what he might need in the coming months: "swimming pool" and "sunbathing," "entertain" and "people who bore me," as well as "shoulders," "breast," "figure," "drunk," and "cockeye" (figure 1.15). Among the more stylish English expressions was the pre-*Casablanca* toast, "here's looking at you," annotating the doodled image of a 1930s cocktail glass cum exclamation point.[221] The relaxed socializing during the transatlantic passage would stand in sharp contrast to the arduous days of the lecture tour ahead.

The debate between modernists and the academy, between factions of the avant-garde, between internationalism and nationalism, between the intellectual and the pragmatic, and between rationalism and social meaning set the tone for Le Corbusier's encounter with America. He would be his own propagandist. Language barriers notwithstanding, he would communicate most effectively through his presence, his forceful personality, and his powerful visual imagery. But his vision and polemical methods would encourage a transatlantic misunderstanding with America, fueled by the disparity between his personal expectations and his disappointment in securing no immediate work. His ambivalence toward America in general and New York City in particular resulted in a distinctive strategy for promoting his ideas. Armed with his preconceptions and these objectives, Le Corbusier began his American campaign.

1.15
English lessons aboard the S.S. *Normandie,* October 1935. (FLC Archive U3(18)142.) © 2001 Artists Rights Society (ARS), New York/ADAGP, Paris/FLC.

A la votre –
cheery-o (anglais)
Here's looking at you
parasseux [sic] – lazy
besoin – need
désire [sic] – desire
wisdom – sagesse
wise
cockeye – louche

**Part I
Public Performance**

2

Le Corbusier Takes New York

On October 21, 1935, Le Corbusier arrived in New York with high expectations. His travel account of America, *Quand les cathédrales étaient blanches: Voyage au pays des timides,* recorded his initial impressions. In two contrasting episodes he experienced both the strengths and weaknesses of Manhattan's architectural and cultural landscape: first, from the ship where he saw through the mist a visionary city, a "temple of the New World"; second, from up close where he encountered the human consequences of urban planning that had produced only chaos. Le Corbusier constructed these polar views to serve his plans for promoting a Radiant City in America. It filled him with hope. "Coming from France at the flat end of 1935," he remembered, "I had confidence."[1]

During the course of his American lecture tour, and especially in New York City, Le Corbusier had his first experience of modern culture. Influenced by the literature of *américanisme,* he shared with other European intellectuals the myth that America was authentically modern. Le Corbusier would lead a double life there. His professional obligations consumed most of his time and diverted him from New York. But his passions drew him back to discover modern life in the city with the young American writer Marguerite Tjader Harris (1901–1986).[2] She revealed to him the mysteries of the Amer-

ican metropolis, and together they explored New York and its environs by car as machine age *flâneurs.* Le Corbusier's experiences with her provided both an empirical confirmation of his preconceptions and the basis for his American synthesis at the same time that they affirmed his own creativity. But his official duties and professional agenda took precedence.

Le Corbusier looked forward to his lecture tour (see appendix A) and to the planned exhibition of his work, both sponsored by the Museum of Modern Art. There was also a traveling exhibit that circulated until 1938 (appendix B), press conferences and a radio broadcast, newspaper and journal articles, meetings with editors to negotiate an American edition of *La Ville radieuse* (*The Radiant City*), and meetings with public officials and potential clients. But the architect and the Modern were operating at cross purposes. Encouraged by the efforts of Schniewind, Frey, and others, Le Corbusier had come in search of commissions. The museum wanted to sponsor this "French genius," as Philip Goodwin once called him, to further the cause of modern architecture in America, but it did not necessarily seek to advance his career as an architect (notwithstanding its later assertions to the contrary).[3] Moreover, even though the museum was willing to incur a small deficit, it had no interest in running up large debts underwriting a lecture tour.[4] But Le Corbusier regarded the Modern as an agent of the Rockefeller Foundation and, despite the warnings of Schniewind and others to the contrary, assumed that both the museum's resources and his prospects were unlimited.[5] Highly skilled at self-promotion, he expected the organization to support his personal objectives.

Le Corbusier's preconceptions affected his encounter with American cities, American society, and American capitalism. It also shaped expectations about how Americans ought to receive him, his relationship with the Modern, his attitude toward the press, and his prospects with potential clients. His triumphant lecture tour of South America in 1929 had fed his rising expectations about North America. Throughout his travels in Brazil, Argentina, and Uruguay he had been treated as an emissary of French culture and given an ambassadorial reception. On his return home aboard the *Lutétia* he had a cabin suite at his disposal where he displayed the colorful drawings with which he illustrated his lectures and prepared notes both for a presentation aboard ship and for eventual publication as the book *Précisions sur un état présent de l'architecture et de l'urbanisme* (1930).[6] If South America had responded with such enthusiasm to him and extended an invitation to return, how much more receptive the affluent and technologically advanced Yankees might be!

His hopes for a similar reception in the United States were emblematic of his general expectations. Even though he professed indifference toward personal publicity, and notwithstanding his disdain for such organs of consumer waste as newspapers, advertising, and pictorial supplements designed, he said, "to take up time," in reality he welcomed self-promotion.[7] Robert Jacobs, his interpreter, experienced this firsthand. The young Jacobs had gone to some length through Howard S. Cullman, a commissioner of the Port of New York Authority and his wife's uncle, to meet Le Corbusier aboard the *Normandie* at daybreak on October 21. At the very least, the visiting architect expected the American press to accord him the same treatment given to celebrities on arrival, and assumed that they would take pictures of him against the iconic skyline of Manhattan. Jacobs recalled,

"I met him [while at Quarantine] . . . And the first thing he said was . . . 'Jacobs, *où sont les photographes?*' So, I took him up to the top deck and one of the photographers was posing a group of *vedettes* . . . chorus girls sitting on the rail with the skyline behind." Jacobs attempted to give one press photographer five dollars to take Le Corbusier's picture but was told, "I've used up all my film." Still, Jacobs appealed to him, "snap the empty camera, I've got to live with this guy for two months." Jacobs remembered how "Corbu ceremoniously [posed]. . . . So I got this picture taken and every morning for two months he'd . . . scan the newspaper [and say], 'Jacobs, *où est mon* [sic] *photo?*'"[8] This awkward, if amusing, episode set a precedent for future relations with the American press.

Le Corbusier's expectations also shaped his first declarations in America. "At two o'clock I disembarked from the ship" and "at four o'clock reporters had gathered at the Museum of Modern Art," then located in a six-story town house at 11 West 53rd Street, which it had leased from John D. Rockefeller, Jr., and refurbished as its headquarters a few years earlier.[9] In contrast to his effort aboard the *Normandie* to engage the photographers, at the Modern he shunned having his picture taken. There, according to Geoffrey Hellman's witty "Profile" in the *New Yorker,* Le Corbusier offered to American newsmen French studio photographs of himself at five dollars each! An embarrassed publicity director at the Modern responded, "My God, you can't do that to the *New York Times.*"[10] At the museum's press conference several days before the opening of Le Corbusier's exhibition, Jacobs experienced some difficulty translating for the architect. Joseph Alsop (1910–1989), the celebrated but controversial reporter of the *New York Herald Tribune,* who "spoke beautiful French, came to my rescue."[11] There Le Corbusier offered a paradoxical opinion that made headlines in a *Herald Tribune* story attributed to Alsop (figure 2.1).

Finds American Skyscrapers "Much Too Small"
Skyscrapers Not Big Enough,
Says Le Corbusier at First Sight . . .
Thinks They Should Be Huge and a Lot Farther
    Apart.[12]

Finds American Skyscrapers 'Much Too Small'

Herald Tribune photo—Acme

Charles Edouard Le Corbusier, the famous French architect, with a model of his Villa Savoye, which he recently designed

Skyscrapers Not Big Enough, Says LeCorbusier at First Sight

French Architect, Here to Preach His Vision of 'Town of Happy Light,' Thinks They Should Be Huge and a Lot Farther Apart

2.1
"Finds American Skyscrapers 'Much Too Small,'" *New York Herald Tribune,* October 22, 1935, p. 21. (FLC Archive B2(16)195, © Artists Rights Society (ARS), New York/ADAGP, Paris/FLC.) Acme Newspictures, Inc. ©1935 The Washington Post. Reprinted with permission.

"My questioners," Le Corbusier wrote, "were speechless! *Tant pis!*"[13] In his characteristically provocative manner, he used paradox and hyperbole to make a self-serving point. He explained his ideal for Manhattan as a *Ville Radieuse,* ineptly translated in the *Herald Tribune* story as a "Town of Happy Light." The "Radiant City" would contain "great obelisks, far apart, so that the city would have space and light and air and order."[14] Later he identified them as Cartesian skyscrapers of steel and glass. But his initial statement that American skyscrapers were "too small" was irresistibly quotable and too aphoristic to elude a headline. Alsop, then a determined young reporter, unfairly sensationalized Le Corbusier's remarks.[15] His article accompanied a news agency photograph of the architect appearing walleyed next to his model of the Villa Savoye, which the museum had had in its collection since the 1932 "Modern Architecture: International Exhibition" (figure 2.2). Le Corbusier later complained that the news photographer's flashbulb produced a caricatured picture.[16] Alsop's less than sympathetic description of the man was calculated to evoke the stereotype of an exotic and peculiar European intellectual. The columnist described "Fernand Léger's strange, mechanistic paintings," on display in the Modern's current exhibition as "an appropriate setting for M. Le Corbusier, whose eggshaped head and face, bisected by a pair of thick spectacles with a heavy black frame, make him look like an up-to-date prophet. He was wearing an orange shirt, a black necktie with red spots and a gray suit. He complained of a headache, but he was able to talk volubly."[17] Indeed, Le Corbusier offered himself to Alsop as a prototypical "egghead," a term Alsop is given credit for coining, that took on invidious associations denoting "a person of spurious intellectual pretensions."[18]

Le Corbusier later explained that his opening comments to the American press were delivered when he was "in a mood for joking." He insisted that he had not intended his remarks to be as controversial as they were considered to be. But such pranks suggest an inclination toward self-destruction that countered his tendency to be arrogant. In pragmatic terms they served to undermine his self-promotion. Of course, his comments on New York were based on preconceptions more than actual experience. Moreover, the pronouncements were reported with the kind of exaggeration and oversimplification that tainted much American journalism in the 1930s. The resulting tempest marked the first of several transatlantic confrontations between the architect and his hosts. The image conveyed by the press reinforced American impressions of Le Corbusier as a visionary architect and also encouraged skepticism of such a controversial guest. For the rest of the tour the public image of the man as an egghead frustrated his dialogue with America.

Le Corbusier's lofty expectations about his reception fueled further American resistance. His encounter with museum officials that first day resulted in a dispute about lodgings, which led to an ongoing feud about the financial arrangements of the tour and his arduous travel itinerary (see appendix A). The Modern had booked a room at the French Institute in New York, but Le Corbusier insisted on a deluxe hotel. "*Je m'en fiche de l'Institut Français,*" he was reported to say, "*Je vais au Waldorf.*"[19] After much wrangling he finally settled for the Park Central Hotel on Seventh Avenue at 56th Street because his close friend Léger was staying there during his own exhibition at the museum.[20] An otherwise banal hotel, the Park Central became infamous in 1928 as the place where gangster Arnold Rothstein was shot to death.[21] Throughout his stay Le Corbusier delighted in branding it the *hôtel des gangsters.*[22]

The Exhibition at the Modern

The Museum of Modern Art officially launched Le Corbusier's tour on October 24 with a preview of the exhibition of his "recent work" in its first-floor galleries. It was not only Le Corbusier's first architectural exhibition in America, but also the Modern's first show devoted to the work of a single European architect.[23] Consisting principally of photographs, it also featured plans, models, and furniture. It was organized by the Department of Architecture and an impressive committee of modernists. Chaired by Philip Goodwin, the committee was composed of Henry-Russell Hitchcock, who wrote a

2.2

News agency photograph of Le
Corbusier beside the model of the
Villa Savoye at the Museum of
Modern Art, New York, 1935.
(Acme Newspictures, Inc.; Library
of Congress, Prints and Photo-
graphs Division, NYWT&S Collec-
tion.) © 2001 Artists Rights
Society (ARS), New York/ADAGP,
Paris/FLC.

short essay for the exhibition catalogue; Philip Johnson, who founded the Department of Architecture in 1932; Alfred H. Barr, Jr., the director; George Howe; and Joseph Hudnut.[24] Ernestine Fantl, a former student of Barr's at Wellesley College now serving as Johnson's secretary (whose salary he paid himself), assisted in the organization, as did Robert Jacobs.[25] The exhibition had a brief run in New York (October 24–November 2, 1935) before a version of it traveled the country.

Committee members shared responsibility for shaping the exhibition. In Paris the previous summer Philip Goodwin had visited Le Corbusier at his atelier and together they made an initial selection of works to be shown. Although much material was then on exhibit in Brussels and other parts of Europe, most of it was

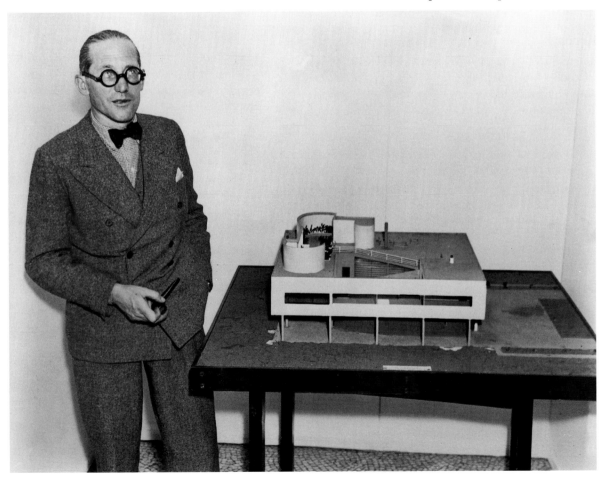

available. Sixty photographs, drawn from the preliminary selection, were shipped to New York in July.[26] Goodwin especially requested the model of the Palais des Soviets.[27] The remaining material formed a general retrospective.

The next month Philip Johnson took it upon himself to conceptualize the exhibition to Fantl. Johnson first met Le Corbusier during his visit to Paris with Hitchcock in the summer of 1930. In the company of Alfred and Marga Barr they visited European sites in preparation for their book *The International Style: Architecture since 1922*. In a letter to his mother Johnson was candid about his opinion of Le Corbusier: "an objectionable man but unquestionably a genius. I would not live in any of his houses but they are certainly exciting to see."[28] Now in anticipation of the forthcoming Le Corbusier exhibition Johnson wrote to Fantl a perceptive, witty, and astonishingly frank letter attuned to the architect's strengths and weaknesses. The letter was pitched in a distinctively supercilious tone remarkable for a young man not yet thirty, even if he had established his reputation as a precocious curator at the Museum of Modern Art.

> Townsend Farm
> New London, Ohio
>
> Aug 15 [1935]
>
> Dear Ernestine,
> How courageous to do L. C. He is almost as difficile as our dear late [sic] lamented F.Ll.W. How much is he having to do with the proposed one man show? His ideas of exhibition are very obscurantist; something like friend Kiesler's Space Theater material. It would seem better to me to have the show approach dullness than unintelligibility.
>
> ∴ (being a sign for summing up) I should recommend, subject to your better knowledge of the material available, that you have *very* large photos of executed work. There is a great deal of new material since '32. It is all in that book Giedion sent me. It is in the library. "L-C depuis 1929" [*Oeuvre complète 1929–1934*]. You could make the key to the show the Internationalism of his work (God help me for

a hypocrite) South American house, France, Swiss, Germany, Algiers, Centrosoyus, Moscow etc. Beware L-C's models. Badly constructed + dirty especially Cité de Refuge. Put his boat in [Asile Flottant de l'Armée de Salut, 1929],[29] it is excellent. As for his Urbanisme it is the bunk as you [k]now. A model of Algiers would of course be inspiring as nonsensical imagination.

> Another angle on the show might be historical. How many people saw his Pavillion [sic] de l'Esprit Nouveau at the '25 Exposition?? Russell didn't. Get early pages of Machine Art out of Esprit Nouveau + blow them way up. How old modern really is 1922 etc. L. C. as the great innovator. Then in small, pictures of houses under the influence of the master, in Italy, Spain, America (the [Donald] Deskey House [for Richard] Mandel) etc.[30]
>
> Another "yangle": Le Corbusier the variety of genius within the strict bounds of style. The wood house [Errázuriz House] in South Am,[31] the first Citroyen [sic] house, the de Mandrot House, the Poissy house.
>
> But I certainly would have a key to the show + stress photos of accomplished houses. Avoid projects. They smell, among American architects. Show them we can compete with the A.I.A. on their own country house level. Don't let your social sense or conscience interfere.
>
> I shall probably be down next month + should simply love to start figuring with you in it.
>
> I pity your arranging L. C. itinerary. Do keep me in touch.
>
> The farm is marvelous, if it weren't for my three nephews who will never leave me in peace. Modern children are worse than guppies or dogs to take care of.
>
> Nice + cool out here. Wish you could come for a visit.
>
> My best to the B-A's. [Alfred and Marga Barr].[32]
> Yours..
> Philip[33]

The most revealing aspects of Johnson's letter demonstrate his attempt to shape Le Corbusier's exhibition according to his own formalist bias and with particular reference to his two previous museum installations, "Modern Architecture: International Exhibition" (1932) and "Machine Art" (1934). Toward that objective Johnson encouraged an emphasis on "internationalism" and "machine art," and yet also a historical perspective on modernism since 1922 to show how influential "the great innovator" had been in both the Americas and Europe. Johnson also advanced "style" at the expense of urban and social concerns. But his suggestion to exhibit four Le Corbusier houses—the Errázuriz ("wood house in South Am"), Citrohan, de Mandrot, and Poissy—to show "the variety of genius within the strict bounds of style" revealed the idiosyncrasies of his formalism. For he may well have considered the stone and timber-frame Errázuriz House project in Chile (1930; figure 2.3) an example of the International Style, as he did the de Mandrot House at Le Pradet near Toulon (1929–1931; figure 2.4), which he included in the 1932 exhibition in spite of its stone rubble wall. However, these two examples departed from many of the aesthetic principles he and Hitchcock assigned to the International Style, especially

2.4
Le Corbusier, de Mandrot House, Le Pradet, near Toulon, France, 1929–1931. (FLC L2(19)16.) © 2001 Artists Rights Society (ARS), New York/ADAGP, Paris/FLC.

"architecture as volume."[34] Moreover, Johnson's emphasis on Le Corbusier's "accomplished houses" promoted his idea of an international alliance of modernists with elite clients to show American architects that "we [modernists] can compete with the A.I.A. on their own country house level."

Aside from the contributions of Goodwin and Johnson, those of Robert Jacobs helped significantly to shape Le Corbusier's exhibition. Having only recently returned from Le Corbusier's atelier, Jacobs was especially familiar with the most recent buildings and projects such as the Weekend House (Petite Maison de Weekend or Villa Félix) at La Celle-Saint-Cloud (1935). He also knew what exhibition material was available. Influenced by his mentor, Jacobs held views that contrasted sharply with Johnson's rhetorical position. For example, Jacobs considered Le Corbusier's "ideas on urbanism almost

2.3
Le Corbusier, Errázuriz House in Chile (unbuilt), 1930. (*Oeuvre complète 1929–1934*, p. 51. Plan FLC 8981.) © 2001 Artists Rights Society (ARS), New York/ADAGP, Paris/FLC.

more important than those on architecture."[35] On the eve of Le Corbusier's arrival he requested on behalf of the Modern the models and plans of the Cité de Refuge (Salvation Army Building), the Rentenanstalt, an insurance company building in Zurich (1933), the Algiers project, and the project for *La Ferme* (Radiant Farm). Of these, Le Corbusier obliged with models of both the Rentenanstalt (in metal) and the town of Nemours in Algeria (1934), the latter a substitute for the Algiers model, which was not available.[36]

Le Corbusier's exhibition at the Modern opened with his lecture at 8:45 P.M. followed by a preview. A formal invitation was sent to all 1,200 members (figure 2.5).[37] The exhibition featured photographs and models of twenty-two buildings and projects. Together they illustrated the development of his design ideas from 1916 to 1935, from the plan of an early house (most likely the Villa Schwob) at La Chaux-de-Fonds, Switzerland, to a photograph of the Weekend House that appeared on the cover of the exhibition catalogue (figure 2.6).[38] In deference to Le Corbusier's use of polychromy in his buildings, the walls of the exhibition room were reported to have been painted "Corbusier pink."[39] Unfortunately, no photographic record of the installation survives.

This survey of Le Corbusier's recent work, like his writings of the 1930s, revealed an evolution in his approach to architecture and planning. During the 1920s he effectively forged an alliance between classicism and mechanization to promote architecture expressive of the machine age. As Francesco Passanti has shown, he employed the vernacular in the 1920s as a "conceptual model for a natural relationship between society and its artifacts," seeking connections between architecture and the "rational and abstract organization of industry and its products."[40] But his concept of the vernacular changed from the 1920s to the 1930s. As Mary McLeod demonstrated, Le Corbusier's political engagement during the 1930s with regional syndicalism (a movement that embraced technocratic ideas but tempered them through local and regional considerations as well as so-called natural hierarchies) caused him to turn away from the culture of capitalism invested in the promise of the machine.[41] Now environmental and sociopolitical factors

The President and the Trustees of

the Museum of Modern Art, 11 West

53rd Street, New York, invite you

to attend an illustrated lecture by

Le Corbusier

and the opening of an exhibition of

his recent work on Thursday evening,

October the twenty-fourth, at eight

forty-five o'clock

Please reply to the Museum

Admission will be by card only

2.5
Invitation to Le Corbusier's first lecture and the opening of his exhibition at the Museum of Modern Art. (Courtesy of the Rockefeller Archive Center.)

2.6
Cover of exhibition cata-
logue *Le Corbusier*, De-
partment of Architecture
and Design, Museum
of Modern Art, New
York, 1935. Photograph
©1999 The Museum of
Modern Art, New York.
Architectural work ©
Artists Rights Society
(ARS), New York/ADAGP,
Paris/FLC.

Le Corbusier

Villa in eastern outskirts of Paris, 1935

Exhibition arranged by the Department of

Architecture of The Museum of Modern Art

principally informed his work; Le Corbusier sought meaning in architecture through an affective relationship between society and building techniques, through collective identity and the real more than the ideal. If the machine was central to his theory and design in the 1920s, man was central in the 1930s. Hitchcock recognized this shift of paradigms. In his catalogue essay he noted that the new work made "free use of curves," responded to the "influence of various natural settings," and incorporated both "traditional materials," and "forms of the past."[42] These were among the regional, vernacular, and earthbound elements that informed the Errázuriz House (see figure 2.3), the de Mandrot House (see figure 2.4), and the Swiss Building (Pavillon Suisse) at the Cité Universitaire in Paris (1930–1931; see figure 3.16), photographs of which appeared in the exhibition.[43]

Failing to distinguish, as Hitchcock had done, between the machine age forms that dominated Le Corbusier's early works and these new references, a *New York Times* reviewer chose instead to emphasize his "extensive use of glass," "buildings mounted on stilts," and "open interior construction."[44] To the still uninitiated, Le Corbusier's architectural models dramatized these earlier innovations. His model of the Villa Savoye, made famous in the "Modern Architecture: International Exhibition" of 1932 (see figure 1.12), and the metal model of the Rentenanstalt demonstrated his modern concerns.[45] A model of the Palace of the Soviets (1931–1932; see figure 3.15), later to become a source of prolonged dispute between the architect and museum officials, was described as "comprehensive." The *New York Times* article commented on the building's program, the large capacity of its auditoria, as well as its structural innovations, including a roof "hung by steel cables from overhead girders" and "a gigantic steel and concrete arch." Notwithstanding Johnson's reservations, a model of the project for Nemours, with its standardized apartment slabs each accommodating 2,000 persons, introduced Americans to Le Corbusier's urban design and mass housing (figure 2.7). The Beistegui Apartment in Paris, shown in a photograph, was probably the work that best described what the reviewer called Le Corbusier's use of "fantasy."[46]

2.7
Model, Le Corbusier project for the town of Nemours, Algeria, 1934. (*Le Corbusier 1910–65*, ed. Boesiger and Girsberger, p. 330. FLC L1(1)104.) © 2001 Artists Rights Society (ARS), New York/ADAGP, Paris/FLC.

In addition to buildings and projects, the exhibition included three pieces of furniture: a chair, a table, and a *chaise-longue* or reclining chair, all from the Wadsworth Atheneum.[47] They had recently been installed in the Avery Memorial, the Wadsworth's newly completed modern wing by architects Morris and O'Connor.[48] The chair was probably the *siège à dossier basculant* or pivoting chair. For his office in the new Avery wing, A. Everett "Chick" Austin, Jr., the Wadsworth's flamboyant director, had himself purchased both the *chaise-longue* and *siège à dossier basculant* in 1933 (figure 2.8).[49] But the table in the exhibition was not by Le Corbusier. No wonder he was coy about its authorship. The furniture, Fantl noted in her letter to Austin, "pleases everybody but the Maestro himself who seems surprised to find that he designed them."[50] For the furniture to arrive at the Modern in time for the critics' preview, Austin personally delivered it by car. Endlessly witty, Austin told Fantl that it was "a pleasure to have a few legs for company on the ride."[51] The *chaise-longue* received the most attention. Its reclining form, Le Corbusier instructed the press, was inspired "by lounging cowboys with their feet on tables, whom he had seen in American motion pictures."[52] In fact, both the *chaise-longue,* whose framework consisted of metal bicycle tubing, and the *siège à dossier basculant* were designed by Le Corbusier in collaboration with Charlotte Perriand and his partner Pierre Jeanneret, although the collaborators were not credited in the exhibition.[53]

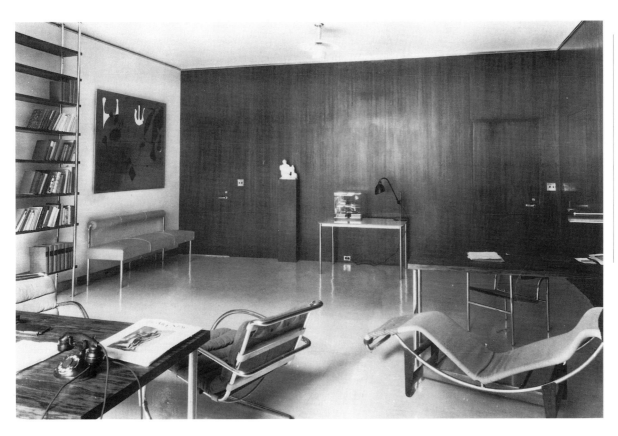

2.8
Director's Office with *chaise-longue* (reclining chair) and *siège à dossier basculant* (pivoting chair behind table to the right), Avery Memorial, Wadsworth Atheneum, 1934. (Wadsworth Atheneum, Hartford.) Furniture by the Le Corbusier atelier © Artists Rights Society (ARS), New York/ADAGP, Paris/FLC.

Encounters and Engagements

At his opening and lecture Le Corbusier met representatives of six groups that the museum considered its audience. In a confidential report of 1933 the Modern identified the constituency that would come to serve Le Corbusier as well. Each of the six groups had its own vested interests and sphere of influence:

1. The avant-garde and intellectuals. Called "the 400," this circle consisted of "a small but powerful minority of professionals and amateurs, critics, collectors, scholars, dealers, who know about modern art and have a passionate interest in it."

2. The socially prominent, known simply as the "social group," comprised the "majority of the members of the Museum [a select club in 1933] and their friends, people who are interested in modern art, are socially inclined, and, in general, earn over $5,000 a year. The group hovers between trying to understand modern art and accepting it as fashionable. From the standpoint of money and interest it is the most important group. In the giving of both it is fickle."

3. Businessmen and industrialists. The Modern designated this sector as the "action group." It was "composed of business people who want to 'do something' about what they see. They are the people who build gasoline stations in the international style . . . to win them over would change the aspect of the entire nation. They have not accepted the proposition that good art is good business but are not absolutely opposed to the idea." Le Corbusier directed his *appel* for work to this constituency.

4. Students.

5. The professional community of architects.

6. The public and the popular press. The museum recognized that its public was "chiefly inspired by a desire to 'know what it [modern art] is all about'—part curiosity, part a vague desire for 'culture.'"[54]

And so Le Corbusier spent the evening of his inaugural lecture and exhibition opening being lionized by the avant-garde and intellectuals, courted by students and young architects, considered a curiosity by businessmen and industrialists, and tolerated by the socially prominent. Because of his need to cultivate prospective clients, his interest in these circles was primarily professional. His sentimental focus was elsewhere.

Far away from his wife, Yvonne, Le Corbusier felt free to engage in romantic involvements outside his marriage that he could not in Paris. He was eager to keep an appointment with the American writer he had met at home in Vevey, who had offered to be his guide in New York. In 1932 Marguerite Tjader Harris had come to Switzerland with her three-year-old son Hilary (figure 2.9). Two years before she had published *Borealis,* a first novel infused with spiritualism, which received little critical notice or enthusiasm.[55] She had recently left a loveless marriage to Overton Harris, a "handsome Southerner" whom she married in 1925 in a fashionable Manhattan wedding, and who was a member of her own social circle.[56] During the early years of their marriage Overton Harris became a successful New York attorney, and later an outspoken and controversial judge magistrate.[57] But their marriage soon shattered. Escaping from her martinet husband on the one hand and her puritanical mother on the other, Marguerite sought Alpine adventure in Blonay-sur-Vevey, where she would come to know Le Corbusier's mother, Marie Jeanneret. Marguerite's Swedish-born father was a successful inventor as well as an ardent evangelist, author, explorer, and sportsman.[58] His death in 1916 deeply affected her. From the father she idolized Marguerite inherited Nordic looks and athleticism. By temperament she was free-spirited, and like him she reveled in skiing and mountain climbing, sailing and swimming. But it was her mother's wealth that provided Marguerite the means to escape to the promise of a new life in Switzerland.

In her unpublished "Portrait of Le Corbusier," Marguerite recalled how she had boldly introduced herself to Madame Jeanneret at Le Lac, the villa he designed for his parents on the shores of Lac Leman (figure 2.10).

In 1932, while living near Vevey, I had felt an odd attraction to this place. Passing the high, cement wall that shielded the low rectangle from the highway, I had often wondered whether it was a dwelling or a boat-house, parallel to the lake. The wall turned

in to form a hidden garden. Was there a beach or rocks on the other side? . . . one day, my curiosity got the better of me. I rang the bell at the garden gate. A small elderly woman with curly, white hair, and wearing African slippers, came gently toward me. Immediately, I felt ashamed of disturbing her. "Is this place, by any chance, for rent?" I faltered. "O [sic] no, Madame, my son built this house for me!" I excused myself, by pleading admiration for the house. "Would you like to see it?" she asked proudly, and opened the gate.[59]

This encounter was the start of Marguerite's lifelong friendship not only with the warm and musically inclined Marie Jeanneret (and her English terrier Nora) but also with her two sons Albert, the mother's favorite, and Edouard. On a visit to the *petite maison* in early March 1932 she met the architect. Indeed, by the second day of that meeting Le Corbusier had reason to regard Mar-

guerite as a client, similar to his American ones in Paris. Marguerite recalled that occasion when they "drove along the green-blue vineyards climbing up from the lake; I said, almost as a subject of conversation, that I wished I could have a house like his mother's along the embankment, or here on these terraces. Immediately, he took me seriously—the idea interested him: To create a house—two steps between the vineyards—If it were possible to buy enough land. *There,* just below the road, or *here*—above it. We continued far along the *Corniche* under *La Crochettaz,* and he promised to think about the project and to return soon." By mid-March he communicated to her the results of his site studies showing that the "land is completely suitable." In April he sent sketch plans of the villa to her in care of his mother and advised her to acquire the land (figure 2.11). But the project was never executed.[60] Although Marguerite returned to America with the intention of making arrangements to live in Switzerland and to secure funds for the house, she

2.10

Madame Jeanneret and Marguerite Tjader Harris by the *petite maison,* Lac Leman, Switzerland, 1934. (Harris family papers.) Architectural work © Artists Rights Society (ARS), New York/ ADAGP, Paris/FLC.

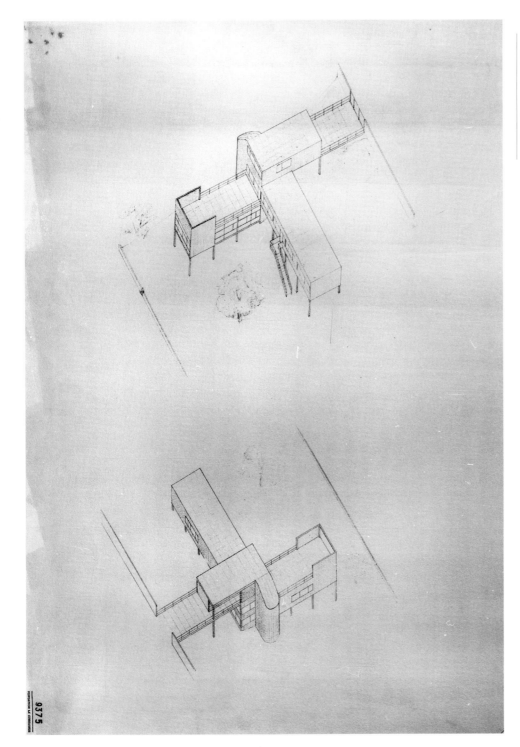

2.11
Le Corbusier, house
project for Marguerite
Tjader Harris, 1932,
axonometric drawing.
(FLC 9375.) © 2001
Artists Rights Society
(ARS), New
York/ADAGP,
Paris/FLC.

was forced to confront the reality of her family's dwindling financial resources, to secure her divorce in 1933, and to wait out the lean years of the Depression at home. It was not until she returned to Vevey during the summer of 1934 that she learned from Le Corbusier of his upcoming trip to America and responded with a practical offer to serve as his chauffeur and interpreter. But the extent of her involvement with him during his American lecture tour was more than she could have anticipated.[61]

By the fall of 1935 she was a 34-year-old divorced mother living in Darien, Connecticut, and was free to show her visitor the town. Their first Saturday together (October 26) marked Le Corbusier's early encounter with New York City and his polar responses to it. "He was like a horse," Marguerite recalled, "fretting against the bridles of his many activities, impatient, eager to see more of this mad city on his own, its suburbs, it[s] transportation. Already, he was trying to formulate some plan of urbanism that could bring order into the confusion he saw." She recorded their excursions "up into the towers of several different sky-scrapers, to study the surrounding terrain." She remembered how they "ducked into subways and rode down to Wall Street, and then up to Harlem. Everywhere, the contrasts appalled him. You could feel how his brain registered every impression, visual and audible; one minute, he was enthusiastic, the next, disgusted with what he saw of our city, our way of behaving on the streets, the quickness of pedestrians, the rush, the nervous, strained faces in the subway—or the indifferent, the crushed,—the gross—all the human condition of our big city."[62]

Their perambulations took them to the tops of the RCA, Empire State, and Chrysler towers, not to observe the buildings themselves, their structure, or cubist imagery, but to use them as lookout sites from which to study the morphology of the city.[63] Of the three, Le Corbusier liked best the observation deck of the RCA building. He surveyed a city of contrasting spectacles, of Wall Street and Harlem, of human achievement and human cost that confirmed his preconceptions. Rockefeller Center held special significance for him. Given his expectations for designing a fragment of his Radiant City on the island of Manhattan, if not then a building complex or a single skyscraper, Rockefeller Center was dramatic evidence that a large but unified group of buildings could be judiciously inserted into the existing urban fabric of the great city.[64]

In the coming weeks Marguerite introduced him to the popular culture of New York and to the complexity of American life in the breadth of its dimensions. She showed him Manhattan by night, downtown to Broadway theaters and burlesque houses, and uptown to jazz and dance clubs. She thus enabled Le Corbusier to experience the realities of the modern American city with its richness and diversity. Through these excursions she revealed to him the culture of America—the built landscape of New York City, the state of the American woman, African-American as well as white popular culture—all of which enabled him to form his own synthesis about the country. Le Corbusier connected with the real, as well as the ideal, in the culture that not only confirmed his preconceptions but also supported his advocacy of social change in America as a precondition for implementing his Radiant City thesis.

Later their first day together, Marguerite brought Le Corbusier to Darien, where she was living in a large late-Victorian house with her evangelical mother and six-year-old son Hilary. For years the Tjaders had rented a cabin on nearby Pratt's Island that they called their "South-Sea Island style" hideaway, "the shack" (figure 2.12).[65] Le Corbusier and Marguerite referred to it affectionately as *la baraque* or sometimes *la cabane*. Its association with the sun and sea, the primitive, the remote, and the romantic served their needs. This simple cabin resonated later in another context when Le Corbusier installed for Yvonne and himself a *petit cabanon* and *baraque* annexed to it on the Mediterranean coast at Cap Martin.[66]

Athletic and free-spirited, Marguerite enjoyed sailing and swimming (figure 2.13). Unseasonably mild weather that October kept the water warm. She recalled how Le Corbusier indulged in his favorite pastime, taking his first *bain de mer* off the waters of Long Island Sound: "he removed his glasses and dove into it as though it were his natural element."[67] He became fascinated with the violet-blue color of beach mussels and

2.12
"The shack" [la baraque], Pratt's Island, Long Island Sound. (Private collection.)

2.13
Marguerite Tjader Harris sailing, Long Island Sound, 1920s. (Private collection.)

made a sketch, *Four Women on the Rocks,* as the basis for a painting and several gouaches.[68] That weekend was also the first of many trysts in the city and at the shore that allowed Le Corbusier to gratify his need for sun and sea, exploration and relaxation, and an adoring and sensual woman.

Their relationship was also significant for Marguerite. In the fall of 1935 she had recently broken off—for the second time—her affair with Theodore Dreiser. She had first met the writer socially in 1928 and worked for him in New York until the end of 1929 when she gave birth to her son Hilary. By then she was torn between her failed marriage and her attraction to Dreiser, who had encouraged her to write *Borealis.* In her biography *Theodore Dreiser: A New Dimension* she described the social realist as a "rebel in thought and feeling . . . [who] had never been a clear thinker," particularly in his relations with women. While separated but still married to a wife in the Midwest, Dreiser carried on an enduring romance in New York with his cousin Helen Richardson. Marguerite felt that she "had no part in his complicated life." With her young son, she established residence in Switzerland intending to obtain a divorce and "start my life over again."[69]

During a three-year separation from Dreiser she began work on another novel, avidly pursued mountain climbing, and met the Jeannerets. In the summer of 1932 and for part of the next year, however, she was "blocked in Connecticut," unable to secure financing for the planned villa in Vevey, yet successful in obtaining her divorce. She left again for Switzerland in the winter of 1933 and was back in Connecticut that summer for what she thought would be a brief visit. But Dreiser waylaid her. "For the second time, he had brought me to a realization that I was a parasite, doing nothing but amuse myself." The confrontation made "an indelible impression" and Dreiser convinced her to work for him. During the next year she served as his literary companion, what she called his literary secretary. To be close to him she took a room near the Ansonia Hotel where he and Helen resided. But by the winter of 1934 Hilary, who was being cared for by his grandmother and a nurse, developed pneumonia. Consumed with guilt for neglecting her child, Marguerite decided to leave Dreiser "for good."[70] During the summer of 1934 she returned to Vevey where she took photographs of the *petite maison* (see figure 2.10) and learned from Le Corbusier of his forthcoming trip to America.[71] By then the transatlantic Marguerite would be back in Connecticut and at his disposal.

Marguerite served as Le Corbusier's mooring in the United States. At the wheel of her 1935 Ford, a little tan-colored V-8, with young Hilary in the rumble seat, she piloted them all around New York City and its distant suburbs.[72] Le Corbusier was at one with the machine and his new family. Marguerite remembered how in awe he was of the George Washington and Brooklyn bridges, the civil engineering of American parkways, then under construction, and "the civic determination behind these efforts to resolve the *crisis* of the automobile." He was impressed with "our very efficient highway net-works, which far surpass anything that European countries have been able to organize," and showed "great enthusiasm for our traffic systems," which he knew from earlier studies.[73] Their excursions led the architect to draw his own conclusions about the modern city that confirmed his vision of a Radiant City. Marguerite wrote that "when we drove over the Pulaski Skyway, that road suspended on bridges and ramps, for twenty miles over the New Jersey swamps, his respect for our achievements turned into real joy. Here was a true *solution* for an enormous problem."[74] Le Corbusier had his own vivid memories of passing "through the Holland Tunnel to the other side of the Hudson and over the Skyway, an elevated road so named because it rises on piles [*pilotis*] or arches high above industrial areas, arms of the sea, railways and roads, over an immense expanse." It was a "road without art because no thought was given to it, but a wonderful tool. The 'Skyway' rises up over the plain and leads to the 'skyscrapers.' Coming from the flat meadows of New Jersey, suddenly it reveals the City of the Incredible Towers."[75] In effect, the Pulaski Skyway and the Manhattan skyscrapers together, as with so many other aspects of American urban form, provided Le Corbusier with an empirical model for his Radiant City and an assumption that his visionary ideas could be adapted to New York. By contrast, however, when Marguerite steered them through the "endless housing developments" of Astoria, Jamaica, and the garden suburbs of Long Island and Connecticut, which he called *cités-jardins,* the architect understood the inadequacy of American planning.[76] This experience affirmed for him the correctness of his Radiant City thesis.

New York City, like its European counterparts, was the domain of the avant-garde because it was here that the artist could be at once loner, outlaw, and prophet. Like Charles Baudelaire in search of modern man, Le Corbusier searched for his own artistic identity in the streets of the great city.[77] But his was a view from above as well as below, and also from without the metropolis as well as from within. For to be modern in the city was to be nomadic, and to be nomadic was to be American. Marguerite was the perfect guide for this exploration. Her transatlantic heritage and persuasion, her liberated status as a woman outside the marital structure that either supported or oppressed women in the 1930s, branded her as truly nomadic, truly American. As urban nomads in the "automobile age," Le Corbusier and Marguerite sought out modernity and aesthetic experience in the flux of the city's mass culture as well as in the infrastructure of the regional city. But Le Corbusier's role as a *flâneur* lacked authenticity because, unlike Adolf Loos who could identify personally with the essence of mass culture in the American city, he could only do so selectively.[78] His experience was more as a voyeur than as a consumer. Moreover, he presented himself as a purveyor of high culture in a land too "timid" to import it. As Marshall Berman showed, Le Corbusier's quest for modernity in the twentieth century allowed him to jettison the nineteenth-century street with all of its human paradox and chaos in favor of the posthumanist highway.[79]

As important as Marguerite's services were as chauffeur, guide, and interpreter, she offered far more than an introduction to the United States. The week after their first days together not only set the brisk pace of Le Corbusier's lectures but also, by consequence, determined the windows of his engagement with Marguerite. On Monday (October 28) he lectured at Columbia University, Tuesday at Wesleyan, and Wednesday at Yale. On

Thursday, the last day of the month, he would visit the Port of New York Authority with Jacobs and Howard Cullman in the morning and the "slums," as he called them, with officials of the New York City Housing Authority in the afternoon. That evening he would dine with Nelson Aldrich Rockefeller (1908–1979), second son of John D. Rockefeller, Jr. (1876–1960), and architect Wallace K. Harrison (1895–1981). But after dinner was reserved for Marguerite. In two letters, both written on Park Central Hotel stationery Thursday morning, Le Corbusier apprised her of his plans. Now using the more intimate salutation "Amie" and signature "v[otre] Ami Corbu," he sent the first to her home in Darien. He informed her that he was back in town, that he had missed her telephone call the previous evening, and, anticipating a busy schedule ahead, would send "this word in haste to let you know the moments of freedom to be wisely employed."[80] The second letter was simply left for her at the hotel in an envelope addressed to "Mrs. Harris," on which was also noted his room number "#2033." Here he tabulated his schedule for her. He would be *libre* that Thursday from 11:30 P.M. until Friday noon, when he would board the train for Vassar College, and again on Saturday from 4:30 P.M. until Monday noon. A sinuous line drawn in red crayon punctuated the free time on his agenda and suggested the steamy possibilities that lay ahead. This was not a love letter or even an invitation to his hotel room.[81] It was a direct summons, Le Corbusier signaling Marguerite when she would be needed and expected.

This pattern of engagement continued in the country as it did in town. On weekends they savored the late fall sun at the shack. Evenings, according to Marguerite, Le Corbusier would sit by the fire in the living room in Darien, poring through the collection of illustrated books in the library. Marguerite's was a surrogate family: her son Toutou (Hilary), her elderly mother Margaret, "who reminded him of his own remarkable mother," and their dog Booby who was like his own schnauzer Pinceau ("Paintbrush"; see figure 1.13). The comforts of home, hearth, and companionship were there.[82]

Between lectures and appointments and travels to them, Le Corbusier planned their rendezvous. Although they saw each other primarily in Connecticut on the weekends, Marguerite drove to town during the week whenever his schedule permitted and she received word. Le Corbusier alerted her in advance, by letter, telephone call, or telegram. There was always great urgency and Swiss precision to his bulletins. In one letter, written on the Friday morning (November 8) of his departure for Philadelphia, he informed her that after his return on Saturday around 6 o'clock he would be free until his first appointment on Monday morning in New York. On the letter itself he drew a view of Long Island Sound from the porch of *la baraque* and added wistfully "this Friday morning sun makes me dream of the beach and of the water and of liquid horizons" (figure 2.14).[83]

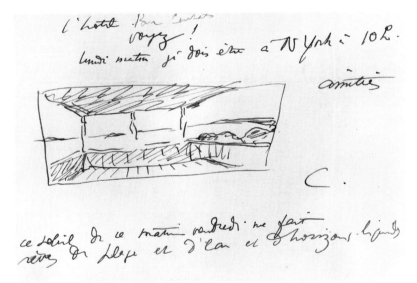

2.14
Le Corbusier, drawing of the porch of *la baraque*, letter, Le Corbusier to Marguerite Tjader Harris, [November 8, 1935]. (Collection Centre Canadien d'Architecture/Canadian Centre for Architecture, Montréal.) © 2001 Artists Rights Society (ARS), New York/ADAGP, Paris/FLC.

In a letter of November 12 dispatched from his lecture venue, identified as "Bowdoin—Brunswick—(*hélas!*)," Le Corbusier was impatient for more stimulating prospects. He sent a detailed itinerary of his next round of lectures, advising Marguerite that he would return from Princeton after midnight on Saturday (November 16) and be "free" and "available" until Monday morning at 11 o'clock.[84] (He intended to visit Mildred and Robert Woods Bliss in Washington, D.C., but preferred a weekend with Marguerite.)[85] His letter indicated that he wanted to be with her after his lecture at Columbia University on November 19 from midnight until 4 o'clock the next afternoon, when he would board the train for the Midwest. He also enclosed two drawings.[86] Even from Kalamazoo (November 22) he gave her his updated itinerary and enclosed a drawing that he called *L'Homme rouge*.[87] And his last act, just before flying home from Chicago on Thanksgiving morning (November 28), was to telegraph Marguerite expectantly: "Arriverai Museum Art Modern Avion Sept Heures PM Aujourd hui = Corbu."[88] In response to all these summons, Marguerite devotedly obliged. She was content to settle for snatched happiness.

During his tour Le Corbusier might have dalliances with other women, or even require a prostitute for a night, but he remained emotionally grounded in Marguerite, as she was in him. In matters of sentiment, the two were well matched. Her relations with men were as complex as his were with women. She was a handsome young woman with fair Nordic features, red hair, freckles, luminous blue eyes, a wide brow, and an athletic physique. She cherished the memory of her creative father who died when he was nearly 48 years old (Le Corbusier's age that fall) and she was a girl of 15. Her marriage to Overton Harris had been acrimonious. She longed to admire and fawn over a man like her father—inventive, artistic, energetic, intelligent, and strong.[89] Feminine and maternal, Marguerite could offer a man her strength and intelligence, her passion and sensuality, her respect, admiration, and devotion. Dreiser appreciated and savored her "dynamic affectionate force."[90] Indeed, he transformed Marguerite from society matron to literary companion and, in the process, his lover. Given

the gender stereotyping implicit in their respective roles, and notwithstanding Marguerite's interludes of independence and reassertion of self, it is natural to conclude that Dreiser schooled her well to assume the role of artist's muse.

Marguerite had her own motives for believing that Le Corbusier "was not a complicated man, not even an *intellectual,* in the narrow meaning of the word [not, she thought, in comparison with Dreiser]. He lived by his faith and his emotions. His desire was to create, to work, to accomplish. Everything in him was united in this intention. If he needed a little relaxation, if he needed affection, it was to work better, afterwards. He cared nothing for a social life, nor for the hundred little subterfuges and gallantries necessary to the pursuit of women. We had found a free companionship without obligations nor demands. . . . The quality of our hours together had been higher because their quantity was so limited."[91] She accepted and embraced Le Corbusier's need to dominate a woman, what one feminist called his explicit misogyny through a "language of mastery."[92] But she also appreciated in him such "female" elements as "his faith and his emotions."

As Le Corbusier later expressed to her directly, he recognized that his understanding of American culture (and its implications for the Radiant City) was inextricably linked to, indeed made possible by, his experiences with her. Without all she had to offer him—her introduction to New York and its suburbs, the solitude of her seaside shack, her commitment to artistic concerns that engaged sociopolitical causes, and her unconditional devotion—his lecture tour would have been shallow and uneventful.

A feminist critique might conclude that without Marguerite's worship, sexual desire, and submission, Le Corbusier would have left America having failed to get commissions and with his male ego irrevocably wounded. But Marguerite's importance transcended the personal because she encouraged the continuing transformation in Le Corbusier's architecture during the early 1930s, characterized by the difference between the Villa Stein-de Monzie (1926–1928) and the de Mandrot House (see figure 2.4). In Nietzschean terms the free-spirited divorcée symbolized (as did Yvonne) the Dionysian attributes of nature, the body, passions, and emotions. These countered the Apollonian male virtues of culture, intellect, soul, order, reason, authority, elitism, and supremacy with which Le Corbusier identified and which he projected onto his architecture and urbanism before 1930. Marguerite's unfettered temperament, her sensuality, her embrace of nature, and her appreciation of Le Corbusier's painting with its own Dionysian associations of the female and the feminine, the cosmic and the cyclical, served as a catalyst for his artistic creativity.[93] Le Corbusier freely confided in her, as she did in him. Through the experiences they shared she understood the different states of his persona more than any other American: his playfulness at the shore and on Broadway; his need to observe and learn from Manhattan's skyscrapers and infrastructure; his contemplative moments by the fireside in Darien; and his passion for making pictures, poetic expression, and physical love. To the end of Le Corbusier's life Marguerite and he remained close friends, exchanging letters and visits but concealing their intimacy. Prudently they had kept their relationship during the 1930s and 1940s a secret. Now Marguerite can be fully appreciated as the person who enabled Le Corbusier to experience the realities of modern life and culture in America that would validate his Radiant City thesis.[94]

3

The American Lectures

Le Corbusier launched his lecture tour with a presentation at the Museum of Modern Art, followed by the opening of an exhibition of his recent work. Hitchcock, then a professor at Wesleyan University and a member of the Architecture Committee, introduced him.[1] In both form and content the lecture was a model for the entire tour. Like each appearance, it was a multimedia event, orchestrated by Robert Jacobs. First, Le Corbusier lectured in French with freehand drawings. Jacobs recalled assisting and observing the speaker: "I would take a roll of tracing paper and stretch it right across the stage. And he was a hell of an artist . . . then in his left hand, he'd take out ten or twelve short pieces of pastel . . . he'd start over at the left hand side and as he talked, he sketched."[2] The impact of Le Corbusier's drawings on his audiences varied tremendously. Max Abramovitz, who was then working in the office of Harvey Wiley Corbett, Wallace K. Harrison, and William H. McMurray, heard the two lectures at Columbia, where he had received his master's degree. Abramovitz remembered Le Corbusier's drawings and "continued to be fascinated by him. . . . He would draw with colored pastels or colored chalk . . . trees . . . water, and different colors for different elements of the site. . . . I was very impressionable."[3] Hitchcock's recollection of Le Corbusier drawing at Yale and Wesleyan and at the Wadsworth Atheneum was more dispassionate: "He would tack up brown paper and sketch very crudely on it—more symbols than architectural details."[4] The drawings were on different papers—tracing (*calque*), manila (*bulle*), or brown—generally one meter (about 40 inches) high and as long as six meters (about 20 feet). Harry Weese, the Chicago architect who attended Le Corbusier's lecture at MIT, considered the drawings "a kind of story board."[5] Le Corbusier claimed that he had produced no less than 300 meters of these "colored frescoes."[6]

Le Corbusier spoke without a prepared text. He regarded his lectures as "improvised," equipping himself with only a synopsis on note cards. These took the form of sequenced preparatory sketches, frequently annotated. Le Corbusier composed his notes at the last minute, sometimes on hotel stationery before a lecture. He kept to this preparation in varying degrees at the Modern, and at Yale, Columbia, Vassar, and Princeton. The method actually originated in 1925 when he began giving lectures around the world. By his own account, the preparatory sketches for these "improvisations" often served a more critical function because the act of drawing became an external confirmation of his ideas.

There [at the lectures] I adopted my own technique which is rather special to me. I would never prepare lectures. You see a small card, about double the size of a calling card . . . with four or five lines on it, that I would improvise. This improvisation is a wonderful thing: I was drawing . . . at first I would work with chalk, colored chalk at the blackboard, provided I could find some. And when one draws around words, one draws with useful words, one creates something. And all my theory—my introspection and my retrospection on the phenomenon of architecture and urbanism—comes from these improvised and illustrated lectures. And so what is characteristic is that the ideas ended up by creating a doctrine—architecture and urbanism make a whole—and so this thesis of architecture and urbanism has now become accepted world-wide, professed everywhere, practiced everywhere, and one does "Corbu" in the entire world. It is perhaps highly regrettable, but it is like that.[7]

A film and sometimes slides augmented the lectures, as much to assist Jacobs as Le Corbusier.[8] Jacobs was the official translator, but he later admitted, "My French was so perfectly terrible."[9] As a survival technique, Jacobs showed *L'Architecture d'aujourd'hui* (1930), a short film of Le Corbusier's work produced and directed by Pierre Chenal, which he had brought to the States.[10] Featuring Le Corbusier's country houses, especially the Villa Stein-de Monzie, Les Terrasses (1926–1928), and the Villa Savoye at Poissy (1928–1930), the film helped to illustrate the applications of functionalism and purism, as well as mechanistic analogies. It also popularized in America his aphorism: "The house is a machine for living in."[11] The film showed dramatic images of the Villa Savoye lifted up on *pilotis* (supporting columns), with shots taken along the ramp, "through the building and then out the window to see the countryside."[12] To help orient Americans to the culture of Paris and its environs, Jacobs arranged for a recording of Gershwin music—then considered chic and urban—to accompany the film.[13]

If Jacobs was apologetic about his French, he was also diffident about his role as translator. Of the lectures at the Modern and Columbia University, he offered a tongue-in-cheek recollection: "I had very little to do in New York. . . . I always made an announcement that there would be a short translation for those that didn't understand. In a very sarcastic voice, I'd say, 'Of course, those of you who understand can leave immediately and those that don't understand could hear the translation.' Those that understood left, those that didn't understand were so ashamed that they didn't speak French, that they left too. So I never had to do a translation until we got to Chicago."[14] It seemed that most architecture students and professionals were able to follow the lectures.[15]

The tour was nothing short of breathless. In just over one month (October 24–November 27) Le Corbusier gave twenty-one lectures in over fifteen locales. By train, car, and plane, he traveled from Maine to Maryland and from New York to Wisconsin. Most of the lectures were given the general title "Modern Architecture and City Planning," but each was actually devoted to one of three specific themes: the first on urbanism explained his concept of the Radiant City; the second was on great works; the third on aesthetics advanced a neo-Platonic "theory of pure forms" (themes that recalled those of his South American tour six years before). Le Corbusier used the lectures and his expressive drawings as rhetorical vehicles of persuasion for the benefit of potential American clients and authorities. They worked in conjunction with photographs and models in the exhibition at the Modern as well as those in the traveling exhibition (in a few cases timed to coincide with the speaker's visit; see appendixes A and B). Le Corbusier's main objective was to convince authorities to adopt the principles and mass housing of the Radiant City, but he also hoped to receive other building commissions, large and small.

The Radiant City

Le Corbusier's emphasis on the Radiant City followed the agenda on urbanism that he set for his most recent lectures in South America (1929), Algiers (1933), and Rome (1934), with one broad exception.[16] During the

South American tour he had presented site-specific plans for cities he visited—Montevideo, São Paulo, Rio de Janeiro. In contrast, due to the rapid pace of the North American tour to cities and towns outside New York—Hartford, New Haven, Boston, Philadelphia, Baltimore, Detroit, Chicago, and Madison, Wisconsin—he made no plans for them. The size and resources of most were too modest. Moreover, their topography did not move him as did the exotic landscapes of South America. Only Manhattan inspired him to propose a scheme employing a new type of Cartesian skyscraper.[17] Implementation of his plan, however, was predicated on revolutionary structural changes in society. From his first press interview announcing the Radiant City he was realistic about the feasibility of any immediate adoption of his urbanism. He professed not to be concerned whether he personally would carry out such planning, for he believed that it would eventually be realized and have a future impact.[18] This was the case with his first formulation of the Radiant City to authorities in Moscow in 1930.[19] To ensure that his ideas would resonate beyond his visit, he tried to secure an American edition of *La Ville radieuse,* which had appeared in France a few months earlier.[20] Based on the success of his previous manifestos, most notably *Towards a New Architecture,* he assumed unrealistically that his book on the Radiant City and his presentations of its ideas during and after the American tour would eventually have a significant impact.

Le Corbusier presented his thesis for the Radiant City in his inaugural lecture at the Museum of Modern Art on October 24. In preparation he executed a remarkable series of annotated lecture sketches and a French text, later excerpted and translated into English by Philip Goodwin (see figures 3.5, 3.6, 3.7, 3.8). Together they provide the most complete narrative of this theme and a template for subsequent lectures. The chalk drawings that accompanied the lecture, however, are among many that do not survive. He opened with a tone of optimism.

The Americans, I am told, are at present finding themselves in a position of doubt: some find that they have gone too far in mechanisation, that they will have to turn back. Mechanisation, they say, is the cause of all the evil. The others think that we must continue to go ahead.

I myself think that the first machine era is passed: violence and tumult; and that the second era of machine civilisation is now beginning: it is harmony which will dominate.

America is confronted with a task which is all its own. It is so strong and so large and it has accumulated such conquests that it is its duty and its honor to continue. It is right here that we have the next great building site of the organisation of mechanistic civilisation.

The Americans are strong. We of Occidental Europe have acquired wisdom. Not having been occupied with our hands, our heads worked. And we are realizing that today the world has attained a new conscience, a modern conscience; certain evolution in the very basis of human need; the necessity of bringing to the totality of humanity the "essential joys." The essential joys raise the problem of leisure of modern society. With the intense mechanisation of to-day, which we should develop even more, leisure will take up the greatest part of the day: a daily occupation. The cultivation of leisure means architecture, urbanisation. Can such spiritual contradictions find a realisation?

Yes, because the revolution of architecture has been accomplished. It has been brought about by modern technique. I will prove it.

The indispensable urban factors I have called the "essential joys": from each room a view of the sky, the sensation of space, sun and trees.

Cities can be constructed in which each window has these factors which I call fundamental. This is a new type of city. I have called this city "La Ville Radieuse" (the Radiant City). These words mean that there is joy in life. This city answers to the coming reorganisation of the solar day of the human being of the mechanistic civilisation. This "Ville Radieuse" represents the first principles of the doctrine of city urbanisation of the machine age. These theses bring with them technical and esthetic factors but at the same time involve questions of biology, psychology, sociology, economics and politics. These theses are strict but they permit a complete diversity of application as follows: climate, topography, customs and even cultural conditions. One must therefore admit that the evolution of cities is similar with that of nature. This evolution proceeds by regular growth up to the moment when a metamorphosis intervenes. This metamorphosis transforms even the very structure of things. New cities will replace old cities.

This is a fatal event and an encouraging promise. I have recognized the necessity of these metamorphoses in all of the cities which I have studied and for which I have established plans: Paris, Sao Paolo [sic], Monte Video [sic], Rio de Janeiro, Moscow, Antwerp, Algiers, etc.

And now, concerning New York: this city which represents the most prodigious problem of optimism, the most striking proof of strength and power where we must face the necessary theses which will permit us to realize by successive and wise steps the transformation of the city, a city which should be as strong as it is today, which should soon become a sign of harmonious grandeur of mechanistic civilisation, a city where harmony and beauty will reign and where each human being will find joy and pride.

All these theses which are marked by a sign of positive development must therefore bring about a prodigious renewal of industry. On the day when the heads of the country and the masters of industry will understand that the evolution means the manufacture of the most indispensable products for consumption. The dwelling must stop using traditional methods of architecture and must be manufactured in a factory just as automobiles and aeroplanes with all the advantages of organisation, of Taylorism and of the impeccable precision of the machines. When the dwelling is regarded from this angle it will mean the end of industrial crisis, for this program is unlimited, innumerable in all countries of the world. It is a program of sane production and not a program of senseless overproduction.

These essential questions are in the hands of the governmental authorities, the responsibility rests with this authority.

This problem is so complex, so synthetic and so manifold that to express it I felt obliged to write a book which is a veritable symphony. To-day's lecture is only a small window open on the expanse of imminent realities. These theses are under the aegis of the word radieux (radiant, luminous). Radiant, joyous, happy, active, optimistic and confident, these are our guides at the beginning of the second era of mechanistic civilisation.[21]

The opening lecture emphasized three commingled objectives for the Radiant City: first, a synoptic explanation of the city as an ideal planning model for social reform (figure 3.1); second, how the city would engender a second machine age of social as well as technological advancement and how it reflected Le Corbusier's new

3.1
Le Corbusier, Ville Radieuse, 1930. (*La Ville radieuse*, p. 221. FLC Archive B2(9)686.) © 2001 Artists Rights Society (ARS), New York/ADAGP, Paris/FLC.

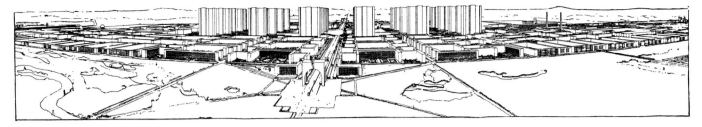

3.2
Le Corbusier, diorama, Ville Contemporaine, 1922. (*Oeuvre complète 1910–1929*, p. 35. Plan FLC 31005.) © 2001 Artists Rights Society (ARS), New York/ADAGP, Paris/FLC.

work and ideas of the 1930s; and third, justification for the plan, the design of a European urbanist, as the best model for American cities, especially New York.

La Ville radieuse elucidated his planning thesis. It was a "doctrine of urbanism" for a new machine age following the American stock market crash. The cities of the first machine age, the century between 1830 and 1930, Le Corbusier explained, were dominated by the railroad and the automobile.[22] There technology advanced at the expense of humanity. To redress the balance, he proposed a second machine age or "second era of machine civilization," grafting human values to technology. The Radiant City would be a rational city analogous to a Ford factory, an allusion he emphasized in his lecture at Cranbrook Academy after a visit to the River Rouge plant near Detroit. It would be technologically advanced and employ rationalized, standardized methods of organization and production. Based on Frederick Winslow Taylor's principles of scientific management and on technocratic assumptions, it would be a Taylorized city, but its formal and social organization would reflect a new priority given to more organic structures and processes. In its emphasis on planning reorganization and on a single-class housing program, it offered a way out of the social dilemma that shifted the focus of his urbanism in the 1930s.

There has been much analysis of Le Corbusier's changing concept of urbanism around 1930, formally, conceptually, and sociologically, from his projects for the Ville Contemporaine (1922; figure 3.2; see figure 1.6) and the Plan Voisin (1925; see figure 6.4) to that of the Ville Radieuse (1930–1935; see figure 3.1).[23] The Radiant City reflected the two earlier more utopian plans but incorporated many of the collective principles and progressive ideals advocated by the delegates to the Congrès Internationaux d'Architecture Moderne (CIAM). In formulating their 1928 manifesto, CIAM delegates were influenced by Le Corbusier's rhetoric when they professed to seek "harmony" in architecture and urban design by abandoning the "sterile influence" of the academy in favor of an "economic and sociological plane." At the same time they endorsed techniques of standardization to increase production, lower costs, and benefit labor.[24]

Still centralized like the Ville Contemporaine, the Radiant City was more regionally dispersed. It was also still formalistic, but now responded to social needs and reflected new organic concerns and models. Le Corbusier first proposed the Radiant City for Moscow in 1930 as a reply to Soviet proponents of urban decentralization (*Réponse à Moscou*). Later that year he presented aspects of his plan at the CIAM III conference devoted to the themes of "Rational Land Use" and "Rational Building Methods," held in Brussels.[25] Departing from his earlier concentric and more centralized plans of 1922 and 1925, the new plan called for a linear city based on a model proposed by Soria y Mata in the 1880s and modified in the 1920s by Russian planner Nikolai Miliutin.[26] The city was axially disposed, expandable, and organized into continuous parallel sectors (figure 3.3).[27] Unlike the bureaucratic schemes for the Ville Contemporaine and Plan Voisin, the cruciform commercial skyscrapers of the Radiant City no longer occupied the center but were relegated to the periphery (see figure 3.1). Now Le Corbusier privileged the residential district. A linear configuration of parallel zones—five sectors—provided for lateral expansion. From top to bottom, the plan was organically composed like the human body. At the top, the business district contained the civic center. A railroad and transportation sector was located between the business and residential districts, and a greenbelt separated residential and industrial areas. Community services included theaters, libraries, and schools in the business district, but no churches. All zones within the city were united by an elevated highway.

As Le Corbusier shifted his concerns around 1930 toward the human elements of town planning, he advanced a new concept of housing that he emphasized in his American lectures. Less hierarchical than his earlier plans, the Radiant City contained one class of apartment blocks, configured on a modular grid to permit a wide range of vistas with southern exposures to maximize sunlight. This housing typology consisted of dense slab blocks called *maisons à redents* (indented houses or set-back apartment blocks), that he demonstrated in a model (figure 3.4). Such housing *à redents* was reminiscent of Victor Considérant's perspective view of Charles Fourier's worker's community or Phalanstère (built in stages from 1859 to 1883), which Peter Serenyi showed to have influenced Le Corbusier.[28] Housing *à redents* had appeared in the Ville Contemporaine (see figure 3.2) and in a project of 1920 called *Les Rues à redents* showing indented apartment blocks along a tree-lined boulevard.[29] Le Corbusier borrowed the typology from Eugène Hénard and from pre–World War I German reformers.[30]

The communal services and amenities for each housing block included child care centers, shopping centers, restaurants, and both playground and roof top recreation. The apartment block prefigured his influential postwar Unité d'Habitation in Marseilles (1947–1953).[31]

The turn toward social engagement in the Radiant City reflected not only Le Corbusier's participation in CIAM and his disillusionment with both communism and capitalism, but also his involvement with regional syndicalism, a group inspired by the pre–World War I French labor movement and committed to social change. As Mary McLeod explained, his commitment extended to both political activism and regular contributions in the neosyndicalist publications *Plans, Prélude,* and *L'Homme Réel*. While the Radiant City synthesized many elements of his earlier plans, it still posed unresolved contradictions that expressed his new political interests. For Le Corbusier and others, regional syndicalism was an answer to the dilemma of capitalism and the economic depression of the post-crash era as it was experienced in France. Its fundamentally egalitarian program advocated a hierarchy of local shops, worker advancement based on merit, and elected management. Yet neosyndicalism still required leadership of a centralized authority. Notwithstanding Le Corbusier's efforts to formulate a more socially responsive urban vision that promised a second machine age of "harmony" and "essential joys" (sky, space, sun, and trees), the Radiant City as a theoretical model was flawed. The plan and accompanying text revealed conflicts between the dense centrality of its urban functions and the decentralized regionalism of the expandable plan, paralleling the sociopolitical contradictions in regional syndicalism between authoritarianism and a technocracy based on collective principles.[32] Moreover the Radiant City, like his modernist visions of 1922 and 1925, used elevated highways to separate roads from people, thereby destroying the nineteenth-century street whose vitality as human theater was central to modern urban life.[33] Le Corbusier was inured to such defects and looked for a case study to confirm his thesis. The lecture tour would provide opportunities for him to convince authorities that the pre-

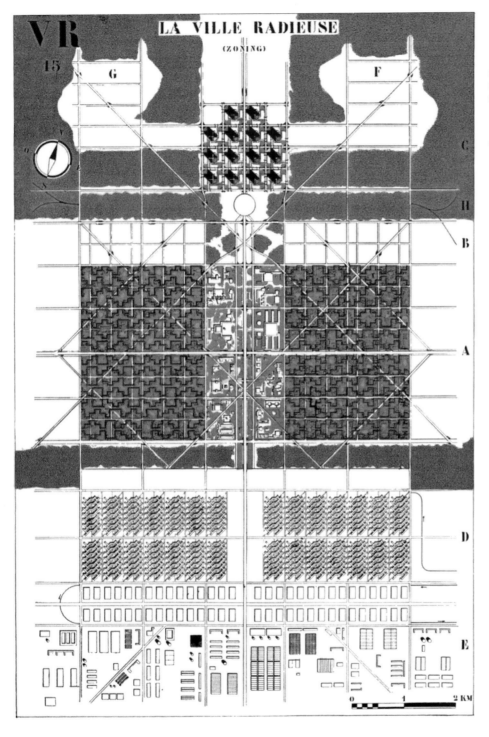

Satellite cities. e.g.: government buildings or center for social studies, etc.

The business center

Railroad station and air terminal

Hotels
Embassies

Housing

Factories

Warehouses

Heavy industry

3.3
Le Corbusier, plan, Ville Radieuse, 1930. (*La Ville radieuse*, p. 170. Plan FLC 24909.) © 2001 Artists Rights Society (ARS), New York/ADAGP, Paris/FLC.

3.4
Le Corbusier with model of hous-
ing *à redents*, Ville Radieuse,
1930. (FLC L1(2)1-13.) © 2001
Artists Rights Society (ARS), New
York/ADAGP, Paris/FLC.

mier American city, namely New York, could lead this endeavor. But its transformation into an empirical model of a Radiant City would have to be predicated on major changes in American economics, politics, and society. Toward these lofty objectives, Le Corbusier directed his rhetoric and assumed a polemical position on issues of leadership, the state of the American city and industrial production, and the culture of capitalism.

In his opening lecture he distanced himself from the strident rhetoric of *La Ville radieuse* and his articles in *Plans, Prélude,* and *L'Homme Réel.* He refrained from continuing to brand America's metropolises "cities of despair," but did characterize them as locked in stasis, without leadership, and paralyzed by indecision.[34] In projecting Radiant City principles for American cities, and particularly for New York, he took a paternalistic position evident in both his text and annotated lecture sketches (figures 3.5, 3.6, 3.7, 3.8).[35] As an outsider, a European, he saw America in 1935 poised at a crossroads between two eras and in "doubt" (see figure 3.5).

During the first machine age, he reasoned, mechanization had not just taken command, it had led America "too far" into overproduction, waste, and "spiritual decadence." If Americans were in doubt about whether to "turn back" or "go ahead," Le Corbusier instructed them, they had only to turn to him for direction and leadership! Americans might be technologically strong but Europeans (*nous*), he claimed, had acquired the wisdom to lead. He had used the argument before. In *Urbanisme* he called on similar cultural stereotyping when he contrasted the Old World with the New. In Europe, he suggested, "our spirits, nourished by past ages, are alert and inventive; their strength is in the head, while America's strength is in its arms and in the noble sentimentality of its youthfulness. If in America they feel and produce, here we think!"[36] More specifically, his feeling for French superiority motivated him in 1935 to recast American cities into radiant ones.

For even though Le Corbusier was born in Switzerland, he chose France as his adopted country, became a French citizen with his marriage to Yvonne Gallis in 1930, and called Paris home. His attitude recalled earlier instances of French hegemony, the kind that appeared in Jacques Gréber's 1920 book *L'Architecture aux Etats-Unis, preuve de la force d'expansion du génie français* (Architecture in the United States, proof of the strength of expansion of the French genius).[37] A solution to the dilemma of American architecture and city planning, Le Corbusier argued, justified the intervention of an intellectual. To redirect a country so technologically determined and misguided required a change of philosophy (*conclusion philosophique*). Only man within a new moral order (*état de conscience moderne*), and not the machine, could secure basic pleasures or essential joys (*joies essentielles*): "from each room a view of the sky, the sensation of space, sun and trees."[38]

To achieve such social benefits, urban life had to be reorganized according to a new "solar day." Drawings from his lectures at Columbia University (October 28 and November 19), Princeton University (November 14, 15, and 16) and the Baltimore Museum of Art (November 18), as well as the published text for one of his talks in Chicago (November 27), demonstrate the way in which his argument formed a stock part of his lecture repertoire. It was only toward the end of the tour, when he had more fully experienced the American city, that he used Radiant City ideas to attack the effects of suburbanization on the city. He did so most fervently in his Baltimore and Chicago talks entitled "The Great Waste." A version of the Chicago talk, subsequently published in *Quand les cathédrales étaient blanches* as "Le grand gaspillage" together with his lecture drawings, explained those ideas.[39] Le Corbusier drew pie charts and a sun graph to illustrate the partitioning of the twenty-four-hour "solar day" (plates 1 and 2; see figure 3.5). In the modern industrial city that day was structured into rigid time periods: eight hours for sleep, two one-and-one-half-hour segments for commuting, eight hours for work, and a meager balance of five hours for leisure. Little time remained for rejuvenation. Urban regions such as New York and Chicago, like Paris and London, extended sixty miles in diameter. At the Princeton (see plate 1), Baltimore, and Columbia (see plate 2) lectures Le Corbusier drew his concept of the present urban region, its contour, center, and ground.[40] Reflecting the infrastructure of nineteenth-century capitalism, these

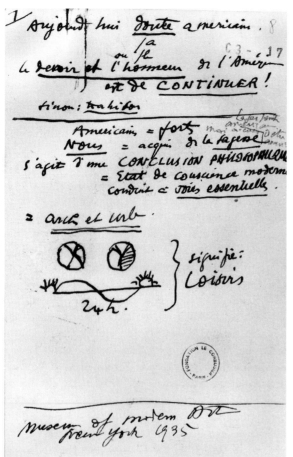

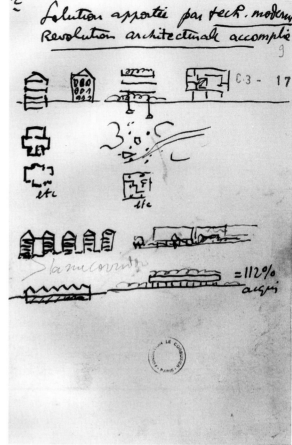

3.5
Le Corbusier, annotated sketches for lecture at the Museum of Modern Art, New York, October 24, 1935. (FLC Archive C3(17)8.) © 2001 Artists Rights Society (ARS), New York/ADAGP, Paris/FLC.

1/ Aujourd'hui doute américain. [today American doubt] // /a ou /b [a or b] // le devoir et l'honneur de l'Amérique est de CONTINUER ! [the duty and the honor of America is to continue] // Sinon: trahison [if not: treason] // Améri-cains = forts [Americans = strong] // [faint pencil:] Léger peintre américain m'accuse d'être américain [Léger, American painter, accuses me of being American] // NO = acquis de la sagesse [we = wisdom acquired] // S'agit d'une CONCLUSION PHILOSOPHIQUE = Etat de conscience moderne conduit à joies essentielles. [It is a question of a philosophical conclusion = state of modern conscience leads to essential joys] // = Arch et urb. [= architecture and urbanism] // 24h. [24 hours] // Signifie = Loisirs [signifies: leisure] // Museum of Modern Art New York 1935

3.6
Annotated lecture sketches, continued. (FLC Archive C3(17)9.) © 2001 Artists Rights Society (ARS), New York/ADAGP, Paris/FLC.

2/ Solution apportée par tech. moderne [solution brought by modern (building) techniques] // Révolution architecturale accomplie [architectural revolution accomplished] // [faint pencil:] la rue corridor [the street corridor] // = 112% acquis [= 112% gained]

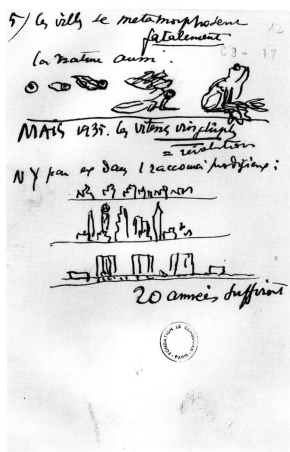

3.7
Annotated lecture sketches, con-
tinued. (FLC Archive C3(17)11.)
© 2001 Artists Rights Society
(ARS), New York/ADAGP,
Paris/FLC.

4/ Il faut un corps de doctrine = V.R
[there must be a body of doctrine = Ville
Radieuse] // infinies combinaisons =
lois naturelles [infinite combinations =
natural laws] // variété des cultures
[variety of cultures] // climats [climates]
// topographie [topography] //
vérités [truths] // coutumes [customs]
// Alors: des propositions: [therefore,
propositions:] // Paris // Sao Paolo
[São Paulo] // Montevideo // [Rio de
Janeiro, Antwerp, and Algiers at bottom, unidentified]

3.8
Annotated lecture sketches, con-
tinued. (FLC Archive C3(17)12.)
© 2001 Artists Rights Society
(ARS), New York/ADAGP,
Paris/FLC.

5/ Les villes se métamorphosent fatalement [cities metamorphose inevitably]
// La nature aussi. [nature too] //
MAIS 1935. [but 1935] // Les
vitesses vingtuples [twentyfold speeds]
// = révolution // N Y par ex dans 1
raccourci prodigieux: [New York for example by a prodigious shortcut] //
20 années suffiront [20 years will be
sufficient]

twentieth-century cities were laced with a network of roads and rails linking commuters in bedroom suburbs to the inner city. Such vast commuting distances robbed workers of family life. Moreover, the burden of paying for this network of services and utilities rested on the taxpayer, weighing heavily on family income.[41] By eliminating suburbs and their infrastructures, the Radiant City promised relief. For the Princeton and Columbia lectures Le Corbusier represented the centralized city as a dense block with satellite housing surrounding it. He assured his audiences that the Radiant City could offer a repartitioned solar day balancing work, sleep, and leisure.

The city required the restructuring and redirection of industrial production. In a series of comparisons between conventional and modern building techniques, Le Corbusier demonstrated the advantages of his "five points of a new architecture." Structures of steel and concrete raised buildings on *pilotis* (see figure 3.6; plate 1). Ferroconcrete construction permitted a *roof garden* to replace the traditional pitched roof and *the free plan* which eliminated bearing walls. *The elongated window* "revolutionized" the placement of windows to extend the length of an entire facade and it encouraged standardized methods of construction. The use of *pilotis* recessed from the envelope of the building, allowed a *free facade* with independently placed windows.[42]

To his audiences at Princeton, Columbia, and Baltimore, Le Corbusier explained that modern building techniques (*techniques moderne*) could bring about an "architectural revolution" that allowed a choice between two contradictory states: suburbs laid out as "horizontal (or sprawling) garden cities" (*cités-jardins en étendue*) or urban centralization employing what he called "vertical garden cities" (*cités-jardins en hauteur*) on "artificial sites" (*terrains artificiels;* see plates 1 and 2).[43] Radiant City principles would transform the traditional relationship between streets and facade-oriented housing, elminating the street corridor (*rue-corridor*) in a residential district (see figure 3.6).

Vertical garden cities would be populated with high-density *à redents* apartment houses for 2,700 occupants (see plates 1, 2, 3). Defined by its siting, configuration and amenities, the apartment house block dominated the residential zone. Le Corbusier designed each slab block to occupy approximately 12 percent of the site (*12% terrain bâti*). Because the blocks were raised on *pilotis,* open park land could extend underneath the buildings. The scheme appropriated 100 percent of the site "free for pedestrians" (*100% libre aux piétons;* see plate 3). Roof gardens with a swimming pool, modeled after the decks of ocean liners, might be used as "beaches for sunbathing."[44] Because the roof area would theoretically increase the site by 12 percent, Le Corbusier further suggested that each block would then capture a total of 112 percent of the flat site (*112% acquis*) for circulation.[45] Continuous bands of such apartment blocks were linked end to end through a corridor (*rue intérieure*). At Bowdoin College, Columbia, and Baltimore Le Corbusier explained how they zigzagged through semienclosed courtyards (see plate 3). Automobiles would be discretely separated from pedestrians. One door serving all 2,700 occupants defined pedestrian access for each block; one parking area or *auto-port* connected each block to the elevated highway only fifty meters away along a branch road. Extensive playing fields, like the ones he admired on the campus of Princeton University, were accessible to each housing block (*sport/s au pied des maisons;* see plate 1). Recreation for all dwellers, not just for a few athletes who performed in stadiums, was a key component of the Radiant City.[46] This point would have been understood on most American campuses where sports were already integrated into the daily culture.

At the Modern and at Columbia University, Le Corbusier made more detailed drawings of the Radiant City apartment block (see plate 2). Anticipating the postwar *Unité,* glazed plate glass walls (*pans de verre*) enclosed each *à redents* slab block of reinforced concrete. The eleven-story building was organized into duplexed units, adjusted to a corridor. Each apartment unit was designed to extend through the entire block, allowing views from windows on the two main facades. Blocks were sealed to permit hermetic conditions for climate control and to provide soundproofing. The structural system ensured that apartment units functioned as "soundproof cells" (*cellules insonorisées*), an idea inspired by his experience of the "soundproof" cabins of ocean liners.[47] Le Corbusier further elucidated the way in which his vertical garden city (*cité-jardin en hauteur*) would be radiant. Each room had its own view, signified by the image of a human eye, like a surrealist *objet*, projecting from the crest of the superblock. This green city (*ville verte*) would ensure "essential joys."[48]

Le Corbusier's program posed a flexible body of doctrine. It was planned for a flat site, but was not site specific. Based on natural laws, the Radiant City could be adapted to "a variety of cultures, climates, topography, winds, and customs," to the Old as well as the New World. Confident of the future application of his planning thesis to North American cities, Le Corbusier presented to his audience at the Modern his earlier schemes for the port cities of São Paulo, Montevideo, Rio, Antwerp, Algiers, and Stockholm (see figure 3.7). Plans for the three South American cities that he published in *Précisions* signaled a new direction in his urbanism, which introduced nature as a generative force.[49] Influenced by French poet Blaise Cendrars as well as by his own experiences flying over the terrain of South America in 1929, Le Corbusier developed a new sense of urbanism from an aerial perspective.[50] The lushness and drama of the topography sensitized him to the importance of adjusting new city plans to variations of climate and region. In response to the vast reaches of sculptured landscape, ports with mountains plunging toward the sea, he designed a megastructure of reinforced concrete with offices and housing that would "glide above the city" without disturbing the existing topography.[51] "From far away I saw in my mind the vast and magnificent belt of buildings, crowned horizontally by a superhighway flying from mount to mount and reaching out from one bay to another."[52] There he proposed a series of linear planning schemes that made dramatic sculptural gestures. For São Paulo, he devised a bold geometric plan for a viaduct cut through the mountains, resulting in what he called a *gratte-terre* (groundscraper). For Montevideo, a T-shaped structure containing a business center thrust out onto the port creating a so-called *gratte-mer* (seascraper).

In his lecture at the Modern Le Corbusier also presented a master plan for transforming the port city of Antwerp with its cathedral and harbor into a "world city" (see figure 3.7).[53] This series of urban "propositions" concluded with the Plan Obus (*obus* meaning an explosive shell) for Algiers, a project he introduced to different American audiences. Influenced by the South American plans and his travels in the developing world, the Plan Obus reflected both the geometry of the superblock and a new organic aesthetic that embraced the "law of the meander."[54] Plan Obus A (1931–1932), the earliest of six versions, was conceived as a redevelopment for the port of Algiers with four components: a business district; a residential district sited on the hilly old Fort-l'Empereur with housing blocks; an elevated highway connecting the two districts that preserved the exotic Casbah underneath; and a sinuous viaduct with an expressway on top that snaked its way along the coast. Le Corbusier's drawings show his emphasis on the residential district, planned for 220,000 persons and composed of curvilinear *à redents* apartment blocks. Such vertical garden cities composed of stacked "artificial sites," raised by *pilotis,* were adjusted to the local terrain (see figure 3.6; and plate 1). This configuration provided communal services and allowed for density without sacrificing an individual's need for "essential joys."[55] In Philadelphia (November 8) and Chicago Le Corbusier produced expressionistic renderings of the *à redents* housing cluster he called a "tiara placed on the head of Algiers" (plate 4 left; figure 3.9).[56] The curved arms of the blocks peeled open toward the landscape.

Le Corbusier also introduced the Philadelphia audience to his plan for Stockholm (1933), which sought to reduce traffic congestion and provide housing on its periphery. It combined notions of the *grand plan* with those of the *ville verte.* The drawing showed the way in which his plan called for the redevelopment of two districts, Nedre Norrmalm and Sodermalm, on opposite banks of the harbor, linked formally and symbolically to the island in between, the site of the Royal Palace (see plate 4 right, above and below). It further specified creation of peripheral traffic arteries. A green promenade defined the axis of Norrmalm's center city framed by a network of housing *à redents*. Together with a similar crest of hill-top housing for the residential district of Sodermalm Island, Le Corbusier's sculptured silhouette for the port city of Stockholm made a dramatic gesture in the landscape.[57]

Le Corbusier's presentation of this wide-ranging and geographically diverse series of projects for the redevelopment of port cities served as a marketing device to introduce his plan for New York. Recalling the biological analogies that shaped nineteenth-century attitudes toward architecture and urbanism, he maintained that transformation of these port cities into radiant cities involved an organic process of growth and evolution. Just as natural life followed a necessary and inevitable metamorphosis, so urban morphology could be restructured (*les villes se métamorphosent fatalement*). In his lecture at the Modern Le Corbusier drew the image of a frog in various states of metamorphosis (see figure 3.8). When he applied this idea to the morphology of Manhattan, he defined its evolution as a function of architectural, cultural, even biological determinism. He envisioned three stages of Manhattan's development—1900 (above), 1935 (middle), and "tomorrow" (below), a concept he elaborated further in *Cathédrales* (see figure 5.32). The three ages of Manhattan in preparatory sketches con-

3.9
Le Corbusier, *Urbanisation de la Cité d'Alger*, 1930–1934. Drawing for lecture "The Great Waste," Stevens Hotel, Chicago, November 26, 1935. Pastel on paper, 39 3/4 × 109 1/2 in. (101 × 278.2 cm.). (The Museum of Modern Art, New York. Gift of Robert Allan Jacobs.) © 2001 Artists Rights Society (ARS), New York/ADAGP, Paris/FLC. Photograph © 1999 The Museum of Modern Art, New York.

300 à 400 vert // par 1000 h[abitants] [by 1000 inhabitants] // ciel [sky] // cités-jardins horizontales [sprawling garden cities] // cités jardins verticales [vertical garden cities] // 220,000 habitants [inhabitants] // à l'ombre fidèle [to the faithful shadow (Robert Allan Jacobs)] // fidèlement Le Corbusier [faithfully Le Corbusier] // Chicago 27 nov 1935

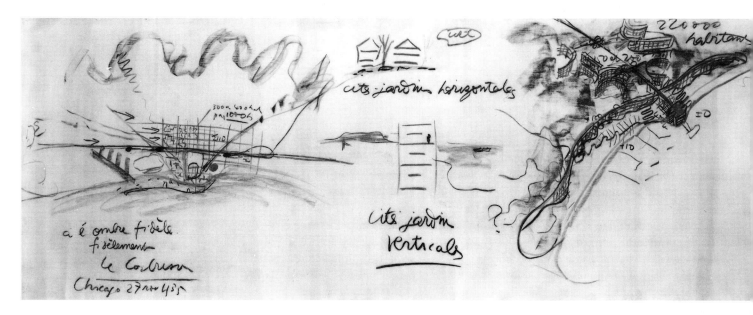

tained the germ of his grand scheme and confirmed his working method. Application of American construction techniques to the Cartesian skyscraper implied a change in the morphology of New York. A twenty-year evolution would be sufficient, he predicted, before "the second era of mechanistic civilization," the "fatal event," would transform the city into a radiant one. Le Corbusier's scheme for three ages of evolution was not restricted to that metropolis but was the result of a preconception. The profile of Manhattan as a necklace of translucent Cartesian skyscrapers was actually an adaptation of earlier studies representing the three ages of Paris, the last showing a site-specific view of a future city with skyscrapers extending from Montmartre to Notre-Dame.[58] That his conclusion for New York was based on such a facile recycling only confirms Le Corbusier's abiding objective to secure an actual site for his Radiant City.

In his second lecture at Columbia University (November 19) Le Corbusier attempted to justify his metamorphosis of Manhattan when he drew the image of two "romantic" setback skyscrapers, which, he explained, would cause "death to the street" between them (see plate 2 right). During the final weeks of his visit and the sea voyage home, this fragment of his plan continued to evolve into a more extensive proposal using Y-shaped skyscrapers for business and potentially also for housing. With these intentions the architect hoped to transform New York from an "enchanted catastrophe" into a Radiant City, a concept he later elucidated in an article in *American Architect* with the title "What Is America's Problem?" (see chapter 5).[59]

As the tour progressed, Le Corbusier articulated more fully the kinds of structural changes that were necessary to change American architecture and urbanism. The metamorphosis called for harnessing industrial production so that dwellings, like automobiles and airplanes, would be manufactured in a factory "with all the advantages of organization, of Taylorism and of the impeccable precision of machines." From 1925 when he first announced his "call to industrialists" (*appel aux industriels*) at the Pavillon de l'Esprit Nouveau, he challenged major industry to take charge of building.[60] Even though by the mid-1930s he had expressed skepticism

about Fordism and Taylorism, his lectures toward the end of the American tour, after he had visited the Ford River Rouge plant (1916–1932) on November 21, reaffirmed the American industrial model with its values of standardization and collaboration. Le Corbusier identified such methods of production in *La Ville radieuse,* but his experiences in Detroit led him to cast the Ford assembly line as a metaphor for the "collective forces" needed in the building industry. His subsequent talks at Cranbrook Academy, in Kalamazoo, in Chicago (Renaissance Society), and in Madison addressed these issues in the heartland of the automobile industry.[61] Because architectural production in America was still dominated by the academy, it remained largely outside the domain of industry and was therefore "paralyzed." His colorful diagrams from these midwestern lectures have not survived in the original but a published drawing from Cranbrook Academy outlines his ideas (figure 3.10). It shows the present state of architecture and planning immobilized by three opposing wills: (A) "individual liberty," (B) "collective forces," and (C) a moribund academy. As Le Corbusier explained, progress would hinge on shedding the academic in favor of a collaboration—biological, economic, political, and technical—that would support at once the rights of the individual and the collective needs of society.[62]

The Cranbrook diagram summarizes the crux of Le Corbusier's ambivalence about American culture during the 1930s. America had once been the fountainhead of production for the first machine age civilization that lasted a century (1830 to 1930). But in recent years the economic and social forces of capitalism had misled the nation. Future industrialization, Le Corbusier recognized, depended on America: "here before anywhere else machines will be mastered."[63] But the social deficit of capitalism, he insisted, had ruined the modern city, causing a schism between architecture and planning. He believed in the possibility of their realliance to form a new urbanism responsive to the individual as well as to society. Given its resources, energy, and evolutionary potential, America was "surely the country first able to bring to fulfillment, and with an exceptional perfection, this contemporary task."[64]

Liberté individuelle

A

Biologie économique

politique

liberté individuelle = architecture

les forces collectives

???

C

technique (physique, chimie, calculs)

B

Puissance Collective

3.10
Le Corbusier, diagram from lecture at Cranbrook Academy, Bloomfield Hills, Michigan, November 21, 1935. (*Cathédrales*, p. 249.) © 2001 Artists Rights Society (ARS), New York/ADAGP, Paris/FLC.

For America to accept the Radiant City, it would have to make revolutionary changes in its social order. Thus, as the tour progressed, Le Corbusier concentrated his efforts on this issue, culminating in his lectures on the "Great Waste." Casting American culture and society as an empirical model for the Radiant City, he developed his proposal for Manhattan into a site-specific case study. Those plans reflected the weaknesses in his general formulation: they were fragmentary and utopian with unresolved contradictions between centralization and decentralization and between authoritarian and participatory intentions. Moreover, whereas most urbanists looked to the traditional configuration of streets, squares, and public spaces to encourage social functions, Le Corbusier considered them impediments. Some of the more visionary aspects of his planning also lacked practicality: the feasibility of implementing collective principles and reorganization of land ownership, and dedicating important industry to the production of housing.

"Great Works"

The lecture tour provided a forum for Le Corbusier to convince American clients that he was capable of designing "great works," both civic and cultural. Within his own architectural career he designated the years between 1929 and 1934 as *L'Ere des grands travaux.*[65] Dur-

ing this "era of great works," he sought important commissions based more on fundamental social needs than on notions of zeitgeist that shaped the previous decade. The projects of these years demonstrated a departure from the taut surfaces and membrane-like forms of the previous decade in favor of more plastic designs. Influenced by his travels, they also reflected new appreciation for vernacular and regional characteristics.

Le Corbusier's concept of great works depended on two interrelated principles that he thought had special significance for the preeminent industrialized society: first, a kind of technological determinism grounded in the idea that modern [building] techniques (*techniques modernes*) would create new and flexible building typologies; and second, an alliance of modern methods of construction and new typologies that would inevitably defeat the academy. He addressed the theme in at least three lectures (Columbia, October 28; Yale University, October 30; and Vassar College, November 7), offering examples from his own repertoire to show Americans the possibilities. He challenged audiences to consider that even though their young country had produced great works of engineering with steel and concrete construction, it had not yet achieved comparable works of architecture because the discipline and the profession were still governed by the Beaux-Arts system. To create them, he inferred, America had to be guided, indeed liberated, by French thought.

For his lectures on "great works" at Columbia, Yale, and Vassar (CYV) Le Corbusier prepared another series of annotated sketches (figures 3.11, 3.12, 3.13, 3.14).[66] He opened with "the evocation of the bridge," the George Washington Bridge (see figure 3.11; plate 5). This "American bridge of the suspension type" with its steel and concrete piers, cables, horizontal platform raised above the river, and approaching ramps, was a "daring" example of such techniques. It was daring not only because the engineering was advanced, but also because the exposed steel towers were "saved" from Cass Gilbert's stone facing "sculptured in 'Beaux-Arts' style."[67] Its structure fully revealed, the George Washington Bridge triumphed over the academy. Le Corbusier pointed out other examples. Like the "American" suspension bridge, the hingeless reinforced concrete arch by French engineer Eugène Freyssinet also confirmed that engineers—French as well as American—produced advanced construction methods resulting in new typologies. In his drawing of one of Freyssinet's twin dirigible hangars at Orly, France (1921), with its parabolic arch of reinforced concrete (see figure 3.11; plate 5), Le Corbusier conveyed his admiration for Freyssinet's work and recalled his earlier use of those structures in *Vers une architecture* to illustrate the polemic "Architecture or Revolution." The bridge, both the American suspension design and the iron two-hinged arch (and also the tower) by Gustave Eiffel, demonstrated a convergence between the engineer's aesthetic and architecture, a postulate of *Vers une architecture* that could provide at once a model and a new direction.[68]

At Columbia, Yale, and Vassar Le Corbusier suggested that the "architectural consequences" of new structural systems, employing a framework of steel or reinforced concrete, and methods of standardization, would result in new typologies.[69] The Cartesian skyscraper and elevated housing *à redents* synthesized his five points of architecture. Moreover, reinforced concrete construction allowed the ramp and the spiral to infuse new typologies with flexible elements adapted to social needs. To illustrate such elements Le Corbusier drew images of a vertical slab, a slab block on *pilotis,* a ramp, and a spiral.

The CYV preparatory sketches and their respective lecture drawings indicate that text followed image. Both suggested an earlier model. In 1929 Le Corbusier illustrated his third lecture in Buenos Aires with similar drawings of Renaissance and neoclassical buildings, dismissing them with the epithet, "This is not architecture. These are 'styles.'"[70] The subject was *précisions* (precisions or finer points), anticipating the title of his book on the South American lectures. His 1929 lecture identified elements and issues that resurfaced in the North American lectures. "I draw things that everyone knows: this Renaissance window flanked by two pilasters and an architrave surmounted by a broken pediment; this Greek temple; this Doric entablature . . ." At the CYV lectures he augmented his images of a French Renaissance palace and a classical temple with those of a mausoleum-like composition from the nineteenth century, a Renaissance window, and, at Columbia, a domed palace, denouncing such relics of the Academy as "no more than corpses" (see figure 3.11; plate 5).[71] His images and rhetoric recalled the great themes of *Vers une architecture*—"eyes which do not see" and "the lesson of Rome." This lesson could be learned in America where the "bad taste of the Roman Renaissance" and the Beaux-Arts legacy continued to inflict architecture, where "styles are a lie," and Vignola was still "god."[72]

In opposing the architecture of the Ecole des Beaux-Arts, Le Corbusier offered new elements and architectural typologies. His five points, along with the ramp and the spiral, formed a modernist vocabulary and grammar of architecture based on standards. And yet his repertoire curiously paralleled and countered those Beaux-Arts elements of architecture and composition that Julien Guadet codified in *Eléments et théorie de l'architecture* (1901–1904). By substituting new elements for old ones, Le Corbusier may have posited a new vocabulary, but he merely replicated the methodology of academic design without its underlying coherence or predictability. His architectural typology effectively if inconsistently severed the earlier relationship between form and function, as Stanislaus von Moos showed. Whereas style and form in Beaux-Arts architecture were contingent on building type and program, in Le Corbusier's

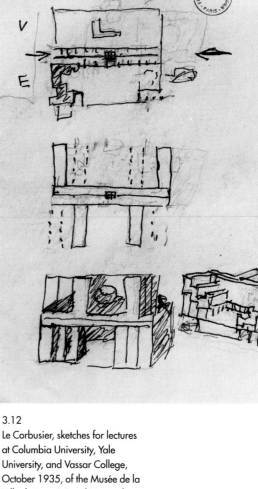

3.11

Le Corbusier, annotated sketches for lectures at Columbia University, Yale University, and Vassar College, October 1935. (FLC Archive C3(17)18.) © 2001 Artists Rights Society (ARS), New York/ADAGP, Paris/FLC.

Voici des combinaisons diverses [Here are the various combinations]
1 Musée art contemporains [sic]
2 Pavillon Suisse
3 Palais des Soviets
5 Musées de l'Etat

3.12

Le Corbusier, sketches for lectures at Columbia University, Yale University, and Vassar College, October 1935, of the Musée de la Ville de Paris (V) and Musée de l'Etat (E). (FLC Archive C3(17)19.) © 2001 Artists Rights Society (ARS), New York/ADAGP, Paris/FLC.

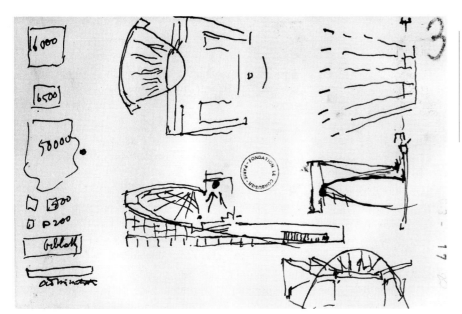

3.13
Le Corbusier, sketches for lectures at Columbia University, Yale University, and Vassar College, October 1935, of the Palais des Soviets. (FLC Archive C3(17)20.) © 2001 Artists Rights Society (ARS), New York/ADAGP, Paris/FLC.

3.14
Le Corbusier, sketches for lectures at Columbia University, Yale University, and Vassar College, October 1935, of the Palais des Soviets. (FLC Archive C3(17)21.) © 2001 Artists Rights Society (ARS), New York/ADAGP, Paris/FLC.

production they developed relatively independently from the functions and social needs of a particular building type.[73]

Le Corbusier offered American audiences four examples of recent great works. His annotations to the CYV sketches specified "1) Musée [d']art contemporain 2) Pavillon Suisse 3) Palais des Soviets 5) [sic] Musées de l'Etat" (see figures 3.11, 3.12, 3.13, 3.14).[74] Once again he used his polemic against the academy to promote them. At Columbia University he contrasted his project for a Museum of Contemporary Art in Paris (1931; see figure 3.12) to the Louvre (plate 6), then considered a standard for an art museum. But to him the colonnaded east facade of the Louvre by Louis Le Vau and Claude Perrault (1667–1670) epitomized the defects of French Renaissance design and its legacy.[75] His new conceptual model of a museum "for living artists" took the form of a prism raised on *pilotis* with a spiral core.[76] It originated in an earlier project for a pyramidal World Museum or Musée Mondial, the focus of his Mundaneum or World City in Geneva of 1928–1929.[77] The Museum of Contemporary Art was the earliest of a type he later called *Musée à Croissance Illimitée* (Museum of Unlimited Growth). He considered its spiral plan a "true form of harmonious and regular growth" based on organic principles, "natural laws," and mathematical proportions. This potentially extendable museum had a skeletal framework of standardized parts and moveable partitions. Combined exhibition and circulatory spaces, which employed a module of seven square meters, rotated around a generous central core. Only the formal axial planning of the museum, like that of the Geneva project, was consistent with Beaux-Arts principles. Rejecting the traditional Beaux-Arts concept of "elevation," he designed it with "no facade" since one "enters the heart of the museum by an underground passage."[78] Moreover, its flexible gallery spaces and spiral circulation employing ramps, that eliminated the traditional corridor system, departed from conventional museum *partis*. The squared spiral form for this museum without walls or *musée sans façades,* as Le Corbusier called it, and many of its features reappeared in a number of his subsequent designs for a Museum of Unlimited Growth. To-

ward the end of his American tour he would make a proposal to Nelson Rockefeller for a museum based on this typology (see chapter 7). In 1939 he made drawings and a model for a project by that name for Philippeville in Algeria.[79] That year he even proposed several similar projects to American patrons including Solomon Guggenheim in New York and Walter Arensberg in Hollywood. His concept may have informed the design of Frank Lloyd Wright's Guggenheim Museum in New York.[80]

At Columbia, Yale, and Vassar, Le Corbusier showed how "diverse combinations" of these same elements could result in an entirely different form of museum, as his competition entry for a Musée de la Ville de Paris et Musée de l'Etat (Museum of the City of Paris and Museum of the State) for the 1937 Exposition Internationale "Arts et Techniques" in Paris demonstrated (see figure 3.12).[81] In a continuing effort to substitute new typologies for traditional ones, he offered drawings for a City Museum and a State Museum, intended for a site on the right bank of the Seine River on axis with the Eiffel Tower.[82] Each had its own exhibition spaces but shared some common services. Six sketches indicated how the two museums, both U-shaped, were joined back to back. A central block, reserved for circulatory spaces and offices, served as a foil to stepped-back wings containing galleries and forming courtyards. The transverse section and plans defined the profile, level change, and juncture of the two buildings: E (Etat) and V (Ville). Two axonometric drawings, from above and from below, exhibited the ingenious nature of the stepped-back galleries and the extent to which provisions for circulation and natural light dominated the entire design. Four sets of ramps leading to the galleries facilitated vertical circulation. Courtyard platforms constructed of reinforced concrete and glass admitted light to the lower floors containing sculpture. At the City Museum Le Corbusier used an elliptical dome to condense light, anticipating a similar element in his Assembly Hall at Chandigarh.

At Columbia, Yale, and Vassar, Le Corbusier explained the way in which he had engaged other "diverse combinations" of elements, especially the acoustical

1.

Le Corbusier, drawing for lecture at Princeton University, November 14 and 15, 1935. (The Art Museum, Princeton University. Lent by the School of Architecture, Princeton University. Photograph by Bruce M. White.) © 2001 Artists Rights Society (ARS), New York/ADAGP, Paris/FLC.

[Left to right: building raised on *pilotis;* existing urban region; existing "solar day"; existing urban region with network of roads and rails; Le Corbusier's centralized modern city with satellite housing; repartitioned "solar day" with greater time allotted to leisure (*loisirs*); existing sprawling garden cities (*cités-jardins en étendue*); Le Corbusier's proposal for vertical garden cities through the creation of artificial sites (*cités jardins en hauteur par création des terrains artificiel[s]*), with space for sports at the base of the buildings (*sports au pied des maisons*) and a separation of cars from pedestrians (*séparation des autos . . . piétons*); a city for 220,000 inhabitants (*220,000 habitants*).]

2.

Le Corbusier, drawing for lecture at Columbia University, November 19, 1935. (Avery Architectural and Fine Arts Library, Columbia University in the City of New York.) © 2001 Artists Rights Society (ARS), New York/ADAGP, Paris/FLC.

24 heures [24 hours] // 24 heures sommeil / transport / transport / loisirs [24 hours sleep / transport / transport / leisure] // liberté indiv (égoiste) [individual liberty (self-centered)] // liberté indiv + puissance civique [individual liberty + strength of the community] // les loisirs = décision de l'autorité / sur plan juste [leisure = decision of the authority / according to an exact plan] // = nouvelle journée de la civilisation machiniste [new day of machine age civilization] // villa = terrain artificiel [villa = artificial site] // cités jardins en étendue [spread-out garden cities] // ville démesurée [?] [scaleless [?]] city] // 80% parc // 12% bâti [12% built] // terrain artificiel superposé [superimposed artificial site] = cité jardin en hauteur [vertical garden city] = ville resserrée [compact city] // [at right: New York City setback skyscrapers and street grid; indented cruciform business tower (Ville Contemporaine model); plan of Y-shaped (new Cartesian) skyscraper]

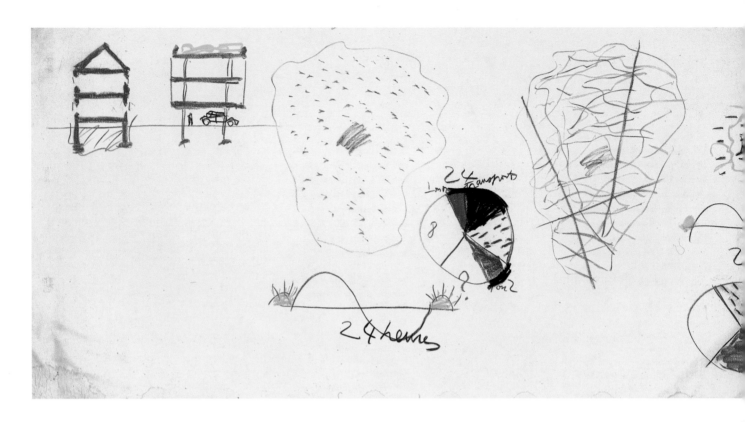

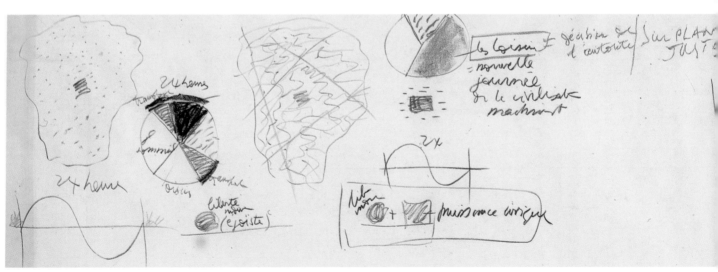

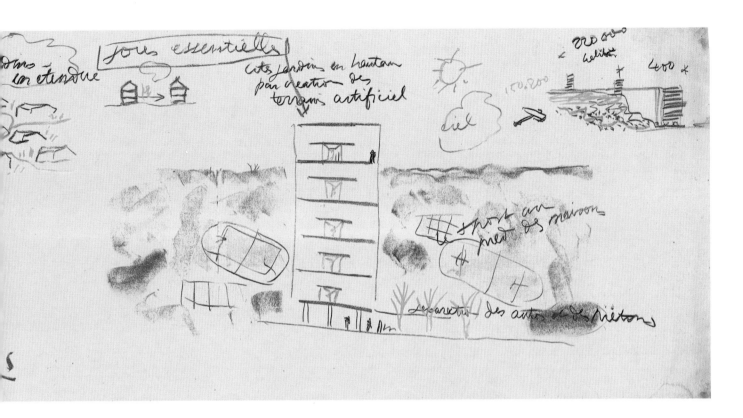

point essentielle

Cités jardins en hauteur
par création des
terrains artificiel

sport au pied des maisons

séparation des autos et des piétons

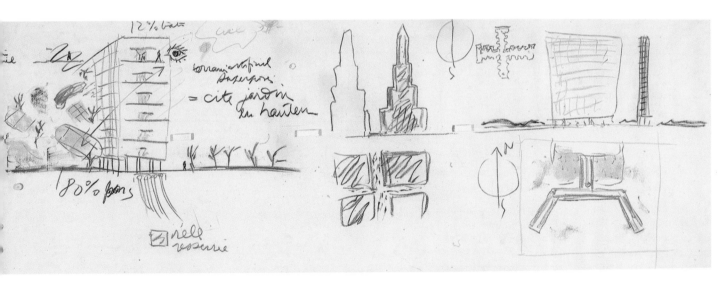

12% bâti

terrain artificiel
superposés
= cité jardin
en hauteur

80% jardins

télé
resserrie

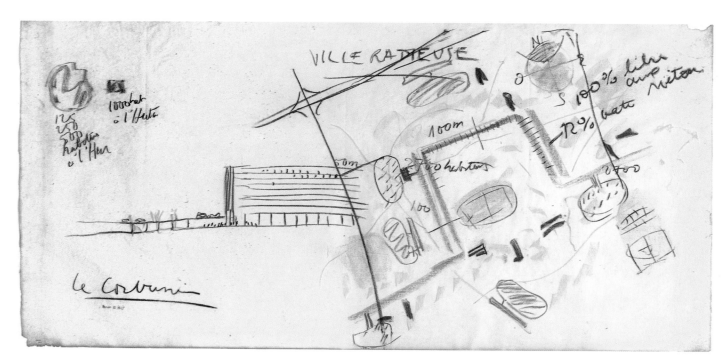

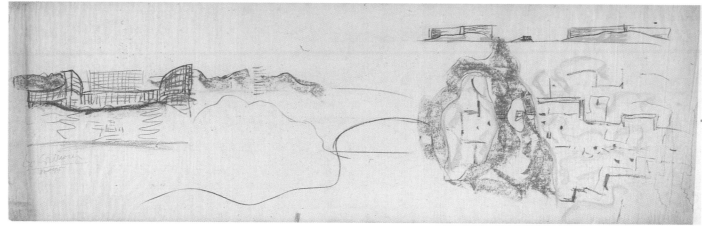

3.

Le Corbusier, drawing for lecture on the Radiant City (Ville Radieuse) at Bowdoin College, Brunswick, Maine, November 12, 1935. (Bowdoin College Museum of Art, Brunswick, Maine.) © 2001 Artists Rights Society (ARS), New York/ADAGP, Paris/FLC.

100% libre aux piéton[s] [100% available to pedestrians] // 12% bâti [12% built]

4.

Le Corbusier, drawing for lecture in Philadelphia, November 8, 1935: housing "tiara," Obus A for Algiers (left, 1931–1932); Royal Palace and plan for Stockholm (top and bottom right, 1933). (The Architectural Archives of the University of Pennsylvania, Philadelphia.) © 2001 Artists Rights Society (ARS), New York/ADAGP, Paris/FLC.

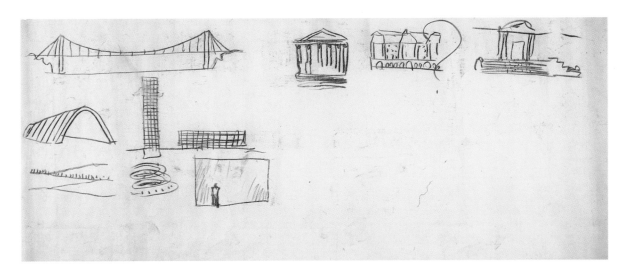

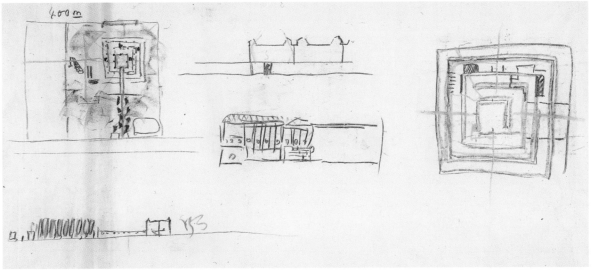

5.
Le Corbusier, drawings of the George Washington Bridge and other twentieth-century structures contrasted with Beaux-Arts design, for lecture at Columbia University, October 28, 1935. (Avery Architectural and Fine Arts Library, Columbia University in the City of New York.) © 2001 Artists Rights Society (ARS), New York/ADAGP, Paris/FLC.

6.
Le Corbusier, project for a Museum of Contemporary Art (1931) contrasted with the Louvre, Paris, for lecture at Columbia University, October 28, 1935. (Avery Architectural and Fine Arts Library, Columbia University in the City of New York.) © 2001 Artists Rights Society (ARS), New York/ADAGP, Paris/FLC.

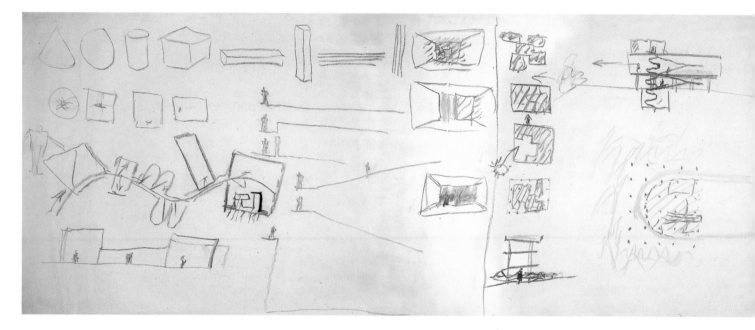

7.
Le Corbusier, drawing for lecture on "Fundamental Principles of Architecture" at Princeton University, November 16, 1935: "pure forms," Phileban or Platonic solids, "law of the meander," Villa Savoye, Poissy (1928–1930), and house at Mathes (Villa le Sextant) on the Atlantic coast (1934–1935). (The Art Museum, Princeton University. Lent by the School of Architecture, Princeton University. Photograph by Bruce M. White.) © 2001 Artists Rights Society (ARS), New York/ADAGP, Paris/FLC.

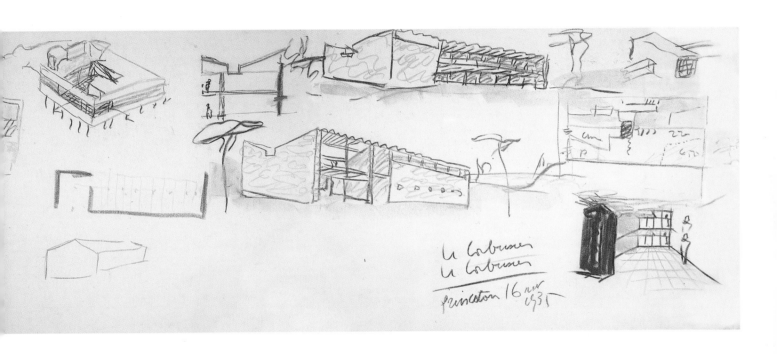

Le Corbusier
Le Corbusier
princeton 16 nov
1935

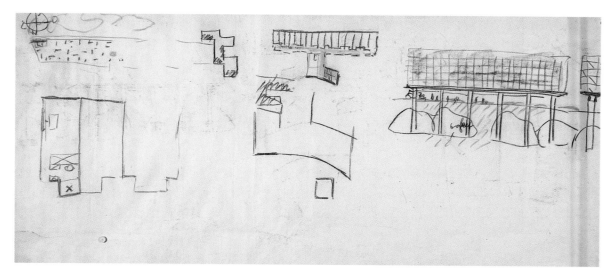

8.
Le Corbusier, Pavillon Suisse,
Paris, 1930–1931, drawing for
lecture at Columbia University,
October 28, 1935. (Avery Archi-
tectural and Fine Arts Library,
Columbia University in the City of
New York.) © 2001 Artists Rights
Society (ARS), New York/ADAGP,
Paris/FLC.

shell and the ramp, in his competition entry for the Palais des Soviets (Palace of the Soviets; 1931–1932) in Moscow (see figures 3.13, 3.14). He underscored the significance of this project when he met Philip Goodwin's bold request to exhibit the fragile model (figure 3.15) and made several drawings of the project during his first Columbia lecture.[83] The building was planned as a center for party congresses, mass meetings, and political rallies. Preparatory sketches (see figure 3.13) indicated specifications for the program on the left, and his daring design solution both on the right and on the next note card (see figure 3.14). The program called for two meeting halls, one for 15,000 (not 16,000 as noted) and another for 6,500 persons, a library, administration block, and an outdoor platform for 50,000 participants in political demonstrations. Here Le Corbusier showed further applications of the new typologies that he introduced to audiences at the Modern. He designed the two halls as megaphone-shaped auditoria, fanning out in opposite directions, each derived from his League of Nations project (1927). The research of Gustave Lyon influenced the design of the roof, an acoustical shell based on Freyssinet's dirigible hangars at Orly, with metal girders attached to a parabolic arch.[84] A network of ramps linked together the assemblage. The innovative design for the Palace of the Soviets, intended as a forum

for political meetings and mass communication, paralleled the daring character and idealism of the burgeoning Socialist state. In emphasizing the flexibility of its typologies Le Corbusier suggested to American audiences that the project might serve the democratic functions of a capitalist society as well as the collective functions of a communist one. Because of its potential resources, the United States offered him more reason to hope for such a commission. The model later created as much controversy as the project, the question of its ownership generating one of the most enduring conflicts of the American tour (see chapter 9).

At his first Columbia lecture Le Corbusier presented his design for the Pavillon Suisse at the Cité Universitaire in Paris (1930–1931; plate 8).[85] In a drawing sequence he showed how his design provided both an economic and an aesthetic solution to a difficult site. The dormitory for Swiss students was built on land above an excavated stone quarry (figure 3.16). He sketched longitudinal and transverse sections to indicate a challenging structural problem. He showed how his design of a four-story structure of steel, stone, and glass was supported on concrete *pilotis* with foundations sunk sixty feet deep to the floor of the quarry cavities.[86] Planned for about fifty students, the building served as one unit of housing *à redents*. Le Corbusier emphasized how the dormitory conveyed Radiant

3.15
Le Corbusier, model, Palace of the Soviets, Moscow, 1931–1932. (*Creation Is a Patient Search*, p. 104.) © 2001 Artists Rights Society (ARS), New York/ADAGP, Paris/FLC.

3.16
Le Corbusier, Pavillon Suisse,
north side, Paris, 1930–1931.
(Photograph by Lucien Hervé, FLC
L2(8)21.) © 2001 Artists Rights
Society (ARS), New York/ADAGP,
Paris/FLC.

City principles, responding to social needs and the character of the site while conveying the fusion of modern building techniques with preindustrial methods. The housing block was raised one story above the ground to accommodate circulation underneath. Paired student rooms extended the length of the glazed south side (a further evolution of the elongated window in the five points) and overlooked a sunny playing field (*parc des sports*). A curved staircase tower annexed to the north side contained halls and toilet facilities. Communal services, including a refectory, kitchen, and library, were housed within a curved block of reinforced concrete, expanded on the ground level and faced with stone. To the architect the concrete and rubble stone wall represented a "modern aesthetic."[87] It also sustained his interest in vernacular and regional identities that he introduced in his Maisons Loucheur project of 1928–1929 (see figure 7.4) and de Mandrot House, Le Pradet, near Toulon in the south of France (1929–1931; see figure 2.4).[88] But the use of rough stonework for the Swiss Pavilion also may have been a symbolic allusion to the quarry that necessitated deeper foundations for the *pilotis* so well defined in his lecture drawings for Columbia.[89]

In promoting these great works to Americans Le Corbusier stressed two issues: first, that important buildings could only result from increased technology within the building industry, a kind of architectural determinism; and second, that the Radiant City required diverse typologies. The presentations on great works offered prototypes: three museums within the artistic and cultural sphere; the Palace of the Soviets as a paradigm for political and state functions; and the Swiss Pavilion as a model for mass housing. Such works demonstrated the transformation in his production from the machine age forms of the 1920s to the more synthetic forms of the 1930s that reflected social and communal functions and expressed an integration of the rational with the organic. Fundamentally experimental, Le Corbusier's new building forms "played the role of laboratories." He suggested to his audiences, but did not identify until later in the tour, what social functions within American culture might require some of these new typologies.[90]

Theory of Pure Forms

The third theme of the American lectures explored primary forms for their aesthetic value as well as their social implications for buildings and cities. Le Corbusier opened lectures at Princeton University (November 16) and the Kalamazoo Institute of Arts (November 22) with illustrations of geometrical forms—circle, sphere, triangle, cone, pyramid, square, rectangle, cylinder, cube, and prism (plate 7). Recalling themes of his early writings, he explained how the fundamental principles of architecture infused such forms. He suggested both their ideal origin and their pragmatic associations. If he used Phileban or Platonic solids to emphasize the idealism of these pure forms and elementary prisms in *Vers une architecture,* he used a page illustrating *lignes, surfaces,* and *solides* from a French primary school book as the frontispiece of *Urbanisme* to demonstrate the practical applications of these forms in building.[91] In *Vers une architecture* he contrasted the purity of the Phileban solids with a "bric-à-brac" assemblage of Roman civic monuments to underscore his contention that the Romans (like the Americans) were "great constructors" but, notwithstanding their capacity to plan on a large scale (viz., Hadrian's Villa at Tivoli), allowed their city to be too congested, "too huddled together."[92]

To emphasize what he considered to be the ethical implications of these geometrical forms on city planning, he showed Princeton and Kalamazoo audiences a sequence of such forms linked to a path. In *Urbanisme* he used similar designs to demonstrate that roads should not determine the siting of buildings. His annotated lecture sketches on a Princeton Inn envelope branded such planning *mauvais* or *indifférent* (figure 3.17).[93] Cities required "surgery" so that streets were straight, rational, and no longer located at the foot of buildings but lifted up onto *pilotis.*[94] During the 1930s he looked increasingly to human as well as to optical factors that guided design.[95] The *Kalamazoo Gazette* reported that Le Corbusier addressed the consequences in architecture of a "psycho-physiological" reaction, an expression he explained in *La Ville radieuse.* That response involved a "sense of movement in space" and a "human scale of im-

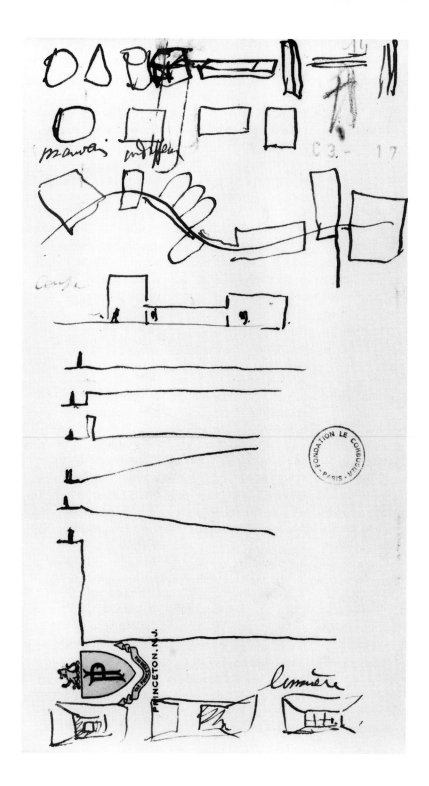

3.17
Le Corbusier, sketches of "pure forms," Phileban or Platonic solids, and "law of meander" on Princeton Inn envelope. (FLC Archive C3(17)14.) © 2001 Artists Rights Society (ARS), New York/ADAGP, Paris/FLC.

mauvais indifféren[t] [bad indifferent] // lumière [light]

3.18
Le Corbusier, Villa le Sextant,
La Palmyre-les-Mathes, France,
1934–1935. (*Oeuvre complète
1934–1938,* p. 135.) © 2001
Artists Rights Society (ARS), New
York/ADAGP, Paris/FLC.

pressions or optical reactions."[96] To elucidate his point for American audiences, he drew a sequence of images of man in relation to such building components as a door or a ramp, ascending or descending.[97]

Le Corbusier's Kalamazoo lecture applied Platonic solids to discussions of both his five points and Radiant City. The Princeton lecture applied them to a study of the villa and seemed to double back on earlier themes. He explained how the free facade would permit glass walls and multiple exposures to natural light (see plates 1, 7). Steel or reinforced concrete construction would eliminate bearing walls and thereby liberate a *plan paralysé.*[98] To show the evolution in his work and ideas over the preceding decade, he revealed "infinite combinations" of these forms in schematic drawings.[99] To Le Corbusier the five points led axiomatically to the iconic image of the building raised on *pilotis* (see figure 3.6). More detailed drawings of the Villa Savoye explained the integration of new elements and typologies: a section drawing emphasized structure and circulation; a ground floor plan indicated vehicular circulation between *pilotis;* a plan of the top floor and an axonometic drawing suggested the importance of siting in relation to sun and views (see plate 7 and figure 2.2).

The striking perspective renderings and section drawing of the house at Mathes (Villa le Sextant) on France's Atlantic coast (1934–1935; see plate 7) showed the Princeton audience Le Corbusier's application of geometrical forms as well as a prominent dihedral elevation. The example of Mathes made the point that, like the Pavillon Suisse, rationalized construction techniques "conforming to a standard" could join with preindustrial methods. Yet it also signaled a new direction in his work away from machine-inspired forms of such villas as the Savoye. At Mathes economic and social factors encouraged Le Corbusier to specify masonry rubble wall construction independent of its timber framing (figure 3.18). Materials were adapted to local construction methods. Like the Errázuriz House project in Chile (1930), the architect designed the house at Mathes without a site visit. Yet he was still attentive to such regional factors as climate and topography, incorporating louvered attic windows for natural ventilation. He was proud to claim that the house was constructed "without a fault, without supervision—by a small village contractor, honest and conscientious—and on an unbelievable budget."[100] Here the faculty of man—the contractor as well as the designer—produced flawless perfection and "good regionalism."[101]

As an addendum to his discussion of villas at Princeton, Le Corbusier presented the problem of the individual housing unit (see plate 7 top right). If a villa might appeal to the Princeton elite, the housing unit could interest the socially responsible student. Calling it a biological unit or cell (*cellule*), Le Corbusier suggested links between the dwelling unit and communal services. He based his worker housing on the monk's cell and also on utopian models.[102] Entering his typology in 1922 with the Immeuble-villas project and the Maison Citrohan, such housing explored the problem of the individual unit or cell in relation to the collective block.[103] Such worker housing now fused independent units into an organization that embraced communitarian principles. Introducing his Kalamazoo audience to the Immeuble-villas, he presented it as a typology based on his theory of pure form but flexible in its adaptation, especially to the city.[104]

Le Corbusier's increasing preoccupation with housing standards and mass production during the late 1920s led him to develop the Maison Minimum (the minimum house) and to submit his findings to the CIAM II conference in Frankfurt in 1929.[105] The theme of the conference, *Die Wohnung für das Existenzminimum* (Housing for minimum habitation), was defined in keynote addresses by the Swiss historian and critic Sigfried Giedion and by Ernst May, as well as in papers by Walter Gropius, Victor Bourgeois, and Hans Schmidt. Le Corbusier based his Minimum House on the five points and on minimum standards—space, sanitation, utilities, and mechanicals—set by the Loi Loucheur, the French law passed in 1928 to allocate large public sums for housing. He was further influenced by the specifications, efficiency, and streamlining of the ocean liner cabin.

During his 1929 South American lecture tour he presented his theorem "a man = a cell; from cells = a city."[106] From a single unit to an entire urban fabric, this principle linked the efficiency of the mechanical world through standardization with the biological and psychological needs of man. Reflecting the concerns of the 1930s, he now hoped to engage machines in the service of humanity. More broadly, this synthesis of man, architecture, and urban landscape approached the objectives of regional syndicalists searching for an integrated utopian society and a new *homme réel*.[107]

At the CIAM III conference in Brussels in 1930, Le Corbusier and other participants, including Gropius, May, and Viennese-born American delegate Richard Neutra, addressed the efficacy of high-rise, low-cost urban buildings, in addition to issues of standardization, land reorganization for housing, urban centralization, and government support for housing.[108] There Le Corbusier exhibited his plans for a Radiant City in which the concatenated *à redents* apartment block functioned as a free-standing slab lifted on *pilotis* above its green space.[109] A corridor (*rue intérieure*) bisected each of the slab's independent units. Through standardization and efficient planning, modest unit sizes of fourteen square meters per occupant would produce the order, harmony, and economy that were lacking in traditionally planned units. Such perspective views of the interior space as the one he presented at Princeton (see plate 7) indicate hermetically sealed walls of plate glass.[110]

With his discussion of the fundamental tenets of modern architectural theory, geometry of pure forms, the biological cell, and standards for the minimum house, as well as their implications for mass housing in the Radiant City, Le Corbusier brought the most comprehensive presentation of his theory and design full circle at Princeton. These lectures, which flowed from aesthetic issues of pure form to the needs of society, addressed the relationship between the single unit and the mass housing block, between individual requirements and collective services, between experimental structural systems and proven construction techniques, between luxury and low-cost, with all the implications of private patronage as opposed to state support.

As he brashly informed the audience in his opening lecture at the Modern, these and other issues affecting the future progress of architecture and urbanism could be resolved only by a new coalition of mind and body: European "wisdom" and American technique. Americans, he suggested, were like their buildings: "strong of force" but "weak of spirit." Of course, he chose to ignore the fact that technique was not simply a matter of raw power but of systematic study and application—the intellectual and the practical. However, at issue was what he considered the misguided application of American technique. Notwithstanding the merits of his insights, his offer to provide his own European wisdom as a key agent in the redirection of American technology, aimed at improving social conditions as well as the formation of an alliance between American government leaders and industrialists, was both naive and presumptuous. His rhetoric and intriguing drawings projected to Americans the controversial notion that an individual from beyond their shores could not only best explain them but also most effectively *lead* them. To the imperious architect from Paris the message in his lectures afforded "a small window" of hope that the New World would enter into a second machine age. But America, then at the low ebb of the Depression, was more inclined to be a passive listener than a committed follower.

4

Le Corbusier Takes America

Three objectives shaped Le Corbusier's tour. The first was to execute the arduous itinerary of lectures. During the first month he kept to the relentless schedule, traveling to different venues but keeping the Park Central Hotel in Manhattan as home base. With the energy of a seasoned politician and the zeal of an evangelist, he completed his formal obligations by Thanksgiving Day. The second objective was to search for commissions. That compelled him to seek out prospective clients and a centralized authority in both the private and public sectors. Le Corbusier's lectures and the publicity associated with them helped to promote his architecture and urbanism, especially the Radiant City. His third objective was to "see the U.S.A." If he could not collect large fees for his lectures, he could at least experience the realities of its modern culture that would inform the book he planned to write about America. And Marguerite Harris largely made that possible.

Of the three goals, the search for commissions dominated. When the lectures were over, Le Corbusier remained in New York City, lodged at the Gotham Hotel, to look for work. Dedicating himself to that search and reserving most of his free time to be with Marguerite, he canceled lecture engagements on the West Coast as well as plans to visit CIAM colleague Richard Neutra in Los Angeles, his Swiss friend Albert Frey who was practicing architecture in Palm Springs, and Washington friends Mildred and Robert Woods Bliss.

From his first days in Manhattan to his last, Le Corbusier's three objectives were closely intertwined. Throughout the tour he engaged his various constituencies: students, avant-garde supporters and intellectuals, the social group, businessmen and industrialists, professional architects, and the press. Each group offered a different response. As a result of visits to cities and towns in the East and Midwest, Le Corbusier identified separate spheres in American culture. In *When the Cathedrals Were White* he once more expressed his bias not only toward urban rather than rural cultures but also toward the largest and most progressive American cities, New York and Chicago. Even then, Manhattan was the only city that truly intrigued him: "For a traveler, New York is the great event of the journey." There he pinned all his hopes and aspirations for work and for realization of Radiant City principles in the New World. With several notable exceptions, most of the lecture sites did not especially interest him. There "in the innumerable cities of the USA," he had found only "average societies," average perhaps because they did not embrace modern life as he saw it elsewhere, and average too because he did not find clients there.[1]

Throughout his visit Le Corbusier took the pulse of America, its cities and suburbs, its buildings and public spaces, its institutions and values. He offered in lectures (especially those in Baltimore and the Midwest), in articles, and in *Cathedrals* some of the most penetrating observations ever written about the nature of American culture and society during the Great Depression, both its virtues and defects. In doing so he joined firsthand experience to his reservoir of preconceptions.

From October 24 to Thanksgiving, his days in Manhattan were dovetailed with lecture commitments out of town. As a result of publicity generated by the Museum of Modern Art, his lectures received gratifying public notice. Professional journals announced the tour. *Architectural Forum* trumpeted the "Coming of Corbusier," who was "indelibly associated with the flat planes and *polychromy* [my emphasis] of the International Style." This dramatic announcement also plunged him into a continuing debate, declaring him on the one hand "a messiah to the moderns" and on the other hand "anathema" to the "traditionalists."[2] *Architectural Record* published an early version of his ambitious lecture schedule.[3] Supplied with press releases from the Modern, local newspapers promoted the lectures and frequently reported on them. In other circumstances, Le Corbusier would have been critical of this typically American "organ of waste." Architects, both moderns and traditionalists, as well as intellectuals and the avant-garde, knew of the man through his controversial writings, but to the vast majority of educated Americans, he was not yet known. Robert Jacobs remembered the consensus of the time that Le Corbusier was "considered avant-garde, which would attract a certain group of people—liberals, intellectuals."[4]

Reaction to the first lecture at the Modern was mixed. Philip Goodwin reported that the talk was too long and suffered from too many "stills" (slides). He responded ambivalently, "I admire the new ideas, and think we are going towards them, but to live in one of his two hundred and twenty thousand human-being-honeycombs—or one of his chairs—would be hell!"[5]

After the opening events at the Modern Le Corbusier traveled to Hartford for his first out-of-town ap-

pearance at the Wadsworth Atheneum on October 25. A. Everett Austin, the Atheneum's charismatic director, arranged the lecture.[6] But unbeknownst to Le Corbusier, it was underwritten by Austin's friend and cousin (by marriage), Philip Goodwin. A native of Hartford, Goodwin wanted to encourage modernism there and also ensure the success of Le Corbusier's tour.[7] Largely through Austin's efforts, Hartford had acquired a considerable reputation for supporting avant-garde art. The new Avery Memorial wing (1934), designed by the firm of Morris and O'Connor, distinguished itself as the first modern museum in America.[8] Le Corbusier later recalled how impressed he was by the design of this "architecturally young" museum addition whose galleries were "joyously lighted" by skylights (figure 4.1).[9] Austin influenced not only the modern elements of Av-

4.1

Avery Court, Wadsworth Atheneum, 1934. (Wadsworth Atheneum, Hartford.)

ery Court, but also the museum's patronage of modern art and culture.[10] Through his efforts, the Avery Memorial held the first Picasso retrospective in America, the first production of Gertrude Stein and Virgil Thomson's *Four Saints in Three Acts* with an all-black cast, and the first surrealist exhibition in America, organized by writer and art critic James Thrall Soby.[11] Austin was also the first American museum director to make significant purchases of seventeenth-century Italian art, including the work of Caravaggio, then considered daring acquisitions. Because of Austin's support of modern art and culture, much against the taste of the museum's old-guard board of directors, Le Corbusier proclaimed the Atheneum a "living museum" and Hartford "a spiritual center in America."[12]

Le Corbusier's fame as well as his notoriety were already well known to Austin's circle of urbane art patrons and supporters. The *Hartford Courant* announced his arrival in its article, "Noted French Architect Is Storm Center." There the architect George Nelson, a native of Hartford, called the controversial Le Corbusier "more widely copied and more bitterly attacked than any living member of his craft."[13] By all accounts the Atheneum lecture was a great success. Its contents were similar to his lecture at the Modern the previous day but, according to Austin, pared down to "a more digestible length." Austin, who had been warned by Goodwin to expect a challenging visitor, reported that "although our lecturer was a little bit difficult before the performance, he afterwards lapsed into an extremely good mood and was most complimentary about the museum, examining it from head to toe." Later that evening the speaker and a small group were invited to Soby's Farmington house. There Austin found his guest "even more sociable," behaving "almost in a courtly manner."[14] He seemed comfortable in Hartford, where he displayed "worlds of charm."[15]

The next morning the group returned to Farmington where Le Corbusier, Jacobs, and Hitchcock joined Soby on the roof of a new addition to his Greek Revival house (figure 4.2). Le Corbusier, then following current French fashion, was conspicuously not wearing a hat, which was a breach of American decorum. The house addition, still under construction, was designed by Hitchcock to be used as a gallery for Soby's expanding collection of modern art. For it, Le Corbusier recommended to Hitchcock square windows on the upper story of the north side.[16] According to Jacobs, Le Corbusier considered this white clapboarded house "typically American—for a rich American."[17] In principle, he opposed its traditional plan and rigid room division. "When I do a house," he emphasized repeatedly during the lecture tour, "I use *les cloisons mobiles*, movable partitions" made possible by a "free plan."[18]

The Hartford event epitomized the social obligations of his lecture tour and his efforts to engage three of his audience groups: local society, avant-garde, and press. He met Hartford's expectation to inform, enlighten, and charm the museum's friends of art. Although Hartford residents may have typified the banal elements in the "innumerable cities in the USA," Austin and Soby's sympathies with avant-garde art distinguished the town and its museum as an oasis of high culture. During the 1930s the museum forged an alliance of support for modern art among avant-garde sympathizers, the social elite, and the business community. Mindful of the economic depression in France and its effects on his artist friends in Europe, Le Corbusier used his influence to promote their work. He deposited with Soby a group of drawings by his cousin Louis Soutter (1871–1942), a surrealist artist. Soby was able to sell a number of them to various American collectors and dealers, and even organized an exhibition the next year at the Atheneum.[19] However, to the city's conservative elite, many of them museum patrons, Le Corbusier's visit was just one more instance of Chick Austin's efforts to promote the *ultra*, which they chose to regard as a purely social occasion. But to Austin, Soby, and their followers, the visit advanced their efforts to create a haven for the avant-garde in that risk-averse insurance capital.

Le Corbusier's subsequent lectures to academic audiences were particularly challenging. These audiences made up another sphere of influence, primarily students and professional architects. As he later told a friend, "the colleges here were in a state of complete architectural slumber."[20] By his standards, of course, they were. Yet, at the same time, he recognized in the schools and their

4.2
Henry-Russell Hitchcock,
Robert Jacobs, James Thrall
Soby, and Le Corbusier on the
roof of Soby house addition,
Farmington, Connecticut,
October 1935. (Wadsworth
Atheneum, Hartford.)

faculty "a sort of fear of seeing the doors open on the unknown of tomorrow."[21] In 1935 the discipline and profession of architecture in the United States would undergo a transition to modernism led by a few progressive educators and practitioners. Although a few early modernists such as Raymond Hood and George Howe, a few foreign-born practitioners including William Lescaze and Richard Neutra, and a few landmark competitions and exhibitions including the 1922 Chicago Tribune competition, the 1932 "Modern Architecture" exhibition, and the 1933 Century of Progress Exposition in Chicago had had a significant impact, educational institutions were slow to transform their curricula and the profession at large was even slower to adjust. By the fall of 1935 the unwieldy Beaux-Arts system of architectural education in America had faltered and was about to be dislodged for the first time. Le Corbusier's presence at architecture schools signaled change.

Joseph Hudnut (1886–1968) was largely responsible for initiating the conversion to modernism in American architecture schools. Dean of Columbia University's School of Architecture and later dean of the Graduate School of Design at Harvard University, he implemented the curricular reforms, policies, and new appointments that transformed the schools.[22] Le Corbusier's visit to Columbia fell between two regimes— a progressive one led by Hudnut and a more conservative one headed by Leopold Arnaud. In 1933–1935 Hudnut helped negotiate Le Corbusier's American tour and, as part of a larger effort to expose students to European modernism, arranged for his lectures at Columbia.

Until Hudnut assumed his post as acting dean at Columbia in 1933 and dean in 1934, the school was dominated by an entrenched faculty trained in the Beaux-Arts system and reluctant to change. Most professors, according to Morris Lapidus who studied there from 1924 to 1927, were unwilling to introduce students to the new architecture from Europe. Only too aware that it would soon overturn the Beaux-Arts system, Lapidus recalled, his professors were "fighting for what they felt was their professional life."[23] During the 1920s such younger faculty members as Wallace K. Harrison, who taught architectural design at Columbia from 1925 to 1927, shared this reluctance, and it was not until 1931 that Harrison demonstrated his conversion to European modernism.[24]

During the 1920s and 1930s growing numbers of students and professors were influenced by the manifestos of European modernism.[25] Students were exposed to the rush of new architectural imagery and design ideas, even though they were given no formal training in analyzing and interpreting them. During his student years, Lapidus recalled, European modernism seemed daring and Le Corbusier's work visionary. "A great revolution was beginning to take place in my profession," Lapidus remembered, "we saw pictures of the Paris World's Fair of 1925, and we were excited by this new architecture. We looked at photographs of Mies van der Rohe's German Pavilion at the Barcelona Fair. Eric Mendelssohn [sic] was creating buildings with free-flowing lines in Germany, lines such as no other building had ever had. Le Corbusier, the Frenchman, was making sketches of wild-looking buildings that we thought no one would ever build. The Dutch architect, Doodok [sic], was creating a new school of design. A group of architects who had founded a school in Germany which they called the Bauhaus . . . But all of this was forbidden territory for us."[26]

During the academic year 1934–1935 Hudnut implemented a series of sweeping curricular reforms based on his own pedagogical position on architecture that emphasized the science of construction, cultural issues, and economic and intellectual developments, as well as on the recommendations of a June 1934 report endorsed by Columbia President Nicholas Murray Butler.[27] That report recommended that the school shed its "stylistic" approach in favor of an "organic" one through the study of "fundamental principles" based "on reality," meaning the practice of architecture. It proposed a new curriculum responsive to social factors in architecture, low-cost housing, methods of construction, appropriate use of materials in relation to problems of design and construction, and economic considerations. In the professional debate between modernists and traditionalists, the report clearly sided with modernists. Moreover, its endorsement of the organic reflected the position of "modernists" and of Frank Lloyd Wright, who would be especially vocal in his opposition to eclecticism during the coming year.[28]

In effect, Hudnut's educational policy initiatives called for an end to the Beaux-Arts system and with it changes in the faculty. His new curriculum substituted pragmatic design courses for *analytiques* and *projets*.[29] Programs would be site specific. Students would acquire knowledge of modern construction methods and "awareness of the social implications" of architecture. Widely published in professional journals, this approach supported practical and technical training, rather than pictorial representation. These reforms began the transformations that eventually recast architectural education in America toward modernism.[30] At their core was the concept of technique, providing students with "a thorough technical knowledge in building construction" including engineering, equipment, legal and business practice, labor, and economics.[31] Hudnut's notion of technique coincided with Le Corbusier's because both considered its socioeconomic implications.[32] But Hudnut's interpretation broke with the more poetic and symbolic aspects of Le Corbusier's rhetoric. "Since Le Corbusier provided the necessary mystifications," Hudnut observed, "the dogma of functionalism has taken on an almost religious character."[33] In the end, the theoretical and pedagogical underpinnings of his curricular reforms of 1934–1935 resulted in a hybrid of design approaches deriving from residual Beaux-Arts teaching and European modernism.[34] In adopting the new curriculum, he concluded, "Columbia stands practically alone."[35]

Hudnut's reforms resulted in the resignation of senior faculty entrenched in the Beaux-Arts, the conversion of existing faculty, and the appointment of young faculty of the new persuasion.[36] Among the latter, Max Abramovitz taught architectural design at Columbia for two years, 1930–1932, where he received a master's degree. As a student at the University of Illinois he "took seriously" his reading of *Vers une architecture* and "decided it backed up my life."[37] Pierre A. Bezy, a young French architect, was also educated at the University of Illinois and at Columbia where he taught design from 1930 to 1936.[38] In 1934 Hudnut recruited Latvian-born Jan Ruhtenberg from his practice in Sweden to teach design and, in Ruhtenberg's words, "help to give the start to the new movement in architecture."[39] New faculty considerably expanded the role of city planning. Hudnut enlisted Henry Wright and Werner Hegemann to teach courses in architectural design and planning.[40]

Hudnut also sought to advance his reforms through Harvey Wiley Corbett and Talbot Faulkner Hamlin (1889–1956), two senior professors who had recently converted from the Beaux-Arts to modernism.[41] In 1931, when Corbett assumed his responsibilities as chairman of the Architectural Commission of the 1933 Century of Progress Exposition in Chicago, he had already denounced historicism in favor of "scientific research" and "new materials" to make "functionalism a basis of design."[42] Hamlin, who taught history and theory courses at Columbia, resisted what today would be called the myth of functionalism in modernism.[43] His review of *Towards a New Architecture* was critical of "propaganda."[44] Moreover, his review of the 1932 "Modern Architecture" exhibition, "The International Style Lacks the Essence of Great Architecture," opposed the contradictions he observed in its philosophy of "strict functionalism."[45] Notwithstanding such reservations, beginning in 1931–1932 Hamlin introduced Columbia students to European modernism. Abramovitz remembered the lectures where "we touched [on] Corbusier and Behrens and Loos and all of that group—the Bauhaus. . . ."[46] Even Hamlin recognized that the Depression required a change of educational focus toward a more pragmatic approach with increasing awareness of social responsibility, housing, city planning, and economics that would challenge the profession.[47]

When Le Corbusier lectured at Columbia, Hudnut had already gone to Harvard's School of Architecture.[48] During the tenure of his successor, Leopold Arnaud, Hudnut's reforms lost momentum, especially with the dismissal of many of his key appointments.[49] Le Corbusier was aware of the winds of change at Columbia and other schools and hoped that he would have a seminal role in the conversion process.[50] In his two Columbia lectures he sought to engage not only receptive architecture students and design professionals, but also potential clients in the New York area. His first talk on October 28 at 5 P.M. was followed by an "official dinner," which provided him with introductions. There were light moments as well as serious ones. His second Columbia appearance on November 19 came near the end of the tour when he had already given over a dozen such talks and his attitude was rather blasé. Robert Jacobs remembered that November evening when he stopped by Le Corbusier's hotel to escort him uptown. The speaker had been sleeping and was hungry, so they stopped at a delicatessen on Broadway for some French bread. When Le Corbusier finally arrived at the amphitheater in Havemeyer Hall, "there were Nicholas Murray Butler, the eminent president of Columbia, and all the dignitaries waiting. Corbu was late. And he walked into the lecture room munching on one end of this loaf of bread tucked under his arm, completely unconscious of anything around him. . . ."[51]

The Columbia audience was sophisticated and knowledgeable about both modern architecture and Le Corbusier's writings. The content of the lectures, therefore, was not as revealing as the speaker's performance. In reviewing the lectures, Hamlin focused on Le Corbusier as a personality but was critical of his urbanism. He identified, on the one hand, the "rigidly logical—character of his thinking" and on the other, his tendency toward "oversimplification," which, when applied to city planning, failed to consider the impact of his theories on a "philosophy of human life." In contrast to his writings, which were deemed "strained and strident," his presence and his ability to elucidate his ideas graphically truly impressed Hamlin. "The dynamic power of his personality—so well expressed in his tall spare form and his long well-modeled head,—the beautiful organization of the material, and especially the swift, nervous drawings with which he so deftly and clearly illustrated his points," recounted Hamlin, "added immensely to the vividness of his theories."[52]

After Columbia, Le Corbusier returned to Connecticut, where he spoke at Wesleyan (October 29) and Yale (October 30). He had come to Middletown at the invitation of Hitchcock who was assistant professor of

art and director of Wesleyan University architectural exhibitions.[53] There Le Corbusier produced what Hitchcock called "large architectural sketches" (*grand* [sic] *esquisses architecturales*). Although they have not survived, the drawings were initially kept as Hitchcock intended to include them, along with an example of Le Corbusier's "work as a painter" (*oeuvre comme peintre*) in one of his avant-garde exhibitions at Wesleyan.[54]

Le Corbusier's lecture at Yale, like those at Columbia, occurred during the school's own transition to modernism. Everett V. Meeks, dean of the Yale School of Fine Arts and chairman of the Department of Architecture, wrote to Le Corbusier in the spring of 1935 inviting him to participate in what came to be known as the Martin A. Ryerson Lectures on Modern Architecture.[55] But traditionalist Meeks, like MIT's dean William Emerson, assumed a staunch antimodernist position until the 1940s when he buckled under considerable pressure, allowing "modernist architecture as the formal basis for teaching design in the school."[56] In anticipation of Le Corbusier's lecture, Meeks wrote to Emerson that the "students are quite excited" about the eight speakers, concluding with a tongue-in-cheek rhetorical comment: "I wonder whether from these they are going to discover the 'new philosophy' of design."[57]

The Ryerson series for 1935–1936 featured other distinguished proponents of modern architecture, among them Frank Lloyd Wright, Ralph Walker, George Howe, and Eliel Saarinen. Yale students regarded the series as "brilliant," claiming that "all the prominent architects of the time had been brought on campus."[58] When campus news reports announced the upcoming lecture by "the eminent French modernist," student interest increased and the event was changed to a larger hall.[59] Le Corbusier's appearance, in the words of one undergraduate at the time, "impressed us very much." Some remember enjoying his "posturing and his accent." Others, however, candidly admitted, that it was "all in French" and they "didn't understand a word of it!"[60]

Wright's lecture, which launched the series, set the tone. He declared America lacking in culture and called for an "organic" architecture, an expression of the individual.[61] When he attacked eclecticism and "imitation in architecture," criticizing James Gamble Rogers's academic Gothic revival buildings, Yale students responded with laughter.[62] Thus even though the students supported change, the kind of change that Le Corbusier offered them was more controversial.[63] They considered Le Corbusier's theories esoteric and treated his concepts with skepticism. The *Yale Daily News* reported that Le Corbusier "claimed that his style was a reflection of the modern machine age." Moreover, he "attempted to prove his theory" that housing "is influenced by the skyscraper, factory, suspension bridge and automobile."[64] Only through the Modern's traveling exhibit (November 4–10) of his work did the Yale community come to appreciate the "sociological" intentions of his work, notably in the Swiss Pavilion and the Nemours project.[65]

Le Corbusier's swing through Connecticut, like his first one to Hartford and Farmington, acquainted him with the American countryside. The trip alerted him to the "bewildering social deficit" of "gigantic suburbs" with their infrastructure of roads and rails for commuters.[66] His return from New Haven in a Pullman car introduced him to the air-conditioned luxury of American trains (even though it was autumn). Yet such club comforts, he thought, belied the underlying waste of suburban commuting, which he considered a social problem resulting from an industrialized system based on capitalism.

Le Corbusier regarded his subsequent visits to Vassar College and Princeton University as parallel experiences shaped by gender and a culture of affluence. He characterized the students in clichés of *américanisme*. He claimed that these students represented a new American youth nurtured by wealthy families and pressed into democratic institutions. To him they symbolized the best and worst aspects of American youth and culture. For even though both institutions had transformed their students into healthy athletes—"Taylorized" by the standards of *américanisme*—these young men and women continued to be afflicted with troubled spirits.

Le Corbusier arrived at Vassar two days after his Yale lecture. Like most American colleges "bathed in verdure," Vassar was located "within a budding grove." It seemed to be a cloistered "temporary paradise" that the

architect sarcastically christened "a joyous convent." So he was not prepared to accept its liberated women. Here he offered his own interpretation of the mind-body conflict that affected educated American women of the 1930s. He enjoyed the athleticism of their "beautiful bodies" and appreciated their "impeccable French." He was confounded by the breadth of their concerns, from frivolous questions—whether he "preferred blonds or brunettes"—to serious issues, ranging from the economic to the sociological and psychological. At once feigning ignorance of such weighty issues and escaping his duties as guest lecturer, he chided these intelligent women, "you are too serious, I must be excused, I am going to join the people who are eating cookies." Yet their intelligence, coupled with their understanding of his "bold theses," he thought, would make them his "best propagandists." "I never had a more responsive audience during my trip," he noted facetiously. But he maligned these intelligent, liberated, cigarette-smoking, athletic women with the epithet "Amazons"—"swollen in mind and body." True to his character, he interpreted their behavior in opposing reactions of shock and delight. He claimed to be appalled by the "mob scene" after his lecture: "they rush onto the platform and seize five or six large drawings . . . rip them apart, tear them up, cut them into small pieces. A piece for each Amazon. Pens in hand, they cry: 'Sign, sign!'"[67] Confirming the incident, one Vassar student recalled that "immediately after the lecture but still during the applause the whole front row erupted, got up on the stage, and the drawings were gone in thirty seconds."[68]

The stereotype Amazons reflects Le Corbusier's mixed feelings about American women at the same time that it reveals a component of *américanisme*. To him Vassar women were free spirits whose elite education and family backgrounds allowed them certain privileges that contrasted sharply with their French counterparts. He acknowledged their intelligence in traditional fields such as languages. But he patronized the liberal political views that armed these women for the "great overturning" of society with "a touching ingenuousness."[69] According to Robert Jacobs, Le Corbusier was "very smitten," with a "statuesque, tall beautiful girl" named

Alma Clayburgh.[70] She was the daughter of New York operatic singer Alma Clayburgh, known as Madame Clayburgh, with whom Le Corbusier socialized in New York City and the next year in Europe (figure 4.3). Young Alma came to symbolize for him a predisposition within the American psyche.

When Le Corbusier delivered his next lectures at Harvard and MIT's schools of architecture (November 5 and 6) he was stepping into Boston's conservative milieu, and he knew it. In *Cathedrals* he alluded to the city's abiding puritanism when he called Boston the "city of thought and meditation."[71] Staying at the Copley Plaza Hotel and dining alone the evening of his Harvard lecture (a situation that would have been inconceivable a generation later), he noted the traditional character of Bostonians that reverberated in the two schools. But what he may only have suspected before his visit was the hostile attitude toward him that prevailed among most of the faculty, especially George H. Edgell of Harvard

and Emerson at MIT. The previous spring the two deans reluctantly signed on to sponsor the architect's lectures at their respective schools. In a letter to Edgell, Emerson wrote that he considered Le Corbusier "a much over-rated individual" and was not disposed to "pay out much good money" for a lecture. Nonetheless, Emerson conceded that "this is a point of view from which many others differ diametrically."[72] In his reply Edgell concurred with Emerson's view, but conceded that the proposed speaker was "an interesting man with interesting ideas" and that Harvard students would be "eager to hear him."[73] Even the reform-minded Hudnut, who succeeded Edgell as dean that fall, sarcastically referred to Le Corbusier as "the great man."[74] Lecturing on town planning at Harvard's Robinson Hall, Le Corbusier was introduced by Jean-Jacques Haffner, the school's distinguished French professor, himself about to be unseated by Hudnut's reforms. A graduate of the Ecole des Beaux-Arts and Prix de Rome winner (1919), Haffner came to

4.3
Madame Alma Clayburgh and Alma Clayburgh sailing on the S.S. *Champlain.* (*New York World-Telegram,* June 20, 1936; Library of Congress, Prints and Photographs Division, NYWT&S Collection.)

Harvard in 1921 where he directed the Beaux-Arts program. But by 1930 he allowed students to follow the work of Le Corbusier, J. J. P. Oud, and other modernists. When Hudnut consolidated the Schools of Architecture, Landscape Architecture, and City Planning into the Graduate School of Design and began to reorganize the school according to his Columbia model during the academic year 1935–1936, Haffner eventually resigned under pressure. Walter Gropius replaced him as professor of architecture in the spring of 1937.[75]

On the afternoon of his second day in Boston Le Corbusier met with journalists and then lectured on "Modern Architecture" at MIT's Rogers Building in Boston, where the school of architecture was then located to be close to the professional community whose offices were near Copley Plaza. If American architects, according to Lawrence B. Anderson, then a young MIT professor of architecture, regarded Le Corbusier as "a kind of curiosity," so did Boston journalists.[76] Like the *New York Herald Tribune,* the conservative *Christian Science Monitor* emphasized the architect's appearance, "attired in a double-breasted suit, brown shirt of geometric design, black bow tie with red spots and wearing glasses with probably the heaviest frames and rims ever seen in these parts . . . " The *Monitor* distorted substantive issues. Unable to distinguish between camps of modernist persuasion, it declared Le Corbusier "the most outspoken exponent of 'functionalism,'" who "'out-wrights' even Frank Lloyd Wright." Providing "clues to the untrammeled ideas" of Le Corbusier, it reported the misconception that he had "never attended school, not even primary school." In a city invested in education, readers of the article must have found that baffling. But the *Monitor* did convey several key elements of Le Corbusier's critique of America: first, that the country had developed methods of mass production but no "philosophy of living," second, that its skyscrapers were not tools of city planning, and third, that America needed "to meet the problem of releasing land for the public's benefit . . . [for] low-cost housing."[77]

Like Harvard during the mid-1930s, MIT's School of Architecture was experiencing what architect Gordon Bunshaft (class of 1935) called "a transition period between the Beaux-Arts and the Modern."[78] But unlike Hudnut, Emerson and a faculty committed to the Beaux-Arts program were resistent to change. According to Anderson, "Emerson represented the old guard in Boston." Even after Jacques Carlu, who headed the design staff, returned to France in 1933, "the faculty was still working in the old mold."[79] For nearly twenty years Harvard, MIT, and the Boston Architectural Club (later Boston Architectural Center) had shared so-called conjunctive problems or sketch problems in the Beaux-Arts curriculum. The endurance of the Beaux-Arts system at the three schools of architecture, according to Anderson, was linked to the city's strong conservative culture. "The art of collectors like Isabella Stewart Gardner—a very connoisseur sort of . . . interest in the Italian Renaissance and in the French Renaissance . . . gave a kind of flavor to Boston culture that was very persistent and very pervasive."[80] But the academic year 1935–1936 marked a watershed at the three schools. Changes in teaching policies at Harvard and MIT resulted in the elimination of conjunctive problems in favor of "interschool problems" shared with such distant institutions as Cornell and the University of Minnesota.[81] By the fall of 1936 Hudnut had begun to reorganize the Harvard curriculum. In shaping the new professional program, he affirmed that "only one subject, *design,* will be taught; but design will be understood as including structural design and the social requirements of architecture."[82] During the academic year 1936–1937 MIT's School of Architecture moved to the main campus in Cambridge and made changes in the curriculum that allowed students to pursue the same general education as those in the sciences and engineering.[83] With the unraveling of the Beaux-Arts system and resulting changes, William Emerson resigned the following year.

When Le Corbusier visited MIT's Rogers Building he saw what he considered to be the toxic effects of a moribund Beaux-Arts program: "huge machines hung on the walls, wash drawings, representing palaces or mausoleums. Boring. Shameful."[84] Ieoh Ming Pei remembered that fall, his first term at the school of architecture when its students were "not inspired" and "groping . . . for a new direction" because they had "no leaders." Students still learned to draw the classical orders and a path to the *analytique,* a pedagogical approach that Pei considered "no longer convincing."[85] Even colonial architecture was still encouraged by some professors.[86] In the face of such entrenched Beaux-Arts pedagogy, Le Corbusier confronted the teachers and students, questioning why they had not "done away with these horrors?"[87]

In the slow transition to modernism at MIT, Le Corbusier's lecture was pivotal. The students felt that they shared an affinity for the architect they regarded as "a strong advocate of 'engineering-building' . . . adapted to present day life."[88] To Harry Weese and the other students, "Le Corbusier was a God."[89] Pei was "mesmerized by the man, by the event," attributing change at the school and in his own work to this visit: "those were the two most important days in my professional life. He was insolent. He was abusive. But he did everything right . . . we had to be shocked out of our complacency."[90] The lectures so impressed Pei that he headed for the library to study the early volumes of the *Oeuvre complète,* which, he later recognized, were the "most important new books for me."[91] In this period at MIT Gordon Bunshaft recollected that "Corbu's books became our bible. What counted more in those books were the drawings, illustrations, and plans, not the written word."[92] But the students' interest often met with frustration. One professor of history, according to Weese, actually "hid all the Le Corbusier books in the library."[93]

In fact, most of MIT's architecture faculty was hostile to the architect. They were "anti . . . all opposed to Corbusier, opposed to Bauhaus," Pei remembered, "particularly William Emerson."[94] According to Weese and others, this explained why no one at MIT saved Le Corbusier's lecture drawings.[95] Faculty support for the modern movement came principally from Lawrence Anderson, later dean of the school.[96] "He would be the only one that would not be prejudiced against it."[97] According to Bunshaft, Anderson was the "head man intellectually and in design."[98] Introduced to Le Corbusier's theory and design during his studies in Paris in the early 1930s, Anderson, together with his partner Herbert L. Beckwith and some of the younger teachers, was respon-

sible for the curricular changes that followed Le Corbusier's visit.

Le Corbusier's appearance in Philadelphia (November 8–9) did not focus on its schools, even though the Architecture Department of the University of Pennsylvania was one of seven organizations sponsoring his lecture.[99] Educational policy at Penn was still resolutely fixed by a cadre of Beaux-Arts architects including Paul Cret, Harry Sternfeld, and John Harbeson.[100] Moreover, its teaching program during the 1930s was still firmly affiliated with the Beaux-Arts Institute of Design.[101] Instead, the Philadelphia Art Alliance was the principal sponsor of the lecture. The Art Alliance, whose impressive honorary committee included Fiske Kimball, director of the Pennsylvania (later Philadelphia) Museum of Art, and architects George Howe, Cret, C. L. Borie, and Clarence Zantzinger, hosted a subscription dinner preceding the talk, both at the Barclay ballroom.[102] Le Corbusier's lecture, entitled "Fundamentals in Architecture," addressed his theory of the Radiant City with drawings for the Stockholm and Algiers projects (see plate 4). Newspaper reports stressed the more controversial aspects of his doctrine, focusing on his plans to launch "garden cities up in the air." They selected quotations from the talk that emphasized the visionary nature of his social message: "Cities all are rebuilt every 50 to 100 years. Let's mobilize property for human good—just as we mobilize in war!"[103] For the war on housing and restructuring of property to do so were themes that Le Corbusier began to address at the CIAM IV congress in 1933 and later in *La Ville radieuse,* in the Pavillon des Temps Nouveaux for the 1937 Paris Exposition "Arts et Techniques," and in his monograph devoted to it, *Des canons, des munitions? Merci! Des logis . . . s.v.p. Pavillon des Temps Nouveaux* (Cannons, arms? No thanks! Housing please).[104]

Le Corbusier's visit to Philadelphia was memorable because of his provocative encounters with three members of the city's diverse artistic community: Cret, who symbolized the enduring Beaux-Arts tradition; Dr. Albert Barnes, infamous collector and founder of the Barnes Foundation in nearby Merion; and Howe, whose modernist work with William Lescaze was well known to Le Corbusier and to the public as a result of its inclusion in the 1932 "Modern Architecture: International Exhibition."[105]

Cret was a distinguished French classicist who promoted the Beaux-Arts method at Penn during his tenure there from 1903 to 1937. Yet, as previously discussed, he endorsed many of Le Corbusier's early ideas.[106] Cret's own work rationalized classical forms and adjusted them to the exigencies of steel frame construction. His alliance of classicism and modernism was also sympathetic to that of Jacques Carlu, his countryman and counterpart at MIT. But Cret did not receive from Le Corbusier the reception he might have expected. When they first met, the affable Cret extended his hand, but Le Corbusier walked by without acknowledging him.[107] At the formal dinner Le Corbusier was seated between Cret and his wife. He was in a puckish mood and insisted on practicing the English colloquialisms and profanities that Robert Jacobs taught him on the train trip to Philadelphia that afternoon. At one point he proudly blurted out "son of a beetch," which, Jacobs recalled, left the Crets "in a state of shock."[108]

Le Corbusier's pranks that evening had unexpected consequences. Dr. Albert Barnes, collector, chemist, and unscrupulous entrepreneur who had made a fortune developing the antiseptic Argyrol, sat at the same table and thought Le Corbusier was conspicuously inebriated.[109] Barnes had a reputation for being ill-tempered and malicious. He clashed with fellow collectors and with museum directors, including John Quinn, respected art patron, and Fiske Kimball.[110] Barnes also had an altercation with Cret who designed his own Barnes Foundation Gallery (1925). Later, Barnes even barred Cret from entering the gallery.[111]

At the Barclay dinner Le Corbusier asked to see Barnes's collection the next morning (Saturday) before his return. He claimed that he had earlier sent a "respectful letter" to Barnes from New York, but presumably received no response. When the Art Alliance tried unsuccessfully to intervene on his behalf through one of Barnes's former students, Le Corbusier withdrew his request but felt humiliated. After all, he considered himself a distinguished visitor and a Barnes supporter. As

coeditor of *L'Esprit Nouveau,* Le Corbusier had promoted Barnes's interests by publishing an informative article on the man, his educational foundation, and his important collection of modern art.[112] Although Le Corbusier did receive a letter from Barnes giving him permission to visit the gallery on Tuesday, November 12, it was long after his scheduled departure from Philadelphia. Le Corbusier returned Barnes's letter writing a caustic message across the front: "I am infinitely respectful of wealth and pride. At the same time, to my great regret, it is not possible for me to wait for four days behind the door of the Barnes Foundation." He signed his note to Barnes, "The founder of *L'Esprit Nouveau* which waged the battle, in 1919–1925, for the artists [whose work] you purchase."[113]

The acid-tongued Barnes shot back a contentious letter in French to the New York hotel addressed to "Master Crow, known as 'Le Corbusier'" (*Maître Corbeau, dit "Le Corbusier"*). The letter offered a new version of Jean de la Fontaine's classic parable *The Crow and the Fox* (*Le Corbeau et le Renard*) in which the crow outsmarts the fox by appealing to his pride. Barnes's letter accused the French architect of being drunk at the dinner of the "alliance of sausages" (*Alliance des Saucissons*) as well as the next day when he "scribbled" his remarks on Barnes's original letter. The episode, suggested Barnes, demonstrated an inversion of Fontaine's characters so that "Master Fox" (*Maître Renard*) now outwitted "Master Crow" (*Maître Corbeau*). Master Fox, Barnes announced, has no respect for the "alliance of fatheads" (*Alliance des Ballots*). The mean-spirited collector signed his letter, "Master Fox, known as 'Albert C. Barnes,'—the founder, before 1910, of l'Esprit Nouveau who seeks to distinguish the true from the false in art and culture."[114]

Le Corbusier was stunned by Barnes's letter, its vitriol and its presumptions. The next day he sent off a conciliatory if defensive reply in which he countered Barnes's accusation, insisting that he was not intoxicated at the Art Alliance. To the contrary, he maintained, "I am a good drinker [*je suis bon buveur*]." In an attempt to pacify Barnes, he maintained that whereas he enjoyed a good "fight in life," he thought that "hostility" was "useless" among people who "love the same things and have the same passions." In an appeasing gesture, he proposed "an end to the duel."[115] But Barnes returned his letter unopened. Instead, he scrawled on the envelope the French profanity *merde*.[116] Still, Le Corbusier had the last word.

In *Cathédrales* Le Corbusier devoted a chapter to the episode, publishing their prickly exchange of letters.[117] He contrasted Barnes with Raoul La Roche, the "affable" Swiss banker whose own house in Paris (designed by Le Corbusier) and collection were open to the public two days a week. The La Roche collection, as previously noted, was particularly strong in purist works by Le Corbusier and Ozenfant.[118] Thus by praising La Roche's "courage" to form a collection "infinitely more 'progressive'" (*allante*) than that of Barnes, Le Corbusier showed his self-serving bias. Drawing on the stereotypes and clichés of European views of America, he concluded that the episode was "evidence of the puffed satisfaction" of men like Barnes who in just a few generations had "made America" (*fait l'Amérique*)—"a bit of a cowboy story." Along with other instances of transatlantic misunderstanding, the Barnes chapter was purged from the postwar American edition either by Le Corbusier or by his editor.[119]

A third encounter in the city, with George Howe, was enriching for Le Corbusier if bewildering for the Philadelphian. This was not their first meeting. According to R. Sturgis Ingersoll, an art collector and close friend of Howe's, the Philadelphia architect "became enamored by Le Corbusier" as early as 1927.[120] According to Howe, the two had met when he visited the Parisian's apartment on the rue Nungesser et Coli soon after its completion in 1933. Le Corbusier was reportedly indifferent to Howe. After ignoring the American for a time, he was said to have inquired if Howe was an architect. When Howe indicated that he was, Le Corbusier allegedly replied, "Oh, I thought you were the naval officer from downstairs."[121] Afterward Howe sent Le Corbusier a letter in admirable French thanking him for the visit.[122] Again in Philadelphia Le Corbusier inexplicably resumed his aloof posture, even though Howe had introduced his lecture.[123] The next day the two visited the Philadelphia Saving Fund Society building (PSFS;

1929–1932). Designed by Howe and Lescaze, it was the city's first modern skyscraper. It was well known to the European avant-garde, having received Sigfried Giedion's enthusiastic endorsement in *Cahiers d'Art*.[124] Full of admiration himself, Le Corbusier baffled Howe when he purportedly exclaimed to him, "*Ah mon vieux, why don't we be partners the next time you have a big job?*"[125] In *Cathedrals* Le Corbusier revealed his esteem for PSFS which, like Rockefeller Center, "affirms to the world the dignity of the new times."[126]

Norman Rice was another of Le Corbusier's young American admirers among the modernists in Philadelphia. Distinguished as the first American student in Le Corbusier's atelier (June 1929), Rice launched his practice in Philadelphia during the early 1930s. His design work showed the influence of his apprenticeship in Paris. In his review of the 1932 "Modern Architecture: International Exhibition" he paid homage to Le Corbusier and several other participants. Entitled "I believe . . . " and published in *T-Square*, Rice interpreted the "New Architecture" as a modernist affirmation of secular spiritualism.[127]

The Barnes episode left Le Corbusier with a bitter memory of his visit to Philadelphia. By contrast, his experiences at Bowdoin College a few days later (November 12) were entirely congenial. Le Corbusier may have considered Bowdoin a provincial New England college, but he found there an audience that appreciated his international celebrity. His lecture was considered the "outstanding event" of the college year, in spite of the fact that it was apparently "lost" on most members of the audience who did not understand French.[128] But to those who did, it offered a vision of future dwellings with uncertain aesthetic, social, and political implications: "modern houses built of concrete and steel on stilts with windows instead of walls" and "community homes built like skyscrapers."[129] A sociology professor at Bowdoin recalled his indifference to Le Corbusier's message because it failed to "stimulate in me and my wife a yearning to move into a *machine à vivre*."[130] Even in the remote reaches of Brunswick, Maine, Le Corbusier remained remarkably in character. Just before the lecture he attended a small gathering at the home of Bowdoin president Kenneth Sills. There at the dinner table, according to a widely circulated story, Le Corbusier responded to a guest's questions about his ideas on city planning. Sweeping aside dishes and silverware, he borrowed a lipstick from one of the women guests and sketched his concept of an ideal town in glossy red.[131]

During his three-day visit to Princeton (November 14–16) he gave a series of three lectures and a seminar. This afforded him a more extended opportunity to communicate his ideas and engage the architecture students.[132] Like other schools, Princeton was in transition from what one alumnus called "traditional" to modern architecture.[133] This confirmed the shift in the discipline that Harbeson identified earlier. During the fall of 1935 Princeton's School of Architecture, more isolated than Columbia and Harvard, was searching for direction. On the one hand, it still used Beaux-Arts Institute of Design programs with such design problems as "A Palace for an Exiled Monarch." On the other hand, "modern architecture was already accepted" through a faculty predisposed to it.[134] Jean Labatut, a French architect who headed the school's design department, and Sherley Warner Morgan, director of the School of Architecture, were instrumental in that acceptance. Labatut and Le Corbusier were friends in Paris, having met through the landscape architect Jean-Claude-Nicolas Forestier.[135] To his students Labatut was a stimulating teacher, the one who had introduced them to Le Corbusier's writings.[136] His colleagues considered him open-minded,[137] and Le Corbusier praised him as an "intelligent and liberal-spirited Frenchman."[138]

The Princeton lectures which had been arranged by Labatut and Morgan, were held on three consecutive days, each at 5 P.M. Entitled "Modern Architecture and City Planning I, II, and III," the first two emphasized planning and the third, modern architecture.[139] They caused considerable excitement. Planner Melville Branch remembered "the skill and ease with which [Le Corbusier] drew . . . very rapidly, expressively, and clearly."[140] G. E. Kidder Smith, historian, writer, and photographer, remembered the students' "effort to grab some of the discarded drawings," two of which were preserved (see plates 1 and 7).[141] Le Corbusier even obliged

his hosts with an unscheduled seminar during the afternoon of Friday, November 15. One alumnus recalled attending the seminar discussion. Le Corbusier appeared to him "a very intense person who wore thick lenses and smoked continuously."[142] In his characteristically ironic manner, Le Corbusier made at least one salty remark (according to his own account in *Cathedrals*). In discussing many possible plans for a villa, he advised the architecture students to choose only one design solution. "Expressing myself (modestly!) in the manner of Montaigne, I conclude: 'Gentlemen, you never have more than one bottom to sit down on!' The teacher and the chairman of the department are present. Silence and embarrassment.—'Will you translate that, please?'—No, you will not translate such a remark in the beautiful, green, Gothic town of Princeton."[143] When Labatut and perhaps also Morgan foiled the translation, Le Corbusier thought their response a sign of the conservative, even prudish, conditions that dominated the precious enclave.

In between the lectures and seminar, Labatut acquainted his visitor with the university, which he described earlier in a letter to Le Corbusier as a "green city and living earth."[144] Labatut offered to show his friend "the famous Rotolactor," an automatic rotary milking machine located nearby that intrigued him.[145] But Le Corbusier, whose concerns had shifted from machine age forms and symbols during the 1920s to social problems of the 1930s, either did not see it or found the apparatus unremarkable.

Le Corbusier extended his sphere of influence to intellectuals and the social circle, groups closely linked in this elite town. Unlike the abstemious academic community in Boston, Princeton's honored its Parisian visitor with various dinners. The first was at the Labatuts'; the second was at the home of Mrs. Junius Spencer Morgan, a local dowager (unrelated to Sherley Morgan). Both were considered prestigious social occasions and reported on the society pages of the *New York Herald Tribune* and *Princeton Herald*.[146]

Of all the Princeton sites, Palmer Stadium (designed by Henry J. Hardenbergh, c. 1920; see figure 10.16) captivated Le Corbusier during a Princeton vs.

Lehigh football game on Saturday afternoon before his last lecture.[147] Like other American stadiums designed, according to Le Corbusier, for "crowds of sixty thousand," this concrete structure was a forum as much for the spectators as for the athletes.[148] Such stadiums later influenced one of his own projects.[149]

Le Corbusier's understanding of Princeton University and Vassar College jelled into stereotypical views that fueled his love-hate relationship with America. The architect regarded Princeton, located "symmetrically south of New York," as a counterpart to Vassar. Each "green city," he understood from Labatut's description, was "an urban unit in itself." If Vassar transformed its women into Amazons, at Princeton the young men, even "the puny ones," developed "solid bodies" (figure 4.4). On these luxurious campuses where he found "everyone an athlete," Le Corbusier was ambivalent about the efforts to nurture both mind and body, where the body seemed more highly developed.[150]

The American system of education posed for him a dialectic in conflict with the French system. The American student, cloistered in his Gothic dormitory and living "in flocks" surrounded by a pastoral setting, was entirely "too timid," absorbed in sports, and spoiled to develop his own mind. By contrast, the French student living in the solitude of a town house garret, suffered "Venetian" summers, "Siberian" winters, and other physical hardships. His life lacked the physical culture of the American student. It was not, Le Corbusier argued, "in conformity" with the aphorism of Taylorism "time for everything."[151] Yet cultivating his mind in the lecture rooms of the "arid city," the Parisian student could develop a remarkable independence of thought. Le Corbusier's critique of the American system of education in *Cathedrals,* based on a myth of architectural and environmental determinism, was self-serving. From his observations of the Vassar woman and the Princeton man, he contrasted the intelligent yet dominating American female with the athletic but submissive American male. By extension, he denounced as "timid" both American skyscrapers and the male architects and industrialists who built them.

4.4
Football practice, Princeton University, 1930s. (Princeton University Library.)

After the Morgan dinner party Le Corbusier took the train back to New York City. He had intended to continue down to Washington, D.C., to visit Robert Woods Bliss and his wife Mildred, but he telegraphed them that his lecture schedule called for his immediate return to Manhattan. In truth, he missed Marguerite Harris and chose to spend the remainder of his weekend in town with her.[152]

Le Corbusier had little more than a day of leisure before he was due to lecture at the Baltimore Museum of Art.[153] From his perspective, the visit to Baltimore was uneventful, but he made a big impression on the city. Sponsored by the Municipal Art Society, his talk presaged the theme of his forthcoming Chicago lecture on the "great waste of modern cities." The *Sun*, Baltimore's sensationalist newspaper, reviewed his lecture favorably. The article publicized Le Corbusier's criticism of the prevailing conditions that removed man from his "natural element" and acknowledged the social dilemma attending modern cities. If the review was uncritical, it reflected a liberal persuasion at the *Sun*.[154]

For a month Le Corbusier's itinerary had kept him on the East Coast. Now the tour broke away for a concluding week in the Midwest (November 20–28) where he traveled to Detroit, Bloomfield Hills, Kalamazoo, Chicago, Madison, and back to Chicago. There Le Corbusier promoted his personal agenda by engaging another sector of his audience: businessmen and industrialists. He made no visits to the iconic grain elevators of the Midwest; instead, he came in search of commissions. His plan was to enlist the leaders of heavy industry in the manufacture of mass-produced housing. Here his lecture tour confirmed a shift in attitude toward America. During the teens and twenties his interest focused on the mythological and symbolic character of American factories, silos, and grain elevators; now he was preoccupied with industrial processes as well as social issues attending American production and consumption, and their inevitable consequences on patterns of land use. Aside from allowing Le Corbusier to experience the reality of the Midwest, its industry, cities, and campuses, the trip was generative. As a result of his visit to Kalamazoo, a locale he considered ludicrously remote,

he produced drawings for the Brewer House, the only project to result from the 1935 tour.

On November 20 Le Corbusier and Jacobs boarded the night train to Detroit. The next morning reporters and photographers, dispatched from the *Detroit News,* met them at the railroad station where Le Corbusier encountered another constituency. It was the reception he had long hoped for, given his disappointing arrival on the *Normandie.* The enthusiastic press gathering was not spontaneous, however, but well orchestrated; the paper was published by George Booth, founder of the Cranbrook Academy of Art where Le Corbusier was to speak that evening.[155] Emerging from the train, Le Corbusier wore a generously lapelled herringbone tweed coat typical of men's fashions of the 1930s and black spectacles but no hat (figure 4.5). Carrying a briefcase, he appeared once more to Americans as "a modern-day prophet," now ready to pursue his visionary agenda in the automobile capital.

On arrival, he "immediately demanded to be taken through the Ford Plant 'to see the mass-production technique that will shortly be applied to the manufacture of houses.'"[156] To a city whose economic destiny was linked to automobile production and one that had not yet recovered from the downturn caused by the Depression, that prediction was encouraging. In its lead story the *Detroit News* announced that Le Corbusier "Thinks Home of the Future Will Be Evolved in Detroit." It reported that the architect considered Detroit "the logical city for the production of the house of tomorrow, the prefabricated efficient mass-production house." Moreover, it would be the automobile manufacturer and not the architect who would be responsible for that task since he was familiar with the methods of production. But achieving this result required a new infrastructure.[157]

That day Le Corbusier visited the Ford Motor Company plant at River Rouge southwest of Detroit (1916–1932), designed by Albert Kahn.[158] The experience was powerful. Le Corbusier later reflected on his sensations as he emerged from the factory. "I am plunged into a kind of stupor," he wrote in *Cathedrals.* He marveled at a machine age spectacle in which a car every 45 seconds, 6,000 cars per day, rolled off the assembly

4.5
Le Corbusier at the railroad
station, Detroit, November 21,
1935. (*Detroit News* Archives.)
Copy print © 2001 Artist Rights
Society (ARS), New York/
ADAGP, Paris/FLC.

4.6
Assembly line, Ford Motor
Company River Rouge plant near
Detroit, 1932. (From the Collec-
tions of Henry Ford Museum &
Greenfield Village.)

line.[159] This tour convinced him of the necessity of adapting automobile assembly line production methods to the building industry (figure 4.6). In a letter to Gordon W. Buehrig, designer of the Cord automobile, Le Corbusier wrote that his visit to Ford "confirmed for me in a lesson of blinding clarity the idea that I have been defending for ten years: heavy industry must become involved with housing, construct assembly line, mass production housing [*le logis en série et à la chaine*] with entirely new industrial processes. Housing must be

made in shops similar to those of the automobile." He concluded that this task would be realized first in the United States because it alone was "equipped with technicians and machines as no one (else)."[160]

Mass-produced houses, he cautioned, could not be effectively integrated within the existing urban fabric where "the automobile has killed the city, as we know it."[161] Such housing required a new infrastructure, a new city plan. Continuing the theme of his Baltimore lecture, Le Corbusier now addressed the "Great Waste" in the modern city. His attack was unrelenting. There was waste in the central city because buildings did not have adequate access to sun and air; there was waste in industry dedicated to the production of useless consumer goods; and there was waste in land resources, particularly evident in the Midwest where conventional dwellings were sited on small suburban plots, decentralized from the city. Thus, although he met neither Henry Ford nor Frank Lloyd Wright during his travels in the Midwest, he courageously challenged these zealous advocates of suburbanization and decentralization on their home turf.

But if America wasted its cities, it also had the power to rescue them. Le Corbusier concluded each of his lectures in the Midwest, as he did his subsequent article in *American Architect,* by offering a heady solution to what he termed "America's problem." He stressed that modern technology should be harnessed for building, that housing should be made in factories that otherwise would produce "sterile consumption goods."[162] In his Cranbrook lecture, he encouraged the United States to be the leader in factory-made shelter. Where he once thought French industry could take the lead, he now realized that it was not adequately equipped. "America is the only country that is ready for it and Detroit, because of the lessons learned in the mass-manufacture of automobiles," he encouraged his audience, "is ideally prepared to take over the task of mass-fabrication of houses." "Houses of the future," he predicted, "will be made in factories and that means a complete reform in methods of construction . . . an entirely new concept of city planning."[163] The twin themes of applying industrial processes to housing and enlisting the help of industrialists to do so dated from his 1925 Esprit Nouveau pavilion with its accompanying *appel aux industriels.* He recalled them again in his speech on "The Minimum House" at the CIAM II congress in Frankfurt (1929).

In Detroit Le Corbusier did meet with Daniel McGuire of General Motors to discuss a program of *grand housing,* but it was only exploratory.[164] His major effort to recruit America's leaders of heavy industry in the manufacture of mass-produced housing came later in New York City. And even if he fervently hoped that

Detroit would dedicate production capacity to housing as it had to transportation, he was skeptical, as he doubted that New Deal housing policies and monies could be redirected toward factory-made shelter. "The tragedy is that these huge funds are not being used intelligently."[165]

On the evening of his arrival Le Corbusier lectured at the Cranbrook Academy of Art in Bloomfield Hills. There he was warmly received by Eliel Saarinen, Finnish-born architect, professor, and president of the Academy.[166] Officially, Le Corbusier and Jacobs were the guests of Richard P. Raseman, Academy secretary.[167] Albert Kahn, internationally renowned Detroit architect long associated with Cranbrook, introduced the speaker rather deferentially.[168] Jacobs recalled that Le Corbusier and Kahn "hit it off very well that night." But what seemed so ironic to the young interpreter was Kahn, "the famous industrial architect" who directed a "600-man office" and designed "millions of square feet of building, introducing Le Corbusier as probably the greatest architect in the world who had done practically nothing."[169] Kahn knew of Le Corbusier's initiatives in the Soviet Union. The Centrosoyuz, for example, was under construction in 1932 when Kahn visited Moscow.[170] Le Corbusier, in turn, admired Kahn's engineering work, especially the River Rouge complex. Although not an engineer, Kahn was cast in that role, having first introduced automated straight-line assembly production in the Ford factory at Highland Park, Michigan (1909–1918).[171] But Le Corbusier was also critical of Kahn's factories. He had once said that Kahn's design work in the USSR "looks like a prison."[172] Their respective approaches to architecture could not have been more different. Whereas Le Corbusier evoked in his buildings a symbolic expression of the machine, Kahn preferred a strictly pragmatic approach to industrial building. At Cranbrook, in the shadow of Ford, Le Corbusier gave one of his most impassioned appeals to an American group. Evoking the model of Ford and the example of Kahn, he maintained that architecture in the Radiant City could employ collaborative methods of production and modern techniques for social ends to fulfill "the essential needs of man."[173]

In spite of favorable publicity attending his visit, the beauty of the fields and woods, and the cordial but reserved reception by Saarinen and Kahn, Le Corbusier was hostile to the whole arts and crafts idealism of Cranbrook. Although he grew up with an appreciation for arts and crafts, he began to reject it first in Germany in 1910 and more emphatically in Paris in 1917. Notwithstanding his recently renewed appreciation for the vernacular and for organic processes, his theory and design did not square with Cranbrook's philosophy because it was simply "cut off from life." Within the environs of Detroit, "the fief of Ford," as Le Corbusier called it, Cranbrook served as a "paradisaic retreat" for "disheartened combatants" of capitalism. Like Princeton and Vassar, it was a convent of sorts, a "monkery." Le Corbusier criticized its ethos as "torn between two fatalities: apostleship and egoism." This retreat from the social function of architecture and planning became fully evident to Le Corbusier only after his lecture. George Booth, "the founder and Maecenes came up to shake my hand and said sadly: 'But art, sir, what do you do about art?'"[174]

Why should Cranbrook, its founder, teachers, and educational system have been the objects of Le Corbusier's contempt? The answer lies in his fervent convictions and petty jealousies. First, the earthy idealism of the arts and crafts tradition ran counter to his own. And although *Cathedrals* never addressed Frank Lloyd Wright directly, the notion of an "apostleship," as Le Corbusier called architectural education in America, alluded not only to Saarinen's Cranbrook, but also to Wright's Taliesen Fellowship.[175] In fact, Le Corbusier's appearance at the school came between two visits by Wright, one in April 1935 and another the following January. Saarinen's comradeship with Wright seems evident in a photograph taken during the April 1935 visit (figure 4.7). Informal, relaxed, and open, they confront the camera side by side. They are kindred spirits. In contrast, when Le Corbusier and Saarinen posed for their photograph before the Cranbrook lecture, the two appear formal, guarded, and distant (figure 4.8). Bareheaded and pipe smoking, the dapper Parisian seems uncharacteristically tenuous and off-balance. The stolid Finn is braced for the unpredictable character of his vis-

itor. Positioned at right angles to one another, they stare out in different directions—eyes which do not meet.

In *Cathedrals* Le Corbusier structured his criticism of Saarinen's community as an ideological assault on the abuse of patronage in a capitalist society. He attributed Saarinen's fame to his celebrated entry in the Chicago Tribune competition of 1922. Although Saarinen did not win the competition, according to Le Corbusier, an "important industrialist" (George Booth) recognized its importance and offered him a site, instructing him: "build what you consider useful for the development of American sensibility." For refuges like Cranbrook were needed to provide salvation to industrialists like Booth and nurture the American character, which he considered "timid."[176]

Le Corbusier had more in common with Saarinen than he wished to admit. On this first visit to America Le Corbusier longed to receive the kind of recognition that he felt had come easily to his Finnish colleague. An uncharitable reading of his narrative suggests that jealousy motivated him to criticize Saarinen's work at Cranbrook. He himself attempted to tap the support of wealthy industrialists in America, not to indulge in Calvinist retreat but to redirect the tools of industry and the spiritual concerns of its people toward the social problems of modern life. However inconsistent or unresolved a philosophy, he carried that message throughout the Middle West.

The architect's peregrinations in Michigan also took him to Olivet and Kalamazoo after his meeting in Detroit the next day with Daniel McGuire at General Motors. Joseph Brewer, president of Olivet College, and some of its faculty members collected the speaker and his interpreter for the drive to Kalamazoo, stopping on the way at Olivet. There Brewer and Le Corbusier discussed the possibility of a new president's house, the former one having recently burned down. During his previous career as an editor and publisher in New York City (1925–1933), Brewer had been a member of an inner circle of early supporters of the Museum of Modern Art.[177] As an editor with Payson and Clarke, he assisted in the publication of American editions of *Towards a New Architecture* and *The City of Tomorrow and Its Planning* as

4.7
Eliel Saarinen and Frank Lloyd
Wright, Kingswood School, Cran-
brook, Michigan, April 1935.
(Courtesy of Cranbrook Archives.)

4.8
Le Corbusier and Eliel Saarinen,
Cranbrook Academy, November
1935. (Courtesy of Cranbrook
Archives.)

well as Henry-Russell Hitchcock's first book, *Modern Architecture: Romanticism and Reintegration* (1929).[178] Brewer recalled that, at the suggestion of Hitchcock, he sought Le Corbusier's assistance: "I took him up to the site and asked if he would be interested to do a quick sketch for a new house. I explained that the College had no money, that a gift would have to be sought, and I could give no assurances of anything. . . . He made some notes of the requirements as I saw them and said he would think about it."[179] Aside from the prospect of a commission, Le Corbusier's reaction to Olivet was in keeping with his views of small-town America. Brewer noted that "he looked around the place, chatted affably enough but was critical and slightly aloof (in fact, rather Swiss!) and clearly wanted to get on."[180] Two days later he produced a drawing of the president's house, signed and dated "Chicago, 24 Nov 1935" (figure 4.9). Brewer recollected that Le Corbusier had given the impression that he "wasn't too keen about the Olivet Building. I was surprised when I got the drawing. He sent it to me from Chicago. He might have done it on the train."[181]

The Brewer project, which was never realized, approached a category of commission—"some elegantly beautiful country house"—that Le Corbusier hoped to garner in America.[182] The project evokes his purist villas of the 1920s and early 1930s, especially those dotting the Paris suburbs. More specifically, the design recalls strongly Le Corbusier's project of 1932 for Marguerite Harris's villa in Vevey, Switzerland (see figure 2.11).[183] Both employ L-shaped wings raised on *pilotis.* Both also suggest modular design and a level of standardization, preoccupations of the 1920s and 1930s. Letters from Kalamazoo indicate that Le Corbusier had Marguerite on his mind, sending her a drawing entitled *L'Homme rouge.*[184] He intended it as a humorous self-portrait, mocking what he considered to be the provincial culture of the Midwest. Although physically absent, Marguerite still provided inspiration to Le Corbusier.

Planned for a site on the southwest corner of the Olivet campus near Main Street (old U.S. 27), the president's house would have stood near the pane of the hill. Oriented to the campus, its views also looked out over the valleys and farmlands below.[185] Hitchcock suggested that the formal elements of the Brewer House recalled Le Corbusier's Dom-ino model and summarized his design development during the 1920s: "The structure is apparently a ferroconcrete skeleton, with large glass areas, ribbon windows on both sides of the lower wing, and tall window-walls, as in the early 'Citrohan' projects, at the end of the living room towards the garden and also at the side of the dining room towards the terrace."[186] Notwithstanding the revival of such forms from the 1920s, references to the vernacular (and to elements that Le Corbusier himself suggested might fulfill "psycho-physiological" needs) place the Brewer House within the typology of the 1930s villas. Its thick stucco walls, and at least one rough stone wall on the lower wing, evoked his most recent villas including the de Mandrot House at Le Pradet near Toulon (1929–1931; see figure 2.4), the Errázuriz House project in Chile (1930; see figure 2.3), the house at Mathes (Villa le Sextant) on the Atlantic coast of France (1934–1935; see figure 3.18 and plate 7), and the Petite Maison de Weekend (Villa Félix) at La Celle-Saint-Cloud (1935; see figure 2.6). Like them, the Brewer House used earth-bound materials derived from the natural as opposed to the mechanical world.[187] If such vernacular elements were sympathetic to the midwestern locale, other elements were not. During the long Michigan winter, for example, the sun terraces would have been caked with snow and the "outdoor living room" that Le Corbusier envisioned would have served no more useful purpose than for storage![188]

Throughout the 1930s Le Corbusier reformulated his theory of design and his concept of the architect's social responsibility so that they might respond more immediately to human conditions. He understood these conditions to be a sort of universal access to what he called "essential joys" or "basic pleasures." In *La Ville radieuse,* as well as in his Kalamazoo lecture the day before he produced the Brewer drawing, he explained them as "psycho-physiological needs" expressed in "the sensation of light with the mass," "a sense of movement in space," and "a human scale of impressions or optical reactions."[189] The Kalamazoo lectures, like the Princeton lectures (see plate 7), emphasized his theory of human scale in architecture and its role in defining an entrance

4.9
Le Corbusier, perspective rendering of the president's house (Brewer House), Olivet College, Michigan, signed "Le Corbusier Chicago, 24 Nov 1935." (*Oeuvre complète 1934–1938*, p. 133. FLC Archive l2(14)122.) © 2001 Artists Rights Society (ARS), New York/ADAGP, Paris/FLC.

or a path.[190] The Brewer project transformed theory into practice.

Le Corbusier interpreted President Brewer's intention to "receive his students in sympathetic surroundings" as a psycho-physiological imperative. This required a hierarchy of order, separating private spaces (on the ground floor) from public spaces (on the floor above) and staging a dramatic entrance. A *corps de logis*, containing the public spaces, was raised on *pilotis*. It suggested a spatial complexity similar to the Harris villa. Living and dining rooms were linked together with a loft space (*soupente*) to serve the college president's office with its adjoining enclosed terrace (*jardin clos*).[191] A balcony terrace off the living room was formed by the cantilevered extension of the concrete floor slab. A long pedestrian ramp that dominated the perspective rendering orchestrated an "architectural promenade."[192] Students and other visitors approaching from the campus would mount the access ramp and turn to traverse the roof terrace leading to the raised *corps de logis*. The ramp, long a familiar element in Le Corbusier's typology of forms, looked back to his early villas in the Paris suburbs while it anticipated his design for the Carpenter Center for the Visual Arts at Harvard University (1959–1963).[193] In effect, the Brewer House ramp was an earlier draft of Le Corbusier's notion linking an individual school building to a campus, both formally and conceptually. The Brewer House is analogous to the Carpenter Center in another way. According to the *Oeuvre complète,* it serves as a "demonstration of Le Corbusier's theories" and "numerous of his typical elements."[194] The two designs, both affiliated with institutions, illustrate the degree to which Le Corbusier was bent on compiling a lexicon of forms from earlier works to serve as instructive prototypes in the New World.

Moreover, in the Brewer project Le Corbusier advanced the formal needs of a college president "imbued with modern ideas."[195] Brewer hoped that the house would instruct a local populace; Le Corbusier intended it to be an object lesson for a "timid" America, in his words, "lagging behind."[196] The Brewer House synthesized the timeless and the timely, as well as revivalism and regionalism. The design folded in the purist forms of his classic villas with the vernacular and regional elements of his more contemporary houses. Le Corbusier's recent experiences at the Ford factory and at Cranbrook were catalytic. The Brewer House assimilated not only the formal qualities of the 1920s and 1930s, but also the assemblage techniques of factory-made housing, including the use of ferroconcrete, plate glass, and *pilotis.* Fresh from Cranbrook too, Le Corbusier was jolted by the impact of Saarinen and Wright in that environment.

In his perspective view he sited the Brewer House overlooking valleys and farmland. A low spreading profile defined the ground floor. The attenuated plan was unmistakably American (figure 4.10). The private domain accommodated an entrance, two-car garage, and four bedrooms *enfilade,* each with its own bathroom. The suite of cell-like bedrooms was linked by a corridor with ribbon windows on both sides of that wing. This prefigured the single-loaded corridor scheme for the center section of the Y-shaped plan of his new Cartesian skyscraper. He proposed this housing block for the American city in 1935–1936 and for the Bastion Kellermann project in 1937.[197] Even the Brewer House ramp, which formally resembled the viaduct of an American motorway, alluded to this strategic component of "cities on stilts" that Le Corbusier addressed in the Kalamazoo lecture.[198] Moreover, the design suggested the way in which the potential for industrially fabricated housing might join handcrafted production using natural stone and also incorporate an expansive plan appropriate to a midwestern terrain. While recalling some of the formal elements of the Harris villa project of 1932 (see figure 2.11), the president's house may even suggest some of the contrasting facets of Marguerite's persona: her assertiveness and athleticism, her tenderness and more passive role as muse.

The Brewer project assumed a central position in Le Corbusier's recurring debates in the 1930s: between Old World and New, between mass-produced and handcrafted, between factory aesthetic and primitivism, between universal and regional, and perhaps even between the masculine and feminine (these themes are examined more fully in subsequent chapters). The resulting prototype suggested a montage, rather than a monolith, that was intended to test American manufacturing and construction practices in the automobile capital.

Nearing the end of the lecture tour, Le Corbusier had no commissions in hand. He counted on this small project and on the support of the *dames de Kalamazoo,* as he called the most promising patrons on Brewer's building committee.[199] Increasingly despondent, therefore, he regarded the Olivet project as a hopeful opportunity to realize his ideas in America; but to the astonished college president who had only asked for "a quick sketch," Le Corbusier's proposal and the task of "converting the infidels" seemed unrealistic. Facing a bleak forecast in

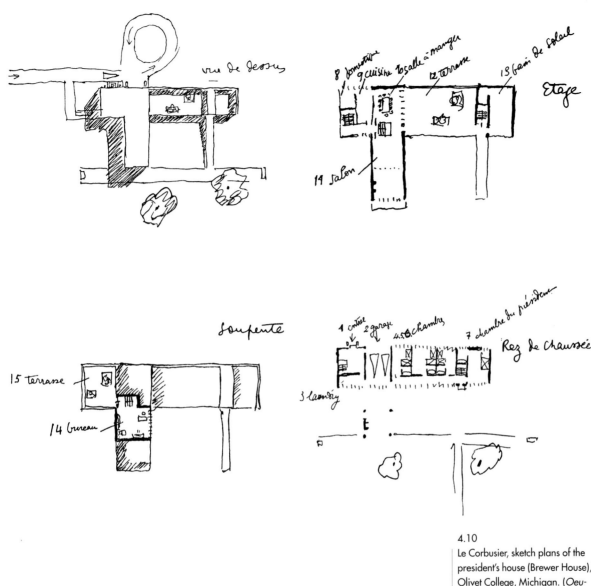

4.10
Le Corbusier, sketch plans of the
president's house (Brewer House),
Olivet College, Michigan. (*Oeu-
vre complète 1934–1938*, p. 132.
FLC Archive I2(14)121.) © 2001
Artists Rights Society (ARS), New
York/ADAGP, Paris/FLC.

the building industry on his return to France, Le Corbusier lost no time in publishing the plans and sending copies to his hesitant client.[200] Had his design been executed, it would have substantially increased his standing and his impact in America, as was the case with the reputations of Walter Gropius and Marcel Breuer after the publication of their house in Lincoln, Massachusetts (1937), and of Mies van der Rohe with his Farnsworth house in Plano, Illinois (1945–1950).[201]

If Le Corbusier was less than enthusiastic about his trip to Olivet, he warmed to the prospect of a commission there and the show of enthusiasm at his lecture later that day. On their arrival Joseph Brewer drove the group to the Civic Auditorium for the event, sponsored by the Kalamazoo Institute of Art. During their brief stay Le Corbusier and Jacobs were guests of Blanche Hull, one of the *dames de Kalamazoo* and an important potential client among the city's modest avant-garde and social elite. In the way in which the Modern defined the American avant-garde to include collectors and supporters of modern art within the establishment, Hull was among Kalamazoo's leaders. A founder and benefactor of the Institute, she was president of its Board of Directors.[202] Le Corbusier's lecture was among the many on modern art and architecture that the fledgling Institute had already sponsored.

News of Le Corbusier's arrival in Kalamazoo reached another constituency: the press. Advanced publicity prepared the public for a discussion of "houses on stilts," similar to what Le Corbusier would propose for Olivet.[203] But that publicity had not prepared them for Le Corbusier's disclosure of his plans for "cities on stilts." Such a radical suggestion made the front page of the *Kalamazoo Gazette,* the article placed strategically below a photograph of a bizarre road accident that landed a car up in a tree (figure 4.11). To a local public anxious to revitalize the automobile industry, the article eagerly pointed out the factory-made components of the Radiant City and its housing. Such a city, according to the *Gazette* account of his Kalamazoo lecture, "would utilize the principle of mass production in which similar individual quarters are multiplied to form a single architectural unit. This would correspond to a comparative

extent to the biological principal [sic] of cells, in which a multiplication of various identical cellular forms comprise a single living body. The apartments, in this plan, would be a 'cell' that would be an integral part of the unified architectural life of the city."[204]

The next afternoon Le Corbusier and Jacobs boarded the train for Chicago where they remained for the next four days until Thanksgiving. They lodged at the Drake, the elegant Swiss hotel on Lake Shore Drive.[205] Le Corbusier spent Sunday afternoon (November 24) completing the Brewer project and embarked on a fast-paced itinerary the next morning. Unlike his visits to Boston and Princeton, he did not address schools of architecture, but rather several arts and professional organizations. He gave one lecture to the Arts Club of Chicago the morning of November 25 and another that evening to the Renaissance Society of the University of Chicago held at the Oriental Institute. The subject of both lectures was "Modern Architecture." Leading Chicago architects and planners, including Nathaniel Owings and Edward Bennett, attended the Arts Club lecture.[206] Chicago society also showed its interest. These included such serious collectors as Elizabeth H. (Mrs. Walter) Paepcke (of modern art), who soon purchased her first Le Corbusier painting, and Bertha (Mrs. Potter) Palmer (of French academic as well as Impressionist art).[207] Le Corbusier's evening lecture was preceded by a formal dinner in his honor at International House.[208]

The next day he and Jacobs drove to Madison for the lecture at the University of Wisconsin's Memorial Union. The scheduled title of his talk was "Modern Architecture," but this was changed to "City Planning."[209] Returning to Chicago on November 26, he gave his final public lecture in the Midwest, his last venue of the tour, to a large gathering of architects and planners.[210] His appearance was sponsored by a number of professional organizations, notably the Illinois Society of Architects and the Chicago chapter of the AIA, which represented the architectural establishment and an important sector of his audience. These groups honored Le Corbusier at a dinner in the resplendent ballroom of the Stevens, which proclaimed itself "the largest hotel in the world."[211] After dinner he took the podium. Le Corbusier considered

Car Climbs Tree After Crash

No one was hurt in this unusual accident, but John Bartunek of Schuyler, Neb., had an exciting few moments when the machine, after sideswiping another, jumped a ditch and a barbed wire fence, turned end over end and landed in a tree as shown here before coming to a stop. Bartunek emerged without a scratch. (Associated Press Photo).

M. Le Corbusier Discloses Plan for Cities on Stilts

Famous French Architect, Talking Here, Suggests Elevated Highways to Accommodate Traffic.

Motor traffic would move on elevated highways and both business centers and living quarters would become an orderly unit of buildings erected on "stilts" to leave the ground area entirely free for the use and advantages of pedestrians, in city plans devised by M. Le Corbusier, the noted French architect whose theories and designs have become a leading international influence in the modern architectural trend.

Conceived in terms of an entire city arranged with the logic of a single architectural movement, this plan was presented by M. Le Corbusier in an illustrated lecture Friday evening at the Civic Auditorium.

SPEAKS IN FRENCH

M. Le Corbusier, who is making his first visit to the United States under the auspices of the Museum of Modern Art, New York City, lectured here in the program spon-

EXILED PRESIDENT RETURNS TO MEXICO

HOLLYWOOD—(INS)—The 12-year exile of Former President Adolfo De La Huerta of Mexico was at an end Saturday.

A charge of rebellion dismissed by his friend, President Lazaro Cardenas, De La Huerta, who had conducted a voice academy here for 10 years, departed for Mexico City with his family.

De La Huerta, provisional president of Mexico in 1920, and minister of finance under President Obregon in 1921-22-23, was exiled following his rebellion against the Obregon and "strong men" Calles regime.

WATCH COURSE OF LAVA IN HAWAII

4.11
Newspaper review of Le Corbusier's lecture in Kalamazoo, Michigan. (*Kalamazoo Gazette,* November 23, 1935, p. 1.)

this his finest hour of the tour, for he transformed his lecture on "City Planning" into his boldest and most comprehensive critique of urban America. Like his Baltimore lecture, it was on the theme of the "Great Waste" and served to promote his Radiant City in the Midwest.

Through secondary sources Le Corbusier, like many Europeans, was well informed about Chicago. From the 1880s to the 1930s Chicago's diverse culture and its history of progressive architecture and planning were closely followed by French writers, journalists, architects, engineers, and planners who journeyed to the city.[212] Their accounts entered into the culture of *américanisme*. Popular clichés about Chicago included its new rich, prohibition, gangsters, slums, stockyards, slaughterhouses, and the Pullman car, as well as standardization and mass production applied to meat packing and other industries. Realism and social commentary left their imprint on the literature of Chicago, both American and French. The city's realism figured in modern American novels that were widely available in French translations. Le Corbusier would have known of Upton Sinclair's writings, especially *The Jungle,* a muckraking novel about the exploitation of immigrant workers in the meat-packing industry.[213] He also knew the social criticism of Sinclair Lewis and others. Lewis's novel *Babbitt* (1922) offered a study of the modern American businessman whose self-congratulatory posture left him socially and morally hollow.[214] And some French observers documented the realism of Chicago's stockyards and slaughterhouses.[215]

In addition to these accounts, France gave widespread attention to Chicago's role in the development of modern architecture and planning: the rise of a Chicago School of architecture, the world's fairs of 1893 and 1933, the Chicago Tribune competition of 1922, as well the work of the city's leading architects, including Sullivan, Wright, and Burnham.[216] Le Corbusier, for example, would have been familiar with developments in Chicago through Werner Hegemann's *Americanische Architektur und Stadtbaukunst* (1925), a book he owned. He certainly knew the Daniel H. Burnham and Edward H. Bennett plan of Chicago (1909).[217] Moreover, he owned a copy of Bennett's *Plan of Minneapolis* (1917) from which he reproduced a "fragment" of the Minneapolis plan in *Urbanisme.* There Le Corbusier extolled the Bennett plan as "a new moral outlook in social life," adding "we must have the courage to view the rectilinear cities of America with admiration."[218]

From at least the early 1920s Le Corbusier's knowledge of Chicago influenced his theory of urban form, mythology about the American engineer, and aspirations for adapting mass production techniques to building construction. The rational planning of the Ville Contemporaine, for example, reflects Burnham and Bennett's plan of Chicago. The glazed cruciform skyscrapers in Le Corbusier's project look back to the Chicago bow window, as D. H. Burnham and Co. employed it in the Reliance Building and Holabird and Roche in the Tacoma Building (1887–1889).[219] Chicago figured in Le Corbusier's writings before 1935. In *Vers une architecture* the allusions to "American grain elevators and factories, the magnificent First-Fruits of the new age," are those long associated with Chicago and the Midwest. Yet with the exception of one silo in Minneapolis, the examples in *Vers une architecture* were located outside the Midwest.[220] In fact, although we might assume that Le Corbusier would have wanted to visit grain elevators (as Gropius did on his first visit to America in 1928), there is no evidence to suggest that he did. And if he viewed silos from his car or train window, he never mentioned them.[221] Moreover, even the illustrations of concrete daylight factories were identified generically as "American factories," together with Gropius's Faguswerk in Alfeld-an-der-Leine (1910–1913).[222] To emphasize the specific affiliation between Chicago and modern industrialization, Le Corbusier included in *Vers une architecture* a section drawing of a Chicago window indicating its standardized parts and its process of assemblage.[223] *Urbanisme* contained at least two allusions to the city. The first was an oblique reference. In the chapter "Our Technical Equipment," Le Corbusier illustrated a "scheme for a skyscraper containing twelve hotels with 6,000 rooms: 190 stories."[224] The source of the image was a news clipping from the journal *L'Illustré* captioned "The dream of an audacious engineer: Sullivan's project."[225] The second was a direct reference. In the chapter "The Urban Scene," Le Corbusier paired an aerial photograph of Chicago's urban sprawl with an axonometric drawing of housing blocks *à redents* to demonstrate that his plan would not lead to "the horrors of the typical American town with its mechanical lay-out."[226] By 1932 Le Corbusier linked Chicago and New York as American cities "utterly devoid of harmony," whose skyscrapers and suburbs were too chaotic to be effective planning tools.[227] He was also aware of the Chicago Tribune competition of 1922. In *Almanach d'architecture moderne* (1926) he paid tribute to the design of Knud Lönberg-Holm, a Danish-born architect who had lived in the Midwest since 1924.[228]

But Le Corbusier would have also known about Chicago through another path entirely, for in 1935 it was the city most closely associated with Frank Lloyd Wright and Louis Sullivan. Just as we might assume, for example, that he was still captivated by grain elevators, we might also assume that he would have expressed interest in meeting Wright. In fact he did not discourage such a meeting. Although he publicly made little acknowledgment of Wright's influence on him, he did admit in a letter to Dutch architect H. T. Wijdeveld in 1925 that he "first saw reproductions of Wright's houses and an office building . . . the sight of these several houses in 1914 strongly impressed me. I was totally unaware that there could be in America an architectural manifestation so purified and so innovative."[229] Before World War I, Wright and Sullivan's work had come to Le Corbusier's attention through H. P. Berlage.[230] In 1929 Le Corbusier expressed his esteem for the two American architects: "In 1913 a bookshop displayed the works of Frank Lloyd Wright, that great pioneer who was the pupil of Louis Sullivan, a still greater one."[231] Le Corbusier had seen photographs of Sullivan's National Farmers Bank in Owatonna, Minnesota (1906–1908), which influenced his design for the La Scala cinema in La Chaux-de-Fonds (1916).[232]

On at least two occasions during the 1935 American tour third parties attempted to arrange a meeting between Wright and Le Corbusier. Jacobs wired Wright in Madison to suggest such a meeting, but Wright responded with a rude refusal.[233] A similar request came from the Fine Arts Department of the University of Wisconsin, but Wright refused again, no doubt provoked that Le Corbusier had come to Wright's home turf to deliver a lecture on "City Planning." Edgar Tafel recalled that Wright came into the drafting room at Spring Green and announced, "Corbu's influence in this country is just terrible, and he has no business here. I don't want to have to shake his hand."[234]

Wright knew of Le Corbusier's trip to the Midwest long in advance. Leo Weissenborn, a Chicago architect who supervised the construction of the Chicago Tribune Tower, invited Wright to attend the Stevens Hotel dinner and presumably hear Le Corbusier's lecture. From Spring Green Wright declined with the perfunctory explanation, "its [sic] a long way to Chicago." In lieu of attending, he offered the European architect and planner a cryptic message: "I hope Le Corbusier may find America all he hoped to find it."[235] It was drafted in the elliptical style of Gertrude Stein, the expatriate American writer who was also on an extended lecture tour of the United States in 1935.[236] By Wright's analysis, American cities from the 1920s had come under Le Corbusier's alarming influence. Wright deduced that if they did not entirely please Le Corbusier, as his criticism of them indicated, then Le Corbusier had only himself to blame. On another tack Wright held that American cities, particularly New York and Chicago, were "disappearing" through increased centralization, congestion, industrialization, and the pollution that accompanied such urban concentrations (figure 4.12). He responded to these developments with a series of publications and presentations intended to promote decentralization, including his dissenting review of *Towards a New Architecture* and his contentious book *The Disappearing City* (1932), and exhibits of Broadacre City at both the Chicago City Club (1932) and the Industrial Arts Exposition at Rockefeller Center (1935).[237] Thus even though both architects stressed the human cost of urbanization, Wright looked for solutions outside the city whereas Le Corbusier looked for them inside. No evidence suggests that Le Corbusier visited any of Wright's buildings. During the fall of 1935 neither Wright nor his work held much interest for Le Corbusier, who underestimated the impor-

4.12
Frontispiece, Frank Lloyd Wright, *The Disappearing City,* 1932. (Private collection.)

tance of the American's authority as a decentralist. But the year 1935 marked a period of increased interest in Wright with his lecture tour, Broadacre City exhibits, and early design work for the Kaufmann House "Fallingwater," Bear Run, Pennsylvania (1934–1937).[238]

Le Corbusier did, however, have an abiding interest in Louis Sullivan's work. Although he left no record of which Sullivan buildings he saw in 1935, he had the opportunity to visit many in the Loop. Apparently he was deeply affected by them, as he subsequently described Sullivan as a "great architect and true architect" (*grand architecte et vrai architecte*).[239] Indeed, Sullivan was an issue to many early modernists and transitional figures of modernism.[240] In this respect, Le Corbusier shared with Wright an admiration for this "great" and "true" architect.

Armed with a broad knowledge of and set of preconceptions about Chicago, Le Corbusier shaped his experiences of the city into a forceful polemic. This "rival to New York" elicited a similar conflict and love-hate relationship. As with New York, Chicago's infrastructure was the focus of his attack. In New York an obsolete gridiron plan and restrictive zoning resulted in an "enchanted catastrophe": the beauty of the skyline above at the expense of the crowded streets below. Chicago suggested a similar set of opposites, only recast and adjusted to a "prairie" landscape. In that city he found both "splendor and horror." Splendor lay in what he called the "importance of the design," referring to both the Burnham plan and "the strong and generously proportioned style of Sullivan [*style fort et ample de Sullivan*]."[241] Horror lay in the city's slums. Like New York, Chicago was a city of extremes. By 1935 its rich and poor were divided into rigidly demarcated zones. The South Side, once prosperous, had been "abandoned" by both the white middle class and the wealthy. This "former paradise," Le Corbusier observed in *Cathedrals,* had once had elegant streets such as "Drexel Avenue which is composed of private houses in the form of German Renaissance Castles." Now the area was afflicted with overcrowding where "a villa becomes a village," where an aggregate of "shanties" and "tuberculous blocks" caused a neighborhood to decline.[242] There was gross disparity between this former "paradise" and the present "physically ugly" slums. Ironically, it was the introduction in 1910 of the Ken-

wood Branch of the elevated railroad at Drexel Boulevard and 40th Street that encouraged development and, by the 1930s, overcrowding (figure 4.13).[243] Socioeconomic and racial divisions separated black Chicagoans living in "misery" within the new slums from the "very comfortable" white inhabitants outside them who, Le Corbusier disparaged, were named in the Social Register that "fixed the notables at 400."[244] He saw in Chicago a "spirit of vanity" and misplaced "pride" where "something" had "gone wrong with the social machine."[245] These observations, echoing misery in the midst of plenty, reflected familiar clichés describing the social and economic conditions of the 1930s.

4.13
South Side Elevated Railroad, Drexel Boulevard and 40th Street, Chicago, c. 1920. (George Krambles collection.)

Le Corbusier's criticism of Chicago emphasized its decentralist policies that privileged the good life in the suburbs over that in the central city. If New York was the vertical city, Chicago was the horizontal city. Notwithstanding their pioneering skyscrapers, Chicagoans were proud of their "drives," especially Lake Shore Drive (figure 4.14). To the architect these thoroughfares evoked two poles: splendor in the free-form expressways from which to view the city, and horror in the capacity of those same roads to sever the *grand plan*.[246] The drives were fundamentally instruments of social alienation. Le Corbusier's argument against them involved issues of gender. Such express routes enabled workers (defined as exclusively male wage earners) to commute fifty miles or more at the expense of family life. Because the American husband (and father) was preoccupied with business, much of his time was lost in commuting. Le Corbusier concluded that with little time left for other pursuits, the man became spiritually impoverished and "timid." If the skyscrapers of Manhattan and drives of Chicago were signs of "youthful power," they were also signs of male impotence. The husband's commitment to capitalism, his devotion to a life of commuting, weakened his position as head of the family. As a result, the American female, the "Amazon," intimidated her man. Such a biased interpretation of male-female roles and family structure reflected European, and particularly French, fears about the Americanization of European women of the mid-1930s, fears that figured in a larger culture of *américanisme*.[247]

In his final lecture, the "Great Waste" (*le grand gaspillage*), Le Corbusier offered his solution for Chicago.[248] Advancing Radiant City ideas, he addressed not so much geographical forces as social and cultural ones to promote centralization. He called for a curb on individual rights associated with capitalism to encourage the collective forces in society. His message was ironic because his audience of potential clients included the same commuters, businessmen, and elite in Chicago's Social Register whom he blamed for causing the waste and human suffering he abhorred. More precisely, his attitude toward them was consistently ambivalent. On one hand, he held most Chicagoans in contempt, considering them to be provincial. On the other hand, he insisted on being taken seriously by them. One anecdote is revealing. In the Midwest Le Corbusier changed his attitude toward the quick English synopsis that Jacobs gave at the end of each of his lectures: "He thought that everybody could speak French in the East," Jacobs recalled. "But out there, he thought . . . that people were still wearing feathers in their hair. He did!" In Chicago, especially for the "jammed packed" audience of architects and planners at the Stevens Hotel the last night, "I had to do a phrase by phrase translation."[249]

By the time he visited Chicago Le Corbusier understood that it was a tenuous moment for launching a campaign for potential clients. Both government and business were exercising caution. The professional community of architects and planners greeted his Radiant City coolly; some Chicagoans even dismissed it to Le Corbusier himself as an *"impossibilité."*[250] But Le Corbusier did meet planner Edward H. Bennett, whose study of Minneapolis he had long admired and whom he identified in his Agenda as the author of a book on the city of Chicago.[251] There he also met Alfred Shaw, a partner in the firm of Graham, Anderson, Probst, and White, who was a member of a committee on the new plan of Chicago. Hoping to interest that committee in his Radiant City, he asked for and later received from Shaw a small-scale plan of Chicago and its suburbs. His proposals would be unsolicited and unremunerated, as Shaw later felt obliged to remind him.[252]

But Chicago's building industry was in a state of near paralysis in spite of the recent Century of Progress Exposition, which had been planned during the late 1920s and was too far committed in the early 1930s to cancel.[253] And notwithstanding progressive contributions of midwestern architects, the 1933 Chicago fair, like its predecessor in 1893, was dominated by eastern architects: H. W. Corbett, Raymond Hood, and Ralph Walker from New York City, and Paul Cret from Philadelphia (with Arthur Brown from San Francisco). Strongly influenced by Frank Lloyd Wright, the fair stressed a "functional, organic and yet festive spirit."[254] According to Corbett, it employed a "thoroughly

4.14
Aerial view, Lake Shore Drive,
Chicago, c. 1935. (Library of
Congress, Prints and Photographs
Division, U.S. Geographical file.)

rational exposition plan in which the design expresses the new construction."[255]

The Century of Progress Exposition coincided with New Deal funding provided by the Public Works Administration (PWA) primarily for roads and housing. The decline in Chicago's real estate values, coupled with demolition-based planning, encouraged decentralization and urban sprawl. Le Corbusier's lecture the "Great Waste" challenged three articles of faith in Chicago: first, that science and progress, themes of the 1933 fair, could promote a higher standard of living and better housing; second, that cheap land could revitalize a city; and third, that the expanding horizontal city, supported by PWA grants, would benefit all Chicagoans by promoting decentralization, alleviating congestion, and encouraging suburbanization. Le Corbusier's Stevens Hotel lecture on November 27 could not have been more ill-timed. That same day plans were announced by Robert Dunham, president of the Chicago park district, to extend the Outer Drive. Funds from the PWA would complete the system, with extensions both north and south to the city limits, making a continuous twenty-six-mile drive along Chicago's lake front.[256] Le Corbusier's suggestions, meant to counter Wright's notion of a "disappearing city" (see figure 4.12) and provide a program of orderly centralized development, were ignored in the rush to implement the federal program and complete the Burnham and Bennett regional plan.[257]

As always, Le Corbusier used the social occasions that attended his lectures to scout for potential clients. Before the Stevens Hotel dinner Elizabeth B. (Mrs. Henry) Field, social editor for the Hearst newspaper *Chicago Herald and Examiner,* who published under the affected pseudonym, "The Dowager," hosted a cocktail party at her home on Lake Shore Drive. There Le Corbusier met Bennett and Shaw, as well as artists, collectors, and other members of Chicago's avant-garde. He also met members of society because, just as in New York and Hartford, arts organizations in Chicago had forged links between the avant-garde and social elite. Vivacious French-speaking Betty Field flirted with Le Corbusier, as he did with her. In her column, she promoted this "lion of the moment" as "one of the most famous of living architects."[258] She also led him to believe that she would give him at least one commission. On his return to New York, Le Corbusier sent Field a drawing. She replied, thanking him in flawed French for "the drawing—the portraits which is sufficient to say that I followed you in the airplane." She spoke of a number of projects: a house in New York, a country house that Le Corbusier would envision as a *ferme radieuse,* a villa in Hawaii where she had spent the previous February, or one in Haiti.[259] Writing to Le Corbusier at the Gotham Hotel the week after his departure from Chicago, she indicated that she wished her villa to be "all in glass." She emphasized that the type of housing he proposed in his Radiant City would not be appropriate as she was not "one [who could] live in a skyscraper for 40,000."[260] Le Corbusier counted on "The Dowager" for at least one building commission, promising that he would purchase Fernand Léger's large painting *The City* (1919) and give it to her.[261] But neither Betty Field nor her husband, an anthropologist and writer, had the means to finance such a commission. Clearly, Betty was a *poseuse* leading him on.[262] During the next six months Le Corbusier continued to correspond, even complying with her excessive request to send a pair of his distinctive glasses. With them, he announced, "you will be gallicized [*francisée*] by the nose." On the eve of his trip to Brazil in July 1936, he even encouraged her to fly down to Rio de Janeiro for a rendezvous. By this time he had finished *Cathédrales.* Hoping to pique her curiosity with a response, he hinted, "there is a word for you in it."[263] But no evidence suggests that their friendship endured.

At other social events attended by supporters of the Arts Club of Chicago and the Renaissance Society, Le Corbusier also engaged the city's elite and its avant-garde art patrons and collectors. He cultivated Elinor Castle Nef, who was on the board of the Renaissance Society, and her husband, John U. Nef, a professor of European economic history at the University of Chicago.[264] He also renewed his association with John Becker, an art dealer who in 1933 gave Le Corbusier his first exhibition in America at his New York gallery. Becker was back in Chicago, as was John Storrs, expatriate artist who had lived in Paris and was a close friend of Léger's.[265] Even after his return home, Le Corbusier continued to pursue the Nefs as potential clients. Early in 1936 he sent from Paris a plaintive letter to Nef complaining, "Life is terribly dull there but perhaps on the eve of important events . . . I would be happy to be able to have the opportunity to construct something in America—in Chicago or elsewhere . . . villas, rental apartments or anything you would like, or the development of a suburb."[266] For want of work he was willing to compromise his most cherished planning principles by proposing a suburb for Chicago.[267]

The Stevens Hotel lecture concluded Le Corbusier's formal duties. At the time he must have been elated over the prospect of possible commissions from Elizabeth Field, the Chicago planners, and the Nefs. He had cause to celebrate. Returning to the Drake Hotel that last night, Jacobs recollected, "Corbu asked me to get him a woman, a prostitute." For European men of his generation, this was not an unusual request. But it was beyond Jacob's responsibilities as translator and it required of him a certain resourcefulness. He turned to his Chicago friend Eddie Robeson, who "got this gal and brought her over" to the hotel suite. "I left them alone," Jacobs vividly recalled "but the next morning we had to get a plane to New York. So, I went in to Corbu's room to wake him up and there they were snuggled in bed together."[268] Over breakfast Le Corbusier was in a puckish mood. He picked up the "silver" dome of the egg dish and crowned himself. Jacobs took a snapshot of "Corbu" in the hotel room wearing striped pajamas, eyeglasses, and the silver dome (figure 4.15). Le Corbusier was "fascinated with the hotel service," Jacobs observed, and thought it "more silver than silver." After breakfast he remarked how "every lump of sugar was sanitarily wrapped in paper. He went into quite a dialogue about getting back to Paris where things are not so clean— more human."[269] As if to underscore the theme of his final lecture on waste, he playfully mocked the hotel's service and sugar wrappers as examples of excessive American consumerism.

To Jacobs the trip back to New York on Thanksgiving afternoon was unforgettable:

4.15
Le Corbusier in pajamas with "silver" dome of egg dish, Thanksgiving morning, November 28, 1935, Drake Hotel. (Photograph by Robert Allan Jacobs; from Jean Petit, *Le Corbusier lui-même*.)

We left at two o'clock on a DC2 . . . a fourteen-passenger plane. . . . There was no stewardess on board. It was a TWA. And it was to go to Newark. . . . As we were traveling along Corbu said, "My God, these things don't move at all." We got up to 10,000 feet which was high for the DC2 to get over the [approaching] storm. But we hit that storm over Pennsylvania and got tossed all over. On the way there was only one other guy on board and he was drunk, passed out. Corbu had written a book called *Avion* [*Aircraft*]. He was crazy about airplanes. It was a hobby with him. He said, "My word, but your American planes don't move." So we put him in the cockpit and put some earphones on him where he could listen to traffic control. And he said to the pilot, "You're way behind us in Europe in aviation . . . this plane is so slow." You see, it was soundproof—double glazing. He was used to the Fokker tri-motor and the Handley Page, which was also a tri-motor plane where the cabin rattled so. There was no insulation. And they went 135 miles an hour. So he said to the pilot, "How fast are we going?" He [the pilot] said, "We're lucky. We have a tail wind. Our ground speed is 240 miles an hour." Corbu almost fell out of the airplane. We made non-stop Chicago to Newark in three and a half hours. And I made Thanksgiving.[270]

A series of snapshots aboard the TWA aircraft "Neptune" captured Le Corbusier in three states of being. The first revived the morning's jubilant mood. Staking a plastic knife and fork behind the arms of his eyeglasses, Le Corbusier mugged at Jacobs's camera (figure 4.16). Perhaps the props suggested the sea god's trident, but the clowning was intended to be satirical. Like the silver dome of the hotel service, TWA's disposable cutlery were not only objects of play but also examples of America's "useless consumer goods." In a second image, Le Corbusier appears to be engaged in activity inside the cabin. With the sunlight streaming in, he is preoccupied—reading, sketching, writing (figure 4.17). A third photograph captures him staring out the window, the remote artist, poet, the man in peaceful seclusion (figure 4.18). Clearly the second two have more in common than either has with the first. The series represents the three mythic roles that Le Corbusier liked to assume: the buffoon (a disguise for the critic and the cynic), the engaged intellectual, and the visionary (the monk in meditation). Students of his published *Sketchbooks* have come to appreciate an abiding theme in his imagery. The airplane seat, with its window on the world outside, stood for the solitary cell. The photographs aboard the TWA bring to mind those of the Caproni explorer and the Tripoli in *Vers une architecture.* The pictures suggest the heroic aviator, and the romance and solitude of early aviation. In contrast to the heady, even hedonistic, sequence of events in Chicago, the flight back fulfilled his inner need, as William Jordy suggested, "to be alone."[271] But Marguerite would be waiting to welcome him in New York; more than any other American, she understood these parts of his persona.

In the early days of commercial aviation, the DC2 hurtled toward the East Coast from Chicago to Newark at a speed even the seasoned European flyer had not experienced. The airplane offered the traveler a unique view from above. In the course of previous flights within South America, Le Corbusier discerned patterns of natural forces and free form sculpture from the rivers, plains, and hilly coastal terrain. From them he developed a quasi-geological theorem, "the law of the meander," which informed his plans for the coastal cities of São Paulo, Montevideo, and Rio de Janeiro.[272] His enduring impression of the flight over Chicago, however, did not fix on the natural forces but man-made ones. This was not an epic landscape of opportunity, as it had been in South America, but a scarred postindustrial landscape. "From a plane," Le Corbusier recorded in *Cathedrals,* "you can grasp more clearly the wretchedness of urban agglomerations and particularly the calamity in the lives of millions of Americans who are thrust into the purgatory of the transportation system."[273] Chicago's drives and railroad tracks, he determined, provided paths of rapid escape for complacent middle-class commuters at the expense of the urban masses strangled by such routes. The waste of prairie commuting paralleled the waste of silver domes for eggs, packaging, and throwaway utensils. In the Corbusian iconography of the early 1920s the airplane symbolized modernity and the virtue of modern technology. From 1929 on it served as a tool for studying urban morphology, for comprehending the social and cultural repercussions of industrialization, and for spreading Le Corbusier's evangelical message across great distances.

Although the American response to Le Corbusier is explored more fully later on, several conclusions may now be drawn about the lecture tour. It was not the general response of Americans that was so compelling to him but the reactions of different constituencies. His most enthusiastic supporters were those disposed to modernism and therefore most open to his ideas. These included students (Amazons at Vassar, Pei and Wesse at MIT) and the avant-garde (Austin and Soby in Hartford, *les dames de Kalamazoo,* the Nefs at the Arts Club of Chicago). Moreover, privileged individuals associated with Le Corbusier because they considered it chic to do so (Elizabeth Field) or because they had a serious interest in art (Marguerite Harris in New York, Elizabeth Paepcke in Chicago). Universities and cultural institutions

4.16
Le Corbusier aboard TWA flight, Chicago to New York, November 28, 1935. (Photograph by Robert Allan Jacobs; FLC L1(1)75.) Copy print © 2001 Artists Rights Society (ARS), New York/ADAGP, Paris/FLC.)

4.17
Le Corbusier aboard TWA flight, Chicago to New York, November 28, 1935. (Photograph by Robert Allan Jacobs; FLC L1(1)74.) Copy print © 2001 Artists Rights Society (ARS), New York/ADAGP, Paris/FLC.

4.18
Le Corbusier aboard TWA flight, Chicago to New York, November 28, 1935. (Photograph by Robert Allan Jacobs; FLC L1(1)76.) Copy print © 2001 Artists Rights Society (ARS), New York/ADAGP, Paris/FLC.

did not provide marketing venues; he would have to create his own back in New York by engaging Nelson Rockefeller and others. The architectural establishment, especially the AIA, did not sponsor the tour at a national level and only selectively at the local level, because some of its most influential members were still opposed to modernism. Nonetheless, many young modernists showed their interest in and support for Le Corbusier (Wallace Harrison, Edward Durell Stone, Lawrence Kocher, George Howe, Nathaniel Owings). Press coverage ranged from enthusiastic promotion (*Detroit News*) and sensationalism (Alsop's story in the *Herald Tribune,* the *Kalamazoo Gazette*) to society chat (The Dowager in the *Chicago Herald and Examiner*) and expository, even probing, accounts of Le Corbusier's ideas (*Christian Science Monitor*).

From his perspective the tour offered him diverse encounters with modern American culture. He experienced the "spiritual center" of Hartford with Austin, Soby, and Hitchcock. He confronted women at Vassar who were both frivolous and informed. He sampled the sobriety of Boston and the "sheltered" character of academic life at Princeton and Cranbrook. He challenged the arrogance of Albert Barnes. He experienced epiphanies at the Ford factory and on encountering Sullivan's architecture in Chicago. Synthesizing the old and the new, his design for the president's house at Olivet College offered a new model. In response to the extremes of wealth and poverty and to the alarming pattern of decentralization that he observed in New York, Chicago, and other metropolises, Le Corbusier launched his most passionate attack on the American city for the purpose of promoting his Radiant City. But for now, the arduous tour was over. He returned to Manhattan and focused his professional efforts on the search for work.

Part II
The Search for Authorities and Commissions

5

The Enchanted Catastrophe

When my ship stopped at Quarantine, I saw a fantastic, almost mystic city rising up in the mist. There is the temple of the new world. But the ship moves forward and the apparition is transformed into an image of incredible brutality and savagery. Here is certainly the most prominent manifestation of the power of modern times. . . . But so much explosive force here in the hard geometry of disordered prisms did not displease me. . . . It is thus that great enterprises begin: by strength. . . . Coming from France at the flat end of 1935, I had confidence.[1]

Through a powerful conjunction of opposing responses, Le Corbusier received his first impression of New York City and, by extension, the United States. On board the ship home only days after concluding his visit, Le Corbusier revealed in a letter to Marguerite Harris his profound ambivalence about the country in general and its cities in particular. He spoke of his heart "torn every day for two months by hate and love of this new world. . . . Hate or love: nothing more, nothing less. Daily debate. Better, debate through every minute in the midst of the stupefying city. Hours of despair in the violence of the city (New York or Chicago); hours of enthusiasm,

confidence, optimism, in the enchanted splendor of the city. . . . I shall come back to America. America is a great country. Hopeless cities and cities of hope at the same time."[2]

The dual nature of his initial impression of New York City—from afar the "mystic city rising up in the mist" but up close transformed into one of "brutality and savagery"—paralleled his eventual experience—"optimism in the enchanted splendor" but "despair in the violence of the city" (figure 5.1). From the celestial to the earthly, from the ideal to the real, from the mythic to the pragmatic, these spheres formed Le Corbusier's vision of New York City as a *catastrophe féerique,* an enchanted catastrophe. It was strong of force but weak of spirit.[3] In effect, the double-edged character of his view of Manhattan paralleled his love-hate relationship with the United States, so intertwined were his associations between the city and the country.

As noted, Le Corbusier employed polemical methods to promote his ideas: his writings on New York and America, his experience of Manhattan, and his statement to the press that American skyscrapers were "much too small." Stanislaus von Moos analyzed this method as "a protest against the ruling state of things . . . a contradiction to the status quo."[4] Le Corbusier himself cited

5.1
New York by day and New York
at night. (From *Rockefeller Center,*
reproduced in *L'Architecture
d'Aujourd'hui* 9 [January 1938],
p. 12.)

Francis Delaisi's observation in *Les Contradictions du
monde moderne* that "the world goes around badly and that
in this century of certitudes we are submerged in incertitudes."[5] Influenced by the writings of Frederich Nietzsche, Le Corbusier cultivated an approach to problem
solving that inevitably shaped his world view. In addition, his preconceptions about the United States and its
cities were drafted within the larger European discourse
on *américanisme.* These methods and this discourse conditioned his analysis of New York and his efforts to promote it as an empirical model for his Radiant City.

Le Corbusier's Preconceptions of New York City

Like the skyscraper, silo, daylight factory, and highway,
the American city symbolized modernity to the European avant-garde. For Le Corbusier and his colleagues

Manhattan represented the model city of the future. Le
Corbusier's writings of the 1920s and 1930s demonstrated the extent to which he had already formed strong
but shifting opinions about the city's architecture and
urbanism. During the mid-1920s his focus was on the
conflict between structure and form in the American
skyscraper. In *Almanach d'architecture moderne* (1926) Le
Corbusier used the example of Ernest R. Graham's Equitable Building (1914–1915) at 120 Broadway to illustrate that it may have achieved "power" through the
use of new technology, but its architectural form was
still not rational.[6] The Equitable's classical design
reflected neither its skeletal frame nor the methods of
mass production used to construct it. In *Vers une architecture* Le Corbusier paired photographs of the Equitable
and a skeletal steel frame by the American Bridge Co., a
subsidiary of U.S. Steel Corporation, to demonstrate that
American architects had not yet learned to use the new
tools to resolve the conflict between structure and form
(figures 5.2 and 5.3).[7]

Le Corbusier's esteem for American skyscraper construction, particularly the tower solution in New York
City, influenced his own projects for skyscraper cities,

Equitable Buildding, New-York.

Construit par la *Steel Corporation*.

5.2
Ernest R. Graham, Equitable Building, New York City, 1914–1915 (*Vers une architecture*, p. 218.) © 2001 Artists Rights Society (ARS), New York/ADAGP, Paris/FLC.

5.3
American steel frame. (Photograph of American Bridge Co. frame, reproduced in *Vers une architecture*, p. 219.) © 2001 Artists Rights Society (ARS), New York/ADAGP, Paris/FLC.

the Ville Contemporaine and Plan Voisin. The Ville Contemporaine reflected his admiration for the aesthetic of the isolated business tower, particularly the Woolworth Building (1911–1913), designed by Cass Gilbert, as illustrations in his *Almanach* suggest (figure 5.4 top).[8] Moreover, the multilevel planning of the Ville Contemporaine was inspired as much by the example of Manhattan as by the prewar visionary designs of Italian futurist Antonio Sant'Elia. Le Corbusier was familiar with New York City's infrastructure, including stacked levels of vehicular circulation wedged between skyscrapers, through an illustration in Werner Hegemann's *Der Städtebau* (1911–1913), which he reproduced in his own publications (figure 5.5).[9]

As a method of promoting the Ville Contemporaine and Plan Voisin in his writings of the mid-1920s, he used New York City repeatedly to identify elements of order and disorder in American urban design. Based in part on publications of his European colleagues, notably Werner Hegemann, the German-born city planner who lived in the United States intermittently from 1913 to 1936, and Walter Gropius (whose first trip to America was not until 1928), Le Corbusier underscored the contradictions in American and particularly New York City planning: skyscrapers promoting rather than decreasing congestion, the potential of tall buildings to block light and air, and chaotic urban development due to real estate speculation.[10] In *Urbanisme* (1925) he admired the rectilinear city plans of such cities as New York, Minneapolis, and Washington, D.C., for their reason and order, confirming "a new moral outlook in social life."[11] Yet however much he endorsed the skyscraper for its technical achievement, he viewed it as an agent of congestion against the order of the plan. In *Almanach* he juxtaposed an image of the free-standing Woolworth Building on Broadway (see figure 5.4 top) with one of lower Manhattan showing a cluster of business towers around it to demonstrate that "the skyscraper foments disorder" (see figure 5.4 middle).[12] If New York's financial district had, in his words, "order for its basis," its aggregate of skyscrapers produced only "confusion, chaos and upheaval."[13] Even the regular rows of skyscrapers that formed the sheer canyon of Wall Street epitomized such

New-York

Le gratte-ciel fomente le désordre.

Le gratte-ciel doit apporter l'ordre. (LE CORBUSIER. Une ville contemporaine, 1922).

5.4
Woolworth Building
(1911–1913), lower Manhattan,
and Ville Contemporaine (1922).
(*Almanach d'architecture
moderne*, p. 186.) © 2001 Artists
Rights Society (ARS), New
York/ADAGP, Paris/FLC.

5.5
Section, New York City street showing infrastructure. (Werner Hegemann, *Der Städtebau* [Berlin, 1913], vol. 2, opp. p. 335.)

5.6
"New-York: congestion," caption to photograph of Wall Street, New York City. (*Urbanisme*, p. 175.) © 2001 Artists Rights Society (ARS), New York/ADAGP, Paris/FLC.

New-York : congestion.

congestion (figure 5.6). Cities like New York, Le Corbusier concluded, had become an "intensely active form of capital for the mad speculation of private enterprise."[14] In *Almanach,* as in *L'Esprit Nouveau* and *Urbanisme,* he paired a perspective rendering of the Ville Contemporaine (see figure 5.4 bottom) with an aerial view of lower Manhattan (see figure 5.4 middle) to sharpen the distinction between the two cities he thought exemplified order and disorder, respectively.[15] The grid plan of Manhattan was orderly and compatible with the scale and building requirements of the early nineteenth century when it was first laid out, but inadequate to meet the demands of automobile traffic and the congestion it produced. His Ville

Contemporaine and Plan Voisin were antidotes to such disordered skyscraper development.[16]

Even if he was sympathetic to the grid as a type of plan, his enthusiasms were not consistently shared by other European writers. In *Internationale Architektur* (1925), Gropius reproduced an aerial photograph of lower Manhattan identical to the cropped one that Le Corbusier published earlier in *L'Esprit Nouveau* and later in *Urbanisme*. Due to the confining geography of lower Manhattan, so Gropius's caption indicated, a modern vertical city of skyscrapers developed in spite of its unsystematic plan.[17] Hegemann was not an advocate of the grid and preferred radial planning. Moreover, he was especially frank in his criticism of the Ville Contemporaine based on the American model. He judged the financial implications of Le Corbusier's concentration of skyscrapers "dangerous" and its design "too monotonous."[18] Furthermore, even though he considered "the office tower capable of the highest artistic effect," he regarded a high tower to be a "big exception" in a cityscape, similar to a "town hall or a single central commercial building."[19] In effect, Le Corbusier isolated and repeated elements of the modern American city—the grid and the tower—as Auguste Perret suggested.[20] Notwithstanding these criticisms, Le Corbusier respected Hegemann's judgment. To promote his own plans he appropriated Hegemann's criticism of New York City's zoning regulations and high-rises as a source of traffic congestion, arguments that appeared in *Amerikanische Architektur und Stadtbaukunst* (1925).[21]

The European discourse on *américanisme* informed Le Corbusier's shifting view of America after 1929 and influenced both his preconceptions about New York City and his decision to select it as a case study for the Radiant City. During the early 1930s his opinions were shaped in part by his engagement with the regional syndicalist movement. Its proponents no longer viewed America, and particularly New York City, as a technocratic model for solving social problems. Le Corbusier and other European intellectuals were disillusioned with that city, as they were with American culture in general, a collective disenchantment that expressed a more pessimistic side of *américanisme*. The 1929 crash and the De-

pression were sober evidence of the failure of capitalism abroad and its effects on a consumer society.[22] In writing of this period Le Corbusier cited the waste inherent in suburbanization and decentralization, with their deleterious effects on family life and human values, the production of unnecessary consumer goods, as well as the consequences of street density and congestion and of business speculation and advertising. Although such themes permeated his writings of the 1920s, they intensified and took on a new political significance during the early 1930s in neosyndicalist publications, especially *Plans* and *Prélude,* in articles, and in his books *Précisions* (1929) and *La Ville radieuse* (1935). Now human and societal costs were factored in. More than ever before Le Corbusier exploited the example of New York City as an object lesson, a counterpoint to his urban visions. Again, his arguments were thoroughly consistent with his polemical methods of problem solving and promotion.

Influenced by Philippe Lamour, editor of *Plans,* Georges Duhamel, and other neosyndicalist colleagues, Le Corbusier adopted a particularly fervent position about American cities during post-crash times.[23] He knew about recent conditions in New York from a wide range of sources as the city had increasingly become the victim of decentralization, congestion, and chaos, and he could use it to contrast with his concept of a Radiant City. In two articles in *Plans* of 1931, entitled "To Live! (To Breathe)" and "To Live! (To Inhabit)," he called for the elimination of suburbs and garden cities because such decentralized and sparse settlements caused inhabitants to lose their "collective force." In contrast, he advocated reintroduction of green spaces into congested urban centers, specifying New York's Wall Street, lower Broadway, and midtown areas.[24] In other articles in *Plans* that year he made more ominous remarks suggesting a causal link, however implausible, between economic chaos and disorder in an urban plan. An aerial view of the New York Stock Exchange at its congested Wall Street site dramatized the futility of merely "Living in order to work" (figure 5.7). He called instead for an urban oasis there.[25] Furthermore, he branded New York "the city of panic," because its dense clusters of setback skyscrapers caused the "death of the street."[26]

5.7
"Living in order to work," caption
to photograph of aerial view of
New York Stock Exchange, Wall
and Broad streets. (*Plans,* no. 3
[March 1931], p. 35.) © 2001
Artists Rights Society (ARS), New
York/ADAGP, Paris/FLC.

DESCARTES EST-IL AMÉRICAIN ?

5.8
"Descartes est-il américain?" (La Ville radieuse, p. 127.) © 2001 Artists Rights Society (ARS), New York/ADAGP, Paris/FLC.

In another article entitled "Descartes est-il américain?" ("Is Descartes American?"), Le Corbusier elucidated the virtues of French thought that could produce such reasoned works as the Cathedral of Notre-Dame in Paris, completed in the thirteenth century, and Gustave Eiffel's bridge at Garabit in the nineteenth century (figure 5.8). By contrast, he denounced as undisciplined the skyscrapers of Manhattan and the Americans who built them. After all, rationalist philosopher René

Descartes was French, and not American. The absence of a cohesive plan in New York's congested financial district, Le Corbusier argued, indicated spiritual decay and lack of human values. He also criticized the quest for individualism, an article of faith in America and a consequence of capitalism. His caption to an aerial photograph of lower Manhattan's jumbled skyscrapers was severe: "Everything here is paradox and disorder: individual liberty destroying collective liberty" (figure 5.9). There was irony in his rhetorical question, "Is Descartes American?" Le Corbusier had consistently stereotyped America as a country of youthful power and France one of reason and intellect. Yet he modeled his own "Cartesian" skyscraper on American towers and the technology that produced them.[27] Tall buildings in America, he maintained, may have achieved record heights, but their stepped-back massing and individualized towers and crests, the result of New York's 1916 zoning ordinance, produced the chaotic forms that Hugh Ferriss and Harvey Wiley Corbett suggested in their setback studies of 1923. This demonstrated a conflict of "spirit" between "a new medievalism" in American architecture and urbanism that encouraged "tumult" and the reasoned French legacy that accounted for the ordered designs of Notre-Dame and his own Plan Voisin (figure 5.10).[28]

Le Corbusier employed similar polemics to promote his ideas in *Précisions* and *La Ville radieuse*. He claimed that other countries less technologically advanced than the United States were already committed to them. His drawing in *Précisions* of a schematic map of the Western Hemisphere indicated that Buenos Aires was "destined for a new city." There, the topography of the port would accommodate his plan for a "Business City" with Cartesian skyscrapers (see figure 3.1). In contrast to that city, New York remained "a pathetic paradox." The tower and setback skyscrapers of Manhattan lacked a sound plan that only encouraged congestion and decentralization.

Tout est paradoxe, désordre; la liberté de ,chacun anéantit la liberté de tous. Indiscipline.

5.9
Aerial view of lower Manhattan. "Everything here is paradox, disorder: individual liberty destroying collective liberty. Lack of discipline." ("Descartes est-il américain?," *La Ville radieuse*, p. 129.) © 2001 Artists Rights Society (ARS), New York/ADAGP, Paris/FLC.

5.10
Le Corbusier, collage for "Descartes est-il américain?" (*La Ville radieuse*, p. 133.) © 2001 Artists Rights Society (ARS), New York/ADAGP, Paris/FLC.

Moreover, such skyscrapers together with the advanced technology that produced them could not respond to the human needs of their inhabitants.[29] Another rhetorical juxtaposition contrasted Algiers with New York. In a series of urban comparisons Le Corbusier annotated a drawing of his *à redents* project for the city of Algiers (Plan Obus A) with harmonious attributes: "precision, organization, order, proportion, beauty, *resplendeur*." In contrast, to a drawing of New York City without the benefit of a plan—a Corbusian plan—he assigned such discordant attributes as "violent, wild, strength, vanity, greed" (figure 5.11).[30]

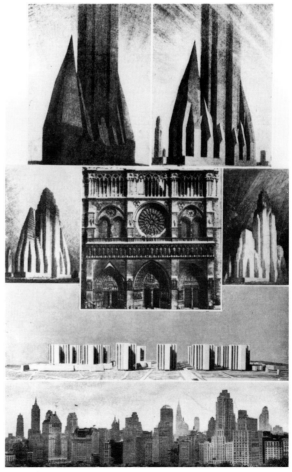

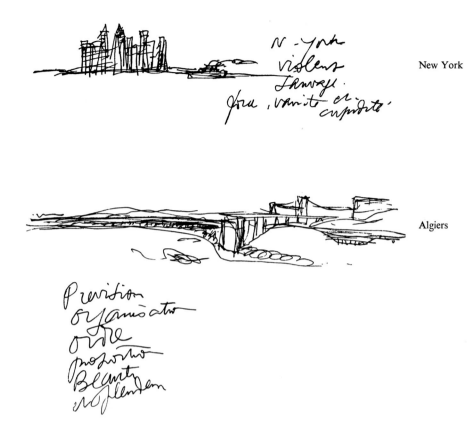

New York

Algiers

5.11
Le Corbusier, lecture drawing comparing the cities of New York and Algiers, 1934. (*La Ville radieuse*, p. 261.) © 2001 Artists Rights Society (ARS), New York/ADAGP, Paris/FLC.

N-York / violent [violent] / sauvage [wild] / force, vanité et cupidité [strength, vanity, greed] // Algiers / précision / organisation / ordre / proportion / beauté / resplendeur

This tactic of promoting his urban design at the expense of existing conditions in New York surfaced again when he addressed the readers of the *New York Times* on the eve of the 1932 "Modern Architecture: International Exhibition." Recently in touch with Lawrence Kocher over one of the early initiatives to bring him to America, Le Corbusier used his article, "A Noted Architect Dissects Our Cities," to advance the Plan Voisin. Promoting his method of antipathy and attraction, he declared American cities "at once so disturbing and yet so admirable." Manhattan and Chicago might be the leading modern cities, he conceded, but their architecture and urbanism did not reflect modern times. In rhetoric based on eschatological notions of decay and rebirth, which surfaced later in *Quand les cathédrales étient blanches,* Le Corbusier indicted these cities as "cataclysms . . . so utterly devoid of harmony." Still, a youthful country like the United States was capable of renewal. "The U.S. is the adolescent of the contemporary world, and New York is her expression of ardor, juvenility, rashness, enterprise, pride, and vanity. So New York stands on the edge of the world like an epic hero."[31] Thus the most likely candidate to accept his ideas was not the entrenched old order of Europe resistant to change but the new order in America.

Representations of New York City and the European Discourse on *américanisme*

Although Le Corbusier's early writings had earned him a reputation as the foremost critic of the modern city and his analysis of the American city was acute and insightful, much of his commentary was neither unique nor original. The arguments he advanced were inextricably linked to the European discourse on *américanisme*. As Gropius, Hegemann, and others transformed images associated with American culture to further their own agenda, so Le Corbusier borrowed liberally from the experiences and observations of avant-garde artists within his circle, as well as French writers, intellectuals, and regional syndicalists who engaged in more strident debate on *américanisme* during the years before and after 1929.

Attitudes associated with *américanisme* reflected shifts in the European position: confidence turning to euphoria during the late teens and early twenties, evident in the pages of *L'Esprit Nouveau,* and caution turning to contempt during the mid-1920s and into the early 1930s. Thus, by the mid-1920s and especially after the debacle of Sacco and Vanzetti in Boston in 1927 followed by the Wall Street crash in New York in 1929, the American city conjured up images of corruption, speculation, materialism, and overproduction.[32] To Europeans, New York City was increasingly viewed as a symbol of America.

Le Corbusier frequently alluded to European attitudes toward America that shaped his preconceptions, especially about New York. Moreover, because he developed his ideas through autodidactic studies, books and other publications in his collection are particularly instructive.[33] Many of them, however, presented the misconception that America could be summarized in the culture of New York City. Le Corbusier read André Maurois's *En Amérique* (1933) as well as a number of anti-American books including Georges Duhamel's *Scènes de la vie future* (1930).

Le Corbusier's assessment of New York was most strongly influenced by Paul Morand, French author and diplomat whose popular book *New-York* (1930) he studied assiduously and may even have brought along on his trip (figure 5.12).[34] From his perspective as a French observer Morand understood the complexities of the modern city and believed that New York signified the state of the nation and its destiny. Paraphrasing French writer Valéry Larbaud in his study of Walt Whitman, Morand perceived in New York "the pulse of the country."[35] As

5.12
Aerial view of Times Square area, New York City. (Paul Morand, *New-York,* cover.)

with Aldous Huxley and Georges Duhamel, he viewed that city as an inevitable path, "a pre-established order which is called the future."[36]

New-York anticipated many of the same arguments and methods as *Cathédrales.* It reflected the European discourse on *américanisme* in its expression of admiration tinged with fear. For example, Morand discovered that skyscrapers created a "starry immensity" as well as congestion and vulgarity that made it resemble a "perpetual thunderstorm." Indeed, "New York's supreme beauty, its truly unique quality," was "its violence . . . in its rhythms."[37]

Because of its emphasis on culture, society, and politics, *New-York* helped to shape Le Corbusier's understanding of the American city that defined modern life; that is, set a new standard for it. A serious student of American history, Morand understood New York's formative events in a way that Le Corbusier did not. Morand was a man of letters. Unlike Le Corbusier, he infused his book with allusions to literary accounts, both American and European.[38] Yet he shared an appreciation for the city's icons: Manhattan bridges, the Subtreasury building, Wall Street. He was also aware of the diversity in its urban life, its ethnic and racial identities as well as its popular culture: the Lower East Side, the Battery, the Bowery, Harlem, the "sky-sign" areas of Broadway and Times Square, the "luxury" of Fifth Avenue, Coney Island, the zoo, the automat, and burlesque houses.[39] With Marguerite Harris and Léger, Le Corbusier experienced some of the same cultural sites, using them to enrich his understanding of the city but only selectively identifying personally with such popular culture.

Like Le Corbusier, Morand viewed the modern city as a biological organism with its own structure and morphology; he also perceived its rhythms as mechanical. He saw Manhattan as the image of a fish, its cross streets connected to major arteries like "fishbones joined to the backbone."[40] He was also attuned to the way in which the city's ethnic groups moved from district to district like "a living organism with shifting cells," a passage that Le Corbusier marked in his copy of *New-York*.[41] For the city, Morand concluded, was "always in process of change." Here the biological met the mechanical. Morand assigned a character to the rhythms of New York in which "all American life is machinery for sensation."[42] If such mechanical rhythms infused white popular culture for Morand, they defined African-American culture for Le Corbusier.

Politics also shaped their respective views. Although Morand counseled his readers in the 1920s to choose the path of democracy in the United States over the path of communism in the Soviet Union, by 1930 he shared Le Corbusier's disenchantment with both systems

and asserted French hegemony instead. Both observers recognized the social deficit of capitalism and its effects on the city, and Le Corbusier endorsed Morand's position on its consequences: overbuilding, obsessive cleanliness, waste of newspapers, and energy consumption. Both men found that most wasteful of all was the American automobile, which divided the urban region into separate spheres. The city remained a haven of multiculturalism while the suburbs prospered as an enclave of Anglo-Saxon intolerance.[43]

Both Morand and Le Corbusier understood that change defined the modern city, that New York derived meaning from its vitality and flux. To Morand it was the "supreme expression of city rush." Whereas Le Corbusier found the city's streets to offer only chaos and disorder, Morand delighted in them. In the end, Le Corbusier shared Morand's eschatological view, for the consequences of capitalism may have destined New York to speculation, volatility, and eventual catastrophe, but the city's dynamic force promised renewal. Morand concluded, "The town spends its all, lives on credit . . . is ruined, starts again and laughs" because it is "inhabited by the strongest race in the world."[44] Le Corbusier's experience of the city as young and powerful allowed him to concur.

Le Corbusier's preconceptions were informed by other French accounts, notably André Maurois's *En Amérique,* a book he owned.[45] This collection of essays assembled two contrasting views of New York as a result of the author's trips to America in 1927 and 1931.[46] On his first trip Maurois discovered the spectacle of the city. He admired the stone walls of new setback skyscrapers whose night lighting turned them "transparent." He compared the island of Manhattan with a "giant steamship." He found discipline and "prodigious order" in the grid plan and in the system of traffic lights. He marveled at the urban infrastructure, mechanization, and utilities. Not predisposed to popular culture, Maurois came to appreciate the vitality of Manhattan, the "necessary folly" of Broadway, and even the "hideous orange taxis."[47] By contrast, his account of a visit in 1931 anticipated Le Corbusier's in 1935 because it turned to questions of ethics and morality. No longer was there an element of wonder in the city. Instead, the effects of over-production and consumption pervaded its streets as they did elsewhere in America during the early years of the Great Depression.[48]

More than *En Amérique,* Duhamel's *Scènes de la vie future* predisposed Le Corbusier to examine the dark side of American culture.[49] Using New York as a case study, the French novelist and physician expressed his revulsion of industrialization and mechanization that influenced Le Corbusier's thinking.[50] Bearing the ominous English title *America the Menace,* Duhamel's account focused on the social problems that resulted from a culture dominated by commerce and materialism. New York and Chicago provided evidence of speculation, greed, and the "tangle of forces in action."[51] Although Le Corbusier shared Duhamel's views, he shed much of this pessimism after

his trip, evident in his allusion to the novelist having visited America with "with his eyes and heart closed."[52]

Le Corbusier's friendship with two other observers of the American scene, Christian Zervos and Fernand Léger, led him to understand a burgeoning argument about the rhythms of the New World versus those of the *vieux Continent.* After a trip to America, Zervos, Greek-born art historian and editor of *Cahiers d'Art,* published a brief account of his impressions in 1926. He illustrated his article with a photograph by Fritz Lang (from Erich Mendelsohn's book *Amerika*) of the electric signage on Broadway at Times Square (figure 5.13) and another of the skyline of lower Manhattan emphasizing the profiles of the skyscrapers, some in the process of construction. He recognized more than just the vitality of urban culture there; he saw in the morphology of the great city a

5.13
"New York. Publicité lumineuse" (New York. Luminous advertising), caption to photograph of electric signage, Times Square, New York City. (Christian Zervos, "Amérique," *Cahiers d'Art* 1 [1926], p. 60.)

"crisis of harmony in modern life." In contrast to a "slow evolution" and gradual transformations in Europe, rapid changes and new rhythms associated with them in America, and especially New York, brought consequences. Le Corbusier accepted Zervos's belief that such changes produced discord between urban growth and social welfare.[53]

Compared with Zervos's measured commentary on disjunctions in the American city, Léger's was bolder. Léger made his first trip to New York in the fall of 1931 to coincide with an exhibition of his work at the John Becker Gallery and at Durand-Ruel.[54] Even more than Morand, Maurois, and Zervos, Léger wrote passionately about New York. On the back of identical picture postcards of the Plaza Hotel, he expressed to Le Corbusier his astonishment at the "vertical thrust of this people drunk on architecture." His response to New York was also dichotomous. "This city is infernal," Léger warned his friend, "a mixture of elegance and harshness."[55] He used its skyscrapers to develop a strident and more complex thesis that must have influenced (and even served to justify) Le Corbusier's later projection of New York as a Radiant City. In an article for *Cahiers d'Art* Léger's image appeared in a photomontage of New York skyscrapers during construction (figure 5.14). Léger concluded that the evolving city was not only the "most colossal spectacle in the world" but also the result of utilitarian objectives and "natural beauty." New York was full of "freshness" and "surprise." And at night a "myriad fantasy of colored lights" transformed the city into a "radiant vision." But in opposition to these notions of natural beauty and new life, the city's "vulgarizations" and its mechanical force left it moribund. Like Morand and Duhamel, Léger regarded its skyscrapers as a consequence of unbridled speculation. They were a "bold collaboration between architects and unscrupulous bankers

5.14
Fernand Léger, photomontage, New York City. (Fernand Léger, "New-York vu par F. Léger," *Cahiers d'Art* 6 [1931], p. 437.)

pushed by necessity." Moreover, they had become symbols of death as well as life. New York resembled a "vast necropolis" of capitalism where skyscrapers were "tombs" of billionaire industrialists—Morgans, Rockefellers, Carnegies. The city offered "a life where one thing follows another in swift succession." Like Morand, Léger anticipated Le Corbusier's view of the city as an "enchanted catastrophe" and his future agenda. For Léger advanced the mistaken idea that New Yorkers would welcome an eschatological event thrust upon their city by French forces. "Destroy New York," as if the city were the site of a World War I artillery attack led by France's Marshal Pétain, Léger fantasized, "it will be rebuilt completely differently. . . . In glass, in glass!" The Americans, he suggested facetiously, "would be the first to applaud."[56]

Le Corbusier's Experience of New York Shapes His Empirical Model for the Radiant City

During the fall of 1935 a more pragmatic approach entered Le Corbusier's urbanism. To cast New York as his empirical model for the Radiant City, he had to experience the metropolis. For him experience served three functions: it allowed him to connect on some level with the reality of that modern city; it validated his own preconceptions that were influenced by *américanisme;* and it evoked in him polemical responses that, in turn, served as rhetorical vehicles of persuasion.

Le Corbusier's exploration of New York put emphasis on recognizance, providing his first personal engagement with the realities of that modern city. New York offered him what Paris, Rome, and other European cities could not. With Marguerite, Léger, Jacobs, housing reformers, and the press he investigated the great metropolis. To formulate his empirical model he matched its problems to solutions in the Radiant City, notwithstanding the fact that his preconceptions served to check a fresh appraisal.

Three interconnected postulates of the Radiant City informed Le Corbusier's investigation of New York's architecture and urbanism: a radically new social system, technical and functional acumen, and organic processes.[57] The Radiant City was predicated on a revolutionary change in modern society. Indeed, as Robert Fishman suggested, Le Corbusier "spoke of the Radiant City as if it had already solved the problems of the Depression."[58] To Le Corbusier no culture was more modern than the American and no city more modern than New York. But because of its political, social, and economic structure and its built environment, it needed the reform he offered. During his days there Le Corbusier sought out the city's technical projects and organic systems. At the same time he criticized weaknesses in existing conditions for the purpose of displacing them with Radiant City solutions. His search, however, seemed tautological, designed to meet a predetermined goal. He concluded that the United States, and by extension New York, had at its disposal the most advanced technical means. Unlike Europe, moreover, America was a young culture predisposed to change. New York could overcome its social deficit, redirect its modern technology, and transform itself. Ironically, the city's enchanted catastrophe offered him "the lever of hope."[59]

Architecture and the Empirical Model: The Functional-Rational and the Biological

Le Corbusier's formulation of New York as an empirical model for the Radiant City countered preconception with experience, the ideal with the real, and the individual skyscraper with a cluster of skyscrapers. These dualities surfaced in his initial responses to Manhattan: an image of enchanted splendor from a distant vantage, but one of brutality up close. This view led him to identify what was "wrong" with the city's architecture and planning. The concepts he advanced in his article "What Is America's Problem?" formed a thesis based on two interrelated models of analogy and analysis that his Radiant City advanced: the functional-rational and the biological with its "psycho-physiological" implications.[60] Here the pragmatic intersected with the somatic. For both models Le Corbusier assumed the roles of advocate for a more human-centered second machine age as well as critic of American culture and society (the latter role is discussed more fully in another chapter).

Le Corbusier used both models to analyze the American skyscraper. The new empiricism in his approach to architecture encouraged him to look to both the actual potential of technology and organic processes. His examination of structural, technical, organizational, managerial, and organic components of the tall building confirmed for him not only its present viability for both commercial and elite residential functions but also its potential adaptation to mass housing on the scale of the Radiant City. He now emphasized the necessity for *techniques modernes,* or modern (building) techniques.[61] But he also assigned a biological order to a skyscraper, whose structural, mechanical, and spatial components might function in ways analogous to organic life. Manhattan furnished proof that the tall building was not an instrument of alienation, for it could be attuned to psychophysiological reflexes, as his friend Dr. Pierre Winter encouraged him to believe.[62] Le Corbusier discovered at heights of twenty stories and more that he did not lose contact with the ground and could still hear street-level noises as they echoed from neighboring buildings.

Le Corbusier singled out Rockefeller Center as a model skyscraper because of its advanced application of the technical and the organic (figure 5.15). Early in his visit he became familiar with the RCA Building (1931–1933) because he gave a radio broadcast in its National Broadcasting Company (NBC) studios. On several occasions he visited business leaders there, including Nelson Rockefeller in the family office at room 5600 (figure 5.16). Only twenty-seven years old at the time, Rockefeller was assisting in the management of Rockefeller Center. This building complex was unprecedented in the history of modern urban architecture. More impressive than its height was the consistency of its performance, like New York's municipal pipelines and street lighting. Here the functional-rational components joined the biological. What made the skyscraper possible was the reliability of its structural and mechanical

5.15
RCA Building and Rockefeller Center, New York City, 1935. (Rockefeller Center Archive Center.)

5.16
Nelson Aldrich Rockefeller,
c. 1935. (Courtesy of the
Rockefeller Archive Center.)

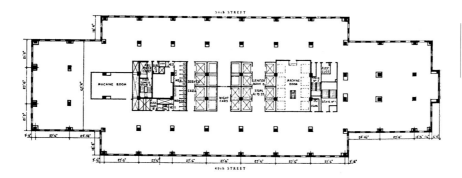

5.17
RCA Building, Rockefeller Center, floor plan. (Sigfried Giedion, *Space, Time and Architecture* [1941], p. 572, fig. 318.)

systems, which Le Corbusier called "rational, logically conceived, biologically normal." Of the RCA Building's spatial and programmatic components, he most admired "its grouped shafts for vertical circulation."[63] His appreciation approached an epiphany. In its elevators, located at the core of the seventy-story slab, he witnessed "moving technical and plastic perfection." The building claimed the fastest elevators in the world (figure 5.17). In *Cathedrals* he described how its banks were "divided into four categories: first, local, from the ground floor to fifteenth floor; second, express, from the first floor to the sixteenth floor, and from there local to the thirtieth floor; third . . . likewise. Finally, express elevators to the sixty-fifth floor where there are living rooms, a restaurant, a large club, a terrace. Speed: thirteen hundred feet per minute. In forty-five seconds you are at the top. Your ears feel it a little at first, but not your heart, so perfect are these machines."[64] His fascination with the elevators later extended to a megastructure he discovered at the port of New York where a block of large-scale freight elevators formed an "immense vertical dock." Le Corbusier defined the elevator as the essential "modern tool" for urban reform, even though many of his colleagues at the 1930 CIAM III congress in Brussels disagreed.[65] While in New York Le Corbusier either met or planned to meet with managers of Otis Corporation to research elevators for the housing blocks of the Radiant City.[66]

At the RCA Building he witnessed other instances of reliable technology. His visit to the NBC studios with Léger confirmed the feasibility of efficient air condition-

ing and soundproofing for the tall building. In that "machine age temple" he experienced for the first time the hermetic environment that he envisioned for the first time the hermetic environment that he envisioned for the Cartesian skyscrapers of the Radiant City: "The temple is solemn, surfaced with somber marble, shining with clear mirrors mounted in stainless steel frames. Silence. Corridors and vast spaces; doors open automatically: they are the silent elevators unloading passengers. No windows anywhere. . . . Silent walls. 'Conditioned' air throughout, pure, clean, at a constant temperature. Am I on the fifth floor or the fortieth?," he wondered.[67] Moreover, he marveled at the "electric circuit" that regulated the "intelligent" entrance door, automatic fire extinguishers, and the "miraculous telephone."[68] The machine age materials that he encountered confirmed what Léger called the "new realism" in America.[69]

At Radio City Le Corbusier was elated by the soundproofed and air-conditioned "glass aquarium" of the broadcasting amphitheater.[70] Thereafter he deferred to the American system and used the term "air conditioning."[71] Even more intriguing was the NBC studio's glass-enclosed main control room (figure 5.18). It evoked in Le Corbusier the dual responses of wonder and fear.[72] He called the master control board by its popular name, "nerve center" (figure 5.19). At once a symbol of the technical and the biological, the functional-rational and the organic, the master control board maintained the pulse of the electrical as well as the heating, ventilating, and air conditioning (HVAC) systems for 100

5.18
Public foyer and main control room, NBC studios, RCA Building, Rockefeller Center. (*Architectural Record* 75 [January 1934], p. 75.)

5.19
"Nerve center," remote central control board, main control room, NBC studios, RCA Building, Rockefeller Center. (*Architectural Record* 75 [January 1934], p. 87.)

rooms in the studios. By remote control technicians would monitor all sounds including the cacophony of city streets outside and the drone of the air conditioning system inside. The acoustical, ventilating, and lighting systems engaged a complex symbiotic relationship that determined thermal conditions.[73] Given his commitment to advanced HVAC systems, it is ironic that Le Corbusier would assign human costs to such mechanization. Yet he regarded the studios' nerve center as a sym-

bol of human alienation: "The glass cage is diabolical."[74] Instead of understanding the dedicated function of the nerve center to monitor the fragile environment of the studios, he distorted its role by assuming that all American skyscrapers were similarly equipped.

In the "glass aquarium" where he broadcast his address Le Corbusier discovered a clock. "I pointed out to my companion, Fernand Léger, a straight red needle turning around a dial marked 1 to 60. They are seconds.

The needle is obsessing; I said to Léger, 'Notice that needle that goes around so fast: it marks the seconds and nothing else. The clock beside it marks the hours; small matter! The hours will return tomorrow. But the dial with the second hand is something cosmic, it is time itself, which never returns. That red needle is a material evidence of the movement of worlds.'"[75] The clock symbolized to him the technical precision and organic processes that dictated both the twenty-four–hour solar day and one complete cycle of the machine age. As one hour or one day replaced another, so a second machine age would replace a first. Le Corbusier infused his broadcast and subsequent lectures with the message that change was necessary and inevitable.

Rockefeller Center also set a new standard for rational organization that had significant implications for the architect. The result of an unprecedented collaboration among architect, engineer, contractor, and manager, it demonstrated "the flawless and rigorous division of responsibilities of technicians grouped as a team."[76] Le Corbusier admired (and CIAM endorsed) such collaborations in the construction process and tried to organize such a team for the production of mass housing in the United States.[77] Although he ran his atelier as a collaborative effort, he was always the master. Publically he eschewed collaboration with other architects. For him a project required but one authority, as his actions on the design team for the United Nations Headquarters later suggested.[78]

Thus on the basis of his on-site inspection of the RCA Building, Le Corbusier concluded that the individual American skyscraper worked effectively. Notwithstanding his interest in that building as an integrated system, however, he regarded its urban design as a failure. If historians consider Rockefeller Center to be an exemplary model of urban design, it is largely for reasons that oppose Le Corbusier's Radiant City thesis.

Urbanism and the Empirical Model: The Ideal and the Real

Le Corbusier's admiration for the functional-rational elements and biological processes of the American skyscraper was not unqualified, and his idealized view of Manhattan did not mean that he endorsed its present conditions. When applied to the whole of New York, the two analogies revealed some of the technical achievements of its infrastructure and organization but they also placed in sharp relief the city's considerable defects. Thus, internally and as an isolated tower, the skyscraper worked comparatively well. But contextually, a city of such skyscrapers did not.

Based on his impression of the city from afar, its geographical conditions, morphological configuration, and island location, Le Corbusier concluded that Manhattan would serve as the ideal "*territoire-type* for a modern city."[79] He considered it to be not just a model city of the future, as it was to the rest of the world, but a global standard against which all urban architecture and planning would be judged. As a Radiant City, it would set the *new* standard. Le Corbusier's experience of the classical world during the course of his now famous *voyage d'Orient* (1910–1911) helped him formulate his ideas of *standard* and *type*, and develop his celebrated quartet of images in *Vers une architecture:* Paestum and the Humbler automobile of 1907 juxtaposed with the Parthenon and the Delage Grand-Sport of 1921. It has been suggested that Le Corbusier regarded these iconic images as standards for subsequent design. The linkage of classicism with mechanization demonstrated that an evolution in architectural design was the result of "progress."[80] The automobile, like the airplane and silo, was not just an objective form, a pure form, but imbued with symbolism and meaning. To emphasize their iconography, Le Corbusier called such forms *objets-types*. His painting during the 1920s suggests a corollary to interpreting these *objets-types*. In formulating their theory of purism, Le Corbusier and Amédée Ozenfant wished to reaffirm those traditional everyday objects—glasses, bottles, pipes—used in cubist still-life paintings. Like the automobiles and silos of the mechanical world, the *objets-types* in purist paintings engendered notions of the timeless, enduring character of everyday life and the daily rituals associated with ordinary objects.[81] With its emphasis on the formal and the ideal, reflecting concerns of the 1920s, Le Corbusier's *territoire-type* invested New York with all the potential of a new archetype. From that standard Manhattan would evolve its architecture and urbanism.

When Le Corbusier encountered America for the first time he retained these ideas from the 1920s as he shifted the focus of his work to a more comprehensive concept of design. From a great distance or in an idealized view from above, New York City appeared iconic and ordered. Visits to the observation deck of the RCA Building as well as to the tops of the Empire State and Chrysler towers confirmed this impression. But when experienced up close at ground level the skyscrapers and streets changed into an image of disorder. There Le Corbusier came to understand reality in the modern city, what he called "the lesson of America," reflecting his belief in the physical and the material that produced great skyscrapers and bridges.[82]

That confrontation of ideal and real continued to shape his experiences as well as his analysis. In *Cathédrales* he announced in *English,* "I am an American." His declaration suggests multiple readings. On a shallow level this textual riddle would indicate that he identified with the country's youthful pride and leadership. A richer interpretation submits that he spoke on behalf of the city, the skyscrapers, the infrastructure, and the businessmen who built them.[83] To the architect, New York's enchanted catastrophe formed a polemic about many enchantments and recurring catastrophes.

A visit to Nelson Rockefeller's corner office on the fifty-sixth floor of the RCA Building provided Le Corbusier with a special vantage from which to view the enchanted catastrophe (figure 5.20). His description in *Cathedrals* was among his most poetic and divided. Whether by day or by night, this view offered a window on "cosmic mutation." By day Manhattan was "a rose-colored stone in the blue of a maritime sky." By night it was transformed into "a limitless cluster of jewels." From this perch he could witness the way in which the "vast nocturnal festival of New York spreads out . . . a titanic mineral display, a prismatic stratification shot through with an infinite number of lights. . . . A diamond, incalculable diamonds." But such a "violent silhouette" read like a "fever chart beside a sick bed." If the skyscraper was "sublime," it was also "atrocious." Extending the biolog-

ical metaphor, Le Corbusier reduced it to an adolescent performing "acrobatic feats." It was constructed with "brute strength" and "youthful enthusiasm," rather than "wise and serious intention." It was merely a "plume," a "romantic . . . gesture of pride," and "not an element in city planning." In their aggregate, skyscrapers were beautiful but their planning was not rational.[84]

If the realities of these defects were not apparent to such "great masters of economic destiny" as Rockefeller, Le Corbusier suggested, it was because they were perched "up there, like eagles, in the silence of their eminences," too lofty to see them.[85] Yet these businessmen and their skyscrapers were still capable of redemption because of their very youth and naiveté. As if to symbolize their unschooled "brute strength," Le Corbusier concluded, "the hand of Nelson Rockefeller is the iron fist of a peasant."[86] That is, this youthful master-builder of the New World, as Le Corbusier considered Rockefeller, lacked the intellectual acumen of old Europe. Indeed, New York reflected its builders. It was a Janus with two faces: one troubled adolescent looking inward, the other a victorious athlete confronting the modern world. The city was poised between two corresponding psyches.[87] Such thoughtless exuberance may have been admirable, but it promoted suburban commuting, slums, and tenement housing that crippled the city. Le Corbusier used his understanding of those realities to enrich his critique of social injustice in America.

The disorder and disjunction of the built environment that first stunned the visitor continued to engage him in a recurring confrontation with New York. Shortly after his arrival he addressed this confrontation at a luncheon Philip Goodwin gave in his honor. It was a select gathering of young modernists (William Lescaze, George Howe, Wallace Harrison), established architects from local professional organizations (Archibald Manning Brown, Ralph T. Walker, Arthur L. Harmon), representatives from the Museum of Modern Art (A. Conger Goodyear, Alfred Barr), architectural editors (Lawrence Kocher, Kenneth Stowell), and Nelson Rockefeller.[88] Le Corbusier spoke about the disjunction he had encountered on an excursion to lower Manhattan with *New York Times* reporter Henry Irving Brock:

5.20
New York City, night view from
RCA Building looking south,
1933. (Rockefeller Center Archive
Center.)

In the intense heart of Wall Street, city of banks at the exciting end of one of the canyons formed by skyscrapers, I experienced the shock of a remarkable architectural spectacle. There, I think, is the strongest and noblest plastic composition (for the moment) in the USA. The bronze statue of Washington stands on the steps of the Sub-Treasury in front of the Doric porch; above are the rough-hewn early skyscrapers, rising vertically. . . . On the right angle formed by the arch of the eyebrow and nose, where the eye is placed, the mask of Washington focuses the whole mass of this immense landscape of stone.

There is disparity: John Ward's Washington; the Doric order of the Theseum in Athens; the walls of American business. . . . The foursquare mask of Washington is at the exact point from which the tumultuous forces of architecture are set in play.[89]

Le Corbusier recognized the distinctive character of this site. It symbolized the chaos of the modern American city in which the skyscraper was not an instrument of judicious city planning. The historic Subtreasury Building (now Federal Hall National Memorial; 1834–1842; figure 5.21) stood next to three reminders of the perilous economic times: the New York Stock Exchange, towering setback skyscrapers, and the dark corridor of Wall Street (see figure 5.6). A statue of George Washington from a more noble past brought into focus this disparate assemblage of buildings and the dynamic forces that generated them. Like so many of his early engagements with Manhattan, Le Corbusier's encounter with this "remarkable architectural spectacle" was suggested to him by Paul Morand. In *New-York* Morand vividly described the Subtreasury, the statue of Washington, and congested Wall Street.[90] Le Corbusier now transformed this iconic image into a symbol of disorder.

When Le Corbusier contrasted the Greek Revival Subtreasury with the skyscrapers of Wall Street, he recalled earlier dialectics in his writings between old and new, between architect and engineer, between spiritual intention and mere technical prowess or business acumen, and more basically between order and chaos. Le

Corbusier viewed George Washington as a symbol of centralized authority. In the *New York Times* article, "Le Corbusier Scans Gotham's Towers," Brock cited the architect's reference to Washington as a "chief" (figure 5.22). Earlier Le Corbusier himself had defined "chief" as "government, authority, the patriarch, the head of the family . . . guardian power."[91] He understood that the first president had been a guiding force in the federal planning of the city of Washington, D.C., designed by Major Pierre Charles L'Enfant (with Andrew Ellicott's assistance). He knew from Hegemann's writings that L'Enfant, a French émigré artist who served in the Corps of Engineers during the American Revolution, employed baroque models including Versailles in the design of his rational plan.[92] It is possible to suggest, therefore, that the statue of Washington (and the president it represented) was a symbol for resolving the "disparity" between Le Corbusier's visions of past and future. He also used the dialectic in his search for American power brokers.

The configuration of Manhattan as an island, a *territoire-type,* made it well suited for developing and testing his Radiant City. Its elevated streets, parkways, and regulation of vehicular traffic indicated proficient organization. Its technical accomplishments were invested in its infrastructure: the Holland Tunnel, Pulaski Skyway, George Washington Bridge (which he christened "the only seat of grace in the disordered city"), and docks.[93] Along the water's edge on Riverside Drive (or Chicago's Lake Shore Drive), vast blocks of well-organized luxury housing already employed such modern techniques as skeletal construction, elevators, and air conditioning.[94] All of this led Le Corbusier to designate New York, and specifically Manhattan, as an empirical model for the Radiant City.

The island of Manhattan, like its skyscrapers, lent itself well to biological metaphors. Le Corbusier was cognizant of the importance of topography and climate as a result of experiences in 1929 cruising by airplane over the cities and rural landscape of South America. Flying over Manhattan, he observed that the island resembled a fish, a "gigantic sole" whose spine was Fifth Avenue. Its fins on both sides were defined by piers that

5.21
Ithiel Town and A. J.
Davis, Subtreasury Build-
ing (originally Custom
House; now Federal Hall
National Memorial),
1834–1842, 28 Wall
Street. (Photo: author.)

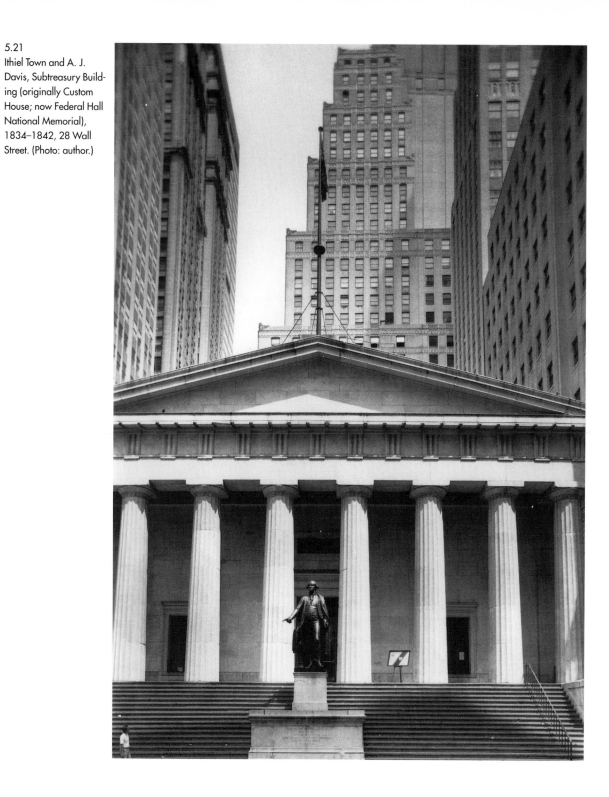

LE CORBUSIER SCANS GOTHAM'S TOWERS

The French Architect, on a Tour, Finds the City Violently Alive, a Wilderness of Experiment Toward a New Order

The City of the Future as Le Corbusier Envisions It.

By H. I. BROCK

THE citizen of the French Republic who is known as Le Corbusier — he was born Jeanneret and his given name is Charles-Edouard — is just now paying his first visit to America and has had his first eyeful of the man-made miracle which is New York. In circles where disputing about art is a major sport, Le Corbusier is identified as the founder and public exponent of the mood in architecture which has been labeled the International Style and which certain stiff conservatives insist does not look like architecture at all.

The basic principle of this style is to regard the architect's function as primarily one of household efficiency engineering. His job is to furnish human creatures with a convenient "machine for living in." As stated, the principle applies specifically to the family dwelling. But it applies also to the multiple arrangement of buildings which takes care of the composite employments and the complex human activities of a city where great numbers of people must live and most of them attend to business.

Since the modern dwelling and the modern city have each new demands to meet, since each has at command a service of machinery and materials which no dwelling and no city has ever had before, Le Corbusier and his school begin by discarding traditions and dismissing prejudices which would perpetuate formulas of building evolved from conditions of life that have ceased to exist.

THE rough idea is that the machine age, with its vast concentrations of population and its prodigious accumulation of mechanical devices for quantity production and for mass movement of goods and men, has created problems which the older architecture is incompetent to solve. The new architecture must face these problems squarely and find a solution on a sound mechanical basis, let the chips of academic estheticism fall where they may.

New York City, for example, is planted thick with skyscrapers — filing cases of millions of human beings at work or stowed away for the night. The streets of New York are jammed with automotive vehicles engaged in distributing the quantity-production output or moving these millions of people about, back and forth between home and business, and generally where they want to go, creating in the process no end of traffic tangles and even seriously endangering in life and limb those who still have to get about on their own feet.

Le Corbusier has built in France and other European countries machines for living in — machines also for doing business in. Whether these machines are, in fact, more efficient than the houses other architects build is a question which will not be argued here. But it is true that, at three years short of 50, he is more famous as the articulate voice of the new architecture than as the executant of its projects. He represents a vision of the future rather than a proved practice of the present.

MODERN architecture — that is, machine-made architecture — was born, as even its most ardent European advocates admit, in this country. The Europeans who have taken it up have made it much more "modern" than we have dared or cared to make it. Nevertheless, New York — the part of it, at least, which enjoys high visibility — is the creation on the greatest scale that the world

knows of the new architecture which is our own. That architecture pierces the sky with pinnacles that lift the level of our rocky little island (which in a state of nature could not boast a really respectable hill) into rivalry with the lesser mountains.

Le Corbusier, from the deck of the giant liner Normandie, looked up the harbor and saw (as he says) afar off a dream city hanging in the blue sky above the horizon of the water — a vision of enchantment. He went below for déjeuner and came up again with the solid substance of the vision right on top of him. He was

appalled by the brutality of the great masses — the "sauvagerie" — the wild barbarity of the stupendous, disorderly accumulation of towers, trampling the living city under their heavy feet, like a herd of mastodons.

As the ship moved up the river and he got the city broadside on, as the clutter of bunched towers of the stronghold of finance thinned out and other towers began to stand out separate, gleaming in the sunlight in the space above the lowlier neighbors, his despondency abated. Hope revived for the future which the first bright vision had seemed to embody. That vision might not, after all, be a mirage.

LATER, while touring the city in the company of the writer, he stood at the base of the steep sheer cliff of Raymond Hood's slat in Rockefeller Center and said that it was good, then began ruefully to rub the crick out of the back of his neck that was the result of trying to look up to the very top of anything so tall and uncompromisingly perpendicular.

He found the smaller buildings on the Fifth Avenue front — dedicated to France and the British Empire — out of scale, both with the upreared mass and the human beings walking about the central plaza. That plaza itself, all bare (as it is apt to be when the tourist season is on the wane), struck him as decidedly dull — in spite of Prometheus and his fountain.

Then he was shot in an elevator (at the rate of 1,200 feet a minute) to the very top of the big slat — the deck under which lurks the Rainbow Room — and looked out upon the map of the city, by that time half veiled in a soft gray mist, which cut off the horizons far short of the two extremes of our narrow island but revealed the bounding ribbons of water on either side.

North, south, east and west, the

skyscrapers nevertheless stood out boldly. Now and again the sun thrust through the thin clouds and bathed their faces in a brief glory of high light or gilded the fancy tops which some of them have borrowed from all the styles — unimportant to M. Le Corbusier — that came before the steel skeleton revolutionized large-scale building. It was excellent theatre — spectacular drama.

BUT the modern architect was not particularly impressed. He was looking for architecture, not theatre, and shy, besides, of succumbing to drama so melodramatic. Moreover, he was looking for architecture in his own sense of the word — in this case, the city that is a machine for living in — not merely frightfully expensive scenery built to knock the beholder's eye out.

"They are too small," he said, looking straight at the Empire State Building, tallest in all the world of filing cases for men and standing on one of the biggest pieces of ground devoted to that purpose in the city.

Somebody pointed out a building with "modern" horizontal lines belting continuous windows about it, down by the Hudson, and a building with "modern" vertical lines, stacking up windows in parallel slits, over, toward the East River.

"I am not interested," said Le Corbusier, "in that sort of thing — both sets of lines are all right as expressing the idea of horizontal and vertical circulation respectively. But what counts is the actual existence in the building of the two kinds of circulation and their efficient coordination. That is the combination which creates adequate machines for business for swarms of people — human beehives — if it is joined, of course, with free circulation among the buildings."

The skyscrapers that thrust up

(Continued on Page 23)

New York Times Studios.

Too Small? — Yes, Says Le Corbusier; Too Narrow for Free, Efficient Circulation.

© Andre Steiner

Le Corbusier Looks — Critically

5.22
"Le Corbusier Scans Gotham's Towers." (*New York Times,* November 3, 1935, 7, p. 10.) NYT Pictures, ©1935 The New York Times Co. Reproduced by permission. Diorama of Plan Voisin by Le Corbusier © Artists Rights Society (ARS), New York/ ADAGP, Paris/FLC.

fanned out from the port.[95] By 1935 this metaphor was common among European travel accounts including Morand's. But Le Corbusier expanded the idea. "A city has a biological life" and "a biological structure," he maintained, but Manhattan is flawed. Its skyscrapers and infrastructure demonstrated the viability of modern techniques, but the city still possessed no "basic pleasures" because it lacked a modern plan, a physical and conceptual structure. Its Euclidean grid might be appropriate to the scale and exigencies of Colonial times (as Le Corbusier inaccurately described the period around 1811, when the commissioners' plan for New York City appeared), but totally inadequate to the needs of the automobile-based culture of the 1930s.[96] Long distances separated the city from the suburbs of Westchester County and Connecticut. Vast arteries of highways, bridges, and elevated roads, Grand Central Terminal, and a "tangled network of railroads" linked "skyscraper elevators" to the commuter's "colonial style cottage" (figure 5.23). Le Corbusier called this daily exodus from the "purgatory" of the city, and both the infrastructure and decentralist planning policies supporting it, the "tumor of the great American waste."[97] He felt compelled to think about the people left behind, about "the strained faces in the subway" that he observed on his excursions with Marguerite. These people would "return in the evening to lodgings that are not like paradise," not like the luxury apartment houses on Fifth Avenue or commuter cottages.[98] The debacle of the suburbs confirmed that America valued "individual liberty" over the collective needs of the society.[99]

What kind of radical retrofitting was required to decongest and revitalize the central city? In "What Is America's Problem?" Le Corbusier determined that America's problem was Manhattan's problem. The city's towers and setback skyscrapers were irrational because their height, density, and massing were largely determined by the New York City zoning ordinance of 1916. For him they confirmed a "romantic digression" (figure 5.24). In response, his plan called for a redevelopment or "cellular reorganization" of the existing grid of streets into larger units to accommodate the automobile (figure 5.25); demolition-based planning to redistribute densi-

5.23
Le Corbusier, "a dream × 2 millions." ("What Is America's Problem?," *American Architect* 148 [March 1936], p. 20, fig. 7; reprinted in *Cathédrales*, p. 283.) © 2001 Artists Rights Society (ARS), New York/ADAGP, Paris/FLC.

ties; displacing setback office towers with Y-shaped slabs (figure 5.26; see plate 2); a program of mass housing; profit recouped from the construction of denser buildings used to build express highways; and government authority to accomplish this metamorphosis.[100]

Manhattan could fulfill this agenda because it met three preconditions for demolition-based planning. It had an excess of "long empty riverbanks" or "wasteland at the edges of the city." It featured Central Park, a large oasis of potentially available green space and other "free areas."[101] Ironically, Le Corbusier attributed the survival of Central Park to "the strength of character of the municipal authorities . . . the sign of a strong society." Finally, Manhattan was cursed with "soulless" tenement streets in its slum neighborhoods. If only Americans

une digagation romantique

5.24
Le Corbusier, "a romantic digression." ("What Is America's Problem?," *American Architect* 148 [March 1936]; reprinted in *Cathédrales*, p. 279.) © 2001 Artists Rights Society (ARS), New York/ADAGP, Paris/FLC.

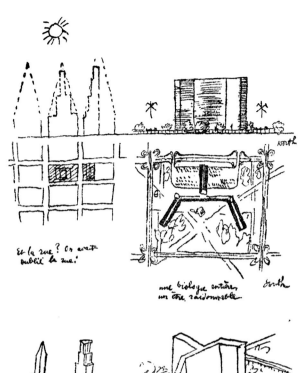

Et la rue ? On avait oublié la rue.

une biologie entière: un être raisonnable.

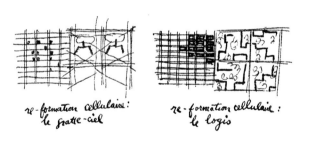

re-formation cellulaire: le gratte-ciel

re-formation cellulaire: le logis

5.25
Le Corbusier, "cellular reorganization: skyscraper [office building]" (left); "cellular reorganization: housing" (right). ("What Is America's Problem?," *American Architect* 148 [March 1936]; reprinted in *Cathédrales*, p. 279.) © 2001 Artists Rights Society (ARS), New York/ADAGP, Paris/FLC.

ré-formation cellulaire de la ville

5.26
Le Corbusier, existing Manhattan setback office tower (top and bottom left); office building transformed into a Cartesian skyscraper (top and bottom right). Elevations, plans, and axonometric drawings. ("What Is America's Problem?," *American Architect* 148 [March 1936]; reprinted in *Cathédrales*, p. 275.) © 2001 Artists Rights Society (ARS), New York/ADAGP, Paris/FLC.

were informed about the slums, "it would make them sick at heart and they would make new city plans."[102]

To reequip American cities during the Depression years, Le Corbusier identified housing as the key issue. He specified three typologies for mass housing in America, all contingent on redevelopment of the block and lot system of the Manhattan grid. The first type followed the *à redents* model (see figures 5.25 right and 3.4) that he described in both *La Ville radieuse* and "What Is America's Problem?" To maintain a linkage between skyscraper and ground he limited housing blocks to sixteen stories of duplex units.[103] By the early 1930s the *à redents* type had evolved into the *cité-jardin en hauteur* or vertical garden city, now configured as a high-rise slab or slab block.[104] The second typology called for a large lozenge-shaped apartment block accommodating from 2,500 to 3,000 people (figure 5.27) that he identified in his lectures on the Radiant City and offered to such government authorities as New York's police commissioner. In 1933 an earlier version of it appeared as a double business tower for Algiers. As his lecture drawings suggest, he planned the housing block as the central feature of a community containing schools, gardens and playgrounds, car parks, a football field, and even tennis courts (figure 5.28; see plate 1).[105] He proposed this high-density solution for the housing crisis in New York, not because it was the option he preferred, but because it was a housing type that maximized the number of apartment units, given limited capital available during the 1930s. A third housing typology that recently entered his lexicon was a sixty-story Cartesian skyscraper, now Y-shaped rather than cruciform in plan, and one he employed for offices (see figure 5.26; see plate 2) but considered "equally valid for *Unités d'Habitation*."[106] This new Cartesian skyscraper was based on a design he referred to as *type Sert*, its Y-shaped plan taking the form of a "hen's foot" (*patte de poule*). Le Corbusier attributed the design to José Luis Sert, even though it was a variant of the cruciform plan. Oriented toward the path of the sun, the facade of the Y-shaped block would receive more exposure to light. It first appeared as office buildings in the Macià master plan for the Casa Bloc development in Barcelona of 1931–1932

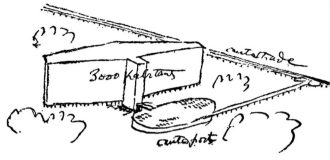

5.27
Le Corbusier, Radiant City apartment block, lozenge configuration. (*Cathédrales*, p. 269.) © 2001 Artists Rights Society (ARS), New York/ADAGP, Paris/FLC.

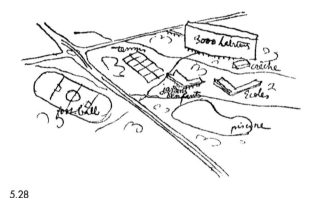

5.28
Le Corbusier, Radiant City community with schools, playgrounds, car parks, swimming pool, football field, tennis courts. (*Cathédrales*, p. 271.) © 2001 Artists Rights Society (ARS), New York/ADAGP, Paris/FLC.

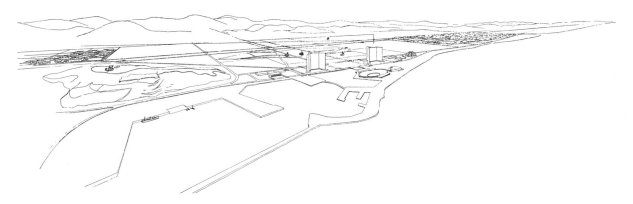

5.29

Le Corbusier and Pierre Jeanneret in collaboration with José Luis Sert and members of GATEPAC, Macià master plan for the Casa Bloc development, Barcelona, 1931–1932. (*Oeuvre complète 1929–1934*, p. 90. Plan FLC 13251.) © 2001 Artists Rights Society (ARS), New York/ADAGP, Paris/FLC.

5.30

Hans Poelzig, project for a skyscraper, Friedrichstrasse, Berlin, 1921. (*Journal of the American Institute of Architects* 11 [September 1923], p. 366, fig. 3.)

by Sert with the GATEPAC group as well as the collaboration of both Le Corbusier and his cousin Pierre Jeanneret (figure 5.29).[107] The Y-shaped block may have looked to such German models as Hans Poelzig's project for a skyscraper (figure 5.30) in the Friedrichstrasse, Berlin (1921). Poelzig's design was widely discussed in the international architectural press.[108]

On the eve of his departure for America Le Corbusier employed the Y shape in projects for housing (Rome suburb of 1934 and Bat'a industries at Hellocourt, France of 1935) as well as for offices.[109] In his Vassar lecture, and most likely in those at Columbia (see plate 2) and Yale, he advanced the typology for housing, calling it "la belle forme pour l'appartement."[110] Throughout the 1930s he promoted the new Cartesian skyscraper, producing a model of it in 1938 (figure 5.31). Although his article designated Y-shaped skyscrapers only for offices, his solution to "America's problem" to "house" 6 million persons at a density of 400 people per acre in Manhattan suggests that he intended to use that high-rise, high-density typology for housing. He made no formal proposal to use the *type Sert* model for public housing, but did suggest it to Rockefeller for an apartment house.

Le Corbusier assigned a kind of evolutionary or biological determinism to his empirical model of New York. The enchanted catastrophe was double-edged and

5.31
Le Corbusier, "Cartesian" skyscraper, model, 1938. (*Le Corbusier 1910–65*, ed. Boesiger and Girsberger, p. 123. FLC L2(19) 3-5.) © 2001 Artists Rights Society (ARS), New York/ADAGP, Paris/FLC.

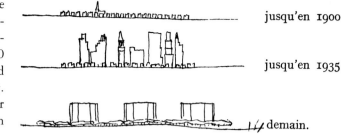

5.32
Le Corbusier, New York City: "to 1900, to 1935, tomorrow." (*Cathédrales*, p. 271.) © 2001 Artists Rights Society (ARS), New York/ADAGP, Paris/FLC.

bittersweet. In its present state, he held, New York was a catastrophe because it was based on the wrong premise. Yet it was also "a beautiful and worthy catastrophe," worthy because it was "a city in the process of becoming" and, therefore, capable of change. It represented an unusual theory of creation. Unlike the cities of Europe, it was "born at once," "when the cathedrals were white." In its brief history it had experienced unprecedented transformations. His lecture sketches showed the metamorphosis of Manhattan in three stages of development: "to 1900," "to 1935," and "tomorrow" (figure 5.32; see figure 3.8).[111] Le Corbusier's self-serving theorem presumed that New York was only a "temporary" city. It owed its existence to change, as Morand and Léger suggested. It defined itself as "a city . . . supplanted by another city."[112] Thus, it was destined to begin all over again. This eschatological view, which was based on preconceptions, guided Le Corbusier's efforts. Announcing the second machine age, he proclaimed once again, "A great epoch has begun. A new epoch."[113] This echoed his earlier call for a first machine age, but the transformations that he envisioned were made possible not by organic processes but by demolition of existing urban fabric.

What then would make the Radiant City plan for New York feasible and the transformations he envisioned possible? Ironically, Le Corbusier's thesis hinged on the very forces that he blamed for undermining the culture and the society: consumerism and capitalism. The metamorphosis of New York would depend on industrial production of affordable housing. His own report at CIAM II indicated that in comparison to the pre–World War I period, the current price of Ford automobiles in the United States, produced by machine labor, had fallen by 50 percent, whereas prices for houses, produced by hand labor, had doubled (figure 5.33).[114] Thus the house had to be transformed into a consumer product through factory production. The growth market for industry would now be housing and not the automobile, making plants productive once again.[115] Even though Europe and America were in a period of economic decline during the early 1930s, he argued, their economies could be revived by factory-made shelter. In effect Le Corbusier resorted to a higher technology to resolve the housing crisis, a method confirmed by his CIAM studies. He insisted that this agenda would take pressure off the consumer and an industry dedicated to automobile production. It would also slow the escalating and alarming trend toward suburbanization and commuting. But once again, his timing was off and his planning ideas delivered too late. In the fall of 1935 the automobile industry was lifting itself out of idleness. Contrary to Le Corbusier's hopes and expectations, consumer interest in new automobiles was reviving, an indication of increased national prosperity.[116] He himself witnessed the large number of visitors to the New York motor show, resulting in record sales.[117] Automobiles encouraged decentralization. Thus Le Corbusier's call for the "cellular reorganization of cities," with its centralist agenda to check suburban commuting, was out of sync with the aspirations of most Americans in the mid-1930s. Moreover, the redirection of industry, especially the automobile industry, toward the production of affordable "standardized" housing necessitated the commitment of big business. Such a transformation would have required not only radical reforms within the housing and automobile industries but also changes in public policy at federal and state levels.

New York, Le Corbusier argued, had the potential for change but it lacked intelligent European leadership that he could provide. Naively, he narrowly focused his efforts on the search for a centralized authority receptive to his services and Radiant City solutions. He called for slum clearance and a new infrastructure with development in the center and along the periphery of Manhattan to recapture the island's best natural sites. Believing in the architect's social responsibility, he advocated communitarian principles including reorganization of land ownership and single-class housing involving new typologies. But many of his assessments of existing conditions, coupled with methods of renewal he advocated, were ultimately misguided and socially untenable. Moreover, his notions of community did not find expression in architecture or urban form. They did not respond to the needs of the public realm to provide adequate public space and what Bernard Rudolfsky later called "streets for people." As Henry-Russell Hitchcock

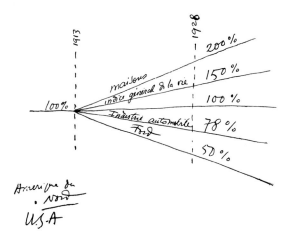

5.33
Le Corbusier, "The Minimum House," changing costs of houses, living, and automobiles in the United States, 1913 to 1928. Report at CIAM II, Frankfurt, 1929. (*La Ville radieuse*, p. 32.) © 2001 Artists Rights Society (ARS), New York/ADAGP, Paris/FLC.

suggested in his translator's note to Le Corbusier's article, "It was an exhortation, a message, not a detailed program."[118] It was driven by his preconceptions and shaped by tensions between his abiding idealism and his first encounter with the realities of the great modern city. Notwithstanding his insightful critique of New York, Le Corbusier's argument for transforming it into a Radiant City in practical terms was deeply flawed. The demolition-based planning that he envisioned may have been considered necessary and feasible in times of economic growth with rising land values, such as in the 1950s and 1960s. But in times of falling land values, such as in the 1930s, economic conditions could not justify it.

Le Corbusier's proposal had absurd inconsistencies. It was only in the execution of the United Nations Headquarters during the late 1940s that the design team, which included Le Corbusier, Oscar Niemeyer, and others, was successful in realizing a fragment of the Radiant City. Although that project may have responded to the technical, organizational, and biological components of his model, it bypassed issues of social reform. There were, of course, social consequences for the UN Headquarters. The midtown location encouraged centralization. As an enclave resulting from the elimination of urban streets, it sought to create an oasis. But at the same time, its demolition-based planning sundered the historic relationship with the evolving city and all the diverse cultures, public spaces, and enriching chaos associated with it. Followers of Le Corbusier succeeded in realizing other urban renewal projects until, at the moment they reached their heyday in the late 1950s and 1960s, they were successfully challenged by Jane Jacobs, Herbert Gans, and like-minded sociologists and planners.[119]

Le Corbusier's invention of New York as an empirical model is significant in the development of his thought because it underscores his efforts to enrich preconception with experience, myth with reality. To a limited but nonetheless significant extent, he was able to connect with the reality of the city in its technical and functional acumen, in its skyscrapers, bridges, and infrastructures, and in the defects of its "wasteland." However, such connections were rare in Le Corbusier's development because his philosophical approach was fundamentally idealist. He lacked both the cultural background and the temperament to engage reality in the United States and elsewhere in a deep or sustained manner. Experience rarely changed his preconceptions; reality rarely challenged his myths. These dichotomies remained in a tense relationship. In the end his *idea* of reality, rather than reality itself, dominated so that it could serve his polemics and rhetoric.

6

Le Corbusier's efforts to realize the Radiant City and its housing program inevitably led him to search aggressively in 1935 for authorities and power brokers in the United States and specifically in New York City, but his initiatives were unsuccessful. It is ironic, therefore, that many American historians, sociologists, and planners have held him responsible for the excesses of midcentury urban renewal and its housing programs. This chapter seeks to inform the debate on Le Corbusier's role in the debacle of public housing in America through consideration of three issues: the diffusion of Corbusian housing typology; American public policy that developed independently of Le Corbusier; and models, American and European, that shaped both American housing and Le Corbusier's projects. The objective, then, is to separate form from public policy.

Le Corbusier's book *La Ville radieuse* was dedicated to *l'Autorité.*[1] Notwithstanding the many contradictions in defining his own identity, Le Corbusier saw himself as a city planner and architect, a technician rather than a politician. This obliged him to seek out authorities with the power to endorse and implement.[2] In America, as in other countries he visited, his search for power brokers followed the often intersecting paths of public- and private-sector work. If a second era of machine civiliza-

tion were to be realized, he assumed, it would depend on the heads of both government and industry. Because the United States had already accomplished a technical revolution in architecture, it could now enter that second machine age and become "the next great building site of the organization of mechanistic civilization."[3] But America, he claimed, was a nation of youth and power that could not solve its complex urban problems. It needed his intellectual leadership to direct the nation's power brokers in the reconstruction of its cities.

Toward this objective Le Corbusier sought to transform Manhattan from an enchanted catastrophe into an empirical model for the Radiant City. It would be a sign of the "écho pratique" he hoped would result from the trip. To accomplish this objective, he fixed his agenda and searched for his own power brokers. He identified three sets. The first was a group of housing administrators and other government authorities within the public sector. These included a number of city officials, especially those in the newly formed New York City Housing Authority. The second was a group of industrial producers who could supply *techniques modernes* and, along with philanthropic investors, offer possible subvention. The third set was Nelson Rockefeller and Wallace Harrison. This chapter considers the first group.

In his initial foray into the public realm Le Corbusier relied on some welcome intervention. Rockefeller, Harrison, and Fernand Léger, as well as local journalists and editors, provided him with introductions to city housing professionals and other officials.⁴ At a luncheon on October 31 he met with Henry Humphrey, a Condé Nast editor for *House and Garden* who introduced him to housing reformers. Humphrey also invited Lawrence Kocher and William Lescaze (1896–1969), Le Corbusier's Swiss friend who was already an insider in the New York public housing circle.⁵ Later Humphrey attempted to meet Le Corbusier's request for an American edition of *La Ville radieuse.*

On November 11, together with Humphrey and others, Le Corbusier made his first professional visit to the city's "slums," as he called them in English.⁶ He was long familiar with such urban conditions in other countries. In Paris he knew well its "tuberculous [housing] blocks" and "rotting neighborhoods."⁷ His moral condemnation of these houses and quarters was, at least in part, self-serving because it sought to rationalize their demolition, promoting instead his own Voisin Plan with its Triumphal Highway (1925). Similarly, on his travels to South America in 1929 he visited the "favelas of the blacks" in Rio de Janeiro and walked the "tragic streets without hope" of Buenos Aires. Even though his colleague Alfred Agache was currently at work on a master plan for Rio, Le Corbusier felt compelled to produce his own plan (see figure 3.7).⁸ In 1932 he observed Barcelona's Barrio Chino district as the "center of prostitution." His Macià master plan for Barcelona (with José Luis Sert and members of GATEPAC, a Catalan wing of CIAM) called for "cleaning" and "purging the old city," leaving a site for Le Corbusier's proposed Civic Center and introduction of new residential districts nearby (see figure 5.29).⁹ The architect's encounter with American slums, like those in other cities, became one of the defining experiences of his tour.

Le Corbusier's early writings demonstrate that he knew much about urban life in America, but his impressions of Harlem and Chicago slums were still affecting.¹⁰ His firsthand experiences there caused him to focus on urban waste and decay for his Baltimore talk and also

for his final lecture of the tour at the Stevens Hotel in Chicago. They also provided poignant reasons for him to dedicate his remaining time in America toward promoting the Radiant City with its large-scale housing program, ostensibly because he believed that it could provide renewal for blighted areas in the nation's most needy cities. A more critical appraisal might conclude that, on the one hand, his urban planning offered no more to the poor neighborhoods of North American cities than it did to those communities in Paris and South American cities: a visionary scheme based on the demolition of existing neighborhoods. On the other hand, his approach to planning and his justification of urban renewal on moral grounds did not differ from the attitudes of most American planning and housing specialists of the period. Although now considered misguided, Le Corbusier's program promised to provide basic affordable shelter for large numbers of urban dwellers. To achieve such low-cost housing, he would also look to the private sector to harness industrial methods and new materials.

Le Corbusier's tour of the slums was arranged by both Humphrey, who was fluent in French, and Langdon W. Post, Chairman of the New York City Housing Authority, the municipal agency charged with building public housing with federal funds. On November 11 they went to sections of Brooklyn and Manhattan where, according to Humphrey, the Authority had "already demolished houses."¹¹ Humphrey met the architect for lunch a few days later and the three met again on November 19.

The New York City Housing Authority (NYCHA) was founded early in 1934 after passage of the Municipal Housing Authority Act by the state legislature. The Act was one of the most ambitious of all New Deal housing measures, encouraging municipalities to establish their own authorities to direct federal monies toward the construction of public housing.¹² It succeeded several earlier federal initiatives, including the 1933 National Industrial Recovery Act, which established the Public Works Administration (PWA) and a vigorous loan program. The Housing Division of the PWA worked closely with the Public Works Emergency Housing Corporation, which in January 1934 made $25 million available to the NYCHA.[13]

The Authority inaugurated its program with First Houses (1935), a series of twenty-four rehabilitated tenements.[14] The project, designed by the Authority's Technical Division headed by Frederick L. Ackerman, marked a significant government initiative because the social housing movement in New York City up to that time had been almost entirely funded by private initiatives.[15] On December 3 Le Corbusier attended the opening ceremonies of First Houses with George B. Cabot, Director of Management Bureau for the NYCHA. Cabot also arranged for him to see building sites that Le Corbusier referred to as "Post's housing."[16]

The Authority planned subsequent projects, but they differed from First Houses because they called for demolition of existing housing. In the spring of 1935 the NYCHA had released a report of its Committee on Long Range Planning, which declared at least ten square miles of slum areas unfit for residential use (over four square miles in Manhattan and five square miles in Brooklyn). The committee further recommended an annual expenditure of $150 million over ten years for slum clearance.[17] Months earlier Mayor Fiorello La Guardia had requested a PWA loan in that amount.[18] Although the federal government did not ultimately endorse and fund the plan, the report nonetheless formed the basis of the Authority's long-range program, which in turn kindled Le Corbusier's expectations.[19] From 1934 to 1937 nine square miles of slums were demolished.[20]

When Le Corbusier, Humphrey, and Post toured project sites, there were only three possible venues where the NYCHA had "already demolished housing": Harlem River Houses (1935–1937) in Manhattan, and Williamsburg Houses (1934–1937; figure 6.1) and Red Hook Houses (1935–1939), both in Brooklyn.[21] Le Corbusier probably visited the Williamsburg site because it was not only the most advanced of the three projects but also of special interest to him. Williamsburg originated as a housing competition in 1934 sponsored by the NYCHA to "qualify registered architects residing . . . in New York City" to design its projects. Written by Frederick Ackerman, the program called for a massive slum

clearance effort to demolish existing city blocks and replace them with larger blocks containing open spaces for parks and playgrounds, a community building, a school, and stores. Of the 277 submissions, twenty-two architectural firms "qualified," according to results of the competition, "for work under the New York City Housing Authority to be financed by loans from the Public Works Administration."[22] In November 1935 no new construction had begun on any project but demolition of the ten-block site for Williamsburg Houses was nearly 90 percent complete.[23]

Aside from its organization, site plan, and program, Williamsburg Houses no doubt intrigued Le Corbusier because William Lescaze had been brought in from the outside to lead the design team. The NYCHA appointed a team of architects headed by Richmond H. Shreve as the project's principal adviser, but Shreve promptly turned over the design to Lescaze, perhaps because of his own preference for modernism.[24] Moreover, Lescaze's experience in advanced housing research made him a desirable choice.[25] Among housing reformers the appointment must have been controversial because of conflicting opinions about modernism. Ackerman's views were generally opposed to European modernism. But others, such as Nelson Rockefeller and his family, "within the highest circle of economic and political power," as Richard Plunz explained, embraced "this new architectural expression . . . as an affirmation of the potential for renewal of the capitalist system along liberal humanitarian lines."[26]

Le Corbusier was keenly aware of Lescaze's success in America, which was predicated on the importation of design ideas derived from his own.[27] Most likely Lescaze was introduced to Le Corbusier's theory and design during his studies with Karl Moser. A close friend of Le Corbusier's, Moser was responsible for sending young Swiss designers to the Paris atelier.[28] Although Lescaze immigrated to the United States in 1920, he made annual trips to Europe and kept well informed about recent developments there.[29] In 1926, for example, he visited Stuttgart where Le Corbusier's housing for the Weissenhof Siedlung was in construction; the next year he met with Le Corbusier in Paris. Early in 1929 Lescaze

·Williamsburg·Houses·
Associated Architects

R. H. SHREVE *Chief Architect*

JAMES F. BLY
ARTHUR C. HOLDEN
GURNEY & CLAVAN
PAUL TRAPANI
HOLMGREN · VOLZ & GARDSTEIN

M. W. DEL GAUDIO
WILLIAM LESCAZE
JOHN W. INGLE JR.
HARRY LESLIE WALKER
IRWIN CLAVAN *Manager*

Consultants
VITALE & GEIFFERT · GILMORE D. CLARKE
MEYER STRONG & JONES INC.
FRED BRUTSCHY GEO. E. STREHAN

FEDERAL EMERGENCY ADMINISTRATION OF PUBLIC WORKS~HAROLD L. ICKES ADMINISTRATOR HORATIO B. HACKETT ASSISTANT ADMINISTRATOR~ANGELO R. CLAS DIRECTOR OF HOUSING~ CITY OF NEW YORK FIORELLO H. LAGUARDIA MAYOR~NEW YORK CITY HOUSING AUTHORITY LANGDON W. POST CHAIRMAN MARY K. SIMKHOVITCH LOUIS H. PINK REV. E. ROBERTS MOORE B. CHARNEY VLADECK

6.1
William Lescaze, chief designer,
and team headed by Richmond H.
Shreve, Williamsburg Houses,
aerial view, Brooklyn, New York,
1934–1937. (New York City
Housing Authority papers, La
Guardia and Wagner Archives,
La Guardia Community
College/The City University of
New York.)

formed a partnership with George Howe who expected to receive the commission for the Philadelphia Saving Fund Society. Lescaze's understanding of European modernism was an asset to Howe. The commission provided Lescaze with the opportunity to work on a skyscraper and satisfied his attraction to the "monumental."[30]

Throughout his partnership with Howe (1929–1933), Lescaze demonstrated his recall of Corbusian theory, especially the "five points of a new architecture," and design, notably in the Ozenfant studio and in villas near Paris. By the late 1920s he had earned a reputation as the "Le Corbusier of America."[31] But he also synthesized elements of Bauhaus design, the De Stijl movement, constructivism, and other European sources of modern architecture.[32] Indeed, he followed the current of Euro-

pean modernism so attentively that his work often lacked originality and vigor.[33] He was still a central figure in what Hitchcock and Johnson considered the transference of European modernism to America. The work of Howe and Lescaze, they suggested in 1932, "represents an increasingly successful attempt to apply in America with full regard for all our conditions, the technical and the aesthetic ideas of modern architecture . . . in Europe."[34]

Among American designers of urban housing during the 1930s, Lescaze's work came closest to imparting the more pragmatic, if not visionary, aspects of Le Corbusier's aesthetics and imagery. To the extent that Corbusian principles did influence the formal design of American housing, it was largely through the efforts of Lescaze and his assistant Albert Frey, a young Swiss architect who had worked in Le Corbusier's atelier (1928–1929). Like other European modernists, especially those associated with CIAM, Lescaze and Frey were committed to mass housing.[35] With Frey respon-

sible for most of the design elements, Chrystie-Forsyth housing project (1931) owed a debt to Le Corbusier (figure 6.2).[36] It called for a series of interlocking L-shaped slab blocks accommodating open corridors, which read as balconies stretched across their facades. The slab blocks were raised on *pilotis* and arranged in crankshaft formation following Le Corbusier's Ville Contemporaine (see figures 3.2, 6.13) and Ville Radieuse (see figure 3.4), the latter exhibited in Brussels at CIAM III in 1930.[37] Lescaze and Frey's blocks, like Le Corbusier's, were recessed (*à redents*) and did not engage the street.[38] Notwithstanding their efforts to increase site coverage, the project was rejected. The socioeconomic realities of the slum clearance program meant that rents at Chrystie-Forsyth would be prohibitive for low-income families, and middle-class workers would be reluctant to resettle there.[39] Still, Chrystie-Forsyth received wide recognition; Hitchcock and Johnson selected it for their 1932 "Modern Architecture" exhibition.[40]

6.3
William Lescaze and Albert Frey,
River Gardens, unexecuted hous-
ing project, Lower East Side, New
York City, 1931–1933. (Lescaze
Archives, George Arents Research
Library, Syracuse University.)

Similarly, Lescaze and Frey's unexecuted project for River Gardens Housing (1931–1933), also intended as a slum clearance project on the Lower East Side, recalled Corbusian models. A bird's-eye rendering of River Gardens, signed by Lescaze, was dated October 4, 1932 (figure 6.3).[41] The cruciform towers, an assemblage of low-, medium-, and high-rises up to thirty-one stories in park land, not only looked to Le Corbusier's Villes-Tours, designated for housing as well as offices (1921; see figure 1.7, chapter 1), but also to an aerial view of the Plan Voisin (figure 6.4) that had been widely circulated in America.[42] However, the varying heights of the towers, according to Frey, illustrated their attempt "to relate [the towers] to the human scale and avoid a stereotyped monotony."[43] By 1935 the image of Le Corbusier's high-rise cruciform tower (and variations of it) was ubiquitous in the United States, and it became especially important for NYCHA projects through Lescaze, who served on its architectural board from the 1930s to the 1960s.[44]

That fall Le Corbusier probably saw Lescaze's working drawings for Williamsburg Houses during one of his frequent visits to Lescaze's newly completed residence and office at 211 East 48th Street. Lescaze was responsible for the project's site plan as well as the design of its exterior.[45] There he made an inevitable break with the long evolution of garden apartment design in America,

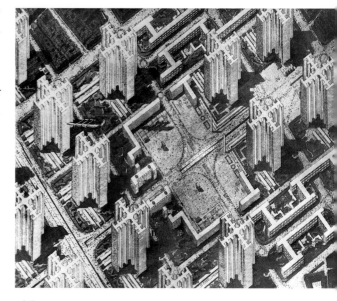

6.4
Le Corbusier, Plan Voisin, 1925.
(*Oeuvre complète 1910–1929*,
p. 117. FLC L2(7)2.) © 2001
Artists Rights Society (ARS), New
York/ADAGP, Paris/FLC.

most notably in the work of Henry Wright, Clarence Stein, and Frederick Ackerman at Sunnyside Gardens in Queens (1924–1928) and the satellite town of Radburn in Fairlawn, New Jersey (1927–1928).[46] Responding to the programmatic requirements of the 1934 NYCHA competition, Lescaze reconfigured the site into four superblocks containing a total of twenty apartment blocks arranged into long crankshafts. This formation was a more complex variant of the German *Zeilenbau* in which parallel rows of slab blocks were open at both ends. Like those at Christie-Forsyth, the crankshafts of Williamsburg Houses were adapted from Le Corbusier's *à redents* model, especially in his Ville Contemporaine (see figures 3.2, 6.13). The monumental apartment blocks at Williamsburg were rotated fifteen degrees, producing a disjuncture with the rectangular city grid around it. Although the blocks were designed to maximize access to light and air, as some critics observed, not all units benefited.[47] As Lewis Mumford noted, "orientation for sunlight works best when you have dwellings in plain rows," rather than in T-units in which one axis is inevitably incorrect.[48] Le Corbusier's early *à redents* schemes were judged similarly. Criticism also came from within the Authority. At Williamsburg and other NYCHA developments, site planning and exteriors were designed by the project architect and unit plans were the work of its technical division. Lescaze clashed with Ackerman's design philosophy opposing the *Zeilenbau* formation and rotation of the blocks that worked against the logic of the unit plans, as well as other aspects of its presumed functionalism.[49] Lescaze was responsible for determining the structural system, a reinforced concrete frame brought to the surface with yellow brick infill.[50] As Talbot Hamlin observed, Williamsburg Houses looked "obstreperously striped" with an incoherent relationship between the concrete bands and the windows.[51]

Finding no economic justification for isolated housing blocks, Richard Pommer argued that it was "characteristic of Lescaze to seek the attention-getting aesthetic of a pseudo-*Zeilenbau* system at the cost of its meaning and function." Lescaze's appeal to the aesthetic principles of the International Style, as Hitchcock and Johnson had

defined it, was clearly at odds with housing professionals in America. Measured against the standard of Le Corbusier, pioneers of the modern movement in Europe, and the housing specialist Oscar Stonorov, Pommer determined that Lescaze was merely a "versatile pasticheur" indifferent to either "social meanings, or comprehension of . . . design procedures."[52] Unlike the first generation of European modernists who were born in the 1880s, Lescaze belonged to a later generation, and specifically to a group of European émigrés in America that included Richard Neutra, Rudolf Schindler, Frederick Kiesler, Alfred Clauss, William Muschenheim, and Knud Lönberg-Holm. These architects became the assimilators in America of European modernism. They worked outside the social and political climate that produced the seminal Weissenhof and Frankfurt housing of the 1920s. Inevitably, like many of his colleagues in America, Lescaze adopted the aesthetic forms but remained indifferent to the social values of the modern movement in Europe.

During his tour with Humphrey and Post on November 11 Le Corbusier most likely also visited another NYCHA site being demolished in preparation for the construction of Harlem River Houses. The project was designed by an NYCHA-approved team that included Archibald Manning Brown, John L. Wilson, Horace Ginsbern, and others. Unlike Williamsburg Houses, Harlem River Houses would reflect "traditionalist" design with bearing-wall construction. Its contextual design and perimeter planning were consonant with Ackerman's values and those of a number of critics including Hamlin.[53] In addition to these features, its affirmation of the traditional street grid increased the distance in design philosophy between Harlem River Houses and Radiant City housing.

In addition to his initiatives with housing reformers, Le Corbusier met with three important government authorities in an attempt to interest them in his ideas for the Radiant City: Adolf A. Berle, New York City Chamberlain; Col. Harold Fowler, First Deputy Police Commissioner; and Howard Stix Cullman, Commissioner of the Port of New York Authority. On December 9 Wallace Harrison arranged a dinner at his home for Le Corbusier to meet Berle.[54] During the early years of the New

Deal, Berle, Rexford Guy Tugwell, and Raymond Moley made up the original trio in the "brain trust." A specialist in law and economics, Berle served as counsel to the Reconstruction Finance Corporation from 1933 to 1938.[55] Le Corbusier considered him to be "an extremely serious man" who held "very great responsibilities," and was "very troubled by urban problems." In *Cathédrales* Le Corbusier described Berle as "one of the 'New Deal' five . . . the five fingers of Roosevelt's hand; the technocrats."[56] He erroneously believed that Berle alone made financial agreements between Washington and New York City for allocation of federal funds for urban projects.[57] Le Corbusier claimed that he spent four hours at dinner with Berle talking about the Radiant City and illustrating his ideas with drawings. He attributed Berle's "uneasy" response to his own political agenda. He believed that Berle would have sent him to Washington to speak to Franklin Delano Roosevelt himself if the president had not been preoccupied that fall with electoral politics. But Berle left no account of his reactions to Le Corbusier's proposals.[58]

Berle's interest in urban architecture and planning in general, and in Le Corbusier's ideas in particular, was undoubtedly influenced by his close association with Tugwell, economist and professor at Columbia University.[59] In the spring of 1935 FDR officially created the Resettlement Administration (RA) and appointed Tugwell as its director. Like FDR, whose ideal was the pastoral community of his hometown Hyde Park, New York, and housing specialists Clarence Stein and Henry Wright, Tugwell supported the "back to the land" movement. Early on he originated the idea of suburban resettlement. The RA had the task of resettling low-income families largely from urban areas through creation of new communities in rural and suburban areas known as greenbelt towns.[60]

In February 1935 while resettlement was still in its planning phase, Tugwell accompanied his friend John Lansill, who soon became director of the RA's Suburban Division responsible for the greenbelt town program, on a site visit to the first community of Beltsville (later Greenbelt), Maryland. There Tugwell described his plan for the construction of a model community in which low-income families would be relocated from Washington's slums to a new project at the periphery of the city.[61] Years later Lansill claimed that for Beltsville, Tugwell originally envisioned skyscrapers resembling those in the Ville Contemporaine (see figures 1.6, 3.2, 6.13), but that he, Lansill, dissuaded his colleague from pursuing the idea.[62] If this unlikely assertion were true, Le Corbusier and Tugwell's joint vision would have anticipated the towers found in many of today's "edge cities."[63] Instead, Lansill endorsed single- and multifamily housing, later influenced by Frank Lloyd Wright's Broadacre City, the model for which he and Tugwell had seen when it was on exhibit at Rockefeller Center in the spring of 1935.[64] Thus, notwithstanding Tugwell's reputation in some camps as an "impractical theorist," his interest in Le Corbusier's ideas was probably academic.[65]

As Tugwell and Lansill molded it, the greenbelt program had two primary objectives: to "provide useful employment for relief labor [semiskilled and unskilled] in the construction of communities" and to relocate "low-income families now inadequately housed in overcrowded industrial centers." Also intended as correctives to rural poverty and unemployment, greenbelt towns sought to provide employment opportunities in the industrial and service sectors within the city as well as the "traditional advantages of life on the land."[66] The automobile would make these communities possible. Tugwell's approach therefore differed from the garden city town of Ebenezer Howard in that Tugwell's dwellers would not be removed entirely from the city with its greater opportunities for work. Like Le Corbusier, Tugwell kept his faith in the metropolis, and especially in New York City. His greenbelt towns, such as those actually built outside Washington, D.C., Milwaukee, and Cincinnati, were not conceived as suburban settlements as much as "small but complete [satellite] cities . . . with schools, stores, water, sewer, and electric systems, streets, parks, community forests and dairies and all the other appurtenances of a modern municipality."[67] Unlike FDR, who supported funding for slum clearance but was otherwise firmly committed to the "back to the land" movement, and Lansill, who opposed renewal of inner-city neighborhoods altogether, Tugwell advocated resettlement communities because they offered an affordable answer to federally subsidized slum clearance where inner-city land values and housing construction costs made urban rehabilitation economically prohibitive.[68]

During the final days of his American stay Le Corbusier's search for authority and a receptive audience for the Radiant City brought him in touch with a second New York City official, one in charge of traffic. On December 13, the day before his departure, he met with Col. Harold Fowler after being introduced by Jean Labatut of Princeton.[69] Le Corbusier knew that Fowler, a close friend of La Guardia, had the mayor's ear. In his efforts to reduce traffic congestion, accidents, and fatalities, Fowler's research the previous summer led him to make a number of aerial reconnaissance flights in a blimp.[70] Over lunch Le Corbusier implored Fowler to consider his plan. For Fowler's benefit he condensed all his lectures on modern architecture and city planning into a rather indigestible course of annotated sketches on a blank restaurant menu.[71] Le Corbusier understood the police commissioner's dilemma of coping with "A million and a half cars every day in a city designed for horse and buggy traffic." He urged Fowler to appreciate the benefits of the Radiant City. As he had done so many times for his American audiences, he sketched the superblock housing 2,500 to 3,000 people and the autoport, all lifted twenty feet above the ground. He also drew his projected transformations in the skyline of Manhattan from 1900 to "tomorrow" (see figures 3.8, 5.32). But according to Le Corbusier's account in *Cathedrals,* the affable police commissioner, like other city officials, only looked at the visitor with "admiring and slightly quizzical eyes" and promptly returned to his mundane duties. Le Corbusier's response to the meeting was defensive: "the authorities are badly informed."[72]

Le Corbusier also met Howard Cullman, introduced by Robert Jacobs who was related to Cullman by marriage.[73] Heir to a tobacco business, Cullman had been in public service since 1927.[74] During his stay in New York Le Corbusier met frequently with him and Jacobs, and concluded that Cullman "knows me well." He regarded Cullman, like Rockefeller, as both an industrialist—in this case "a cigar manufacturer"—and a public servant.

Although the Port Authority had six commissioners in 1935, Le Corbusier chose to believe that Cullman alone "built the George Washington Bridge."[75] And the bridge held a certain fascination for him as an icon of *techniques modernes* and the sign of a native spiritualism sympathetic to his urban vision. He confirmed this in his Columbia lecture (see plate 5) as well as in his homage to the bridge, "A Place of Radiant Grace."[76] According to Jacobs, Le Corbusier considered Cullman important because he was not only "very powerful and very wealthy," but also "a friend of Roosevelt."[77] Like other authorities and industrialists he met, Le Corbusier looked upon Cullman as a potential builder and client. Long after his return to France, he still hoped for a commission from Cullman. He even sent an accusatory letter to Jacobs reminding him that his uncle was "supposed to have me do a study of a large rental building." Needling Jacobs that he was a "good businessman" and might therefore be reserving the commission for himself, the Parisian whined, "you know that it would interest me to do something [like that] in the United States."[78]

Le Corbusier's experiences with NYCHA administrators Post and Cabot, as well as with Berle, Fowler, and Cullman, convinced him that government officials did not have "the time to keep themselves informed and reflect." Consequently they made the wrong decisions. The culture of capitalism infected the young society, and coping with its inevitable problems left little time for leaders to make thoughtful decisions. Le Corbusier's enchanted catastrophe was an omen of things to come, and his book describing it served to warn France whose public officials were also "unaware."[79]

Government authorities in America were cordial but cool to the visiting architect. Contrary to Le Corbusier's claims, if Post and others failed to engage him, it was not because they were "badly informed" or indifferent to his contributions, particularly in urban housing. Indeed, by 1935 most of the conceptual, programmatic, and design elements of the housing program for the Radiant City, as well as Le Corbusier's specific recommendations for urban housing in America, were already components of New York City housing and public policy, or known to reformers through a range of

American proposals. They had in common at least five such elements: demolition-based planning, disregard for the traditional configuration of streets, large-scale planning and block development, a comprehensively planned community, and a variety of housing typologies. In America the first four elements resulted from policies that developed independently of Le Corbusier. In the case of housing typologies, Le Corbusier's series of urban visions from the 1920s served as only one of several models from a European tradition that joined with pragmatic American developments. When united, these components promoted what in recent years has been roundly denigrated as urban renewal with Le Corbusier mistakenly cast as its sole villain.

Demolition-based planning, the first component, had long been accepted practice in American cities. Slum clearance for housing in New York was governed by legislation dating back to around 1800.[80] The model tenement house movement there during the nineteenth and early twentieth centuries was closely associated with condemnation of existing buildings and destruction of neighborhoods, increasingly mandated by law.[81] During the first half of the twentieth century unprecedented numbers of tenements were demolished.[82] By the early 1930s condemnation proceedings, routinely followed by destruction of housing deemed unfit for habitation, was fully accepted as the norm, and chronicled by such planners as Werner Hegemann.[83] In conjunction with the Tenement House Department, which authorized condemnation and demolition, the NYCHA followed an established pattern of large-scale slum clearance.

During the 1930s three positions governed public policy toward slums and urban shelter in America: rehabilitation, demolition-based renewal, and resettlement of inner-city populations to the periphery. The more enlightened approach of rehabilitating neighborhoods, preserving traditional street patterns, and integrating new housing following contextual guidelines has become accepted practice only in relatively recent years. Such NYCHA projects as First Houses and Harlem River Houses were successful efforts to achieve some of these objectives. But First Houses and projects like it were later repudiated by Post, who considered slum re-

habilitation, or "modernization of old existing structures," both socially indefensible and economically untenable.[85] He favored renewal rather than rehabilitation. He and other American housing specialists sought a more radical mode of intervention than preservation of existing blocks and streets that defined them. Here Post advocated disregard for the configuration of existing streets, a second element in common with the Radiant City. This attitude favoring elimination of the street grid for parklike settings reflected late nineteenth- and early twentieth-century garden city ideals of Ebenezer Howard and Patrick Geddes. Adopted by Mumford, Stein, Henry Wright, Catherine Bauer, and others, garden city planning influenced the policies of American housing authorities during the 1920s. When applied to metropolitan centers, garden city principles that favored parks over streets, as sociologist Jane Jacobs observed, actually influenced the Ville Contemporaine, Plan Voisin, and Radiant City.[86] To achieve renewal with "the introduction of open spaces, parks, and playgrounds," as well as lower coverage, Ackerman wrote in the program for the 1934 housing competition, the "existing street pattern must . . . be changed."[87] Williamsburg Houses in Brooklyn (see figure 6.1) followed this directive. If these first two positions were centralist, the third was decentralist: to many, slum clearance meant resettlement at the periphery. Although Roosevelt supported programs for improving slums through economic assistance, his model was not urban renewal but rural resettlement. However, Tugwell's plans for suburban and rural resettlement still relied on cities for employment opportunities.

Large-scale planning and block development, made possible by eliminating existing city streets, was a third element in common with the Radiant City. After World War I a new housing pattern employing large-scale blocks emerged in Europe, especially in Paris and Berlin, as it did in the United States. Encouraged by continental developments as well as garden city planning ideals, a new housing typology surfaced in New York City in which the long sides of an entire block were lined with tenement buildings, reserving the interior for gardens and playgrounds. A precedent for the later superblock, the perimeter block plan was used by such innovative practitioners as Andrew J. Thomas and others for both model tenement houses in Manhattan and middle-class garden apartments in Manhattan and other boroughs. Large-scale U-shaped blocks were employed for the Amalgamated Clothing Workers Union (1930) by Springsteen and Goldhammer that brought modernist elements of German expressionism and Viennese worker housing to New York's Lower East Side.[88]

New York City housing policy favored the comprehensively planned community, a fourth element shared with the Radiant City. Independent of Le Corbusier, the public housing movement in New York had long advocated the social and material elements that promoted neighborhood and community, particularly so in the NYCHA program. The garden city movement and New Deal policies of Roosevelt, Berle, and Tugwell's Resettlement Administration were as dedicated to communitarian principles and comprehensive planning as they were to decentralization.

American housing typology was a fifth element in common with the Radiant City. Indeed, Le Corbusier's housing typologies—the block à redents, slab block, high-rise slab, and skyscraper—had been employed by American housing specialists and architects promoting their own urban visions. American housing typologies reflected both the pragmatic elements of native practice and the impact of European developments. Moreover, even though they shared formal elements of design with Corbusian projects, those elements often had a common origin in American and European models.

In the United States the meander pattern of housing à redents had been successfully employed by Clarence Stein in his plan for Hillside Homes (1932–1933; figure 6.5) in the Bronx, the first project financed by a loan from the PWA.[89] In his article "Vers un renouveau architectural de l'Amérique," Sigfried Giedion noted that the configuration at Hillside recalled "the disposition of the meander pattern in Le Corbusier's quarters."[90] Lescaze and Frey also used blocks à redents for both their Chrystie-Forsyth project (see figure 6.2) and the low-rise structures of their River Gardens project (see figure 6.3). However, American housing specialists and Le Cor-

6.5
Clarence Stein, Hillside Homes, Bronx, New York, 1932–1935. (*Architecture* 71 [May 1935], p. 252.)

busier shared a mutual indebtedness to Eugène Hénard's à redans model and the work of German housing reformers including Paul Mebes.[91]

Development of the slab for housing was not used only by Le Corbusier, although he came to be most closely associated with it after construction of his Unité d'Habitation in Marseilles of 1947–1953. During the 1920s German architects developed projects for slab blocks that emerged from research in garden apartments or *Siedlungen*. Le Corbusier's housing blocks differed in fundamental ways from their German counterparts (whose engagement with the ground was among those features Le Corbusier opposed), but both emerged from the new modernist vision in Europe that emphasized functional elements of design, particularly exposure of blocks and apartment units to the sun. The German plan called *Zeilenbau*, formally presented at CIAM III in 1930 devoted to "Rational Division into Building Lots" (*Rationelle Bebauungsweisen*), figured prominently in the 1932 "Modern Architecture: International Exhibition" and in professional journals.[92] Early in the history of public housing in the United States architects of modernist persuasion introduced the slab block and *Zeilenbau*

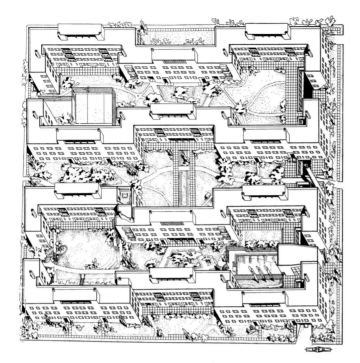

6.6
Oscar Stonorov and Alfred Kastner, axonometric drawing, Mackley Apartments (A Community Development for Hosiery Workers), Philadelphia, 1931–1933. (*Journal of the Society of Architectural Historians* 37 [December 1978], p. 241, fig. 5.)

project. Oscar Stonorov and Alfred Kastner were proponents of *Zeilenbau* planning in America. An early design for the Carl Mackley Apartments (A Community Development for Hosiery Workers) in Philadelphia (1931–1932) adapted Le Corbusier's studio apartments and duplex plan to *Zeilenbau* formation. The final design of 1933 indented the central sections and returned the ends to form courtyards (figure 6.6).[93]

During the 1920s the skyscraper designated for housing was a feature of American cities. In New York, real estate interests, combined with the city's zoning regulations, promoted the tower solution for residential as well as commercial use. The Ritz Tower on 57th Street (Emery Roth and Carrère and Hastings, 1925; see figure 10.2) was an early high-rise residence that Le Corbusier came to know well in 1935 because Alma Clayburgh and her daughter lived there. The Multiple Dwelling Law of 1929 encouraged high-rise housing. By the early 1930s apartment towers, which responded to the new law, dotted the periphery of Central Park. They included the San

Remo (Emery Roth, 1930) and Eldorado (Emery Roth with Margon and Holder, 1931), as well as the Majestic (1930–1931) and Century Apartments (1931), twin towers by Irwin S. Chanin (an acquaintance of Le Corbusier), and Jacques Delamarre and Sloan and Robertson. With its nineteen-story base and fourteen-story tower, the Century Apartments (figure 6.7) took advantage of the law's new massing potential.[94] These towers on Central Park West respected the traditional relationship between buildings and streets in Manhattan. Moreover, some apartment towers, even those in the city, were planned within a park setting. For the St. Mark's-in-the-Bouwerie Tower project of 1929–1930 Frank Lloyd Wright designed a cluster of high-rise apartment towers in a park, its construction predicated on demolition of existing buildings on the Lower East Side.[95]

Another Corbusian typology is more intriguing, if more problematic, because its use in America reflects an inherent contradiction in the identification of its program: the cruciform tower sited in an open green space. In 1935 Le Corbusier did not propose the high-rise tower (where height exceeds breadth) for American mass housing. But he did advocate a variant of it in the form of a Y-shaped high-rise slab or Cartesian skyscraper that could be adapted to either apartments or offices and provide a solution to "America's problem" (along with lozenge-shaped blocks housing 2,500 to 3,000 persons, also situated in a park; see chapter 5, figures 5.27, 5.28). However, before 1930 Le Corbusier proposed a cruciform tower dedicated either to housing or to business. As discussed earlier, in 1921 when he published his Villes-Tours (see figure 1.7) in *L'Esprit Nouveau,* he had

6.7
Irwin S. Chanin, Jacques Delamarre, and Sloan and Robertson, Century Apartments (1931), Central Park West, New York City. (Milstein Division of United States History, Local History and Genealogy, New York Public Library; Astor, Lenox, and Tilden Foundations.)

modeled it "after the theories of Auguste Perret," specifically his skyscraper apartment houses for Paris (see figure 1.8). Le Corbusier had long known of Perret's research and especially of his intention in 1915 to concentrate housing into twenty-story towers aligned to a boulevard, a metropolitan infrastructure, and also to a green space.[96] This probably introduced the modern notion of the "tower in a park." Like Perret, Le Corbusier designated the Villes-Tours in 1921 for housing. It was a large-scale project. Each of six towers would be sixty stories (250 meters) high with thirty-six apartments per floor, and a total of 2,160 apartments per tower.[97] But when Villes-Tours appeared in *Vers une architecture* two years later, it was still the same project with the same drawings except that its program had undergone a transformation. Le Corbusier now identified it as a "development . . . devoted exclusively to business offices" whose "proper place would therefore be in the center of great cities." As a result, he recognized that "family life would hardly be at home in them, with their prodigious mechanism of lifts."[98] Early on he used the typology interchangeably for residential and commercial use. But by 1923 he understood that the high-rise elevator tower was not the best solution for mass housing. In his projects for the Ville Contemporaine (see figures 1.6, 3.2, 6.13) and Plan Voisin (see figure 6.4), he dedicated cruciform towers to business. He also designated high-rise cruciform towers of the Radiant City for offices, illustrated in his drawing of a projected business center for Buenos Aires (1930; see figure 3.1). At one of his Columbia lectures he drew a cruciform plan for such a tower (see plate 2). In the three published projects, *à redents* extensions were reserved for housing.

Especially after publication of *Towards a New Architecture* (1927) and *The City of Tomorrow and Its Planning* (1929), modernists in the United States embraced the imagery of Le Corbusier's cross-shaped towers and visionary plans for them. If they appropriated these towers for housing, it was because the English text of *Towards a New Architecture* encouraged them to do so. In those editions, translator Frederick Etchells misled his readers and obscured Le Corbusier's intentions in 1923 to use the cruciform towers in Villes-Tours for business.

6.8
Edwin Rorke, The Manor, The Kenilworth, The Cambridge, Alden Park, Germantown, Pennsylvania, 1925–1928. (*Architectural Record* 67 [March 1930], p. 212.)

Instead of translating *Proposition de Lotissement* as a "subdivision" or "development proposal," Etchells reverted to the earlier description of Villes-Tours in *L'Esprit Nouveau* and identified it as "A Project for Apartments or Flats" (see figure 1.7).[99] This must have been especially confusing to readers of the English and American editions because Etchells then faithfully translated Le Corbusier's description of the project destined for office towers and unsuitable for housing. Similarly, Francisco Mujica, Latin American architect and skyscraper chronicler, misunderstood the programmatic function of the business towers in the Ville Contemporaine (see figures 1.6 and 3.2). Referring to the project's "residential skyscrapers" in his 1929 *History of the Skyscraper*, he envisioned them as "the cradle of to-morrow's strong race."[100]

There were, of course, American precedents for cruciform towers both in residential and nonresidential buildings, in city and country. As noted, Louis Sullivan's Fraternity Temple in Chicago (1891; see figure 1.9) is a cogent example that may have influenced Le Corbusier. Moreover, the cruciform plan had long served American housing specialists, as it had Le Corbusier, Perret, and

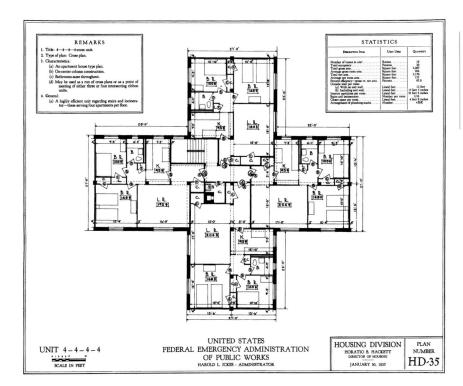

6.9

Cross plan, Housing Division model unit plan HD-35, Public Works Administration, 1935. (*Unit Plans,* Housing Division, United States Federal Emergency Administration of Public Works [Washington, DC: GPO, 1935].)

earlier European architects.[101] Among the repertory of plans that evolved in America since the previous century, the cross unit and cross plan were frequently designated for urban housing, especially during World War I.[102] Another American precedent for cross-shaped as well as both attached and free-standing Y-shaped housing blocks is Alden Park (1925–1928; fig. 6.8), a cooperative apartment complex (with three clusters: the Manor, the Kenilworth, and the Cambridge) in suburban Germantown, Pennsylvania, designed by Edwin Rorke (with Kenneth M. de Vos in charge of design). While the Manor (1925–1926) contained three cruciform housing blocks, each nine stories high, the Kenilworth (1926–1927) comprised two Y-shaped towers (joined together on the ground floor), each thirteen stories high with twenty-two or more rooms on most floors. Widely published, especially by housing specialist Henry Wright, Alden Park was well known to American urban reformers.[103] It too may have looked to European as well as American precedents.[104]

Because the Multiple Dwelling Law of 1929 did not distinguish between an apartment and a tenement, transposition from private development to public and low-income housing was axiomatic. Yet the shift was not without controversy. Whereas such housing specialists as Fred F. French argued for housing towers exceeding twelve stories in congested lower Manhattan, opponents countered that towers would only create "vertical sanitary slums."[105] The economic advantages of these high-rises were recognized by most housing professionals, especially those bent on renewal rather than rehabilitation.

By 1935 the cross plan had become a well-established model for the Housing Division of the PWA under the direction of Horatio B. Hackett and its technical consultant Frederick Ackerman (figure 6.9).[106] Henry Wright promoted a small-scale version of the cross type as the most efficient plan for vertical circulation and, therefore, one that "forms the best basis for free-standing skyscraper apartments."[107] But what separated most American public housing using the cross plan from the Corbusian model was the scale and density of the plan. For reasons of economy the American model typically had a small number of apartments (four or eight) per floor, frequently without an elevator, whereas the Corbusian plan arranged thirty-six apartments along two intersecting double-loaded corridors with an elevator and service core (see plate 2). In 1925 Auguste Perret proposed a similar large-scale use of the cruciform plan for his Maison-Tour, a skyscraper designated for both housing and offices (figure 6.10) that Le Corbusier endorsed.[108] In their scale, density, and typology, Le Corbusier's and Perret's projects have much in common with Alden Park and Sullivan's cruciform tower, as they have with European models including Hans Poelzig's skyscraper project for the Friedrichstrasse in Berlin (1921; see figure 5.30).

As mentioned, Lescaze and Frey were among the first to embrace the vision of Le Corbusier, Perret, and others when they appropriated the cruciform model for housing in their River Gardens project (see figure 6.3). Intended as a slum clearance project without reference either to the scale and street grid of the existing city or to the logic of Corbusian planning, they designed such towers, specified at heights of eight, seventeen, and even thirty-one stories, dispersed across the site. In 1929 Lawrence Kocher and Gerhard Ziegler employed the cross plan for an urban version of Sunlight Towers (figure 6.11), their thirty-two story apartment house project raised on supports above a multilevel circulation system and clearly inspired by Le Corbusier's skyscraper projects of the 1920s.[109] A large-scale cruciform tower also appeared in such mixed-use projects as Raymond Hood's City under a Single Roof of 1929, which combined offices and apartments with stores and other services (figure 6.12), and Wallace Harrison's "city of the future" of 1931 where a "modern school" dominated each crest (see figure 7.7).[110]

In 1933 the Housing Study Guild, a private group founded by Henry Wright, Lewis Mumford, and Albert Mayer, responded to the pragmatic needs of rehousing urban America with proposals for high-rise towers. The next year the Guild advocated the cruciform tower up to twelve stories over the slab block because of its economic advantages.[111] Its position, as Eric Mumford has shown, was influenced in part by the efforts of Gropius and Le Corbusier in promoting high-rise urban building, which were also presented at CIAM III in Brussels in 1930. Toward this objective the Guild even published English texts of Gropius's paper "Low Buildings, Medium-High or High Buildings?" and Le Corbusier's "The Sub-Division of Land in Cities," as well as those of other participants.[112] Le Corbusier's call for such elements of communitarian planning as "a complete reorganization of the way building lots are divided . . . and . . . laid out," as well as "communal services," would not have met with Guild approval. But his advocacy of "vertical public transportation" meant that a single shaft containing four elevators together with the corridors or "interior streets" (*rues intérieures*) could serve a fifteen-story apartment block with 100 apartments per floor.[113] Although this magnitude of density (together with its more radical components) was dismissed by most American reformers, the possibilities of high-rise housing resonated within and without the Guild.

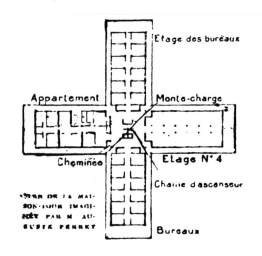

6.10

Auguste Perret, cruciform plan for Maison-Tour, 1925. (*Almanach d'architecture moderne*, p. 97.)

SUNLIGHT TOWERS
(An Apartment House)

A. LAWRENCE KOCHER AND
GERHARD ZIEGLER,
ARCHITECTS

Diagram of sawtooth units vertically repeated. The building is diagonally planned so as to give space back to the streets and to admit sunlight and air to all rooms. Each apartment is given a garden and all rooms have exposure and view in two directions. (See ARCHITECTURAL RECORD, March, 1929, p. 307–310.) There is a clear definition between traffic, stores, dining living space and recreation areas. The building is designed not as sculpture with a flat facade and accidental setbacks but as a direct utilization of rooms for city life. The separation of auto and foot traffic is imperative

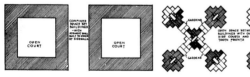

6.11
A. Lawrence Kocher and Gerhard Ziegler, Sunlight Towers, project, 1929. (*Architectural Record* 67 [March 1930], p. 286.)

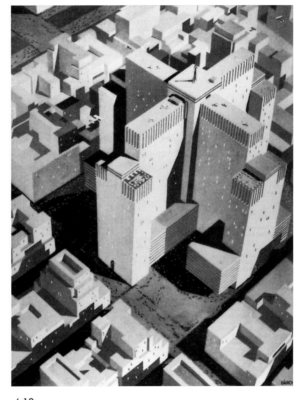

6.12
Raymond Hood, A City under a Single Roof, project, 1929. (*Nation's Business* 17, no. 12 [November 1929], p. 18; photograph courtesy of the Trustees of the Boston Public Library.)

If fragments of Le Corbusier's housing program for the Radiant City and his more customized proposals to meet American needs were already established practice in America, why did housing reformers oppose his suggestions on philosophical, economic, and moral grounds? What barriers prevented him from engaging a public authority and receiving a housing commission? Le Corbusier must have been chagrined, if not understandably jealous, of Lescaze's success in designing public housing modeled so conspicuously on his own ideas. Le Corbusier was eager for the commissions and recognition he felt were owed to him. But at least six impediments prohibited him from securing work in America.

The first was the widespread perception in the country that he was a partisan of the International Style. This was a result of the Museum of Modern Art's 1932 "Modern Architecture" exhibition that effectively factionalized architects concerned with aesthetic issues as opposed to others of technocratic persuasion as well as to social reformers. In the fall of 1935, just as the debate between traditionalists and modernists had run its course, new tensions emerged between promoters of the International Style and pragmatic housing reformers. By this time Hitchcock and Johnson's book *The International Style* was widely read. Moreover, the popular traveling exhibition of "Modern Architecture" had completed its tour. To advance the curators' world view, their book reduced all of the complexity and diversity of avant-garde developments in European architecture from 1922 to 1932 into a formula of three aesthetic principles: volume, irregularity, and lack of applied ornament. In identifying the new architecture with the simple tag International Style, they promoted "the style," and by definition also "style" in the formalist sense, at the expense of political intentions and social meaning.[114] European as well as American examples of progressive currents were evaluated a priori according to fixed categories. They included only examples of European and American work that would support their aesthetic principles. For example, the curators chose to feature Frank Lloyd Wright's Mesa house project (1932), with a model that emphasized the horizontality of its boldly cantilevered slab roof, over his Millard House (1921–1923)

whose concrete block construction projected a temple-like structure of mass rather than volume. In a similar nod to the Style and to its potential advancement in America, the curators emphasized J. J. P. Oud's house for Philip Johnson's family at Pinehurst, North Carolina (1931), by exhibiting a model of that project instead of one of his executed works.[115]

Although Johnson originally intended to include a section on industrial architecture with American examples, he did not seriously consider native technocratic and pragmatic developments, with the exception of work by the Bowman Brothers. The curators excluded on the basis of style Buckminster Fuller's industrially produced prefabricated housing, notably his celebrated Dymaxion House of 1927, and the work of the modernist Knud Lönberg-Holm.[116] The American strain of functionalism and pragmatism, as exemplified by Fuller's housing research and Ackerman's technical studies, were not considered International or part of the Style.

To further their positions Hitchcock and Johnson distanced the architecture of the seminal decade 1922–1932 from its political and social underpinnings. In their choice of works for the exhibition they sought to demonstrate the political detachment of most American modernists—both European influenced and technical pragmatists—from socialist and collectivist leanings of their many European counterparts. Moreover, they did not address capitalist assumptions of industrialized housing, those that considered Fuller's prefabricated housing or Le Corbusier's *maisons en série* (mass-produced houses) as agents of consumerism.

Hitchcock and Johnson isolated social housing in a separate section at the exhibition, unofficially curated by Mumford (with assistance from Bauer, Stein, and Henry Wright).[117] The marginal role given to mass housing only confirmed the bias that it could not be properly legitimized within the canon of high culture Hitchcock and Johnson projected for the International Style. The curators' decision to exhibit a model of Chrystie-Forsyth (see figure 6.2) at the entrance to work by Howe and Lescaze, rather than in the housing section, confirmed their admiration for the stylistic rather than social merits of the project.[118]

Hitchcock, Le Corbusier's most influential supporter in America, found a strategic role for the architect. Even though he included much of Le Corbusier's finest work in the exhibition (and Johnson commissioned a model of the Villa Savoye that confirmed his own elitist persuasion), Hitchcock cast him as "a theorist," "the most erudite," but not a practitioner. That honor went to Oud as city architect at Rotterdam.[119]

Thus the far-reaching effect on the profession of Hitchcock and Johnson's exhibition, catalogue, book, and traveling exhibition, along with criticism surrounding them, divided the community of modernists into three camps: proponents of European modernism represented by Hood, Neutra, Howe, Lescaze, Clauss and Daub, and others; proponents of a technocratic and pragmatic approach to architecture represented by Fuller and Lönberg-Holm, which included the group associated with the Philadelphia journal *Shelter;* and proponents of social reform, which included critics and housing specialists Veiller, Mumford, Bauer, Stein, Henry Wright, Post, and Ackerman.[120] Frank Lloyd Wright was a conspicuous exception to this triad, as his insistence on "organic" rather than modern architecture placed him in a self-imposed separate sphere.

By 1935 the issue of the International Style had jelled within the professional community. Most American housing reformers were not philosophically disposed to European modernism, especially its use of the slab block and *Zeilenbau* planning. As a group, they were averse to individuality and creative expression in public housing design. They avoided innovation and favored conformity. Instead, PWA's Housing Division and technical department put a premium on such "detailed standards of planning" as the model unit plans it published, which, according to one commentator in *American Architect,* effectively limited the "architect's job . . . [to] one of synthesis."[121] Le Corbusier's association with the International Style and its emphasis on aesthetics further isolated him from American social reformers and technical pragmatists.

The second barrier that Le Corbusier faced in securing work was his commitment to *techniques modernes.* Ironically, while Manhattan's middle-class and luxury apartment towers of the 1920s and 1930s relied on advanced systems of construction that were pioneered in the United States, American public housing did not always take advantage of such modern building practices as skeletal steel construction. Harlem River Houses, for example, employed load-bearing walls. In contrast to most American housing reformers who relied on innovations in planning rather than construction techniques to produce economic savings and social benefits, Le Corbusier subscribed to the myth that higher technology would result in lower construction costs. His concepts, for example, collided with those of Ackerman who firmly believed that technique alone could not solve the problem. Critical of *Zeilenbau,* Ackerman demonstrated through technical analyses of sites that low-cost housing could be calculated only on a long-term "cost of use" basis, which he determined would result from simple low-rise forms.[122]

Le Corbusier's status as a foreigner turned out to be third impediment. Not only was individual expression in public housing design discouraged, but there were also bureaucratic obstacles to and bias against hiring foreign, and specifically European, architects. This reflected both the realities of unemployment during the Depression and a broader current of nationalism, even xenophobia, that permeated housing policy. The program of the 1934 NYCHA competition, for example, specified that its objective was "to qualify Registered Architects residing, or having their principal office, in New York City."[123] The Authority's approved list of twenty-two architects drawn from the submissions did not include the names of foreign-born architects, even though German-born Alfred Clauss was an entrant.[124] For although the list was intended to confirm residency status for project architects, it was also a device to screen applicants. Lescaze, whose residence and office were both in New York City, was barred from the list only to be later engaged personally by Richmond Shreve for Williamsburg Houses. Lescaze was particularly sensitive to his uncertain status. In 1930 the Museum of Modern Art had not seriously considered him for a building commission because, notwithstanding the trustees' earlier bid to Howe and Lescaze for conceptual plans, one board member now objected to Lescaze as a foreigner.[125] Mayor La Guardia also kept a list. Selected by a jury of architects representing professional organizations, the names of fifty architects eligible to work on municipal projects favored insiders and included no foreign born.[126]

Le Corbusier's commitment to the centralized city and his efforts to redirect housing resources to it suggest a fourth obstacle. As mentioned, the NYCHA and other agencies were guided by decentralist policies of garden city planning under the leadership of Mumford, Stein, Henry Wright, and other American followers of British theorist Patrick Geddes. Thus even though Le Corbusier concurred with proponents of garden cities in advocating comprehensively planned communities, he was at odds with them over the issue of decentralization that placed most new projects in the outer boroughs and at the periphery of the city, or in suburbs.

A fifth impediment to Le Corbusier's contributions to and collaboration on housing in American cities involved the titanic scale of the slab blocks and high-rises he proposed. Large-scale development was fully consonant with housing policy during the 1930s, but the lozenge-shaped block (like the Y-shaped skyscraper), accommodating at least 2,500 people, which he described in his proposal to New York City's police commissioner and in his article on "America's problem," far exceeded local precedents. Because the United States had not yet engaged in a housing program on this scale, its policy makers and technocrats were reluctant to entertain such an experiment without technical analysis. Such analysis was not forthcoming.

Inevitably Le Corbusier's large-scale housing was associated with the more visionary aspects of his planning and deemed unacceptable to pragmatic housing reformers. That association formed a sixth barrier. On one hand, the Radiant City, like his urban visions of the 1920s, was linked to a tradition of utopian planning that thrived in America during the 1920s and early 1930s. Such projects and proposals by Raymond Hood, Richard Neutra, Kocher and Ziegler, Wallace Harrison, Hugh Ferriss, Harvey Wiley Corbett, Ernest Flagg, and others enjoyed wide circulation.[127] On the other hand, what separated the Radiant City (and Le Corbusier's projects

of the 1920s) from many of its American visionary counterparts was his radical treatment of urban infrastructure and his advocacy of cooperative ownership, thus mandating not only material changes in the structure of the city but also political changes in a free-market economy that historically promoted individual property rights. Henry Wright's succinct dismissal of the Ville Contemporaine suggests that he viewed these differences as obstacles. In 1930 he published an illustration entitled "The City of Tomorrow" with the caption: "It would require a revolution in our ideas of city building and land ownership" (figure 6.13).[128] As a pragmatic reformer, he would have been opposed in theory to Le Corbusier's visionary plans. American "ideas of city building," as Wright understood them, developed in response to principles of land values where high-rise office towers occupied the central city and residential buildings were preferably dispersed to the periphery. By contrast, Le Corbusier's proposals called for a closer proximity of commercial and residential buildings. Moreover, even though the American city had begun to integrate two infrastructures—skyscrapers and transport—it had not yet developed the macrosystem specified in either the Ville Contemporaine or Radiant City.

Ironically though, Le Corbusier's urban vision was predicated on the American model of the technically advanced skyscraper integrated with multilevel transportation systems: the railroad and the subway (Grand Central Terminal), as well as the city street (see section of Manhattan street, figure 5.5). Such skyscrapers as the Woolworth Building (see figure 5.4) and later the Rockefeller Center complex (see figure 5.15), which sought to integrate these infrastructures, served as models for him. Also ironic is the fact that many visionary projects produced in America were influenced by Le Corbusier's urban imagery before 1930. As observed, the cruciform towers of Hood's City under a Single Roof (see figure 6.12) recalled those in the Ville Contemporaine (see figures 1.6, 3.2, 6.13), Villes-Tours (see figure 1.7), and Plan Voisin (see figure 6.4). Hood conceived of his mixed-use project as an aggregate plan covering three city blocks, with buildings supported on columns to leave the space beneath them open for automobiles,

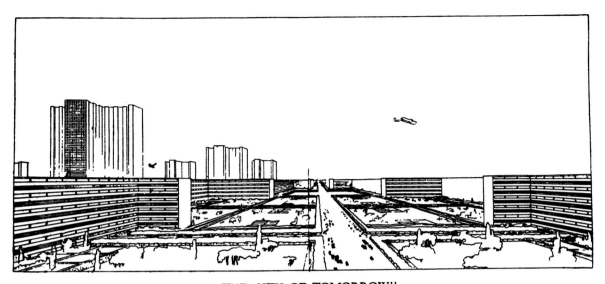

"THE CITY OF TOMORROW"

A SCHEME BY THE EUROPEAN ARCHITECT LE CORBUSIER

"It would require a revolution in our ideas of city building and land ownership"

6.13

Le Corbusier's Ville Contemporaine, 1922, as illustrated and captioned by Henry Wright. (*Architectural Record* 67 [March 1930], p. 237. Plan FLC 30827.) © 2001 Artists Rights Society (ARS), New York/ADAGP, Paris/FLC.

pedestrians, and parking. This attitude toward open space and urban infrastructure reflected his reading of *Urbanisme* in January 1928.[129] But Hood's emphasis on mass and dramatic shadows revealed his Beaux-Arts training, and perhaps also a debt to Perret's urban vision (see figure 1.8) that earlier influenced Le Corbusier.[130]

Moreover, some American architects and visionaries believed that if skyscrapers created inner-city congestion, multilevel planning combined with rapid transit would alleviate it. The Rush City Reformed project of the late 1920s by Neutra, the Viennese modernist who practiced in America, also had an affinity with Le Corbusier's urban visions (figure 6.14). With its severe highrise slabs in *Zeilenbau* formation and new circulation system separated by level changes, Rush City Reformed reflected modern European developments rather than a contemporary American tradition.[131] Similar to the multilevel planning of Hood's City, Kocher and Ziegler's Sunlight Towers project of 1929 accommodated the disparate functions of the apartment house to separate levels through the use of skeletal construction (see figure 6.11). But housing specialists and public officials did not consider the multilevel projects of Hood, Neutra, or Kocher and Ziegler, much less those of Ferriss and Corbett, to be practical solutions to urban congestion. When Henry Wright criticized Le Corbusier's Ville Contemporaine in his *Record* article, he also criticized Sunlight Towers for the same reasons. He may

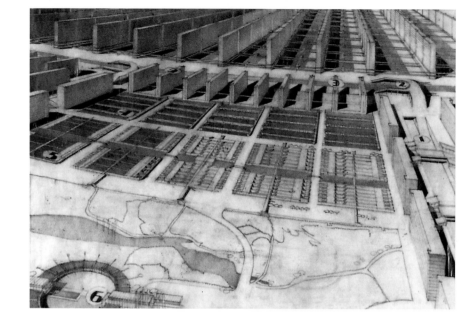

6.14
Richard Neutra, Rush City
Reformed, project, aerial view,
1928–1931. (Department of
Special Collections, Young
Research Library, UCLA.)

have appreciated both projects as "imaginative" and "rational," but unlike his pragmatic proposals for urban housing, they could not be "built up step by step from existing conditions and habits" precisely because they relied on a radical sea change in what Wright considered "our ideas of city building and land ownership" (see figure 6.13).[132]

Housing reformers did not take such urban visions seriously. Ackerman may have been willing to alter traditional configurations of existing streets, but not to introduce a large-scale infrastructure. To Wright and other reformers the visionary character of Le Corbusier's macrosystem of centralized skyscraper towers and housing blocks linked to an exposed and elevated highway network implied a transfer of authority from the private to the public sector. Such solutions seemed beyond the practical limits of urban renewal during the mid-1930s.

Thus aside from de facto injunctions barring innovative nonconformist solutions and foreign architects, housing reformers harbored deep philosophical differences with what they considered to be Le Corbusier's nearly totalitarian approach to urban design. Henry Wright's criticism reflects these reservations. Lawrence

Veiller called for "chloroform" when confronted in 1932 with Le Corbusier's proposed city of the future; moreover, he was a consistently vocal critic of modern architecture. When Lescaze and Frey's Chrystie-Forsyth project (see figure 6.2) was exhibited at the Museum of Modern Art, Veiller denounced it as "'battleship' design."[133] Others also regarded Le Corbusier as too radical, too visionary, too destructive. In his book *The Challenge of Housing* (1938), Langdon Post tried to insulate the Authority's program from such visions: "This is no picture of a fantastic Utopia. . . . it fits within . . . our present economic system. It does not require the wiping out of our cities . . . as do the pictures conjured up for us by Hugh Ferris [sic] or Le Corbusier. It is based on the theory that our cities must be salvaged, not destroyed."[134] Mumford was more contentious. Late in his career he recalled that "from the time I read the first edition of his *Vers une architecture*, I knew that we were . . . predestined enemies: he with his Cartesian clarity and his Cartesian elegance but also—alas!—with his Baroque insensitiveness to time, change, organic adaptation, functional fitness, ecological complexity; and, not least, with his sociological naivete, his economic ignorance, and his political indifference."[135]

During the course of his tour, Le Corbusier became increasingly aware of the divisions within the modern movement in America and the opposition of housing reformers both to the International Style and to his own proposals. He made no effort to reconcile these diverse camps, but increased his efforts to lobby all potential clients and patrons. He went directly to housing administrators, he engaged the public through articles in the popular press, and he enlisted the aid of prominent architects and editors. But housing administrators were united in their opposition to Le Corbusier and reformers were repelled by his association with the International Style and the formalist canons of Hitchcock and Johnson. His approach to design emphasized creative expression rather than synthesis. His housing relied on high technology, then considered uneconomical. He was also a foreigner. Le Corbusier's commitment to the inner city and his housing program for it were diametrically opposed to the thrust of federal and state efforts to create suburban garden cities and satellite towns. Notwithstanding the obvious reservations of Post and Mumford to the scale and visionary character of Le Corbusier's housing proposals, their views and those of other housing reformers reflected the broader consequences of the American Depression: isolationism, detachment in international affairs, reaction against the idealism of the First World War, and a burgeoning nationalism that favored the native-born. This phase of self-examination and self-discovery that deeply affected foreign affairs, therefore, also shaped art, architecture, culture, and society.[136]

Housing reformers and public officials rejected Le Corbusier's efforts in 1935 to engage a centralized authority and recast New York as a Radiant City. As noted, the formal elements of Corbusian design had already entered into the lexicon of options for American architects and housing specialists. But such housing typologies as the cruciform tower and other forms of high-rises had their origins in both American building practice and other European models. Moreover, Le Corbusier clearly preferred the low-rise *à redents* scheme for housing; he admitted the high-density slab, lozenge block, and Y-shaped Cartesian skyscraper only when the demand for housing necessitated it. Notwithstanding Le Corbusier's influence, American housing typology and the policies governing it before World War II developed independently of him, for most of the conceptual and design components of the Radiant City had long been accepted practice. After World War II the misguided path of urban renewal and promotion of housing towers persisted until they were challenged in the late 1950s and early 1960s by urban sociologists and planners who mistakenly blamed Le Corbusier alone for what were actually American planning policies and market forces.

7

The Private Sector

Besides public authorities, Le Corbusier hoped to collaborate with industrial producers and with Nelson Rockefeller and his architect Wallace Harrison. In the past, private industry rather than government leaders had been more favorably disposed to Le Corbusier's plans and projects. From the mid-1920s the architect had sounded an *appel aux industriels* (call to industrialists) to support his objectives for modern building techniques and equipment that could produce a new order. Such entrepreneurs as Gabriel Voisin, Henry Frugès, and Thomas Bat'a responded with support for actual construction.[1] Le Corbusier's *appel,* first announced within the Pavillon de l'Esprit Nouveau and in its catalogue *Almanach d'architecture moderne* (1926), constituted both a summons to potential clients and an appeal to industry to adapt modern techniques of mass production for building (figure 7.1). It embraced the range of Esprit Nouveau theory including Fordism and Taylorism.[2]

In the wake of the American stock market crash and its consequences in France, Le Corbusier lost confidence in his vision of an industrial utopia based on the American model, as Mary McLeod has argued. However, he continued to believe in the social values of American methods of production, adapted to building and to housing in particular, coupled with the promise of artistic expression. His participation in political groups and movements encouraged his activism and showed his commitment to social change. These included both Le Redressement Français, an organization that advocated a technocracy or government headed by technical experts and an economy based on enlightened practices of mass production.[3] As an editor of and contributor to *Plans* and *Prélude,* he assumed a more activist role.[4] He signaled his new combative position by a shift in rhetoric from advocating "architecture or revolution" in the 1920s to "architecture and revolution" in the 1930s.[5] He drew greater attention to his theory and design by publishing more strident articles, particularly in France and America.[6]

In the fall of 1935 Le Corbusier directed his efforts along two paths. First, he attempted to form a consortium of industrial producers for which he proposed to serve as technical and artistic coordinator, however implausible an expectation this may have been. This venture was consonant with both the teamwork approach to construction practices considered normative in America and the collaborative process advocated by CIAM.[7] Second, he launched an investigation into how the American building industry was structured and managed, as well as how it might be retooled to use the designs and

APPEL
AUX INDUSTRIELS

7.1
Le Corbusier, "Appel aux industriels," catalogue of the Pavillon
de l'Esprit Nouveau. (*Almanach
d'architecture moderne*, p. 102.)
© 2001 Artists Rights Society
(ARS), New York/ADAGP,
Paris/FLC.

techniques he proposed. He was especially interested in
what building methods were available as well as in
building products and their applications. If his European *appel* of the 1920s was characterized by idealism,
his American *appel* of the 1930s was characterized by
pragmatism. Le Corbusier directed his efforts not only
toward a search for commissions, therefore, but also toward research into industrially produced building components and structural systems that were far ahead of
their French counterparts. In doing so he operated on the
assumption that unlike the power brokers in "old Europe," those in "young America" would be receptive to
change and the new spirit of the times.[8]

The "Call" to American Industrialists

During his first days in New York Le Corbusier renewed
his acquaintance with Irwin S. Chanin, the builder and
engineer whom he had met in Paris in 1929, and sought
to interest him in his projects. With the intention of ac-
cepting the Architectural League's invitation and hoping to secure new work, Le Corbusier wrote to the
American builder about his own "enormous [and] truly

revolutionary interest in the subject of skyscrapers
([providing] daylight and ventilation to the interior)."[9]
During the 1920s and early 1930s Chanin was fully
committed to New York City, its mass culture and spirit
of modern life. In less than a decade he had built the
Chanin Building (1928), eight theaters (1925–1927), as
well as the twin thirty-story Majestic and Century apartment towers on Central Park West (1930–1931 and
1931; see figure 6.7), all of which expressed the exuberance of the modern city.[10] But by 1935 he had turned his
interests away from urban building and toward a Long
Island housing project called Green Acres (1936–1939).
With its ribbons of connecting highways, Green Acres
was touted as the "community for the motor age."[11] In
the fall of 1935 Le Corbusier's meetings with Chanin
about his Radiant City were unproductive. Although he
continued to consider Chanin a potential client, Le Corbusier did not count on their earlier association to ensure
him new work.[12] Besides, Chanin's enterprise was modest; the architect had greater expectations.

Le Corbusier's search for authority and a new urban
order compelled him to go directly to the leaders of
American industry. He hoped that some would commission work and others would involve their companies in
his more advanced research ideas. To achieve his objectives he called on the leaders of big business to redirect
American heavy industry to develop standardized equipment and adapt prefabricated methods of dry assembly
to the large-scale housing components of a Radiant City.
He also enlisted the help of Rockefeller and Harrison;
the former responded to the call with the possibility of
philanthropic investment, the latter with potential interest in collaboration.

Le Corbusier also enlisted corporate leaders in his
agenda for the Radiant City, including petrochemical,
steel, aircraft, and automobile executives. Like his encounters with the public sector, his methods of involving the private sector were rhetorical and proselytizing.
André Jaoul, a French steel and electrochemical executive who later became a client, constructed a primary
network of industrialists.[13] As head of his company's foreign relations department, Jaoul traveled frequently to
America and met Le Corbusier serendipitously aboard

the *Normandie* en route to New York. Soon after their arrival Jaoul convened a lunch at the Plaza Hotel where he introduced Le Corbusier to James A. Rafferty, president of Carbon and Carbide Chemical Corporation (CCCC), a subsidiary company of Union Carbide, and George W. Davison, a director of Union Carbide who was also president of the Hanover Bank.[14] In *Cathedrals* Le Corbusier describes this curious event, the American business lunch awash in cocktails. It gave him an opportunity to explain his Radiant City, much as he had to public officials Berle and Fowler. He recalled the occasion at the "handsome" and "substantial" Plaza: "Introduction, cocktails while the hor d'oeuvres are being served. In a few precise words he [Jaoul] explains the purpose of our meeting. Immediately I submit my proposals. The back of the menu serves for graphic illustrations whose eloquence avoids the ambushes of language. Questions, replies. It is finished in a quarter of an hour . . . a story . . . a good joke. . . . Business matters are put aside. . . . A gay lunch facilitates business transactions."[15]

As a result of Jaoul's introduction Le Corbusier pursued these businessmen, calling on them at their New York office on 42nd Street. He even intended to visit the Union Carbide plant near Chicago. On December 6 he met again with James Rafferty, and possibly also with Morse G. Dial, vice president and treasurer of Union Carbide, who told him about the company's synthetic materials with diverse building applications. Among the newest was a resin product called Vinylite.[16] Transparent or opaque, this thermoplastic could be dyed any color. Le Corbusier was interested in Vinylite because of its versatility. It could be extruded or molded into sectional wall panels so that an entire apartment—partitions, ceiling, floor tiles, wall finishes, and building materials—might be produced in a factory using dry-assembly processes. In 1933 a three-room apartment called the Vinylite House was exhibited in the Hall of Science at the Century of Progress Exposition in Chicago.[17] A color photograph of the living room was featured in *Architectural Record* (figure 7.2).[18] The Vinylite House tapped the color preferences and experimental use of materials associated with the mid-1930s: glossy aqua paneling, green and yellow checkerboard floor tiles.

7.2
Living room, Vinylite House exhibit, Hall of Science, Century of Progress Exposition, Chicago, 1933. (*Architectural Record* 75 [January 1934], frontispiece, opp. p. 3.)

Union Carbide was not the only petrochemical producer that Le Corbusier approached. He also renewed an earlier association with Howard Huston, assistant to the president of American Cyanamid who directed its public relations and advertising.[19] During the late 1920s Huston served as Secretariat and Chief of Internal Services for the League of Nations. Le Corbusier believed that Huston had "defended" his project during the debacle that enveloped the competition.[20] The two men did maintain a sympathetic and cordial relationship, but there is no evidence to support Le Corbusier's claims that Huston had defended his project and also had "called him" to the United States.[21] It is clear, however, that their meetings during the fall of 1935 were substantive. In Huston's office at 30 Rockefeller Plaza they spoke about the broad applications of Cyanamid by-products, especially gypsum-based materials, for floors, partitions, supplies, and cabinets.[22]

An early proponent of standardization and prefabrication, Le Corbusier was the object of considerable interest among some of the more progressive American researchers in building technology. For example, they sought his approval on the results of a *House and Garden* symposium on American methods of prefabrication. Le Corbusier enthusiastically pronounced them, "very significant of the incomparable American strength."[23] Among the participants, Robert L. Davison, director of the Housing Research Division of the John B. Pierce Foundation, was especially eager to meet Le Corbusier. *House and Garden* editor Henry Humphrey responded with a luncheon.[24] In effect, the Connecticut-based philanthropic organization was the research arm of the American Radiator and Standard Sanitary Corporation.[25] One of the leading centers of housing studies, the Pierce Foundation specialized in technical research in new building materials and methods of construction, as well as HVAC systems and sanitation. Davison himself pioneered the concept in America of housing "completely fabricated in a plant on the same basis as the automobile," and predicted that such efficient and economical manufacturing methods could produce a *machine à habiter*, thus promoting Le Corbusier's objective as a goal of American industry.[26] In 1932 the Pierce Foundation exhibited one of its experimental houses, complete with General Electric fixtures, on the roof of the Starrett-Lehigh Building in New York.[27] The foundation also sponsored research on the development of a metal frame used in conjunction with panels of calcium hydrosilicate called Microporite that were especially strong in compressive strength.[28] But it was designed for single-family units rather than mass housing.

Other technical researchers for heavy industry were interested in Le Corbusier's proposals, among them Dr. Rufus E. Zimmerman, a vice president of United States Steel Corporation. Jaoul arranged for Zimmerman to meet Le Corbusier who, in turn, initiated subsequent meetings.[29] As director of research for U.S. Steel, Zimmerman pioneered new applications for its products, some supplied by its subsidiaries including American Bridge, Carnegie-Illinois Steel, and Universal Atlas Cement.[30] In 1935 U.S. Steel was investigating the use of steel and other products in the "construction of residences."[31] Anticipating the market for steel and cement in the "evolution of prefabricated sections for housing," the company intensified its research during the mid-1930s.[32] But it was not until the next decade, with the acquisition of Gunnison Homes, Inc., that it committed its resources to the production of single-family housing units of "standardized, interchangeable parts."[33] Apprised of the research and development being conducted, Le Corbusier proposed designing *maisons en série* or mass production houses for the corporation.[34]

Le Corbusier also met with aircraft and automobile manufacturers. During the early days of his American tour he called on Samuel S. Bradley, general manager of the Manufacturers Aircraft Association, in his office at 30 Rockefeller Plaza. The architect had learned from a Swiss friend that Bradley was interested in building a house in the area around Vevey. Aside from the prospect of that commission, Le Corbusier hoped to interest Bradley in adapting aircraft-manufacturing techniques to the production of housing, for Bradley's responsibilities included shaping aviation policy and stimulating aircraft production. In the end neither prospect sustained Bradley's interest.[35]

Le Corbusier was more successful in engaging automobile manufacturers. On several occasions he met with managers at General Motors. Diversifying its operations in the 1930s, GM already had a considerable stake in the domestic market with housing, home products, and real estate.[36] In New York Le Corbusier conferred with John O. Downey, director of the Economic Research Department at GM. A physician by education, Downey had worked as a chemist and metallurgist before joining General Motors as an economist.[37] Architects and journal editors were especially interested in his research on the cost benefits associated with the standardization and integration of housing components. But Le Corbusier was wary of Downey and sought to interest him in his ideas only because the economist was a recognized authority on prefabrication.[38]

These overtures to American industrialists continued Le Corbusier's long-standing interest in the technology of industrial housing that began around 1910

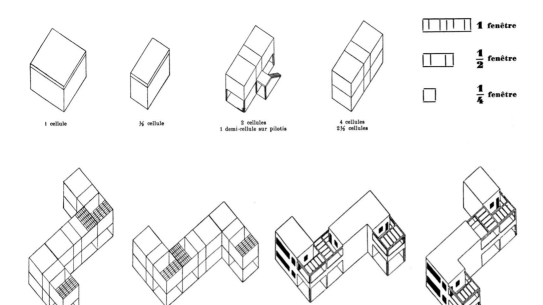

1 cellule   ½ cellule   2 cellules
1 demi-cellule sur pilotis   4 cellules
2½ cellules

1 fenêtre

½ fenêtre

¼ fenêtre

when he first came under the influence of Gropius, the Deutscher Werkbund, and German technocracy.[39] During the teens and twenties Le Corbusier's projects, especially his *maisons en série,* employed principles of standardization, Taylorism, and mass production.[40] The Quartiers Modernes Frugès at Pessac near Bordeaux of 1924–1926 provided his only opportunity to realize a large-scale project for standardized housing (figure 7.3).[41] The Pessac units, together with his Pavillon de l'Esprit Nouveau and both single-family and double villas for the Weissenhof Siedlung exhibition in Stuttgart (1927), served as ideas for industrially produced housing.[42] In 1929, as the housing crisis in Europe grew increasingly severe, he proposed a sophisticated version of the Dom-ino House in response to a French law sponsored by Minister of Labor Louis Loucheur. The Loi Loucheur, as it was called, was intended at once to assist public housing in France and to stimulate the steel industry. Le Corbusier's houses called for a factory-produced metal skeleton.[43] His designs for mass-produced houses were reasonably well known in America from 1927 with the publication of *Towards a New Architecture,* followed in 1937 by the first volume of

7.3
Le Corbusier, "La Maison standardisée." (*Oeuvre complète 1910–1929,* p. 69.) © 2001 Artists Rights Society (ARS), New York/ADAGP, Paris/FLC.

the French edition of *Oeuvre complète 1910–1929*.[44] The Loucheur Houses were featured in Norman Rice's article in *Architectural Record* in 1930 (figure 7.4) and his houses for the Weissenhof Siedlung in his own article "Architecture, the Expression of the Materials and Methods of Our Times" in 1929.[45]

Le Corbusier's applications of standardization and mass production became increasingly known in America during the late 1920s and early 1930s when housing was the subject of intense research and experimentation. The Hoover administration encouraged industry to adopt such methods to increase consumption and create jobs. Now that Le Corbusier was finally in the land of mechanization and commanded the attention of American industrialists, now that he could see that American factories were already dedicated to mass-produced houses, he could envision on an unprecedented scale his earlier prediction of "conceiving," "constructing," and "living in mass-production houses" that were "built on the same principles as the Ford car."[46] Far from abandoning his earlier concerns, he now dedicated much of his remaining time in the United States toward engaging authorities in his program. He envisioned houses being made in "steel workshops" employing "metal, wood, or synthetic materials, as cars are made in series at the factory."[47]

Because he knew that he alone could not rally the support of American industrialists, he enlisted the help of Henry Sipos, a little-known European-born, French-speaking draftsman who identified himself as a "craftsman in architecture." Le Corbusier first encountered Sipos after his inaugural lecture at the Museum of Modern Art. Sipos was neither a registered architect nor a member of any of the leading professional and social organizations for architects in New York City. He claimed that he was trained in economics.[48] He was one of several hundred unemployed architects and engineers engaged by Columbia University's Housing Orientation Study group (later Housing Research Bureau).[49] Led by Carol Aronovici, a professor in the School of Architecture from 1933 to 1940 and a housing expert, the Housing Orientation Study was devoted to technical research in the building industries. Under Aronovici's direction, the group initiated research and published reports on housing in a number of countries, but focused on New York City.[50] It provided the NYCHA and other government agencies with survey work and data on the "necessity of slum clearance and improvement of the housing conditions" as well as on the "most suitable locations for housing."[51] Aronovici and the Housing Research Bureau made a significant impact on public housing in the fall

7.4
Le Corbusier, drawing of the Loucheur House. (*Architectural Record* 68 [August 1930], p. 133. Plan FLC 18252.) © 2001 Artists Rights Society (ARS), New York/ADAGP, Paris/FLC.

THE MINIMAL HOUSE: A SOLUTION
By LE CORBUSIER and P. JEANNERET, ARCHITECTS

of 1934 as organizers of the exhibition "America Can't Have Housing" at the Museum of Modern Art.[52]

Beyond his interest in housing Sipos promoted a larger urban agenda predicated in vague terms on a "cooperative society" living and working in the city. His politics were decidedly leftist and did not always square with Le Corbusier's fluctuating positions. Even though both men called for economic and technocratic reorganization of the city as well as land reform, Le Corbusier did not advocate a complete ban on private ownership of land as Sipos did. Moreover, Le Corbusier's call for authority flowed from his engagement with Redressement Français, but was more diffuse and yet more sustained a position, underscoring his differences with Sipos's more socialist objectives. Yet Sipos deemed his own economic plans and Le Corbusier's urbanism to be a common vision because both relied on technocratic reform. On a personal basis they were bound by language and a mentor-protégé relationship. Sipos addressed Le Corbusier as "cher Maître" and heralded him as "a Man of destiny," all the while insisting that he was no flatterer. Claiming that he had been raised in the Parisian workers' quarter of Faubourg Saint-Antoine, Sipos could assure Le Corbusier that his intentions to assist him were genuine. Sipos looked to Le Corbusier as an authority. Dismissing New Deal efforts, he identified the need to "inaugurate a national building program." Recalling Duhamel's *Scènes de la vie future,* he warned that this "menaced civilization" would not survive. In concluding an appeal to Le Corbusier for his intervention, Sipos argued that America was "pregnant with immense actions," only in need of a "good obstetrician."[53]

Addressing American industrialists, Le Corbusier proposed the formation of a consortium of producers for which he would serve as technical coordinator. Together with Sipos, they convened a press conference on November 19 and issued a statement entitled "The Necessity and Possibility of Inaugurating Immediately a Rehousing Program on [a] National Scale in the United States" (appendix C). The statement was both a formal address to public authorities and an *appel aux industriels.* It was intended as a call to action "to stimulate the creation of new plans for homes and districts." The press statement

outlined three components of his program: first, heavy industry should undertake the mass production of housing through industrial methods; second, this large-scale program would reconstruct both urban and rural areas; and third, achieving these ends required an unprecedented collaboration among public agencies, technical organizations, and industrial producers and manufacturers.[54] Le Corbusier envisioned that the program would engage the entire U.S. work force. But conceived in isolation from the political climate of the New Deal, the lofty objectives were either regarded as idealistic rhetoric or totally ignored. The statement was not carried in the daily press, perhaps because Le Corbusier's views had already received much attention. To Hitchcock and proponents of the International Style, he was upheld as a "new pioneer," but to leftist technical professionals in America he was later dismissed as a "lost pioneer."[55]

The morning of November 20, Sipos staged a meeting for Le Corbusier with a number of industry executives and engineers: Downey from General Motors, three structural engineers with U.S. Steel, and a representative from American Radiator.[56] Later that afternoon the architect boarded the night train for Detroit to resume his lecture tour and reach the long-anticipated land of Ford. But Henry Ford (1863–1947) was not the industrialist he had arranged to meet in Detroit. Instead, on November 22, the morning after his Cranbrook lecture, Le Corbusier met with Daniel C. McGuire, one of Downey's colleagues. McGuire headed both GM's Modern Housing Corporation and the Argonaut Realty Company, which directed GM's real estate operations in the United States. They discussed at length Le Corbusier's plans for housing on a large scale, which the architect called "le grand housing." Once again, like the industrialists in New York, McGuire may have been earnest and serious in his interest but he was also noncommittal.[57]

Before Le Corbusier returned to New York, Sipos set to work publicizing his ideas. He sought to interest the Architectural League of New York in featuring Le Corbusier's architecture and urbanism in their fiftieth-anniversary exhibition the next February.[58] But in spite of his efforts, Sipos lacked the influence and charisma of his mentor. In the end it was up to Le Corbusier.

Initiatives with Nelson Rockefeller and Wallace Harrison

Aside from industrial producers who could supply *techniques modernes,* Rockefeller and Harrison offered Le Corbusier both access to authority and possible subvention. While in New York Le Corbusier was frequently in touch with Harrison and met with Rockefeller on a number of occasions. Although both men responded positively to the *appel aux industriels,* Rockefeller's reaction was tempered by duty, perhaps because of his affiliation with the Modern, and Harrison's enthusiasm was influenced by his sense of being in the presence of the master. But whatever their motivations, their meetings fueled Le Corbusier's mounting expectations for work in America.

Rockefeller's interests in real estate and social investment as well as politics and government made him a potentially ideal authority, patron, and client. Harrison, because of his close personal and professional association with Rockefeller, promised to be Le Corbusier's most likely American collaborator, although in the end he would be his archrival. From his first days in the United States to his last, Rockefeller remained Le Corbusier's single most likely authority, and Harrison was his key liaison for "housing by heavy industry."[59] At the outset these two men held much promise for the visiting architect.

During the fall of 1935 Rockefeller was deeply involved in the real estate operations of Rockefeller Center and devoting considerable energy to the Museum of Modern Art. He had far-reaching aspirations. At Dartmouth College he had emphasized the practical and majored in economics. But because he struggled with dyslexia, his actions and behavior were generally more intuitive. He was not an intellectual but became a tenacious learner.[60] He also pursued an interest in art, shaped by his mother, Abby Aldrich Rockefeller, who seems to have been his most important influence. At Dartmouth he developed an interest in architecture but received no encouragement from her to pursue it as a profession.[61] In 1932 when he became a trustee of both the newly founded Museum of Modern Art and the Metropolitan Museum of Art, he offered his father an explanation: "My justification for spending the time which I do in this work is that I feel that the aesthetic side of a person's life is almost as important as his spiritual development or his physical well being."[62]

Nelson Rockefeller's engagement with Rockefeller Center launched his professional career and stimulated his interest in real estate, design, and development. In 1929 while still at Dartmouth, his father, John D. Rockefeller, Jr., placed him on the board of the Rockefeller Center.[63] Two years later the young Rockefeller went into his father's office at 26 Broadway where he worked on family business, especially real estate. In 1931 he formed a partnership in a general brokerage firm called Turck and Co., which brought tenants into Rockefeller Center, as did Special Work, Inc., the firm he later established.[64] During the 1930s Nelson Rockefeller continued to assert his influence in the management of the Center.[65] Able and amiable, but also ambitious and calculating, he gained a reputation for shrewd dealings.[66] In October 1933 he joined his father and brother John D. 3rd in room 5600, their new office in the RCA building at 30 Rockefeller Plaza. More and more the extrovert, Nelson Rockefeller concerned himself not only with the Center's real estate operations but also with its development, both artistic and promotional.[67] In the early 1930s he became embroiled in a well-publicized dispute between his family and Mexican artist Diego Rivera over a fresco mural for the lobby of the RCA building.[68]

When Rockefeller encountered Le Corbusier in 1935 he was involved in a wide range of projects at the Center including real estate, labor-management relations, and public relations as well as commercial interests and local politics. He had already held several minor government posts.[69] With a vested interest in the Center, he attempted to assume more and more control over its operations. In 1934 he initiated and subsequently failed in an attempt, together with his brother John, to take control of the Center away from its managing agents Todd, Robertson, and Todd (figure 7.5).[70] That year Nelson Rockefeller came into a large portion of his inheritance. Although the assets in his trust were substantial, valued at as much as $12 million, access to both principal and income was restricted until 1938 when he

7.5
Nelson Rockefeller (left) and
Rockefeller Center managers
John R. Todd (middle) and
Colonel Arthur Woods (right),
c. 1933–1934. (Rockefeller
Center Archive Center.)

reached the age of 30.[71] Historians disagree over the amount of his income in 1935. One estimate places it over $150,000, but a more conservative one puts it well below $50,000.[72] By the spring of 1934 it was substantial enough for him to buy and maintain a grand apartment at 810 Fifth Avenue.[73] In spite of the impediments he encountered in his effort to take control of Rockefeller Center management during the mid-1930s, he eventually prevailed. In 1938 he became president of the Center, although his responsibilities were shared with Hugh Robertson as executive manager.[74]

When Rockefeller attended Philip Goodwin's luncheon for Le Corbusier he did so in his capacity as a trustee of the Museum of Modern Art and its newly appointed treasurer.[75] With these activities he followed the lead of his parents, the Modern's principal benefactors.[76] Even Le Corbusier recognized Abby Aldrich Rockefeller's role in founding and "guiding the destiny" of the Modern.[77] The Rockefellers were also responsible for providing first quarters and then a site for the new museum. In 1932 the Modern leased a Rockefeller house at 11 West 53rd Street, and in the spring of 1936 Nelson Rockefeller's parents made possible the acquisition and purchase of land on West 53rd Street for the construction of a new building.[78] Given the family's role in

founding, guiding, and providing venues for the Modern, it may not be an exaggeration to suggest, as Le Corbusier did, that during the 1930s the Rockefellers *were* the museum.[79]

From the beginning, Rockefeller's close friendship with Wallace Harrison frustrated Le Corbusier's efforts to secure Rockefeller as a client and supporter. In fact, at the time of the luncheon Harrison was part of an intimate group of Rockefeller's advisors at the Center. Harrison's wife, Ellen, was a member of the Rockefeller family circle. In 1925, a year before her own marriage, Ellen's older brother David Milton married Nelson's sister Abby.[80] But Harrison's friendship with Rockefeller developed only after 1931 when, as a partner in the firm of Corbett, Harrison and MacMurray, he joined the Rockefeller Center design team as its junior member. Together with L. Andrew Reinhard and Henry Hofmeister, as well as Raymond Hood (until 1934), Frederick Godley (until 1931), and J. André Fouilhoux, they formed the Associated Architects (figure 7.6). It was not an easy alliance but their client, John D. Rockefeller, Jr., made it work.[81]

Harrison's background and education could not have been more different from Rockefeller's. Harrison was thirteen years older than Rockefeller, who regarded

7.6

Wallace Harrison (behind) and
members of the Rockefeller Center
design team Raymond Hood and
L. Andrew Reinhard, c. 1931.
(Rockefeller Center Archive
Center.)

him as a mentor. Harrison had little formal education and was in most respects self-made.[82] During his apprenticeship in architecture, he held several drafting jobs in Worcester, Massachusetts, before moving to New York City in 1916 where he worked in the office of McKim, Mead and White and joined the atelier of Harvey Wiley Corbett.[83] In 1921 he received formal training at the Ecole des Beaux-Arts in Paris. There he read Le Corbusier's manifestos in *L'Esprit Nouveau,* despite the objections of his atelier *patron* Gustave Umbdenstock. He became further acquainted with Le Corbusier through his friendship with American-born architect Paul Nelson.[84] Later he returned to the Umbdenstock atelier on a Rotch Traveling Scholarship. Back in New York he worked in a number of offices (Bertram Goodhue, Corbett, Hood, and the Board of Education) while teaching architectural design and rendering at Columbia.

Harrison confirmed his commitment to modernism when he joined Corbett and Frank Helmle in 1927 as a junior partner. By then he knew that he wanted to be a "modern architect" and to "utilize the best principles of design and the advances of our modern technology."[85] Like Corbett, he made the transition from traditionalist to modernist during the early 1930s.[86] As co-author (with C. E. Dobbin) of *School Buildings of Today and Tomorrow,* he confirmed his sympathies with the modern movement. In his chapter "The Design of the Modern School," Harrison specifically invoked Corbusier's aphorism *machine à habiter* when he contended that school design must be "industrial in character as it is a machine for education." His mixed-use project for a "city of the future with a school on top of each building" (with office space on the lower floors and apartments above) employed cruciform towers (figure 7.7), recalling Le Corbusier's Ville Contemporaine (see figures 1.6, 3.2, and 6.13), Villes-Tours (see figure 1.7), and Plan Voisin (see figure 6.4) that Harrison knew through Le Corbusier's publications.[87] Because Harrison's towers were isolated and laid out in rows on a traditional street grid that did not call for multilevel planning, they suggested the influential perspective view of 1922 associated with Auguste Perret (see figure 1.8), which also influenced Le Corbusier.[88] Rotated from the grid, the glazed skyscrapers of Harrison's project also recalled Lawrence Kocher and Gerhard Ziegler's Sunlight Towers project of 1929 (see figure 6.11).[89] But perhaps Harrison's "city of the future" was shaped most directly by the work of Raymond Hood, his partner for Rockefeller Center. Harrison's cruciform towers resembled Hood's project of 1929 for a City under a Single Roof (see figure 6.12), except that they emphasized volume over mass. Harrison's perspective also evoked earlier visionary schemes by Hood. Moreover, the setback blocks and horizontal bands of glazing suggested an even closer association with Hood's newly completed McGraw-Hill Building (1931) on West 42nd Street in New York, which was included in the 1932 "Modern Architecture: International Exhibition."[90]

Harrison's alliance with Hood and their joint sympathy with Corbusian theory and design also extended to mass-produced houses. In January 1933 the two men,

7.7
Wallace Harrison, project for a
"city of the future with a school
on top of each building," 1931.
(Wallace Harrison and C. E.
Dobbin, *School Buildings of
Today and Tomorrow*, p. 2.)

with Joseph Urban, exhibited their plan for a "country home development" at the New School for Social Research. Six-room houses would be factory-produced and built principally of steel, their flat roofs and terraces now part of the idiom of American modernism that reflected the principles of Le Corbusier's five points.[91] Later that fall Harrison, then in partnership with Corbett and Mac-Murray, taught a course in architecture at the New School for Social Research in which he presented design problems that were intended to be "entirely modern in their scope."[92]

As the junior member in the Rockefeller Center design team and overshadowed within his own firm by the brilliant Hood and also by Corbett, Harrison had paid his dues. With at least seven of the Center's buildings completed, he left Corbett and MacMurray in the spring of 1934 to launch his own practice.[93] Then in the fall of 1935 he teamed up with architect and engineer André Fouilhoux, who was left on his own after Hood's death in 1934, to form what became a compatible partnership. When Le Corbusier visited Harrison he was still in his office on the fifty-second floor of the RCA Building.[94]

During the construction of Rockefeller Center Harrison and Rockefeller developed a strong mentor-protégé relationship, but in reverse. The ebullient Rock-

efeller described Harrison about this time as "an extremely delightful person."[95] They thought alike on most things, shared similar interests, and kept close company.[96] According to Harrison, "We spoke the same language."[97] When Max Abramovitz joined the Harrison office in 1934, he recalled that some of the older Rockefeller Center architects resented "the boss's son." But to Abramovitz, "Wally didn't act that way and I think that was the beginning of this great friendship that turned out to have Nelson essentially be his patron."[98] Rockefeller often sought Harrison's advice on matters of art and architecture. For example, at his request Harrison invited Fernand Léger, whom he had known in Paris, to design a mural for the lobby of the RCA Building.[99] It has been suggested that Nelson Rockefeller satisfied his passion for architecture through his association with Harrison and the various projects he commissioned. Harrison even characterized Rockefeller as a "frustrated architect."[100] As Rockefeller sought control over the operations of the Center, he surrounded himself with his own inner circle of advisors, Harrison among them. Harrison became more and more identified as the family architect, the obvious implications of which Le Corbusier never fully appreciated or understood.

During the fall of 1935 Rockefeller and Harrison had already joined forces on two projects just north of Rockefeller Center that fed Le Corbusier's ambitions to collaborate with them. The development of Rockefeller Center in the area between Fifth and Sixth avenues from 48th to 51st Street was not merely an exercise in civic art, but a real estate venture. Historians have suggested that the Rockefellers sought expedient means to preserve their property values. As Nelson Rockefeller assumed more authority in the mid-1930s he attempted to provide the Center with good neighbors to the north and thereby stabilize its market value.[101]

The first project involved two eleven-story apartment buildings (17 to 23 West 54th Street and 24 to 38 West 55th Street) in which Nelson Rockefeller performed his father's role as client (figure 7.8).[102] Its midtown location was intended to provide housing for "business executives and wealthy commuters."[103] Designed by Harrison and Fouilhoux, the Rockefeller Apartments appealed to critics who considered them French. Through the use of planar walls punctuated with convex bays (for dining), undoubtedly inspired by the Parisian apartments of Michel Roux-Spitz, the apartments achieved elegance, urbanity, and sophistication. They gave Harrison the critical attention that Nelson Rockefeller felt was important to his family. Even Lewis Mumford, who had been especially disparaging of Rockefeller Center, called them "the most brilliant and most successful example of modern architecture in the city." Forwarding Mumford's article to his father, Nelson Rockefeller noted that praise from this "very severe critic" was unusual and should strengthen his mother's "confidence in Wally's ability."[104]

The second project was a master plan for the northern extension to the Center that Harrison and Rockefeller formally developed in 1935–1936. In an attempt to fulfill his father's original intentions to provide a site for the Metropolitan Opera at the Center, Rockefeller envisioned the extension as the location for a new opera house.[105] As agents for John D. Rockefeller, Jr., acquired more land, Nelson Rockefeller became the driving force behind the effort to extend the Center north of 51st Street along its private street.[106]

7.8

Harrison and Fouilhoux, Rockefeller Apartments, West 54th and West 55th streets, New York, 1935–1936. (Museum of the City of New York, Wurts Collection.)

But in January 1935, independent of the Rockefeller initiative, Mayor La Guardia announced his own plans for a public art center that would contain a large opera house, a municipal symphony orchestra, and a high school for the study of music. He had already appointed a Municipal Art Committee charged with that mission. La Guardia was committed to the idea of providing opera and concerts at popular prices because he considered them key elements of civic culture.[107] Soon private and public interests faced a standoff.[108] In the fall of 1935, just before Le Corbusier's arrival, La Guardia's committee unveiled elaborate plans by Benjamin Wistar Morris and Robert O'Connor for a Municipal Art Center located at Columbus Circle, which the mayor favored.[109] But earlier that summer and again later that fall these plans collided with Nelson Rockefeller's plans for the northern extension of Rockefeller Center, because both hoped to provide space for the new Museum of Modern Art. The Municipal Art Committee suggested to the Rockefeller people and the Modern that the new museum might be incorporated in the proposed Municipal Art Center.[110] In December the mayor publicly announced that intention.[111]

Le Corbusier had not been in New York very long before he learned of the mayor's plans. He used his encounters with Rockefeller, Harrison, and other influential New Yorkers to advance his interests in both the Rockefeller scheme and the Municipal Art Center.[112] Le Corbusier scheduled office meetings and used social occasions to engage Rockefeller and Harrison in his projects. Harrison encouraged the association for the ideas it might bring to him. He also genuinely wanted to assist Le Corbusier. On the evening of October 31 Nelson Rockefeller hosted a dinner party at his Fifth Avenue apartment, which Harrison had redesigned in 1934–1935.[113] Together the three proposed to meet with urban planners in late November once the visitor completed his lecture tour. Le Corbusier considered the dinner a working session, but it is unclear the extent to which Rockefeller gave any serious thought to engaging him. For one thing, Rockefeller may have given the impression of having authority and the backing of Rockefeller Center, but in fact, as his dealings with his father and the Rockefeller managers the previous year showed, at that time he had very little direct power in the organization. And even though he held minor posts in local government, he did not yet have real political power in the public sector.

Yet undoubtedly persuaded by Nelson Rockefeller's semblance of power, Le Corbusier was filled with high expectations. At the dinner party he learned from Rockefeller and Harrison that La Guardia had committed $150 million the previous February toward "urban initiatives," specifically housing.[114] During the course of their discussions, private and public interests were commingled. There was talk of future Rockefeller initiatives, often overlapping with those of La Guardia, which Nelson Rockefeller envisioned at the Center and its proposed northern extension. According to Le Corbusier's notes, Rockefeller suggested the creation of model schools, including a research center for urban studies with an emphasis on housing. The visitor was led to believe that Rockefeller also planned to create "an office of urban research and realize one model apartment block."[115] Another project involved La Guardia's plan for a music school and children's orchestra in the Municipal Art Center. Le Corbusier hoped that the organizers would engage his brother Albert Jeanneret, a musician, composer, and instructor committed to musical education who intended to found his own music school for children.[116]

Le Corbusier had reason to believe that Nelson Rockefeller, whose father had already been petitioned, would support his case in Geneva over his entry in the League of Nations competition.[117] If the intervention were successful, Le Corbusier intended to donate his model of the League of Nations to the Museum of Modern Art. During the course of his visit Le Corbusier pressed Rockefeller to direct the museum to publish a translation of *La Ville radieuse*. He even tried to interest Rockefeller in sponsoring a so-called tonic steamship that would be modeled after the *Normandie,* whose scale, he emphasized, was American rather than French. He intended the proposed ship to adopt the *Normandie*'s emphasis on health but not its "enervating luxury."[118] Throughout his stay in New York, he explored all these possibilities with Rockefeller and Harrison, but did not approach La Guardia directly.

Of the projects they discussed, Le Corbusier was most interested in and committed to housing, which would realize at least a fragment of his Radiant City. He envisioned a Rockefeller-sponsored model apartment block based on the *type Sert.* The design of this *gratte-ciel moderne* would be a new Cartesian skyscraper, Y-shaped, and oriented toward the sun (facing south), the type that he had also proposed to aid New York's enchanted catastrophe. With the addition of communal services, the project would be based "on radiant city ideas but a model sufficiently *authentic* to *earn* money in agreement with Post." Thus Le Corbusier expected to follow his earlier method of developing an experimental design and testing it in the private sector, as he did with the Maisons Loucheur. Rockefeller's philanthropy and authority, he hoped, would support the construction of a model block. Based on Radiant City principles, the prototype would be both practical and economical enough to receive the endorsement of NYCHA chairman Langdon Post.[119]

When Le Corbusier returned from the Midwest on Thanksgiving day he had no more lecture commitments. At last he could direct his efforts to secure architectural commissions and interest public authorities in the Radiant City, with its housing program produced by the consortium of industrialists he had been actively assembling. But on December 2 the Museum of Modern Art abruptly curtailed his visit when it notified him that his expenses would not be assumed beyond November 30 and advised him to return home.[120] His plans now hinged on the support of Rockefeller and Harrison. On December 6 he addressed two "notes" on Gotham Hotel stationery to Harrison summarizing their conversation the previous day.

To Harrison Le Corbusier directed both his large-scale housing program in the New York area and his plan for a consortium of industrialists to realize it. His "Note p. [our] Wallace Harrison" contained his program for "Housing by leading industry." It specified the constituents of the consortium and their respective contributions: skeleton: [U.S.] Steel Corporation; partitions and cabinets: CCCC; and mechanical equipment: General Electric. It reviewed the substance of his talks with Rafferty and Davison of Union Carbide about CCCC's Vinylite. The note also suggested that Otis elevator might contribute studies on vertical transportation for "une unité d'habitation" and assist with lobbying efforts for housing on a large scale.[121] It outlined his meetings with Downey and with McGuire of General Motors on the subject of "le grand housing." It identified other potential collaborators and clients including Huston of American Cyanamid and Dr. Frank Safford, Jr., a friend

of art dealer John Becker who was engaged in recreational buildings for the middle class.[122]

The second set of notes, labeled "Concernant Mr Nelson Rockefeller pour Wallace Harrison," served as the agenda for his meeting with Rockefeller on December 12. Clearly Le Corbusier intended Harrison to be a liaison with Rockefeller not only for his program of "grand housing" but also for projects that did not involve the American architect. These proposals flowed from his first talks with the men on October 31. By December, with no other commissions in sight, Le Corbusier pressed an increasingly unrealistic agenda on Rockefeller.[123] He continued to expect Rockefeller's support for an American edition of *La Ville radieuse* that could be "useful," he claimed, "to authorities and to students and professionals." He proposed that the book be published under the aegis of the Museum of Modern Art because it had sponsored his tour of lectures primarily on the Radiant City. Mistakenly he assumed that this sponsorship would signify the Modern's endorsement of his ideas. But during the months that followed, Philip Goodwin, whom Harrison and Rockefeller consulted, declined to give the museum's approval, because he hoped to avoid further tensions in what by then had become a tangled misunderstanding with the visiting architect.[124]

Le Corbusier's other proposals to Rockefeller were more ambitious. He offered to collaborate on a pavilion for the 1939 New York World's Fair, the organization of which was still in its early stages.[125] He envisioned his exhibition pavilion as an "eloquent demonstration" of the new planning theses he later outlined in "What Is America's Problem?" and an essay, "The Theme of a World's Fair." He probably intended the pavilion as a provisional version of the research center for urban studies, which he had earlier discussed with Rockefeller. In proposing to build a demonstration model of a Radiant City housing block (*type VR*), Le Corbusier shared George Fred Keck's intentions. At the Chicago Century of Progress Exposition in 1933 Keck exhibited his House of Tomorrow (and the Crystal House a year later) that was inspired by machine metaphors in *Vers une architecture*. In both exhibit houses Keck employed such industrially produced building materials and consumer products as U.S. Gypsum flooring, Holland Furnace air conditioning, and General Electric appliances.[126] For the 1939 initiatives Le Corbusier proposed to serve as technical and artistic coordinator in collaboration with American industrialists. He may also have intended to intervene in a process that Neutra observed in *Wie baut Amerika?* (*How America Builds*), namely, that architecture was being driven by manufactured building materials with the architect relegated more and more to the periphery.[127] Le Corbusier would not be left out of the process. Rather than allowing industrial designers and manufacturers to dictate standards, he demanded a central role for the architect, asserting both aesthetic judgment and technical acumen.

His proposal to Rockefeller called for a pavilion demonstrating through various exhibits his ideas on urbanism in general and the Radiant City in particular. In an effort to engage Rockefeller and other potential supporters Le Corbusier later attempted unsuccessfully to publish "The Theme of a World's Fair" in the American popular press. His proposal specified larger objectives for the propaganda pavilion: "to give the leadership [*l'Autorité*] lines of necessary guidance in order to reform the laws and undertake the essential work" of reconstructing cities. This demonstration, Le Corbusier maintained, would instill in "timid" American leaders the "will" he felt they lacked.[128] But between May and October 1936 organizers of the fair moved swiftly. A seven-member design board was formed. It established the fair's theme of "Building the World of Tomorrow" and, reversing an earlier decision, held an architectural competition restricted to registered architects with practices in the New York metropolitan area.[129] In October 1936 Le Corbusier engaged photographer Thérèse Bonney, his agent in America, and enlisted the help of Alma Clayburgh to represent his interests and secure his participation in the fair.[130] His expectations remained high. The June 1938 issue of *Direction,* the leftist journal of arts and letters that Marguerite Harris had begun to publish, announced that Le Corbusier would design the French Pavilion and return to the United States in 1939.[131] Now more than ever his participation would depend on

Wallace Harrison, who designed several of the fair's key buildings.

Even John Downey of General Motors suggested that Nelson Rockefeller ought to take the lead in a series of studies and a call to industry.[132] Le Corbusier urged Rockefeller to support not only his work in America but also the international cause of modern architecture and urbanism. He hoped that Rockefeller could arrange subvention from the Rockefeller Foundation for CIAM in the amount of $6,000 to $7,000 every year for five years. The sum was large, but CIAM was worthy, Le Corbusier reasoned, because it was "currently the only organization studying the serious problems of housing and urban planning." Le Corbusier urged the foundation to fund the proposed CIAM VI congress to be held in New York to coincide with the 1939 fair.[133]

In a final complex proposal to Rockefeller, Le Corbusier requested support to enable American artists to participate in the 1937 Exposition Internationale "Arts et Techniques." He indicated that he had been commissioned to design for the exposition a Museum of Contemporary Art, what he called a *musée sans façades* (museum without walls). This would become project "C" of 1936 or a project for a *Centre d'esthéthique contemporaine* (center of contemporary aesthetics) that eventually was rejected.[134] Le Corbusier intended the museum to exhibit works demonstrating a synthesis of the arts or "alliance of urbanism, architecture, statuary [and] painting." He proposed Nelson Rockefeller's association with the Paris exposition through an unusual scheme in which Le Corbusier himself would choose the American participants, suggesting that he would impose *French* judgment. It was his way of ensuring that the selection would be both rigorous and international. Then Rockefeller would enter into a contract with artists of Le Corbusier's choice to provide support for materials and the fabrication of works exhibited there, in addition to honoraria for them over a three-year period. At the same time Rockefeller would "undertake the progressive construction of a museum *type: sans façades,*" like the one in Paris, but built in New York. After the Paris exposition, the works would be shipped to New York and reside in the new Rockefeller-sponsored art museum. "This museum," Le Corbusier envisioned, "would be an entirely new type: *collection d'esprit nouveau*."[135] He conceived it *"en type M.A.C."* or Musée à Croissance Illimitée (Museum of Unlimited Growth) whose typology as discussed earlier, he introduced to American audiences in his lecture at Columbia University on October 28, which Rockefeller did not attend (see figure 3.12; plate 6).[136] Originating in his project for a pyramidal World Museum for the Mundaneum in Geneva of 1928–1929, the squared spiral form resurfaced in a number of projects including a Museum of Contemporary Art in Paris (1931).[137] Le Corbusier's proposal was timely because Rockefeller was then in the midst of convincing the trustees of the Museum of Modern Art to authorize a new building, and he knew it.[138]

In response to the note, and perhaps at Harrison's urging, Rockefeller met the persistent visitor in his office on December 12, two days before Le Corbusier returned to France. Rockefeller's reaction to Le Corbusier's proposals was mixed. Initially he endorsed the request for an American edition of *La Ville radieuse,* forwarding his copy to Philip Goodwin at the Modern. But Goodwin flatly refused to sponsor the publication. As Harrison told Le Corbusier, "relations between you and the Museum are not as yet on a very satisfactory basis."[139] Rockefeller referred Le Corbusier's request for support for CIAM to the Rockefeller Foundation, which would later decline it for unknown reasons.[140]

Rockefeller must have been intrigued by Le Corbusier's idea for a museum without walls, but he was already committed to plans for a more conventional building for the Modern. At a meeting of the museum's Board of Trustees on December 19, 1935, he urged the trustees to "consider independent plans for a new building."[141] Public disclosure of the plans after the meeting was timed in response not to Le Corbusier but to La Guardia's announcement a few days before about his grand scheme for a Municipal Art Center with "space for the Museum of Modern Art, the Museum of the Public Library, a music library, and exhibition halls," as well as a large auditorium for opera and symphony concerts. The new complex would be financed by city revenues, but neither a definitive site nor an architect had been

chosen.[142] Rockefeller's intention was to extricate the Modern from the mayor's project. At the same time he hoped that advocates for the Municipal Art Center would commit to the site north of Rockefeller Center and give the commission to Harrison, who had worked on the northern extension since the spring of 1935.[143]

After that meeting, A. Conger Goodyear and the Board of Trustees moved decisively. Goodyear expressed to La Guardia the museum's reservations about the potential conflict between its need for "independent control" and the mayor's concern for the public interest.[144] Then in January 1936, at Nelson Rockefeller's suggestion, the Modern purchased three lots on the south side of 53rd Street as the site for its new building.[145] Notwithstanding the mayor's assurances to the museum and even a plea to Abby Aldrich Rockefeller to consider other options, Nelson Rockefeller and the museum pulled out, leaving the mayor and his Municipal Art Committee to face an uncertain future.[146] Rockefeller still envisioned the Municipal Art Center as part of an extension to Rockefeller Center on the blocks north of 51st Street between Fifth and Sixth avenues. Now he could suggest a new site for the Museum of Modern Art that would crown the complex at the head of the proposed mall on the north side of 53rd Street. Toward that objective he arranged for the Modern to exchange its parcel on the south side for three lots owned by his father, as well as for the acquisition of contiguous lots on the north side to form a parcel with 150 feet of frontage for a new building.[147] In March 1936 museum trustees appointed Philip Goodwin as architect. Goodyear subsequently appointed Nelson Rockefeller, Alfred Barr, and himself to the Building Committee.[148]

Back in Paris, Le Corbusier continued to advance his interests with Rockefeller through Harrison. At the same time Rockefeller continued to promote the extension site, attempting to join the private interests of both Rockefeller Center and the Museum of Modern Art with the public interests of La Guardia's Municipal Art Center. In July 1936 Rockefeller sent Harrison to Europe on a "mission" to secure the support of Solomon R. Guggenheim, who had promised to donate $6 million for the museum buildings in the Municipal Art Center.[149] That fall Rockefeller sought to engage Guggenheim directly by arranging for him to meet with Harrison, now designated as architect, together with principals of the Municipal Art Committee, Guggenheim's lawyer Lewis Levy, and his curator and advisor Baroness Hilla Rebay.[150] Le Corbusier himself later attempted to interest Guggenheim and Rebay in his Museum of Unlimited Growth.

In the fall of 1936 Harrison prepared two master plans for the Municipal Art Center, the first a more ab-breviated version that accompanied plans by Goodwin for a new building for the Modern, and a comprehensive report to its Board of Trustees on November 12, 1936 (figure 7.9).[151] Harrison's second plan was more comprehensive. A perspective rendering indicates that, as in the first version, the Museum of Modern Art would terminate the northern axis of a private street and proposed plaza extending from 51st to 53rd Street (figure 7.10). In that second, more ambitious scheme, separate buildings for various cultural organizations occupied four

7.9
Wallace Harrison and Nelson Rockefeller, master plan for Municipal Art Center and northern extension of Rockefeller Center to West 53rd Street, 1936. (*The Museum of Modern Art* [New York, 1984], p. 34, chart 8; photograph courtesy of the Rockefeller Archive Center.)

7.10
Wallace Harrison, perspective view, northern extension of Rockefeller Center with Museum of Modern Art, opera, a museum building (intended for the Guggenheim collection), Columbia Broadcasting Company studios, and undesignated commercial building, 1936. (Wallace K. Harrison Papers, Avery Architectural and Fine Arts Library, Columbia University in the City of New York.)

blocks on either side of the plaza: the opera and a museum building (intended for the Guggenheim collection) were sited on the two western blocks, and a building for the Columbia Broadcasting Company studios and an undesignated commercial building were on the two eastern blocks. The Beaux-Arts arrangement of the new museum and buildings on either side of the plaza suggested the axial arrangement formed by the RCA Building and the International Buildings at Rockefeller Center. Until 1940 the mayor entertained a series of increasingly ambitious projects for the Municipal Art Center on the northern extension to Rockefeller Center, but the city could afford none of them.[152] Moreover, with La Guardia's announcement in late December 1935 of an approved list of fifty architects for municipal projects, similar to the NYCHA's list, Le Corbusier had little chance of receiving a commission. But because Harrison's name was on the list for municipal work, he might have been in a position to form a collaborative relationship with Le Corbusier similar to the one between Richmond Shreve and William Lescaze.[153] All this, however, was academic. The legacy of the mayor's art center resurfaced in the Rockefeller-sponsored Lincoln Center for the Performing Arts (1958–1966) by Harrison and Abramovitz, whose early schemes employed a wedge-shaped auditorium for the opera house that recalled Le Corbusier's formal imagery. In a separate development, La Guardia's project evolved into the New York City Center of Music and Drama.[154]

Le Corbusier's Initiatives Meet with Indifference

Given Le Corbusier's wide-ranging efforts to urge industrial producers to implement his ideas on modern building techniques and to secure clients among American power brokers, why did his initiatives meet a consensus of indifference? First, his expectations were unrealistic. In a technical age, an authority had special obligations. In the early 1930s Le Corbusier called for "revolutionary" acts to change the system; the times were revolutionary because technology itself was revolutionary, constantly overturning past uses and transforming society.[155] He concluded that it would take a "courageous" and farsighted authority to harness the "spirit of the times" and undertake "great works."[156] Second, his methods were philosophically opposed to those generally practiced in America. If Radiant City principles determined that "the plan must rule," that "the plan is dictator," then the planner would seek unilateral power.[157] This posed a dilemma for American authorities who pursued more democratic processes. Le Corbusier said that he searched for an authority already invested with the "means" and powers to regulate and implement.[158] But with himself as planner and the Radiant City as the plan, albeit in the form of guidelines rather than a rigid structure with fixed policies, such a program struck American industrialists and public officials as both autocratic and idealistic. Pragmatic Americans, who were cautious about their investments, did not "pay" for ideas, as Goodwin informed him, and that was principally what Le Corbusier offered them in 1935.

Consequently, most American authorities in the private sector, as in the public sector, were unresponsive to Le Corbusier's "call." To industrialists and government authorities, the architect's personality was bewildering. His European background and his need to communicate through an interpreter signaled mistrust. And even though progressive technical researchers and corporate executives recognized him as a pioneering advocate of industrially produced housing they, like their counterparts in the public sector, hesitated to commit their resources to his visionary proposals.

Le Corbusier advocated two types of housing on a large scale. The first type employed techniques of prefabrication and dry assembly that resulted in a kit-of-parts approach to building on site. He envisioned these methods applied to high-rise, high-density housing prototypes.[159] To achieve this he proposed a consortium of manufacturers whose products, methods, and research he considered sufficiently advanced and consonant with his ideas. The second type was the *maison en série,* or mass production house that was already in line with American production methods. But by 1935 scores of housing prefabricators, either individual researchers often with their own independent companies or subsidiary companies of large corporations, were already engaged in experimental mass production houses. Systems employing precast concrete, metal frames, and panels, often using experimental building materials such as Vinylite, replaced traditional frame houses.[160] The most successful experiments during the early 1930s replicated the unit production of automobiles, so that entire houses would be ready for transportation to a site. At first these houses, built like Fords, had the potential to rejuvenate the beleaguered automobile industry. So promising was such industrially produced housing that by the early 1930s it seemed to have the potential to displace the automobile in leading the U.S. economy out of the Depression. Although research and development continued into the post–World War II period, most of these enterprises failed because factory retooling was costly and industrially produced housing could not endure extreme market fluctuations. Industrial methods of housing production were not accompanied by new methods of distribution and appropriate market analysis. Whereas houses lent themselves to long-term investment, automobiles with their limited lifetimes implied short-term investment. Buyers accustomed to traditional design and conventional methods of construction, not to mention conservative financing institutions, were cautious about commitments to factory-made shelter. During the mid-1930s as the automobile industry began to be revitalized, it was primarily at the expense of the construction industry; automobile production cut costs in half while building costs doubled. The high cost of transporting such heavy preassembled units as metal frame houses, for example, made them uneconomical. Finally, while industry might produce housing units, it could not produce neighborhoods and did not assume any social responsibility.[161]

Although Le Corbusier had designed and built several metal frame houses and housing prototypes, his experience was limited. In 1935 his choice of prefabricated dry-assembly methods, which involved a consortium of manufacturers rather than a single producer, complicated production procedures. Like most of his American counterparts, he gave little thought to market analysis, methods of distribution, questions involving real estate and land reform, and industry's social responsibility.

Furthermore, his reliance on Henry Sipos, a fringe member of a group of housing reformers, proved ineffective. Sipos's leftist sociopolitical persuasions, and perhaps also his foreign background, had more in common with Le Corbusier than with American authorities, public and private. Given Le Corbusier's short visit and his failure to form a consortium of industrial producers, his proposals met with indifference.

In his search for authority among American power brokers, Le Corbusier focused his efforts on securing the support of Rockefeller and the collaboration of Harrison. The name Rockefeller was widely known in France as signifying wealth and power, and the Rockefeller Foundation had financed many buildings, including post–World War I reconstruction projects in France, with which Le Corbusier had been associated.[162] Before 1935 Le Corbusier included John D. Rockefeller, Jr., in a list of names to solicit support for his causes. Appearing face to face with Nelson Rockefeller in his office, Le Corbusier appealed directly to this promising authority whose personality suggested his capacity for leadership. Le Corbusier viewed him in the somewhat inflated position of heir to the dynasty, notwithstanding his youth, inexperience, and position as only one of five sons of John D. Rockefeller, Jr. Nelson Rockefeller and his father, Le Corbusier later wrote in *Cathédrales,* "administer the mountain of gold, but work toward making it a source of as many social benefits as possible. . . . They dedicate a large part of their heart to it. They still have heart." Remaining ambivalent about his lofty new friend, with an "iron fist of a peasant" and yet also the object of his esteem, Le Corbusier claimed special insight: "I observed Nelson Rockefeller up close and often, enough to catch a glimpse of the psychology of this man whose destiny is as burdensome as it is privileged."[163] Indeed, he viewed Nelson Rockefeller at once as a modern version of Louis XIV (or of his finance minister Colbert) and as a potential source of patrimony needed to realize his own grand planning ideas. Although Louis XIV may have been a "despot," he "conceived immense projects and realized them" such that "his noble works still fill us with admiration."[164] Le Corbusier defined his ideal authority thus: "A well-informed man, strong in his convictions, passionate, breaks through obstacles." His model was centralized and French, not American. Recalling the French symbol of authority, Le Corbusier concluded that such a "genius" would be the "Colbert of today."[165] As he had earlier pinned his hopes on such leaders as Francesc Macià, president of the Catalan Republican government and empowered to implement his new plan for Barcelona, so his new Colbert would be Nelson Rockefeller.[166]

If Le Corbusier was ambivalent about "this man of destiny," Nelson Rockefeller was equally ambivalent about the quixotic visitor but still intrigued by his ideas and eager to respond to him. Rockefeller, however, was too young and inexperienced; although he was influential, real power was just beyond his grasp. Even when he had the opportunity to involve Le Corbusier in such projects as the Museum of Modern Art, he demurred, already predisposed toward Wallace Harrison whose design abilities he overestimated. Le Corbusier may have invested Harrison with authority, but his power came from his association with Rockefeller. Harrison did provide Le Corbusier with promising introductions to industrialists and government leaders, however, even if he was reluctant to collaborate directly. For Harrison was an architect who, according to Max Abramovitz, "ran an office almost like an atelier" where design ideas and decisions came from many sources within the office.[167] After all, he had been the junior member of the Rockefeller Center design team that provided him with a working model. More important, Harrison had no pride of authorship, whereas Le Corbusier was fanatical about authorship.[168] Their respective attitudes resonated later in designing the United Nations Headquarters: Harrison insisting on teamwork and collaboration; Le Corbusier insisting on individual recognition. Although Rockefeller and Harrison gave marginal support to Le Corbusier's ideas and projects, they were far more committed to their own mutually affirming compact. They valued Le Corbusier's vision largely for what it could bring to their own collaboration, later confirmed by Le Corbusier's engagement with the United Nations.

Aboard the S.S. *Lafayette* on his return to France Le Corbusier came to the bitter conclusion: "There is not an imaginable regime which goes ahead with its plan."[169]

At that moment he was not speaking exclusively about his disappointments in the United States, but about a consistent pattern of rejection of his urban vision and the industrial components for it. At least his experiences in France (Ville Contemporaine, Plan Voisin), the Soviet Union (plan for Moscow), and Algeria (plans for Algiers) prepared him for the likely conclusion. His considerable efforts in 1935 to engage the leaders of American government and industry outside conventional political channels represent a lost episode in a succession of disappointment and rejection. That pattern was not broken until 1950–1951 when authorities in the Punjab called British architects Jane Drew and Maxwell Fry who, in turn, recommended that Le Corbusier prepare a master plan and design the Capitol complex for Chandigarh.

In the end Le Corbusier's efforts to enlist American industrialists and authorities confirmed that his idealism of the 1920s had given way to his pragmatism of the 1930s. He may have rejected capitalism as a complete system, flawed by its social structure, unbridled individualism, and consumption-based economics, but he was still invested in its production-based assumptions. The American tour functioned as a journey of research and discovery. His strategy immersed him in a complex network of industrialists. He tested the American market through direct encounters with big business and heavy industry. He deployed his resources and used his experiences in America in an attempt to achieve practical results. Following many previous efforts, this renewed interest in factory-made shelter marked a significant, if unproductive, episode in 1935 at the fountainhead of industry in the land of Ford. After his return to France he incorporated in his projects design elements based on American industrial models and products. Le Corbusier's investigations of 1935, therefore, suggest previously unexplored sources that helped to shape the architecture of his late career.

Part III
The Transatlantic Misunderstanding

8

Le Corbusier's Reaction to the
"Country of Timid People"

Le Corbusier's visit did not generate commissions, but it did enrich his appraisal of American culture and society. Because social change was a prerequisite for Radiant City planning, Le Corbusier needed to advance his critique of the American system. His polemical view of New York City as an enchanted catastrophe, therefore, served his objective to persuade authorities to adopt his proposals. When he cast New York as his empirical model, he instinctively matched real-life experiences to his preconceptions and Manhattan's problems to solutions in the Radiant City. But those preconceptions, viewed through the lens of *américanisme,* dominated his experiences, and what remained for him was principally his *idea* of the reality he encountered. Le Corbusier's idealistic methods and views, common to modernists of his generation, inevitably resulted in a transatlantic misunderstanding between him and Americans.

Three important considerations influenced the relationship between Le Corbusier's enunciations on America and the timing of his visit. First, his attitude toward the United States changed as his enthusiasms shifted from emphasis on mechanization and modernity in the 1920s to society, culture, and politics in the 1930s. During the teens and twenties Le Corbusier had promoted the automobile as a symbol of mechanization and stan-

dardization. But by the 1930s he denounced the automobile as an agent of decentralization and suburbanization because it promoted the destruction of family life and spiritual values. When he toured the River Rouge Ford plant, he did not experience it as a symbol of machine age modernity alone. He considered the urban consequences and human costs of automobile production. The visit assured him that such factories could be retooled to produce mass housing and that a new collaboration between industry and government could redress the urgent need for affordable shelter.[1] This was the central theme of both his Pavillon des Temps Nouveaux for the 1937 Exposition "Arts et Techniques" and his book *Des canons, des munitions? Merci! Des logis . . . s.v.p. Pavillon des Temps Nouveaux* (Cannons, arms? No thanks! Housing please).[2] In America he found empirical evidence to justify deconstruction of his first machine age in favor of a more human-centered approach to urban architecture and planning. He considered the United States to be precariously suspended between two ages: a first machine age that had become moribund through overmechanization, and a second machine age, or second phase of modernity more harmoniously attuned to human needs, based on his idealized projections for the Radiant City.

Second, this visit to the United States, and his three earlier trips to the USSR from 1928 to 1930, were efforts to engage the "two great systems which are truly new and whose products are revolutionary."[3] Both countries had the raw materials and requisite industrial capacity. By the early 1930s Le Corbusier perceived that the communist system had failed to solve unemployment. His trip to America and his search for work signaled a shift in his aspiration toward the uncertain possibilities of a democratic system enmeshed in capitalism but still capable of change. Like Paul Morand and the regional syndicalists, he had shed his illusions and expectations about either system. But after years of negotiations he accepted his invitation to visit the fountainhead of industrial production and the land of opportunity at a time when it seemed to offer greater prospects than elsewhere. His engagement with American industrialists was proof of his expedient but uneasy compact with the agents of capitalism.

Third, it must be remembered that the American initiatives coincided with the financial crash of 1929 and the early years of the Depression. Inevitably, Le Corbusier's moral duty to level criticism at American capitalism conflicted with his objective to secure work and his inner need to be true to himself. At a deeper level his conflict between morality and self-expression reflects the dilemma faced by the individual whom Colin Wilson labeled the "outsider."[4] This conflict invariably complicated Le Corbusier's relations with Americans as potential patrons and clients. It permeated every aspect of his visit and caused him to examine closely the structure of American society.

The debate on America was conducted primarily in his book *Quand les cathédrales étaient blanches: Voyage au pays des timides* (and in its American edition). Completed in June 1936, it drew on his American experiences and also promoted his mythological view of the country. Originally intended for French readership, a small portion of *Cathédrales* first appeared as an article in 1934 in *Prélude*. But just before his departure Le Corbusier decided to expand the article, presumably in anticipation of his trip, and to redirect his message to an American as well as a French audience. He informed Louis Carré, the

French art dealer then living in New York City, of his plans. Carré responded enthusiastically to his projected *livre des cathédrales*. "I envisage a 'novel-book,'" the dealer encouraged him, "sold [at] the price of an average book, more compelling than a murder mystery."[5]

Although *Cathédrales* was passionate, it was no novel. Like so many of his earlier publications, especially *Vers une architecture, Urbanisme,* and even *La Ville radieuse,* its narrative was disorganized, fragmentary, repetitive, and peppered with textual riddles. Similarly, its methods were polemical and rhetorical. Le Corbusier structured *Cathédrales* in two parts: "Atmospheres" and "U.S.A." In "Atmospheres" he set the scene, *his* scene, by opening up old wounds. He revisited lost commissions including the Palace of the League of Nations (1927) and the Bastion Kellermann housing project (1934–1935). He railed against the academy. He assigned blame for the debacle of the Pessac housing project (Quartiers Modernes Frugès) near Bordeaux (1924–1926). On one hand, he expressed pessimism about the ominous military threat of the Third Reich (omitted in the American edition of 1947), the American obsession with money, and waste as a consequence of capitalism. On the other hand, he expressed optimism about American technology, especially air conditioning, and the promise of modernism that CIAM had helped to launch. By contrast, in "U.S.A." he explored present conditions. He cast his analysis as a social critique divided into five sections. Like *Précisions* (1930), *Cathédrales* addressed the structure and conditions of a new culture and society; but it also shifted his focus from formal and aesthetic practice to challenge the existing political, social, and moral order of American culture. In that respect it departed from his seminal books of the 1920s and early 1930s, which may account for its marginalization in Le Corbusier studies until recent times.

The author conceived *Cathédrales* as a didactic report on the state of America. His purpose was fourfold: he wanted to identify defects in the culture of capitalism and expose its consequences; he sought to inform Americans about inequities of gender, class, and race that he observed in their social structure; he identified signs of redemption in American culture; and he showed how

Radiant City planning could correct flaws in the social system and existing architectural and urban conditions, thereby meeting the needs of all Americans. Its lessons could apply also, but to a lesser extent, to French culture and society. Le Corbusier assigned a level of determinism to his plan to make New York the model for the Radiant City. He assumed, for example, that single-class housing would erase social and racial inequities, and yet his assumptions had a teleological quality because his planning was, in fact, predicated on structural changes in society.

The book was shaped by both his first impressions and his enduring critique of New York's enchanted catastrophe: poles of "love and hate," "hours of enthusiasm, confidence, optimism" countered by "hours of despair in the violence" of a city "strong of force" but "weak of spirit." The city further evoked polarization of opposites between the Subtreasury with its statue of George Washington and the skyscrapers of Wall Street, the contrast between the old order and the new, between spiritual intention and business acumen, between centralized authority and free market forces, and between order and chaos. Le Corbusier's view also embraced elements of good and evil: "hopeless cities and cities of hope" (see chapter 5). The same was true of his general response to America.

The argument Le Corbusier employed for his study of America, however, differed from the one he advanced for New York City because he cast the nation in external opposition with France. Even though he frequently alluded to distinctions between New York City and Paris, he did not pose them in that antinomic relationship. Rather, his intention was to find common ground between them to advance his Radiant City. Yet he still used the polemical methods of his European counterparts. He pitted America's decadence, a consequence of capitalism, against its virtues and possibilities for redemption precisely because it was the youngest and freest of countries. In the process he made penetrating observations about the country and its diverse people, institutions, and values while elucidating some of the deep divisions within it. He did this with the self-assurance that he was probing the psyche of a strong nation beset by timid people,

as both the subtitle and subtext of his book suggest.[6] At the same time he vented his frustrations.

The Consequences of Capitalism: Decadence of American Culture

By 1935 Le Corbusier had largely fixed his ideological position on America. His political engagement with regional syndicalism during the early 1930s exposed him to vehement anti-American sentiment. Like these colleagues, as Mary McLeod observed, he no longer viewed America as the utopia of advanced technology and efficient production that it had seemed in the 1920s. Even though he still believed in the lessons of Taylor and Ford with their techniques of standardization and assembly line production, he deplored the amount of labor engaged in producing unnecessary and wasteful consumer goods. The Wall Street crash and the Depression were sober evidence of the failure of capitalism and its misguided consumerist society.[7]

Inevitably, American problems reverberated throughout Europe during the 1930s. French intellectuals countered with an avalanche of anti-American literature. Among them Robert Aron and Arnaud Dandieu held America responsible for "the decadence of the French nation," as they called their book of 1931, which Le Corbusier read and heavily annotated.[8] Moreover, in their article in the regional syndicalist review *Plans* entitled, "Le Cancer américain," Aron and Dandieu cited American imperialism as the cause of world instability and uncertainty. During the interwar period they charged that America pursued a course of self-interest at France's expense. The dominance of American industrial and financial hegemony coupled with political expansionism, they concluded, would inevitably have consequences for "the true progress of man."[9] Le Corbusier kept well informed on these issues and positions. In addition to Aron and Dandieu's work, he read Georges Duhamel's *Scènes de la vie future* (*America the Menace,* 1930), Louis-Ferdinand Céline's *Voyage au bout de la nuit* (1931), and Jean de Pierrefeu, *Contre la vie chère* (1933).[10] He also was a frequent contributor to *Plans,* which fervently promoted its anti-American position in a blitz of

CRISE AUX...   ...ÉTATS-UNIS

« Valentine massacre » quatre hommes abattus à la mitrailleuse dans un garage. Prohibition, puritanisme, bootleggers, gangsters, royauté du crime, corruption de la justice et de la police. Les U. S. A. n'en restent pas moins une grande aventure humaine. Mais crise...

8.1
Photographs of Chicago gangsters from *Plans,* no. 3 (February
1931), pp. 108–109.

articles during the early 1930s.[11] Illustrations in *Plans* exposed and mocked the "Crise aux . . . Etats-Unis." One issue contained graphic photographs of the victims of the Chicago gangland Valentine's Day Massacre, captioning them "Prohibition, puritanism, bootleggers, gangsters, the royalty figures of crime, corruption of justice and of the police" (figure 8.1).[12] In addition to such books and reviews, Le Corbusier read the less partisan critical accounts of Morand, André Maurois, and others that shaped his views.

Thus the literature of *américanisme* with its anti-American component prepared Le Corbusier for the all

too obvious excesses of capitalism he found on his arrival. Everywhere he confronted social and spiritual "poverty in the midst of plenty," a cliché employed by the *Plans* group.[13] He structured his critique of American culture and society as a series of didactic pedagogical sketches, a method emphasizing organic process that he may have borrowed from Paul Klee's *Pädagogisches Skizzenbuch,* a book he owned.[14] The substance of his critique instructed Americans in the correctness of French ways and established four standards based on hegemony: French restraint in the face of capitalism and consumerism; French culture and civilization; French aesthetics; and French spiritualism or, more precisely, secular spiritualism.

Thus he was predisposed to find America in a state of decadence. On the surface, the economic consequences were most apparent. Production was misdirected toward "useless" rather than "useful" consumer goods with their inevitable waste, a set of themes he sounded in earlier writings, especially in *Vers une architecture, L'Art décoratif d'aujourd'hui, Plans* (and other regional syndicalist reviews), and *La Ville radieuse* (figure 8.2).[15] Consumerism demanded a "product" and an "antiproduct," advertising and publicity. In effect, the capitalist system created an economy of abundance that in turn bred chaos and a "fatal American waste" of material resources, time, and money, with devastating effects on cities and suburbs.[16]

Daily Le Corbusier confronted these excesses of overproduction and consumption, which he contrasted to French restraint. American newspapers fed the local appetite for features on crime and gangsters. Moreover, its advertising and pictorial supplements were designed "to take up time." Such 100-page papers nourished the

8.2

"Useless consumer goods." (*La Ville radieuse*, p. 10.) © 2001 Artists Rights Society (ARS), New York/ADAGP, Paris/FLC.

"barbarian" consumer. His conclusion: "the Indian raids are not far away," meaning that either the course of American civilization had not developed beyond an age of pioneers, or it had reached a state of excess that would inevitably result in its fall and rebirth. He maintained that French papers, by contrast, touched the human spirit. They "skillfully balanced . . . serious things" with stories that "touch the depths of human psychology," stories as "true" as Balzac's. The American deification of advertising and publicity had spun out of control. Taking his cues from Aron and Dandieu, he called this a cancer. With its "limitless seductions," advertising was simply materially manifested "narcissism." As evidence, he recounted a tale in *Cathedrals* about Swiss banker Raoul La Roche refusing to loan his collection to the Museum of Modern Art in exchange for mere publicity.[17] The object lesson in Le Corbusier's admonitions was that French art and culture did not *need* publicity.

Like the regional syndicalists, Le Corbusier viewed advertising as a dehumanizing consequence of capitalism: "a man is a company, a company is a poster, a gag in a magazine, an immense colored billboard." By contrast, French poster kiosks had "charm." With their "walls decorated by those remarkable frescos," he puffed, they were "masterpieces of wit and plasticity." But the electric dazzle of Broadway, especially at Times Square, nearly overcame his reservations about American publicity. He was mesmerized by "that incandescent path cutting diagonally across Manhattan" and the "sexual excitement" of its wares (see figures 5.13, 5.20). But true to his preconceptions and love of polarities, Le Corbusier found "the things behind" Broadway's "luminous advertising" truly decadent. He was torn by his own labile "feelings of melancholy and lively gaiety."[18] However, his position was contradictory; notwithstanding his objections to advertising, he sought to enlist these agents for his own self-promotion. The irony was that French art and culture may not have needed publicity, but *he* did. When Le Corbusier arrived at Quarantine he expected to be courted by the American press. Moreover, to ensure a measure of control in shaping his transatlantic image, he distributed for a fee the studio portraits he had brought from Paris.

The material world of American culture also intrigued and repelled him. He showed contempt for fashion and product design determined by late Beaux-Arts taste. He mocked the hotel service, especially the nickel-plated silver dome on his breakfast egg dish (see figure 4.15). Such products were signs of a lifeless culture. He viewed everyday American consumerism and packaging with the same mix of curiosity and revulsion: "food wrapped up in bright cellophane," "boxes of cellophane toothbrush containers, ticket slots in the backs of train seats, paper wrappers on lump sugar."[19] Attacking consumption was also the focus of Jean de Pierrefeu's *Contre la vie chère,* a book Le Corbusier found especially sympathetic. The capitalism of consumption in America had two consequences. First, such packaging typified the production of useless goods whose deceptive appearance only obscured reality. Second, the underlying obsession with cleanliness created hygienic but culturally sterile conditions.[20] "In Paris," Le Corbusier was reported to have said, "food hangs around unsanitarily but appetizingly."[21] Yet America's obsession with cleanliness and sanitation, he thought, might also be redemptive because it signified a country predisposed to renewing itself. That was a welcome sign to an architect proposing no less than the sudden overturning of a nation's built environment. Distancing himself from his French model, he confessed that on his return from America, the "faded charm" of the Paris bistro would "disappoint" him, along with the people who "cultivate dust and filth" as if "to prove that they possess an age-old culture."[22] His critique was characteristically unresolved and contradictory. Moreover, like the electronic lure of Broadway, packaging and appearances in America masked a dark side, for in the public realm, as in the private one, there lurked a "funereal spirit."

Aside from advertising and consumerism, the New World showed other signs of waste. Le Corbusier's condemnation of capitalism and reappraisal of Fordism and Taylorism caused him to focus on social deficits embodied in such aphorisms and tropes as "time is money," "almighty dollar," and "make big money." He observed how Americans depended on radios, telephones, newspapers, and popular magazines, especially while traveling in the comfort of a Pullman car or even in a Ford, "to fill up all the vacant time" leaving none for making "appraisals."[23] To Le Corbusier waste was deplorable, but these forms of waste were signs of a deeply troubled society. He argued his case for the Radiant City as if his ideal plan could correct such defects.

The Consequences of Capitalism: A Dysfunctional Society and Its Built Environment

If such excessive comforts, abundance, and waste were signs of decadent prosperity, bread lines and unemployment, isolation, and alienation were the human consequences of a dysfunctional capitalist system. For Le Corbusier French culture defined the standard against which to judge American culture and society. Only the depth and character of French culture had managed thus far to immunize it from full-scale Americanization. A keen observer of gender, race, and class differences in America, Le Corbusier had his own theory to account for the country's social inequities and his own solution to right them. The American tour provided him with opportunities to evaluate the state of those relations among men and women as well as among European-Americans and African-Americans within the family unit, and among the elite, the intelligentsia, and the underclass. Individually and collectively as a society, all were victims of capitalism, which explained the tensions among them.

To Le Corbusier the dominant culture (European-American or white males) and the marginalized subcultures (women and African-Americans) existed in separate spheres. The European-American man was a victim of the stock exchange, business enterprises, and suburbia with its cycle of commuting that Le Corbusier denigrated in his Baltimore and Chicago lectures on the "Great Waste." Driven by his quest for money, this man was doomed to a long daily commute, resulting in a fractured "solar day," "sterile business activity," business lunches and dinners, and stand-up cocktail parties with no time for the kind of conversation, thought, and reflection that would ensure his cultural and spiritual well-being. The system that promoted individualism had isolated and alienated him. These were consequences of the "unbalance of machine age times." Such encounters as his "business lunch at the Plaza" with André Jaoul and the Union Carbide managers led him to that conclusion: when Le Corbusier was given only fifteen minutes to explain his proposals, the lunch was somber (and unproductive), but when Jaoul injected wit into the conversation with his "back-room story," his *joie de vivre* finally injected a brief human element.[24]

Le Corbusier used other comparisons with France to confirm America's discordant social relations and its excessive but immature culture. If lunch with industrialists was dominated by business interests, two meals in the company of American engineers, one at his hotel in Boston and another at a club in New York City, produced no conversation at all. When he dined alone at the Copley-Plaza Hotel the evening of his Harvard lecture, he observed three Boston engineers at a nearby table. Their handsome heads, he assumed, must reflect the character of their country: "balanced, strong, energetic." But because the men dined in silence, "they have not yet tasted the joys of . . . ardent thought." If "conversation is a sign of culture," the French who converse at meals have attained what the Americans have not. Similarly, meaningful exchanges at large cocktail parties were impossible because of the amount of alcohol consumed. Such social engagements struck "cudgel blows on spirits wearied by hard work in the city." In contrast, the French aperitif, sipped slowly while seated and enjoyed in a select group, was valued as a "social institution." Yet true to his contradictions, Le Corbusier may have endorsed the social rites of his culture but he rarely had time or inclination for such conversation.[25]

If the European-American man was enslaved by his quest for money, the woman was similarly victimized. However, because of the social networks she developed, Le Corbusier reasoned, she was less isolated and alienated. He stereotyped American men by profession and privilege: businessmen, engineers, professors, and millionaires. He stereotyped American women by their sexual roles, mythic character, and "feminine fetishes": the Vassar Amazon; surrogate "wax manikins" in Fifth Avenue shops with their "square shoulders, incisive features, sharp coiffure," red or "metallic blond hair" that "make women masters, with conquering smiles"; "little blonds of the movies"; the "vamp"; and the "pretty" girl—"a healthy . . . very beautiful animal"—in the burlesque show who is "never joyous, but rather tragic or desperately sentimental."[26]

This caricatured woman, a manifestation of *américanisme*, lived outside the family.[27] But what about the woman who lived within it? To Le Corbusier this meant exclusively the woman of privilege. Because of her associations with high culture he found her more compatible. Unlike her husband and more than her working sisters, this woman had leisure time, better organization, more disposable income, and more inclination to "take an interest in the things of the spirit," which to him meant aesthetic sensibilities. As a result, she was out of harmony with her husband whose time and resources were devoured by the waste and futility of all the social deficits of the culture. Although "worn out," Le Corbusier insisted, the American husband still "showers her with attentions—money, jewels, furnishings, comfort, luxury, vacations." Defeated by his struggle, the husband becomes "intimidated," while the wife "dominates." "Such different voltages" would spark a chain reaction to divide the family.[28] He identified with this woman of high culture because his mismatch with the executive was precisely the same as hers. He understood Marguerite Harris in these terms. Intelligent and sensual, the free-spirited woman chose divorce over a discordant marriage.

As a result of this imbalance, American men were victims of their own sexual inferiority. Women too, especially those intelligent Vassar women, were also victims of sexual tensions. They sought satisfaction in the culture of surrealism. To Le Corbusier this explained why the "brilliant student" Alma Clayburgh was so infatuated with Caravaggio, the sixteenth-century Italian painter whose mannerist tendencies he associated with surrealism.[29] At Vassar, Clayburgh studied the painter in her art history classes with Professor Agnes Rindge. "I always loved Caravaggio's work," she later recalled, because it was "so sensual."[30] Le Corbusier may have fantasized that this infatuation was a Freudian sign of an "unsatisfied heart" he hoped to capture. The student was "troubled" because of her attraction to a painter who he claimed had a "very disquieting mentality." Alma Clayburgh's enthusiasms both fascinated and repelled him, reflecting his own reservations about the painter's turbulent life and perhaps also an unenlightened attitude toward Caravaggio's alleged homosexuality. In *Cathedrals* Le Corbusier offered a lugubrious description of the artist's studio. Its black walls were relieved only by a small amount of light entering through an opening overhead. Caravaggio's art, another manifestation of the funereal spirit, and the student's attraction to it, allowed him to discover within "a corner of the American soul . . . the tangled catacombs of consciousness frequented by troubled, youthful hearts."[31]

By extension, therefore, a youthful American society was "hesitant and troubled" because of its interest in surrealism, a vogue in avant-garde circles both exhibited and assiduously collected by such museum directors as Chick Austin. In 1930 the Wadsworth Atheneum had held an important exhibition, "Italian Painting of the Sei- and Settecento," that included a small painting *Head of a Young Boy* attributed to Caravaggio which Austin later acquired (figure 8.3).[32] The vogue for surrealism, Le Corbusier contended, opposed the "lucid gesture" of European cubism and purism that genuinely reflected the "new times." To assuage the funereal spirit attending Caravaggio and contemporary surrealism that afflicted the Vassar student and retarded the maturation of the American psyche, Le Corbusier offered his personal diagnosis. "Under well-bred external appearances, a complex disturbance and the anxieties of sexual life" could be detected. "The cultivated American [male], once he is pulled away from his business affairs," he observed at the annual Beaux-Arts ball in New York, "talks freely about his inferiority complex. Each time I am embarrassed by that gesture of humility; I see an erect Manhattan, the drives of Chicago, Ford in Detroit, and so many clear signs of youthful power."[33]

By such spurious Freudian reasoning Le Corbusier formulated another indulgent analysis. The sexual anxiety and insecurity of the American male resulted in not only imbalance within the family, but also distortions

8.3
Exhibition "Italian Painting of the Sei- and Settecento," with *Head of a Young Boy* attributed to Caravaggio (left), January–February 1930, Wadsworth Atheneum. (Wadsworth Atheneum, Hartford.)

within the built environment. Extending his biological model to architecture and urbanism, Le Corbusier was overcome by the machismo of the American skyscraper. Only a sexual metaphor would explain its "brute strength" and the businessmen who built it. The New York skyline marked the "first time that men have projected all their strength and labor into the sky." One starry night on the roof of James Johnson Sweeney's penthouse apartment near the East River, Le Corbusier experienced the virile but uncontrollable forces that produced it: "Feeling comes into play; the action of the heart is released; crescendo, allegro, fortissimo . . . we are intoxicated; legs strengthened, chest expanded, eager for action, we are filled with a great confidence."[34] He most likely formed these views as a result of his friendship with Dr. René Allendy, whose ideas found sympathy in avant-garde circles associated with *L'Esprit Nouveau*. René and Yvonne Allendy's *Capitalisme et sexualité,* a book the architect owned and heavily annotated, was especially influential.[35]

Some contemporary feminists hold that American skyscrapers and commentaries on them have been historically invested with a language of male identity and sexual prowess.[36] "The architecture we see," Louis Sullivan explained in *Kindergarten Chats,* "shall be as a man active, alert, supple, strong, sane. A generative man."[37] Even that definition emphasized the skyscraper's organic and expressive forces: "It must be every inch a proud and soaring thing, rising in sheer exultation that from bottom to top it is a unit without a single dissenting line."[38] Critic Montgomery Schuyler conferred sexual authority to the new towers of Manhattan when he called them "Titanian erections."[39]

Le Corbusier proposed that the skyscraper's "brute strength" actually resulted from an architectural mishap, like an adolescent male with a growth spurt that left him with a normal torso but abnormally long legs. The skyscrapers of New York and Chicago, he maintained, were flawed by ill-proportioned setback massing. Like the American man, they suggested sexual dysfunction because they were powerful but not masterful. The skyscraper might be a potent force, but the formal and functional elements of its design were unresolved and unconsummated, the result of a ruptured mind-body connection. Such excesses as the American love of expressive height and the legislated setback towers paralleled the love of Caravaggio and surrealism. Surrealist tendencies in his own work aside, Le Corbusier judged this love to be both sexually and spiritually troubled.[40] The "veil which discloses devotions to Caravaggio . . .

well thought of in the intellectual circles of the USA" brought him fresh insight: "the grandeur of the skyscrapers is suddenly explained. I realize that I am in the country of the timid people."[41] He inferred that such towers masked the fundamental insecurity of "timid" builders who lacked courage to connect with the natural forces in the culture, those he associated with the second machine age.

For similar reasons American urbanism was equally unresolved and dysfunctional. "In its gigantomachy," caused by the distortions of decentralization, "American city planning betrays a timidity" at the very moment when the country ought to act.[42] If Americans were timid about their architecture and urbanism, Le Corbusier reasoned, it was because they were timid about their sexual relations. The skyscraper was not the invention of just any man; it was a conceit of the *American* man. A product of the New World, it lacked the wisdom of the Old. The Parisian assured his American hosts that *he* was not "timid" about, and therefore not sexually inadequate to, the task of designing "correctly" proportioned towers at great heights to replace Manhattan's existing setback buildings. His claim that "The Skyscrapers of New York Are Too Small" and timid was meant to promote his mature Cartesian skyscrapers and confirm his sexual persona. His pursuit of Marguerite and other women during his tour formed a corollary to the language of male identity he employed to criticize the skyscraper for the purpose of advancing his own work. However, in their discourse on sexuality and building height, contemporaneous American architects, modern feminist critics, and Le Corbusier himself all failed to take into account the principles of land values and other empirical conditions that shaped them.[43]

Inequities of Class and Race in the Dysfunctional Society

Le Corbusier presumed to inform Americans about inequities in their own social structure and instruct them about principles to correct them. If the family was divided, he argued, so the society was divided by class, race, and attitudes toward them. This social dysfunction manifested itself directly in the built environment. For suburbanization resulted in more than just a divided family; it destroyed the inner cities left behind. During his tour Le Corbusier circulated mostly among the country's elite, but he made efforts to experience the conditions of the underclass. As a visitor, he alerted European readers of *Cathedrals*, "you will be shown only the handsome quarters; you will never be entertained except by hosts in comfortable circumstances; very comfortable, terribly comfortable in the midst of pathetic masses. The slums of Chicago are terrible." But what troubled him was not that the slums were "physically ugly," but that they could morally imperil the lives of their inhabitants. "This slum, then, is sinister not because of the place itself but because of the kind of spirit which has sown death . . ." He considered the African-American the greatest victim because the European-American condemned him to slums and shunned him as a "pariah." He announced, "Americans are eminently democratic—except about Negroes." They and their national leaders might also be "good-natured, cordial, and companionable," but they were entirely "ignorant of the great charnel house of human misery" because they cocooned themselves in a treadmill of commuting, cocktail parties, and colonial suburban houses, all of which bypassed the reality of the American city.[44] Only when Le Corbusier escaped from the tour itinerary—in Harlem and along Broadway with Marguerite, in the chaos of the metropolis with Fernand Léger, in the depressed areas of New York with housing reformers or those of Chicago with Jacobs—could he experience that reality.

The "Funereal Spirit" and Its Effects on the Built Environment

In one of his most bizarre critiques in *Cathédrales* (judiciously excised in the American edition), Le Corbusier claimed that American culture was the victim of its own agent of repression through what he metaphorically called *salpêtre* (saltpeter), an antiaphrodisiac. Broadway and burlesque as well as the freely passionate forces within the African-American community, especially music and dance, not only kept the white intelligentsia from recognizing the physical decay of the Harlem slums but also diverted and deflated its sexual energy.

Moreover, the bold flirtations of college students, the "violent morality" he witnessed, workers building skyscrapers, suburbanization resulting in dislocation and a crushing work day for commuters, and even business itself were repressive forces. These deliberately distorted elements served as erotic surrogates to assuage an underlying sexual inhibition, psychological repression, and timidity within the culture. Such forms of saltpeter kept America from reaching an age of maturity.[45]

To Le Corbusier the waste of advertising and consumption, obsession with cleanliness, enslavement of the nuclear family, inequities of class and race, and urban slums confirmed that American culture was rapidly declining into a moribund state. This new machine age civilization, he thought, was dominated by the same funereal, even decadent spirit in Caravaggio and surrealism. The culture was funereal because it had created something "black" and lifeless, a "solemnity which has not yet succeeded in coming alive." Signs of this were all around him: in the "heavy and overstuffed" American car, in the entrances to the Empire State Building with their "walls faced with dark, gleaming slabs" (figure 8.4), in the "wax manikins" of Fifth Avenue shops (figure 8.5), and in the absence of trees in the city.[46] Le Corbusier's visit to the automobile show at Grand Central Palace convinced him that the 1936 models, such as the lugubrious Cadillac Fleetwood Town Sedan (figure 8.6) or the staid Chevrolet Standard Sport Sedan that emphasized "service and safety," only made the streets "oppressive." His thesis, however, was not supported by the show's biggest hits: the stylized New Cord (whose inventor was inspired by Le Corbusier) and the aerodynamic De Soto Airstream convertible.[47]

The American, as opposed to the French, Beaux-Arts ball illustrated another funereal rite. In an effort to make it "the most colorful New York has ever seen" and to escape the sober realities of their dwindling practices during the low ebb of the Depression years, the Beaux-Arts architects staged a "Quat'z Arts Night in India" pageant at the Waldorf-Astoria. On December 6 New York society rose to the occasion with 2,500 of its ranks *en costume* (figure 8.7). Ringling Brothers and Barnum and Bailey Circus provided exotically athletic acts of

8.4
Entrance, Empire State Building.
(F. S. Lincoln Collection, Historical
Collections and Labor Archives,
Pennsylvania State University.)

8.5
"Wax manikins," surrealist window
display at Bergdorf Goodman and
Co., 1930s. (Photograph by Russell
Lee; Library of Congress, Prints
and Photographs Division, Farm
Security Administration Collection.)

8.6
Cadillac Fleetwood town sedan, 1936 model. (Courtesy of the Detroit Public Library, National Automotive History Collection.)

tightrope walkers, Balinese tumblers, Abyssinian pole balancers, and Scandinavian weight lifters. At midnight, 2 A.M. and 3:30 A.M. they performed under the "big top" of the Waldorf ballroom before a costumed "Royal Indian family" including the Maharajah of Rajput played by Arthur Ware, former president of the Beaux-Arts Society of Architects.[48] As Le Corbusier described it, "there were elephants [called Jazzbo and Razzbo], bears [which gyrated], clowns, and acrobats. Everyone was bedecked, covered with brocades, with plume turbans, Indian scarfs, shimmering silk." But the spectacle's cacophony of color seemed "lusterless and flat." Amid the confetti, Le Corbusier thought the only "luxurious costume" was the gray skin of the elephant.[49]

At the Waldorf Le Corbusier was in the company of Alma Clayburgh, the singer and mother of the Vassar student so infatuated with Caravaggio.[50] Some New Yorkers may have considered her a society matron but Madame Clayburgh, as she called herself, was neither a socialite nor very wealthy. However, she liked to function as a patron of the arts, giving frequent parties at her apartment in the Ritz Tower where she introduced members of high society to theater people, musicians,

artists, and writers including Theodore Dreiser and Franz Werfel. Le Corbusier attended at least one of these soirées, no doubt with the expectation of meeting potential clients.[51]

Le Corbusier probably never met the celebrities at the ball that night, including Mayor La Guardia, Babe Ruth, and the honorary chairman Whitney Warren.[52] But he did take the pulse of New York society, concluding that Quat'z Arts was the product of a decadent culture victimized by its own illusions. From such heady heights, he claimed, one could not grasp reality. In contrast, the Parisian ball reflected a spirited realism in French culture, an ironic argument that privileged nationalism over modernism. In Paris, Le Corbusier boasted without an inkling of political correctness, "little nude women brighten the affair." But at the Waldorf, he announced coyly, "there will be no little nude women, oh never!"[53] To the Parisian, nudity in the 1930s was reality; absence of nudity at the New York Quat'z Arts was a breach of the norm. That defect in the American character vividly illustrated both its funereal spirit and abiding puritanism. Le Corbusier's efforts to gauge the spiritual dimensions of a culture by a costume ball

BEAUX-ARTS BALL IS FEAST OF COLOR

Spangled Circus Setting and Baroque Magnificence of East Indian Rajah Blended.

EXOTIC COSTUMES NOTED

More Than 3,000 Persons at Dance Given by Society of Architects.

With all its traditional glamour and festive spirit, marked this year by many striking and colorful innovations, the annual Beaux-Arts Ball was held last night in the grand ballroom suite of the Waldorf-Astoria. Framed in a setting flashing with the spangled trappings of a circus "big top" and the baroque motif of East Indian decoration, the event was given under the auspices of the Society of Beaux-Arts Architects to further that organization's extensive educational program.

In some respects last night's ball recalled an earlier fête of the architects' society, the "Cirque d'Hiver" ball of many years ago, but a fanciful legend attached to this, the seventeenth ball of a brilliant series begun in 1913, brought forth an exotic display of Oriental costumes and decorative effects which combined in a kaleidoscopic manner with the circus element of the party.

A brilliantly costumed throng of 3,000 persons, representative of society and the fine arts, reveled in the ballroom suite throughout the night, one and all dedicated to the now internationally known Beaux-Arts Ball spirit of conviviality, which was not a little heightened last night by the ballroom début of several real elephants and dancing bears.

Police Facilitate Traffic.

The gay influence of the ball was not confined solely to the entertaining suite of the hotel. The guests arriving in costume attracted an interested and amused crowd to the hotel lobbies and foyers, as well as to the sidewalk entrances. A spe-

SOCIETY TURNS TO THE ORIENT FOR BEAUX-ARTS BALL COSTUMES.

New York Times Studio Photo.
Mrs. S. Stanwood Menken as the Sacred White Peacock of the tableaux which featured last night's fête at the Waldorf-Astoria.

New York Times Studio Photo.
Leonard J. Cushing as Colonel, the Hon. Buxton Bridgeley, and Mrs. Cushing as Mayura, a member of the Maharajah's court.

Oriental Incense Marks Dinner Given for Subscribers to Ball

'A Night in India,' at the Weylin, Is Attended by 200 Costumed Members of Beaux-Arts Spectacle—Many Other Events Precede the Dance.

8.7
"A Night in India," Beaux-Arts
Ball, Waldorf Astoria, December
6, 1935. (*New York Times,*
December 7, 1935.) NYT Pictures,
© 1935 The New York Times Co.
Reproduced by permission.

seems absurd when placed in comparison with such French domains of popular culture as the Folies Bergère and the Lido. From the American perspective these spectacles were like Fred Astaire films of the 1930s. Their fantasy provided momentary relief from the anxieties of the Depression.[54] Once again, Le Corbusier preferred his *idea* of reality over the reality he actually experienced.

As for his own masquerade, he would have none of the proud and pretentious trappings of a moribund culture, "no usurped title," or rajah's "turban and a brocaded robe." Refusing to conform to the Beaux-Arts code of expectations, he preferred to play the role of outlaw, "a sore thumb," a critic.[55] He dressed as a convict or a clown, a safe pose that he invariably adopted for parties.[56] His costume formed a collage announcing his affiliation with modernism: "I insist on white and blue striped convict's trousers and an Indian army guard's vermilion coat; I find an enormous gold epaulette which I fasten on the left side. No military cap, sir, a white, pointed clown's hat, please. For color balance I put on a dark blue sash as a shoulder-belt, cut by a gold band. . . . To finish off, three differently shaped spots of white on my cheeks and forehead, to perplex the curious." Expecting to receive the same attention that reporters had given his everyday appearance, he was not prepared to be ignored. "I did not arouse the slightest smile, the slightest interest," he sulked; "I left ingloriously, thrust aside by respectability."[57]

If Americans were indifferent to his avant-garde costume it was a sign of not only a lifeless culture but also one ignorant of modern color theory. They had not learned the lessons of Picasso's costume designs for Diaghilev's Ballet Russe, that brilliance is not a matter of luxurious silks or bright colors, but the use of neutral tones with only a dash of color. The pageant reflected a society whose illusions and false pride kept it from appreciating the spontaneous joys of the "spirit" or the "feeling for contemporary life."[58] Architects in America had merely appropriated the rites of the ball, as they had the Beaux-Arts *grand projet*. In France such idealized projects were never meant to be realized; but in America all things were possible and the *grand projet* came to dominate its City Beautiful architecture and planning

plus royaliste que le roi. Notwithstanding the degree to which Le Corbusier's preconceptions impeded his ability to connect with the reality that he experienced, much of his criticism of the pageant was both perceptive and witty.

But a more serious consequence of the funereal spirit was embodied in American thought that Le Corbusier deemed slow, "hesitant" and preoccupied with meditations on "the moral support of life." In contrast, French thought was quick and simply the "strongest," a position that confirmed his attitude of French superiority. The architect claimed that unlike the French who were proficient in "Cartesian reason," an ideal he long promoted, Americans were unaccustomed to deep thought. As a consequence, theirs was underdeveloped and the thought process itself unappreciated. In no segment of American society was this more evident than in its youth whose education on "Elysian" campuses could not equip them for the realities of adult life. American education might prepare youth athletically, but not intellectually and spiritually. This posed a mind-body conflict that Le Corbusier observed on the campuses he visited: the "sadness of strong-armed, full-hearted young men [and women]," whose "spirits have not set out in search of the inner joys which are the fruit of civilization." Moreover, "troubled by the incapacity of their age . . . they are grieved and melancholy."[59]

The funereal spirit, Le Corbusier instructed readers of *Cathedrals,* had consequences for the built environment. It defined another dimension of the dysfunctional American society. The defects in American buildings seemed to symbolize to him the paradox between athletic programs and educational policy, especially at institutions with schools of architecture. For, in spite of their feats of athleticism, the skyscrapers of Manhattan and Chicago were actually weak and timid. The buildings, and the architects who designed them, reflected architectural education in America that lacked "intellectual gymnastics which make minds supple." And if the discipline of architecture was intellectually deficient, it reflected weaknesses in the practice of architecture as well as in the general culture: misuse of height, money, and publicity. "Animated by an architectural spirit which is manifest in everything, skyscrapers, machines, objects, bars, clothes," Le Corbusier concluded, American life fluctuates "between the impulses of will and power, between incontestable success and a funereal sadness." Materialism had suppressed spiritualism. In a culture where "time is money," where there is little appreciation for or tolerance of reason for the sake of reason, the character of American thought is "grave."[60] This perspective was particularly French, going back to Alexis de Tocqueville, the French politician and writer whose *Democracy in America* (1835) attributed the "gravity of Americans" to "pride" and their lack of "high ambitions" to the democratic system.[61]

Le Corbusier concluded that the funereal spirit and the misguided morality he called a "hazardous Puritanism" left American culture suspended between the academic and the modern, between a soulless first machine age and the possibility of a second machine age with more humanist concerns. To lift the country out of stasis and redeem it from the decadence of capitalism, the dysfunctions of its society, and the moribund state of its culture, Le Corbusier instructed Americans to seek spiritual renewal as well as physical rebirth. It is ironic that he should denounce the puritan strain in American culture when his own culture and thinking were so strongly rooted in the Calvinism of the region around his native La Chaux-de-Fonds.[62]

Signs of Redemption in American Culture

What virtues and signs of hope might redeem and renew the country? Le Corbusier saw obvious ones in the culture at large: the "honest" character of New York and its people, preoccupation with cleanliness that signaled a healthy predisposition toward renewal, the boldness of technology, evidence of collaboration in assembly line production, and the success of business enterprises in which Americans were "champions."[63] These virtues would have to overcome the decadent and the funereal.

But did the culture and society possess the requisite spiritualism, namely, a secular spiritualism? Le Corbusier saw signs of hope and redemption in the nation's

pluralism, especially in white popular culture, African-American popular and folk culture, and high culture originating from or associated with France. He was ambivalent about the white popular culture because he viewed it through the lens of *américanisme*. Between the wars the European avant-garde saw it as both a threat to and a means of renewing its own culture. Le Corbusier recognized that Hollywood movies, burlesque shows, revues, and the musicals he attended with Marguerite had the capacity to reveal what was "true." Thus, if the society was dysfunctional, the popular culture would expose its true condition. The social consequences of capitalism, Le Corbusier suggested in *Cathedrals*, undermined the integrity of the individual. A case in point was Billy Rose's lavish circus musical *Jumbo* at the Hippodrome, starring comedian Jimmy Durante. Critic Robert Benchley described the orchestra leader Paul Whiteman as "ravishing in baby blue raiment astride a white charger at the head of his musical myrmidons."[64] To Le Corbusier *Jumbo* may have been "an admirable theatrical spectacle, as detailed, precise, as the organization of a skyscraper" but, like the Beaux-Arts ball and the country itself, this Broadway "triumph" revealed a deficit because "the individual is crushed by the masses" and, as a consequence, no "philosophy of life" or "of pleasure" is yet apparent.[65]

Along with the Broadway spectacle and the ball, Hollywood comic movies supported Le Corbusier's position about the state of American culture. On one hand, comic movies were leavening agents to the "grave" in American life. "To shake the people out of their seriousness, Hollywood has invented some astonishing types" that reveal man's alienation within a spiritually bankrupted culture: "Charlie Chaplin, the imperturbable ordinary man, Buster Keaton, tragically isolated in his individual activity, Laurel and Hardy, indifferent to circumstances." Le Corbusier was particularly sympathetic to Chaplin whose films, especially *City Lights* (1931; figure 8.8), had been the subject of debate among the regional syndicalists in *Plans*. Chaplin's urban tramp played the role of outsider. In the end comic movies were not comic at all. The ordinary heroes in these films, like "sensitive persons" in society at large, were overwhelmed

8.8
Charlie Chaplin in *City Lights*, 1931. (Library of Congress, Prints and Photographs Division, NYWT&S Collection.) © Roy Export Company Establishment.

by the "inhuman dimensions" of American life.[66] Le Corbusier probably identified with the comic hero, especially the outsider, as he engaged power brokers and faltered in his efforts to reach common ground.

If his notion of popular culture focused on the individual and his relation to society, it was because he associated the individual with the heroic and the ideal. His claim that the individual both revealed the problems of an entire culture and provided solutions to them is evident in his prescription for America: "through the individual reformation of consciousness . . . the reformation of collective consciousness will be accomplished."[67] Within the society he identified groups of individuals most predisposed to renewal and to his initiatives.

The first of these groups, marginalized by the dominant white male culture, was the African-American. Le Corbusier assigned special significance to African-Americans because they were part of the underclass, because their own cultural heritage had helped to shape the development of modernism, and because their present folk culture synthesized the modern and the ancient. In Paris Le Corbusier had been influenced by avant-garde interest in African art, but he came to it late. During the teens and twenties avant-garde artists led by Picasso and others, as well as European writers and intellectuals, sought to purify their culture through *art nègre*. Notwithstanding an undercurrent of the vernacular in his theory and design during those years, Le Corbusier largely eschewed such interests, advancing purism based on machine age forms.[68] As *L'Esprit Nouveau* and *Vers une architecture* suggest, he directed his enthusiasms more toward the art of classical antiquity in order to make a formal and symbolic linkage between the "pure" forms of the machine and those in ancient art, which shared an honesty and directness resulting in functional clarity. Such formal, aesthetic, and symbolic elements in Greek and Roman art shaped his interest in "primitivism" within the rhetoric of modernism.[69]

By 1920, however, under the influence of Amédée Ozenfant and Léger, Le Corbusier embraced African art. Like them, he admired its geometrical, formal, mechanistic, decorative, and expressive properties.[70] When Léger relied on the formal elements of African sculpture for his 1923 *ballet nègre, The Creation of the World,* he cast them as "high art" and played into the myth of modernism.[71] But James Clifford has offered a counterargument suggesting that it was the language of African-American popular culture that attracted Léger, Picasso, Guillaume Apollinaire, and other members of the Parisian avant-garde. During this period of *négrophilie,* a strong popular culture emerged that included such "evocative black figures" as the jazzman, the boxer, and Josephine Baker, all of whom satisfied a search for "something primitive, *sauvage* . . . and completely modern."[72]

It is significant for Le Corbusier that after World War I neither the Parisian avant-garde, much less the bourgeoisie, made a meaningful distinction between African and African-American art and culture. As Parisians had been exposed increasingly to exhibitions, concerts, performances, ballets, and theater, the two cultures became invariably interconnected. Thus *art nègre* could encompass modern American jazz with its associations of the mechanical and mechanistic, Oceanian sculpture, and pre-Columbian material culture as well as African artifacts, which collectively represented the myth of an "other" exotic world.[73] As a received tradition in Europe, this engagement of African culture also shaped Ozenfant's art theory. In his *Foundations of Modern Art* (1931) Ozenfant freely juxtaposed images of African art and material culture with those of the machine not only to show the formal elements common to them but also to recast African artifacts into the language of modernity.[74] Le Corbusier absorbed the duality of African folk culture and the machine that infused the work of Ozenfant and others.

By the late 1920s the European avant-garde had developed a mythology associated with *art nègre* and with African and African-American culture. America was at once a country of noble savages and high technology, of the primitive and the modern. This metaphorical fusion

produced jazz.[75] In Weimar Germany African-American music and dance, particularly jazz, served the formal language of expressionism and joined together "instinctual, savage, and sexual forces" with American technology.[76] In France, Léger was compelled by the mechanistic elements he saw in both African sculpture and American jazz to express this alliance of primitive vitality and power in the costumes and stage sets for *The Creation of the World.*[77] Thus, Ozenfant, Léger, and others freely coopted representations of African and African-American art and artifacts as metaphors for the exotic, vital, primitive, and mechanical. Such coded messages, long separated from their cultural and anthropological contexts, now served the interests of modernism.

Although Le Corbusier had been aware of *art nègre* for some time, his serious engagement with folk culture and non-Western traditions emerged in the late 1920s when a confluence of events—artistic, social, cultural, political, and ideological—encouraged him to make a significant reassessment. The American crash and its threat to Europe caused regional syndicalists to search for a new order. This search, as McLeod has explained, included "proposals for new administrative units based on regional groupings and natural hierarchies; the restructuring of the economy along noncapitalist lines; and the development of a new spiritual and emotional life."[78] The period around 1930 marked a parallel shift in the direction of Le Corbusier's production. Now man and not the machine was central. Influenced by the formal and aesthetic concerns of the Parisian avant-garde and the regional syndicalist agenda, his new work incorporated vernacular, topographical, and regional elements as well as traditional materials, especially the use of rustic stone. The culture of the Americas and the African-American would take on special significance for him because it achieved a synthesis of the folk and the mechanical.[79]

Le Corbusier's trip to South America in 1929 celebrated his personal introduction to the New World and with it a new understanding of the importance of region, topography, climate, and folk culture. The exotic terrain of that continent with its vast expanses of sculpted landscape and the scenographic drama of such ports as Rio de

Janeiro and São Paulo, offered a new plastic conception and topographical model for his urbanism. Moreover, his experience of the slums of Rio de Janeiro and Buenos Aires produced an affective response to the human condition and a call for "valorization of a poor neighborhood" through demolition-based planning.[80]

During the 1930s Le Corbusier also intensified his interest in the primitive. He loved jazz, like Ozenfant, and also enjoyed ethnic music.[81] In 1935 his apartment at 24 rue Nungesser et Coli served as a gallery for Louis Carré's exhibition of *art primitif*. On view were Benin bronzes and an archaic Greek statue exhibited alongside a Léger tapestry and his own painting. As with Ozenfant and other avant-garde artists of his generation, Le Corbusier converted this assemblage of "primitive art" into a fusion of modernist expression and collective memory. "The technique of groupings" in the exhibition, he explained in the *Oeuvre complète 1934–1938,* "is in some way a manifestation of modern sensibility in the understanding of the past, of exoticism, or of the present."[82] During his time in New York City he continued to pursue his interest in African sculpture, attending Louis Carré's exhibition at the Knoedler gallery of bronzes and ivories from Benin, which he called "sumptuous," "noble," and "solemn" (figure 8.9).[83] In the collections of the Brooklyn Museum he discovered the ancient art of the Americas, a "great and magnificent art, dominating, exalting the sun and cosmic powers" that could invigorate the modern spirit.[84]

Travels in South America also marked his firsthand engagement with African-American folk and popular culture. There he developed a close friendship with Josephine Baker, whom he had seen in Paris revues and now met aboard the *Giulio Cesare.*[85] While traversing the continent he had several encounters with the music hall star. He saw her perform in public and in private; he shared intimate moments in her cabin. On several occasions he made tender drawings of her, one showing a sleeping Josephine (figure 8.10).[86] He invested in her not only symbols of purity, innocence, and nobility, but also a kind of *sauvage* vitality, all of which he associated with the folk and popular culture of the American Negro, but that more fundamentally reflected the language

8.9

"Portrait of a Princess," bronze, Benin, 1360–1500, Louis Carré exhibition at M. Knoedler and Co., New York City, November 25–December 14, 1935. (*Bronzes and Ivories from the Old Kingdom of Benin,* pl. 1; courtesy of M. Knoedler & Co.)

and myths of "primitivism," modernism, and *américanisme.* "In a ridiculous music hall in Sao Paolo [sic] Josephine Baker sang 'Baby' with such an intense and dramatic sensibility," he revealed in *Précisions,* "that I was moved to tears."[87] In addition to these encounters, he and Baker spent the last days of their respective South American visits together in Rio.

The degree to which Le Corbusier recast Baker into the modernist view of "primitivism" is embodied in a ballet script he wrote for her during the South American trip. The narrative conveys tangled images of the music

8.10

Josephine Baker, drawing by Le
Corbusier, 1929. (FLC.) © 2001
Artists Rights Society (ARS), New
York/ADAGP, Paris/FLC.

hall star and the woman he knew in the New World, purist forms, and racial stereotypes, the mythical, the ideal, and the real.[88] His description of "a modern man and woman + New York" suggests her affinity with the modern city. It may also reflect his interest in pursuing their personal relationship with the prospect of future meetings in the United States.[89] In December 1929 the two returned to Paris aboard the ship *Lutétia.* At a costume party the night they crossed the Equator, Le Corbusier reversed roles and appeared as Josephine herself.[90] In remembrance of their days in Rio together, he made a drawing of the two of them as a stylish couple dressed in chic European clothes posing in front of the city's dramatic skyline.[91]

In letters to Baker both before and after his tour of the United States, he recalled their time together in South America, mixing, as he invariably did, the personal and the professional. Early in 1935 he had heard through friends that Baker was about to build a series of houses, in effect a village for children. He reminded her to recall their travels together "when you asked me so sweetly to collaborate with you in your building projects on returning to Europe."[92] Although Baker was in New York City that fall rehearsing a musical revue for the Ziegfeld Follies, the two did not meet. On his return from America Le Corbusier wrote to her, apologizing for having left her New York address at home and claiming that it had prevented him from getting in touch with her. He explained to her somewhat unctuously, "what pleasure it would have been to see you, you who are so pretty, so nice and we would have been able to recall in North America the good memories of South America." Then he reproached her for broken promises. Wounded that she had neither kept up their friendship nor hired him for her proposed projects, he chided her. "I said that I had no luck with you. Because you made me promise in Rio de Janeiro that I would not drop you; now it is you who have thoroughly dropped me and I would not excuse you if I did not know what a hard worker you are."[93] Although his marriage to Yvonne kept him from liaisons with women in Paris, he felt free to pursue them abroad. A plausible explanation for his failure to communicate with Baker in Manhattan, and one that supports the view that they were once lovers, may be that he did not want to rekindle their relationship in deference to Marguerite. Once again, Le Corbusier allowed professional gain to test a friendship. But Baker's tastes ran counter to his. As one biographer observed, "When push came to shove Baker did not want to live in a hard-edged modern house . . . she preferred traditional upper-middle-class comforts and charm."[94]

Le Corbusier's intimate friendship with Baker helped him to appreciate the character of the American woman and that of the African-American, at once descended from an early culture and yet also inextricably a part of the New World. By the 1930s he was predisposed to look upon African-American culture as a more noble one. He held that if the dominant culture relegated the Negro to the underclass, to be the servant (a Grand Central or Pullman car porter) in a capitalist society limited only to served and servant classes, or to be crowded into oppressive slums, the Negro's intrinsic culture, his art of movement and music, liberated his spirit and his soul. Le Corbusier regarded Baker's music as not merely "intense" and "dramatic"; it shared with his own architecture the primal, modern, and universal. For he discovered in American Negro music "a lyrical 'contemporary' mass so invincible that I could see the foundation of a new sentiment of music capable of being the expression of the new epoch."[95]

While in the United States Le Corbusier pursued his interest in African-American folk and popular culture and was particularly drawn to the Harlem Renaissance.[96] He admired the way in which "Negroes showed their remarkable abilities in plays, in musical programs, in stage design."[97] He attended at least two Manhattan performances of what he called *opéra nègre*, including a stunning production of George Gershwin's opera *Porgy and Bess* at the Alvin Theater with a cast of singers from Harlem (figure 8.11).[98] Like the original play by DuBose and Dorothy Heyward, Gershwin's *Porgy and Bess* treated "the Negro as a serious subject" although, according to Nathan Huggins, "in stereotyped ways."[99] Moved by the actors and the productions, Le Corbusier called such musicals a "revelation" because they allowed him a deeper understanding of the culture, even though the productions often involved collaborations with white males and employed stereotypes.[100] While in Hartford he may have seen photographs of the modernist sets in colorful cellophane for the Wadsworth Atheneum's production of *Four Saints in Three Acts*, the first American opera with an all-black cast.[101]

African-American music and dance intrigued Le Corbusier even more than theater. But like Duhamel and Morand, he tended to regard them as part of a more general confusion between African and African-American culture.[102] He cast Harlem in Morand's image of a "miniature Africa" with many of the same racially charged stereotypes that also informed the literature of *américanisme.*[103] "Taught on the plantations of Louisiana," he explained, Negro hymns and songs were an authentic "folklore of the best quality." Yet he imagined "in them the depths of equatorial Africa rise again."[104] More enlightened than Duhamel and Morand, he understood

8.11
Catfish Row, scene from *Porgy and Bess*, Alvin Theater, New York City, 1935. (Museum of the City of New York, Theatre Collection.)

that African-American culture was inextricably bound to the destiny of modern America.

Le Corbusier experienced African-American music and dance as both modern and mechanical, savage and spiritual, symbolic and universal. It contained "the past and the present, Africa and pre-machine age Europe and contemporary America." It confirmed, as McLeod cogently argued, the synthesis of folk culture and mechanical forms that had helped to shape Parisian modernism and regional syndicalist ideology.[105] "Negro music," he wrote in *Cathedrals,* "has touched America because it is the melody of the soul joined with the rhythm of the machine. It is in two-part time: tears in the heart; movement of legs, torso, arms and head." It was "the music of an era of construction," of skyscrapers, subways, and cities, the "sound of modern times" that would overturn conservatories. To Le Corbusier a night club performance by Louis Armstrong at Connie's Inn (actually the Great White Way) on Broadway at 48th Street symbolized this best: "He sings, he guffaws, he makes his silver trumpet spurt. He is mathematics, equilibrium on a tightrope. He is Shakespearean! . . . he roars and puts the trumpet to his mouth. With it he is in turn demoniac, playful and massive. . . . The man is extravagantly skillful; he is a king" (figure 8.12). On Broadway and in Harlem "the Negro orchestra is impeccable . . . a beautiful turbine running in the midst of human conversations. Hot jazz."[106]

African-American dancing in the night clubs of Broadway and Harlem also brought out Le Corbusier's preconceptions on race. Marguerite remembered taking him up to Harlem to introduce him to the Savoy Ballroom at a time when "Blacks and Whites mingled freely" and the atmosphere was as "relaxed and happy as it was exciting" (figure 8.13).[107] To Le Corbusier the dance hall had the power to transform the movements of ordinary African-Americans into "nearly savage rites." Even tap dancers, "as mechanical as a sewing machine," demonstrated that "the old rhythmic instinct of the virgin African forest has learned the lesson of the machine." Similarly, Le Corbusier allowed race to dominate his description of the stage show that accompanied Louis Armstrong's performance: "a series of dances . . . stimulating the body to frenzied gesticulation. Savagery is constantly present, particularly in the frightful murder scene which leaves you terrified; these naked Negroes, formidable black athletes, seem as if they were imported directly from Africa where there are still tom-toms, massacres, and the complete destruction of villages or tribes." Moreover, the Negro had "virgin ears" and "fresh curiosity." But such night club performances also dramatized for him the isolation of the African-American. At the Savoy he noticed the way in which "an ingenious

8.12
Louis Armstrong, publicity photograph, 1935. (Library of Congress, Prints and Photographs Division, NYWT&S Collection.)

projector throws on the wall behind the orchestra what seem like black strips of broken clouds." The projection produced a "somber atmosphere," symbolizing the indifference of natural forces to man.[108] Although he was sensitive to inequities affecting African-Americans, he

8.13
Savoy Ballroom,
Lenox Avenue at
140th Street, Harlem,
1935. (Collection
Frank Driggs.)

allowed the excitement of the music and dance spectacles to support racial stereotyping and to distract him
from recognizing the social injustice these night clubs
encouraged. Like most white Americans, he was probably unaware that such Harlem institutions as the Savoy
Ballroom and Apollo were both white-owned and open
shops. In the 1920s and 1930s black performers were
routinely exploited by white managers and theater own-
ers. As writer and poet Claude McKay explained in
1940, "behind the exciting baroque fantasy of Negro en-
tertainment lies the grim reality of ruthless jobbery."[109]

To Le Corbusier such music was both American and
universal. It transcended barriers of race, ethnicity, national origin, class, and gender. "In spite of the impla-
cable color line, through his music the Negro has
entered the chapel of hearts and, through his music, the
whole fashionable world of balls and drawing rooms—
from the working girl to the millionaire's daughter—is
delighted." Its appeal to the spirit, he suggested, made
the music "stir up consciousness in a profound way" and
"introduce new values into the depths of the heart."[110]

Enthusiastically received in Europe, the mechanical
rhythms and soulful expressions of the music, he
claimed, stimulated transatlantic exchange.[111]

Le Corbusier endorsed African-American theater,
music, and dance because their modernity made them
catalysts for cultural and spiritual renewal. Drawing an
analogy between the city and this music, between individual building and modern rhythms, he announced:
"Manhattan is hot jazz in stone and steel." Like the skyscraper, jazz was another expression of the "forces" of
modern American life. But the architecture was not as
"advanced" as jazz because it lacked "contemporary renewal."[112] He believed that unlike other groups in
American society, blacks were predisposed to change.
He endorsed the widely held European belief that they
were more primitive, more unspoiled, more noble, and
open to new ideas. In reality these Americans had the
most to gain by change and renewal. But if they had
brought about a spiritual and cultural "reformation" in
music, Le Corbusier concluded, other outside forces
could bring about a reformation in architecture.

Le Corbusier also saw signs of hope for American culture and society in its strong and free-spoken women. They too were marginalized by the dominant white male culture. Most of the women Le Corbusier met were well educated, privileged, and white. At Vassar, he observed, women who had spent a year abroad where they lived individually, rather than in groups on their home campuses, developed independent thinking. Physically athletic and mentally agile, they, like other American women, were not timid. To Le Corbusier these young women, some with "communistic sympathies," represented "the good society intelligentsia, well to do and liberal spenders." They were already "prepared for the great overturning with a touching ingenuousness."[113] In 1935 these women were among the most liberated in the world. They were accustomed to initiating reforms and, Le Corbusier assumed, poised for change.

Josephine Baker and Marguerite Harris, the two American women he knew best, shared some common ground with Vassar women. They all were strong and independent, free-thinking and free-spirited, sophisticated and well traveled. All spoke French. Indeed, French culture, he thought, made them truly enlightened. But unlike most of the Vassar women, Josephine and Marguerite lived outside the family structure that Le Corbusier believed enslaved women. Both women had managed to elude their respective societies: Josephine the underclass and Marguerite the bourgeois. Josephine was exemplary because she escaped the limitations American society had placed on her race and gender by achieving status as a celebrity and living as an expatriate in Paris. Marguerite escaped the expectations of her class and gender because her education and family gave her exceptional opportunities. Governesses taught her to speak fluent French, but Dreiser encouraged her to rebel. Marguerite's allowance supported her writing and work with Dreiser; her family helped to raise her son. Naturally athletic and inclined, under Dreiser's influence, toward intellectual and political engagement, she possessed a strength and spirit that drew Le Corbusier to her. Through him she developed an interest in avant-garde art.

Le Corbusier entrusted a third group, often connected to the first two, with the reform of American culture and society. This was a special cadre of privileged Americans who embraced French culture, but in ways different from the women he knew. He identified it as a group of professional men in the arts. But why should associations with France be a prerequisite for cultural and spiritual reform in America? Le Corbusier took a conservative, hegemonic, and self-serving position that only an infusion of French culture, which he considered to be of a higher order, could ensure the required renewal. Without any associations with France, a youthful America could "act" but not "know," possess physical strength but not spirituality. Immodestly referring to himself and Frenchmen of his generation, "we have reflected and have perhaps discovered the philosophy of things." Oblivious to any contradiction, he insisted that only the French were at once worldly and spiritual. "The spiritual strength of Frenchmen" and their "feeling for contemporary life" acquired through travel abroad made them leaders of modern art and culture. In *Cathedrals* he enumerated ways in which America had already benefited from its exposure to French culture: through publicly held collections of French art in Chicago (Seurat's *Grande Jatte* at the Art Institute); the "sparkling purity" of such "French art events" in Manhattan as the exhibitions at the galleries of Louis Carré and Pierre Matisse, as well as Léger's show at the Museum of Modern Art and Jacques Lipschitz's at the Brummer Gallery. Le Corbusier attended all these events. Without exposure to French culture, he presumptuously assumed, Americans would purchase "false Rembrandts."[114]

While in this country he witnessed one comprehensive model of renewal in which French culture was catalytic. Largely due to avant-garde activities at the Wadsworth Atheneum under the progressive direction of Chick Austin and James Thrall Soby (see figures 4.1, 4.2), both educated in French language and culture, Hartford became "a spiritual center."[115] Through the leadership of these cultured men, the museum offered exhibitions, performances, and screenings of avant-garde productions that synthesized American, African-American, and French culture, as well as the modern and the folk.

Assuming his antideterminist position, Le Corbusier maintained that the reform of American culture could be accomplished only by individuals, those like Austin and Soby. "The responsibility for fruitful action rests on a few shoulders" because the "inert bloc" of "American masses" remains "indifferent." Renewal in the New World would depend on the engagement of its elite and intelligentsia who have recognized France as the fountainhead of art, culture, reason, and the spirit. Like Austin and Soby, this educated elite comprised "Americans who are kept very well informed by men who have come to study among us, in Paris." Other French-speaking men he met, especially those in avant-garde circles, included Hitchcock, Sweeney, and George Howe. With an elite of such men and women, Le Corbusier announced, "America is full of a violent desire to learn."[116] However, his conclusions only underscored the weakness of an argument premised on the renewal of American civilization through the influence of an outside culture deemed superior, and the agent of a privileged corps of bilingual Americans who embraced all things French.

The Paradigm of the Middle Ages

This was not the only country in need of a spiritual tonic during the lean years of the 1930s. Ultimately even France required nourishment and rejuvenation. Notwithstanding his use of Paris as a model for New York City—an argument underscored by contradictions—Le Corbusier considered his adopted city a candidate for renewal. By 1932 Paris and its public officials had filled him with "despair" because they refused to undertake his audacious proposals for the city center. Instead, decentralist policies had promoted the development of low-income housing on the periphery of the city that Le Corbusier denounced as "cancerous." As a result, he demoted Paris to the rank of a "once admirable city . . . [with] nothing left inside it but the soul of an archeologist. No more power of command. No head. No powers of action. No genius."[117] To achieve renewal for French as well as American cities, Le Corbusier looked to the historical model of spiritualism: the

Middle Ages. *Quand les cathédrales étaient blanches* contains a fundamentally Calvinist message of morality in that model.

To Le Corbusier the Middle Ages formed a sympathetic analogy to the 1930s. The Great Peace was shattered by World War I; economic and social welfare declined after 1929. Like the Middle Ages, the culture of the 1930s constituted an ironic rite of passage, at once a beginning and a collapse, as the new order—the uncouth popular culture of America—threatened an entrenched old order and high art of Europe. Le Corbusier was drawn to the culture of the Middle Ages because he considered it collective and participatory.

He mythologized the Middle Ages in all its dimensions, but most notably its architecture and urbanism, which he deemed international, preacademic, and both conceived and executed through collective processes. Moreover, by overturning previous building traditions, medieval architecture achieved "exceedingly daring technique . . . which led to unexpected systems of forms." There "reason and poetry co-exist," moving architecture and civilization along uncharted paths. An "international style" developed that favored "the exchange of ideas and the transfer of culture," carrying "the passionate stream of spiritual delights: love of art, disinterestedness, joy of living in creating." When the cathedrals were white, that is when they were new, Le Corbusier believed, "people were direct and raw, frank." When the cathedrals were white, there was no Academy to govern builders; "spirit was alive," "participation was unanimous," and building was a collective enterprise. The new language of design "expressed a new society." "Cities were new" because "they were constructed all at once, in an orderly way, regular, geometric, in accordance with plans." But "the Cathedrals of our own time," he concluded, "have not yet been built."[118]

Those cathedrals, of course, would be his Cartesian skyscrapers and urbanism to support them. But why did he specify cathedrals, rather than other building types, and why did he associate them with renewal? On a superficial level the towers of New York had long been seen in the French and American press as accolades to business. The Woolworth Building (1911–1913) was widely known as the "Cathedral of Commerce."[119] But when Le Corbusier thought of steel and glass skyscrapers as cathedrals, he considered them spiritual. In doing so he invoked a cultural discourse of German origin. The cathedral was a collective building type. It crowned the medieval city, defined the focus of the community, and embodied its society. This discourse infused Le Corbusier's early writings on urbanism. When he evoked the spiritualism of the medieval cathedral for the modern steel and glass skyscrapers he envisioned in the New World, he recalled the expressionist ideas in both Bruno Taut's *Die Stadtkrone* (City Crown) of 1919 and Ludwig Mies van der Rohe's projects for glass towers in 1921.[120] A counterpart to the idealism of Mies van der Rohe's skyscraper projects, Taut's post–World War I vision of a new society would emerge from the ruins of a past civilization of the alienated and rootless, just as Le Corbusier's Radiant City would rise from the disorder and nomadic culture of New York.

Why did he use the Middle Ages as a paradigm? One answer is his quest to find our common origins as well as our identity as inheritors of Western culture. As Umberto Eco observed, "all the problems of the Western world emerged in the Middle Ages: Modern languages, merchant cities, capitalist economy . . . the rise of modern armies, of the modern concept of the national state . . . the struggle between the poor and the rich, the concept of heresy or ideological deviation. . . . the technological transformation of labor." The Middle Ages reflects ourselves and our origins. "Looking at the Middle Ages," according to Eco's post-Freudian interpretation, "means looking at our infancy . . . the same way that the psychoanalyst, to understand our present neuroses, makes a careful investigation of the primal scene."[121] So a return to the Middle Ages for Le Corbusier signified a return not only to the roots of modern Western culture but also to first principles. The Middle Ages was the childhood of modernity as well as an alternative to classicism.

Another answer lies in Le Corbusier's return to the theories of John Ruskin and Eugène-Emmanuel Viollet-le-Duc that were so formative to his early education and thought.[122] Under Ruskin's influence he viewed nature and architecture as emblems of a spiritual and moral order. "Ruskin," he acknowledged, "has deeply moved our hearts."[123] Moreover, Ruskin's view of the Middle Ages was man-centered. His "Lamp of Life" celebrated the craftsman, building process, and social concerns.[124] After 1910 Le Corbusier abandoned Ruskin, but when he proposed a second machine age of harmony in the early 1930s, when he wanted to go back to first principles for the purpose of reforming the first machine age that had left Ruskin behind, it was to introduce into the new age of modernism design concepts based on morality, an integrated social order, respect for craft and process, and a spiritualism that were fundamentally Ruskinian. Moreover, his call for a return to the Middle Ages in the twentieth century was motivated by the same reason that had propelled Viollet-le-Duc's in the nineteenth century. Le Corbusier's objective to employ modern building techniques for the Cartesian skyscrapers of his Radiant City recalled Viollet-le-Duc's efforts to apply the principle of structural rationalism in Gothic architecture—that is, a reasoned approach to architecture as decorated construction—to new building.[125]

Still another response suggests that Le Corbusier's enchantment with the Middle Ages reflected modernist discourse. Henry-Russell Hitchcock, for example, maintained that the International Style was the first new style since the Gothic to emerge from a new type of construction. Advancing the mythology of a universal language, Hitchcock claimed that the International Style had crossed borders and found common ground.[126]

Where, then, would the new cathedrals of the twentieth century be built first? By 1935 Le Corbusier pinned his hopes on the United States. Like Europe in the Middle Ages, America in modern times had "daring technique," experimentation ("people who were not fossilized"), and models of collaboration and teamwork in production. If cathedrals were to appear there first, the country would have to acquire spiritual direction and be reborn. It was all a matter of "intention" or that which "touches the deepest recesses of our heart, the quality of the spirit brought to the creation of the work of art." Looking for signs of conviction and enthusiasm in America, Le Corbusier found them in the "reality" of such *grands travaux* as the Brooklyn Bridge because they were truly "American and not 'Beaux-Arts.'" He valued that reality because "it gives our boldest speculation the certainty of imminent birth."[127]

America in the mid-1930s, he warned readers of *Cathédrales,* was stalled at a critical juncture where "a fork has appeared on the road of architecture."[128] Unlike his compatriot Duhamel who was "irritated" and pessimistic about the new country, Le Corbusier broke from his own preconceptions to express hope and optimism.[129] This departure underscored the shift in his concerns from the ideological to the pragmatic. And he was most hopeful about New York City, which "is ready to begin over again [because] those people have courage!"[130] America may have been a country of timid people without "high ambitions," according to Tocqueville, but the behavior of New Yorkers and the promise of their city, Le Corbusier hoped, would be an exception. In fact, he originally had not intended to use *timides* in the title of *Cathédrales.* It was only when he was unable to secure a publisher for the American edition in the spring of 1936 that he made the change from the original title, *Quand les cathédrales étaient blanches: Premier voyage en U.S.A.* (When the Cathedrals Were White: First Trip to the U.S.A.).[131]

If groups of individuals were responsible for renewal, and if renewal could be accomplished only through an infusion of French culture, Le Corbusier knew he had to collaborate with American authorities in the public and private sectors. In a larger sense, of course, he envisioned collaborations between France and America as well as transatlantic joint ventures involving teamwork among architects, producers, and contractors. Indeed, this was his conclusion to the dilemma of the enchanted catastrophe. "Let's work together," he suggested. "Let's throw a bridge across the Atlantic. New York is the city nearest to Paris." Like the *Normandie,* "constructed on an American scale," he might also serve as "an ambassador of France in America" and bring about a "crescendo" of collaboration on future projects. In addition to his memos to Harrison and Rockefeller, the text of *Cathedrals* specifies the kinds of joint ventures in which he hoped to interest American authorities, both

during his visit and again on his return to France. "Some day I hope to collaborate in the planning of a tonic steamship," he announced. In addition, he proposed "communal enterprises [to] build housing" and Cartesian skyscrapers as well as to "reform the cellular system of cities."[132]

Why did he consider himself to be the man of the hour, America's designated French collaborator? Immodestly, he says in *Cathedrals,* "My life, by its active adventurousness and by the nature of my character and origins, allows me to get close to ideas brought into relation with the steadiness of the general human scheme, without the obstruction of a too marked regionalism. In the course of years, I have felt myself become more and more a man of everywhere with, nevertheless, one strong root: the Mediterranean, queen of forms under the play of light; I am dominated by the imperatives of harmony, beauty, plasticity . . . in my background . . . freedom in thinking normally conducted above the level of passing events."[133] Le Corbusier promoted the illusion that his Swiss heritage and acquired French citizenship allowed him to function as an architect and urbanist without borders—intellectual or regional—"a man from everywhere." He considered his own work, based on a Mediterranean aesthetic, to be truly universal. However, the idealism in that declaration was also deceptive because it was motivated more by self-promotion than by altruism.

To realize joint ventures, Le Corbusier proposed a bridge of collaboration with "well-informed" individuals. In fact, he even envisaged himself as *the* bridge. In a letter to Jean Labatut shortly before his departure he thanked his Princeton host and expressed to him his *désir très vif* to return to America. In an accompanying drawing the visitor depicted himself as a colossal *piéton de Princeton* (Princeton pedestrian) with derby, pipe, and glasses, one foot lunging forward to touch base with Paris and the Eiffel Tower, the other still anchored tenuously to the skyscrapers of the Manhattan skyline, objects of his ambivalent affection (figure 8.14).[134] The enchanted catastrophe of New York City continued to remain his "lever of hope." Notwithstanding the paradox in this conviction, he persisted in his feeling that "France and America could exchange a solid handshake

8.14
Le Corbusier drawing, *piéton de Princeton* (Princeton pedestrian), December 4, 1935. (Princeton University Library.) © 2001 Artists Rights Society (ARS), New York/ADAGP, Paris/FLC.

de revenir et de vous serrez à nouveau la main [to come back and once more shake your hand] / au revoir / Le Corbusier / 4 dec 1935 and do each other an infinite amount of good."[135] His preliminary drawing for the cover of *Cathédrales* (figure 8.15), executed early in 1936, confirms those intentions. He depicted himself as the knight rider positioned above the New York skyline and the George Washington Bridge. As with his earlier juxtapositions (see figures 5.8, 5.10), this assemblage brought together the medieval and the modern. The skyscrapers and bridge symbolized the raw power of New World technology, its possibilities for new construction, and his longing for joint ventures.

Le Corbusier's optimistic predictions for collaboration, however, were undermined by the polemical language and methods he employed to advance his ideas and ideals. In *Cathedrals* he cited Francis Delaisi's observation in *Les Contradictions du monde moderne* that "the world goes around badly and that in this century of certitudes we are submerged into incertitudes."[136] As seen in his evocation of America, based on both preconceptions and experience, he consistently employed polarities to shape his arguments. To promote the Radiant City at the expense of existing metropolises, he defined America's two largest cities in polar terms: the enchanted catastrophe of New York and the "splendor and horror" of Chicago. To advance his theory of centralization and demolition-based planning, he resorted to powerful images of disorder and decay. In lectures on the "Great Waste" he described the process of suburban commuting as "the mad movement of these millions of beings in the circle of their hell."[137] Thus his efforts to reject the past through eschatological imagery were calculated to promote a new urban vision and his own role as prophet.

Le Corbusier's approach to his art, favoring the intellectual and idealistic, has its origins in the autodidactic studies of his formative years. His notions of the necessary and inevitable destruction of the past to create the future was compatible with the central theme of Nietzsche's *Also sprach Zarathustra* (*Thus Spake Zarathustra*), the French edition (1908) of which greatly influenced him. Le Corbusier's view of himself as a messianic spiritual reformer, a prophet, and even a martyr sacrificing himself to noble ends (the spiritual regeneration of the modern world) was reinforced by selected

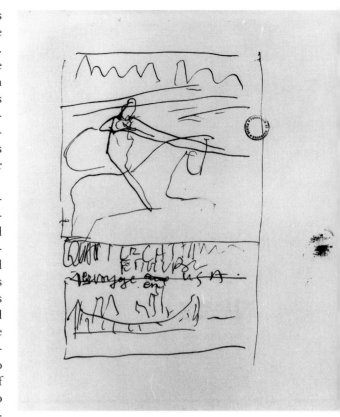

8.15
Le Corbusier, drawing for the cover of *Quand les cathédrales étaient blanches*, 1936. (FLC Archive B2(17)1.) © 2001 Artists Rights Society (ARS), New York/ADAGP, Paris/FLC.

readings from *Zarathustra*, Henry Provensal's *L'Art de demain*, Edouard Schuré's *Les Grands Initiés*, and Ernest Renan's *La Vie de Jésus*, as Paul Turner demonstrated.[138] His idea that heroic individuals, especially artists and intellectuals, were inevitably misunderstood was strongly rooted in Ruskinian thought.

For rhetorical effect the final cover of *Cathédrales*, a collage of images from the fifteenth and twentieth centuries, conveys the polemics of Le Corbusier's idealism (figure 8.16) as it employs the techniques of dada, Russian constructivist photomontage, and American

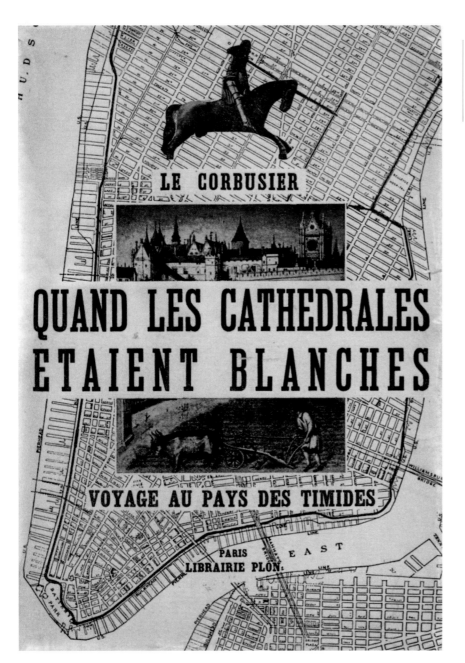

8.16
Cover, *Quand les cathédrales étaient blanches: Voyage au pays des timides* (Paris: Librairie Plon, 1937). © 2001 Artists Rights Society (ARS), New York/ADAGP, Paris/FLC.

advertising.[139] Two scenes are taken from the early fifteenth-century calendar of Pol de Limbourg's *Très riches heures* of Jean, Duc de Berry: above, an image of the walled and centralized city of medieval Paris with a "white" Sainte-Chapelle, is taken from the month of June (figure 8.17); below, a peasant scores the soil in orderly furrows with a plow, an image from the month of March (figure 8.18). The medieval scenes are superimposed on a 1922 plan of Manhattan, with elevated drives along its periphery to accommodate its ever-expanding automobile traffic (figure 8.19). This use of the Manhattan plan proposed by Nelson Lewis suggests several readings. Its expressways seem to represent the kind of advanced infrastructure that the Radiant City required. However, the drives allowed direct access to bridges linking the city to its suburbs, thereby promoting the decentralization that the Radiant City would correct.[140]

This assemblage of images offered two conceptual models. On one hand, Le Corbusier understood that such American cities as New York were based on a rational gridiron plan that he erroneously believed had been "established in colonial times." For this reason Manhattan was "a model of wisdom and greatness of vision." But to the visitor the model was flawed, for the country that had "established the skyscraper, set up cities thrusting into the sky, thrown highways across the country, built bridges over . . . rivers" still lacked spiritual intention.[141] Such a city might provide early precedents for reasoned planning and centralization, yet the demands of the automobile, coupled with decentralist policies and garden city planning, undermined them. On the other hand, the modern cities of France might lack rational gridiron plans but their medieval counterparts offered centralized planning as well as a culture infused with spiritual concerns. Thus Le Corbusier envisioned a new society based on two patterns of "colonialization": Manhattan would supply the empirical model for rational planning, and the centralized city of medieval Paris would serve as the model of a collectivized (and spiritual) French society where the functions of town and country were discrete. His collage, like his preliminary drawing, depicted himself as the white knight, now assigned to unite the two models. Like the crusader and

preacher Peter the Hermit, with whom he identified at the outset of his American campaign, he fought for a noble cause that brought spiritual rather than worldly rewards.

To Le Corbusier the period of the 1930s marked the beginning of "a new epoch . . . [in which] machine civilization breaks forth," similar to the medieval epoch seven centuries earlier when "a new world was being born, when the cathedrals were white."[142] This eschatological view of a civilization reborn reflects the millennialist beliefs common to Christian faiths and may be associated with his Calvinist heritage. If *Cathedrals* recorded "a journey to the country of timid people," its dedication to his mother, "woman of courage and faith," acknowledged her Calvinist teachings that helped shape his attitudes toward morality and social values.[143] In this instance Le Corbusier believed that spiritual regeneration could be achieved through an educated citizenry led by a centralized authority in charge of the public welfare. The superimposed image of the knight conveyed his aspirations. As medieval monks crossed Europe transmitting new ideas, so he would perform the role of a modern crusader carrying a message of spirituality and renewal, this time across America.

But his paradigm for the American city was not without its own paradox and mythology; for the medievalism that Le Corbusier saw as the salvation to the city was actually at the root of its current dysfunction. Like a medieval society dominated by clan allegiance and segregated neighborhoods, the modern city was subjected to fragmentation within its physical and social fabric, resulting in extremes of urban decline versus suburban prosperity. Le Corbusier's union of the Middle Ages and the modern ignored these contradictions. Instead, he idealized his notion of a new Middle Ages in America when he called for a social and cultural revolution in which the architect, like the monk or knight errant, would bring a reasoned assemblage of order out of disorder and bricolage. When he delivered his message to American architecture schools, he attempted to transfer his ideas directly to the next generation of individuals responsible for shaping its future cities. He intended *Cathédrales* as a spiritual reawakening. It was an urgent

8.17
Pol de Limbourg, June, *Très riches heures* of Jean, Duc de Berry (1413–1416), Musée Condé, Chantilly. (Giraudon.)

8.18
Pol de Limbourg, March, *Très riches heures* of Jean, Duc de Berry (1413–1416), Musée Condé, Chantilly. (Giraudon.)

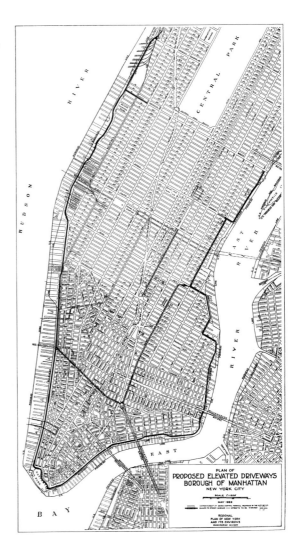

8.19
Nelson Lewis, plan of Manhattan, 1922. (Thomas Adams, *The Building of the City,* vol. 2 of *Regional Plan of New York and Its Environs* [New York: Regional Plan of New York and Its Environs, 1931], p. 300; private collection.)

call for France to reassert its hegemony and for America to overcome its timidity by adopting Radiant City principles. At the same time he cast *Cathédrales* as a modern morality tale of betrayal as well as one of hope and salvation that chronicled a partisan account of his transatlantic misunderstanding with America.

9

The American people may have been timid about endorsing Le Corbusier's vision, but they were not timid in their response to him. Reactions were mixed because the receptors were so varied. Students, the avant-garde, and intellectuals—the less entrenched sectors of American society and also those whom the Modern counted among its supporters—welcomed him and his ideas. By contrast, public and private authorities, the architectural establishment, the general public, and the press found his program controversial or altogether untenable and his behavior exasperating. In part their response reflected the broader consequences of the Depression: isolationism, pragmatism, and renewed nationalism. The bilateral difficulties in communication that Le Corbusier and many Americans experienced were questions of language and culture as much as of temperament, preconceptions, and expectations. During the 1930s these impediments, as well as an architectural and urban agenda out of sync with American practice, help to account for Le Corbusier's failure to find work in the United States. Together they were components of the misunderstanding between the man and the country that reverberated on its shores to the end of his career.

It is no surprise that Le Corbusier's most enthusiastic reception came from the institutions where he lectured, from architecture students, particularly at MIT and Princeton, and from Vassar women who recognized him as the intellectual leader of European modernism. If most professors at the American architecture schools he visited were cool or even hostile, as I. M. Pei reported was the case at MIT, that response backfired. His visit to MIT, for example, only made the students more resolute. But students were not yet enfranchised with authority.

During his American tour Le Corbusier assiduously pursued clients among the avant-garde, architects committed to modernism, the socially prominent, and businessmen. He seemed most compatible with and most understood by the elite group of collectors and supporters of modern art. The founder's circle of the Museum of Modern Art, including Barr, Soby, Hitchcock, Chick Austin, Joseph Brewer, as well as Kocher, Hudnut, Howe, and others, were openly receptive to the visitor, even if Philip Goodwin and Philip Johnson resisted Le Corbusier's aura. In Chicago the Arts Club and the Renaissance Society gathered their ranks in support of his visit. Le Corbusier's highest hopes for securing commissions came from both supporters of modernism and intellectuals, either directly or indirectly through their intervention and influence. In addition to the Modern's inner circle, potential clients in this group included

Richard Mandel, a client of Edward Durell Stone's who expressed interest in Le Corbusier's work, John and Elinor Nef in Chicago, and Joseph Brewer and Blanche Hull in Kalamazoo.[1] Yet their depleted or insufficient resources checked their enthusiasm to have Le Corbusier design single-family houses.

Encouraged by museum directors and other enthusiasts of modern art, the avant-garde sought to enlist the support of the elite and socially prominent. With the help of Madame Alma Clayburgh, mother of the Vassar student, Le Corbusier attempted to cultivate the social group. In New York and Chicago he was courted by society figures, a group to which he responded with alternating charm and petulance. Editors at Condé Nast (*Vogue, Vanity Fair,* and *House and Garden*), as well as newspaper society editors in the locales he visited, pursued him vigorously. The Hearst publication *Town and Country* labeled him "Europe's Best Known Architect." Le Corbusier's lectures and other engagements were duly noted in the society pages of New York, Chicago, and Princeton papers. A number of wealthy New Yorkers entertained him, including Mrs. Charles I. Liebman, whom Edward Durell Stone and others had tried unsuccessfully to interest in commissioning Le Corbusier to design a house (see chapter 10). Apart from the enthusiasm of what the popular press called "lion-hunting socialites" at his lectures and social engagements, the "social group," whom the Modern had labeled "fickle," was indifferent to his message and his services.[2] For his part, Le Corbusier had limited success with American high society because he liked to mock its "moribund culture" by playing the outlaw and critic, as he did through his costume and demeanor at the Beaux-Arts ball. But high society was neither impressed with his mode of critique nor interested in giving him commissions.

Notwithstanding Nelson Rockefeller's position among the elite, he could not be considered squarely within the social group since his family distanced itself from its conspicuous trappings.[3] Rockefeller was most closely identified in Le Corbusier's mind as a member of a powerful industrialist family committed to philanthropy. Of all the businessmen he pursued, Rockefeller was the most receptive to Le Corbusier's ideas because he already supported modernism in art and architecture. He was also young and enthusiastic, but inexperienced and without access to capital. More significantly, when he was able to secure work for an architect of his choice, as seen in an earlier chapter, he selected Wallace Harrison who designed two houses for him before World War II.[4] Unlike the many industrialists whom Le Corbusier attempted to engage, Rockefeller did hear his call but was committed to Harrison.

Both the public sector and the public at large were wary of a foreign architect considered to be a theorist and intellectual. Although Adolf Berle and Rexford Tugwell, both former professors, had been brought into government as New Deal experts, signaling a brief alliance between the intellectual and the public sector at the federal level, their concerns gravitated toward the pragmatic rather than the visionary.[5] If they considered Le Corbusier's proposals it was for their value as ideas. At the local level, such authorities as Langdon Post and Harold Fowler were more typical of the general public who found what Le Corbusier offered to be especially suspect. Public perception identified the architect as an abstract thinker, an idealist, and an internationalist, as opposed to a pragmatist and nationalist. But as Richard Pells has shown, the intelligentsia had long recognized among average Americans what Harold Stearns called a "contempt for mere intellectual values."[6] Together with industrialists, the public and the popular press were among the most ideologically conservative. Following Alsop's lead in the *Herald Tribune,* the press cast him as a visionary at odds with practical American ways. *Time,* the right-wing Luce publication that championed Frank Lloyd Wright during the 1930s, summarized the view of middle America when it published a French studio photograph of Le Corbusier, captioning it "He supplied the philosophy, left practicality to others" (figure 9.1). However, the magazine did recognize the architect's importance in some camps. Notwithstanding his use of "great expanses of glass that . . . may occasionally turn his rooms into hothouses . . . flat roofs [that] may leak," and "plans [that] may be wasteful of space," this "philosopher and phrasemaker," *Time* acknowledged, "has had more effect than any living man on the development of

André Steiner

CHARLES-EDOUARD JEANNERET

*He supplied the philosophy, left practical-
ity to others.*

9.1
Photograph of Le Corbusier from
Time magazine. ("Corbusier-
ismus," *Time* 26 [November 4,
1935], p. 36; photograph by
André Steiner.)

modern architecture, and has become the patron saint of
a whole school of ardent practitioners who write tomes
on the subject of *Corbusierismus.*"[7]

American architects expressed considerable curiosity about their European colleague. Many professional
organizations, including local chapters of the AIA, sponsored his lectures and planned events in his honor. But
the national organization of the AIA ignored the visit.
The professional community was often perplexed by
Le Corbusier. Henry Saylor's encounter with the architect "whose name has been of such significance in the
modern movement" must have been typical. Saylor's Oc-

tober 24 entry in his "Editor's Diary" for the journal *Architecture* recorded that "Lawrence Kocher brought Le
Corbusier to the Architectural League for luncheon today, when I had the pleasure of meeting him. . . . Since
Le Corbusier knows little English and Lawrence Kocher
little French, their continued conversation together. . . .
provoked considerable discussion as to how they were
making themselves understood. . . . Tonight Le Corbusier . . . lectured in French at the Museum upon his theories of building and town planning. My own difficulty
in following his French was somewhat offset by his habit
of drawing on a great pad of paper at the rear of the platform, illustrating almost every thought. In this drawing
he uses a fistful of colored chalks, and by the time he has
covered one of the great sheets of paper behind him, the
pattern is interesting even if one does not know just
what it is all about."[8]

Within the architecture community the critical response to Le Corbusier was especially intense. During
the 1920s and early 1930s, as discussed, his theory and
design entered into larger debates between modernists
and traditionalists, between advocates of European modernism and supporters of a native technocratic movement, and between proponents of internationalism
versus nationalism within architectural discourse as well
as within the social and political climate. By 1935, however, these issues and contentions were commingled. For
the duration of his tour they enveloped the archpolemi-
cist along with two other debates: the first on the culture
of man in the postindustrial age, with Le Corbusier
caught in the crossfire of critical exchange between
Henry-Russell Hitchcock and social historian Lewis
Mumford; the second a controversy affecting political
factions within the profession, between the forces of capitalism and those of socialism and trade unionism. That
fall Le Corbusier's architecture engaged Hitchcock and
Mumford in a further episode in their continuing
contretemps.

The opposition between the two critics first surfaced in 1925 when Mumford cast Frank Lloyd Wright
and Le Corbusier as adversaries.[9] By 1935 Hitchcock had
assumed the role of Le Corbusier's principal champion
and apologist. The irony was that from 1928 Hitchcock

had also supported the work of Frank Lloyd Wright and even introduced it to the French.[10] *Time* described Hitchcock as Le Corbusier's "burning defender" in America.[11] In his essay for the catalogue of Le Corbusier's exhibition at the Modern, Hitchcock emphasized the architect's latest work, identifying his shift away from the centrality of the machine in the 1920s to the centrality of man, nature, and folk culture in the 1930s. Thus, because Le Corbusier's recent architecture had moved in another direction, it now differed from practitioners in both Europe and America who based their work on his earlier theory and design. When Hitchcock identified the evolution in Le Corbusier's architecture and urbanism, he also elucidated the doctrine of the Radiant City that affirmed human needs as well as poetic and spiritual sensibilities. The exhibition demonstrated to Hitchcock that the mature Le Corbusier had entered "the middle of the century not only undiminished in stature but actually more advanced in thought and achievement." Applauding the new direction and implied growth in Le Corbusier's recent work, Hitchcock recognized the significance of its "increasingly free use of curves," emphasis on "traditional materials," and response "to the influence of various natural settings," which demonstrated topographical, regional, and vernacular characteristics. Moreover, he understood Le Corbusier's concept of "joy" as "a spiritual matter" based on material, psychological, and biological well-being. At the same time Hitchcock admitted that the architect's executed works were not "in an everyday sense, always practical." His recognition of the new elements in Le Corbusier's work of the 1930s indicated his ability to transcend narrow formal and stylistic analysis, as he had also done in his examination of American urban issues within other critical domains, which only a few years before had dominated his and Johnson's suppositions about the International Style.[12]

Mumford's criticism of Le Corbusier's exhibition at the Modern stands in sharp contrast. Ironically, the social historian used formalist analysis to counter Hitchcock's support for Le Corbusier's recent work. Writing in his *New Yorker* column "The Sky Line," Mumford acknowledged a shift in Le Corbusier's architecture and urbanism. Unlike Hitchcock, he did not attribute it to a new humanism, but to Le Corbusier's attempt "more and more pathetically to escape the weaknesses of his early rationalism and mechanization." Mumford branded the architect's recent departure from the "rigorous restrictions of his formula" as merely "frivolous." For example, he regarded the barrel-vaulted roof and stone walls of the Weekend House (see figure 2.6) as "curious stylistic atavisms," recalling New England carriage houses of the 1840s. Though Mumford could admit that Le Corbusier's "influence as a polemical writer has been challenging and healthy," his architecture waffled between "formula" and "sheer caprice." In the end, Mumford, who could not yet come to terms with the evolution of Le Corbusier's work toward man and nature, left his readers with the dismissal, "I prefer his bleakest rationalism to his 'poetry,' even though the latter acknowledges belatedly the excellent principle that good building seeks not only efficiency but joy." A testament to the limitations of his critical lexicon based on nationalism, relentless antagonism, and a stale polemic reconstituted from *Sticks and Stones,* Mumford found no cause to assign any significance to that "principle" in Le Corbusier's recent architecture because it was already present in the work of Richardson, Sullivan, Gill, and Wright.[13] In mocking the new directions in Le Corbusier's work and depreciating them as mere mannerisms, Mumford denied the architect's growth intellectually, politically, socially, and artistically.

This critical exchange about Le Corbusier's work is significant because it not only identifies a pervasive American response but also provides a rare instance of Mumford's direct engagement with Hitchcock. There was more irony in Mumford's criticism; his "Sky Line" essay conveniently omitted a discussion of Le Corbusier's urbanism, even though he was impressed by the model of Nemours, Algeria (1934), that was featured in the exhibition. In a letter of 1937 to Le Corbusier, written in rusty French, Mumford spoke of his admiration for the plan, "the best, I think, that anyone has produced for contemporary urban design." In his *Culture of Cities* (1938) Mumford illustrated the Nemours plan, endorsing its "combination of concentration social and openness [sic] which is one of the marks of the new urban order."[14]

Le Corbusier's call for a "housing program on a national scale" fueled a second debate that opposed capitalism to socialism and trade unionism within the profession. Because Le Corbusier directed his new *appel aux industriels* to American industry, the political left was suspect. Due to his recent political activities with regional syndicalism and the group associated with *Plans,* Le Corbusier had railed against the effects of American capitalism. His quarrel was not against its theory of production, but against its mindless consumption. There was irony in the fact that his theory of design concepts of the 1920s, like those of Gropius, had been labeled "Bolshevized" by the conservative press.[15] In *La Ville radieuse,* for example, he proclaimed an end to the capitalist-dominated first machine age, denouncing it as "a savage era of civilization—that of money, money, money!"[16] Many of the collective principles in the Radiant City, including a single-class society, reorganization of land ownership to exclude single-family lots, and government support for housing, were attempts to counter capitalist forces. The Radiant City still required modern construction techniques, but only a collaboration between government authorities and manufacturers could achieve such a nationwide housing program. Le Corbusier's objectives, however, were too unresolved, and the production methods he intended too unspecified, to resonate in the American public sector. And even though industrial leaders found his conditions too radically proscripive, his appeal to them made him especially vulnerable to a backlash of criticism from socialists and trade unionists in the architecture community.

The most hostile response to these initiatives came from the Federation of Architects Engineers Chemists and Technicians (FAECT), an American trade unionist group founded in the early 1930s to "improve the economic status of the technical professionals and subprofessional employee in private industry, work relief or unemployed."[17] In his essay "Le Corbusier—Lost Pioneer" (figure 9.2), Gerald Price presented the FAECT rebuttal to the housing program that Le Corbusier proposed in both his "statement for the press" (see appendix

9.2
"Le Corbusier—Lost Pioneer."
(*Bulletin* 1 [January 1936], cover.
Avery Architectural and Fine Arts
Library, Columbia University in
the City of New York.)

C) and second Columbia lecture on November 19. "To the multitude of technical men in this country," Price wrote in the FAECT *Bulletin,* Le Corbusier "remains an enigma."[18] On the one hand, the Federation counted this "artist and thinker in terms of aesthetics" as a "profound student of architecture, form and structure." It endorsed his Weissenhof housing, presumably because it was an example of government-sponsored and technically advanced modern shelter.[19] In addition, FAECT appreciated those elements of Le Corbusier's present housing program that confirmed its own agenda. It considered the technocratic elements of the program "more native, more faithful to our industrial developments." Moreover, it deemed Le Corbusier's "scientific urbanism" with its "application of modern industrial technique and materials; new plans formulated on the basis of light, air, sun exposure, convenience and utility" to be "akin, in fact, to the *form follows function principle.*"[20] On the other hand, the Federation claimed that Le Corbusier's social planning was misguided. Like Mumford and others, Federation leaders failed to acknowledge the new direction in Le Corbusier's architecture and urbanism. Ironically, Gerald Price used Le Corbusier's rhetoric of the previous decade to support the FAECT position: "building . . . is at the root of our social unrest of today: Architecture or Revolution."[21] By the early 1930s Le Corbusier had distanced himself from purely technocratic solutions toward political activism and changes in the social system, but still relied on the production-based assumptions of capitalism. The Federation acknowledged the contradiction that Le Corbusier recognized in his call for the collaboration of authorities in industry and government to implement new plans, and his own admission that those "plans may be unrealized because the laws of society, institutions and authority oppose them."[22] It dismissed Le Corbusier's plan as an effort to promote manufactured housing while ignoring the larger social concerns of employment, health insurance, and recreational and cultural programs.

On another tack, contributors to FAECT had reason to dissociate the organization from Le Corbusier on purely ideological grounds. When Percival Goodman, leftist architect and professor at Columbia, first asked Le Corbusier to reply to a "questionnaire" intended for the FAECT *Bulletin* (published in *Cathédrales*), he regarded him as a fellow supporter.[23] Goodman, who considered himself a "communist, parlor pink," recalled that he directed his questions "to get out of him that he was a communist." From Le Corbusier's response, however, Goodman found him to be "proto-fascist," one who "believed in a strong man up at the top."[24] Moreover, Le Corbusier's demand to be compensated for his response, which Goodman claimed would compromise the organization's nonprofit status, may also have contributed to FAECT's resistance to his ideas for American cities.[25]

In its review of Le Corbusier's article, "What Is America's Problem?," editors of the FAECT *Bulletin* focused their attack. They did support his concept of "a city of towers set in park lands" that would effectively end suburbanization and promote centralization. "Stacking citizens in vertical piles instead of buttering them over the landscape is good land economy." But FAECT rejected Le Corbusier's proposal for Manhattan because it failed to address viable social planning. Instead, the Federation favored Clarence Perry's "workable theories for vast city blocks, each block comprising an organic neighborhood."[26] In its criticism of Le Corbusier's plan of Manhattan FAECT also revived the debate between pragmatism and idealism, which Fuller, Henry Wright, and the *Shelter* group had championed earlier in the decade. Strong partisans of pragmatism, FAECT's editors took issue with the visionary nature of the Parisian architect's proposal. Notwithstanding "the fact that it was beautifully said and drawn," the editors concluded, Le Corbusier's "sketchy ideal" for New York, like his earlier schemes for Paris, Moscow, and Geneva, was merely "old stuff" that turned "dreams" into "nightmares." Federation supporters also rejected the proposal because it had appeared in *American Architect,* an organ of the reactionary Hearst publishing empire, and saw irony in the publisher's endorsement. "Willie Hearst, having made profits out of keeping his Manhattan lands in speculative disorder, having made profits by luring populations to disordered suburbs, is now exploiting a quaint technical personality who proposes *Order!*"[27] In the end, the FAECT quarrel with Le Corbusier's program served principally to promote its own economic and social agenda favoring trade union activism to ensure government intervention. Its reaction also signaled a more diffuse opposition from socialists and the left in America, particularly the Communist party, to fascism. Fascism had already destabilized Europe and caused a collapse of international order.[28] Paradoxically, in 1935 FAECT considered the communitarian and socialist aspects of the Radiant City as totalitarian. But when Percival Goodman reflected on Le Corbusier's subsequent involvement in France's Vichy government, he concluded, "I was later found to be right."[29]

Aside from resistance within the profession, bilateral impediments kept the large commissions he sought and so urgently needed to sustain his large atelier just beyond his reach. External factors—economic and political as well as ideological and cultural—accounted for the fundamental discord between Americans and Le Corbusier. Internal factors associated with his personality and behavior held some clients at bay.

External factors conspired against Le Corbusier. Politically and culturally the United States during the 1930s charted a deeply entrenched path toward nationalism and isolationism, first as a response to the idealism of World War I and second as a consequence of the Depression. This affected not only foreign policy but also cultural relations between the United States and Europe. The 1930s marked a new nationalism in which the country sought to define its own culture. Untainted by European intervention, the United States would serve as its own model.[30] American authorities were as resistant to Le Corbusier as they were to William Lescaze because of their general proscriptions against foreigners. But they were particularly wary of Le Corbusier because he was cast as an intellectual and his solutions were considered aesthetic and idealistic. In general, Americans resisted an intellectual offering mere ideas and visionary schemes, as opposed to an architect with practical solutions.

Economic considerations affecting the building industry also frustrated Le Corbusier's opportunities in the United States. Hitchcock remembered that the year 1935 was "a very bad moment to come here. Although the worst of the Depression was over, the building block did not end until 1938."[31] Le Corbusier traveled to America to promote his Radiant City and its Cartesian skyscrapers at a time when the future of tall buildings was in question. New construction was halted and the recently completed Empire State Building, then the world's tallest skyscraper, was only half rented. Even Nelson Rockefeller resorted to unorthodox promotional schemes at Rockefeller Center to secure tenants. Many architects and critics mistrusted skyscrapers. Mumford vehemently opposed them, primarily on social grounds. In *The Brown Decades* (1931) he called attention to the inherent "defects of the tall building . . . the shutting out of sunlight and air, and the intensification of congestion on the streets and in the subways." Moreover, he contended, "Socially, the skyscraper gave encouragement to all our characteristic American weaknesses: our love of abstract magnitude, our interest in land-gambling, our desire for conspicuous waste."[32]

American building and planning practice was ideologically opposed to much of Le Corbusier's theory and design. Even though most of the requisite components of the Radiant City were in place—visionary schemes, demolition-based planning, disregard for the configuration of existing streets, housing blocks, and modern construction techniques—his social policy was not consonant with American political conditions or the views of housing administrators. Jan Reiner, a member of Le Corbusier's atelier from 1932 to 1935 who later practiced architecture in the United States, suggested that the communitarian components of the Radiant City accounted for its failure.[33] Moreover, most American critics and journalists still cast Le Corbusier as the intellectual leader of the International Style whose work continued to promote the symbolism and idealism of machine age forms. Like Mumford, they failed to recognize the shift within Le Corbusier's theory and design toward regionalism and vernacular concerns. In retrospect, no one recognized this more than the architect himself. In his introduction to *Cathedrals,* written in 1946, he recounted how, when he was invited to America a decade earlier by the Museum of Modern Art, "I was considered the man of 'the machine for living.'" But Le Corbusier's largely unrecognized position of the 1930s explains only part of the "misunderstanding" that he himself acknowledged.[34]

There was a more fundamental ideological opposition to the Radiant City by those who defined the nation's path to recovery through agrarian values. For Frank Lloyd Wright, Henry Ford, and others, land symbolized stability and rootedness, the common man and democratization. America's response to Le Corbusier's urbanism, therefore, touched on its ambivalent, even hostile, attitude toward the city. During the early part of the century the city offered economic opportunity and the fruits of popular culture, but by 1930 it had failed in its promise. By contrast, the country and the suburb offered the simple virtues of agrarian life (or the illusion of it) as well as rugged individualism and self-determination. Further support for this position came from the top with Franklin Delano Roosevelt subscribing to the nostalgia of this popular conception; the Hyde Park of his childhood remained his enduring model.[35]

Le Corbusier's radical and comprehensive plans for American cities called for a change in public policy toward centralization at the very moment in which there was a renewed commitment to increasing decentralization at both local and national levels. His proposals urging Americans to reverse their addiction to suburbanization and commuting occurred during an upswing in consumer confidence in the fall of 1935 when new car sales reached a post–Wall Street crash high (see chapter 5) and the automobile industry had its first evidence of a strong rebound. As a result, Le Corbusier's centralized planning was perceived as unrealistic and his efforts untimely.

At the national level, politics under the Roosevelt administration moved toward a new period of federal centralization. But centralization in America was different from centralization in Europe. When Germany or Italy centralized in the 1930s it did so with dictators. When the United States centralized, it federalized in a manner that distributed monies to the states. America would be as unlikely to look to Europe (and Europeans) for models of political centralization as it would be to look there for models of urban centralization. Moreover, New Deal planning efforts were not comprehensive. Although technocrats of the 1930s sought to achieve order in city and regional planning, notwithstanding the work

of the National Planning Board, these efforts involved only "piecemeal experimentation." Mumford, a vocal critic of New Deal planning, denounced it as "aimless experiment, sporadic patchwork, total indifference to guiding principles or definite goals."[36] In effect, central planning was deemed un-American. "Most Americans," wrote conservative journalist George E. Sokolsky, "regard the intellectual planner as a strange creature . . . There is something Russian or Italian [or Swiss] about him that will not fit Toledo, Ohio . . ."[37]

In addition to external factors, Le Corbusier's personality and behavior were often impediments to working with clients and authorities. In social situations with French-speaking Americans, he could be charming and engaging. His persona as hero and prophet served him well in his relations with some American women. Marguerite Harris cast him in romantic, even idolized, roles of artist and poet. In the intimacy of their friendship he found himself most appreciated, his mission in America most fully validated.

But in his professional relations, almost exclusively with men, Le Corbusier's guise of hero and prophet seemed exotic, anomalous, and excessive. On a practical level he spoke very little English and had difficulty communicating with American colleagues. He had to rely on young and inexperienced intermediaries, especially Robert Jacobs and Henry Sipos, to interpret his ideas. Even his most ardent supporters were confounded by his attitude and behavior. To Henry-Russell Hitchcock, who was frequently in his company that fall, "Le Corbusier was very hard-boiled and particularly abrasive toward Americans."[38] Philip Johnson, who met Le Corbusier with Hitchcock in Paris in 1930, later wrote, "I never found him a sympathetic person to be with. His pathological bitterness, his self-isolation from his own world of art and architecture, his downright rudeness kept him from the position of personal leadership he might have had." Hitchcock concurred with Johnson's assessment, adding, "Europeans may doubt that this expresses, outside France, a general attitude towards Le Corbusier, but it understates the American reaction."[39] Professionally, Le Corbusier expected his colleagues abroad to pay homage, but only Princeton's Jean Labatut, students, and a few young architects indulged him. Hitchcock put the issue of commissions rather bluntly: "The chances of this rather disagreeable man, scornful of America, getting any work was very slight."[40]

Unlike Joseph Brewer and other potential private clients, the corporate executives and public officials Le Corbusier encountered were servants of complex and entrenched bureaucracies. They relied on teamwork with developers. Max Abramovitz attributed Le Corbusier's lack of success in these circles not only to his "brashness" and "aggressiveness" but also to his difficulty in "breaking through bureaucracy right here." Even when executives from Union Carbide, U.S. Steel, and General Motors or government leaders were interested in his design work, according to Abramovitz, "they didn't know how they could sell it to their superiors, or to the party."[41]

Even Wallace Harrison and George Howe, to whom Le Corbusier expressed an interest in collaborating in 1935, must have been wary of his methods. Teamwork and partnership in design, management, and construction was the American way but not necessarily Le Corbusier's. Abramovitz came to understand this in 1946 during the planning stages of the United Nations. He felt obliged to remind this European member of the site committee that in an American democracy architects respect consensus planning. Le Corbusier responded, perhaps playfully and certainly dismissively, "ah, you *démocratie* people. Only I'm *dictateur*."[42]

Thus his brand of individualism was bound to fail in a country that valued teamwork and consensus. Unfortunately, his quest to implement the Radiant City and its housing program diverted him from seeking more aggressively clients who were able to commission "an office building or rental property or some elegantly beautiful country house" that would have met his minimal expectations.

From his perspective one episode symbolized best the transatlantic misunderstanding between himself and America: his bitter relations with the Museum of Modern Art. The events that followed the completion of his arduous itinerary of lectures and the remainder of his visit in New York City form a compelling narrative. On

December 2, Thomas Dabney Mabry, the Modern's executive director, informed Le Corbusier by letter that according to the terms of their agreement, "our responsibility in connection with this tour ends with your return to Paris upon the date originally set by you, i.e., as near the first of December as possible." Mabry stated that the Modern would pay his expenses through the end of November and purchase his steamship passage home. He also reviewed the Modern's understanding of their financial agreement that entitled it to offset the tour expenses with the architect's lecture fees. From its perspective the Modern had not "invited" Le Corbusier to give a lecture tour, but it had agreed to sponsor the tour and stand ready to assume any deficit. Thus Mabry informed Le Corbusier, "we were very glad indeed to be able to make possible your first visit to this country by arranging this series of lectures to defray the expenses of your trip." Because the Modern's preliminary account showed a small surplus, however, Mabry told Le Corbusier somewhat patronizingly that the museum would turn it over to him "as an acknowledgment, inadequate though it may be, of your generous cooperation on this tour."[43]

But this was not Le Corbusier's understanding of their agreement. He believed that the Modern had invited him and that he was entitled therefore to receive the lecture receipts free of expenses. Indeed, Carl Schniewind had led Le Corbusier to that assumption during the early stages of negotiations the previous spring by telling him, "you have been invited by the Museum of Modern Art of New York."[44] On December 10, Le Corbusier had a contentious final meeting with Philip Goodwin to review the account, which the visitor disputed. After an adjustment, the museum informed him that lecture receipts of $1,775 would be offset by expenses of $1,226.95, leaving a balance of $548.05.[45] The Modern had assumed a large number of additional expenses itself (publicity, general overhead, exhibition, and lectures), totaling $1,789.32.[46] With Mabry and Goodwin standing behind the account, the architect appealed to the Modern's director Alfred Barr. Unfortunately, the tone and sometimes the language in Le Corbusier's letter to Barr was acerbic. "In the land of dollars," he explained, "accounting is a strict science, precise, indisputable . . . I am the happy beneficiary of very benevolent intentions." Le Corbusier also related to Barr how Goodwin had stipulated "with mathematical precision 'that it was necessary for me to know that the U.S.A. never paid dollars for ideas or for the arts, in contrast to South American gentlemen who know how to appreciate the joys of the spirit.'" He insisted that he was only a "worker . . . obliged to earn his living." But what was particularly galling to him was that the Modern, which he considered to be an instrument of, if not synonymous with, the Rockefeller Foundation, had not done right by him and met the standard he expected of it. "I note with curiosity," he needled Barr sarcastically, "that the Museum of Modern Art, Rockefeller foundation . . . paid the extremely modest fee of $50 for my lecture which was held in front of New York high society. Kalamazoo paid $100. *Vive Kalamazoo!* Buenos Aires paid me $400 per lecture for a series of ten—$4,000 and all expenses paid from Paris to Paris and in luxury hotels."[47] Thereafter he took every opportunity to broadcast the injustice. He was even purported to have appeared at a dinner party "waving a dollar bill," sneering, "This is what the Rockefeller Foundation paid me for my lecture tour."[48] In the final accounting Le Corbusier received the sum of $683.53.[49]

With marching orders from the Modern, Le Corbusier had no other choice than to book passage for his return to France; he would leave on December 14. He spent his final two weeks in New York searching unsuccessfully for work, pursuing potential clients who might provide the basis for his return. His good-byes to Marguerite Harris were sweet, but his last exchanges with Mabry, Goodwin, and Barr were acrimonious. Le Corbusier concluded his visit in a state of dejection. At the moment of his departure aboard the *Lafayette,* now occupying a humble cabin instead of a luxury stateroom, Robert Jacobs recalled, "Stamo [Papadaki] and I were the only two to see him off."[50]

Le Corbusier wanted to leave well, but his pride was at stake. He felt the conflict common to outsiders between the need to earn his living, in his case to sustain the Paris atelier, and his equally valid need for self-expression. He wanted to garner commissions, but they eluded him. Instead, he confided to Léger that he returned home from America with "empty pockets" only to find a "deplorable situation in the apartment house at 24 rue Nungesser" that required a large expenditure. "Paris seems to me like a village," he told Léger who was still living in New York, "life here is bleak. Louis Carré suffocates here."[51] And to Carl Schniewind he described the "calm and stagnation in Paris," urging his friend at the Brooklyn Museum to "keep watch over the question of a *musée en spirale* with the director."[52]

Le Corbusier closed the year by pressing once more his case to Goodwin in an effort to secure all his lecture fees. Going over old ground and attempting to bolster his case, he even sent Goodwin excerpts from his correspondence with Schniewind during the spring of 1935. At the same time he tried to set a conciliatory tone because he did not wish their differences over the account to obscure his "American horizon." He told Goodwin of his intention to "return one time to America to see a good season [for honoraria and commissions] and truly to make a trip that would not be a source of heavy fatigue."[53]

But Goodwin held fast to the Modern's position. He was a New Englander, patrician by birth and serious by temperament (see figure 1.14). Le Corbusier described him as a "true transatlantic gentleman."[54] As one family member suggested, he "would not have anything to do with people he didn't like."[55] He countered Le Corbusier's overtures, spelling out the terms of their agreement and politely but firmly refusing to alter the account. Having brokered the original agreement with Schniewind, he was not prepared to concede much ground. In a manner Le Corbusier interpreted as cruel and somewhat cynical, Goodwin emphasized how "extremely correct the Museum has been." Quoting excerpts from Le Corbusier's correspondence with Schniewind the previous spring, Goodwin reminded the visitor that he himself had agreed that "for me the essential thing is to see the U.S.A., being paid for the out-of-pocket expenses of the trip and to leave large honoraria for another occasion."[56]

What emerged from the correspondence between Le Corbusier and Goodwin during the winter and spring of

1936 were unfortunate consequences resulting from differences over money and other issues, which degenerated into a dialogue about cultural stereotyping. Goodwin blamed Le Corbusier's "false impression of North America" for his misinterpretation of the Modern's agreement with him. "Foreigners . . . have been blinded by the money reputation that the country has got" and uninformed about "our methods of doing and living." Moreover, "our actually democratic methods have almost ignored official welcomes to distinguished foreigners." But he expressed the hope that Le Corbusier would return to the United States to enjoy "something more than its mechanical and flashy aspects."[57] It was at this time that Goodwin notified Nelson Rockefeller, who in turn wrote to Le Corbusier, that the Modern would not publish an American edition of *La Ville radieuse*. When Le Corbusier received the news, he exploded in a letter to Léger, "Sacré Goodwin!" Revealing to his friend a degree of self-knowledge about his own delusions, he confided, "my dealings with Goodwin and the Museum remained exactly as they were in New York . . . it is perhaps fair since I had no formal agreement, but in the end it leaves me rather perplexed. The second time I will not be had by them."[58]

In a reply to Goodwin Le Corbusier revisited the account, raising new questions while insisting that he could not dismiss his claim with a "generous gesture" because of his real financial needs. "I am not rich, I am even poor, because all that I earn is employed in the disinterested studies that I make. For me, small sums are large sums. A 'cent' for you is a dollar for me." In pressing his case he tapped the deeper source of their misunderstanding. He reminded Goodwin of their last "friendly" conversation when Goodwin said to him on the eve of his departure, "In short, you believe that we were somewhat petty." Then Le Corbusier recalled for Goodwin, "And I answered you, 'Bravo, you have put your finger on the issue.' I would like you to appreciate why I did not have the very generous gesture of the man completely detached from questions of money."[59]

Le Corbusier thought the Modern especially mean since he considered it an organ of the Rockefeller Foundation, which functioned as a charity to assuage the "guilt" of machine age American capitalism. He wanted to have it both ways. He thought he was entitled to benefit from the patronage of "hazardous Puritanism." He also wanted to continue to criticize Americans for their materialism and to subject them to cultural stereotyping: men were cowboys, women Amazons. He used tropes and clichés associated with *américanisme* to deflate the culture of a youthful but impotent country, together with its architects and builders, to promote the mature, wise and "spiritual" culture of Europe and, by extension, his own leadership. In contrast, reports of Le Corbusier, especially the *Herald Tribune* description attributed to Joseph Alsop, illustrated the tendency of Americans to stereotype the architect as the exotic intellectual whose culture and ideas were inherently foreign. By such xenophobic standards, Le Corbusier was suspect.

Like Alsop and others, Goodwin resorted to cultural stereotyping in a misguided and portentous effort to explain his side of the dispute, even though he considered his overtures conciliatory. "The real basic difference between ourselves, and also your point of view and the Museum's with regard to the lecture tour, boils down to one of race." "Good common-sense," he stated flatly, "seems petty to you, and the reaching out for glory does not appeal to me." He concluded, "It is the difference between Latin and Anglo-Saxon, which I hardly believed in, but which seems to have existed strongly in this case."[60] Le Corbusier answered him in kind.

None of Goodwin's pretense to mend transatlantic fences, however, affected his, and by extension the Modern's, decision not to publish an American edition of *La Ville radieuse* or to provide further sponsorship. Le Corbusier felt compelled to have the last word. As he did in his quarrel with Barnes, he used *Cathédrales* to hurl a parting shot. In effect, his chapter "Orgueil" ("Pride"), written in the spring of 1936 after their most heated exchange of cultural stereotyping, served as a response to Goodwin. He refused to accept the American's account of their differences. Instead, he asserted that neither "common sense" nor "glory" was the exclusive domain of Anglo-Saxons and Latins, respectively. The two were not mutually exclusive. Using the same stereotypes, Le Corbusier built his case for the supremacy of Latins who could rapidly achieve "order" out of confusion through "good old common sense," as opposed to Anglo-Saxons whose actions were slow and uncertain because decisions were made on a "battlefield" where "Time is Money." And to counter Goodwin's argument about Latin glory, Le Corbusier instructed him that the United States was especially preoccupied with glory and publicity because its system of capitalism made them necessary. He concluded that in both countries "glory and good common sense are Siamese twins."[61] He could match Yankee pride with Gallic pride, but the exchange did not win him favors in Goodwin's camp. The tendency to stereotype individuals by culture, race, or ethnicity, so prevalent in the 1930s, ultimately reflected the darker side of each man's character.

In spite of his difficulties with Goodwin, Le Corbusier persisted in his efforts to gain the Modern's eventual support by pressing William Lescaze to intervene with the institution and by encouraging Hitchcock to have a word with Nelson Rockefeller.[62] But by the fall of 1937 Le Corbusier found new reason to continue his dispute with the museum: compensation for or return of the architectural models he had lent for his solo exhibition.[63] To settle the issue of the three maquettes—the Palace of the Soviets (see figure 3.15), which Goodwin especially prized, the Rentenanstalt Insurance Company Building in Zurich, and the project for the town of Nemours, Algeria—he sought the help of Barr and the intervention of Albert Frey, Wallace Harrison and wife Ellen, Stamo Papadaki, and Léger.[64] During the summer of 1938 he saw Barr in Paris and later reported the conversation to Harrison. Le Corbusier suggested to Barr that instead of returning the maquettes, it would be "simpler" for the Modern to purchase them, especially the Palace of the Soviets, which is "certainly a work of modern architecture which can remain in the annals of architecture if the components are conserved." But Barr maintained that the Modern was without funds. Le Corbusier asked Harrison to persuade Rockefeller to purchase the Palace of the Soviets model for the Modern at a cost of $2,000.[65] In an attempt to bring the matter to closure in 1940, he enlisted the commercial consul at the French Embassy in New York, who wrote to Barr. John McAndrew, newly appointed curator of the Department of Architecture, responded on Barr's behalf requesting that the consul inform Le Corbusier that because he "never requested the return of his three architectural models, they are still in our store-rooms." Barr offered either to return them to the architect or to sell them for him.[66] Barr may possibly have been stonewalling or even bluffing, since he, Philip Johnson, and others associated with the Modern particularly valued architectural models and Barr was well aware of the Parisian's limited resources during that period.[67] Le Corbusier subsequently sold the maquettes to the Modern for $600 but later complained to Johnson that he was inadequately compensated for them because the transaction had occurred during "the worst moment of German occupation and of the resulting misery for him because his architecture," he claimed, "was banned by the Germans."[68] Thus, long after he received a modest compensation for the models, he continued to be resentful about the transaction. He preferred to believe that the Modern retained unlawfully what was still his property.

The Goodwin affair served as an object lesson to enrich the larger moral message that Le Corbusier promoted in *Cathédrales*. That account of his travels in America was composed in the language of a medieval morality tale. It was a matter of simple ethics: good versus evil. Le Corbusier believed that he had come to the United States not because his atelier was in need of work, not because of the rejection of his projects for the 1937 Exposition Internationale in Paris, not even to learn from America, although he learned much in spite of himself. He believed that he had come to *save* America— as well as France and other countries threatened by the culture of American capitalism—from the present ill-fated course of its architecture and urbanism. His morality tale was inevitably intertwined with Nietzschean mythology. On the one hand, his deeds were those of the knight errant wandering in search of adventures (and commissions), especially those that would redress past wrongs and demonstrate his acumen. On the other hand, his actions were calculated to promote the myth of the superhero whose martyrdom was contingent on the kind of failure he experienced with Goodwin and, more ambivalently, with Rockefeller.

His struggle was primal because he believed that he was looking back to first principles at the same time that he pursued millennialist objectives associated with Calvinism. He told his tale in an Edenic language of saved versus damned, order versus disorder, collapse and destruction. In 1935 American architecture and urbanism, Le Corbusier believed, was poised at a perilous juncture. Without intervention, they were doomed. Rebirth was possible, but the path to it was mined by impediments personified by Goodwin and Barnes. Only a redeemer, a Christ-like figure could ensure the salvation, rebirth, and metamorphosis of the New World. America was experiencing, if it had not already experienced, a collapse of its culture at the same time that it was ready to begin again. Here, as elsewhere, Le Corbusier used eschatological predictions and catastrophe theory for the explicit purpose of advancing his own work. New York City, he predicted, was already poised to undergo the third phase of its metamorphosis (see figure 5.32). Tomorrow would bring his "program of great public works, on the scale of modern times."[69] In the opening pages of *Cathedrals* he recalled his first machine age trope, "A great epoch has begun. A new epoch." At the end of the book he was compelled to refine his idea: "A new age has begun. A new Middle Age."[70] These aphorisms remain important rhetorical devices, securing like bookends the idealism as well as the polemic of his narrative.

Although complex, the book does not obscure an explicit moral message. At the same time that he assumed the roles of knight errant and martyr to a cause he deemed spiritual, Le Corbusier attempted to form a new secular order, a modern "guild" of New Deal technocrats and industrial leaders dedicated to his objectives. But his efforts to forge such an alliance were unsuccessful and, in Nietzschean terms, destined to be ill-fated.

Interpreted as a morality tale, *Cathédrales* allows us to understand Le Corbusier's agenda as well as his experiences in America. But because its text is an "open work," this interpretation must stand as only one of many possible meanings.[71] In a most elemental way, Le Corbusier's view of American culture and society was divided into good and evil. Schniewind, Hitchcock, and

Huston, Marguerite Harris, the young Alma Clayburgh, and her mother Madame Clayburgh, all symbolized the "good" men and women of America largely because they sympathized with and supported him. But there were hostile forces in the culture. Goodwin was capable of uncharitable acts, Barnes of malevolence; Rockefeller was victimized by inherited wealth.

Although Le Corbusier used most of these men and women as characters through which to develop the episodic narrative of his plot, the last three men were especially significant. In keeping with the medievalism of his theme, Le Corbusier shaped character sketches of them in the form of three parables. The first parable engaged Goodwin as the principal antagonist of his chapter "Pride." In Goodwin's match between Latins and Anglo-Saxons, Le Corbusier was defeated by home rules but emerged morally triumphant. The second parable identified Barnes as the malicious antagonist of his narrative "Mr. C. Albert Barnes de Philadelphie." In the story of his dispute over access to Barnes's art collection, Le Corbusier cast himself as the martyred hero. If Goodwin's sin was pride, Barnes's was a false sense of possession and self.[72]

The third parable concerned Nelson Rockefeller. There his character was more sympathetic, but Le Corbusier still felt some degree of ambivalence and conflict about him. In fact, the parable was not solely about Nelson Rockefeller, but embraced the family dynasty and other American millionaires. Le Corbusier claimed that capitalism had entrapped the Rockefellers, and called them "victims of the unlimited piles of gold which they have heaped up in the vicious circle of their own bank accounts." It was "cruel and false" to say that the object of their social philanthropy was "to dissimulate their crimes." And even though John D. Rockefeller, Sr., engaged in "the battle of gold," he was not the "criminal" that he was in the public eye.[73] Given his own self-interest, Le Corbusier found it expedient to regard the Rockefellers as victims, rather than profiteers, of capitalism. Nelson Rockefeller had youth, energy, and enthusiasm as well as a position of wealth and a history of good works. He had already shown acts of altruism and social benefit. As with Goodwin and Barnes, he was dedicated to the cause of modernism. Le Corbusier saw them as promising attributes for a potential client and patron, yet he was candid enough to be wary of the "psychology" of a man whose access to power shaped his persona.[74] This parable cast Nelson Rockefeller as his most promising future client even if he was flawed, like other Americans, by a lack of conviction that made him "timid" about giving Le Corbusier a commission. In reality, the young Rockefeller was not yet invested with sufficient power.

In effect, Le Corbusier's love-hate relationship toward America was symbolized best in his relations with Rockefeller. Together, Rockefeller and Harrison remained Le Corbusier's "lever of hope" because the Parisian counted on Rockefeller's patronage for collaborative projects with Harrison in America as well as support for projects in France, for books, and for CIAM. During the spring of 1936 he expressed to Rockefeller his impatience for an economic recovery in America so that he could return to New York for the "execution of a building" with Harrison.[75]

By his own mythology he interpreted his American tour as an experience that catapulted him into a series of encounters and events, misfortunes and reversals, with Goodwin, Barnes, and Rockefeller rejecting him. Out of this fatal plot Le Corbusier could emerge a tragic hero. Yet, notwithstanding his poignant and often severe critique of American culture and society, with frank appraisals about Barnes and Rockefeller that were excised from the American edition, Le Corbusier intended *Cathédrales* to convey a message of hope. Nearing the completion of his text during the spring of 1936, he affirmed to Rockefeller that "this book is optimistic."[76] If the trip did not result in fulfillment of his own personal ends, it also did not dampen his enthusiasm for the promise of America or his expectation to return.

Le Corbusier spent the last night of his visit with Marguerite Harris. In her "Portrait of Le Corbusier" she recalled that final week of the tour when "he had not had much time for his personal life." Instead, he was preoccupied with the mixed messages he received from his American hosts. "He had been almost bored by his success as a lecturer, but he was disillusioned to think that

he must leave without a serious order or commission in his pocket. . . . Violent reactions were still boiling in his head."[77] He recorded their conversation that last evening in New York in his essay, "I Am an American," written aboard the *Lafayette* and published in *Cathédrales*. "Come back to America, my friend," Marguerite beseeched him, "America is a great country." And it was to her that he spoke of his divided feelings about America, of "despair in the violence of the city," "optimism, in the enchanted splendor of the city."[78]

The drawing he made the next day aboard ship summarized in one image his bittersweet feelings for America and for the sensual woman he left behind (figure 9.3). Marguerite's profile stands tall against the skyline of Manhattan. Still on shore, she looks stoically toward the *Lafayette* already steaming through the harbor. This is an imaginary scene (she did not actually see him off) and she is both a person and a symbol. The skyline of New York is Le Corbusier's skyline as he envisioned its three transformations (from right to left): the skyscrapers of Wall Street depicting old New York of 1900; the setback tower skyscrapers of midtown in 1935; and the Cartesian skyscrapers of the Radiant City, an image of tomorrow. Le Corbusier poignantly positioned the silhouette of Marguerite between a setback tower, a Chrysler or Empire State building, and his own Cartesian towers, between the present and the future. She may also have symbolized to him another transatlantic beacon in the harbor, a modern Statue of Liberty. His message to her was simple, "au revoir, Amie!" (see you again, my friend!). In a farewell letter, which accompanied the drawing (on the back of Gotham Hotel letterhead), he told Marguerite, "my last gesture was for you." There Le Corbusier countered his tender sentiments toward her with his visceral response to America. Recalling the nature of their love, he confided to her,

> Everything was beautiful and good and clean, worthy and loving. Why shouldn't the heart have the right to love, there where things make it open up, discover itself, and receive a full measure of joy and benefit? . . . You are strong, right-minded, fair and good. You are loving and open. Not closed up.

au revoir, amie!

14 Dec
1935

9.3
Le Corbusier, drawing of Marguerite Tjader Harris against the skyline of Manhattan, December 14, 1935. (Collection Centre Canadien d'Architecture/Canadian Centre for Architecture, Montréal.) © 2001 Artists Rights Society (ARS), New York/ADAGP, Paris/FLC.

Around you are gathered many affections. . . . I can't imagine—because I can't imagine the unknown—what would have been my New York and my U.S.A. without you, without the sea, without your mother, without Toutou and Booby, without the cabin and without the colonial [sic] house, without the roadways of Connecticut and the red-haired amazon who drives. It would have been something, but what? Risqué adventures on Broadway, or some other escape along Park Avenue or wherever. You were the peasant woman of New York, Corbu's little Jeanne d'Arc fencing clumsily in the void. A support. The peasant woman, in opposition to the other of Chicago and who is the woman of the skyscrapers, courageous but fearful, reckless but irrational, another Jeanne d'Arc [in Chicago] without possible victory, because artifice leads to defeat, whereas health and goodness go toward the light. Blond sweet light . . . Let us imagine instead of the cold, the heat of summer, or the mildness of spring. The sea gentle, the water near at hand, and soon deep. Nights in the water and on the sand. Frolics. Honest joy and tender gestures. Tenderness! What a rare event, thing, word. Tenderness in the country of skyscrapers, so close to New York. The future does not belong to us. The years pass, will continue to pass. Poor old *Corbu,* so near the autumn of his life, and whose heart is that of a child.[79]

Marguerite could not resist a reply to his letter even though, she cautioned herself, "we do not much like words." With Le Corbusier's departure, winter had come. "*La baraque* shivers under the snow. The sea is crusted with large waves of ice. But there is nothing like the harsh winter to make one dream of spring, leisure, love." And true to her nature to salute the artist she adored, she closed with a lofty *hommage,* "Au revoir, Corbu, peintre, poète, rêveur en composition."[80] Le Corbusier, in return, valued Marguerite's appreciation of his transatlantic aspirations. In 1947 he would inscribe her copy of *When the Cathedrals Were White* "for Marguerite Tjader Harris the friend who understood, the first in the U.S.A., the interplay of strength and harmony which is

the law of life that brings together within this book, and across an ocean, two cultures that can aid one another."[81]

During the fall of 1935 Marguerite became Le Corbusier's American muse. That December he was obliged to leave her, their trysts at the shack and by the sea, and their exploits in town. Stoically he returned to Paris and to Yvonne, his other life. As Yvonne was his *gardienne du foyer* in Paris, so Marguerite was his "guardian of the hearth" in New York, poised to welcome him back.[82] She remained his earthy Amazon, fair Jeanne d'Arc, and radiant symbol of his future in America. She was the "woman of skyscrapers"—all health and goodness—in New York. Le Corbusier situated her "in opposition to the other of Chicago" whose "artifice leads to defeat," a possible allusion to the prostitute with whom he shared his last night in that city and to such deceptive "Gothic" skyscrapers as the Tribune Tower, the product of timid people.

Le Corbusier vowed to return and renew his campaign. "Everywhere there is an immense hope," he recorded in *Cathedrals.* "And at the same time, all the doors seem to be closing everywhere: defenses are thrown up because an attack is being made. Everywhere all the doors are opening."[83] Thus, returning home to Paris full of bitterness and yet fervent love and resolve, full of transatlantic understandings and misunderstandings, he confronted the mystique about America that the French people aboard ship had already accepted: "Once you have opened the door on America you cannot close it again."[84] And because he continued his liaison with Marguerite in encounters outside Paris during the years that followed, he too could not close that door.[85]

**Part IV
Epilogue**

While directed toward an interdisciplinary critique, this study examines Le Corbusier in America in the context of biography, transatlantic exchange, and cultural criticism as well as the various manifestations of *américanisme* associated with it. The investigation now turns to the impact of Le Corbusier's encounter with America on the evolution and diffusion of his architectural ideas after 1935. Le Corbusier's enunciations on America reached three receivers: himself, the French and other Europeans, and Americans. The architect was the author and sender of his message; the other receivers were the principal but not exclusive addressees.

From Le Corbusier's perspective, the meaning and significance of the trip hinged on two questions: did the trip fulfill his objectives? and to what extent did his experience of America influence his theory and design? As it turned out, the tour affected his own work as well as architecture in the United States, but had little immediate consequence in France beyond the work of his own atelier.

While planning the trip, Le Corbusier articulated three objectives: commissions, large lecture fees, and experience of the United States. With respect to commissions the tour might be considered a failure, if toward the end of his visit Le Corbusier had not held out hope for a return trip that would yield him important work. By the standard of large lecture fees, the trip was also a

failure but for his earlier concession that he was willing to forgo significant fees and be content with experiencing the country. With regard to the third objective, his visit was indeed compromised by his preconceptions and prejudices, by language difficulties, and by the obligations of an arduous itinerary. Moreover, when he did have free time he spent much of it searching for commissions rather than exploring other regions of the country.

Yet Le Corbusier did fulfill unstated objectives that made his visit both instructive and productive. His network of contacts and encounters with business and industrial leaders enabled him to study the American market, and he focused his energy on achieving practical results when his visionary goals met with indifference. Thus he learned about American manufacturing methods from his discussions with industrialists and from his investigations of the building industry. His research into structural systems and building products, especially steel and plastics, enabled him to employ these systems and products in his work.

A Second Machine Age

Quand les cathédrales étaient blanches: Voyage au pays des timides was Le Corbusier's most compelling rhetorical tool for the diffusion of his ideas. An unstated objective of his American trip forms the subtext of his book (elucidated more fully later in this chapter) and indicates a dramatic shift of focus in his internal development: the quest for a second machine age. At the Ford factory and in large cities Le Corbusier encountered the possibilities of unprecedented power, technology, and organization. But he also confronted the consequences of capitalism. The economic, political, social, and moral implications of that system on the leading industrial society of the 1930s confirmed his preconceptions. It allowed him to demythologize his theory of the first machine age in favor of a humanistic design strategy. From this new understanding of machine and man he forged an American synthesis, not without contradictions, that had important consequences in his work. This synthesis did not provide a fusion of preconception and experience; for Le Corbusier the two would always remain in tension. Rather, it was a synthesis of the technical and the biological, of substance as well as metaphor, that informed his case study of New York as the empirical model for the Radiant City.

By 1935 Le Corbusier had suggested the concept of a second machine age. But it was his experience of North America that supported his new appraisal, embracing the moral values of folk and popular culture without betraying his core of modernism.[1] Marguerite Harris made it possible for him to explore a more diverse arena of American culture. It was largely through his experiences with her that he arrived at his synthesis about "the country of timid people" and validated his destiny for creative work. Le Corbusier advocated a more humanistic approach to design as a result of his trip to South America in 1929. He shared with the Parisian avant-garde greater formal and aesthetic concerns for the folk and the modern at the same time that he intensified his political engagement with regional syndicalism. He may also have revised his views in response to the social criticism of the program he presented at the founding CIAM conference at La Sarraz in 1928. America confirmed his hypothesis, giving him the illusion that he could have it both ways. A second machine age would attempt to mediate between, but not resolve, the ambiguity inherent in the dichotomy between the extremes of machine versus man, industrial versus preindustrial civilization, the twentieth century versus the Middle Ages, a consumerist culture fed by capitalist pressures versus a folk culture with vernacular traditions and regional ideals, and the timely versus the timeless. His myth was based on John Ruskin and preindustrial concerns for nature and culture, joined with Viollet-le-Duc, Tony Garnier, Auguste Perret, and modernist assumptions about progress in technology. The response to American culture that reflected issues of *américanisme* confirmed that it was a model of both admiration and fear. Le Corbusier considered himself "the man of 'the machine for living,'" with America holding out the possibility for him to benefit from the machine age. He did not want to destroy the first machine age but rather to revisit it for the purpose of correcting its flaws. When he called for a second machine age, therefore, he did so with the intention of perfecting the first through an infusion of humanism that synthesized the technical and the poetic, regional concerns, and social needs. Notwithstanding the machine-man paradox, this millennialist reawakening might usher in a second coming and with it a mythical "era of harmony" and "basic pleasures." It also promised to provide Le Corbusier with the commissions his office so desperately needed. Yet he used the rhetoric of the second machine age to promote an idealism that Americans found untenable.

The CIAM Debate

To identify the American contributions to his theory of the second machine age, it is important to examine briefly his architectural and urbanistic objectives during the years preceding the 1935 tour. These objectives are articulated in his formulations for three CIAM congresses: CIAM I at La Sarraz (1928), CIAM III in Brussels (1930), and CIAM IV in Athens (1933). From the debate, polemics, and program offered by Le Corbusier, as Giorgio Ciucci cogently demonstrated, emerged four themes: a position against the academy, a proponent of authority and the power of the state, an advocate of mechanization to solve social problems, and a design strategy based on aesthetics and poetry. His agenda was often in conflict with those of other CIAM delegates, especially the Germans, but for the greater good of their cause and despite considerable internal dissension, the participants were committed to presenting a unified vision that, by the 1933 congress in Athens, contributed to the myth of the modern movement.[2]

When Le Corbusier arrived in New York he was still smarting from the recent rejection of his Bastion Kellermann housing project (1934–1935) for the 1937 Exposition "Arts et Techniques," on the grounds that it was "anti-French" and presumably not "academic." He was also still bitter about the rejection of his projects for the Palace of the League of Nations and the Palace of the Soviets. What especially rankled was that Beaux-Arts architects won those competitions. It was ironic and especially disillusioning to him that a socialist state preferred an idealized classicism associated with Western materialism when Boris Iofan's design won the Palace of the Soviets competition.[3] Le Corbusier speaks of these rejections in the opening chapters of *Cathédrales*.[4] In the United States he was forced to encounter the dominant culture of the academy all over again: in the buildings of New York ("the Customs House . . . done in pure 'Beaux-Arts' strikes a disagreeable note"), in the "German Renaissance castles" of Chicago, in the schools of architecture he visited (at MIT "huge machines hung on the walls, wash drawings, representing palaces or mausoleums. Boring. Shameful"), and at the Waldorf "Quat'z Arts" ball.[5] In the face of Beaux-Arts authority and solid resistance to modernism, which he had not encountered in South America six years earlier, his experiences in North America gave him pause. Confronted with the realities of the most industrialized nation in the world, he used each encounter during the tour to reformulate his position and advance his methods, policies, and principles, unencumbered by the opposition he encountered at CIAM congresses.

The dominance of the academy in America only strengthened Le Corbusier's resolve to undermine it on both sides of the Atlantic. By 1935 he reasoned that if the ideology of the first machine age could not defeat the academy in the 1920s, a more elemental and more social message was required to defeat it in the 1930s.[6] He now turned to the paradigm of a preindustrial age before the academy. His models of the Middle Ages and those of primitivism and folk culture represented basic truths and human concerns that might overturn what the machine could not. By uniting the best of the first machine age with an infusion of folklore, Le Corbusier hoped to crush a moribund academy. His invocation of African-American culture, especially its music ("the melody of the soul joined with the rhythm of the machine . . . turned the page on the conservatories"[7]), as well as the "true" in American popular and folk culture signified that America had already achieved a synthesis of machine and man for the second machine age. In the new culture, as in the archaic culture of the Americas, Le Corbusier concluded that "modern consciousness finds here an eternal vigor."[8] The United States offered conclusive proof that its modern spirit could defeat the academy.

If his rhetoric against the academy in America replayed a schism within the CIAM congresses, so did his efforts to engage political power there. Once again, this imperative flowed from his defeats at Geneva and Moscow. Whereas many of his CIAM colleagues proposed structural changes through economic and legal means, Le Corbusier endorsed a direct relationship among architecture, urbanism, and the state in the belief that social reform would follow. Discussions at CIAM III sharpened the debate, with Gropius advocating zoning laws to regulate "low buildings, medium-high or high buildings" and Le Corbusier arguing for the architect to formulate proposals, fix housing specifications, and engage political authorities to implement them. In other words, Le Corbusier wanted to bypass building regulations and other laws of state. He allowed his designs to be unfettered by local restrictions, appealing directly to authorities in the public and private sectors to realize them in spite of their inevitable infractions. He had been vehemently opposed to New York City's zoning law of 1916 because, among other things, it mandated form. Hugh Ferriss's massing studies for the Manhattan skyscraper were flatly unacceptable to him because they were determined by provisions in the law rather than aesthetic considerations.[9] As a consequence of these "quite absurd zoning regulations," New York City promoted setback skyscrapers that Le Corbusier dismissed as "irrational from top to bottom."[10] Thus when he proposed his solution to Manhattan's enchanted catastrophe, he deliberately circumvented the 1916 ordinance.

It is important to consider the relationship of mechanization and standardization to Le Corbusier's theory and design. The French and German texts for the program at CIAM I, as Ciucci has argued, underscored different conceptions of the role of architecture in society. Unlike many of his German colleagues, Le Corbusier viewed architecture as independent of economic and legal structures. His advocacy of mechanization and social change was behind his program for CIAM I and his solution to "America's problem." Simply put, mechanization could solve social problems and result in economic benefits without legislation. Le Corbusier employed his five points to form an inexorable link between architecture and urbanism. The architect was in charge; he, rather than building laws or authorities, would initiate both program and plan. He emphasized the architect's autonomy in his response to Percival Goodman's questionnaire, intended for the FAECT *Bulletin,* but published in *Cathédrales.* Recalling the rhetoric of *La Ville radieuse,* he announced, "The Plan is dictator! Let each specialist establish plans which are in conformity with the new times."[11] Application of the five points to industry ensured production of standardized structural units that would still permit the flexible configuration of exterior elevations and interior spaces.

Le Corbusier's emphasis on formal architectural elements stood in sharp contrast to the program of German participants at CIAM I who advocated unlimited use of standardization to produce the most technologically expedient solutions.[12] Le Corbusier used his American tour and his engagements with industrialists as a platform for advancing his position in the CIAM debate about the role of the architect in the production process. Whereas the German position cast the architect as a technician captive to industrial production, Le Corbusier sought a more creative role for the architect as an autonomous consultant directing the production process. His reply to Goodman about the architect's role in the "science of

shelter" elucidated his position about standardization and its relationship to other design issues, including aesthetic and cultural ones: "The problem is to see what standard is in question and what may properly be standardized. That is research whose conclusions can lead housing and cities to their ruin through inhumanity and oppressive boredom, or can, on the contrary, bring grace, variety, suppleness, and the infinite manifestations of personality . . . those standards, from folklore, are the basic expression of what is necessary and sufficient."[13] It is easy to understand why the FAECT position, which was closer to that of the German delegates at the early CIAM congresses, was at odds with Le Corbusier's emphasis on formal elements and concerns that were external to technique. In this respect, Le Corbusier's experiences in America did little to change either his or the American position on standardization.

In addition to the importance of American culture in the issues that engaged Le Corbusier during this period—the academy, authority, mechanization, and standardization—the lecture tour allowed him to reaffirm in his work a position that favored aesthetics, poetry, and concerns of the spirit. Throughout his career that emphasis remained constant, as did his identification with Mediterranean forms. But even as aesthetics and poetry continued to dominate, their expression in his work evolved from the machine-centered forms of the 1920s to the human-centered forms of the 1930s. The more radical CIAM participants, especially the Germans, opposed aesthetic solutions in favor of structural changes in society largely based on economics and politics.[14] During the early CIAM congresses Le Corbusier advanced his five points as the basis of his design strategy. His program for urban transformations at CIAM I and his subsequent theses for the Radiant City (a Taylorized rational city) called for significant redirection of industry to produce autonomous structural units, following the specifications of the five points. At CIAM IV he emphasized the importance of "air, sound, light," themes from a questionnaire drawn up by CIAM III, as well as "irreducible truths" learned from his 1911 *voyage d'Orient,* all cast in a language of aesthetics and poetry.[15]

He continued to promote this agenda in his American lectures and in his case study of Manhattan. At the Museum of Modern Art lecture he affirmed that mechanization would not be a mere technological goal but a vehicle for achieving formal and aesthetic solutions. These, in turn, might address social problems. It was a selective kind of mechanization, in which the architect would provide not only the five points but also aesthetic and poetic answers to basic human concerns in architecture and urbanism. The theses he proposed for the Radiant City—the application of modern technique to city building, reorganization of the solar day, provisions for "essential joys" (human entitlement to space, sun, trees, a view)—could be adjusted to "climate, topography, customs and even cultural conditions." Art and poetry, rather than structural changes in economic, political, or social systems, would achieve "harmony" in a second machine age. "These theses are under the aegis of the word 'radieux'. . . . Radiant, joyous, happy, active, optimistic, and confident, these are our guides."[16]

Le Corbusier also assigned spiritual roles to both architecture and the architect that gained their authority in a hierarchy predating both the academy and the machine age. Although he expressed concerns of the spirit in his response to the questionnaire for CIAM III, they assumed new importance after one American tour.[17] In his reply to Goodman, Le Corbusier defined architecture at the level of metaphysics as "superior spiritual intervention." The architect now assumed a paradoxical identity, at once more spiritual and more worldly. Le Corbusier invested him with ancestral roots in a vernacular building tradition: "He is an architect like those who built the 'houses' of earlier days in which everything was present: the best techniques, the most efficient, desirable, fruitful, and economical dimensions and plans, in which wisdom was in control and expressed itself through *poetry*." The architect was also endowed with an identity as a "naturalist" (one who finds "the appropriate response to all truly human needs, needs on every social level") and "engineer" (one who has "a proper understanding of all the imperative though infinitely supple demands of industrial production"). In this formulation, the architect synthesized these attributes with those of the enlightened manager. Distinguished from all other technicians, only the architect was capable of "superior ordering."[18] The mythology of a second machine age was based on this program and these intentions.

As a result of divisions that were more apparent inside than outside CIAM, Le Corbusier must have considered it necessary to stay the course—alone. His trip to the United States, therefore, was a personal crusade to realize his own theses, rather than those that represented the wider spectrum of CIAM debate. His was also a personal myth about the promise of the modern movement: that the aesthetics and poetry of his theses had the capacity to renew industry and thereby transform the city. In America he came to appreciate the first mature and instinctual fusion of modernism and folklore in African-American music and dance, especially jazz. Together with other redemptive forces in the culture, this synthesis identified the new country, and more specifically New York City, as the promised site for the cathedrals of the second machine age. But the expectation that the production of urban housing based on Radiant City theses would bring about the "prodigious renewal of industry" in America was checked in the fall of 1935, as seen, by many factors including a coincidental resurgence of the automobile industry.

The Americanization of Le Corbusier's Architecture

Le Corbusier's experiences in the United States changed the course of his own design development. The new country would provide an empirical model and the first site for cathedrals of the twentieth century. His encounter with its culture confirmed his synthesis of machine and man. It is important, therefore, to examine briefly some of the largely unexplored roots of his architecture as it matured in the years after 1935, but with caution because, as Stanislaus von Moos determined, no "consistent formal development" defines either Le Corbusier's design method or his use of typology.[19]

After Le Corbusier returned to France his design work underwent an Americanization: the introduction of the textured skyscraper, which articulated its functions and reflected the plasticity, monumentality, and classicism in detailing and proportions he admired in America's early tall buildings; a new attitude toward the skyscraper as an integrated system, inspired by the RCA Building at Rockefeller Center and by Howe and Lescaze's PSFS Building; the introduction of tension structures directly influenced by New York's suspension bridges and the possibilities offered by American industrial products; and a new typology for the sports stadium influenced in part by American design and the response of American spectators.

Le Corbusier's trip occurred during a transitional period in his design development in which he had already shifted away from the machine-inspired volumes and taut surfaces of the 1920s toward more massive facades incorporating such regional and vernacular elements as stone walls and the *brise-soleil* (sun-breaker). But his encounter with the American skyscraper, as Peter Serenyi first suggested, was a defining experience.[20] The organic character of America's dense business districts made an enduring impression on him; they were like medieval cities, analogous to those Ruskin admired. Le Corbusier discovered that New York and Chicago were not cities of steel but of masonry with their skyscrapers "made of stone and not of glass." The architect marveled at the way in which "whole quarries have been fastened to their steel skeletons by means of cramps [sic], quarries suspended in empty space." His response was emotive. He was struck by the "grandeur and intensity" of the Wall Street towers that formed a sheer "cliff" with "canyons surging up, deep and violent fissures" resulting in "a very strong architectural sensation . . . calculated to inspire courage." Like Ruskin, the French impressionists, and even the German expressionists, he perceived the painterly effects of natural light on stone buildings. "The sunsets are very moving. The sunrises (I saw them) are admirable: in a violet fog or dull atmosphere the solar fanfare bursts forth like a salvo, raw and clean, on the surface of one tower, then another, then many others. An Alpine spectacle which lights up the vast horizon of the city. Rose crystals, rose stone."[21]

But it was not New York's most recent art deco skyscrapers—Empire State, Chrysler, and Irving Trust Company buildings—that appealed to him.[22] They were the "weak ones." Their facades appeared "flat and false." Moreover, their "plumes" seemed "irrational" because they were mandated by the 1916 zoning law rather than by aesthetic judgment. By contrast, buildings designed before the impact of the Exposition Internationale des Arts Décoratifs et Industriels Modernes (1925), when "Brunelleschi and Palladio were in control," Le Corbusier maintained, were the powerful and compelling ones. "In New York, then, I learn to appreciate the Italian Renaissance. It is so well done that you could believe it to be genuine. It even has a strange, new firmness which is not Italian but American! The maritime atmosphere and the potential of the American adventure have lifted the Tuscan graces to a new tone." In such early tall buildings as Trowbridge and Livingston's Bankers Trust Building at 16 Wall Street (1910–1912) he discovered a new classicism (figure 10.1). He admired the way in which "The oldest skyscrapers of Wall Street add the superimposed orders of Bramante all the way up to the top with a clearness in molding and proportion."[23] The Bankers Trust and other Wall Street skyscrapers conveyed the language and principles of academic classicism as they were understood in America. Like the tall buildings of George B. Post, Bruce Price, Adler and Sullivan, Daniel Burnham, and others, Wall Street's oldest skyscrapers were composed of well-proportioned and horizontally stacked elevations or "superimposed orders." Some employed tripartite divisions reflecting the column analogy of base, shaft, capital; but Le Corbusier was not invested in mere academic formulas.[24] He was interested in the way in which the facades were richly articulated with classical elements to establish proportions and demarcate the organization of functions within. Most of these buildings conveyed Beaux-Arts principles of composition, including the rational correspondence between elevation and plan so that exteriors might articulate legible volumes of interior space. Louis Sullivan's influential essay of 1896, "The Tall Office Building Artistically Considered," defined the divisions for the commercial skyscraper. Aside from the classicism of its tripartite divisions, a Sullivan skyscraper articulated its proportions and programmatic functions in a way that Le Corbusier would have found compelling: a ground

10.1
Trowbridge and Livingston,
Bankers Trust Building (the nearest
of the three skyscrapers shown),
16 Wall Street, 1910–1912.
(Library of Congress, Prints and
Photographs Division, U.S. Geo-
graphical file.)

floor devoted to stores, banks, and other enterprises re-
quiring abundant space and light; a middle section for
offices "piled tier upon tier . . . an office being similar to
a cell in a honey-comb"; and an attic story "purely physiological in its nature" for mechanical equipment.[25]
Thus, notwithstanding his criticism of American
Beaux-Arts architecture and his earlier efforts to denounce the "chaos" of Wall Street skyscrapers that symbolized the "mad speculation" of capital, Le Corbusier
came to endorse their visual language.[26]

Among New York's "Italian Renaissance" skyscrapers he found "a perfection strictly American." That perfection was also evident "in certain hotels," including the
Gotham on Fifth Avenue (1905) where he stayed after
his return from the Midwest, and "in numerous vast
apartments on Park Avenue," most notably the Ritz
Tower by Emery Roth with Carrère and Hastings (1925;
figure 10.2) where he attended Madame Clayburgh's
soirées. The forty-story Ritz Tower must have impressed
him. When completed it was the world's tallest residential structure.[27] He would also have valued its boldly articulated stone facade, adapted from sixteenth-century
Italian Renaissance design, and the expression of its duplex units and double-height living rooms on the upper
floors through a differentiated window treatment. But
he would not have condoned the "plume" of the Ritz
Tower's stepped-back profile.

Le Corbusier also came to appreciate the use of "cottage or private-house windows" in the RCA Building
and in Sullivan's skyscrapers in Chicago. For even
though he deemed this American "type of window" both
"anachronistic" and "annoying," it imparted human
scale to a monumental facade. Such "cottage windows"
also denoted anthropocentric functions within: "they
express the presence of a normal man, a man behind an
old-fashioned window."[28]

As a result of his visit to Chicago, Le Corbusier
found special inspiration in Sullivan's "strong and generously proportioned style," which was examined in
chapter 4. He was long familiar with the Owatonna
bank and other Sullivan works. In Adler and Sullivan's
commercial buildings, which he presumably visited in
the Loop, he recognized the character that John Ruskin

10.2
Emery Roth and Carrère and
Hastings, Ritz Tower, Park Avenue
and 57th Street, 1925. (Library
of Congress, Prints and Photographs Division, Irving Underhill
Collection.)

called the "Lamp of Power" or "governing" factor of architecture.[29] Sullivan's work conveyed a bold sense of
monumentality, a robust sculptural treatment of mass,
lively "organic" ornament in the tradition of H. H.
Richardson and classical proportions derived from
Beaux-Arts principles. Because of these design attributes Le Corbusier called Sullivan a "great architect and
true architect." Moreover, his preoccupation with what
Philip Johnson called the "third dimension, the shadow,
[that] was coming in in the 1930s" allowed him a fresh
appraisal of the commercial architecture of Sullivan and
his contemporaries.[30] Their plasticity or "firmness," as
discussed above, their well-proportioned facades and
classical detailing that revealed programmatic functions
("clearness in molding and proportion"), their sense of
scale in relation to man as well as to the city, influenced
Le Corbusier's subsequent work.

The most dramatic evidence of his shift toward plasticity is the project for the Admiralty Building for the
Quartier de la Marine in Algiers (1938–1942; figure
10.3).[31] This skyscraper marks the mature development
of the textured and emphatically proportioned facade
made possible by the use of the *brise-soleil* fully integrated into a reinforced concrete skeleton. Introduction
of the *brise-soleil,* a sixth "point," produced a weblike
honeycomb facade. It had actually appeared before his
American tour (e.g., projects for an apartment house in
Algiers of 1933 and for "petites maisons" in Oued
Ouchaïa in Algeria of 1933–1934), conceived as a response to southern climates and strong light. The *brise-
soleil* functioned as a modern counterpart to past regional
and vernacular building traditions.[32] But the Admiralty's new sense of scale and proportions, at once monumental and human, as well as its more classically
articulated facade, demarcating on the exterior the cell-
like offices of the interior, reflected the impact of his recent encounters with Beaux-Arts and Sullivan
skyscrapers, together with respect for selective elements
of American design.[33] The Admiralty Building, as
Serenyi suggested, may also have been influenced by the
principles of academic classicism in Albert Kahn's 1922
First National Bank Building (Fisher Building) in Detroit (figure 10.4), which Le Corbusier illustrated in

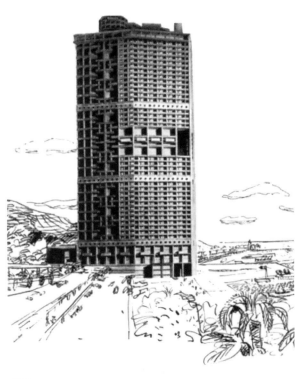

10.3
Le Corbusier, Admirality Building
for the Quartier de la Marine in
Algiers, 1938–1942. (*Oeuvre
complète 1938–1946*, p. 64. FLC
L3(1)5-82.) © 2001 Artists Rights
Society (ARS), New York/ADAGP,
Paris/FLC.

10.4
Albert Kahn, First National Bank
Building (Fisher Building), Detroit,
1922. (*L'Art décoratif d'aujour-
d'hui*, p. 83.)

L'Esprit Nouveau and later in a chapter on utilitarian design in *L'Art décoratif d'aujourd'hui*.[34] He must also have appreciated Kahn's treatment of the bank building's faceted facade whose attic story was boldly capped by a flat cornice molding. But if he saw the building during his visit to Detroit, he left no record. Similarly, he must have been impressed by D. H. Burnham and Co.'s flat-topped and equally "Renaissance" Fuller ("Flatiron") Building in New York City (1901–1903; figure 10.5), having received several postcards of it from Blaise Cendrars in 1926.[35] But in terms of its urban character the "Flatiron," like other American skyscrapers, was no tool of city planning and served only as an object lesson.[36] However, the common visual language of both the American Beaux-Arts skyscraper and the Admiralty later emerged in Le Corbusier's design of such works as the Unité d'Habitation in Marseilles (1947–1953) and the Secretariat at Chandigarh (1951–1958).[37]

A second path toward the Americanization of Le Corbusier's design development is suggested by his new attitude toward the skyscraper as an integrated system, much as he viewed the ocean liner. His project for the Admiralty Building in Algiers also marked a new direction in his conceptual approach that later informed his design for the Unité d'Habitation and, to a lesser extent, the Secretariat buildings at both the United Nations and Chandigarh. The structure, program, and systems of the Admiralty were fully integrated, uniting the functional-rational and biological models that he admired in Rockefeller Center's RCA Building (see figure 5.15) and Howe and Lescaze's PSFS structure. As if to belie his indebtedness to American building, Le Corbusier expressly disassociated his design for the Admiralty from that model: "The Skyscraper is no longer an accidental form as it is in America; it is a veritable biology in itself, containing determined organs in their precise ordering. An independent frame, the entire facade of glass, a 'sun-breaker' . . . a complete ordering of the vertical circulation, a system for the efficient distribution of pedestrian and automobile traffic at the foot of the sky-scraper; vehicular parking . . . the installation of a hotel and restaurant at the summit of the sky-scraper, with private access from the high point of the site."[38] Other than the *brise-*

10.5
D. H. Burnham and Co., Fuller ("Flatiron") Building, New York City, 1901–1903. (Library of Congress, Prints and Photographs Division.)

soleil, elements he identified in the Admiralty were those which he valued in the RCA Building and PSFS, the two most technologically and artistically advanced American skyscrapers. Notwithstanding the question of regulated setbacks, Le Corbusier admired the RCA Building's rigorous (and markedly Beaux-Arts) hierarchical ordering: "It is rational, logically conceived, biologically normal, harmonious in its four functional elements: halls for the entrance and division of crowds, grouped shafts for vertical circulation [elevators], corridors [internal streets], regular offices." As previously discussed, he appreciated the building's control or nerve center that monitored the mechanical systems ("the eye that sees everything, the brain that perceives everything"); the efficient vertical circulation made possible by an arrangement of banks of elevators, so perfectly orchestrated in the seventy-story slab that he concluded that they reached "a moving technical and plastic perfection."[39] His appreciation for these high-speed elevators and his projected meeting with Otis Corporation managers confirmed his intent to employ such reliable American technology.[40] Acoustically engineered "silent walls" with "'conditioned' air throughout" and electric-eye mechanisms for operating doors automatically, the RCA Building was his model for a "machine age temple."[41] It also had a complex network of corridors as well as separate ramps for pedestrians and vehicles, a subway connection, and vehicular parking, all of which all must have impressed him. Rockefeller Center, and to a lesser extent PSFS, provided the kind of spatial organization that he envisioned for the Admiralty project and later realized in the Marseilles Unité. At the RCA Building Le Corbusier observed "express elevators to the sixty-fifth floor where there are living rooms, a restaurant, a large club, a terrace," and at PSFS a well-defined social organization with shops on the ground floor, a banking hall reached by escalators, and an office tower reached by a separate entrance and banks of elevators. In both, the "quality of workmanship" impressed him.[42]

Moreover, Le Corbusier's solution to effective pedestrian and vehicular circulation at the base of the skyscrapers required elevated expressways modeled on the American parkway system. During his drives with Marguerite Harris he experienced at once the Pulaski Skyway and the distant towers of Manhattan. "The 'Skyway' rises up over the plain and leads to the 'skyscrapers.'"[43] Le Corbusier did recognize in the RCA Building the close relationship between form and function, between tower slabs made possible first by the clustering of office space around a central core of elevators and utilities, and second by the elevator core coordinated with setbacks so that, as William Jordy explained, it "becomes progressively thinner as the building rises and elevators serving the lower tiers are eliminated" (see figures 5.15, 5.17).[44] The RCA and PSFS buildings confirmed that the skyscraper, in conjunction with the elevated parkway, would enrich the conceptual model that Le Corbusier had used to shaped his Radiant City.

Introduction of bridgelike tension structures suggests a third development in his design work after 1935 and demonstrates his intention to apply his research on American technology to projects on both sides of the Atlantic. Excluding the wide range of bridge designs in the United States, he categorically declared in Cathedrals, "American bridges are of the suspension type."[45] His admiration for two of New York's suspension bridges, the George Washington and the Brooklyn (figures 10.6, 10.7, 10.8, plate 5), stimulated his interest in exploring the aesthetic as well as architectonic possibilities of such structures in his own architecture. He had actually produced his first "suspension" design for the Palace of the Soviets project (see figures 3.13, 3.14, 3.15); its structural system employed both a concrete parabolic arch and a series of metal girders fixed to metal rods that supported auditoria below. His design made reference to Eugène Freyssinet's bridge at Saint-Pierre du Vauvray (1923), which used both concrete arches and metal tie-rods.[46] American suspension bridges differed from concrete arch bridges because they employed thin cables suspended from tall stone or steel piers, thus inverting their parabolic arches.[47] To Le Corbusier the George Washington Bridge was no less than "a place of radiant grace" dominated by twin towers of riveted steel with wide approach ramps. Its profile was unforgettable (see figure 10.6). Merely drawing the bridge, an act that launched his first Columbia lecture (see figure 3.11,

10.6
Othmar Hermann Ammann,
George Washington Bridge,
spanning the Hudson River,
New York and New Jersey,
1926–1931. (Museum of the City
of New York, Print Archives.)

10.7
John A. Roebling and Washington
Roebling, Brooklyn Bridge, New
York, 1867–1883. (Library of
Congress, Prints and Photographs
Division.)

10.8
John A. Roebling and Washington
Roebling, Brooklyn Bridge, New
York, 1867–1883. (Milstein Divi-
sion of United States History, Local
History and Genealogy, The New
York Public Library; Astor, Lenox
and Tilden Foundations.)

plate 5), "cannot give you the inexpressible sensation of a work thus suspended between water and sky," but "through personal experience I knew that it is necessary to have seen [it]." The bridge engendered somatic as well as aesthetic and poetic responses. "When your car moves up the ramp the two towers rise so high that it brings you happiness," Le Corbusier waxed, "innumerable vertical cables, gleaming against the sky, are suspended from the magisterial curve which swings down and then up." The structure was an inspiring example of modern building technique because its concrete and steel piers were spared a stone facing originally intended for them. If the George Washington Bridge "smiles like a young athlete," the Brooklyn Bridge "is as strong and rugged as a gladiator." Together these bridges confirmed the virtues of America's "daring" spirit as well as a "conviction and enthusiasm" necessary to produce the new and, therefore, "white cathedrals" he hoped to build.[48]

Le Corbusier's research on American building products and components, especially those intended for industrially produced housing, encouraged him to expand his language of architecture after 1935. Through meetings with American manufacturers, including the American Bridge Company whose engineers had attended the Lexington Hotel meeting of journalists on November 20, he learned about the uses of these products, which suggested to him previously unexplored design possibilities. Moreover, his meetings with specialists in prefabricated housing, including Robert L. Davison of the Pierce Foundation and managers of Manufacturers Aircraft Association, General Motors, and U.S. Steel, helped inform him about production methods in which houses were assembled on site from factory-made parts.

The use of tension structures employing dry-assembly processes and building products based on American models found expression in Le Corbusier's work after 1935, principally in the Pavillon des Temps Nouveaux (with Pierre Jeanneret) for the 1937 Exposition Internationale "Arts et Techniques" in Paris (figure 10.9) and in other projects involving prefabricated components. Le Corbusier's early intentions for the exposition, as discussed in chapter 7, emerged two years earlier

when he asked Nelson Rockefeller to commission him to build a Museum of Contemporary Art for the Paris fair and to support the participation of American artists. He also proposed a demonstration of CCCC (Union Carbide) products at the fair's CIAM exhibit as well as Rockefeller Foundation support for a projected CIAM congress.[49]

Although this and other proposals, both to Rockefeller and to the counsel for the 1937 exposition, never panned out, Le Corbusier did realize his Pavillon des Temps Nouveaux (Project D).[50] Recent scholarship has credited Pierre Jeanneret with the design of the pavilion based in part on a suggestion by the exhibition's chief architect Jacques Gréber to replace fibrocement panels with canvas.[51] However, because many of its formal and conceptual elements appear to be "Americanized," it seems reasonable to suggest that Le Corbusier handed them to Jeanneret to refine and execute. The Temps Nouveaux pavilion is a large-scale tension structure that recalls the suspension bridges (see figures 10.6, 10.7) Le Corbusier admired in New York. If he applauded the George Washington as a frank demonstration of structure, he conceived the Temps Nouveaux pavilion on those terms. Like the bridge, his design operates on the principle that steel works as effectively in tension as in compression. Its colorful tent of red, white, and blue canvas with a roof of yellow canvas (allowing a diffuse natural light to enter) was supported entirely by steel open-truss pylons, resembling those he had seen at the Ford River Rouge plant (figure 10.11), as well as tension cables held in place by anchors and turnbuckles secured to concrete footings. The appearance in America of open-truss pylons, similar to those used in France, confirmed them as normative technology, a *standard*. Indeed, in his monograph on the pavilion, *Des canons, des munitions? Merci! Des logis . . . s.v.p. Pavillon des Temps Nouveaux,* he suggested that the form was adopted from the canvas circus tent.[52] But the structure was based on the American suspension bridge. Le Corbusier's description of the skeleton of the Temps Nouveaux pavilion "in all its purity: a spidery veil [*une toile d'araignée*]," recalled the constructivist imagery of his earlier evocation of the Brooklyn Bridge: "The vertical cables are black and not silver, but in perspective their vertical fall fixes a spidery

10.9
Le Corbusier and Pierre Jeanneret,
Pavillon des Temps Nouveaux,
entrance facade, Project D, 1937.
(*Oeuvre complète 1934–1938*,
p. 158. FLC L2(8)2-73.) © 2001
Artists Rights Society (ARS), New
York/ADAGP, Paris/FLC.

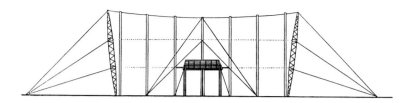

10.10
Le Corbusier and Pierre Jeanneret, Pavillon des Temps Nouveaux, *façade principale*, Project
D, 1937, line drawing. (*Oeuvre
complète 1934–1938*, p. 160
top. Plan FLC 647.) © 2001
Artists Rights Society (ARS),
New York/ADAGP, Paris/FLC.

10.11
Ford Motor Company River Rouge
Plant, near Detroit, c. 1932. (From
the Collections of Henry Ford
Museum & Greenfield Village.)

veil" (*une voilette arachnéenne;* see figure 10.8).[53] More precisely, the exhibition structure suggests the George
Washington Bridge as it appeared in Le Corbusier's lecture drawings (see figure 3.11; plate 5). The interior of
the pavilion contained a progression of ramps and land-
ings supported independently on a steel framework
(figure 10.12).[54] Although Le Corbusier had employed
ramps in his work before 1935 (thought to have been inspired by American buildings, parkways, and similar infrastructures), those that threaded through the pavilion's
exhibit spaces suggest his American experiences, especially the George Washington approach ramps. In *Cathedrals* he also expressed his admiration for the functional
and scenographic disposition of the ramps of Grand Central Terminal: "cars come up carefully planned ramps to
the ground level for departures; they go down to the
basement for arrivals. The traveler will go everywhere
without stairs."[55] At Rockefeller Center Le Corbusier
also saw an extensive matrix of underground ramps that
directed pedestrians from the RCA to adjacent buildings
and vehicles to subbasement-level facilities.[56] Reflecting
the increasing Americanization of his work, the Temps
Nouveaux pavilion joined a tension structure with a
complex circulation system. In that way it anticipated
the postwar development of such tension structures.
Conceived as a pilot project for a "museum of popular
education" devoted to urbanism, its exhibits recalled the
platform of educational and professional reform of Le
Corbusier's American tour.[57]

Moreover, the Temps Nouveaux pavilion devolved
from the earlier project for a *musée sans façades* that Le
Corbusier proposed to Nelson Rockefeller. It was constructed under the aegis of CIAM-FRANCE with the
collaboration of CIAM groups from other countries. It
employed dry-assembly processes and building products
including cables, anchors, and turnbuckles (figure
10.13), similar to those offered by such American sup-
pliers as CCCC and U.S. Steel, which Le Corbusier
specified in his earlier proposal to Rockefeller and also in
a memorandum to Union Carbide executives James Rafferty and George W. Davison.[58] The Temps Nouveaux
pavilion is significant, therefore, because it provides

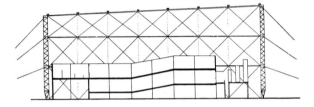

10.12
Le Corbusier and Pierre Jean-
neret, Pavillon des Temps Nou-
veaux, steel structure and ramps,
Project D, 1937. (*Oeuvre
complète 1934–1938,* p. 161.
Plan FLC 783.) © 2001 Artists
Rights Society (ARS), New
York/ADAGP, Paris/FLC.

both an assemblage of design elements and an alliance of the arts as an instrument for educational reform.

Similar analogies might be suggested for a number of later designs employing tension structures. A second pavilion project, originally intended for a "Saison de l'Eau" or water exhibition intended for a site on the banks of the Meuse River in Liège, Belgium (1938–1939), took the form of a bridgelike structure with steel lenticular trusses. It was proposed as a Pavillon Français for the Golden Gate International Exposition in San Francisco of 1939 (figure 10.14). The formal elements of the pavilion's Americanized structure were also appropriate for a fair held in celebration of three new bridges linking the Bay area.[59] Used in both tension and compression, the pavilion's trussed steel frame emulated the structure of an airplane wing. Because its load is carried at the center of each structure, the pavilion has been linked typologically to "the roof as an umbrella." Moreover, it seems to respond to constructivist tendencies. The San Francisco project shares similarities with Le Corbusier's portable Nestlé pavilion of 1928 for a commercial fair in Paris. The architect boldly predicted that its innovative form, modeled after the bridge and the

10.13
Le Corbusier and Pierre Jeanneret, Pavillon des Temps Nouveaux, anchor, cables, and turnbuckles, Project D, 1937. (Le Corbusier, *Des canons, des munitions? Merci! Des logis . . . s.v.p.,* p. 18.) © 2001 Artists Rights Society (ARS), New York/ADAGP, Paris/FLC.

10.14
Le Corbusier, "Pavillon Français, San Francisco 1939 ou Liège 1939." (*Oeuvre complète 1934–1938,* p. 173.) © 2001 Artists Rights Society (ARS), New York/ADAGP, Paris/FLC.

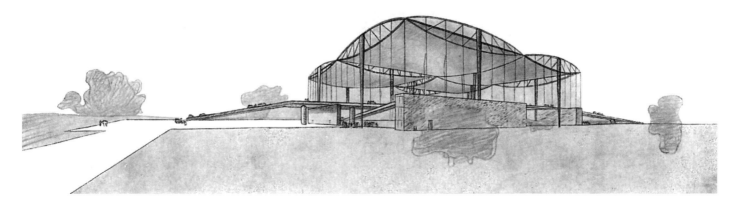

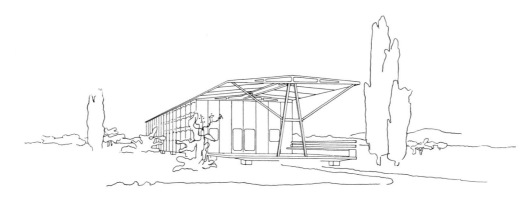

10.15

Le Corbusier with Jean Prouvé, "portable schools for the refugees from the first part of the 1939–40 war." (*Oeuvre complète 1938–1946,* p. 100. Plan FLC 18066.) © 2001 Artists Rights Society (ARS), New York/ADAGP, Paris/FLC.

airplane, would take its place among "the grand tradition of nineteenth century world's fairs."[60] Scholars have suggested that the Pavillon Français is an important project because it "anticipated post-war developments in its welded steel construction."[61]

Le Corbusier's late work suggests further references to his American experiences. His Philips Pavilion for the 1958 Exposition Universelle in Brussels, for example, employs a curvilinear tension structure of tubular steel and cables. There the architect incorporated an "Electronic Poem," a sound and light show synthesizing "color, imagery, music, words and rhythm." This production as well as the use of neon signage recall Le Corbusier's scenographic experiences on Broadway ("that incandescent path cutting diagonally across Manhattan") and in such popular spectacles as the Hippodrome production of *Jumbo.*[62] In Heidi Weber's Maison de l'Homme in Zurich (1961–1965; completed posthumously in

1967), Le Corbusier also employed a tension structure for a pavilion devoted to a synthesis of the arts.[63]

At the beginning of World War II he collaborated with Jean Prouvé, a builder from Nancy, in designing "portable schools for refugees." The prototype they developed in 1939–1940 called for dry-assembly modular units, each of which had a trussed structure with folded sheet steel and timber panels (figure 10.15).[64] Encouraged by such American methods of dry assembly, Le Corbusier might have extended his research, as he attempted to do in his transatlantic tour, to persuade European airplane and automobile manufacturers to produce these mobile units.

A fourth path toward Americanization is suggested by Le Corbusier's introduction of a new typology, as Stanislaus von Moos proposed, for the sports stadium in the form of a bowl. When attending a football game at Princeton, Le Corbusier was impressed by both the con-

10.16
Henry J. Hardenbergh, Palmer
Stadium, aerial view, Princeton
University, 1914. (Princeton
University Library.)

10.17
Le Corbusier, Project for a National Sports Center for 100,000
Spectators, preliminary study,
1936–1937. (Le Corbusier, *Des
canons, des munitions? Merci!
Des logis . . . s.v.p.*, p. 98. Plan
FLC 21140.) © 2001 Artists
Rights Society (ARS), New
York/ADAGP, Paris/FLC.

crete structure of Palmer Stadium (1914; figure 10.16) and the enthusiasm of the crowds. During the 1930s American college athletics dominated major sports and attracted large numbers of spectators. Participation in such sports as football reflected a growing movement toward a more broadly expressed culture of commitment.[65] Le Corbusier observed, "The whole country takes part in it with an unimaginable fervor. Sixty thousand, a hundred thousand spectators participate at these remarkable jousts, in which everything is conducted with propriety, style, enthusiasm, in gigantic concrete bowls, uncluttered and clean."[66]

More than the formal character of their design, his experience of such university stadiums as the majestic one at Princeton informed his project for a national sports center for Paris (1936–1937).[67] At a time when mass rallies were being held in Berlin, Rome, and Moscow, the projected stadium for Paris would have pro-

vided a spectacular new arena for sports, speeches, theater, gymnastics, music, and dance. The design called for a vast concrete shell with a seating capacity of 100,000 approached by an extensive system of ramps reminiscent of American bridge infrastructure. On the one hand, his project for the Palace of the Soviets had employed ramps, large amphitheaters, and other programmatic elements to serve mass audiences.[68] Moreover, in collaboration with Pierre Jeanneret, José Luis Sert, and the GATEPAC group, Le Corbusier had planned a stadium for the Macià master plan for the Casa Bloc development in Barcelona (1931–1932; see figure 5.29).[69] On the other hand, his response to American stadiums suggests that he was inspired by them. His early study for the stadium project in Paris (figure 10.17) indicates an awning suspended by cables from two masts (but later changed to a single mast), another striking evocation of the American suspension bridge (see figure 3.11, plate 5).[70]

The French Response to *Cathédrales*

Among European readers, the French were intended as the principal audience for Le Corbusier's cultural criticism of America largely because of the publication of *Cathédrales* by Plon in January 1937.[71] Ever the polemicist, Le Corbusier criticized the French for lacking authority and failing to adopt his proposals. Returning from America he found Paris "bleak." As a rhetorical device to persuade the French to renew, he shamed them with talk of a people who "cultivate dust and filth"; he appealed to their intellect; he spoke of French hegemony and "Cartesian reason"; he flattered and beguiled them with discussions about a nation possessed of "spiritual strength," a people who have "reflected" and acquired "wisdom," and whose culture possessed "the spirit of tradition and feeling for contemporary life." Yet in spite of its virtues France had no central authority, "no genius." Only a new leader could shed the entrenched old order of the academy. And, in a reversal, only an infusion of American culture with its "daring technique," experimentation, and teamwork could achieve the kind of renewal that cities experienced in the Middle Ages. With France and America exchanging "a solid handshake," bridges of collaboration would benefit both countries. By adopting Radiant City principles during the lean years of the Depression, he assured his readers that France could reassert its supreme judgment and its hegemony, while America might overcome its timidity.[72] As with his more strident *Des canons, des munitions?*, directed primarily to a French audience, *Cathédrales* elucidated the great themes of his agenda during the 1930s: opposition to the academy, support for authority and the power of the state, design informed by aesthetics and poetry, endorsement of mechanization to solve social problems, and mass housing advocacy.[73]

How then was *Cathédrales* received by French audiences? What was the critical reception to the book? In spite of its polemics, it met with a certain amount of indifference. Where French response was strongest, however, it was based on ideological concerns. A very few progressive and leftist journals, in both the architectural and general press, focused on Le Corbusier's critique of the American skyscraper and on his more broadly based assessment of American culture. Of those French observers who did respond, most had reservations.

Under the editorship of Le Corbusier's friend André Bloc, *L'Architecture d'Aujourd'hui* was committed to advancing the architect's ideas but not necessarily endorsing them. Considered the leading avant-garde architectural journal in France, it also extensively promoted what it considered to be progressive developments in American architecture and urbanism during the 1930s. It published several abridged chapters from Le Corbusier's expository section, "I Am an American": "La Catastrophe féerique" (The enchanted catastrophe), "Dans les caves!"[72] (In the caves), and "Les Gratte-ciel sont plus grands que les architectes" (The skyscrapers are greater than the architects). In so doing Bloc and other editors advanced Le Corbusier's criticism of the American skyscraper as an object of misplaced pride because it did not promote judicious city planning. The reprinted chapters saved André Fouilhoux, the journal's correspondent from America then serving on the Rockefeller Center design team, from sanctioning a position critical of American zoning policies favoring setback and tower skyscrapers that it helped to promote in France.[74]

Lucien Metrich's review in the left-wing newspaper *Vendredi* sympathized with the cultural criticism in *Cathédrales*. Although *Vendredi* had formerly denounced the negative effects of mechanization, it updated its position on Le Corbusier, no longer associating it with him. Metrich was exceptional in his understanding of the shift in Le Corbusier's work from idealism and mechanization to humanism. He recognized in Le Corbusier's criticism of the American response to art, architecture, and urbanism the architect's efforts to address issues affecting "mankind."[75] But such insights were rare.

Most French observers distorted Le Corbusier's intentions when they interpreted *Cathédrales* as an agent of Americanization rather than a critical response to American culture. Cast in language of dichotomies, *Cathédrales* reflected attitudes closely associated with *américanisme*. Ironically, French reactions to it were defensive, based on fears of Americanization that flowed from its own long-standing nationalism and reinforced by isolationism during the 1930s. Unlike *Vendredi,* more moderate and conservative journals deemed *Cathédrales* a manifesto on the machine age, as they had the architect's earlier books, and therefore a cause for concern. If the United States continued to regard Le Corbusier as the "man of the machine," the French were no exception. In *Les Annales Politiques et Littéraires,* a popular French magazine of opinion, one reviewer reproached the architect for promoting air conditioning, which it characterized as "mechanization in the American way."[76] In fact, many French critics regarded the Ville Radieuse, as they had his Ville Contemporaine and Plan Voisin, as being *plus américain que les américains.* Denigrating those visions as examples of Americanized planning, they considered such modernist dogma a serious threat to France's culture, aesthetics, traditions, identity, and inevitably its hegemony. Louis Hautecoeur, eminent French art historian and editor of the conservative journal *L'Architecture,* reproached Le Corbusier for infusing his urbanism with such "radicalism": "He regrets, for example, that France did not do to Morocco what America did to New York. . . . He denies the concept of Nation." Hautecoeur may have sympathized with Le Corbusier's efforts to eliminate suburbanization and urban waste, but he criticized his failure to "discuss the means of realizing it" and other forms of political engagement.[77]

Le Corbusier returned to France to confront some of the same impediments he had encountered in the United States. French critics questioned his motives. One reviewer for the moderate architectural journal *La Construction Moderne* ridiculed "M. Le Corbusier 'from France,' in making his eulogy, on the occasion of a propaganda round of visits in America, criticizes our institutions on a mode which would not be acceptable if one did not feel behind each one of his attacks, a deceptive ambition."[78]

In the end, for all of its rhetorical power, its intriguing title, and the artistry of its cover, the book drew very little response in France.[79] But this may have been in part because it appeared after the most strident debate on America during the early 1930s had run its course. One more octavo volume on the New World with no photographs and only a few dreamy sketches, *Cathédrales*

failed to touch the recesses of a people deeply entrenched in isolationism and more pragmatic concerns attending economic crisis.[80] Some French reviewers and readers objected to its didactic tone. The French did not appreciate being dictated to by a Swiss-born architect in a language of Calvinism any more than Americans did. Moreover, Le Corbusier completed *Cathédrales* in the years after his American tour during a period in which his architectural work received little attention in France. Published outside the channels of the architectural press, the general readership was largely indifferent to his message. Had Bloc given his imprimatur by allowing *L'Architecture d'Aujourd'hui* to publish *Cathédrales,* the response might have been more sympathetic.

The American Response to *Cathédrales*

And what of the American response to Le Corbusier's criticism? Despite the efforts of the author, Marguerite Harris, and others, American publishers were as reluctant to produce an edition of *Cathédrales* as they were of *La Ville radieuse.* It was not until 1947, and after Le Corbusier's return to New York as part of an international team of architects to help establish a headquarters for the United Nations, that Reynal and Hitchcock published *Cathedrals.* With the appearance of *Cathédrales* in 1937, Harris began work on an English text in hopes of securing an American publisher. On one of their encounters in Europe that spring, she and Le Corbusier collaborated on the translation. They chose to rendezvous at the Hôtel de la Cloche in Dijon, a midway point from Switzerland where she had been at work on the translation.[81] There he annotated Harris's copy of *Cathédrales* with marginal drawings. While still hoping to interest a publisher, Harris printed the excerpts she translated in four issues of *Direction.*[82]

For the most part the architectural press in America ignored *Cathédrales,* perhaps because it did not regard it as a book on architecture. Under Lawrence Kocher's editorship, *Architectural Record,* which had formerly championed the European modernist, did not publish a review, even though it did print a sympathetic one by Carl Schniewind of *La Ville radieuse.*[83] However spare, the critical response nonetheless plunged Le Corbusier's book into the same debate that shaped his earlier reception: intellectualism versus antiintellectualism, nationalism versus internationalism, totalitarianism and fascism versus democratic values, centralization versus decentralization, and idealism versus pragmatism. Because of its ideology and politics, *Cathédrales* received mixed reviews. Some critics appreciated Le Corbusier's intellect and his intellectualism. For "most Americans," wrote historian and critic Frederick Gutheim in 1938, it is "the best introduction to one of the really first class minds of our time."[84] The partisan Franco-American review *Légion d'Honneur Magazine* applauded "the logic of the Latin mind as he weighs the virtues and defects of American character and life."[85] Politically affiliated editors responded. For example, FAECT editors had already charged Le Corbusier with totalitarianism and identified his "proto-fascist" tendencies; they would not review the book. In contrast, the Christian right criticized *Cathédrales* because its position on property rights for the poor in the Radiant City involved "communal ownership of their dwelling." That "city of man," denounced a writer in *Catholic World,* was "secular and mechanized" and therefore antithetical to its Christian readers.[86]

The most insightful criticism came from Gutheim and George Howe, both predisposed to define Le Corbusier as Frank Lloyd Wright's European counterpart. These critics chose to use Wright's attack on the central city as a foil to their analysis. This interjection signaled Wright's new authority in the late 1930s as a proponent of nationalism and democratic values, in contrast to Le Corbusier's internationalism and visionary ambitions. A Wright supporter, Gutheim thought it improbable for a "Paris intellectual . . . identified with his abstract architectural utopias, to rejoice fully in the United States." And like Wright, Gutheim held Le Corbusier accountable for the "inseparable difficulties" of American cities because they were "the realizations of his [Le Corbusier's] airy improbabilities: the swift and efficient elevators, air-conditioning, skyscrapers, elevated highways, etc."[87]

Howe's review found some common ground between Wright and Le Corbusier because both were "prophets" concerned with advancing architecture beyond the realm of mere functionalism to human concerns and to the "poetic." But Howe placed the two architects in sharp opposition not only because their use of "social-technological architecture" was directed toward different ends but also because "the American" was a decentralist and "the Frenchman" a centralist. Wright "sings the glory of socio-technology as a promise of release from the trammels of the city, of a return to a glorified pioneer age. Le Corbusier prophesies the extension and amplification of Megalopolis." Neither "poet" could be expected to be "factual and logical." If Le Corbusier was critical of New York and Paris, he may be excused for his "bold solutions," which gave us "a sense of the poetic content of the machine to look upon the superhighway and . . . the skyscraper . . . as poetic-spatial symbols of a social-technological way of life, rather than as mere utilities." Howe could excuse Le Corbusier's criticism of the modern metropolis, his "rude answer" (an allusion also to his controversial visit to Philadelphia), because he understood and appreciated the Parisian's contributions to his "humanization of great cities" as well as to the poetic and aesthetic dimensions of his modernism.[88] Yet, because of Le Corbusier's idiosyncratic interpretation of the social over the technical, *Cathédrales* failed to resonate, as did the historically based sociotechnological explorations of Mumford's two studies, *Technics and Civilization* and *Culture of Cities,* and Sigfried Giedion's *Space, Time and Architecture* (1941), which emphasized the technical over the social.[89] During the late 1930s Le Corbusier's failure to interest American publishers offered further evidence of a transatlantic misunderstanding. In his 1938 review Gutheim concluded that because of Le Corbusier's "personal appraisals and interpretations and sophisticated indiscretions . . . no American translation is likely to appear."[90] Thus because *Cathédrales* was not available in an English translation until a decade after its publication, it did not capture the readership or publicity that the author expected.

Le Corbusier's Impact on the Discipline and Practice of Architecture in America after 1935

Given Le Corbusier's unsuccessful efforts to obtain commissions in the United States, the polarized American response to his theory and design, the tendency to view avant-garde elements in his architecture and urbanism in opposition to those of Frank Lloyd Wright, and limited interest in his publications, where did the impact of his lecture tour on the discipline and practice of architecture in America reach fertile ground? It seems to have had the greatest impact on those predisposed to modernism, especially on students in the architecture schools he visited. But his ideas did influence, in varying degrees, American architecture, planning—especially visionary planning—housing reform, and attitudes toward urban centralization. Because a full investigation is outside the scope of this study, such conclusions are only speculative.

American Schools

Le Corbusier's lecture tour brought Americans up to date on his theory and design of the 1930s as well as the 1920s. In this respect his visits to schools of architecture were especially instructive. His impact on students came from his publications and personal encounters, rather than through curricula or pedagogy. For however much Harvey Wiley Corbett at Columbia, Jean-Jacques Haffner at Harvard, and Jean Labatut at Princeton may have introduced their students to his theory of architecture, and however progressive and emancipating students may have considered his ideas, Le Corbusier was still marginalized by the prevailing Beaux-Arts system. Yet his appearances at American schools during the critical years of transition in the mid-1930s gave Joseph Hudnut and other reformers leverage to advance the cause of modernism. So his visit was affective. The man's intellect and vitality stunned American students and practitioners long anesthetized by the stasis of the early 1930s. Le Corbusier communicated powerfully through his charismatic persona and through his gestural drawings that transcended language. With the demise of the Beaux-Arts curriculum by the late 1930s and early

1940s, either rapidly at Harvard or gradually at Columbia, Yale, Penn, and elsewhere, the most enduring reform came from the Bauhaus and the impact of émigrés Gropius and Mies van der Rohe, rather than from Le Corbusier.[91] Indeed, to some it was difficult to distinguish the impact of Le Corbusier from the larger influence of European modernism. It was only during the postwar years that a resurgence of interest in him enabled Hudnut to report that "in the minds of the thousand students of architecture to whom he is prophet and missionary," his influence "saturates the schools of architecture . . . its strength is the strength of idea."[92] Le Corbusier's visit reinforced the impact of his widely read publications, as his writings generated considerable interest in his lectures. In evaluating the reception of his ideas after 1935, it must be emphasized that American students and practitioners, who had only recently been introduced to the architect through English and American editions of his publications, were inclined to integrate his theory of the first machine age with that of the second.

Students receptive to modernism, those for whom the Beaux-Arts system had little to offer in 1935, were most affected by Le Corbusier's lectures. To them the visit was an epiphany, an experience that irrevocably changed the course of their design work. To others it provided direct contact with the intellectual leader of twentieth-century architecture. In the vacuum caused by the weakened Beaux-Arts system and a shifting design curriculum at MIT, I. M. Pei and Harry Weese (class of 1938) were among those who found direction in the modernist's work. For Pei, Le Corbusier's appearance at MIT and Dean Emerson's influence were important factors that propelled his conversion from architectural engineering (MIT course IV-A), away from the technical, "purely to architecture."[93] By consulting the *Oeuvre complète* in the library, Pei could use Le Corbusier's projects as sources for his own work. Pei's "Standardized Propaganda Units for War Time and Peace Time China," his bachelor of architecture thesis in 1940 (figure 10.18), is a fascinating example of his ability to assimilate Le Corbusier's theory and design. Pei's project for a portable theater complex responded to the social need to disseminate information about education, sanitation,

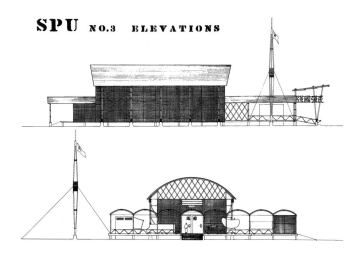

SPU NO.3 ELEVATIONS

10.18
Ieoh Ming Pei, "Standardized Propaganda Units for War Time and Peace Time China," B.Arch. thesis, Massachusetts Institute of Technology, 1940. (MIT Museum.)

and agriculture to a migratory population in China, often located in remote areas after the outbreak of war in 1937.[94] His prefabricated units, whose shallow vaults were made of steamed and bent bamboo, were inspired by a town hall and other buildings in Le Corbusier's project of 1934 for a cooperative village called the Radiant Farm (figure 10.19).[95] In its design concept and use of materials the project also demonstrated that Pei shared Le Corbusier's new concern for regionalism. Moreover, the provisional nature of the bamboo and canvas theater, designed for rapid assembly and disassembly, recalled the steel and canvas tension structure of the Pavillon des Temps Nouveaux (see figures 10.9, 10.10). Both the Radiant Farm and the pavilion were illustrated in the *Oeuvre complète* and other Le Corbusier publications.[96]

Le Corbusier's visits to other schools of architecture, however, rarely resulted in the awakening that Pei experienced. At Harvard, where Hudnut had begun to implement curricular reforms and Haffner introduced students to the work of Le Corbusier and other European modernists, his visit encouraged such students as Robert Woods Kennedy (M.Arch. 1937) to form a life-long admiration for his work.[97] The residual impact of his visit was still strong in the fall of 1936 when landscape architect Daniel Kiley (class of 1938) arrived at Harvard. He "remembered poring over Le Corbusier's plans" and appreciating the "wonderful structural spatial thrusts in his work . . . [which] opened the door."[98] By contrast, Carl Koch (M.Arch. 1937) claimed that "Le Corbusier didn't affect me while in school. . . . Frank Lloyd Wright was my hero in those days."[99] Le Corbusier's brief visit did not have an enduring impact at Harvard because Gropius's arrival in the spring of 1937 gave the school its dominant pedagogical direction.[100]

Although the lecture at Yale's School of Fine Arts caused considerable excitement, it failed to resonate in part because Dean Everett Meeks continued to keep a firm rein on the Beaux-Arts curriculum. As Yale alumni Carroll L. V. Meeks and George Nelson confirmed, architecture students by the late 1920s "knew about Le Corbusier."[101] But, like students at Cranbrook Academy who preferred the "Craftsman" tendencies of Wright and Saarinen, Yale students considered Le Corbusier and the

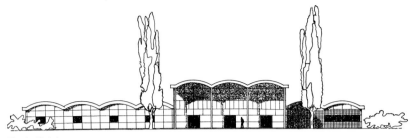

10.19
Le Corbusier, *la mairie*, coopera-
tive village, 1934–1938, Ferme
Radieuse. (*Oeuvre complète
1934–1938*, p. 110.) © 2001
Artists Rights Society (ARS), New
York/ADAGP, Paris/FLC.

Facade d'entrée

European modernism of the International Style too esoteric. As one alumnus explains, Le Corbusier's "philosophy runs foreign to my loves and gods in the world of
architecture, namely Wright, Saarinen," two other Ryerson lecturers in the 1935–1936 series.[102] It was only after Gropius's arrival at Harvard that Yale took much
notice of the new pedagogy and appointed the young
modernist Wallace Harrison as associate professor of design (1939–1942). Still the exposure to modernism that
Nelson and other students received at Yale was also due
to a tradition of bringing Europeans into the drafting
rooms.[103] During his postgraduate years of study at the
American Academy in Rome, Nelson conducted interviews with leading European modernists and published
them in a series for *Pencil Points* called "Architects of Europe Today." In July 1935 he published a candid interview with Le Corbusier cautioning Americans to be
skeptical of him.[104]

At Columbia, as at most other schools except Harvard, the transition to modernism was gradual and often
halting. When Dean Leopold Arnaud took direction of
the school in 1937 he reasserted its conservatism by
largely abandoning Hudnut's curricular reforms. Yet
most Columbia student projects of the late 1930s still
reflected the new modernism, though not specific Corbusian models.[105]

In spite of Jean Labatut's influence at Princeton, Le
Corbusier's visit failed to cultivate a large following. On
one hand, according to Melville C. Branch (M.C.P.
1936), his lectures had less impact because "we were familiar with his ideas through his writings." On the other
hand, the school still used the Beaux-Arts Institute of
Design programs. Thus, notwithstanding Labatut's en-

dorsement of modernism, student projects that reflected
Le Corbusier's design ideas would have been unacceptable to jurors. Branch, who would become president of
the City Planning Commission in Los Angeles, later acknowledged that Le Corbusier's "new treatment of architectural space . . . [and] an awareness of large or
mega-buildings was probably the only influence for me."
But other students recalled no debt whatsoever.[106]

Beaux-Arts Institute of Design programs also prevailed at the University of Pennsylvania, where Joseph
Esherick was a student in the Department of Architecture, School of Fine Arts (1932–1937). But by the fall of
1935 when Le Corbusier visited Philadelphia, Esherick
had found a new "direction . . . toward Le Corbusier."
Esherick recounted that in his fourth year, "Le Corbusier,
not only in his buildings and projects and drawings but
also in his writing, became a major influence, and I and
several others devoured everything we could get our
hands on." For his fifth-year project for a summer hotel,
Esherick "designed it as a wooden pole structure with a
simple warehouse-like frame with partitions and walls,
also of wood, floating around independent of the
frame—Le Corbusier again." He received a "mention"
for this BAID-generated project but realized that compared with the prize-winning designs, he would "never
make it."[107] Because of the entrenched Beaux-Arts system, therefore, he and other students at Penn found Le
Corbusier's theory and design liberating to their creative
work but limiting to their professional development.

Le Corbusier's influence in American schools of architecture was neither consistent nor in any sense governing. Students reacted to both his visit and his
writings individually rather than collectively. Except at

Harvard and briefly at Columbia, this occurred under still-dominant but threatened Beaux-Arts regimes. At their respective institutions Pei, Weese, Kennedy (and Kiley), Branch, and Esherick were exceptional in their awareness and appreciation of Le Corbusier, who offered them an idiosyncratic path to design rather than the formal pedagogical one that the Gropius model provided at Harvard and elsewhere.

American Practice

Before 1935 Le Corbusier influenced the practice of architecture in the United States through the three groups discussed in chapter 1: young architects who had passed through his atelier (both Europeans who later emigrated and North Americans), European-born modernists who worked there, and American avant-garde practitioners. As European modernism moved from avant-garde circles to the mainstream during the 1930s and as the English and American editions of *Towards a New Architecture* and *City of Tomorrow* reached a wide readership, Americans came to understand Le Corbusier's notion of the first machine age.

After 1935 Le Corbusier's influence on American architecture continued to be inextricably linked to the reception of the International Style because his theory and design were central to it. In this sense Americans were more inclined to identify with his production of 1925 than of 1935. Most critics in the 1930s continued Hitchcock and Johnson's earlier practice of conferring the label International Style on all European modernism. As a result, they commingled still further the work of Le Corbusier with that of other Europeans.

In the years after the 1932 "Modern Architecture: International Exhibition," the concept as well as the practice of an International Style enjoyed a strong following in America, in effect its Americanization. This was due in part to the formalist bias of Hitchcock and Johnson, which encouraged appropriation of forms without reference to underlying social and political structures that had shaped their European counterparts. America also became the principal site for the evolution of the International Style after the arrival of Gropius, Mies van der Rohe, Marcel Breuer, and others during the late 1930s. Paradoxically, some maintain, the advancement of an International Style in continental Europe effectively ended after 1932 in the sense that individual practitioners either made few contributions to it, as in the case of Oud, or departed from the canons prescribed by Hitchcock and Johnson, as in the case of Le Corbusier. Others emigrated to England and later to America.[108]

To International Style proponents Hitchcock and Elizabeth Mock (later Kassler), American developments after 1932 paled in comparison with European achievements during the seminal decade before 1932. By 1937 Hitchcock could distance himself from the International Style in America, calling it "aesthetically second rate." Mock later made her assessment that "as the dominant movement of the 1930s" the International Style "produced no buildings of intrinsic value in this country."[109] Le Corbusier's visit, therefore, occurred during a time that Hitchcock considered a "vacuum." In contrast to the "aesthetic canons" of the International Style during the decade before 1932, Hitchcock now saw a "bankruptcy . . . of the sense of form." He could not yet envision the reemergence of Frank Lloyd Wright, or that another American architect might "lead the world with all the originality of Wright's best work."[110]

During the 1930s many critics in America tended to use the terms "International" style and "Functional" style interchangeably because, as Mock explained, "In a period of depression the popular slogan of 'functionalism' was valuable promotion for modern architecture."[111] In 1936 Sheldon Cheney tagged European modernists and participants in the 1932 exhibition as "Functionalists." He characterized their impact in this country as "a great slide toward the rational ideas of Le Corbusier, Gropius, [Mies] Van der Rohe, and Oud."[112] And even as late as 1940 John McAndrew continued to advance the mythology of an "'International' or 'Functional' style" having been brought to America from Europe a decade earlier. Yet McAndrew and other critics were fully aware of Richard Neutra's conviction that modernism in America would develop from the exigencies of its own technology, as well as the importance of the native technocratic movement that Buckminster Fuller raised to new heights of popularity.[113] But the formalist interpretation of style, championed by Hitchcock and Johnson, continued to dominate the historiography of the modern movement in America. Moreover, just after 1932 the work of some American modernists had not codified as much as calcified into a formulaic representation of the International Style, as in projects by Raymond Hood and Harvey Wiley Corbett for the Forward House exhibition sponsored by R. H. Macy and Co. in 1933.[114]

Thus Le Corbusier's impact on the practice of architecture in the United States from 1932 to World War II occurred during a period of transition. Critical debate in the 1930s focused on the architect's design within an aesthetic formulation of the International Style such that the work of its "theorist" and "propagandist" became synonymous with it. During the 1930s elements of Corbusian theory, especially his aphorisms of the 1920s, entered architectural discourse. Well into the decade such critics as Cheney popularized Le Corbusier's earlier advocacy of the machine, with allusions to his "barbed and argumentative essays" and quotations from *Towards a New Architecture,* long after the architect had shifted to a humanist rhetoric.[115] Similarly, Henry Humphrey, the *House and Garden* editor responsible for Le Corbusier's

meetings with New York City housing officials, continued to advance the stereotype of the 1930s when he characterized the architect as the "emotional polemicist for modern [who] says 'the house is a machine for living.'"[116] Thus, if American practitioners were learning about Le Corbusier from critics and journalists in the late 1930s, they were receiving outdated rhetoric and models from which the architect had already distanced himself.

One measure of the diffusion of Le Corbusier's ideas in the work of an American closely associated with the canons of the International Style is the domestic architecture of Edward Durell Stone. Philip Johnson recognized Stone's debt to Le Corbusier when he urged organizers of the Modern's Le Corbusier exhibition to use a photograph of the Richard Mandel House, Mt. Kisco, New York (with Donald Deskey, 1934–1935; figure 10.20), as an example of American work "under the influence of the master."[117] Stone himself identified his houses of the 1930s with the International Style.[118] These included a project for Mrs. Charles I. Liebman in Mt. Kisco (1937; unbuilt) that Le Corbusier had tried unsuccessfully to secure for himself, purportedly with the help of Stone who was then working in the office of Wallace Harrison. Another is Stone's residence for Museum of

10.20
Edward Durell Stone and Donald Deskey, Richard Mandel House, Mt. Kisco, New York, 1934–1935. (*Architectural Forum* 63 [August 1935], p. 81; John Gass Photos.)

Modern Art president A. Conger Goodyear in Old West-bury, New York, of 1938, a commission that would also have eluded Le Corbusier because the Modern then considered him persona non grata.[119]

If Stone's houses of the 1930s quoted broadly from the International Style and more specifically from Le Corbusier, his design with Philip Goodwin for the Museum of Modern Art (1936–1939) was a veritable pastiche of Le Corbusier's buildings from the 1920s and 1930s. The irony was not lost on Le Corbusier. In December 1935, toward the end of his tour, the Rocke-fellers, together with Museum of Modern Art trustees, were at odds with Mayor Fiorello La Guardia over the proposed Municipal Art Center. In hopes of securing the Art Center job himself, Le Corbusier sought assistance from Nelson Rockefeller and Harrison. The next spring plans for a new museum, independent of the mayor's intentions, moved forward when John D. Rockefeller, Jr., acquired the necessary land. And although Le Corbusier tried to mend fences with Goodwin during the winter and spring of 1936 and may have entertained the hope of the Museum of Modern Art commission, as he did the Municipal Art Center, his efforts were unsuccessful.

It is all the more ironic, then, that not only did Le Corbusier's work inform the design of the new Museum of Modern Art but also that his transatlantic misunderstanding with Goodwin encouraged the selection of Stone as associated architect and helped to exclude the participation of Europe's leading modernists. By March 1936 the Board of Trustees selected Goodwin as architect; Goodyear, Barr, and Nelson Rockefeller were named to the building committee. But later that spring when John D. Rockefeller, Jr., acquired more land for an imposing museum site on 53rd Street to crown the northern extension to Rockefeller Center (see chapter 7, figure 7.10), Barr felt compelled to find a leading European architect to assist Goodwin. During his travels in Europe Barr consulted with Gropius, Mies van der Rohe, and Oud, but not with Le Corbusier whom he and Nelson Rockefeller "eliminated as impossible temperamentally."[120] Looking back on those discussions, Barr's wife, Margaret, recalled that Frank Lloyd Wright had been dismissed from consideration as "too much of a prima

donna, too extravagant and hard to work with," and the same could be said for the "disruptive Le Corbusier, whose show the previous year is remembered with shudders in the architecture department."[121] Coincidentally, Barr was also on a mission for Harvard's Hudnut. He sounded out Gropius, Mies van der Rohe, and, at his own suggestion, Oud about their respective interest in an appointment as professor of design at Harvard. But Goodwin resolutely opposed collaboration with any foreign architect and Barr understood that some of the Modern's trustees were "strongly nationalistic in feeling." By June 1936 the building committee agreed to authorize Goodwin to proceed, with the assistance of Stone who was still in the Harrison office. But Barr hoped to avoid a "mediocre building." Rallying the support of Abby Aldrich Rockefeller, he pursued on his own discussions with the three European architects. Of them, only Mies van der Rohe expressed definitive interest in both the museum collaboration and the Harvard professorship.[122]

In spite of Goodwin's resistance to a European collaborator, Barr pressed his case for Mies as "the greatest architect of our generation (granting that Corbusier is the most original and brilliant)." And whereas "Mies is no Corbusier," Barr conceded, "he is charming, affable and used to working with others."[123] But Goodwin stood firm with Barr, as he had months earlier with Le Corbusier on the finances of his visit. With the backing of Goodyear and Nelson Rockefeller, Stone was brought on board as Goodwin's associate.[124] Barr still hoped to bring Mies van der Rohe to the United States. By the fall of 1936 Harrison had even met with Mies in Berlin to interest him in becoming consulting architect for the Municipal Art scheme (on which Stone was working).[125] But Barr was not able to secure Mies's collaboration on the Modern's new design or on the Municipal Art Center project, which was soon abandoned.[126]

These events shed light on Le Corbusier's tacit role in the selection of an architect. Evidently Goodwin found working with Le Corbusier on his exhibition and lecture tour so disagreeable that he refused to collaborate with any foreign architect on the Modern's new building. Similarly, Lescaze, who worked on an earlier design for the Modern (1929–1931), was excluded from further participation because one member of the Board of Trustees had objected to him as foreign-born. Goodwin and others had that kind of influence.[127] And if it is true that Le Corbusier's dispute with representatives of the Modern poisoned the well for any European collaborator, it had far-ranging consequences that affected the unfolding of Mies van der Rohe's career. Had Mies received the prestigious Modern assignment, he might have been assured a successful practice on the East Coast. It also would have strengthened his candidacy at Harvard, which Hudnut finally had to abandon in November 1936.[128]

The development of Goodwin and Stone's design for the new Modern suggests the irony (and perhaps also the duplicity) of Goodwin's relationship with Le Corbusier. Barr's comment about Le Corbusier as "most original and brilliant" underscores his admiration for the Parisian architect as a form-giver, not just a "theorist" and "propagandist." The preliminary design of April 15, 1937 (figure 10.21), confirms that Goodwin and Stone shared this appreciation. Their treatment of the museum facade is an assemblage of quotations from Le Corbusier's recent buildings and projects, especially those shown at his solo exhibition. The design specified smooth white walls of marble punctuated with strip windows that recalled the south facade of the Pavillon Suisse and, together with one asymmetrically placed window, suggested the front elevation of the Villa Stein-de Monzie at Garches (1926–1928). Plate glass factory

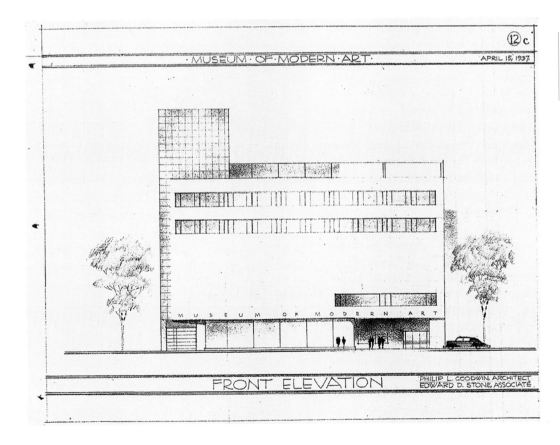

10.21
Philip Goodwin and Edward Durell Stone, preliminary design for the Museum of Modern Art, April 15, 1937. (Frances Loeb Library, Harvard Design School.)

windows and glass brick (on the proposed rear elevation) were reminiscent of Le Corbusier's designs for his Salvation Army Building (1929–1933) and his apartment house on the rue Nungesser et Coli (1933; figure 10.22), both in Paris. The recessed penthouse of the Museum of Modern Art design suggests a further debt to Le Corbusier.[129] Goodwin and Stone's executed design (figure 10.23) used an even more complex assemblage of forms borrowed from Le Corbusier's Pavillon de l'Esprit Nouveau and other iconic examples of modernism at the 1925 Paris fair, including Konstantin Melnikov's USSR Pavilion, presumably influenced by Stone's association with the Harrison office whose Trylon and Peristyle reflected constructivist influence.[130] Their museum building suggests a further paradox. Barr had supported Goodwin's appointment in the hope that he would agree to work with Mies van der Rohe, a collaboration preferable to "the half-baked modernistic designers who have helped bedizen our cities since Paris 1925." Now, for all of Barr's efforts to achieve authenticity, he was left with the kind of derivative design he tried so hard to avoid.[131]

As the modern movement in America reached its maturity during the late 1930s, it underwent three transformations, as William Jordy suggests. First, technological advances, including reliable heating systems that made glass walls feasible, and prefabricated building products caught up with the machine age metaphors of the International Style. These were the result of American inventions and processes. Second, vernacular and regional traditions provided modern architecture with the denser appeal and denser meanings possible from form called forth by concern for historical values."[132] Third, a more humanist approach to design emerged, closely linked to vernacular and regional concerns, that addressed social needs. Le Corbusier was instrumental in shaping the last two transformations.

With the assimilation of European modernism in the United States during the 1930s came a central question: how to Americanize modern architecture, to endorse the machine age metaphors and aesthetic ideals of European architecture and yet also be true to itself by reflecting the native traditions in American culture, both technical and vernacular? The trick was for archi-

10.22
Le Corbusier, apartment house, rue Nungesser et Coli, Paris, 1933. (*Oeuvre complète 1929–1934*, p. 147.) © 2001 Artists Rights Society (ARS), New York/ADAGP, Paris/FLC.

10.23
Philip Goodwin and Edward
Durell Stone, Museum of Modern
Art, New York, 1936–1939.
(Photograph by Wurts Brothers,
courtesy The Museum of Modern
Art, New York.)

tects to be inclusive. This issue raises the larger one of internationalism versus nationalism, the latter becoming as much a European as an American concern. For the shift in American architecture, as in politics, culture, and the arts, toward vernacular and regional traditions paralleled a similar shift in Europe. Sigfried Giedion characterized such developments as the new regional approach or the new regionalism.[133] Embraced within the new preoccupation was emphasis on social needs that had been the focus of CIAM debate, especially at the 1930 congress in Brussels. During the decade the evolution of modernism in both Europe and America, therefore, reflected a new humanism.

Committed to a *representation* of the symbolism and aesthetics of the machine over the *use* of advanced technology, Le Corbusier subscribed to what William Jordy called "symbolic essence" and Stanford Anderson "the fiction of function." So when Le Corbusier advocated a synthesis of the technological and the aesthetic, he was actually revisiting some of his earlier concerns of the 1920s that Francesco Passanti has recently elucidated.[134]

In the 1930s Le Corbusier turned out to be among the most creative of European modernists. He reinvented himself so that his own work engaged environmental as well as sociopolitical concerns. His Maisons Monol of 1919 anticipated the shift away from the "strong objectivity of forms" in the work he himself characterized as "*male* architecture" (which Peter Serenyi associated with the Citrohan House of 1920–1922) toward the "limitless subjectivity" in the work he characterized as "female architecture."[135] His "free use of curves, responsiveness to the influence of various natural settings [and] . . . traditional materials," as Hitchcock suggested in his catalogue essay for the Le Corbusier exhibition, "opened again many avenues for artistic exploration."[136] In the Monol House project a continuous flow of space and arched concrete vaults replaced machine-inspired forms. His Loucheur Houses of 1928–1929 combined factory-produced steel-frame construction with stone rubble walls—the machine-made and the man-made. Le Corbusier also used regional and vernacular elements to emphasize the more earthbound character of his new work and materials sympathetic to their

10.24

Le Corbusier, farmhouse, Ferme
Radieuse. (*Oeuvre complète
1929–1934*, p. 190. Plan FLC
28618.) © 2001 Artists Rights
Society (ARS), New York/ADAGP,
Paris/FLC.

respective sites: masonry walls and a podium of local stone (combined with a metal frame to ensure a free plan) at the de Mandrot House (see figure 2.4) and massive concrete *pilotis* and a curved masonry rubble wall at the Pavillon Suisse (see figure 3.16). As his affiliation with regional syndicalism deepened during the 1930s, so did his interest in folk culture as well as local economies and social hierarchies. Both the Errázuriz House (1930; see figure 2.3) and the house at Mathes (1934–1935; see figure 3.18, plate 7) employed timber framing and rough masonry walls.[137] By 1935 Le Corbusier had built his first Monol-type Maison de Weekend (Villa Félix) in La Celle-Saint-Cloud (see figure 2.6). But unlike its prototype of 1919 whose thin walls seemed to resist gravity, the Weekend House anchored stone walls and heavy concrete vaults firmly to the ground. And even the Brewer House project of 1935 employed thick stucco walls and a rough stone wall, which signaled a return to vernacular traditions he thought appropriate to the Midwest (see figure 4.9). Le Corbusier's Ferme Radieuse (figure 10.24), followed by his Village Coopératif, addressed

agrarian reorganization for a rural community in the French province of Sarthe that was consonant with the regional syndicalist agenda. Shaped by the involvement of the "peasant activist" Norbert Bezard, as Mary McLeod showed, Le Corbusier's project was cooperative in its political and social structure, and rational in its organization. Whereas the larger Village Radieux contained a number of farm structures, the glass-walled model farmhouse raised on *pilotis*, and based on the Maison Loucheur model (see figure 7.4), revealed Le Corbusier's intentions to adapt prefabricated building techniques to rural needs.[138] Although he proposed a country house based on the Ferme Radieuse type to Chicago society columnist Elizabeth Field, he offered it more seriously to the American public as part of a reconstruction plan he intended for rural areas.[139]

Taken as a whole, these developments transformed Le Corbusier's production. Moreover, although some were only projects and others were isolated geographically, they became well known in America through the early volumes of the *Oeuvre complète, La Ville radieuse,* numerous articles in American art and architecture journals, the Le Corbusier exhibition at the Modern and the traveling exhibition with its accompanying catalogue, and his popular lecture tour.[140] In the aggregate these works demonstrated his new humanism: a synthesis of poetic expression of technology, vernacular, and regional influences, and responsiveness to social needs. At the same time modern building techniques were not forgotten. The use of a metal frame and especially prefabricated elements, as in the Loucheur model and Ferme Radieuse, were incorporated whenever viable, even if they were not technically advanced.

Humanism in the Second Machine Age

By the late 1930s the effects of the Depression in America encouraged such humanist concerns in design and with them a relaxation of the canons of the International Style. These developments caught up with Le Corbusier's work of the 1930s. In Hitchcock's view, "no one has done more than Le Corbusier ever since [the 1932 'Modern Architecture: International Exhibition'] to extend and loosen the sanctions of the International Style." Le Corbusier's new synthesis also influenced several of the more inventive and nuanced developments in American architecture before World War II.[141] In this sense some American critics understood the new directions in his work, even if Lewis Mumford was not among the first to do so.

From the mid-1930s Le Corbusier's concept of the second machine age infused *American* discourse and developments. By now Carl Schniewind and Albert Frey were freely alluding to his notion of "essential joys" and other elusive elements of Le Corbusier's humanism in reviews of his publications.[142] But it was Sheldon and Martha Cheney who saw the impact of Le Corbusier's ideal of "human service" when they defined the second machine age in America as "less impersonal in expression than the early Functionalists admitted: less standardized, less stripped, more humanly individualized . . . making the rationalist house more intensely expressive of human function . . . signs that the self-conscious and dogmatic Functionalism of the days of Le Corbusier's first dictum is likely to be modified in various interpretations and brought closer to 'man's essential pleasures.'"[143]

In *Built in USA 1932–1944* Elizabeth Mock found the course toward humanism especially significant. Before "the new architecture" had been assimilated and de-mocratized, she stated in 1945, it had undergone a "process of humanization" and shed its "romanticization of the machine which had produced . . . cold abstractions." In America that had been achieved through the influence of Frank Lloyd Wright, traditional vernacular building, and "Le Corbusier's experiments with natural materials," as in the de Mandrot House and Swiss Dormitory in Paris. Together Wright and Le Corbusier "stimulated" Americans to look at their own native folk architecture—Pennsylvania stone and timber barns or late-nineteenth-century California redwood houses—not so much for "picturesque detail" but for "their straightforward use of material and their subtle adaptation to climate and topography." By following the example of these two architects, one could find "local encouragement for the growing international movement towards a friendlier, more differentiated contemporary architecture."[144]

But unlike Mock, most critics and historians writing in the late 1930s continued to advance Mumford's divisive position of the previous decade, casting Wright and Le Corbusier as adversaries. If Mumford refused to recognize in Le Corbusier's exhibition of 1935 the transformations in his work that Hitchcock identified as poetic and spiritual, it was because he saw no reason to alter his earlier position.[145] Walter Curt Behrendt extended that stale debate when he polarized Le Corbusier's abstract principles derived from cubism and Wright's "organic forms." "Le Corbusier, *l'homme géometrique,* is in every respect the antithesis and antagonist of Wright. Le Corbusier's art is based on an experience of Education, that of Wright on an experience of Nature."[146] As late as 1940 John McAndrew opposed the International Style to Wright's "warm humanitarian approach to architecture . . . and even romantic escape from the very Machine Age the functionalists were domesticating."[147] And when James and Katherine Morrow Ford asked architects that same year to define "at what points American work in modern design and construction departs from European methods," several chose to pit the tradition of Wright against the International Style, but most looked more dispassionately at national differences and formalist concerns, some eschewing the label altogether.[148]

By the 1940s most architects, critics, and historians, however, concurred with Mock that the opposition of Wright to Le Corbusier was a false debate. They preferred to find in their work synthesis and common ground rather than antithesis and antagonisms.[149] Looking back on the late 1930s Mock perceived a reconciliation between "Le Corbusier's experiments with natural materials and open forms," bringing him "closer to Frank Lloyd Wright," whereas Wright's house Fallingwater at Bear Run (1936–1939) ironically brought him "considerably closer to the Europeans." Le Corbusier's "free plan" allowed the architect to use "diagonals and non-geometric curves appropriate to control the flow of human activity," as did the "curving rubble wall" and "diagonal stair-tower in the Swiss Dormitory." If Le Corbusier was "attacking the rectangle" and demonstrating "a new freedom of action" in the 1930s, so was Wright. The concrete vaults of Le Corbusier's Weekend House (see figure 2.6) and multiplane tile roof of his Errázuriz House project in Chile brought a new freedom to interior space. Similarly, the "oblique planes which defined the living space" of Wright's "honeycomb" Paul Hanna House in Palo Alto (1936) "seem remarkably unforced."[150] Finding consensus between Wright and Le Corbusier was also an objective of the Fords. Attentive to the subtleties of history, they preferred to view Wright as a powerful influence on European architecture during the first three decades of this century, which then returned to America "under a new group of teachers and practitioners, modified by experiments and developing experience under Gropius and Mies van der Rohe . . . Le Corbusier . . . Oud."[151]

A brief examination of a few single-family houses built before World War II illustrates the new humanist concerns (synthesizing standardization and mass production, vernacular traditions, and social needs) within the context of Le Corbusier's influence on the development of American architecture. Le Corbusier-inspired houses of the late 1930s reflect a renewed interest in mass, although often contrasted with volumes and planar surfaces that had been so dominant in the early years of the decade. Moreover, around 1940 the Fords observed in "the present phase" an "increasing technical proficiency associated with greater naturalness of design and above all with planning that is truly organic."[152] Although organic architecture was associated most closely with Frank Lloyd Wright, Mock recognized Le Corbusier's "initiative" in using "the free curve and the diagonal" and consequently contributing to the "new freedom" in American design.[153] Unfortunately, because the United States lacked a Corbusian model—a house for Joseph Brewer, Elizabeth Field, or Mrs. Charles Liebman—the architect's impact was more nuanced and certainly less authoritative than it might otherwise have been.[154]

During the late 1930s house design in the United States conveyed modernism in transition as many architects sought to integrate these new developments—some from Wright and other American sources as well as some from Le Corbusier and the residual International Style—and still define itself as American. European émigrés understood best the shifts that occurred in Le Corbusier's work. William Lescaze's designs for single-family houses as well as for public housing in the 1930s borrowed forms from Le Corbusier's first and second machine ages, confirming his skill as a "versatile pasticheur." His 1933–1934 studio and garage for Roy F. Spreter in Lower Merion Township, Pennsylvania (figures 10.25, 10.26), indicate the way in which he mined Corbusian models to create the desired hybrid. The white walls and studio corner window recall the forms and factory glazing of Le Corbusier's Ozenfant Studio of 1922. But the juxtaposition of plain stucco walls for the Spreter Studio and local fieldstone for its garage suggest similar juxtapositions in Le Corbusier's Errázuriz and de Mandrot houses as well as the Swiss Dormitory (see figures 2.3, 2.4, 3.16). Lescaze's house for Alfred L. Loomis in Tuxedo Park (1936–1937) also reflects Le Corbusier's innovations. Its expressionist canopy supported by V-shaped struts is reminiscent of the entrance to Le Corbusier's Cité de Refuge in Paris.[155]

Le Corbusier similarly influenced Wallace Harrison's houses of the late 1930s. In Harrison's house for Julian and Narcissa Street in Scarborough, New York (1938; figures 10.27, 10.28), smooth stucco contrasted with fieldstone retaining walls, engaging the landscape in the Corbusian manner. In fact, Robert Jacobs was

10.25
William Lescaze, Roy F. Spreter studio and garage, Lower Merion Township, Pennsylvania, 1933–1934, view from the drive. (Private collection.)

10.26
William Lescaze, Roy F. Spreter studio and garage, Lower Merion Township, Pennsylvania, 1933–1934, view of studio corner window. (Private collection.)

10.27
Wallace Harrison, Julian and Narcissa Street House, Scarborough, New York, 1938. (F. S. Lincoln Collection, Historical Collections and Labor Archives, Pennsylvania State University.)

10.28
Wallace Harrison, Julian and Narcissa Street House, Scarborough, New York, 1938. (F. S. Lincoln Collection, Historical Collections and Labor Archives, Pennsylvania State University.)

responsible for the design. Fresh from his apprentice-ship in the Le Corbusier atelier and his assignment as interpreter on the lecture tour, Jacobs joined the Harrison office in 1936. "Wally was always interested in new ideas and thought that I might bring some of Corbu's ideas into the shop," Jacobs remembered.[156] The Hawes Guest House for Nelson Rockefeller at Pocantico, New York, demonstrated Harrison's original and whimsical juxtaposition of textures and forms. There he used a white cut-out canopy designed by Fernand Léger to light the entrance between two fieldstone pavilions of contrasting geometries.[157]

During the 1930s Marcel Breuer, like Lescaze, came under the influence of Le Corbusier's new humanist synthesis and more plastic expression. Breuer's Ganes Exhibition Pavilion in Bristol, England (1936), employed rough masonry walls, some curved and some configured on a diagonal, in addition to large plate glass walls recalling Le Corbusier's Swiss Dormitory as well as the de Mandrot, Errázuriz, and Mathes houses.[158] Breuer's

American work with Gropius, especially their house for Mrs. Josephine Hagerty in Cohasset, Massachusetts (1938; figure 10.29), and their own Walter Gropius (1938) and Marcel Breuer (1939) houses, as well as the James Ford House (1939), all in Lincoln, Massachusetts, shared a fusion of International Style representation with juxtapositions of smooth and textured surfaces, local materials, and more complex forms.[159] When Walter F. Bogner, a colleague at Harvard's Graduate School of Design, built his own house in Lincoln (1939; figure 10.30), he followed the example of Gropius and Breuer. Bogner's use of traditional balloon frame construction with rough fieldstone walls recalled everyday New England practices as well as forms from both Wright and Le Corbusier. But the sculptural treatment of its rubble wall construction, open planning, and curved garage unit suggested closer affinities to Le Corbusier.[160]

The work of Alfred and Jane West Clauss in Knoxville, Tennessee, is another example of the diffusion of Le Corbusier's ideas in the United States. Two

10.29
Marcel Breuer (with Walter Gropius), Mrs. Josephine Hagerty House, Cohasset, Massachusetts, 1938. (Ford and Ford, *The Modern House in America*, p. 45; George H. Davis Studios.)

10.30
Walter F. Bogner, Bogner House,
Lincoln, Massachusetts, 1939.
(Photograph by Ezra Stoller,
© Esto.)

10.31
Alfred and Jane West Clauss,
Hart House, Knoxville, Tennessee,
1943. (Photograph by Billy M.
Glenn.)

years before her marriage to Alfred (Zeppel) Clauss in 1934, Jane West worked in Le Corbusier's atelier on the design of the Swiss Dormitory.[161] From 1934 to 1945 the couple collaborated on seven houses sponsored by the Tennessee Valley Authority as part of Franklin D. Roosevelt's New Deal program.[162] Into the 1940s the Clausses remained faithful to Le Corbusier's example. Of all their Knoxville work, the Hart House on Holston Hills Road (1943; figure 10.31) best reflects Le Corbusier's synthesis and West's experience working on the Swiss Dormitory. Commanding a hilltop site, the Hart House used wood frame construction faced with asbestos tiles. Both the garage and retaining walls employed local stone. The "contrast" between the rough stone below and smooth walls above, noted *Architectural Review,* "has become popular in the United States in the wake of Le Corbusier and Breuer."[163]

Some American architects readily accepted not only the formal elements of Le Corbusier's production but also his communitarian ideas. During the late 1930s his Ferme Radieuse (see figure 10.19), for example, had an impact on social housing in the West. The San Francisco office of the Farm Security Administration (FSA) sponsored a number of housing communities for migrant farm workers and resident farmers. After the 1937 U.S. Housing Act the FSA was responsible for building two

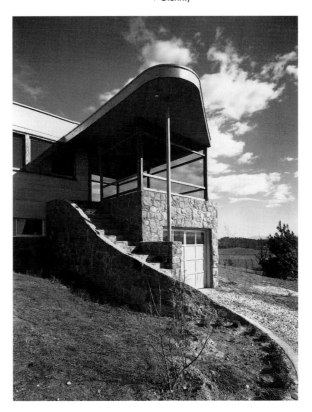

10.32
Vernon De Mars and Burton D. Cairns, FSA agricultural workers' community, Yuba City, California. (*Architectural Forum 74* [January 1941], p. 7.)

agricultural communities: Yuba City (1939; figure 10.32) and Woodville (1939–1941). In both, architect Vernon De Mars maintained that he was influenced by Le Corbusier's theory and design, specifically his Ferme Radieuse. Both communities emphasize communitarian planning and a reliance on local materials. At Yuba City the multifamily apartment blocks supported by *pilotis* are reminiscent of Le Corbusier's more sophisticated and complex design for the Oued-Ouchaïa housing project in Algiers. Other FSA-sponsored farm communities included one at Chandler, Arizona (1936–1937), designed by Burton D. Cairns and Vernon De Mars, in which Le Corbusier's example influenced authorities to be responsive to regional needs. In 1942 Philip Johnson recognized in these communities an architecture that engaged as much nationalism as internationalism: "though they owe something in design to the great Swiss pioneer of contemporary architecture, Le Corbusier, [they] are very clean, very neat, and very American." What also made these communities American may have been the impact of Wright's project for the San-Marcos-in-the-Desert Hotel (1928–1929), planned for a site on the Phoenix South Mountains not far from Chandler, Arizona.[164]

New York World's Fair

Much of the planning and many of the buildings and exhibits of the New York World's Fair of 1939–1940 reflect the further spread of Le Corbusier's ideas, notwithstanding Nelson Rockefeller and Wallace Harrison's lack of interest in sponsoring and collaborating with him on the theme pavilion or his efforts to secure a commission for the French pavilion.[165] When the idea of the fair was first discussed, a group of young modernists supported by Henry Wright and the Museum of Modern Art sought to design an entire community. Le Corbusier's work was brought in as a model. "The aim," according to Lewis Mumford, "was to make as decisive an innovation in city building as Le Corbusier made in his individual 'machine for habitation' at the Decorative Arts Exposition in Paris in 1925."[166] But even though a large tract of land was reserved, the project was defeated.

As early as May 1936 Le Corbusier's ideas on housing figured in the debate over the fair's theme. Robert D. Kohn, former AIA president who later became chairman of the fair's Board of Design, advocated housing as a central theme, based on the Weissenhof Siedlung model.[167]

But Walter Dorwin Teague, an influential member of the design board, promoted the theme "Building the World of Tomorrow," with a key role given to the industrial designer.[168] There would be a housing exhibit, but restricted to single-family demonstration houses and displays targeted to consumers. The Town of Tomorrow may have been a model village with a few modernist houses, including those by Lawrence Kocher and others, but it was largely historicist and decidedly suburban.[169]

Of the many pavilions and exhibit buildings at the 1939 New York World's Fair, the Trylon and Perisphere, Harrison and Fouilhoux's dramatic Theme Center, did not turn out to be especially Corbusian. However, Le Corbusier himself believed that the Trylon showed that his ideas on urbanism had taken hold in New York City. Notwithstanding its needle-like form—evidence, Le Corbusier thought, of the prevailing romanticism that still afflicted American skyscraper design—the Trylon was a dense high-rise; its rational site emphasized the restoration of order in the metropolis of tomorrow that Le Corbusier endorsed.[170] But it was the work of foreign architects, especially Brazilians, and of Norman Bel Geddes that signaled acceptance of Le Corbusier's ideas on architecture and urbanism.

As at most international exhibitions, the foreign pavilions at the New York fair were among the most architecturally innovative. The Brazilian Pavilion (figure 10.33), designed by Oscar Niemeyer and Lúcio Costa (with interiors and exhibits by the German-born American architect Paul Lester Wiener), demonstrated the spread of Corbusian design ideas in the Americas. It followed Niemeyer's first collaboration with Costa and others in 1936 on the headquarters of the Ministry of

10.33
Oscar Niemeyer with Lúcio Costa and Paul Lester Wiener, Brazilian Pavilion, New York World's Fair, 1939. (F. S. Lincoln Collection, Historical Collections and Labor Archives, Pennsylvania State University.)

Education and Public Health in Rio de Janeiro, where Le Corbusier was a consultant and had provided the *parti*.[171] As much as Costa, Le Corbusier served as Niemeyer's mentor. The Brazilian Pavilion (like the Ministry of Education and Public Health building) interpreted Le Corbusier's most recent lexicon of forms. Its open plan and *brise-soleil*, its ramps and curvilinear forms translated Le Corbusier's sculptural expression into Latin rhythms and what David Underwood has called "free-form Modernism."[172]

In the Futurama and the "Highways and Horizons" exhibit for General Motors, Norman Bel Geddes presented an ideal city of the future principally inspired by Le Corbusier's plans of the 1920s and 1930s. To a large extent Bel Geddes's work reflected an earlier apprecia-

tion in some circles of Le Corbusier's urbanism. During the early 1930s landscape architect and highway engineer Charles Downing Lay, for example, attempted to introduce America to the expressways found in Le Corbusier's urban schemes. In 1933 he published a view of the Ville Contemporaine (see figure 6.13) whose multi-lane "highway scheme" might serve as a model for his own "high-speed trunk highway through a suburban or city district." As an advisor to the New Jersey Highway Department, Lay was successful in promoting high-speed roads linked to new towns.[173]

Bel Geddes's Futurama was a 35,000-square-foot model of a projected American landscape whose transcontinental highway system linked a metropolis of the future to the country beyond (figure 10.34). With the help

10.34
Norman Bel Geddes, Futurama, General Motors exhibit, New York World's Fair, 1939. (The Norman Bel Geddes Collection, The Theatre Arts Collection, Harry Ransom Humanities Research Center, The University of Texas at Austin, by permission of Edith Lutyens Bel Geddes, Executrix.)

10.35
Norman Bel Geddes, Futurama, General Motors exhibit, New York World's Fair, 1939. (The Norman Bel Geddes Collection, The Theatre Arts Collection, Harry Ransom Humanities Research Center, The University of Texas at Austin, by permission of Edith Lutyens Bel Geddes, Executrix.)

of the automobile this vision could be realized. Like Le Corbusier, Bel Geddes intended his city of the future not only to be developed in relation to highways but also to follow the tenets of demolition-based planning. The General Motors exhibit elucidated his vision: "Here is an American city replanned around a highly developed modern traffic system.... Whenever possible the rights of way of these express city thoroughfares have been so routed as to displace outmoded business sections and undesirable slum areas."[174] In this "great metropolis of 1960" sleek skyscraper towers were widely spaced to allow "sunshine, light and air" and accommodate multi-level "express boulevards . . . for through city traffic" (figure 10.35). The metropolis with its projected highway and transportation system promising "new social horizons . . . leading to new benefits for everyone" recalled the imagery of Le Corbusier's schemes of the 1920s and the rhetoric of his Radiant City, even though its formal elements and social planning raised legitimate questions.[175] Bel Geddes's Futurama also borrowed from Frank Lloyd Wright's Broadacre City of the 1930s and Walter Dorwin Teague's redevelopment project for San Francisco (itself inspired by the cruciform business towers of Le Corbusier's ideal cities), sponsored by U.S. Steel.[176]

Notwithstanding its affinities to many of the formal and conceptual elements of Le Corbusier's centralized plans, Bel Geddes's was fundamentally a decentralized scheme. Whereas Le Corbusier employed highways to increase centralization, Bel Geddes and other American visionaries used them to encourage decentralization and unite city with region. It is ironic that in promoting garden city ideals the Futurama adopted the imagery of Le Corbusier's first machine age and the humanist language of the second machine age intended to support only centralization. Bel Geddes's vision sustained a late-nineteenth-century pastoral ideal and endorsed the automobile as the new "machine in the garden." But like Le Corbusier, he was controversial. Mumford ignored the Futurama's sympathies with the Garden City. He criticized Bel Geddes's city as an "old-fashioned" vision of a "jumbled world of yesterday" that, like the ground plan of the fair, lacked "order," in effect because he associated it with Corbusian order.[177]

On one hand, Bel Geddes's prototypes threatened American industrialists and planners in the same way as Le Corbusier's did because, if adopted, they would have involved expensive factory retooling and radical changes in infrastructure.[178] On the other hand, Bel Geddes's models did stimulate the development of a new national highway system. His vision in the Futurama exhibit, as in the model for the Shell Oil Company and book *Magic Motorways,* based on the example of Le Corbusier and others, helped to establish what Richard Guy Wilson called "the great American post–World War II achievement, the Interstate Highway System."[179]

The Debate on American Housing Reform

Collectively Le Corbusier's housing typologies, including the skyscraper designated for housing, was one of several influences on the development of public housing in New York City before 1935. However, as examined in chapter 6, most of the elements of his housing program—demolition-based planning, disregard for the traditional configuration of streets, large-scale planning and block development, and comprehensively planned communities—developed independently of Le Cor-

busier and were already components of New York City public housing and the policies that governed them. Issues dividing housing reformers from Le Corbusier included their resistance to European modernism and to his proposals for superblocks on a scale exceeding American precedent (i.e., more than 2,400 persons), to his proposals for factory-made housing, and to his plans that involved a radical treatment of infrastructure and cooperative ownership. Their own policies favoring decentralization and restricting commissions to those on approved lists effectively precluded collaboration with him. Lawrence Veiller dismissed Le Corbusier's utopianism and Mumford his centralized agenda. Henry Wright had more specific reservations. He objected to such visionary plans, as previously discussed, because they could not develop from "existing conditions and habits." Yet the policies of his own Housing Study Guild did support the economic benefits of high-rises (eight, ten, and twelve stories).[180] By enlisting the arguments of Le Corbusier and Gropius in favor of high densities and promoting them in its publications, the Housing Study Guild could strengthen its own position.[181]

Thus even though popular consensus among such sociologists and urban historians as Jane Jacobs, Vincent Scully, and Peter Hall held Le Corbusier largely responsible for the debacle of post–World War II high-rise housing and urban renewal in the United States, their arguments must be reevaluated in light of prewar housing typologies, public policy, opposition from housing reformers to his proposals, and market forces.[182] Public housing in the United States is distanced from Le Corbusier in another important respect. With the passage of the Wagner Housing Act in 1937, federal regulations played a greater role in restricting costs, building coverage, and other factors affecting housing. These mandates dictated increasingly banal designs that lacked most of the formal, technical, and social components of Le Corbusier's models. Such is the case with two NYCHA projects affected by the new law. Red Hook Houses in Brooklyn (1935–1939) adopted the cruciform plan but restricted the height of its buildings to six stories.[183] Similarly, the Queensbridge housing project in Queens (1936–1940; figure 10.36), whose design team was

10.36
William F. R. Ballard,
chief architect, and
Frederick G. Frost,
Sr., Henry S. Chur-
chill, and Burnett C.
Turner, associated
architects, Queens-
bridge Houses, ren-
dering, Queens, New
York, 1936–1940.
(New-York Historical
Society, 1940
McLaughlin AS.)

headed by William F. R. Ballard (chief architect) and Frederick G. Frost, Sr., Henry S. Churchill, and Burnett C. Turner (associated architects), employed attached Y-shaped "unit plans" around the perimeter of superblocks with central courts. The housing blocks, configured at angles of 120 degrees under the technical supervision of Frederick Ackerman, sought to "provide each apartment with the greatest possible cross ventilation, light, air and privacy." Although their plan recalls both the *type Sert* model (see figure 5.29) and Hans Poelzig's skyscraper project for the Friedrichstrasse in Berlin (1921; see figure 5.30) that was widely published in American architectural journals, the six-story units at Queensbridge were far from the large-scale high-rise metal and glass Cartesian skyscrapers that Le Corbusier had proposed in his American lectures and privately to the NYCHA.[184] Moreover, Ackerman's preliminary design for Queensbridge, which employed three- and four-story buildings largely in *Zeilenbau* formation (1936), showed little Corbusian influence. Ballard himself maintained that Queensbridge had little in common with the Sert–Le Corbusier model.[185] Rather, its design resulted from the Authority's reliance on empirical studies and the economic advantages of low-rise units joined together where land values were stable. Frost was responsible for the plan of the Y-shaped units taking "maximum advantage of the New York City Multiple Dwelling Law which permitted up to 21 rooms served by a single open stair and a single elevator in a six-story fireproof building."[186] It seems far more likely that Frost was inspired by the Y-shaped apartment towers at Alden Park (see figure 6.8), which Henry Wright and other New York-based housing reformers promoted, since Frost and Ballard were both in Wright's camp.[187]

As the heights and densities of New York City housing projects increased during the late 1930s, especially where land was restricted and values were high, architects and planners used cruciform and Y-shaped towers for the same pragmatic reasons. Two case studies illustrate this point. The public-sector East River Houses, completed by the NYCHA in 1941, has been called by Richard Plunz "the first high-rise tower project in the history of New York housing philanthropy" (figure 10.37).[188] Slum clearance provided for a parklike superblock along the East River Drive in Harlem from 102nd to 105th streets. Designed by Voorhees, Walker,

Foley and Smith, East River Houses employed housing typologies ranging from low-rise blocks approximating *Zeilenbau* formation similar to Lescaze's Williamsburg Houses (see figure 6.1) to cruciform towers, both freestanding and attached, up to ten and eleven stories (like Lescaze and Frey's River Gardens Housing; see figure 6.3). The rotation of the apartment blocks, set at an angle to the city's street grid, was meant to conform with a triangular park along East River Drive, mandated by Park Commissioner Robert Moses. Thus, at East River Houses its configuration was determined not so much by solar orientation but by the aesthetics of the site planning, as Plunz showed. The tower scheme was chosen in preference to uniformly disposed six-story elevator buildings because it was more economical. Along with pragmatic considerations and empirical studies that de-

10.37
Voorhees, Walker, Foley and Smith, East River Houses, New York City Housing Authority, Manhattan, 1941. (*East River Houses*, New York City Housing Authority, July 1941.)

termined the use of cruciform towers, East River Houses looked to the more visionary scheme of Lescaze and Frey's River Gardens housing and thereby indirectly engaged Corbusian aesthetics. Through the influence of Lescaze, an important member of the NYCHA architectural board during the 1930s and 1940s, Le Corbusier's cruciform towers and variations of them had an increasing impact. Plunz determined that "the high-rise, government-subsidized precedent set by East River Houses remained the exclusive model for housing development in East Harlem," so its own design owed a debt to the projects of Le Corbusier, Lescaze, and Frey.[189]

In the private sector as well, designers were guided by both empirical studies and visionary plans. In 1938 when architects Richmond H. Shreve and Irwin Clavan and town planner Gilmore D. Clarke designed housing for Parkchester (figure 10.38)—what Eric Mumford called "the first large-scale realization of the 'tower in the park' idea in the United States"—they looked to native as well as European precedents.[190] Roberta Moudry suggested that Parkchester "represented a hybridization of certain modernist ideas, and their blending with standard American housing forms."[191] Built by the Metropolitan Life Insurance Co. for 42,000 people on 129

10.38
Richmond H. Shreve, Irwin Clavan, and Gilmore D. Clarke, Parkchester, south quadrant, Metropolitan Life Insurance Co., Bronx, New York. (MetLife Archives.)

acres in the Bronx, Parkchester employed fifty-one cruciform towers up to thirteen stories high because they offered economic advantages as well as more access to light
and air. Like Williamsburg Houses and other NYCHA
projects of the 1930s, Parkchester ignored the existing
street grid. But it did emphasize the "neighborhood unit
concept" of sociologist Clarence Perry. In so doing its
planners brought once more the garden city ideals of
Clarence Stein and Henry Wright to the dense borough.[192] Yet Parkchester's dispersal of cruciform towers
within a green space recalls not only River Gardens (see
figure 6.3) and East River Houses (see figure 10.37) but
also the imagery of the Radiant City (see figure 3.1).[193]
Endorsed by *Architectural Forum* as an example of "sound,
conservative design," the banality of its brick facades,
however, had little in common with Corbusian design.[194]

Historians may have held Le Corbusier accountable
for the mistakes of housing reform in the United States,
but their view was not shared by those within the movement, including both Frederick G. Frost, Jr., a partner in
the office of his father Frederick G. Frost, Sr., and
William Ballard. When asked to assess Le Corbusier's
influence on New York City housing, the younger Frost
concluded that except for one NYCHA project by
Lescaze (and Frey, either Chrystie-Forsyth or River Gardens), "it was minimal certainly in the early days of public housing." Ballard was equally skeptical about Le
Corbusier's impact during those years, emphasizing
instead the contributions of Ackerman and Henry
Wright.[195] An informed view of public housing as it developed both before and after World War II suggests that
American housing specialists used Le Corbusier's typologies, formal imagery, and aesthetics only when they
confirmed their own empirical models.[196] Moreover,
notwithstanding similarities between Le Corbusier's
projects and New York City public housing, the planning policy that shaped that housing developed independently of Le Corbusier. Significantly, what American
housing specialists of the 1930s did not criticize in Le
Corbusier's plans were those defects that today seem
most socially untenable: their failure to engage the street
and contribute to its vitality as well as other elements of
city-making. For both Le Corbusier and American hous-

ing reformers had endorsed an idealized image of the
tower in a park, a legacy of garden city planning. These
considerations encourage a fresh appraisal of such New
York City housing developments as Eggers and Higgins's Alfred E. Smith Houses (1948), Metropolitan
Life's Stuyvesant Town (1943–1947), NYCHA's Baruch
Houses (1953–1954) by Emery Roth and Sons, and especially Ballard, Todd and Associates' Polo Grounds
Houses (1964–1968). More than just Voisin or Radiant
City schemes come to life, these high-rise housing projects have a far more complex history that suggests shared
accountability.[197]

Urban Centralization

Le Corbusier may have played a more direct role in the
maturation of America's urban centers because he called
for centralization during a period of increasing decentralization. This was especially true for New York City.
In an effort to check decentralization during the 1930s
and 1940s, he called for redevelopment of the central
city to achieve order. That effort reinforced the interests
of urban real estate developers and entrepreneurs as well
as enlightened municipal authorities. During the early
1930s arguments favoring centralization were consonant with the vested interests of the Rockefeller family;
they also stimulated the urban vision of Raymond Hood
and his associates who were predisposed to European
modernism. After publication of *Cathédrales* with its endorsement of Rockefeller Center as both a functional-
rational and a biological model, Hitchcock agreed that
it "does point a new way for urban architecture." Rockefeller Center was significant, he maintained, not on account of its style but because "here for the first time the
bold ideal of such European theorists of the skyscraper as
Le Corbusier was approached." For this mixed-use but
largely commercial complex the Associated Architects
introduced demolition-based planning to the center city
in an "attempt to construct in one coherent scheme a
whole urban quarter, to provide for that quarter its own
streets and squares and to place the tall buildings so that
they do not get in each other's light and air." But Hitchcock also noted its social and collective life, "integrating

© 1936 The Washington Post. Reprinted with permission.

10.39

"Nelson Rockefeller Warns Real Estate to Check Business Decentralization," *New York Herald Tribune*, June 21, 1936, 10, p. 1. (Courtesy of the Rockefeller Archive Center.) © 1936 The Washington Post. Reprinted with permission.

thus the architectural expression with a multitude of urban needs so that the rich and the middle classes at least, can find within its limits, offices, shops, recreation, and even instruction."[198] The success of Rockefeller Center made it a cultural and commercial anchor for midtown, stabilizing the center city by increasing property values and slowing the migration of commercial development northward.[199]

As Nelson Rockefeller made his swift ascent to the presidency of Rockefeller Center during the years after Le Corbusier's visit, he appropriated the architect's ideas on centralization and his program for rebuilding New York City. In June 1936 he delivered a radio speech advising "real estate interests of this city to check decentralization before it was too late." Rockefeller's warning made headlines in the *New York Herald Tribune* (figure 10.39). To maintain the city's "position in the business and social world," he called for "lower taxes, replacement

of obsolete buildings, and a wholesale rehabilitation." Much as Le Corbusier directed his agenda to Rockefeller in fall of 1935, the next spring the young "authority" urged real estate investors to undertake "a concentrated program of reconstruction." In elucidating his arguments about the dangers of decentralization and the importance of rebuilding, Rockefeller drew on his many conversations with Le Corbusier about the Radiant City. He made direct reference to the architect when he unabashedly paraphrased the view "expressed by a friend" that "to get green grass, trees, fresh air and sunlight, millions of human beings pay the penalty of traveling by train or bus from one to more than two hours daily." Rockefeller maintained that "such a building program would soon make it possible for New York to offer modernized living and working quarters on a large scale and enable it to re-assert its position of pre-eminence."[200] If real estate interests would follow the example of Rockefeller Center and the Rockefeller Apartments, he implied, they could use commercial and residential development to revitalize Manhattan. By adopting Corbusian rhetoric, Rockefeller formulated proposals in support of centralization that would benefit not only the interests of the city but also those of the Rockefellers.

The success of Rockefeller Center as well as strategies learned from Le Corbusier for achieving urban centralization were foremost in the mind of Nelson Rockefeller a decade later when he negotiated with his father, leaders of the United Nations organization, municipal authorities, and real estate developer William Zeckendorf to secure a site in the New York area for the United Nations Headquarters.[201]

Le Corbusier and the Planning of the United Nations Headquarters

It was not until after World War II that Le Corbusier would return to New York, to collaborate on the design of the United Nations Headquarters. There he realized a fragment of the Radiant City project that had so long eluded him. For the U.N. Headquarters, he condensed his ideas on centralization, building typology, and program, as well as his *parti* for the Radiant City. His ambivalence about collaborations notwithstanding, he was compelled to work as a member of a large design team. His formal involvement followed his arrival in New York in May 1946, having been appointed by France as its delegate to the U.N. Permanent Headquarters Commission.[202] The Commission was responsible for securing a permanent site for the new U.N. offices.[203] While Le Corbusier participated actively in the meetings of both the Commission and two subcommittees on requirements and site, he pressed his personal agenda on U.N. officials and submitted his own *Report of the French Delegate* in June 1946.[204] Cast in the language of the second machine age, his report emphasized the benefits of centralization and recommended Manhattan as the new site. Over the objections of New York City Park Commissioner Robert Moses and others, the Manhattan site prevailed.[205]

By December 1946 Nelson Rockefeller had facilitated his father's gift of $8.5 million to purchase from William Zeckendorf a seventeen-acre East River parcel between 42nd and 48th streets. For that site Wallace Harrison submitted a controversial proposal to the U.N. General Assembly of a recycled scheme for a mixed-use complex of office skyscrapers, cruciform apartment towers, and an auditorium called X-City.[206] In justifying the high-rise scheme, Harrison prepared a brochure appro-

priating arguments from *Cathédrales*. Senator Warren Austin, chief of the U.S. Mission, advanced Le Corbusier's position that the modern skyscrapers of the New World, like the medieval cathedrals of Europe, might offer cultural renewal.[207] Thus, Le Corbusier played an important role in the selection of a site for the U.N. Headquarters. His position on centralization was influential to Nelson Rockefeller, his preference for Manhattan over other sites was persuasive to U.N. delegates, and his defense of the modern skyscraper invoking the spiritualism of the cathedral was successfully deployed by advocates of Harrison's scheme.

With the approval of the X-City site Secretary General Trygve Lie established the U.N. Headquarters Planning Office and named Harrison Director of Planning. Harrison in turn assembled an international team to the U.N.'s Board of Design Consultants, including Le Corbusier (who returned to New York toward the end of January 1947), Oscar Niemeyer from Brazil, Sven Markelius from Sweden, and special consultants including the Russian-born engineer Vladimir Bodiansky who had worked in Le Corbusier's atelier.[208] On the dynamics of the design team during its formative weeks, Max Abramovitz recalled, "We thought we all were affected by Corbu. . . . Wally was really behind him until he made life difficult for Wally."[209]

Under Harrison's direction the Board was committed to collaborative design work, based on the model of Rockefeller Center's Associated Architects whose team of technical experts Le Corbusier had applauded in *Cathédrales*.[210] But in spite of a pledge of support for collaboration, presenting a formal "Declaration" at the April 18, 1947, meeting of the Board and assuring the Director of Planning that "all will work anonymously," Le Corbusier challenged Harrison's leadership at every turn.[211] Intent on controlling design decisions, he attempted to have CIAM delegates appointed to the Board. He continued to cultivate high-ranking U.N. officials because he considered them, rather than Harrison and Rockefeller, in his camp.[212] From the start he and the Harrison team worked at cross purposes, each with competing agendas and divergent views on the issue of authorship.

10.40
Hugh Ferriss, bird's-eye view of
Scheme 46G, U.N. Headquarters.
(Avery Architectural and Fine Arts
Library, Columbia University in
the City of New York; Jean Ferriss
Leich Collection.)

The collaborative nature of the design process under
Harrison's executive control, and the Board's practice of
leaving drawings unsigned, encouraged anonymity, thus
frustrating later attempts to assign authorship of the
U.N. Headquarters. But recent studies by Victoria Newhouse, George Dudley, and Linda Phipps, documenting
an extensive chronology of events and the respective contributions of architects on the Board, as well as those in
the office of Harrison and Abramovitz, now make it possible to understand Le Corbusier's participation and assess his later claims of authorship.[213] These studies
suggest that Le Corbusier influenced the final design for
the U.N. Headquarters, Scheme 46G as it appeared in
Hugh Ferriss's rendering (figure 10.40), in three important ways: building typology and program, formal components of the Radiant City *parti,* and collaboration on
the design. First, Scheme 46G employed a trapezoid

10.41
Le Corbusier, project for the World Library (slab raised on *pilotis*) and the International Association (slab-block/trapezoid), 1946. (*UN Headquarters*, p. 36, pl. 10.) © 2001 Artists Rights Society (ARS), New York/ADAGP, Paris/FLC.

10.42
Le Corbusier, high-rise slab and block with *cafés-terrasses*, drawing for U.N. Headquarters, January 28, 1947. (*Carnet de poche*, p. 1; FLC Archive W1(6)1.) © 2001 Artists Rights Society (ARS), New York/ADAGP, Paris/FLC.

Plans // 28/1/47 // faire pour gde [grande] Salle [make for large hall] // I Av [First Avenue] // cafés terrasses // east River // ici [here] // Créer 1 séparation [create a separation] // on entre dans la cité mondiale [one enters the world headquarters]

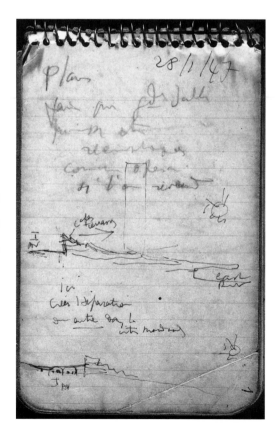

form and tower for the General Assembly and Secretariat, respectively, recalling the slab lifted on *pilotis* for the World Library (*la Bibliothèque*) and the slab-block/trapezoid for the International Association that Le Corbusier had developed the previous year, working alone and without a program or site, for his *Report of the French Delegate* (figure 10.41).[214]

Second, Scheme 46G recalled the Radiant City *parti* that Le Corbusier envisioned in his unpublished *carnet de poche* or sketchbook containing his studies of the project from January 28 to May 11, 1947. Le Corbusier proposed a number of schemes but his first, a cross section of the site, was generative (figure 10.42).[215] Dated January 28, 1947, the first day he visited the East River parcel and nearly three weeks before the first meeting of the Board of Design, the drawing shows the image of a single high-rise tower beside a sculpted block (topped by *cafés-terrasses*) standing in the sun. It flowed naturally from his long-deferred ambition to design a Cartesian skyscraper and fragment of the Radiant City in Manhattan. The simplicity of his idea contrasted sharply with the complexity of Harrison's scheme derived from X-City.

Third, the drawings presented at the forty-five meetings of the Board of Design from February 17 to June 9, 1947, reveal the extent of Le Corbusier's collaboration and how his initial ideas were folded into the design development.[216] They also demonstrate how his proposals reworked the ideas of other architects on the team, especially Scheme 17 by Niemeyer and Oscar Nitzchke, the latter a designer in Harrison's office.[217] When team members challenged Le Corbusier's authority, he responded with Scheme 23.[218] As a counterproposal Niemeyer presented Scheme 32, which the Board endorsed.[219] Le Corbusier in turn teamed up with Bodiansky to design Scheme 23A, an alternative version.[220] Harrison resolved the debate by selecting the best design himself. His solution was diplomatic: "The only scheme that gets complete satisfaction is an early idea of Le Corbusier's as carried out, drawn up, by Oscar Niemeyer." According to Dudley, "Harrison pointed to Niemeyer's Scheme 32. 'This could be the original Le Corbusier February 21st sketch: [the Secretariat] building [freestanding] down to [the] ground; the open ground scheme!'" In fact, Harrison was referring to an early conceptual drawing by Le Corbusier, dated February 21, 1947 (figure 10.43), rather than to his Scheme 23 or 23A. This, Dudley remembered, "had stayed in Harrison's mind as the first time Corbu had loosened up his meeting-hall block, letting the Secretariat stand free, beginning to open up the center of the site."[221] The sim-

10.43
Le Corbusier, drawing for U.N. Headquarters, February 21, 1947. (Plan FLC 31678.) © 2001 Artists Rights Society (ARS), New York/ADAGP, Paris/FLC.

plicity of the free-standing slab (the Secretariat) in the February 21 drawing recalled the tower skyscraper in Le Corbusier's *carnet* (see figure 10.42).

Le Corbusier's most effective collaboration came when he joined with Niemeyer and engineers Bodiansky and Ernst Weissmann to form one of two teams to work toward a final design. With a cadre of former students and associates, including Weissmann, Le Corbusier assembled his own atelier in New York, but was still forced to make concessions. At the Board meeting of May 7 Weissmann presented Scheme 23/32, a hybrid of Schemes 23 and 32 that he and others had drawn up.[222] Scheme 23/32 formed the basis of the final design Scheme 42G, as it was worked out by Harrison's office and submitted in a report to the General Assembly on July 1, 1947 (see figure 10.40). It still reflected Le Corbusier's insistence on positions of authority for the General Assembly (near the center of the site) and the Secretariat (near the south end of the site), which characterized his Scheme 23. Here too the extended trapezoidal form emerged, evolved from Scheme 23A. But most of the other key elements, including separation of the General Assembly and the other three constituents (Secretariat, conference wing, library) of the "central four" that clustered around a public plaza, evolved from Niemeyer's Scheme 32. The final design for the U.N. Headquarters has been judged harshly as Harrison's assemblage of elements from different schemes. However, recognition must be given to Le Corbusier for developing the initial *parti* and to Niemeyer and others for redirecting and enriching it.[223] "After all," Abramovitz reflected, "as a great architect to be remembered, it would be Corbu and not Wallace Harrison or Abramovitz.... He was the innovator.... Shook us all up."[224]

Notwithstanding competing claims of authorship, especially from Le Corbusier, architects and critics of the period recognized that, for better or worse, Le Corbusier's ideas dominated the U.N. *parti.*[225] In his review, José Luis Sert identified the importance of Le Corbusier's contributions to the conceptual and programmatic development of the complex. For, instead of proceeding with plans for the "world capital" that most politicians would idealistically project for the U.N. ironically it

would be the "Utopian Planner" who pragmatically "defines the needs and outlines the general program that made it possible to choose a site" for a future headquarters.[226] From his experience with the League of Nations competition, Le Corbusier was able to identify various programmatic elements for the new U.N. offices, as yet unspecified by the organization. To Joseph Hudnut the Headquarters was the realization of the design principles and typologies that Le Corbusier had long advanced.[227] But Lewis Mumford reproached Le Corbusier for the commercial character of the high-rise Secretariat, which "symbolizes the worst practices of New York."[228] The Headquarters, Mumford charged, "is a combination of Le Corbusier's breezy City of the Future and the businesslike congestion of Rockefeller Center."[229]

Le Corbusier's participation in this project allowed him to realize both a civic model of "great works" and a fragment of the Radiant City. Harrison wanted him on the team to advance the cause of modernism in the belief that it would provide the United Nations with a compelling symbol of a New World order. Had Le Corbusier not made his initiatives to Rockefeller and Harrison in 1935, had Harrison not assimilated Le Corbusier's theory and design of the 1930s, Le Corbusier's role on the team as well as the design of the U.N. Headquarters would have taken a different course. Some critics contend that the Headquarters is a sterile common denominator of the postwar International Style, advancing Hitchcock and Johnson's emphasis on form and style. Its design may have incorporated formal elements of the Radiant City but not its social agenda. A parcel of urban intervention, the Headquarters was flawed because its public space was isolated from rather than integrated with the street.

The U.N. Headquarters was important to Le Corbusier because it left his imprint on New York City, although not as he had hoped, because in the end it was a work of collaboration. He wanted to dominate the Design Board to confirm that America could achieve spiritual and cultural renewal in the postwar years, as in 1935, through the agent of French culture and specifically his own initiative.[230] But such confirmation required recognition. In spite of his efforts to assert his ideas and to circumvent Harrison's consensus planning by both appealing to higher authorities and claiming proprietary authorship, credit for the final design of the Headquarters must be shared. Like the debacle of the League of Nations and his disappointments of 1935, this episode was destined to be ill-fated, according to his own mythic narrative, so that Le Corbusier could emerge morally triumphant. He continued to adopt the mantle of tragic hero in order to create.

Through Harrison's skillful diplomacy, the design development of the U.N. Headquarters took ideas as they emerged from scheme to scheme. Working for four months, Le Corbusier pursued his designs and made changes in his own schemes, notably 23, 23A, and 23/32, that reflected the ideas of Niemeyer, Nitzchke, and others, as well as the criticism of Board members. Conversely, Niemeyer, Nitzchke, and other modernists on the team employed typologies that Le Corbusier had either invented or advanced, including the tall slab and slab-block as well as trapezoidal and paraboloid forms. The project demonstrated that, in spite of himself, Le Corbusier was capable of collaboration, bringing a new dimension of reality to his work. The consortium he proposed to Rockefeller and Harrison in 1935 set a precedent for collaborations with them on planning and designing the U.N. Headquarters. Such collaborations, including his attempt to form a consortium of transatlantic industrialists in 1935, helped prepare him for the teamwork involved in designing and executing the Carpenter Center for the Visual Arts at Harvard University (1959–1963). The United Nations project gave him the opportunity to return to the great city of towers and bridges that he had reluctantly left in 1935 (figure 10.44).

Outcome

Le Corbusier's 1935 lecture tour to America evoked reciprocal responses. Although he received no commissions, he still found his visit highly affective and generative. His experience of America, now grafted to received ideas, contributed to his development. His theory and design, in turn, influenced the discipline and

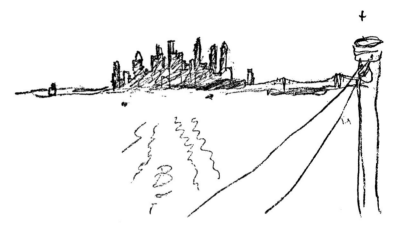

10.44
Le Corbusier, drawing of lower Manhattan and Brooklyn Bridge from S.S. *Lafayette*, December 13, 1935. (*Cathédrales*, p. 320.) © 2001 Artists Rights Society (ARS), New York/ADAGP, Paris/FLC.

practice of architecture in the United States. Yet the tour caused a transatlantic misunderstanding between him and the country that symbolized a clash of two cultures. Le Corbusier's criticism resulted in a penetrating, if idiosyncratic, analysis of America. He applied an outsider's perspective that brought the culture of the New World into high relief, although publication of *Cathédrales* in 1937 had little direct impact in either America or France.

An important and unresolved question remains. Did this visit change his preconceptions? In an ideological sense, it did not; in a pragmatic sense, it did affect his theory and design in significant ways. His experiences at the Ford plant and in American cities enriched his concept of a second machine age that would synthesize modern building techniques and humanist concerns. As a result of his encounters with the skyscrapers, bridges, and slums of New York and Chicago, Le Corbusier exchanged a measure of the ideal for the real. But his inability to communicate effectively in English, the demands of the lecture tour, and his pressing search for work compromised his ability to make deep connections. Moreover, his study of American history and culture was selective. His philosophical predisposition toward the visionary also limited his ability to engage mere facts. And the same temperament that impeded his previous efforts to make connections with politics and industry in France and in other countries reasserted itself in the United States. For these reasons Le Corbusier's preconceptions of America remained in tension with his experiences, allowing his idealism to dominate.

Notwithstanding these limitations, his subsequent work showed the impact of America. He introduced in his skyscrapers greater monumentality and plasticity, well-articulated functions, and integrated systems; and he employed tension structures and explored a new typology. On another level, Le Corbusier may have been disillusioned with the economic and social inequities of capitalism, but he was still invested in its production-based assumptions. His research into basic industries, their processes, and products, enabled him to bring to his architecture after 1935 an infusion of design elements based on American models. As a result, his late works reveal an interest in more pragmatic concerns.

From an American perspective Le Corbusier's visit encouraged the transition to modernism that was previously initiated within the discipline and practice of architecture. His theory and design continued to serve promoters of the International Style who emphasized form. The tour introduced Americans to his new work, which synthesized technical, vernacular, regional, and humanist concerns. Moreover, American housing reformers employed Le Corbusier's typologies, but largely as formal elements to confirm their own empirical models. The public policies, and the economic and political conditions that mandated them, developed independently of the architect. An advocate for the central city, Le Corbusier helped to counter the trend toward increasing decentralization in the New York region. His ideas influenced not only Nelson Rockefeller's thinking but also the United Nation's decision a decade later to locate in Manhattan. In helping to shape the design for the U.N. Headquarters Le Corbusier would offer New York a case study of Radiant City planning.

But Le Corbusier's Mediterranean forms and the ideas that sustained them could not be easily communicated to North American students and practitioners as they had to their South American counterparts. Instead, Gropius provided a pedagogy for modernism and Mies van der Rohe an approach to standardization that could be adapted to American building techniques. For Gropius, Mies, and Breuer brought with them German system and method that joined with American pragmatism and efficiency. With no system or method to offer, Le Corbusier had few prospects for work. Moreover, in comparison with Le Corbusier, Frank Lloyd Wright offered Americans a formal language and rhetoric of "organic architecture" more sympathetic to their aesthetics, values, and politics. Yet Le Corbusier's lecture tour made him the best-known European modernist on American shores before the German design migration.[231]

Le Corbusier's ambivalent obsession about American culture reflects the volatile conflicts that shaped his own aspirations to be a modern man. At the core of the idea of the modern lies the notion of mélange. He believed that America's impact on Europe, and especially on France, would increasingly dilute the culture of the

Old World; that prospect, offering both good and bad, seemed inevitable. However, France's impact on the United States could enlighten the culture of the New World; but that prospect was not inevitable. After 1935 Le Corbusier increasingly linked his destiny to the notion of the modern. To be modern was not to work in an arena of a pure national culture, but in a more globalized one. Inevitably his debate on America, the result of both preconception and experience, defined his expression of the modern and shaped design in the Old and New World. In the twentieth century no other European architect matched the breadth of Le Corbusier's contributions to transatlantic exchange, both architectural and cultural.

Appendix A
Itinerary of Le Corbusier's 1935 American Lecture Tour

Source: Based on undated "Itinerary" (FLC).

As of August 12, 1935

October	24	Thursday	Museum of Modern Art
	25	Friday	Wadsworth Atheneum
	30	Wednesday	Yale University
	31	Thursday	Columbia University
November	1	Friday	Vassar College
	4	Monday	Princeton University
	5	Tuesday	Princeton University
	6	Wednesday	Princeton University
	8	Friday	Philadelphia Art Alliance
	12	Tuesday	Bowdoin College
	14	Thursday	Massachusetts Institute of Technology
	15	Friday	Harvard University
	18	Monday	Municipal Art Association of Baltimore
	21	Thursday	Cranbrook Academy, Michigan
	22	Friday	Kalamazoo Institute of Arts (pending)
	27	Wednesday	Wisconsin Union ⎤
	28	Thursday	Wisconsin Union ⎬ (pending)
	29	Friday	Wisconsin Union ⎦
December	2	Monday	Kansas City
	5	Thursday	Denver Art Museum (pending)
	9	Monday	Seattle Art Institute
	11	Wednesday	Portland Art Association ⎤
	12	Thursday	Portland Art Association ⎦ (pending)

Christmas holidays	Mexico City
January	The Dallas Art Museum, Columbia, and possibly Vassar requested lectures toward the end of Le Corbusier's tour.

Institutions that expressed interest but were awaiting decisions of committees or directors:

Smith College
Buffalo Fine Arts Academy
University of Minnesota
Detroit Institute of Arts
Dartmouth College
Pittsburgh Chapter of the AIA
Brown University
Rhode Island School of Design
Stanford University

As of August 28, 1935

October	24	Thursday	Museum of Modern Art
	25	Friday	Wadsworth Atheneum, Hartford
	30	Wednesday	Yale University
	31	Thursday	Columbia University
November	1	Friday	Vassar College
	4	Monday	Princeton University
	5	Tuesday	Princeton University
	6	Wednesday	Princeton University
	8	Friday	Philadelphia Art Alliance
	12	Tuesday	Bowdoin College
	14	Thursday	Massachusetts Institute of Technology
	15	Friday	Harvard University
	18	Monday	Municipal Art Association of Baltimore
	21	Thursday	Cranbrook Academy, Michigan
	22	Friday	Kalamazoo Institute of Arts, Michigan (pending)
	27	Wednesday	Madison ⎤
	28	Thursday	Madison ⎬ (pending)
	29	Friday	Madison ⎦
December	2	Monday	Kansas City
	5	Thursday	Denver (awaiting decision on date)
	9	Monday	Seattle
	11	Wednesday	Portland ⎤ (awaiting decision
	12	Thursday	Portland ⎦ on date)
	16–January 1936		Mexico City

Source: Based on undated "Schedule" (FLC).

Final Itinerary

October	24	Thursday	Museum of Modern Art
	25	Friday	Wadsworth Atheneum
	28	Monday	Columbia University
	29	Tuesday	Wesleyan University
	30	Wednesday	Yale University
November	1	Friday	Vassar College
	5	Tuesday	Harvard University
	6	Wednesday	Massachusetts Institute of Technology
	8	Friday	Philadelphia Art Alliance
	12	Tuesday	Bowdoin College
	14	Thursday	Princeton University
	15	Friday	Princeton University

	16	Saturday	Princeton University
	18	Monday	Municipal Art Society of Baltimore
	19	Tuesday	Columbia University
	21	Thursday	Cranbrook Academy
	22	Friday	Kalamazoo Institute of Arts
	25	Monday	Arts Club of Chicago
	25	Monday	Renaissance Society, University of Chicago
	26	Tuesday	Memorial Union, University of Wisconsin, Madison
	27	Wednesday	Illinois Society of Architects and American Institute of Architects, Chicago

Source: Author's reconstruction of final itinerary.

Appendix B
Itinerary of the Traveling Exhibit
"Recent Work of Le Corbusier"

1935	November 5–November 12	Yale University, New Haven
	November 18–November 25	Cranbrook Academy of Art, Bloomfield Hills, Michigan
	November 26–December 10	Wisconsin Union, Madison
1936	February 18–March 18	Colorado Springs Art Gallery, Colorado Springs
	March 30–April 13	Henry Gallery, University of Washington, Seattle
1937	May 10–May 31	College of William and Mary, Williamsburg, Virginia
	August 9–August 23	Fox Theatre, St. Louis
	October 1–October 22	M. H. de Young Memorial Museum, San Francisco
	November 8–November 22	Texas State College for Women, Denton
	November 29–December 20	State University of Iowa, Iowa City
1938	January 24–February 14	Pittsburgh Architectural Club, Pittsburgh
	February 29–March 14	Dartmouth College, Hanover, New Hampshire

| | April 25–May 9 | Wells College, Aurora, New York |
| | May 16–June 6 | Wesleyan University, Middletown, Connecticut |

Source: The Museum of Modern Art Archives, NY: Records of the Department of Circulating Exhibitions, II.1/71 (7), album A1.

Appendix C
Le Corbusier's Statement for the Press,
November 19, 1935

STATEMENT MADE BY MR. LE CORBUSIER, FRENCH AR-
CHITECT AND CITY PLANNER ON THE NECESSITY
AND POSSIBILITY OF INAUGURATING IMMEDIATELY A
REHOUSING PROGRAM ON [A] NATIONAL SCALE IN
THE UNITED STATES.

In the destiny of nations, the United States is the first to be
in a position to realize immediately the equipment of the second
era in the machine civilization.

The second era of the Machine Age must be erected on the
ruins of the last hundred years, Chaos and absurdity will be followed by Harmony through social, economic and political organization. This misfortune in which we were plunged by the frantic
squandering of the last twenty years will be remedied as a result
of WISE PLANNING. The eminently wise plan is the FABRI-
CATION OF HOMES. To provide proper housing, both in the
cities and the country, is answering the most urgent demand of the
consuming public all over the world. BIG INDUSTRY SHOULD
UNDERTAKE THE FABRICATION OF HOMES. But the rou-
tine practices in architecture and construction must be abandoned. The new dwellings can and should be dry-fabricated in the
factory with all the marvelous machines including the conveyor
and with the full cooperation of the engineers and technicians.

A short time ago the U.S.A. constituted a formidable production equipment for efficient methods of work. The U.S.A. has
the spirit of enterprise, the strength of youth and in its immense
territory it possesses an unlimited program.

Housing; there lies the program of American Big Industry
and not in the purposeless manufacture of innumerable super-
fluous products, perfectly needless in modern Society and which
Society cannot pay.

Today, in 1935, owing to the preparations made in the last
years, the possibility is given in this United States of the immediate inauguration of a housing program on a national scale for the
gradual reconstruction of the American cities and rural districts.

For this we must have completely new plans, and must take
important measures of public welfare. Suitable plans must be prepared for the reformation of the overcrowded cities and a decent
occupation of the soil.

The Authorities, governmental and municipal, together
with the necessary technical organizations, the manufacturers of
metal products and other materials, the builders of machines for
the equipment of the home must collaborate to stimulate the creation of new plans for homes and districts. As a matter of fact, the
entire population will have to be shown how to participate in this
work of regeneration that is to be done for them very largely by
themselves.

But the science of urbanism must dominate and lead the inhabitants of the cities to the cessation of waste, to the full enjoy-
ment of the freedom that these new methods can produce.

Until now cities have rebuilt themselves without conscious
purpose. Today we must introduce the new plan (for habitation
and circulation) which will regulate the future transformation of
our cities.

Source: Fondation Le Corbusier, document in English titled as
above; English translation attributed to Henry Sipos.

Notes

Abbreviations

Agenda   Le Corbusier, Agenda, 1935–1936, Fondation Le Corbusier, Paris.

Almanach   Charles Edouard Jeanneret-Gris, *Almanach d'architecture moderne* (Paris: Editions G. Crès, [1926]).

Cathédrales   Le Corbusier, *Quand les cathédrales étaient blanches: Voyage aux pays des timides* (Paris: Librairie Plon, 1937).

Cathedrals   Le Corbusier, *When the Cathedrals Were White: A Journey to the Country of Timid People,* trans. Francis E. Hyslop, Jr. (New York: Reynal and Hitchcock, 1947).

Century   *Le Corbusier, Architect of the Century* (London: Hayward Gallery, 1987).

City of Tomorrow   Le Corbusier, *The City of Tomorrow and Its Planning,* trans. with an introduction by Frederick Etchells (New York: Payson and Clarke [1929]).

DAD, MoMA, NY   Department of Architecture and Design, Museum of Modern Art, New York.

Encyclopédie   *Le Corbusier une encyclopédie* (Paris: Centre Georges Pompidou, 1987).

EN   *L'Esprit Nouveau.*

FLC   Fondation Le Corbusier, Paris.

JSAH   *Journal of the Society of Architectural Historians.*

Le Corbusier 1910–65   *Le Corbusier 1910–65,* ed. W. Boesiger and H. Girsberger (London: Thames and Hudson, 1967).

OC 1910–1929   Le Corbusier and Pierre Jeanneret, *Oeuvre complète 1910–1929* (Zurich: Girsberger, 1937; reprint, 1964). Orig. pub. as *Ihr Gesamtes Werk von 1910–1929,* ed. O. Stonorov and W. Boesiger (Zurich: Girsberger, 1930).

OC 1929–1934   Le Corbusier and P[ierre] Jeanneret, *Oeuvre complète de 1929–1934,* ed. Willy Boesiger (Zurich: Girsberger, 1935; reprint, 1964).

OC 1934–1938   Le Corbusier and Pierre Jeanneret, *Oeuvre complète 1934–1938,* ed. Max Bill (Zurich: Girsberger, 1939; reprint, 1964).

OC 1938–1946   Le Corbusier, *Oeuvre complète 1938–1946,* ed. W. Boesiger (Zurich: Editions d'Architecture, 1946).

Précisions   Le Corbusier, *Précisions sur an état présent de l'architecture et de l'urbanisme* (Paris: Editions G. Crès et Cie, [1930]).

Precisions   Le Corbusier, *Precisions on the Present State of Architecture and City Planning,* trans. Edith Schreiber Aujame (Cambridge: MIT Press, 1991).

RC   Le Corbusier, *The Radiant City,* trans. Pamela Knight, Eleanor Levieux, and Derek Coltman (New York: Orion Press, 1967).

Record   *Architectural Record.*

Towards a New Architecture   Le Corbusier, *Towards a New Architecture,* trans. with an introduction by Frederick Etchells (New York: Payson and Clarke, 1927).

Vers une architecture   Le Corbusier-Saugnier, *Vers une architecture* (Paris: G. Crès [1923]).

VR   Le Corbusier, *La Ville radieuse* (Paris: Editions de l'architecture d'aujourd'hui [1935]).

Introduction

1. On the social and political implications of Taylorism, see Charles S. Maier, "Between Taylorism and Technocracy: European Ideologies and the Vision of Industrial Productivity in the 1920s," *Journal of Contemporary History* 5 (1970), pp. 27–61.

2. Werner Hegemann, *Der Städtebau nach den Ergebnissen der allgemeinen Städtebau-Ausstellung in Berlin, nebst einem Anhang: Die Internationale Städtebau Ausstellung in Düsseldorf,* 2 vols. (Berlin: Wasmuth, 1911–1913), and *Amerikanische Architektur und Stadtbaukunst* (Berlin: Wasmuth, 1925); Walter Gropius, "Die Entwicklung moderner Industriebaukunst," *Jahrbuch des deutschen Werkbundes,* 1913, pp. 17–22; Paul Morand, *New-York* (Paris: Flammarion, 1930); Georges Duhamel, *Scènes de la vie future* (Paris: Mercure de France, 1930); André Maurois, *En Amérique* (Paris: Flammarion, 1933); René et Yvonne Allendy, *Capitalisme et sexualité* (Paris: Editions Denoël et Steele, 1932); Robert Aron and Arnaud Dandieu, *Décadence de la nation française* (Paris: Editions Rieder, 1931); Jean de Pierrefeu, *Contre la vie chère* (Paris: Magasins à prix uniques, décembre 1933), pages cut and annotations (FLC). For Mary McLeod's analysis of *Plans, Prélude,* and other neosyndicalist literature, see "Le Rêve transi de Le Corbusier: l'Amérique 'catastrophe féerique,'" in J.[ean]-L.[ouis] Cohen and H.[ubert] Damisch, eds., *Américanisme et modernité* (Paris: EHESS and Flammarion, 1993), pp. 208–227.

3. Louis-Ferdinand Céline, *Voyage au bout de la nuit* (Paris: Gallimard, 1931); Blaise Cendrars, *Les Paques à New York* (1912); "New-York vu par F. Léger," *Cahiers d'Art* 6 (1931), pp. 437–439, reprinted in Fernand Léger, *Fonctions de la peinture* (Paris: Gonthier, 1965), pp. 186–193; Christian Zervos, "Amérique," *Cahiers d'Art* 1 (1926), p. 60; S.[igfried] Giedion, "Vers un renouveau architectural de l'Amérique," *Cahiers d'Art* 8 (1933), pp. 237–243.

4. For facsimile reproductions of drawings and watercolors in Le Corbusier's 1907 Tuscan sketchbook, see Giuliano Gresleri, ed., *Le Corbusier, il viaggio in Toscana 1907* (Florence and Venice: Marsilio, 1987). On the "voyage d'Orient" of 1911, see "En Orient," *La Feuille d'Avis de La Chaux-de-Fonds* (1911); Le Corbusier, *Le Voyage d'Orient* (Paris: Editions Forces Vives, 1966); for a facsimile edition of Le Corbusier's sketchbooks of his "voyage d'Orient," see Le Corbusier, *Voyage to the Orient,* ed. Giuliano Gresleri, 6 vols. (New York: Rizzoli, 1988); Giuliano Gresleri and Italo Zannier, *Le Corbusier, viaggio in oriente: gli inediti di Charles Edouard Jeanneret, fotografo e scrittore* (Venice and Paris: Marsilio and Fondation Le Corbusier, 1984); Le Corbusier, *Journey to the East,* ed. and trans. Ivan Žaknić with Nicole Pertuiset (Cambridge: MIT Press, 1987). On his travels in Germany, see Charles-Edouard Jeanneret, *Etude sur le mouvement d'art décoratif en Allemagne* (La Chaux-de-Fonds: Haefeli, 1912); facsimile editions of the sketchbooks from his travels in Germany are published in Le Corbusier, *Les Voyages d'Allemagne: Carnets* (Paris and New York: Fondation Le Corbusier and Monacelli Press, 1995); see also Werner Oechslin, "Alle-

magne: Influences, confluences et reniements," in *Encyclopédie,* pp. 33–39. Jean-Louis Cohen documents Le Corbusier's travels in Moscow most comprehensively in his book *Le Corbusier and the Mystique of the USSR* (Princeton: Princeton University Press, 1992). On his South American lectures, see Le Corbusier, *Précisions;* Elizabeth Davis Harris, "Le Corbusier and the Headquarters of the Brazilian Ministry of Education and Health 1936–1947" (Ph.D. diss., University of Chicago, 1984); see also Jean-Pierre Giordani, "Territoire," in *Encyclopédie,* pp. 402–406. Seventy-three sketchbooks from travels between 1914 and 1964 are reproduced in facsimile in *Le Corbusier Sketchbooks,* 4 vols. (New York and Cambridge: Architectural History Foundation and MIT Press, 1981–1982).

5. For references to his *carnet,* see *Cathédrales,* pp. 89, 230; *Cathedrals,* pp. 63, 155. The published *carnets* indicate a gap in the chronology between 1933 (Algiers) and 1936 (Rio de Janeiro). See *Le Corbusier Sketchbooks,* vol. 1, 1914–1948, C10, pp. 27–29, C11, pp. 31–32.

6. On his lectures in Algiers, see Mary Caroline McLeod, "Urbanism and Utopia: Le Corbusier from Regional Syndicalism to Vichy" (Ph.D. diss., Princeton University, 1985); and McLeod, "Le Corbusier and Algiers," *Oppositions* 19/20 (Winter/Spring 1980). On the Rome lectures, see Giorgio Ciucci, "A Roma con Bottai," *Rassegna* (I Clienti di Le Corbusier) 3 (March 1980), pp. 66–71.

7. Mary McLeod, review of Le Corbusier, *Precisions on the Present State of Architecture and City Planning,* the 1991 English translation, *JSAH* 90 (March 1996), pp. 89–92.

8. Mardges Bacon, "Le Corbusier et l'Amérique: Première rencontre," pp. 190–207; Francesco Passanti, "Le Corbusier et le gratte-ciel: Aux origines du plan voisin," pp. 171–189; McLeod, "Le Rêve transi de Le Corbusier: L'Amérique 'catastrophe féerique,'" pp. 208–227, all in Cohen and Damisch, eds., *Américanisme et modernité.* Passanti's article appears in English translation in "The Skyscrapers of the Ville Contemporaine," *Assemblage* 4 (October 1987), pp. 53–65.

9. Colin Rowe, "Chicago Frame" (1956), reprinted in *The Mathematics of the Ideal Villa and Other Essays* (Cambridge: MIT Press, 1976), pp. 89–117. Joan Ockman makes this point in her exhibition review, "Scenes of the World to Come: European Architecture and the American Challenge, 1893–1960 (Canadian Centre for Architecture, Montreal)," *JSAH* 55 (June 1996), p. 179.

10. Reyner Banham, *A Concrete Atlantis* (Cambridge: MIT Press, 1986).

11. Mary McLeod, "'Architecture or Revolution': Taylorism, Technocracy, and Social Change," *Art Journal* 43 (Summer 1983), pp. 132–147.

12. Isabelle Jeanne Gournay, "France Discovers America, 1917–1939 (French Writings on American Architecture)" (Ph.D. diss., Yale University, 1989).

13. Jean-Louis Cohen, *Scenes of the World to Come: European Architecture and the American Challenge, 1893–1960* (Paris and Montreal: Flammarion and Canadian Centre for Architecture, 1995).

14. VIIes Rencontres de la Fondation Le Corbusier 1996–1997, "Le Corbusier, Travels and International Influence: Le Corbusier and North America," co-sponsored by Fondation Le Corbusier and Harvard University, October 11–12, 1996.

15. Miles David Samson, "German-American Dialogues and the Modern Movement Before the 'Design Migration,' 1910–1933" (Ph.D. diss., Harvard University, 1988), and "A World Like a Ford: Amerikanismus and the Modern Movement in Architecture, 1893–1936" (unpublished manuscript).

16. Beeke Sell Tower, *Envisioning America: Prints, Drawings, and Photographs by George Grosz and His Contemporaries, 1915–1933* (Cambridge: Busch-Reisinger Museum, Harvard University, 1990).

17. On the meaning of "open work," see Umberto Eco, *The Role of the Reader* (Bloomington: Indiana University Press, 1984), pp. 57–59.

18. On "new history" as a methodology postulating a new paradigm, in contrast to the "traditional paradigm," see Peter Burke, "Overture: The New History, Its Past and Its Future," in Peter Burke, ed., *New Perspectives on Historical Writing* (University Park: Pennsylvania State University Press, 1992), pp. 1–23.

19. Michel Foucault, *The Archaeology of Knowledge* (New York: Pantheon, 1972), and *The Order of Things* (New York: Vintage Books, 1973). Eco, *The Role of the Reader.*

20. Sigfried Giedion, *Léger and America* (Chicago: Institute of Design, 1944), p. 2.

1   Le Corbusier and Transatlantic Exchange

1. After 1920 Charles-Edouard Jeanneret became known as Le Corbusier, the name he used to sign his articles on architecture for *L'Esprit Nouveau.* He reserved the use of his real name for his work as a painter. On the origin and use of the name Le Corbusier, see H. Allen Brooks, *Le Corbusier's Formative Years* (Chicago: Chicago University Press, 1997), pp. 8–9, 498; J.-P. R. [Jean-Paul Robert], "Pseudonymes," in *Encyclopédie,* pp. 316–317.

2. Le Corbusier, *Quand les cathédrales étaient blanches: Voyage aux pays des timides* (Paris: Librairie Plon, 1937).

3. Le Corbusier, *When the Cathedrals Were White: A Journey to the Country of Timid People,* trans. Francis E. Hyslop, Jr. (New York: Reynal and Hitchcock, 1947).

4. H. Allen Brooks recounts this amusing episode in *Le Corbusier's Formative Years,* pp. 178–179.

5. Le Corbusier first met Osthaus during the period from April to September 1910, while working in the Berlin office of Peter Behrens, and visited him in May 1911 in Hagen. Postcard, Ch.-E. Jeanneret to Karl Ernst Osthaus, August 7, 1913. Herta Hesse-Frielinghaus, *Briefwechsel Le Corbusier–Karl Ernst Osthaus* (Hagen: Karl Ernst Osthaus Museum, 1977). See also Peter Stressig, "Le Corbusier," in Herta Hesse-Frielinghaus, *Karl Ernst Osthaus: Leben und Werk* (Recklinghausen: Verlag Aurel Bongers, 1971), p. 453.

6. Roberto Gabetti and Carlo Olmo, *Le Corbusier e "L'Esprit Nouveau"* (Turin: Einaudi, 1975), pp. 233–234. The editors of *L'Esprit Nouveau* envisioned trips across the Atlantic in 1921 and again in the summer of 1922 to arrange for an American edition of the journal. Letter, Walter Pach to Amédée Ozenfant, June 23, 1922 (FLC), cited in S.v.M./S.R. [Stanislaus von Moos and Simone Rümmele], "Pages choisies: L'Amérique," in *L'Esprit nouveau: Le Corbusier et l'industrie 1920–1925* (Zurich: Ernst & Sohn, 1987), pp. 191, 193; Mary Patricia May Sekler and Eduard F. Sekler, "Le Corbusier," in Adolf K. Placzek, ed., *Macmillan Encyclopedia of Architects,* vol. 2 (New York: Free Press, 1982), p. 635.

7. Les Terrasses was built in 1927–1928. Gabrielle de Monzie was the divorced wife of Anatole de Monzie, Ministre des Travaux Publics. For details on the financing of the villa, see Tim Benton, *The Villas of Le Corbusier, 1920–1930* (New Haven and London: Yale University Press, 1987), pp. 164–189, 219. See also James Michael Ward, "Le Corbusier's Villa 'Les Terrasses' and the International Style" (Ph.D. diss., New York University, 1984); Alice T. Friedman, *Women and the Making of the Modern House: A Social and Architectural History* (New York: Abrams, 1998), pp. 106–111.

8. James Ward analyzes these objectives in two such films depicting the Villa Stein-de Monzie: a home movie of 1928 attributed to Julian Stein, Michael's cousin, and *L'Architecture d'aujourd'hui* of 1930, a film by Pierre Chenal in collaboration with Le Corbusier. A third film by Abel Gance (codirected by V. Ivanoff) of 1931 depicts the villa as an icon of capitalism. James Ward, "Les Terrasses," *Architectural Review* (London) 177 (March 1985), pp. 64–69.

9. James R. Mellow, *Charmed Circle: Gertrude Stein and Company* (New York: Praeger, 1974), pp. 330–331.

10. The Cooks first met Gertrude Stein while they were vacationing in Majorca in 1915. Mellow, *Charmed Circle,* pp. 218–220. See also Benton, *The Villas of Le Corbusier, 1920–1930,* pp. 118–119, 154–163, 219.

11. *OC 1910–1929,* pp. 128–35.

12. Charlotte Perriand joined the Atelier Le Corbusier in October 1927 and remained there for a decade. She was responsible for a number of furniture designs including the *siège tournant* ("swivel chair"), shown in 1928 at the Salon des Artistes Décorateurs, Paris, and a number of collaborations with Le Corbusier and Jeanneret including the *siège à dossier basculant* (chair with tilting back or pivoting chair), the so-called *grand confort,* and the *chaise-longue,* all of 1928–1929. Mary McLeod, "Charlotte Perriand: Her First Decade as a Designer," *AA Files* 13 (Summer 1987), pp. 3–13. See also *Charlotte Perriand: Un art de vivre,* exhibition catalogue (Paris, 1985).

13. *OC 1910–1929,* pp. 201–203. For a discussion of the three projects that the Villa Church commission comprised, see Benton, *The Villas of Le Corbusier, 1920–1930,* pp. 8, 51–52, 104–112, 121–127, 218–219. Le Corbusier owned two books by Henry Church: *Indésirables* (Paris: Librairie de France, 1923) and *Les Clowns* (Paris: Editions des deux amis, 1922), both inscribed to him (FLC).

14. "Princess de Polignac," *New York Times,* November 27, 1943, p. 13. Unpublished drawings for the Neuilly house are in the collection of the Fondation Le Corbusier.

15. *OC 1910–1929,* pp. 124–125.

16. Brian Brace Taylor, "Technology, Society, and Social Control in Le Corbusier's Cité de Refuge, Paris, 1933," *Oppositions* 15/16 (Winter/Spring 1979), pp. 168–185; *Le Corbusier: La Cité de refuge, Paris, 1929/1933* (Paris: Equerre, 1980); *Le Corbusier, the City of Refuge, Paris 1929–33* (Chicago: University of Chicago Press, 1987). See also Howard Robertson, "The Salvation Army 'Cité Refuge,'" *American Architect* 137 (February 2, 1934), pp. 165–169. "Corot Exhibition Opened in Paris," *New York Times,* January 18, 1931, 2, p. 6.

17. This private philanthropic tradition was consonant with a long-established practice among earlier Singer Company beneficiaries including Mrs. Alfred Corning Clark. See Mardges Bacon, *Ernest Flagg: Beaux-Arts Architect and Urban Reformer* (New York and Cambridge: Architectural History Foundation and MIT Press, 1986), pp. 65, 72, 107, 247–250. The Princess Edmond de Polignac was also a patron of the 1932 "Modern Architecture: International Exhibition" at the Museum of Modern Art.

18. Le Corbusier referred to the orphanage as "un village pour les petits enfants." Letters, Le Corbusier to Josephine Baker, February 4, 1935, and January 2, 1936 (FLC). Baker was also on board the *Lutétia* when he returned from Rio de Janeiro in December 1929. Le Corbusier's sketchbook of this trip contains several drawings of her: one is a nude study; another is a self-portrait with Baker against the skyline of Rio. *Le Corbusier Sketchbooks* (New York and Cambridge: Architectural History Foundation and MIT Press, 1981), vol. 1, 1914–1948, B4, pp. 13–14, nos. 239, 261. Jean Petit, ed., *Le Corbusier lui-même* (Geneva: Editions Rousseau, 1970), pp. 68–69. "Baker (Joséphine)," in *Encyclopédie,* p. 59. Elizabeth Davis Harris, "Le Corbusier and the Headquarters of the Brazilian Ministry of Education and Health 1936–1945" (Ph.D. diss., University of Chicago, 1984), p. 20. See also Le Corbusier, *Precisions,* pp. 12–13; Phyllis Rose, *Jazz Cleopatra: Josephine Baker in Her Time* (New York: Vintage Books, 1991), pp. 152–153.

19. Sarah and Michael Stein's vast collection of modern art contained no paintings by either Le Corbusier or Ozenfant. See Lucile M. Golson, "The Michael Steins of San Francisco: Art Patrons and Collectors," in *Four Americans in Paris: The Collections of Gertrude Stein and Her Family* (New York: Museum of Modern Art, 1970), pp. 34–49. On Le Corbusier, Ozenfant, and purism, see Susan L. Ball, *Ozenfant and Purism: The Evolution of a Style, 1915–30* (Ann Arbor: UMI Research Press, 1981); Peter Serenyi, "Le Corbusier's Art and Thought 1918–1935" (Ph.D. diss., Washington University, 1968). Kenneth E. Silver, "Purism: Straightening Up after the Great War," *Artforum* 15 (March 1977), pp. 56–63; chapter 8, "Perchance to Dream," in his *Esprit de Corps: The Art of the Parisian Avant-Garde and the First World War* (Princeton: Princeton University Press, 1989), pp. 362–399. Françoise Ducros, "Le Purisme et les compromis d'une 'peinture moderne,'" in *L'Esprit nouveau: Le Corbusier et l'industrie 1920–1925,* pp. 66–79. For other articles on Le Corbusier and purism, see Darlene Brady, *Le Corbusier: An Annotated Bibliography* (New York and London: Garland Publishing, 1985), p. 267.

20. *Four Americans in Paris: The Collections of Gertrude Stein and Her Family* (New York: Museum of Modern Art, 1970). Brenda Richardson, *Dr. Claribel and Miss Etta: The Cone Collection of the Baltimore Museum of Art* (Baltimore: Baltimore Museum of Art, 1985).

21. In 1936, for example, the permanent collection of the Museum of Modern Art contained no paintings by Le Corbusier ("The Museum of Modern Art, New York," report of 1936 produced by the Museum, p. 52). Mary Patricia May Sekler is engaged in a study of Le Corbusier's paintings and drawings in American collections.

22. Katharina Schmidt and Hartwig Fischer, eds., *Ein Haus für den Kubismus: Die Sammlung Raoul La Roche: Picasso, Braques, Léger, Gris—Le Corbusier und Ozenfant* (Basel: Kunstmuseum, and Ostfildern-Ruit: Hatje, 1998).

23. Norman Rice, interview with author, August 5, 1985. Norman N. Rice, "I Remember 35 Rue de Sèvres" [1961] (FLC). For a record of Americans and other foreigners in Le Corbusier's atelier, see "Répertoire des collaborateurs de Le Corbusier ayant travaillé à l'atelier 35 rue de Sèvres ainsi qu'aux travaux exécutés à l'étranger" (FLC). On Le Corbusier's atelier, see Marc Bédarida, "Rue de Sèvres, 35: L'Envers du décor," in *Encyclopédie,* pp. 354–359. See also J.-L. C. [Jean-Louis Cohen] "Kolli Nikolaj Dzemsovic," in *Encyclopédie,* pp. 216–217; "Le Corbusier l'atelier 35 rue de Sèvres," *Bulletin d'Informations Architecturales,* supplement to no. 114 (Summer 1987); Joseph Rosa, *Albert Frey, Architect* (New York: Rizzoli, 1990), pp. 15–18, 26.

24. On the Canadian-born Hamilton Beatty, who practiced in Madison at the time of Le Corbusier's visit in 1935, see letters, Hamilton Beatty to Le Corbusier, September 24, 1930 and July 24, 1935 (FLC). See also Hamilton Beatty, "The Urbanism of Le Corbusier," in C. W. Thomas, ed., *Essays in Contemporary Civilization* (New York: Macmillan, 1931), pp. 311–325. Matthew B. Ehrlich was a contributor to *Shelter* magazine. See "The Renaissance of Reason in Architecture," *Shelter* 1 (January 1931), pp. 18–19; "Our Russian Correspondent," *Shelter* 2 (November 1932), p. 93. On the importance of *Shelter* and its contributors, see Marc Dessauce, "Contro lo Stile Internazionale: 'Shelter' e la stampa architettonica americana," *Casabella* 57 (September 1993), pp. 46–53, 70–71.

25. Letters, Hugh D. McClellan to "Secretary, Harvard School of Architecture," October 1, 1935 (courtesy of the Harvard University Archives); Hugh D. McClellan to Le Corbusier, October 1 and 18, 1935 (FLC). Later he became an architect for the New England Regional Planning Commission and held a government post in Washington, DC.

26. Beatty (spelled "Beathy"), [Matthew] Ehrlich, [Hugh] McClellan (spelled Mac-clellan), [Norman] Rice, [Elroy] Webber (spelled Weber), [Jane] West, and [?] White were the only Americans to appear in a list of assistants at 35 rue de Sèvres (before 1935); *Le Corbusier 1910–65*, p. 8. In 1932 an American architect identified only as White worked in the atelier. In 1932 and 1933 Andreas Feininger worked as a photographer in the atelier. "Répertoire des collaborateurs de Le Corbusier ayant travaillé à l'atelier 35 rue de Sèvres ainsi qu'aux travaux executés à l'étranger" (FLC).

27. Robert Allan Jacobs, interview with author, Pawling, NY, November 21, 1984 (hereafter cited as Jacobs interview). "Robert Jacobs," obituary, *New York Times,* November 5, 1993, D, p. 17. See also Le Corbusier, Certificat, Robert Allan Jacobs (FLC).

28. Aldous L. Huxley, quoted in André Maurois, *En Amérique* (New York: American Book Company, 1936, pub. in French; orig. pub. Paris: Flammarion, 1933), p. 11.

29. Richard Neutra, the American delegate to CIAM, engaged Le Corbusier on the issue of building height at the Brussels meeting in 1930 where they both presented papers. See Thomas S. Hines, *Richard Neutra and the Search for Modern Architecture* (New York and Oxford: Oxford University Press, 1982), pp. 96–97. Judith Applegate, "Paul Nelson: An Interview," *Perspecta* 13 (1971), pp. 78–79, 128. Letter, Le Corbusier to George Ford, January 11, 1924 (FLC). I am indebted to Francesco Passanti for information on Le Corbusier's misperception about George Ford. On Ford's post–World War I reconstruction efforts in Reims with La Renaissance des Cités, see Jean-Louis Cohen, *Scenes of the World to Come: European Architecture and the American Challenge, 1893–1960* (Paris and Montreal: Flammarion and Canadian Centre for Architecture, 1995), pp. 49–50.

30. For example, French urbanist Donat-Alfred Agache published articles on American city planning in *L'Intransigeant,* "Comment Chicago est devenu l'une des plus belles cités du monde," August 15, 1929; "New-York, splendide monstruosité," August 17, 1929, newspaper clippings (Frances Loeb Library, Harvard Design School). For examples of Le Corbusier's use of newspaper clippings, see "Coupures de journaux," in his *Urbanisme* (Paris: Editions Crès, 1925), pp. 119–133.

31. French journals *L'Architecture, La Construction Moderne,* and *L'Architecture d'Aujourd'hui* were among the most prominent. For a series of articles by Paul Nelson that extends from 1904 to 1913, see especially "Courrier des Etats-Unis," *L'Architecture* 17 (July 2, 1904), pp. 256–258; (December 3, 1904), pp. 449–450; 19 (May 26, 1906), pp. 165–169; 24 (November 18, 1911), pp. 377–381;

and "Choses d'Amérique," 26 (May 10, 1913), pp. 149–151. Randolph W. Sexton, editor of *American Architect,* published in the French journal *La Construction Moderne.* See his "Le developpement du 'gratte-ciel américain,'" 39 (August 24, 1924), pp. 553–554; "Y a-t-'il un style américain?," 40 (February 15, 1925), pp. 229–230; "Urbanisme et architecture en U.S.A.," 40 (April 27, 1925), pp. 317–319; "Les effets de la loi zonière sur l'architecture américaine," 41 (April 18, 1926), pp. 343–345. See also E[ugène] Beaudouin, "Urbanisme et architecture en U.S.A.: Notes de voyage de M. E. Beaudouin," *L'Architecture d'Aujourd'hui* 4 (November-December 1933), pp. 54–68. See Isabelle Jeanne Gournay, "France Discovers America, 1917–1939 (French Writings on American Architecture)" (Ph.D. diss., Yale University, 1989), and her bibliography *Américanisme et modernité bibliographie raisonnée,* 2 vols. (Paris: Institut français d'architecture, 1984).

32. In *L'Esprit Nouveau,* Le Corbusier (under the names Le Corbusier and Le Corbusier-Saugnier) published over forty articles, and he and Ozenfant together published over fifteen. For a list of them, see Simone Rümmele, "L'Esprit Nouveau 1–28 Index," *L'Esprit nouveau: Le Corbusier et l'industrie 1920–1925,* pp. 284–286, 290.

33. On the image of American machine age forms and methods of mass production in Le Corbusier's publications, see Reyner Banham, *A Concrete Atlantis* (Cambridge: MIT Press, 1986). For images of American safes, file cabinets, desks, and offices, see Le Corbusier, *L'Art décoratif d'aujourd'hui* (Paris: Editions Crès, 1925). On the use of American advertising techniques, see *EN* 18 (November 1923), [p. 5]; *EN* 19 (December 1923), [p. 7]. For an analysis of Le Corbusier's use of industrial products in *L'Esprit Nouveau,* see "Pages choisies: Produits industriels," in *L'Esprit nouveau: Le Corbusier et l'industrie 1920–1925,* pp. 244–281. On Le Corbusier's use of industrial products in advertising and their links to the avant-garde, see Beatriz Colomina, "Architecture et publicité," in *Encyclopédie,* pp. 140–145, and Colomina, *Privacy and Publicity: Modern Architecture as Mass Media* (Cambridge: MIT Press, 1994). For Le Corbusier's fascination with American multilevel, multifunctional circulation system, see *Urbanisme,* p. 144.

34. Walter Gropius, "Die Entwicklung moderner Industriebaukunst," *Jahrbuch des deutschen Werkbundes,* 1913, pp. 17–22. Gropius, "Memories of Le Corbusier," in *Apollo in the Democracy* (New York: McGraw-Hill, 1968), p. 174. Le Corbusier-Saugnier, "Trois rappels à MM. les architectes. Premier rappel: Le Volume," *EN* 1 (October 1920), p. [95]; *Vers une architecture,* p. 17; Stanislaus von Moos, *Le Corbusier: Elements of a Synthesis* (Cambridge: MIT Press, 1979), pp. 48–49, 62–63, figs. 35, 36; Paul Venable Turner, *The Education of Le Corbusier* (New York and London: Garland, 1977), p. 81, figs. 30, 31. Banham noted that Le Corbusier miscaptioned the Bunge y Born elevator in Buenos Aires as "Canadian"; *A Concrete Atlantis,* pp. 207, 219–222.

35. *Vers une architecture,* p. 29; *Towards a New Architecture,* p. 42. The Spreckels Building was published in *American Architect and*

Building News 57 (August 28, 1897), p. 75, pl. 1131. I made this observation in my paper "The Trans-Atlantic Misunderstanding: Le Corbusier's First Visit to America in 1935," symposium, *L'Américanisme et la modernité,* Ecole des Hautes Etudes en Sciences Sociales and the Institut Français d'Architecture, October 24, 1985. See also Banham, *A Concrete Atlantis,* pp. 228–229.

36. *Urbanisme,* p. 185; *Almanach,* p. 13.

37. Le Corbusier, *Urbanisme,* pp. 178–179. Although it was published in the *Oeuvre complète 1910–1929* as the Plan Voisin of 1925, the perspective view of the "central station" is that of the Ville Contemporaine. The airport that appears in the perspective view and in the program for the Ville Contemporaine, for example, does not appear in the Plan Voisin. Notwithstanding inconsistencies between the perspective view and the plan, both clearly indicate the curvilinear landing platform. Having identified this discrepancy, I am grateful to Francesco Passanti for his role in the attribution and for suggesting that the perspective view was probably not drawn until 1925. Further analysis is beyond the scope of my study except to note that the inconsistency is one of many that occurs in the publication of Le Corbusier's work. If the architect endorsed the discrepancy, he preferred publicity over accurate documentation. *OC 1910–1929,* p. 109.

38. S.v.M./S.R., "Pages choisies: L'Amérique," pp. 190–193. See also Colin Rowe, "Chicago Frame,' in *The Mathematics of the Ideal Villa and Other Essays* (Cambridge: MIT Press, 1976), pp. 89–117.

39. Le Corbusier-Saugnier, "Trois rappels à MM. les architectes," *EN* 4 (January 1921), pp. 465–466; *Vers une architecture,* pp. 42–43.

40. The Lambert drawing is captioned "d'après les esquisses de l'architecte Auguste Perret." J. Labadié, "Les Cathédrales de la cité moderne: Un audacieux projet pour résoudre en hauteur la crise de logement et les problèmes de confort et d'hygiène," *L'Illustration* (August 12, 1922), pp. 131–135. Von Moos, *Le Corbusier: Elements of a Synthesis,* pp. 190–191, 352, 14n, 15n. On press reports as well as Le Corbusier's knowledge of Perret's studies and their impact on him, see Francesco Passanti's groundbreaking study "Des gratte-ciel pour la 'Ville contemporaine,'" in *L'Esprit nouveau: Le Corbusier et l'industrie 1920–1925,* pp. 58–59; "The Skyscrapers of the Ville Contemporaine," *Assemblage* 4 (October 1987), pp. 56–60. For an insightful analysis of Perret's Tower Cities and his efforts to link tower blocks with infrastructure, see Cohen, *Scenes of the World to Come,* pp. 117–119.

41. The Perret-inspired perspective view of masonry-clad towers linked by elevated roads recalls "King's Dream of New York," a visionary scheme drawn by Harry M. Pettit and published by Moses King in his *King's Views of New York* (1908), and also a setback skyscraper city project of 1891 by Louis Sullivan. The cruciform plan of the first tower in the Perret-influenced project recalls Sullivan's Fraternity Temple as well as the Woolworth Building (1911–1913) and Beaux-Arts skyscrapers of New York before World War I. But, as Francesco Passanti observed, the second sky-scraper in the drawing after Perret makes explicit reference to the massing of McKim, Mead and White's widely published Municipal Row Building (1909) and other American towers. On the Fraternity Temple, originally Odd Fellows Temple, and the setback skyscraper city, see Louis Sullivan, "The High-Building Question," *Graphic* 5 (December 19, 1891), pp. 404–405; Donald Hoffmann, "The Setback Skyscraper City of 1891: An Unknown Essay by Louis H. Sullivan," *JSAH* 29 (May 1970), pp. 181–187; Willard Connely, *Louis Sullivan as He Lived* (New York: Horizon Press, 1960), pp. 148–149. See von Moos, *Le Corbusier: Elements of a Synthesis,* p. 191; "Urbanism and Transcultural Exchanges, 1910–1935: A Survey," in H. Allen Brooks, ed., *Le Corbusier* (Princeton: Princeton University Press, 1987), p. 223.

42. On Perret's claim that he rejected the model of American cruciform skyscrapers, see Cohen, *Scenes of the World to Come,* pp. 117, 119. On Perret's use of American cruciform plans, see Roberto Gargiani, *Auguste Perret 1874–1954* (Milan: Electa, 1993).

43. Wilhelm Worringer, *Abstraktion und Einfühlung* (Munich: R. Piper, 1959, orig. pub. 1908); Banham, *A Concrete Atlantis,* pp. 194–199; Mardges Bacon, "Introduction" to Society of Architectural Historians session "In Search of a Transatlantic Culture: European Travel Accounts of American Buildings and Civic Spaces, 1900–1925," Boston, 1990. By the late 1920s Worringer had a darker view of American production: see Worringer, *Egyptian Art* (London: G. P. Putnam's Sons, 1928).

44. Mary McLeod, "'Architecture or Revolution': Taylorism, Technocracy, and Social Change," *Art Journal* 43 (Summer 1983), pp. 132–133; "Taylorisme," in *Encyclopédie,* pp. 397–400.

45. Henry Ford, *Ma vie et mon oeuvre* (Paris: Payot, 1925). Le Corbusier also owned copies of Hyacinthe Dubreuil, *Standards* (Paris: B. Grasset, 1929) and *Nouveaux standards* (Paris: B. Grasset [1931]) (FLC).

46. *Almanach,* p. 188.

47. Georges Duhamel, *America the Menace,* trans. Charles Miner Thompson (Boston: Houghton Mifflin, 1931), p. xiv. Georges Duhamel, *Scènes de la vie future* (Paris: Mercure de France, 1930), p. 19 (FLC).

48. Yale University, the University of Pennsylvania, and the University of California, Berkeley, were among the few institutions that subscribed to *L'Esprit Nouveau;* such institutions as Harvard and Columbia universities, the Metropolitan Museum, and the Art Institute of Chicago did not. I am grateful to Marc Dessauce for providing me with a list of subscribers to *L'Esprit Nouveau* (1920–1923) compiled from files of the FLC, Paris.

49. Victoria Newhouse, *Wallace K. Harrison, Architect* (New York: Rizzoli, 1989), pp. 15–16.

50. Irving K. Pond, "From Foreign Shores," *Journal of the American Institute of Architects* 11 (December 1923), p. 475; *Journal of the American Institute of Architects* 12 (March 1924), p. 122. On the Ribot House, see H. Allen Brooks, ed., *The Le Corbusier Archive,* vol.

1, *Early Buildings and Projects, 1912–1923* (New York, London, and Paris: Garland and Fondation Le Corbusier, 1982), pp. 467–471. On the Villa Ker-Ka-Ré (Besnus), see *OC 1910–1929,* pp. 48–52; Benton, *The Villas of Le Corbusier, 1920–1930,* pp. 22–29; Brooks, ed., *The Le Corbusier Archive,* vol. 1, pp. 401–425.

51. G. F. Sebille, "Paris Letter," *Journal of the American Institute of Architects* 13 (January 1925), pp. 27–28.

52. See John F. Harbeson, "Design in Modern Architecture: 4—The Modern Interior," *Pencil Points* 11 (April 1930), p. 262.

53. On the American response to the 1925 Paris exposition, see Cervin Robinson and Rosemarie Haag Bletter, *Skyscraper Style: Art Deco New York* (New York: Oxford University Press, 1975), pp. 44–48; Rosemarie Haag Bletter, "Modernism Rears Its Head—The Twenties and Thirties," in Richard Oliver, ed., *The Making of an Architect: 1881–1981* (New York: Rizzoli, 1981), pp. 108–110.

54. For the location of the Esprit Nouveau pavilion, see *Catalogue général officiel,* Exposition Internationale des Arts Décoratifs et Industriels Modernes, Paris, April–October 1925, Cours-la-reine map G-72 [before p. 183], p. 211.

55. Henry Russel [sic] Hitchcock, "Le Corbusier and the United States," *Zodiac* 16 (1966), p. 8. For Le Corbusier's account as well as images of the pavilion, see *OC 1910–1929,* pp. 98–108; and his catalogue of the Pavillon de l'Esprit Nouveau, *Almanach.*

56. *Encyclopédie des arts décoratifs et industriels modernes au xxème siècle,* vol. 2 (New York: Garland, 1977; orig. pub. Paris: Office Central d'Editions et de Librairie, [1925]), pp. 12, 13, 45–46, pl. 65. Le Corbusier *L'Art décoratif d'aujourd'hui.* Giuliano Gresleri, *L'Esprit nouveau* (Milan: Electa Editrice, 1979). See chapter 3, note 103.

57. Lewis Mumford, "Decoration and Structure," *Commonweal* 2 (October 7, 1925), p. 533. See also Robert Wojtowitz, *Lewis Mumford and American Modernism* (New York: Cambridge University Press, 1996), pp. 86–87.

58. Hitchcock, "Le Corbusier and the United States," pp. 8–9. In a subsequent account the date 1926 appears as a misprint; Henry-Russell Hitchcock, "Modern Architecture—A Memoir," *JSAH* 27 (December 1968), p. 229.

59. Although the United States had been invited to participate in the 1925 Paris fair, there was no American exhibit. Government officials, including Secretary of Commerce Herbert Hoover, felt that the country could offer no appropriate building design responding to the official French ban against eclecticism. Hoover named a commission that appointed 108 American delegates sent to France. "Changing Styles in Architecture," *New York Times,* February 21, 1926, 10, p. 2. The commission report gave an account of the "Genesis and Development of [the] Modern Movement," but did not mention any of the fair buildings. *Report of Commission Appointed by the Secretary of Commerce to Visit and Report upon the International Exposition of Modern Decorative and Industrial Art in Paris 1925,* pp. 5–18, 42–47. See also "New York Architects at Paris Exhibit," *New York Times,* May 24, 1925, 11, p. 17.

60. On Howe's visit to the 1925 Paris fair, see Robert A. M. Stern, *George Howe* (New Haven: Yale University Press, 1975), p. 78n67. Wallace Harrison did not publish an account but was critical of the Esprit Nouveau pavilion, which "looked as if it had left history too far behind, it made a complete cut with the past." Newhouse, *Wallace K. Harrison, Architect,* p. 28. Raymond Hood sailed for Europe in October 1926; "Meet Foreign Architects, R. M. Hood Sailing to Arrange for European Exhibitions," *New York Times,* October 10, 1926, 11, p. 19. Ely Jacques Kahn, Alfred C. Bossom, and Ralph Walker also visited the fair.

61. D. Everett Waid, "A Report on the Paris Exposition," *American Architect* 128 (November 20, 1925), p. 458.

62. Richardson Wright, "The Modernist Taste," *House and Garden* 48 (October 1925), p. 77.

63. "Art of the Day in Many Galleries," *New York Times,* March 7, 1926, 8, p. 12. Frank Leslie Baker was probably the author. Oliver P. Bernard published notes from his 1925 visit in *Creative Art* 5 (September 1929), p. 612.

64. *Yearbook of the Architectural League of New York and Catalogue of the Forty-First Annual Exhibition* (1926). "The Forty-First Annual Exhibition of The Architectural League of New York," *Pencil Points* 7, January 1926, pp. 105, 129. "French Architects' Studies Arrive in New York," *New York Times,* (February 14, 1926), 4, pp. 12–13. A loan exhibition of French decorative arts at the Metropolitan Museum of Art ran concurrently with the League exhibition: H. I. Brock, "The Art of Ensemble Is Revealed, *New York Times,* February 28, 1926, pp. 12, 22. See also Ely J. Kahn, "The Architectural League Exhibition of 1926," *Record* 59 (March 1926), pp. 226–227.

65. "[Alfred Bossom] Sees Europe Entering upon New Era of Art," *New York Times,* July 25, 1925, p. 5. Bossom excluded the Esprit Nouveau pavilion from his report on the Paris fair, "The Rebirth of Art and Architecture in Europe," *American Architect* 128 (August 26, 1925), pp. 161–166.

66. Lewis Mumford, "Notes on Books," in Mumford, *Sticks and Stones* (New York: Liveright, 1924), p. 246.

67. "French Modernist Urges New Art in Architecture," *New York Times,* November 28, 1926, 8, p. 19.

68. Paul Cret, "Modernists and Conservatives," presented to the T-Square Club, Philadelphia, November 19, 1927 (Paul Cret Papers, Rare Book and Manuscript Library, University of Pennsylvania). David B. Brownlee, *Building the City Beautiful: The Benjamin Franklin Parkway and the Philadelphia Museum of Art* (Philadelphia Museum of Art, 1989), pp. 10–11.

69. The article was written in February 1927 and published the next year. Paul Cret, "The Architect as Collaborator of the Engineer," *Architectural Forum* 49 (July 1928), pp. 97–104. For further

examination of Cret's view of Le Corbusier, see Elizabeth Greenwell Grossman, *The Civic Architecture of Paul Cret* (New York: Cambridge University Press, 1996), pp. 156, 244.

70. Samuel Chamberlain, "In Search of Modernism, Concerning the Dearth of Material in France for the Enquiring Reporter," *American Architect* 131 (January 20, 1927), p. 73. See also Robert A. M. Stern, "Relevance of the Decade," in "Modern Architecture Symposium (MAS 1964): The Decade 1929–1939," *JSAH* 24 (March 1965), p. 8.

71. The American edition was actually printed in England from sheets supplied by the English publisher.

72. See, for example, Frederick Etchells, "Le Corbusier: A Pioneer of Modern European Architecture," *Studio* 96 (1928), pp. 156–163. On the awareness of Le Corbusier in England, see Anthony Jackson, "The Politics of Architecture: English Architecture 1929–1951," *JSAH* 24 (March 1965), pp. 97–107.

73. "On Our Library Table," *Architect* 9 (December 1927), p. 287.

74. T-Square [George Chappell], "The Sky Line," *New Yorker* 3 (November 12, 1927), p. 97.

75. "Modernism and Tradition," *Pencil Points* 6 (September 1925), p. 41.

76. "Architectural League Exhibition Develops Interesting Discussions," *Real Estate Record and Guide* 117 (February 13, 1926), p. 10.

77. In addition to Bossom, Corbett, and Hood, supporters of the "new style of architecture" included Howard Greenley, Arthur Corey, and Julian Clarence Levi. "Changing Styles in Architecture," *New York Times,* February 21, 1926, 10, p. 2.

78. "French Architects' Studies Arrive in New York," *New York Times,* February 14, 1926, 4, p. 13.

79. "Changing Styles in Architecture," p. 2.

80. "Changing Styles in Architecture," p. 2. See also Kahn, "The Architectural League Exhibition of 1926," pp. 226–227.

81. On the fragmentation of academic discourse, see Hyungmin Pai, "From the Portfolio to the Diagram: Architectural Discourse and the Transformation of the Discipline of Architecture in America, 1918–1943" (Ph.D. diss., Massachusetts Institute of Technology, 1993), pp. 87–106.

82. Ralph T. Walker, "A New Architecture," *Architectural Forum* 48 (January 1928), pp. 1, 4. The caption to the photograph of the Barclay-Vesey Telephone Building (1923–1926) by the firm of Voorhees, Gmelin and Walker read simply "The Telephone Building, New York"; *Towards a New Architecture,* frontispiece. Hitchcock, "Le Corbusier and the United States," p. 8.

83. Talbot Faulkner Hamlin, "Review of *Towards a New Architecture,*" *Nation* 229 (July 10, 1929), p. 46. On Hamlin's view of Le Corbusier, see Kenneth Frampton, "Slouching toward Modernity:

Talbot Faulkner Hamlin and the Architecture of the New Deal," in Oliver, ed., *The Making of an Architect,* pp. 153–154.

84. John F. Harbeson, "Design in Modern Architecture: I—What Is Modern?," *Pencil Points* 11 (January 1930), pp. 3, 45.

85. Harbeson, "Design in Modern Architecture: I—What Is Modern?," p. 4.

86. Harbeson, "Design in Modern Architecture: I—What Is Modern?," pp. 6–7. See also *OC 1910–1929,* p. 174; von Moos, *Le Corbusier: Elements of a Synthesis,* p. 98. Perceptively, Harbeson also recognized Le Corbusier's reliance on the plan and, by inference, his debt to Beaux-Arts theory; see "Design in Modern Architecture: II—The Modern Plan," *Pencil Points* 11 (February 1930), pp. 91, 93.

87. "Contemporary Architecture: A Symposium," *Proceedings of the Sixty-third Annual Convention of the American Institute of Architects,* May 21–30, 1930 (American Institute of Architects, 1930), pp. 23, 25, 31. Henry-Russell Hitchcock also used the labels conservative and liberal. See his "The Brown Decades and the Brown Year," *Hound and Horn* 5 (January–March 1932), p. 275.

88. "Contemporary Architecture: A Symposium," *Proceedings,* p. 33.

89. "Contemporary Architecture: A Symposium," *Proceedings,* p. 27. Excerpts of Howe's talk appear in "Modernist and Traditionalist," *Architectural Forum,* 53 (July 1930), p. 49; and in *T-Square Club Journal* 1 (March 1931), [p. 3]. Richard Guy Wilson identified the significance of the AIA symposium in his essay "Architecture in the Machine Age," in Richard Guy Wilson, Dianne H. Pilgrim, and Dickran Tashjian, eds., *The Machine Age in America, 1918–1941* (New York: Brooklyn Museum, 1986), p. 149.

90. George Howe [transcript], "Contemporary Architecture: A Symposium," *Proceedings,* pp. 25, 28.

91. "Modernist and Traditionalist," p. 49; C. Howard Walker's criticism was eliminated from the published transcript of his paper in "Contemporary Architecture: A Symposium," *Proceedings,* pp. 29–33.

92. Everett V. Meeks [transcript], "Contemporary Architecture: A Symposium," *Proceedings,* p. 48. See also Ralph T. Walker [transcript], "Contemporary Architecture: A Symposium," *Proceedings,* p. 43.

93. See, for example, Howell Lewis Shay, "Modern Architecture and Tradition," *T-Square Club Journal* 1 (January 1931), pp. 12–15; Paul P. Cret and others, letters to the editor in response to Shay, "Modern Architecture and Tradition," *T-Square Club Journal* 1 (February 1931), pp. 14–15.

94. William H. Jordy, "The Symbolic Essence of Modern Architecture and Its Continuing Influence," *JSAH* 22 (October 1963), pp. 177–187.

95. *Towards a New Architecture,* p. 4.

96. On these developments see Pai, "From the Portfolio to the Diagram: Architectural Discourse and the Transformation of the Discipline of Architecture in America, 1918–1943," pp. 116–133.

97. On the technocratic camp and opposition to the canon of the International Style among journalists in the American architectural press, see Dessauce, "Contro lo Stile Internazionale: 'Shelter' e la stampa architettonica americana," pp. 46–53, 70–71.

98. Hitchcock, "Modern Architecture—A Memoir," p. 229.

99. Alfred Barr gave this account, which Hitchcock published in "Le Corbusier in the United States," p. 9, and in "Modern Architecture—A Memoir," p. 229.

100. Henry-Russell Hitchcock, Jr., "The Decline of Architecture," *Hound and Horn* 1 (September 1927), pp. 28–35, and "Modern Architecture—A Memoir," p. 229. See also Helen Searing, "Henry-Russell Hitchcock: Architectura et Amicitia," in Helen Searing, ed., *In Search of Modern Architecture: A Tribute to Henry-Russell Hitchcock* (New York and Cambridge: Architectural History Foundation and MIT Press, 1982), pp. 2–9.

101. Henry-Russell Hitchcock, Jr., review of *Towards a New Architecture, Record* 63 (January 1928), pp. 90–91.

102. Henry-Russell Hitchcock, Jr., "Six Modern European Houses," *House Beautiful* 64 (September 1928), p. 254.

103. Douglas Haskell, review of Fiske Kimball, *American Architecture, New Republic* 55 (June 20, 1928), pp. 126–127; Henry-Russell Hitchcock, Jr., "American Architecture," *Creative Art* 3 (August 1928), p. xiv.

104. A.[lfred] Lawrence Kocher became a contributing editor of *Architectural Record* in 1926, and an associate editor after he joined the staff in 1927. "Contents," *Record* 60 (August 1926); "Prof. Kocher Joins the Architectural Record Staff," *Record* 62 (August 1927), p. 167; "Contents," *Record* 62 (September 1927); "Contents," *Record* 63 (January 1928).

105. Henry-Russell Hitchcock, Jr., "Modern Architecture II. The New Pioneers," *Record* 63 (May 1928), pp. 452–60; Hitchcock, *Modern Architecture: Romanticism and Reintegration* (New York: Payson and Clarke, 1929), pp. 163–171. The Villa Stein-de Monzie was also the subject of an early Hitchcock article, "Houses by Two Moderns," *Arts* 16 (September 1929), pp. 33–40. Unfortunately in his many writings on the architect, Hitchcock does not mention the first time he met him. Frederick Etchells followed Hitchcock's lead in identifying Le Corbusier as a pioneer; see his "Le Corbusier: A Pioneer of Modern European Architecture," *Creative Art* 3 (September 1928), pp. 156–163.

106. Letter, A. Lawrence Kocher to Le Corbusier, May 8, 1928 (FLC).

107. Letter, Le Corbusier to "Messieurs, the Architectural Record," February 20, 1929 (FLC).

108. Le Corbusier, "Architecture, the Expression of the Materials and Methods of Our Times," *Record* 66 (August 1929), pp. 123–128.

109. Norman N. Rice, "The Minimal House: A Solution," *Record* 68 (August 1930), pp. 133–137.

110. "Planeix House, Paris," *Record* 68 (October 1930), p. 338.

111. On these themes, see Sigfried Giedion, *Mechanization Takes Command* (New York: Oxford University Press, 1948); Thomas P. Hughes, *American Genesis: A Century of Invention and Technological Enthusiasm, 1870–1970* (New York: Penguin Books, 1989).

112. Douglas Haskell, review of *Towards a New Architecture, Creative Art* 2 (March 1928), p. xxv.

113. Lewis Mumford, "Mass-Production and the Modern House," *Record* 67, part 1 (January 1930), pp. 13–20; part 2 (February 1930), pp. 110–116; Mumford, *Sticks and Stones,* p. 181.

114. Stern proposes 1927 as the key year in his "Relevance of the Decade" in "Modern Architecture Symposium (MAS 1964): The Decade 1929–1939," pp. 6–10. A version of the argument appears in Stern, *George Howe,* pp. 71–78. See William E. Leuchtenburg, *The Perils of Prosperity, 1914–32,* (Chicago: University of Chicago Press, 1958).

115. For a comprehensive discussion of modernist exhibits in New York City between the two world wars, see Robert A. M. Stern, Gregory Gilmartin, and Thomas Mellins, "Exhibitions," in *New York 1930: Architecture and Urbanism between the Two World Wars* (New York: Rizzoli, 1987), pp. 328–355.

116. Stern, Gilmartin, and Mellins, *New York 1930,* pp. 335–336. See also "Three Rings and a Stage," editorial, *Architecture* 55 (April 1927), p. 201.

117. *Machine-Age Exposition,* New York, May 16–28, 1927. The exhibition was held at 119 West 57th Street.

118. Jane Heap visited the Esprit Nouveau pavilion in 1925 and returned home with this objective. Susan Fillin Yeh, *The Precisionist Painters 1916–1949: Interpretations of a Mechanical Age* (Huntington, NY: Heckscher Museum, 1978), p. 12. Hughes, *American Genesis,* p. 343.

119. Heap wrote, "I am not prepared to say what returns would be beyond the educational and the propaganda value." Letter, Jane Heap to Pierre Jeanneret, October 5, 1925 (FLC). André Lurçat curated the French section and Le Corbusier's work is mentioned only briefly, "French Architecture," *Machine-Age Exposition,* p. 23.

120. Herbert Lippmann, "The Machine-Age Exposition," *Arts* 11 (June 1927), p. 326.

121. S.[zymon] Syrkus, "Architecture Opens Up Volume," *Machine-Age Exposition,* New York, p. 30.

122. J. H. [Jane Heap], "Machine-Age Exposition," *Machine-Age Exposition,* New York, p. 37.

123. Louis Lozowick, "The Americanization of Art," *Machine-Age Exposition,* New York, p. 18. Hughes, *American Genesis,* pp. 10–11, 345–346. Louis Lozowick also subscribed to *L'Esprit Nouveau.*

124. Philip Johnson, *Machine Art* (New York: Museum of Modern Art, 1934).

125. Catherine Bauer, "Machine-Age Mansions for Ultra-Moderns," *New York Times,* April 15, 1928, 5, pp. 10, 22.

126. Dessauce, "Contro lo Stile Internazionale: 'Shelter' e la stampa architettonica americana," pp. 49–50, 71.

127. As Douglas Haskell explained, the full-scale Aluminaire House was "not sponsored by the committee but was a 'commercial' exhibit sponsored by manufacturers and contractors." "The Architectural League and the Rejected Architects," *Parnassus* 3 (May 1931), p. 12. For a discussion of Philip Johnson's objectives, see Stern, Gilmartin, and Mellins, *New York 1930,* p. 343. See also Philip Johnson, "Rejected Architects," *Creative Art* 8 (June 1931), pp. 433–435; reprinted in *Philip Johnson Writings,* ed. Peter Eisenman and Robert A. M. Stern (New York: Oxford University Press, 1979), pp. 44–47.

128. "Rejected Architects," April 21–May 5 [1931 exhibition brochure] (FLC). Barr was also associated with the "Rejected Architects" exhibition. For an analysis of the relationship between that exhibition in 1931 and the "Modern Architecture: International Exhibition" in 1932, see Terence Riley, *The International Style: Exhibition 15 and the Museum of Modern Art* (New York: Rizzoli, 1992), pp. 40ff. On the origins of the term "International Style" see Riley, *The International Style: Exhibition 15 and the Museum of Modern Art,* pp. 89–93; "International Style," Alfred H. Barr, Jr., preface to Henry-Russell Hitchcock, Jr., and Philip Johnson, *The International Style: Architecture since 1922* (New York: W. W. Norton, 1932), pp. 11–16; Henry-Russell Hitchcock, "The International Style Twenty Years After," *Record* 110 (August 1951), pp. 89–90.

129. *Le Corbusier und Pierre Jeanneret, ihr Gesamtes Werk von 1910–1929,* ed. Willy Boesiger and O. Stonorov (Zurich: Girsberger, 1930).

130. "Répertoire des collaborateurs de Le Corbusier ayant travaillé à l'atelier 35 rue de Sèvres ainsi qu'aux travaux exécutés à l'étranger" (FLC). Hazen Sise attended McGill School of Architecture in Montreal and graduated from the MIT School of Architecture in 1930. "College of Fellows: New Members, 1967 Convention," *Architecture Canada* 44 (June 1967), p. 9.

131. "Rejected Architects," April 21–May 5 [1931], inscribed by Henry-Russell Hitchcock (FLC). Johnson's ironic title to the exhibition was a calculated allusion to two celebrated French art exhibitions, one of Gustave Courbet in 1855 and another of Edouard Manet and the impressionists in 1863.

132. Haskell, "The Architectural League and the Rejected Architects," *Parnassus,* p. 12. See also Douglas Haskell, "The Column, the Gable, and the Box," *Arts* 17 (June 1931), pp. 636–639.

133. Catherine K. Bauer, "Who Cares about Architecture?," *New Republic* 66 (May 6, 1931), p. 327.

134. Rona Roob, "1936: The Museum Selects an Architect," *Archives of American Art Journal* 23 (1983), p. 27.

135. Riley, *The International Style: Exhibition 15 and the Museum of Modern Art,* p. 51. "Circulating Exhibitions," *Bulletin of The Museum of Modern Art* 1 (March 1, 1934), p. 2.

136. According to Terence Riley, "Hitchcock and Johnson conceived of the International Style project first as a book and later as an exhibition." On the discrepancies between the catalogue and the exhibition, see *The International Style: Exhibition 15 and the Museum of Modern Art,* pp. 9–10.

137. Alfred H. Barr, Jr., foreword to *Modern Architecture: International Exhibition* (New York: Museum of Modern Art, 1932), p. 16.

138. Philip Johnson, "Historical Note," in *Modern Architecture: International Exhibition,* p. 20.

139. Presumably because of its early date, the Citrohan House model was not shown in the exhibition. Hitchcock and Johnson, *International Style: Architecture since 1922,* p. 31. See also Johnson's discussion in "Historical Note," *Modern Architecture: International Exhibition,* p. 20. These quotations also appear in Henry-Russell Hitchcock, "The International Style Twenty Years After," pp. 89–97; reprinted in *International Style: Architecture since 1922* (New York: W. W. Norton, 1966), p. 245.

140. Lewis Mumford, "Housing," *Modern Architecture: International Exhibition,* pp. 179–192. Letter, Lewis Mumford to Le Corbusier, September 18, 1937 (FLC). On his 1932 trip with Bauer, see Wojtowicz, *Lewis Mumford and American Modernism,* pp. 95–96.

141. H. I. [Henry Irving] Brock, "Architecture Styled 'International,'" *New York Times,* February 7, 1932, 5, p. 11. See also Edward Alden Jewell, "In the Realm of Art: Important Current Shows," *New York Times,* February 14, 1932, 8, p. 10.

142. Harold Sterner, "Architectural Chronicle: International Architectural Style," *Hound and Horn* 5 (April–June 1932), p. 456. See also John Wheelwright, "The Grand Manner in Contemporary Lintel Construction," *Hound and Horn* 5 (July–September 1932), pp. 702–708.

143. Fiske Kimball reviewed the traveling exhibition at the Pennsylvania Museum of Art (March 30–April 22, 1932). See "Modern Architecture: An Exhibition in the Galleries of the Museum," *Pennsylvania Museum Bulletin* 27 (April 1932), pp. 131–133. Catherine K. Bauer, "Exhibition of Modern Architecture, Museum of Modern Art," *Creative Art* 10 (March 1932), pp. 201–206.

144. Frank Lloyd Wright, "Towards a New Architecture," *World Unity* 2 (September 1928), pp. 393–395. In *Towards a New Architecture* Etchells mistranslated *volume* as "mass" instead of "volume," pp. 21–31 (*Vers une architecture*, pp. 11–20).

145. Buckminster Fuller, "Universal Architecture," *T-Square* [*Shelter*] 2 (February 1932), pp. 22, 35. On Fuller and the Shelter group, see Dessauce, "Contro lo Stile Internazionale: 'Shelter' e la stampa architettonica americana," pp. 46–53, 70–71.

146. Robert W. Marks, *The Dymaxion World of Buckminster Fuller* (New York: Reinhold, 1960), p. 22.

147. Reyner Banham, *Theory and Design in the First Machine Age* (New York: Praeger, 1960), pp. 326–327.

148. Franz Schulze, *Philip Johnson: Life and Work* (New York: Alfred A. Knopf, 1994), p. 86.

149. Stern, Gilmartin, and Mellins, *New York 1930*, p. 344.

150. For the proposed "Itinerary for Exhibition of Modern Architecture, Museum of Modern Art, New York" and the publication of talks from a symposium on the 1932 show, see *Shelter* 2 (April 1932), pp. 3–10, 36. In her memorandum, Elizabeth Mock lists the institutions at which the traveling exhibition was actually shown. The itinerary includes Chicago (Sears, Roebuck and Company, June 9–July 8, 1932) and Los Angeles (Bullock's Wilshire, July 23–August 30, 1932), with Dartmouth College in Hanover, NH (November 17–December 15, 1933) as the last venue. See memorandum, Elizabeth Mock, Museum of Modern Art, May 26, 1944 in Riley, *The International Style: Exhibition 15 and the Museum of Modern Art*, p. 222.

151. Norman N. Rice, "I Believe," *T-Square* 2 (January 1932), pp. 24–25, 34–35. On Le Corbusier's plans for a World Museum or Mundaneum within a Cité Mondiale, see Waldemar Kaempffert, "Vital Museums of the New Era," *New York Times Magazine,* March 20, 1932, pp. 12–13, 22. "Corbusier's City of the Future," *Housing* 21 (October 1932), pp. 239–240. C. Mauclair, "Bolshevized Architecture," *Living Age* 344 (July 1933), pp. 441–443. Elizabeth B. Mock, "Le Corbusier's Swiss Pavilion," *American Magazine of Art* 27 (January 1934), pp. 18–19. Harry Kurz, "Joyously Comfortable," reply to Elizabeth Mock, *American Magazine of Art* 27 (February 1934), p. 50. Howard Robertson, "The Salvation Army 'Cité-Refuge,' Paris," *American Architect* 137 (February 2, 1934), pp. 165–169. S.[igfried] Giedion, "Swiss Pavilion: Cité Universitaire," *Record* 75 (May 1934), pp. 400–403.

152. Pond, "From Foreign Shores," *Journal of the American Institute of Architects* 12 (March 1924), p. 122.

153. Le Corbusier, *The City of Tomorrow and Its Planning,* translated from the 8th edition of *Urbanisme* with an introduction by Frederick Etchells (New York: Payson and Clarke [1929]).

154. R. L. Duffus, "A Vision of the Future City," *New York Times Book Review,* October 27, 1929, 4, p. 1; [R. L. Duffus] "Municipal and Civic Publications," *American City* 41 (December 1929), p. 172.

155. No doubt Harbeson had read *Vers une architecture* because he identified Villes-Tours as "a project for 60-story office buildings," rather than as per the Etchells translation, which had identified the project "for Apartments or Flats." John F. Harbeson "Design in Modern Architecture: 3—The City of Tomorrow," *Pencil Points* 11 (March 1930), pp. 168–169.

156. John F. Harbeson, "Design in Modern Architecture: 10—Some Things in Which We May Learn from Europe," *Pencil Points* 12 (February 1931), p. 103.

157. Oliver P. Bernard, review of *The City of Tomorrow, Creative Art* 5 (September 1929), pp. 612–624.

158. Henry R. Hitchcock, Jr., "Conflicting Views on Modern Architecture," review of *The City of Tomorrow, International Studio* 48 (March 1931), pp. 68, 70.

159. Henry Wright, "The Place of the Apartment in the Modern Community," *Record* 67 (March 1930), p. 237.

160. [Lawrence Veiller], *Housing* 21 (October 1932), p. 40.

161. Le Corbusier, "A Noted Architect Dissects Our Cities," *New York Times,* January 3, 1932, 5, pp. 10, 11, 19. Reprinted as "We Are Entering upon a New Era," *T-Square* [*Shelter*] 2 (February 1932), pp. 14–17, 41–42.

162. "Le Corbusier's City," *Art Digest* 6 (February 1932), p. 7.

163. Hitchcock noted only that the Plan Voisin of 1925 was exhibited in the Pavillon de l'Esprit Nouveau. Intended as a supplement to rather than a record of the exhibition, the catalogue did list as "unexecuted projects" the "*Voisin* Plan for Rebuilding Paris" and "Project for Skyscraper City of Three Million." See Henry-Russell Hitchcock, Jr., "Le Corbusier," in *Modern Architecture: International Exhibition,* pp. 73, 80.

164. Mumford's annotated bibliography on "Housing" refers to Le Corbusier's book as *The City of the Future.* See *Modern Architecture: International Exhibition,* p. 191. On its functional planning, see Lewis Mumford, "The City of Tomorrow," *New Republic* 61 (February 12, 1930), p. 333.

165. Edward Alden Jewell, "Art in Review," *New York Times,* October 27, 1933, p. 17.

166. Amédée Ozenfant and Charles-Edouard Jeanneret, *Après le cubisme* (Paris: Editions des Commentaires, 1918). Amédée Ozenfant and Charles-Edouard Jeanneret, *La Peinture moderne* (Paris: Editions Crès, 1925).

167. Hitchcock's essay is actually a letter to Le Corbusier. *Le Corbusier, Paintings, Watercolors, Drawings,* exh. cat. (New York, John Becker Gallery, October 16–November 5, 1933).

168. Jewell, "Art in Review," p. 17.

169. "In the Realm of Art: Comment on Current Exhibitions," *New York Times,* October 29, 1933, 9, p. 5.

170. [Henry McBride] ". . . Exhibition Open Le Corbusier as Painter," *New York Sun,* October 21, 1933, newspaper clipping

(FLC); "Le Corbusier as a Painter," *Art Digest* 8 (November 1, 1933), p. 12.

171. The exhibition resulted in the sale of only one small drawing. Letter, John Becker to Le Corbusier, April 4, 1924 [read 1934] (FLC). In 1930 Philip Johnson tried unsuccessfully to purchase "some plans" but could not agree on a price. Riley, *The International Style: Exhibition 15 and the Museum of Modern Art*, pp. 35, 204–205n22. For "Cubism and Abstract Art," his 1936 exhibition at the Modern, Alfred Barr asked Le Corbusier for the loan of a still life. Letter, Le Corbusier to Alfred Barr, January 10, 1936 (FLC).

172. A. J. Raspetti, the New York correspondent of the Association Française d'Expansion et d'Echanges artistiques, acted as the League's representative in Paris. Letter, Louis Bouchet to Le Corbusier, November 1929; letter and cable, A. J. Raspetti to Le Corbusier, November 8, 1929 (FLC).

173. Letters, Robert Woods Bliss to Lawrence Grant White, and Robert Woods Bliss to Vernon Kellogg, both November 12, 1929 (FLC).

174. Harris, "Le Corbusier and the Headquarters of the Brazilian Ministry of Education and Health 1936–1945," pp. 19–24.

175. Letters, Le Corbusier to A. J. Raspetti, January 2 and 8, 1930 (FLC).

176. Joseph Brewer was a partner in the publishing firm of Brewer and Warren, formerly Payson and Clarke, which published the American editions of *Towards a New Architecture* and *City of Tomorrow*. Le Corbusier communicated to his publisher through expatriate American journalist William Aspenwall Bradley. Letters, Joseph Brewer to William Aspenwall Bradley, February 14, 1930; William Aspenwall Bradley to Le Corbusier, February 26, 1930 (FLC).

177. Letter, Raymond M. Hood to Le Corbusier, January 16, 1930 (FLC).

178. Letters, A. J. Raspetti to Le Corbusier, January 30, 1930; A. Lawrence Kocher to Le Corbusier, October 3, 1930; A. J. Raspetti to Le Corbusier, October 15, 1930; Arthur [Hamilton] Beatty to A. J. Raspetti, October 3, 1930; Fred L. Plummer to A. J. Raspetti, October 11, 1930 (FLC).

179. Letter, Le Corbusier to Lawrence Kocher, October 22, 1930 (FLC).

180. Letter, Le Corbusier to A. J. Raspetti, October 27, 1930 (FLC).

181. Chanin was president of the Chanin Construction Co. Le Corbusier, Agenda, 1928–1929, p. 45 (FLC). Letter, Le Corbusier to Chanin, January 27, 1930 (FLC).

182. See letters, Melville M. Easterday to Le Corbusier, April 18 [postmarked], June 26, August 12, and December 5, 1929; Le Corbusier to Melville M. Easterday, June 28 and September 15, 1929, and January 2, 1930 (FLC).

183. Letters, A. Lawrence Kocher to Le Corbusier, November 27, 1930, and January 5, 1931 (FLC).

184. By this time the Architectural League had dropped out, possibly because Beaux-Arts architect Julian Clarence Levi had replaced Hood as its president.

185. After 1953 Harvard's Graduate School of Architecture was called the Graduate School of Design. Joseph Hudnut was made acting dean during the academic year 1933–1934 and dean the next year. Joseph Hudnut, "The Education of an Architect," *Record* 69 (May 1931), pp. 412–414. Judith Oberlander, "History IV 1933–1935," in Oliver, ed., *The Making of an Architect 1881–1981*, pp. 119–126. Bletter, "Modernism Rears Its Head—The Twenties and Thirties," pp. 110–116. "Joseph Hudnut, Architect, Dead," obituary, *New York Times*, January 17, 1968, p. 47. See also Jill Perlman, "Joseph Hudnut's Other Modernism at the 'Harvard Bauhaus,'" *JSAH* 56 (December 1997), pp. 452–477.

186. Letter, Joseph Hudnut to George Harold Edgell, November 4, 1933 (Graduate School of Design, Records of the Office of the Dean, 1932–1935, courtesy of the Harvard University Archives).

187. Letter, Joseph Hudnut to George Harold Edgell, November 13, 1933 (Graduate School of Design, Records of the Office of the Dean, 1932–1935, courtesy of the Harvard University Archives).

188. Letters, G. H. Edgell to Joseph Hudnut, November 7, 1933; Joseph Hudnut to George Harold Edgell, November 13, 1933 (Graduate School of Design, Records of the Office of the Dean, 1932–1935, courtesy of the Harvard University Archives).

189. In 1924 Frey received his diploma in architecture from the Institute of Technology in Winterthur, Switzerland. He worked in Le Corbusier's atelier from October 1928 to July 1929. Joseph Rosa, *Albert Frey, Architect* (New York: Rizzoli, 1990), pp. 12, 16–17.

190. Letter, Albert Frey to Le Corbusier, February 20, 1931 (FLC). *Yearbook of the Architectural League of New York 1931* (New York: Architectural League of New York, 1931). A. Lawrence Kocher and Albert Frey, "Aluminaire: A House for Contemporary Life," *Shelter* 2 (May 1932), pp. 54–56.

191. Letter, Albert Frey to Le Corbusier, February 20, 1931 (FLC).

192. Letter, Albert Frey to Le Corbusier, October 10, 1934 (FLC).

193. Peter the Hermit, born in Amiens, France, was a leading preacher of the First Crusade during the late eleventh century. Letter, Le Corbusier to Albert Frey, October 26, 1934 (FLC).

194. During the period from November 1929 to October 1934 the value of the French franc in relation to the dollar increased by over 40 percent. On November 8, 1929, the date of A. J. Raspetti's first letter to Le Corbusier, the French franc was valued

at 3.91 cents. On October 26, 1934, the date of Le Corbusier's letter to Albert Frey, the French franc was valued at 6.63 cents. See "Foreign Exchange," *New York Times,* November 9, 1929, p. 31, and October 27, 1934, p. 23. On French monetary and economic policy during this period, see Alfred Sauvy, *Histoire économique de la France entre les deux guerres,* vol. 1 (Paris: Economica, 1984), pp. 125–160; Jean-Pierre Patat and Michel Lutfalla, *A Monetary History of France in the Twentieth Century* (London: Macmillan Press, 1990), pp. 68–79.

195. Letter, Carl Schniewind to Le Corbusier ("Cher Monsieur Jeanneret"), June 4, 1928 (FLC). Schniewind was born in New York City of German parents. See "Carl Schniewind, Art Curator," obituary, *New York Times,* August 30, 1957, p. 19.

196. Letters, Carl Schniewind to Le Corbusier, August 7, 1929; Le Corbusier to Carl Schniewind ("Cher M. Schniewindt"), August 16, 1929; Carl Schniewind to Le Corbusier, February 13, 1932; [Le Corbusier] to Karl [sic] Schniewind, September 17, 1934 (FLC). In February 1935 Schniewind described Le Corbusier as a "close personal friend of mine." Letter Carl Schniewind to Dean G. H. [Harold] Edgell, February 8, 1935 (Graduate School of Design, Records of the Office of the Dean, 1932–1935, courtesy of the Harvard University Archives).

197. Letter, Albert Frey to Le Corbusier, February 7, 1935 (FLC).

198. Schniewind tried to placate Le Corbusier on the issue of his lecture fees, suggesting that he consult Léger. Letter, Carl Schniewind ("Votre Charlie") to Le Corbusier ("Mon cher Corbu"), February 6, 1935 (FLC).

199. The Cornell engagement was still tentative. Letter, Carl Schniewind to Le Corbusier, March 7, 1935 (FLC).

200. Letter, [Le Corbusier] to Carl Schniewind, February 15, 1935 (FLC).

201. Letter, Carl Schniewind to Le Corbusier, March 7, 1935 (FLC). Harvard's Dean Edgell, for example, informed Schniewind that he had been "instructed by the Corporation not to spend a cent of money beyond the budget this year." Letter, G. H. Edgell to C. Schniewind, February 13, 1935 (Graduate School of Design, Records of the Office of the Dean, 1932–1935, courtesy of the Harvard University Archives).

202. James Johnson Sweeney and Oscar Stonorov were included in the group, but could not attend the meeting. Letter, Carl Schniewind to Le Corbusier, March 7, 1935 (FLC). On Jan Ruhtenberg, who had previously worked with Mies van der Rohe in Berlin and came to Columbia in 1934 to fill the post of professor of architectural design, see Bletter, "Modernism Rears Its Head— the Twenties and Thirties," p. 113.

203. Letter, [Le Corbusier] to Carl Schniewind, April 8, 1935 (FLC).

204. Le Corbusier also received from Sweeney the names and addresses of such dealers. Letter (fragment), Carl Schniewind to [Le Corbusier], May 5, [1935] (FLC).

205. The deficit reserve was projected for $700 to $1,000. Letter, C. O. [Carl] Schniewind ("F. d'A") to Le Corbusier, May 30, 1935 (FLC). Letters, C. O. [Carl] Schniewind to William Emerson, May 30, 1935; C. O. [Carl] Schniewind to G. H. Edgell, May 30, 1935 (Graduate School of Design, Records of the Office of the Dean, 1932–1935, courtesy of the Harvard University Archives).

206. Letters, Le Corbusier to Carl Schniewind, June 25, 1935; Carl Schniewind to Le Corbusier, July 3, 1935; Le Corbusier to Carl Schniewind, July 12, 1935 (FLC).

207. Georges Huismans had supported Le Corbusier's League of Nations project in 1927. For Algiers, Huismans assisted Le Corbusier in his appointment to the Comité du plan régional in 1938. Mary McLeod, "L'Appel de la Meditérranée," and Richard Quincerot, "Palais des Nations: Le Concours international, 1926–1931," in *Encyclopédie,* pp. 30, 285.

208. Le Corbusier to Georges Huisman [sic], July 19, 1935. Schniewind suggested several times to Le Corbusier that he write to Huismans. Letters, (fragment), Carl Schniewind to [Le Corbusier], May 5 [1935]; Carl Schniewind to Le Corbusier, July 3, 1935; Le Corbusier to Carl Schniewind, July 12, 1935 (FLC).

209. Letters, Le Corbusier to Carl Schniewind, July 26, 1935; Carl Schniewind to Le Corbusier, August 28, 1935 (FLC).

210. Letters, Ernestine M. Fantl to G. H. Edgell, July 17, 1935 (Graduate School of Design, Records of the Office of the Dean, 1932–1935, courtesy of the Harvard University Archives); Le Corbusier to Carl Schniewind, July 26, 1935 (FLC); Philip Goodwin to Le Corbusier, August 12, 1935 (FLC); Philip Goodwin to Ernestine M. Fantl, August 12, 1935 (DAD, MoMA, NY). Ernestine Fantl, a former student of Alfred Barr at Wellesley College, was the staff member in charge of the exhibition and lecture tour at the Department of Architecture at the museum. See Hitchcock, "Le Corbusier and the United States," p. 10.

211. Robert Jacobs insisted that his official position was to serve as translator for Le Corbusier's lectures. Unofficially he served as his interpreter during the lecture tour. Letter, Robert Jacobs to [Philip] Goodwin, July 14, 1935 (DAD, MoMA, NY). Although Le Corbusier thought Jacobs "un garçon très gentil" and "d'accord en principe" with him, he wondered whether Jacobs knew enough French to translate before the public. He would have preferred Carl Schniewind to do the translations "for the good of the cause." But when Schniewind met Jacobs at the museum in late August, he was convinced that the young architect could translate the lectures, especially since "he knows a little your ideas and he has worked with you." Letters, Carl Schniewind to Le Corbusier, July 3, 1935; Le Corbusier to Carl Schniewind, July12, 1935; Carl Schniewind to Le Corbusier, August 28, 1935 (FLC).

212. Letters, Carl Schniewind to Le Corbusier, August 28, 1935, September 11, 1935 (FLC).

213. Le Corbusier wrote to museum administrators, "Je répète formellement que je n'ai pas le gout . . . de faire d'innombrables conférences. C'est tout à fait inutile. Mon désir est d'être utile à

quelque chose en parlant dans certains cercles autorisés et j'ai l'intention de me limiter esclusivement [sic] à NEW-YORK et ses satellites, CHICAGO, SAN FRANCISCO, LOS ANGELES et MEXICO." Letter, Le Corbusier to the Modern Art Museum ("Messieurs"), September 10, 1935 (FLC).

214. Letters, Le Corbusier to Carl Schniewind, September 10, 1935; Carl Schniewind to Le Corbusier, September 11, 1935 (FLC).

215. Letter, [Le Corbusier] to Carl Schniewind, February 15, 1935 (FLC).

216. Gournay, "France Discovers America, 1917–1939," pp. 20–21.

217. From the proceeds of the lecture tour, the Museum of Modern Art required Le Corbusier to pay for his first-class ticket, which was discounted at 30 percent. See [Museum of Modern Art], "Le Corbusier Lecture Tour Statement of Receipts and Expenditures" (FLC).

218. Inexplicably the entry actually read "The Architect L. Le Corbusier," [first-class passenger list], "Paquebot 'Normandie'" (FLC). "Un grand ami de la France: Mr Whitney Warren," L'Amérique (September 15–22, 1917), p. 40n56. See also "Un ami de la France. Mr Whitney Warren," L'Illustration (July 14, 1917), pp. 32–33. Among his efforts to preserve French architecture and culture, Whitney Warren played a major role in the reconstruction of France and restoration of its monuments after World War I. See Gournay, "France Discovers America, 1917–1939," pp. 72–73, 103–104, 111n. André Jaoul's name does not appear on the list. I thank Nancy Austin for information on Le Corbusier's first encounter with Jaoul.

219. Rose, Jazz Cleopatra: Josephine Baker in Her Time, pp. 152–153.

220. Brooks, Le Corbusier's Formative Years, pp. 21, 182. Marguerite Tjader Harris, interview with author, Darien, CT, October 23, 1984; Jacobs interview, November 21, 1984.

221. See lists on S.S. Normandie stationery (FLC). Abraham Rattner was a surrealist painter living in Paris who returned to America, probably aboard the Normandie, in time for the opening of his exhibition on November 1, 1935, at the Julien Levy Gallery. Julien Levy, Memoir of an Art Gallery (New York: G. P. Putnam's Sons, 1977), p. 159. For a comparison with other examples of Rattner's handwriting, see letter, "Abe Rattner" to "M Corbusier" undated, on Barbizon Plaza Hotel stationery, and invitation to his exhibition at the Julien Levy Gallery, signed "A Rattner" (FLC).

2   Le Corbusier Takes New York

1. Le Corbusier, Quand les cathédrales étaient blanches: Voyage au pays des timides (Paris: Librairie Plon, 1937), hereafter cited as Cathédrales; and the American edition, When the Cathedrals Were White: A Journey to the Country of Timid People, trans. Francis E. Hyslop, Jr. (New York: Reynal and Hitchcock, 1947), hereafter cited as Cathedrals, pp. 34, 186–187. Most quotations and citations are from the Hyslop translation, except where noted.

2. I owe a special debt of gratitude to Tim Benton for alerting me to Marguerite's love relationship with Le Corbusier and for sharing so generously his views on it. Century, p. 181.

3. Letter, Philip Goodwin to Ernestine M. Fantl, August 12, 1935 (DAD, MoMA, NY).

4. In the spring of 1935 the Museum of Modern Art (MoMA) agreed to incur a modest deficit for the entire tour, which Schniewind estimated to be in the range of $700 to $1,000; Letter, Carl Schniewind to Le Corbusier, May 30, 1935 (FLC). According to Geoffrey Hellman's article in the New Yorker, "Goodwin said that the Museum would sponsor the tour and pay all expenses, and that the entire favorable difference, if any, between these costs and the lecture fees would go to Le Corbusier." Geoffrey T. Hellman, "Profiles: From Within to Without—II," New Yorker 23 (May 3, 1947), p. 37. Letters, Thomas Dabney Mabry, Jr. (Executive Director, Museum of Modern Art), to Le Corbusier, December 2 and December 13, 1935 (FLC).

5. Cathedrals, pp. 99, 125. See also [Le Corbusier] "Note pour Mlle Thérèse Bonney" [c. 1936] (FLC).

6. Elizabeth Davis Harris, "Le Corbusier and the Headquarters of the Brazilian Ministry of Education and Health 1936–1945" (Ph.D. diss., University of Chicago, 1984), p. 24.

7. Cathedrals, p. 106. In response to a letter from the publicity director of the Modern sending clippings from American newspapers on his work, Le Corbusier expressed his indifference, "you know how much that sort of literature is deceiving and offers little interest." Letters, Sarah Newmeyer to Le Corbusier, April 17, 1936; Le Corbusier to Sarah Newmeyer, May 28, 1936 (FLC and DAD, MoMA, NY).

8. This recounting conflates two versions of the story, one told by Robert Allan Jacobs, interview with author, Pawling, NY, November 21, 1984 (hereafter cited as Jacobs interview), and another contained in Hellman, "Profiles: From Within to Without—II" (May 3, 1947), p. 37.

9. Cathedrals, p. 51. Press release, Museum of Modern Art, 351018–35 (DAD, MoMA, NY). Russell Lynes, Good Old Modern (New York: Atheneum, 1973), pp. 95–96.

10. Hellman, "Profiles: From Within to Without—II" (May 3, 1947), pp. 37–38.

11. Jacobs interview, November 21, 1984.

12. "Finds American Skyscrapers 'Much Too Small,'" New York Herald Tribune, October 22, 1935, p. 21.

13. Cathédrales, p. 72; Cathedrals, p. 51.

14. In reality Le Corbusier did not envision his skyscrapers as obelisks with pointed crests. "Finds American Skyscrapers 'Much Too Small,'" p. 21.

15. On Alsop's persona as a journalist, see Edwin M. Yoder, Jr., *Joseph Alsop's Cold War* (Chapel Hill: University of North Carolina Press, 1995); "Joseph Alsop Dies at Home at 78," obituary, *New York Times,* August 29, 1989, B6.

16. *Cathedrals,* p. 51.

17. "Finds American Skyscrapers 'Much Too Small,'" p. 21. The *New York Times* report was more generous to Le Corbusier, indicating that he was not yet able to speak on New York, "having seen the city so far only from the ship's deck and hurrying taxicabs. . . . However, he feels that the average city leaves much to be desired . . . and he has definite ideas about what should be done." "Venice 'Best City,' Le Corbusier Finds," *New York Times,* October 22, 1935, p. 35.

18. Joseph and Stewart Alsop, *The Reporter's Trade* (New York: Reynal and Company, 1958), p. 188; Louis Bromfield provided the definition of "egghead" in his essay "The Triumph of the Egghead," *Freeman* 3 (December 1, 1952), p. 158, quoted in Richard Hofstadter, *Anti-intellectualism in American Life* (New York: Alfred A. Knopf, 1964), p. 9.

19. Hellman, "Profiles: From Within to Without—II" (May 3, 1947), p. 37.

20. The Léger exhibition closed on October 24. Edward Alden Jewell, "In the Realm of Art," *New York Times,* October 6, 1935, 11, p. 9. See "Fernand Léger Exhibition," *Bulletin of the Museum of Modern Art* 3 (October 1935), pp. 1–8. Le Corbusier called that exhibition "the best one which had been organized" of Léger's work, *Cathedrals,* p. 127.

21. The character of Meyer Wolfsheim in F. Scott Fitzgerald's novel *The Great Gatsby* was allegedly modeled after Rothstein. Robert A. M. Stern, Gregory Gilmartin, and Thomas Mellins, *New York 1930: Architecture and Urbanism between the World Wars* (New York: Rizzoli, 1987), p. 206.

22. Jacobs interview, November 21, 1984. See also Hellman, "Profiles: From Within to Without—II" (May 3, 1947), p. 38.

23. Letter, Ernestine M. Fantl to Le Corbusier, September 17, 1935 (DAD, MoMA, NY).

24. Henry-Russell Hitchcock, Jr., *Le Corbusier,* "Exhibition arranged by the Department of Architecture of the Museum of Modern Art" (New York: Museum of Modern Art, 1935), unpaged.

25. Franz Schulze, *Philip Johnson* (New York: Alfred A. Knopf, 1994), p. 71.

26. Letter, Le Corbusier to "Monsieur Levy" [photographer], July 28, 1935 (FLC).

27. Letters, Philip Goodwin to Le Corbusier, August 12, 1935 (FLC); Philip Goodwin to Ernestine Fantl, August 12, 1935 (DAD, MoMA, NY).

28. Schulze, *Philip Johnson,* p. 63.

29. A reference to Le Corbusier's Asile Flottant de l'Armée du Salut (1929), a boat moored along the Seine in Paris that served as a Salvation Army shelter for the homeless. *OC 1929–1934,* pp. 32–33.

30. A reference to the Richard Mandel House in Mount Kisco, New York (1933–1934) by Edward Durell Stone with interiors by Donald Deskey. The house had just been the subject of an extensive review in *Architectural Forum* 63 (August 1935), pp. [78]–88.

31. A reference to the Errázuriz House project in Chile of 1930 (see figure 2.3). *OC 1929–1934,* pp. 48–52.

32. Letter, Philip Johnson to author, September 5, 1991.

33. Letter, Philip Johnson to Ernestine Fantl, August 15 [1935] (DAD, MoMA, NY).

34. Henry-Russell Hitchcock, Jr. and Philip Johnson, *International Style: Architecture since 1922* (New York: W. W. Norton, 1932), pp. 40–49.

35. Letter, Robert Jacobs to Ernestine Fantl, August 16, 1935 (DAD, MoMA, NY).

36. The Algiers model was then in Algeria. Letter, Adrian Waldorf to "Museum of Modern Art," October 1, 1935 (DAD, MoMA, NY). Unfortunately the model of the Radiant Farm had been destroyed. Letter, Le Corbusier to "Messieurs" MoMA, September 24, 1935 (FLC).

37. Members received free admission to all lectures and previews of exhibitions. "Museum of Modern Art Catechism" [Summer 1935] (Rockefeller family archives, R.G. 2, Cultural Interests, box 20, folder 198, Rockefeller Archive Center).

38. The exhibition catalogue incorrectly identified the Weekend House as a "Villa in eastern outskirts of Paris." La Celle-Saint-Cloud is located west of Paris.

39. "Design: Modern Architecture's Father Shows Brain Children," *Newsweek* 6 (October 26, 1935), p. 31.

40. Francesco Passanti, "The Vernacular, Modernism, and Le Corbusier," *JSAH* 56 (December 1997), p. 447.

41. Mary Caroline McLeod, "Urbanism and Utopia: Le Corbusier from Regional Syndicalism to Vichy" (Ph.D. diss., Princeton University, 1985); Mary McLeod, "Le Rêve transi de Le Corbusier: L'Amérique 'catastrophe féerique,'" in J.[ean]-L.[ouis] Cohen and H.[ubert] Damisch, eds., *Américanisme et modernité* (Paris: EHESS and Flammarion, 1993), pp. 208–227.

42. Hitchcock, *Le Corbusier.*

43. *OC 1929–1934,* pp. 48–52, 58–62, 74–89.

44. "French Architect Shows Work Here," *New York Times,* October 25, 1935, p. 23.

45. [Le Corbusier], "Note pour Mlle Thérèse Bonney" (FLC).

46. "French Architect Shows Work Here," p. 23. A photograph of the model appears in *OC 1929–1934,* pp. 179, 184.

47. Letter, A. Everett Austin Jr. to John Eckstrom, undated (DAD, MoMA, NY).

48. C. A. Cochran [Morris and O'Connor], "Wadsworth Atheneum, 'Avery Extension,' Tentative Miscellaneous Furniture Budget" August 8, 1933, and letter, C. A. Cochran to Flint-Bruce Company, August 17, 1933 (Wadsworth Atheneum, Hartford).

49. For this information I thank Eugene Gaddis, archivist, Wadsworth Atheneum. See Helen Searing, "From the Fogg to the Bauhaus: A Museum for the Machine Age," in Eugene Gaddis, ed., *Avery Memorial, Wadsworth Atheneum* (Hartford: Wadsworth Atheneum, 1985), pp. 18–30.

50. Letter, Ernestine M. Fantl to A. Everett Austin, October 26, 1935 (DAD, MoMA, NY).

51. Letter, A. Everett Austin to Ernestine Fantl, November 1, 1935 (DAD, MoMA, NY).

52. "French Architect Shows Work Here," p. 23. Le Corbusier described the origin of the chair in *Précisions,* pp. 118–121.

53. In her article on Charlotte Perriand, Mary McLeod identified the collaborative roles of these designers for three chairs, the *siège à dossier basculant, grand confort,* and *chaise-longue:* "Perriand credits Le Corbusier with setting the problem. Typically, she worked out the designs and details, sometimes with the assistance of Jeanneret." Mary McLeod, "Charlotte Perriand, Her First Decade as a Designer," *AA Files* 15, p. 7. See also Charlotte Benton, "Furniture Design," in *Century,* pp. 158–163. In their book *The International Style,* Johnson and Hitchcock were careful to recognize Perriand's collaboration in the furniture design. They identified the designers of the annex to the Villa Church: Le Corbusier and his cousin Pierre Jeanneret as architects with "furniture by Le Corbusier and Charlotte Perriand." See *The International Style: Architecture since 1922,* p. 127. "L'Art de Vivre: Charlotte Perriand and New Conceptions of Modern Life," conference at Columbia University, January 24, 1998.

54. The museum report specified "trustees" as one of its groups, rather than "the professional community of architects." *Present Status and Future Direction of the Museum of Modern Art: Confidential Report to Executive Committee* (1933), pp. 1–6 (Rockefeller family archives, R.G. 2 OMR, Cultural Interests, box 20, folder 197, Rockefeller Archive Center).

55. As with all of her subsequent writing, *Borealis* appeared under her maiden name Marguerite Tjader (New York: Logos Publishing Company). In it the protagonist, Signe, confronts good and evil and is "overcome by a religious ecstasy." One critic deemed the novel "interesting" but not "particularly successful." "A Swedish Novel," *New York Times,* May 31, 1931, 4, p. 6. See also "Marguerite Tjader Harris," obituary, *Darien News Review,* April 10, 1986, and "Marguerite Tjader," *Contemporary Authors,* 17 (Detroit: Gale Research Company, 1976), p. 732. Marguerite Tjader Harris, interview with author, Darien, CT, October 23, 1984.

56. "Harris–Tjader," *New York Times,* May 24, 1925, p. 29.

57. Hilary Harris, interviews with author, Woodstock, NY, May 20 and December 6, 1994. See Marguerite's characterization of Overton Harris in her book *Theodore Dreiser: A New Dimension* (Norwalk, CT: Silvermine Publishers, 1965), p. 6. Harris's tenure as magistrate was controversial. See, for example, newspaper reports "Rebukes Magistrate in Court as Unfair," *New York Times,* September 23, 1932, p. 2; "Harris Caustic on Police," *New York Times,* January 23, 1935, p. 8; "Relief Officials Rebuked," *New York Times,* April 20, 1935, p. 14; "Magistrate Harris Assailed as 'Unfair,'" *New York Times,* August 3, 1935, p. 28.

58. "Charles Richard Tjader," *National Cyclopaedia of American Biography* 17 (New York: James T. White and Company, 1920), pp. 144–145. "Charles Richard Tjader," obituary, *New York Times,* December 29, 1916, p. 9. Hilary Harris, interview with author, December 6, 1994.

59. Marguerite Tjader, "Portrait of Le Corbusier," unpublished manuscript, 1984 (Harris family papers).

60. Tjader, "Portrait of Le Corbusier" (Harris family papers). Letters, Marguerite Tjader Harris to Le Corbusier, March 18, April 25, and May 2 [1932] (FLC); Le Corbusier to Marguerite Tchader [sic] Harris, March 15 and April 23, 1932 (DR 1984: 1701, 1702, Collection Centre Canadien d'Architecture/Canadian Centre for Architecture, Montréal; Le Corbusier to Marguerite Tjader Harris, September 27, 1934 (FLC). Le Corbusier retained a small sketch of the villa (FLC). Designs for the Harris villa (incorrectly dated) appear in H. Allen Brooks, ed., *The Le Corbusier Archive,* vol. 7, *Villa Savoye and Other Buildings and Projects, 1929–1930,"* (New York, London, and Paris: Garland and Fondation Le Corbusier, 1984), pp. 241–246.

61. Le Corbusier's relationship with her at that time was still formal. He addressed a letter to her "Cher [sic] Madame." Letter, Le Corbusier to Marguerite Harris, September 27, 1934 (FLC).

62. Le Corbusier notes on this day that he made a "visite de New York." Agenda, Samedi [October 26, 1935] (FLC). Tjader, "Portrait of Le Corbusier" (Harris family papers).

63. Marguerite Tjader Harris, interview with author, Darien, CT, October 23, 1984.

64. Marguerite Tjader Harris, interview with author, Darien, CT, October 23, 1984. For the significance of Rockefeller Center, see chapter 5.

65. Hilary Harris, interviews with author, Woodstock, NY, March 26 and May 20, 1994.

66. He built the *petit cabanon* overlooking the Mediterranean at Cap Martin in 1952 and the *baraque* adjacent to it in 1955. On the significance of both structures and photographs of them, see Bruno Chiambretto, "Cabanon," in *Encyclopédie*, pp. 81–83. For a Nietzschean interpretation of the *petit cabanon*, see Charles Jencks, *Le Corbusier and the Tragic View of Architecture* (Cambridge: Harvard University Press, 1973), pp. 25–27.

67. Tjader, "Portrait of Le Corbusier" (Harris family papers).

68. Tjader, "Portrait of Le Corbusier" (Harris family papers).

69. Marguerite Tjader, *Theodore Dreiser*, pp. 10, 40.

70. Tjader, *Theodore Dreiser*, pp. 47, 60–63; Tjader, "Portrait of Le Corbusier" (Harris family papers). See also Richard Lingeman, *Theodore Dreiser: An American Journey 1908–1945* (New York: G. P. Putnam's Sons, 1986), pp. 324–325.

71. Letter, Le Corbusier to Marguerite Tjader Harris, September 27, 1934 (FLC); Tjader, "Portrait of Le Corbusier" (Harris family papers).

72. Hilary Harris, interviews with author, Woodstock, NY, March 26 and May 20, 1994.

73. On Le Corbusier's studies of American elevated streets, traffic patterns, and automobile intersections see, for example, *VR*, p. 34; "Mort de la rue," *Plans* (May 1931), p. 49; reprinted in *VR* [and *RC*], pp. 119–126.

74. Tjader, "Portrait of Le Corbusier" (Harris family papers).

75. Le Corbusier uses the word *pilotis* in *Cathédrales*, pp. 59–60; *Cathedrals*, pp. 42–43.

76. Tjader, "Portrait of Le Corbusier" (Harris family papers).

77. On the avant-garde in the city, see Walter Benjamin, "On Some Motifs in Baudelaire," in *Illuminations*, ed. Hannah Arendt (New York: Schocken Books, 1968), pp. 170–174, 192–194.

78. On Adolf Loos as *flâneur* in America, see M. David Samson, "A World Like a Ford: Amerikanismus and the Modern Movement in Architecture 1893–1936," unpublished manuscript, pp. 75–79. See also Adolf Loos, "The Leather Goods and Gold- and Silversmith Trades," 1898, in *Spoken into the Void: Collected Essays 1897–1900* (Cambridge: MIT Press, 1982), p. 7; Benedetto Gravagnuolo, *Adolf Loos: Theory and Works* (New York: Rizzoli, 1982), pp. 29, 42.

79. Marshall Berman, *All That Is Solid Melts into Air* (New York: Penguin Books, 1988), pp. 164–171.

80. Letter, Le Corbusier to Marguerite Tjader Harris, "jeudi matin" [October 31, 1935] (Frances Loeb Library, Harvard Design School).

81. Letter, Le Corbusier to Marguerite Tjader Harris [to Park Central Hotel, New York, October 31, 1935] (Frances Loeb Library, Harvard Design School).

82. Tjader, "Portrait of Le Corbusier" (Harris family papers).

83. Letter, Le Corbusier to Marguerite Tjader Harris [November 8, 1935] (Collection Centre Canadien d'Architecture/Canadian Centre for Architecture, Montréal).

84. Letter, Le Corbusier to Marguerite Harris, Brunswick, ME [November 12, 1935] (Frances Loeb Library, Harvard Design School).

85. Agenda, November 17 and 18, 1935 (FLC).

86. Letter, Le Corbusier to Marguerite Tjader Harris [November 22, 1935] (Frances Loeb Library, Harvard Design School). The present location of the drawings is unknown.

87. Letter, Le Corbusier to "Amie" [Marguerite Tjader Harris; [envelope postmarked November 23, 1935] (Frances Loeb Library, Harvard Design School). In an earlier version of the manuscript of her biography entitled "Le Corbusier: Letters and Commentary," Marguerite confirmed that he sent from Kalamazoo a brief note to signal his return and enclosed the drawing *L'Homme rouge* (present location unknown). Marguerite Tjader Harris, interview with author, Darien, CT, October 23, 1984.

88. Telegram, Le Corbusier to Marguerite Tjader Harris [November 28, 1935] (Frances Loeb Library, Harvard Design School).

89. Hilary Harris, interviews with author, Woodstock, NY, March 26 and May 20, 1994.

90. Lingeman, *Theodore Dreiser: An American Journey 1908–1945*, p. 452.

91. Tjader, "Portrait of Le Corbusier" (Harris family papers).

92. For an analysis of Le Corbusier's misogyny and "language of mastery," see Margalit Shinar, "Feminist Criticism of Urban Theory and Design: Case Study: Le Corbusier," *Journal of Urban and Cultural Studies* 2, no. 2 (1992), pp. 29–39.

93. On Le Corbusier's use of Nietzsche's apollonian virtues in his urbanism, see Shinar, "Feminist Criticism of Urban Theory and Design: Case Study: Le Corbusier," pp. 34–39. On the Dionysian view of nature, see Alexander Nehamas, *Nietzsche, Life as Literature* (Cambridge: Harvard University Press, 1985), pp. 146–147.

94. Jacobs, for example, did not know her or know of her. Jacobs interview, November 21, 1984. During her lifetime Marguerite Harris concealed her intimate relationship with Le Corbusier. Her motive was probably twofold: first, to shield Yvonne, whom she considered a friend (as well as to shield herself and Le Corbusier from Yvonne!); and second, to ensure that her relationship with Le Corbusier did not cause her to lose her rank as Dreiser's preeminent mistress and muse. In her "Portrait of Le Corbusier," written long after the deaths of both Le Corbusier and his wife, she continued to conceal her long affair with him. Her decision in 1984 to sell her extensive correspondence with him, therefore, remains a mystery. It supports the view that she intended future biographers and historians to know about their liaison.

3 The American Lectures

1. Press release, Museum of Modern Art, New York, October 24, 1935, #351022–37 (DAD, MoMA, NY).

2. Robert Allan Jacobs, interviews with author, Pawling, NY, November 21, 1984, and June 7, 1987 (hereafter cited as Jacobs interview/s).

3. Max Abramovitz, interview with author, New York City, June 2, 1987.

4. Henry-Russell Hitchcock, interview with author, New York City, December 13, 1984.

5. Harry Weese was a student at MIT in the class of 1938. "War Stories from the Educational Front," *Inland Architect* 31 (September–October 1987), p. 112. Harry Weese, interview with author, December 8, 1987.

6. *Cathédrales*, p. 204; *Cathedrals*, p. 137.

7. "Là, j'ai adopté une technique à moi qui est assez particulière. Je ne préparais jamais de conférences. Vous voyez une petite carte comme une carte de visite double à peu près, n'est-ce pas, avec quatre ou cinq lignes dessus que j'improvisais. Cette improvisation est une chose formidable: je dessinais . . . au début je travaillais avec des craies, des craies de couleur au tableau noir, encore fallait-il qu'il y en ait. Et quand on dessine autour des paroles, on dessine avec les paroles utiles, on crée quelque chose. Et toute ma théorie—mon introspection et ma rétrospection sur le phénomène Architecture et Urbanisme—vient de ces conférences improvisées et dessinées. Et alors ce qu'il y a de caractéristique, c'est que les idées ont fini par faire une doctrine—ça fait un tout Architecture et Urbanisme—et alors cette thèse Architecture et Urbanisme est devenue maintenant mondialement acquise, professée partout, pratiquée partout, et on fait du Corbu dans le monde entier maintenant. C'est peut-être désespérant—mais c'est comme ça." Excerpt from Le Corbusier audiotape, from the exhibition "L'Aventure Le Corbusier," Centre National d'Art et de Culture Georges Pompidou, Paris (October 1987–January 1988).

8. Le Corbusier showed "stills" (slides) at his first lecture at the Modern. Letter, Philip Goodwin to A. Everett Austin, October 25, 1935 (Wadsworth Atheneum, Hartford). His lectures at the Wadsworth Atheneum, Bowdoin, and Baltimore, and at least one at Princeton, were also reported to have been illustrated with slides. But Hitchcock, who attended his lectures at Yale and Wesleyan, maintained that "Corbusier did not lecture with slides." Henry-Russell Hitchcock, interview with author, New York City, December 13, 1984.

9. Jacobs interview, November 21, 1984.

10. Jacobs interview, November 21, 1984. Letter, Robert Jacobs to Philip Goodwin, July 14, 1935 (DAD, MoMA, NY). See also James Ward, "Les Terrasses," *Architectural Review* (London) 177 (March 1985), p. 65.

11. Le Corbusier, *Towards a New Architecture,* trans. Frederick Etchells (New York: Payson and Clarke, 1927), p. 14; Ward, "Les Terrasses," p. 67.

12. Jacobs interview, November 21, 1984.

13. Jacobs interview, November 21, 1984.

14. Jacobs interview, June 7, 1987.

15. Weese, "War Stories from the Educational Front," p. 112; Max Abramovitz, interview with author, New York City, June 2, 1987.

16. See lecture sketches in *VR,* p. 173; *Précisions; Giorgio Ciucci, "A Roma con Bottai," *Rassegna* (I Clienti di Le Corbusier) 3 (March 1980), pp. 66–71.

17. On the new Cartesian skyscraper, see chapter 4.

18. "Venice 'Best City,' Le Corbusier Finds," *New York Times,* October 22, 1935, p. 23.

19. *VR,* p. 90.

20. The American edition did not appear until a generation later. Le Corbusier, *The Radiant City,* trans. Pamela Knight, Eleanor Levieux, and Derek Coltman (New York: Orion Press, 1967).

21. Philip Goodwin, "Excerpt from lecture, delivered at the Museum of Modern Art, New York, by Le Corbusier, October 25 [sic], 1935. . . ." (DAD, MoMA, NY). Goodwin notes, "this excerpt is the gist of all subsequent lectures he will—Le Corbusier—deliver in the United States this year."

22. Le Corbusier defined this period in *VR,* title page, p. 340.

23. On changes in Le Corbusier's urbanism, see Robert Fishman, *Urban Utopias in the Twentieth Century* (New York: Basic Books, 1977), pp. 188–242; Mary Caroline McLeod, "Urbanism and Utopia: Le Corbusier from Regional Syndicalism to Vichy" (Ph.D. diss., Princeton University, 1985), pp. 208–272; Tim Benton and C. B. [Charlotte Benton], "Urbanism," in *Century,* pp. 200–237; Stanislaus von Moos, "Urbanism and Transcultural Exchanges, 1910–1935: A Survey," in H. Allen Brooks, ed., *Le Corbusier* (Princeton: Princeton University Press, 1987), pp. 219–232; Manfredo Tafuri, "'Machine et mémoire': The City in the Work of Le Corbusier," in Brooks, ed., *Le Corbusier,* pp. 203–218; Kenneth Frampton, "The Rise and Fall of the Radiant City: Le Corbusier 1928–1960," *Oppositions* 19/20 (Winter/Spring 1980), pp. 2–25; Mary McLeod, "Le Corbusier and Algiers," *Oppositions* 19/20 (Winter/Spring 1980), pp. 54–85.

24. "Declaration of the First Congress, La Sarraz, June 28, 1928: Aims of the C.I.A.M.," reprinted in José Luis Sert, *Can Our Cities Survive?* (Cambridge: Harvard University Press, 1942), p. 242. On CIAM, see Martin Steinmann, ed., *CIAM: Dokumente 1928–1939* (Basel and Stuttgart: Birkhäuser Verlag, 1979); Sigfried Giedion, "The Work of CIAM," *Circle* (1937), 272–278; Reyner Banham, "CIAM," in Wolfgang Pehnt, ed., *Encyclopedia of Modern Architecture* (New York: Abrams, 1964), pp. 70–73; Giorgio Ciucci, "The In-

vention of the Modern Movement," *Oppositions* 24 (Spring 1981); Giorgio Ciucci, "CIAM," in *Encyclopédie*, pp. 90–92.

25. For an English translation, see Le Corbusier, "The Sub-Division of Land in Cities," in Housing Study Guild, ed., *Abstract of Papers at the 3rd International Congress at Brussels of the International Committee for the Solution of the Problems in Modern Architecture*, pp. 3–11. On the "Reply to Moscow," see McLeod, "Urbanism and Utopia: Le Corbusier from Regional Syndicalism to Vichy," pp. 225–234; Jean-Louis Cohen, *Le Corbusier and the Mystique of the USSR* (Princeton: Princeton University Press, 1992), pp. 126–163.

26. Carlos Flores Lopez and Arturo Soria y Puig, *Arturo Soria y la ciudad lineal* (Madrid: Revista de Occidente, 1968). On Miliutin and the linear city, see Nikolai Miliutin, *Sotsgorod: The Problem of Building Socialist Cities*, ed. George R. Collins and William Alex (Cambridge: MIT Press, 1974); Cohen, *Le Corbusier and the Mystique of the USSR*, pp. 160–163.

27. For analyses of the Ville Contemporaine and Plan Voisin, the influence of Ebenezer Howard and Raymond Unwin's garden city planning, as well as Tony Garnier's use of rationalized construction techniques in his Industrial City, see Fishman, *Urban Utopias in the Twentieth Century*.

28. Peter Serenyi, "Le Corbusier, Fourier, and the Monastery of Ema," in Peter Serenyi, ed., *Le Corbusier in Perspective* (Englewood Cliffs, NJ: Prentice-Hall, 1975), pp. 103–116 (orig. pub. *Art Bulletin* 49 [December 1967], pp. 277–286).

29. *Vers une architecture*, p. 46.

30. Both the typology and the term *à redents* are derived from Eugène Hénard's use of "boulevard à redans" in his multivolume *Etudes sur les transformations de Paris* (1903–1906). Stanislaus von Moos, *Le Corbusier: Elements of a Synthesis* (Cambridge: MIT Press, 1979), pp. 151, 189, 348n17.

31. Influenced by Russian models of communal dwelling, Le Corbusier's new mode of mass housing was used first at the Salvation Army hostel Cité de Refuge and at the Pavillon Suisse. See von Moos, "Apartment Houses after 1930," and "Unité d'Habitation à Grandeur Conforme," in von Moos *Le Corbusier: Elements of a Synthesis*, pp. 151–163; on the Unité d'Habitation in Marseilles and its relationship to other Unités, see J. S. [Jacques Sbriglio], "Unité d'habitation," in *Encyclopédie*, pp. 422–431.

32. On regional syndicalism, see McLeod, "Urbanism and Utopia: Le Corbusier from Regional Syndicalism to Vichy," pp. 94–207; McLeod, "Le Corbusier and Algiers," pp. 54–85; Jean-Louis Cohen, Politique," in *Encyclopédie*, pp. 309–313; Mary McLeod, "Bibliography: *Plans*," *Oppositions* 19/20 (Winter/Spring 1980), pp. 184–201.

33. For a social critique of Le Corbusier's planning, see Marshall Berman, *All That Is Solid Melts into Air* (New York: Penguin Books, 1988), pp. 164–171.

34. *RC*, p. 44.

35. Annotated lecture sketches, Museum of Modern Art, October 25, 1935; six note cards (FLC).

36. Le Corbusier, *Urbanisme*, p. iv; *City of Tomorrow*, p. xxvii.

37. Jacques Gréber, *L'Architecture aux Etats-Unis, preuve de la force d'expansion du génie français* (Paris: Payot & Cie, 1920), 2 vols.

38. On *joies essentielles*, see *VR* and *RC*, pp. 86–87.

39. *Cathédrales*, pp. 252–261; *Cathedrals*, pp. 171–178. In the *Oeuvre complète 1934–1938*, "Le grand gaspillage" appears as "The Inefficiency of the Modern City," pp. 20–21.

40. These diagrams correspond to those in his Chicago talk entitled the "Great Waste," *Cathédrales*, pp. 253, 254; *Cathedrals*, pp. 172–173. For a discussion and diagrams of the "solar day," see also *VR* and *RC*, pp. 77, 78, 173, 190–191.

41. *Cathedrals* excludes passages from *Cathédrales* that explain Le Corbusier's understanding of government culpability ("Vos statisticiens nous disent: 'Le Gouvernement de l'U.S.A. prélève le 54 pour 100 du fruit du travail général.' Tel est le fait": *Cathédrales*, pp. 256–258; *Cathedrals*, pp. 174–175).

42. The five points first appeared in print under the joint signature of Le Corbusier and Pierre Jeanneret in Alfred Roth, *Zwei Wohnhäuser von Le Corbusier und Pierre Jeanneret* (Stuttgart: Wedekind 1927). See also Le Corbusier, *OC 1910–1929*, pp. 128–129; *VR* and *RC*, p. 295; and W. O. [Werner Oechslin], "5 Points d'une architecture nouvelle," in *Encyclopédie*, pp. 92–95. For drawings of the five points from the South American tour of 1929, see *Précisions*, opp. pp. 42, 44.

43. *VR* and *RC*, p. 38.

44. *RC*, p. 109.

45. *RC*, pp. 108–118.

46. For a partial explanation of the program, see *RC*, p. 161. The emphasis on participatory rather than spectator sports reflected the influence of Dr. Pierre Winter with whom Le Corbusier played basketball every week. Through Winter, Le Corbusier had come to advocate daily physical exercise. Among his many articles on sports and physical culture in *L'Esprit Nouveau*, *Plans* and *Prélude*, see P. Winter, "Le Sport au pied des maisons," *Prélude*, no. 3 (March 15, 1933), p. 3; *RC*, pp. 67–68.

47. On soundproofing and references to the theory and practice of the French acoustical engineer Gustave Lyon, see *RC*, pp. 36, 39, 45, 49–50, 113–114. In his publications Le Corbusier suggested comparisons between the roofs of his apartment blocks and the decks of both passenger ocean liners and aircraft carriers. Pairing cross sections of housing blocks and ships, he perceived the ocean liner with its functional decks, efficient cabins, and communal services as "a floating apartment house." A picture of an ocean liner deck appears in *RC*, p. 59. Aircraft carriers with their platform decks are illustrated in *Urbanisme*, p. 152; *RC*, p. 109. Pho-

tographs of cabins appear in *RC*, p. 115. For cross sections of an ocean liner, see *RC*, p. 118.

48. A similar drawing appears in *VR*, p. 36.

49. *Précisions*, pp. 241, opp. p. 244. *VR*, pp. 222–225. In *Oeuvre complète de 1929–1934*, Le Corbusier described these as "several sketches evoking entirely new conceptions of urbanism," harnessing "modern [building] techniques . . . to establish important vehicular thoroughfares in cities" and "creating substantial housing blocks" on "artificial sites," p. 138. See also McLeod, "Le Corbusier and Algiers," pp. 54–85.

50. On Cendrar's influence, see *Précisions*, pp. 19–20; *VR*, p. 220; Elizabeth Davis Harris, "Le Corbusier and the Headquarters of the Brazilian Ministry of Education and Health 1936–1947" (Ph.D. diss., University of Chicago, 1984), pp. 12–19.

51. *RC*, p. 224.

52. *Précisions*, p. 244, translated in von Moos, *Le Corbusier: Elements of a Synthesis*, p. 201.

53. *VR*, pp. 284–287.

54. As a result of his South American travels in 1929, Le Corbusier reversed his attitude toward the meandering path. For his earlier assessment, see "The Pack-Donkey's Way and Man's Way," in *City of Tomorrow*, pp. 5–12. See also McLeod, "Urbanism and Utopia: Le Corbusier from Regional Syndicalism to Vichy."

55. *RC*, pp. 234, 246. The Princeton drawing (November 16, 1935; top right) is similar to others illustrated in *The Radiant City*, pp. 57, 235.

56. The Philadelphia drawing of the Algiers housing is similar to those Le Corbusier published in *OC 1929–1934*, p. 141 (top right), and *VR*, p. 260.

57. Plan 3067, *VR* and *RC*, pp. 297–303. See also Le Corbusier's discussion of the project in Le Corbusier and François de Pierrefeu, *The Home of Man*, trans. Clive Entwistle and Gordon Holt (London: Architectural Press, 1948), p. 154.

58. *Cathédrales*, p. 271; *VR*, p. 101. With photographs of the Manhattan skyline and Hugh Ferriss's drawings of setback skyscrapers juxtaposed with the model of the Voisin plan for Paris, Le Corbusier suggested that the Cartesian skyscraper stood "in opposition to New York, to Chicago"; *RC*, p. 133.

59. The Columbia drawing (plate 2) indicates that Le Corbusier proposed to substitute a cruciform business tower for the Manhattan setback skyscraper. His program for New York is contained in the article "What Is America's Problem?" *American Architect* 148 (March 1936), pp. 16–23; later reprinted in *Cathédrales*, pp. 273–291, and *Cathedrals*, pp. 186–201. Additional components of the program are contained in the section "The Authorities Are Badly Informed," in *Cathedrals*, pp. 178–186; *Cathédrales*, pp. 262–272.

60. *OC 1910–1929*, p. 77; *Almanach*, pp. 102–103.

61. Annotated lecture sketches for the Kalamazoo, Chicago (Renaissance Society), and Madison lectures appear in Le Corbusier, *Creation Is a Patient Search,* trans. James Palmes (New York: Praeger, 1960), p. 205; note cards (FLC).

62. *Cathédrales*, pp. 248–249, and *Cathedrals*, pp. 168–169.

63. On the first machine age, see *RC*, p. 340. "Skyscrapers Not Big Enough Says LeCorbusier [sic] at First Sight," *New York Herald Tribune*, October 22, 1935, p. 21.

64. *Cathedrals*, pp. 34–35.

65. *OC 1929–1934*, p. 11; *Précisions*. Le Corbusier referred to *L'Ere des grands travaux* in a speech in Algiers in 1934; *VR*, p. 261. See Tim Benton's essay, "The Era of Great Projects," in *Century*, pp. 164–199.

66. Card no. 1 (figure 3.12) indicates that he prepared the sequence for the Columbia and Yale lectures; card no. 3 verso (not illustrated) indicates that he also used them for his lecture at Vassar College (FLC).

67. *Cathedrals*, pp. 74–76. Aymar Embury II, consulting architect for the project after Gilbert's death in 1934, was responsible for omitting the granite facing. See Aymar Embury II, "The Aesthetics of Bridge Design," *Pencil Points* 19 (February 1938), pp. 116–117; see also Carl W. Condit, *American Building Art: The Twentieth Century* (New York: Oxford University Press, 1961), pp. 135–138; Hans Wittfoht, *Building Bridges* (Düsseldorf: Beton-Verlag, 1984), pp. 73–77.

68. See *VR*, p. 340; *Towards a New Architecture*, pp. 263–266; *Almanach*, p. 18.

69. *VR*, pp. 20–21.

70. *Precisions*, [p. 69].

71. *Précisions*, p. 70 (author's translation). Le Corbusier's drawings for the third lecture in Buenos Aires, October 8, 1929, are illustrated in *Précisions*, opp. p. 70 and on pp. 72, 75, [77], 79, 80, 82.

72. *Towards a New Architecture*, pp. 81, 88, 160–161; *Precisions*, p. 219.

73. For an analysis of the relationship between style and building type or program during the early Third Republic, see Mardges Bacon, *Ernest Flagg: Beaux-Arts Architect and Urban Reformer* (New York and Cambridge: Architectural History Foundation and MIT Press, 1986), pp. 42–48. Stanislaus von Moos analyzes the inconsistencies between form and purpose in Le Corbusier's work in *Le Corbusier: Elements of a Synthesis*, pp. 101–104.

74. His list omitted a fourth building (no. 4). This was most likely the housing development for Oued Ouchaïa in Algiers (1933–1934), a project he discussed at Vassar College. Vassar College lecture note card (FLC). Amelia Thompson Vose lecture notes (see chapter 4).

75. The Louvre became a museum in 1793.

76. *OC 1929–1934*, pp. 72–73.

77. Le Corbusier and Paul Otlet, *Mundaneum* (Brussels: J. Lebegue & Cie, 1928). *OC 1910–1929*, pp. 190–197.

78. Letter, Le Corbusier to Christian Zervos (editor of *Cahiers d'art*) December 8, 1930, published in *OC 1929–1934*, pp. 72–73. In an earlier letter to Zervos, Le Corbusier described the museum's *spirales carrées* (squared spirals). Letter, Le Corbusier to Christian Zervos, February 20, 1930 (FLC), quoted in Gilles Ragot, "Musée à croissance illimitée," in *Encyclopédie*, p. 267.

79. *OC 1938–1946*, pp. 16–21.

80. Through an intermediary, Le Corbusier offered his project for "un centre d'esthétique contemporaine," project C 1936 (originally intended for the 1937 Exposition Internationale in Paris) to Solomon Guggenheim for his new museum. Letter, Le Corbusier to "Monsieur Sides," March 28, 1939 (FLC). *OC 1934–1938*, pp. 152–155. For a discussion of Le Corbusier's postwar application of this typology, see Ragot, "Musée à croissance illimitée," p. 267. Neil Levine suggested possible links to Frank Lloyd Wright's Gordon Strong Automobile Objective and Planetarium project, Sugarloaf Mountain, near Dickerson, MD, 1924–1925; see *The Architecture of Frank Lloyd Wright* (Princeton: Princeton University Press, 1996), pp. 302, 480n17.

81. *OC 1934–1938*, pp. 82–89.

82. The Musée de la Ville and Musée de l'Etat were intended to replace the Petit Palais and the Luxembourg Museum, respectively. Robert Jacobs, unsigned article on the City and State museums, Paris (DA, MoMA, NY).

83. For his lecture Le Corbusier made a second sheet of drawings for the Palace of the Soviets (Avery Architectural and Fine Arts Library, Columbia University).

84. Cohen, *Le Corbusier and the Mystique of the USSR*, pp. 164–203; von Moos, *Le Corbusier: Elements of a Synthesis*, p. 246; C. B. [Charlotte Benton] in *Century*, pp. 174–175; *OC 1929–1934*, 123–137.

85. For a series of drawings and construction photographs, see *OC 1929–1934*, pp. 74–89.

86. William J. R. Curtis, "Ideas of Structure and the Structure of Ideas: Le Corbusier's Pavillon Suisse, 1930–1931," *JSAH* 40 (December 1981), pp. 295–310. The Pavillon Suisse does not appear in the CYV notes.

87. *OC 1929–1934*, p. 83.

88. *OC 1910–1929*, pp. 198–200; *OC 1929–1934*, pp. 58–62.

89. On the controversy over the structural efficacy of *pilotis* see Curtis, "Ideas of Structure and the Structure of Ideas," pp. 302–303.

90. *OC 1929–1934*, p. 11, as cited in T. B. [Tim Benton] in *Century*, p. 180; Curtis, *Le Corbusier: Ideas and Forms*, p. 106.

91. *Vers une architecture*, p. 128; *Urbanisme*, p. v.

92. *Towards a New Architecture*, pp. 153–159.

93. Princeton University annotated lecture sketches (FLC).

94. *City of Tomorrow*, pp. 270–273.

95. For an earlier discussion of "sensibility," perception, and optics, see "Le Sentiment Déborde," in *Urbanisme*, pp. 29–37.

96. *Kalamazoo Gazette*, November 23, 1935, pp. 1, 8; on "psycho-physiological needs," and similar expressions, see *VR* and *RC*, pp. 7, 86.

97. The concept of man in relation to these elements prefigured his later formulations in the *Modulor*.

98. A similar drawing from the second lecture in Buenos Aires (October 5, 1929) is given the same identification; *Précisions*, opp. p. 44.

99. *RC*, p. 82. Similar schematic plans are identified in *Précisions*, p. 135; *OC 1910–1929*, p. 189.

100. *Le Corbusier 1910–65*, p. 70. On this unbuilt house, see Christiane Crasemann Collins, "Le Corbusier's Maison Errázuriz: A Conflict of Fictive Cultures," *Harvard Architecture Review* 6 (1987), pp. 38–53.

101. Le Corbusier used the term *bon régionalisme* (good regionalism) to describe Algiers. See *VR* and *RC*, p. 247.

102. Le Corbusier modeled his monk's cell on a unit within the Carthusian monastery at Ema near Florence that he had visited in 1907. The Immeuble-villas project of 1922 was also informed specifically by J. B. André Godin's factory housing, the *familistère*, at Guise, which in turn was based on the theories of Fourier and his *phalanstère*. Serenyi, "Le Corbusier, Fourier, and the Monastery of Ema," in *Le Corbusier in Perspective*, pp. 103–116. *Jean-Baptiste André Godin, 1817–1888: Le Familistère de Guise ou les équivalents de la richesse* (Brussels: Archives d'Architecture Moderne, 1980).

103. For a discussion of the origins of the Immeuble-villas, see Pierre-Alain Croset, "Les Origines d'un type," in *Encyclopédie*, pp. 178–189. In 1925 a cell from the Immeuble-villas project served as a unit of his Esprit Nouveau pavilion. As Tim Benton showed, the Esprit-Nouveau pavilion was a prototype for both the "mass housing cell" and the "bourgeois villas of the 1920s." Tim Benton, "Six Houses," in *Century*, p. 45–46.

104. See Kalamazoo sketches, *Creation Is a Patient Search*, p. 205. *Vers une architecture*, pp. 206–209; *Almanach*, pp. 126–128; *Urbanisme*, pp. 213–216; H. Allen Brooks, ed., *The Le Corbusier Archive*, vol. 1, *Early Buildings and Projects, 1912–1923* (New York, London, and Paris: Garland and Fondation Le Corbusier, 1982), pp. 355–397.

105. Pierre Jeanneret read the paper since Le Corbusier was in South America at the time and was not present at CIAM II (October 24–29, 1929). Le Corbusier and Pierre Jeanneret, "Analyse des éléments fondamentaux du problème de la maison mini-

mum," in Steinmann, ed., *CIAM: Dokumente 1928–1939,* pp. 60–63.

106. "Un homme = une cellule; des cellules = la ville," lecture in Buenos Aires to Amigos del Ciudad, October 24, 1929, in *Précisions,* pp. 141–156.

107. McLeod, "Le Corbusier and Algiers," pp. 54–85; McLeod, "Urbanism and Utopia: Le Corbusier from Regional Syndicalism to Vichy."

108. Le Corbusier, "Air-son-lumière," in Steinmann, ed., *CIAM: Dokumente 1928–1939,* pp. 82–85. See also Walter Gropius's paper, "Flach-, Mittel- oder Hochbau?" ("Low-, Middle-, or High-Rise Apartments?"), in Steinmann, ed., *CIAM: Dokumente 1928–1939,* pp. 92–97. See also "Die Wohnformen: Flach-, Mittel- oder Hochbau?" in Martin Wagner, ed., *Das neue Berlin* (Berlin: Deutsche Bauzeitung, 1929), pp. 74–80; and "Low Buildings, Medium-High or High Buildings?" in Housing Study Guild, ed., *Abstract of Papers,* ser. 1, no. 1 (1935), pp. 3–7.

109. See "Die Ausstellung von Le Corbusier 'La ville radieuse,'" in Steinmann, ed., *CIAM: Dokumente 1928–1939,* pp. 98–101.

110. *VR,* pp. 114, 143–146. Similar perspective renderings appear on p. 144.

4 Le Corbusier Takes America

1. *Cathedrals,* p. 84.

2. "Coming of Corbusier," *Architectural Forum* 63 (October 1935), pp. 34, 64.

3. At Le Corbusier's insistence, these cities were dropped. "Le Corbusier," *Record* 78 (October 1935), p. 26. To defray the cost of its proposed lecture, the Portland (Oregon) chapter of the AIA even planned to sell 100 tickets at 50 cents each. See "With the Chapters and State Associations," *Octagon* 7 (October 1935), p. 15.

4. Robert Allan Jacobs, interview with author, Pawling, NY, June 7, 1987 (hereafter cited as Jacobs interview).

5. Letter, Philip L. Goodwin to A. Everett Austin, Jr., October 25, 1935 (Wadsworth Atheneum, Hartford).

6. Although Austin was in Paris in 1932–1933, he seems not to have known Le Corbusier there. Letters, Philip L. Goodwin to A. Everett Austin, Jr., October 14, 1935; A. Everett Austin, Jr. to Philip L. Goodwin, October 16, 1935 (Wadsworth Atheneum, Hartford).

7. Goodwin was a member of one of the city's leading families and one of the Atheneum's principal supporters. The Rev. Francis Goodwin, an amateur architect, was his uncle and grandfather of Austin's wife, Helen Goodwin Austin. Charles A. Goodwin, Helen Austin's rather conservative uncle, was president of the Atheneum Board (1925–1954) during Austin's entire tenure as director (1927–1945). For a genealogy of the Goodwin family and a history of its buildings, see Philip Lippincott Goodwin, *Rooftrees*

or the Architectural History of an American Family (Philadelphia: J. B. Lippincott, 1933). When Austin told him that the Atheneum was "practically on the rocks until the first of January," Goodwin reimbursed the museum for Le Corbusier's lecture fee of $50 plus expenses. Letters, Philip L. Goodwin to A. Everett Austin, Jr., May 27, October 7, and November 11, 1935; and A. Everett Austin, Jr. to Philip L. Goodwin, May 28, October 10, November 5, and November 12, 1935 (Wadsworth Atheneum, Hartford).

8. Avery Memorial's place in the modern movement is the subject of Helen Searing's essay, "From the Fogg to the Bauhaus: A Museum for the Machine Age," in Eugene R. Gaddis, ed., *Avery Memorial, Wadsworth Atheneum* (Hartford: Wadsworth Atheneum, 1984), pp. 19–30.

9. *Cathedrals,* p. 129.

10. Henry-Russell Hitchcock, excerpts from interview recorded in 1974, published in Gaddis, ed., *Avery Memorial, Wadsworth Atheneum,* p. 13.

11. On Austin's contributions, see Eugene R. Gaddis, "'The New Athens': Moments from an Era," in Gaddis, ed., *Avery Memorial, Wadsworth Atheneum,* pp. 33–58; "James Soby, 72, Art Connoisseur and Trustee of Modern Museum," obituary, *New York Times,* January 30, 1979, D19.

12. *Cathedrals,* pp. 128, 130.

13. "Noted French Architect Is Storm Center," *Hartford Courant,* October 25, 1935, p. 24. In identifying him as "one of the greatest controversial figures of this age," the *Hartford Times* emphasized also that "there is virtually no corner of the globe where his influence is not felt." See "Lecture Tonight by Le Corbusier," *Hartford Times,* October 25, 1935 (Wadsworth Atheneum, Hartford).

14. Letter, A. Everett Austin, Jr., to Philip L. Goodwin, October 29, 1935 (Wadsworth Atheneum, Hartford).

15. Mrs. John L. Bunce [Eleanor Howland Soby, former wife of James Thrall Soby], interview with author, West Hartford, CT, January 29, 1985. See also "Le Corbusier Visions Future City on Stilts," *Hartford Times,* October 28, 1935 (Wadsworth Atheneum, Hartford).

16. Henry-Russell Hitchcock, interview with author, New York City, December 13, 1984. Hitchcock's addition to and remodeling of the Soby House was published in two articles: "House at Farmington, Connecticut: Remodelled by Henry-Russell Hitchcock, Jr., Architect," *Architectural Review* (London) 81 (January 1937), pp. 19–20; "Farmington, Conn., House Remodelled by Henry-Russell Hitchcock, Jr.," *American Architect* 151 (July 1937), pp. 67–68. See also Helen Searing, "Henry-Russell Hitchcock: Formative Years," *Skyline* (December 1982), pp. 10–11.

17. Jacobs interview, June 7, 1987.

18. Jacobs interview, November 21, 1984.

19. Ten Soutter drawings were sold: Soby purchased six for himself; Paul Cooley, Austin's assistant, purchased two; and Hitchcock purchased two (one for the Wadsworth Atheneum and one for Kirk and Constance Askew). Letter, James Thrall Soby to Le Corbusier, December 9, 1935 (FLC). Soutter sent via Le Corbusier a shipment of fifty drawings for the Wadsworth Atheneum exhibition (and also one to the Arts Club of Chicago, which declined a Soutter exhibit). Letters, Le Corbusier to Louis Soutter, December 24, 1935, and January 10, 1936 (FLC); Le Corbusier to [A. Everett] Austin, October 1, 1936 (Wadsworth Atheneum, Hartford). Le Corbusier's support of Soutter extended beyond friendship and family ties to deep personal conviction in his work. See Daniel Joseph Naegele, "Drawing-over: *une vie decanté* [sic], Le Corbusier and Louis Soutter," in "Le Corbusier's Seeing Things: Ambiguity and Illusion in the Representation of Modern Architecture" (Ph.D. diss., University of Pennsylvania, 1996), pp. 298–323.

20. Geoffrey T. Hellman, "Profiles: From Within to Without—I," *New Yorker* 23 (April 26, 1947), p. 36.

21. *Cathedrals,* p. 142.

22. Joseph Hudnut, biographical file (Central Files, Columbia University). See also Jill Perlman, "Joseph Hudnut's Other Modernism at the 'Harvard Bauhaus,'" *JSAH* 56 (December 1997), pp. 452–459.

23. Morris Lapidus, interview in John W. Cook and Heinrich Klotz, *Conversations with Architects* (New York: Praeger, 1973), p. 148.

24. Theodor K. Rohdenburg, *A History of the School of Architecture Columbia University* (New York: Columbia University Press, 1954), p. 94. Charles Savage dates Harrison's conversion to modernism to his designs for school buildings and the publication that documents them. W. K. Harrison, "The Design of the Modern School," in W. K. Harrison and C. E. Dobbin, *School Buildings of Today and Tomorrow* (New York: Architectural Book Publishing Co., 1931), pp. 1–20. Charles C. Savage, "The Rockefeller Apartments: Siedlung für die Wohlhabenden," abstract, annual meeting of the Society of Architectural Historians, Pittsburgh, 1985. See also Victoria Newhouse, *Wallace K. Harrison, Architect* (New York: Rizzoli, 1989), pp. 29–30, 293n22, n23.

25. Rosemarie Haag Bletter analyzes architectural education at the School of Architecture at Columbia University under its curriculum adapted from Beaux-Arts teaching. "Modernism Rears Its Head—The Twenties and Thirties," in Richard Oliver, ed., *The Making of an Architect 1881–1981* (New York: Rizzoli, 1981), pp. 103–110; see also essays by Steven M. Bedford, David G. De Long, and Susan M. Strauss in Oliver, ed., *The Making of an Architect 1881–1981,* pp. 5–48, 87–102.

26. Morris Lapidus, *An Architecture of Joy* (Miami: E. A. Seemann, 1979), pp. 55–57.

27. [Joseph Hudnut], "Report of Dean Hudnut, June 30, 1934," *Architectural Forum* 62 (February 1935), pp. 166–167. For changes that Hudnut introduced at the beginning of the academic years 1934–1935 and 1935–1936, see his letter to Nicholas Murray Butler, July 10, 1934 (Central Files, Columbia University). The June 1934 report was based on Hudnut's pedagogical position; see "The Education of an Architect," *Record* 69 (May 1931), p. 412. See also Bletter, "Modernism Rears Its Head—The Twenties and Thirties," p. 110.

28. *Report of Committee on Columbia School of Architecture,* May 1, 1934 (Central Files, Columbia University), pp. 1–6. See also Judith Oberlander, "History IV 1933–1935," in Oliver, ed., *The Making of an Architect 1881–1981,* p. 120n9. For Wright's comments on "organic" architecture during the fall of 1935, see Yale lecture criticism, "Wright Decries Lack of American Culture," *Yale Daily News,* October 17, 1935, pp. 1, 4; "Frank L. Wright Hits 'So-Called' U.S. Education," *New York Herald Tribune,* November 5, 1935, p. 13; Henry W. Kneeland, "Traditional Architecture Assailed as 'Betrayal' by Frank Lloyd Wright to Crowd in Gothic Hall at Yale," *Hartford Courant,* October 17, 1935, pp. 1, 24.

29. Letter, Joseph Hudnut to Frank D. Fackenthal, June 7, 1935; [Joseph Hudnut] "Notes on Educational Policy in the School of Architecture" June 7, 1935 (Central Files, Columbia University). A comparison between the School of Architecture's course offerings for the academic years 1934–1935 and 1935–1936 indicates that Hudnut's reforms effectively eliminated a series of courses in architectural drawing that specialized in "elements of classic architecture," "rendering," and "shades and shadows." He substituted for them "a series of progressive exercises in the design of three-dimensional forms" taught in two courses in "introduction to design" (originally scheduled for Hudnut to teach in 1935–1936) and in "drafting." He replaced courses in the "Theory of Architecture: Plan and Composition," "*analytique,*" and "*projets*" with courses in "architectural design," including one that began with "problems in the design of simple buildings and in site planning . . . [that] furnish practical applications. . . ." He also substituted courses in "Modern Buildings" (originally scheduled for Hudnut to teach) for those in the theory of architecture, beginning with "fundamental principles governing the composition of plans" and progressing to "advanced composition." *Columbia University Bulletin of Information, School of Architecture,* 1934–1935, pp. 24–29, and *Columbia University Bulletin of Information, School of Architecture,* 1935–1936, pp. 22–31.

30. "Columbia Changes Her Methods," *Architectural Forum* 62 (February 1935), p. 168; Bletter, "Modernism Rears Its Head—The Twenties and Thirties," pp. 110–111n23, n26.

31. [Hudnut], "Notes on Educational Policy in the School of Architecture," June 7, 1935 (Central Files, Columbia University).

32. On the socioeconomic implications of technology see, for example, Le Corbusier's chapters "Maisons en série" and "Architecture ou Revolution" in *Vers une architecture,* and his more strident

argument in the early chapters of *La Ville radieuse,* especially "2e partie: Les Techniques modernes," pp. 18–61.

33. Hudnut, "The Education of an Architect," p. 413. See also Bletter, "Modernism Rears Its Head—The Twenties and Thirties," p. 111.

34. The curriculum for the academic year 1935–1936 still included a course in the applications of descriptive geometry, which taught among other problems associated with the Beaux-Arts, "shadows by elevation and plan, shade . . . shadows in perspective." *Columbia University Bulletin of Information, School of Architecture,* 1935–1936, p. 22. See also Bletter, "Modernism Rears Its Head—The Twenties and Thirties," pp. 111–112.

35. [Hudnut], "Notes on Educational Policy in the School of Architecture," June 7, 1935 (Central Files, Columbia University).

36. Hudnut called for the resignation of Lemuel C. Dillenback who remained committed to the Beaux-Arts system. For a description of Dillenback's courses, see *Columbia University Bulletin of Information, School of Architecture,* 1934–1935, pp. 28–29. Earlier in 1930 George Licht, a member of the Beaux-Arts firm of Delano and Aldrich, left Columbia; Rohdenburg, *A History of the School of Architecture Columbia University,* pp. 92, 95; see also Oberlander, "History IV 1933–1935," p. 122.

37. Abramovitz received his B.S. degree from the University of Illinois in 1929. Abramovitz, interview with author, New York City, June 2, 1987. Rohdenburg, *A History of the School of Architecture Columbia University,* p. 91. Ironically, in 1932 Abramovitz received a Columbia University fellowship to study at the Ecole des Beaux-Arts, where he remained until 1934 when he joined the firm of Corbett, Harrison and McMurray. Victoria Newhouse, "Harrison and Abramovitz," in Adolf K. Placzek, ed., *Macmillan Encyclopedia of Architects,* vol. 2 (New York: Free Press), p. 325. See also Newhouse, *Wallace K. Harrison, Architect,* p. 58.

38. Rohdenburg, *A History of the School of Architecture Columbia University,* p. 92.

39. Letter, Jan Ruhtenberg to Nicholas Murray Butler, May 29, 1936 (Central Files, Columbia University). Ruhtenberg worked for Mies van der Rohe in Berlin in 1931 and then practiced in Stockholm before coming to America in 1933. His approach was more practical, advocating that architectural models be substituted for graphic presentations and that students gain experience in the building trades. According to Hudnut, Ruhtenberg was born in Riga, Latvia, in 1896 of Swedish parentage, and educated at the University of Leipzig. Letter, Joseph Hudnut to Nicholas Murray Butler, June 12, 1934 (Central Files, Columbia University). See also Bletter, "Modernism Rears Its Head—The Twenties and Thirties," p. 113n35; Rohdenburg, *A History of the School of Architecture Columbia University,* pp. 38, 97.

40. *Columbia University Bulletin of Information, School of Architecture,* 1935–1936, pp. 26, 27, 31.

41. Corbett, a distinguished proponent of the Beaux-Arts system of education, first came to Columbia in 1907 as Associate Director of Atelier. Rohdenburg, *A History of the School of Architecture Columbia University,* p. 92.

42. Harvey W. Corbett, "Dawn of a New Architecture Is Here," *Architect and Engineer* 105 (April 1931), pp. 79–80. A few years before Corbett could endorse "the new movement" only in terms of a transformation of decoration, rather than form. "The wheel, straight line and angle," he observed, reflect a basis of decoration in machines and industrialism that expresses "the condition today." Harvey Wiley Corbett, "The Meaning of Modernism," *Architect* 12 (June 1929), p. 272 (revised address originally delivered at a meeting of the Architectural League of New York, March 7, 1929).

43. Talbot Faulkner Hamlin was the son of A. D. F. Hamlin (1855–1926), eminent professor of architecture at Columbia University. He received a Beaux-Arts education at Columbia's School of Architecture (1910–1914) and returned there in 1926 to teach courses in the history and theory of architecture. Kenneth Frampton, "Slouching toward Modernity: Talbot Faulkner Hamlin and the Architecture of the New Deal," in Oliver, ed., *The Making of an Architect 1881–1981,* p. 154.

44. Talbot F. Hamlin, "Review of *Towards a New Architecture,*" in *Nation,* quoted in Frampton, "Slouching Toward Modernity: Talbot Faulkner Hamlin and the Architecture of the New Deal," p. 153n6.

45. Talbot Faulkner Hamlin, "The International Style Lacks the Essence of Great Architecture," *American Architect* 143 (January 1933), pp. 12–16.

46. Max Abramovitz, interview with author, New York City, June 2, 1987.

47. Talbot Hamlin, "The Architect and the Depression," *Nation* 137 (August 9, 1933), p. 154, quoted in Oberlander, "History IV: 1933–1935," p. 120n6.

48. Letter, Nicholas Murray Butler to Joseph Hudnut, May 31, 1935 (Central Files, Columbia University).

49. By the spring of 1936 Arnaud had dismissed Jan Ruhtenberg, Russell M. Krob, and Walter B. Sanders and other modernists and replaced them with a more conservative group of critics, including Donald Fletcher, Edgar Williams, and John C. B. Moore, even though he did arrange for such visiting critics as George Howe, André Fouilhoux, and William Lescaze. Hudnut was appalled to hear about the dismissals. Letters, Joseph Hudnut to Frank D. Fackenthal, February 11 and March 16, 1936; Leopold Arnaud to Frank D. Fackenthal, May 15, 1936; Frank D. Fackenthal to Leopold Arnaud, May 18 and May 20, 1936 (Central Files, Columbia University). Arnaud's position on educational policy is summarized in his article "History and Architecture," *Columbia University Quarterly* 27 (December 1935), pp. 409–414. Arnaud was made acting dean in February 1936

and dean the next academic year, a post he held until 1957. Letter, Frank D. Fackenthal to Joseph Hudnut, February 8, 1936. See also Diane Boas, "History V: 1935–1959," in Oliver, ed., *The Making of an Architect 1881–1981,*" pp. 137–148.

50. Letter, P. le Astrillo to Le Corbusier, November 24, 1935. In *Cathédrales* Le Corbusier makes reference to Columbia students.

51. Jacobs interview, November 21, 1984.

52. T. F. H. [Talbot Faulkner Hamlin], *Columbia University Quarterly* 28 (March 1936), pp. 68–69.

53. Le Corbusier and Jacobs traveled by car to Middletown where they lodged at a local hotel.

54. Letters, Henry-Russell Hitchcock to Le Corbusier, November 14 and 22, 1935 (FLC). "Le Corbusier Speaks at Shanklin Tuesday," *Wesleyan Argus,* October 31, 1935, p. 1 (Wesleyan University Archives). On one of Hitchcock's exhibitions promoting modernism at Wesleyan, see Janine A. Mileaf, *Constructing Modernism: Berenice Abbott and Henry-Russell Hitchcock* (Middletown, CT: Davison Art Center, Wesleyan University, 1993). See also Mardges Bacon, exhibition review, "Constructing Modernism: Berenice Abbott and Henry-Russell Hitchcock," *JSAH* 53 (June 1994), pp. 232–234.

55. Letter, Everett V. Meeks to "Mr. Charles-Edouard Jenneret [sic] Care of Carl O. Schniewind," May 27, 1935 (FLC).

56. Robert A. M. Stern, *George Howe: Toward a Modern American Architecture* (New Haven: Yale University Press, 1975), p. 210.

57. Letter, Everett V. Meeks to Dean William Emerson, October 3, 1935 (Yale University, School of the Fine Arts, Administrative Records, YRG 16-E, RU 189, Manuscripts and Archives, Yale University Library).

58. George Nichols, Yale Class of 1938, interview with author, September 3, 1991. The other lecturers in the Ryerson series were John A. Holabird, Eric Gugler, and Philip N. Youtz. *Yale University News Statement,* September 23, 1935 (Yale University, School of the Fine Arts, Administrative Records, YRG 16-E, RU 189, Manuscripts and Archives, Yale University Library).

59. Le Corbusier's took place in the auditorium of the Yale Law School (Sterling Law Building), holding 800 persons. *Yale University News Statement,* October 30, 1935 (Yale University, School of the Fine Arts, Administrative Records, YRG 16-E, RU 189, Manuscripts and Archives, Yale University Library); "French Architect Speaks Here Today," *New Haven Journal-Courier,* October 30, 1935, 2, p. 9.

60. George Nichols, interview with author, September 3, 1991. Letter, Richard G. Creadick, Yale Class of 1938 (1941 Arch.) to author, September 12, 1991.

61. "Wright Decries Lack of American Culture," pp. 1, 4. Kneeland, "Traditional Architecture Assailed as 'Betrayal' by Frank Lloyd Wright," pp. 1, 24.

62. "Yale Applauds as Wright Hits Its Architecture," *New York Herald Tribune,* October 17, 1935 (Yale University, School of the Fine Arts, Administrative Records, YRG 16-E, RU 189, Manuscripts and Archives, Yale University Library); "Wright Decries Lack of American Culture," p. 4.

63. "Le Corbusier Lectures Here Wednesday; Free Tickets to Be Distributed Monday," *Yale University News Statement,* n.d. (Yale University, School of the Fine Arts, Administrative Records, YRG 16-E, RU 189, Manuscripts and Archives, Yale University Library). The statement quoted the Modern's press release that Le Corbusier's aphorism, the "house is a machine for living in," had "aroused a storm of controversy." Moreover, his infamous statements about New York's skyscrapers—"much too small" and "too many of them"—were reprinted from the acerbic *Herald Tribune* article attributed to Joseph Alsop, news release, Museum of Modern Art, #5909-29 (DAD, MoMA, NY). "Famous Architect Will Lecture Here," *Yale Daily News,* October 30, 1935, pp. 1, 3.

64. "Le Corbusier Shows Origin of Modernism," *Yale Daily News,* October 31, 1935, p. 2.

65. "Yale Gallery Exhibits Le Corbusier's Work," *Yale Daily News,* November 6, 1935, p. 1. The exhibition opened at the Yale School of Fine Arts on November 4 and closed on November 10, 1935.

66. *Cathedrals,* pp. 80–83.

67. *Cathedrals,* pp. 135–137.

68. Amelia Thompson Vose, Vassar class of 1938, interview with author, June 23, 1999.

69. *Cathedrals,* p. 138.

70. Jacobs interview, November 21, 1984. Alma Clayburgh, Vassar class of 1936, was the daughter of Alma Clayburgh (1882–1958). Obituary, *New York Times,* August 6, 1958, p. 25.

71. *Cathedrals,* p. 83.

72. Letter, William Emerson to George H. Edgell, June 4, 1935 (courtesy of the Harvard University Archives).

73. Letter, George H. Edgell to William Emerson, June 8, 1935 (courtesy of the Harvard University Archives).

74. Edgell resigned during the summer of 1935 to become director of the Boston Museum of Fine Arts. Letters, Sally S. Raabe to Ernestine Fantl, July 19, 1935; Joseph Hudnut to Ernestine M. Fantl, October 21, 1935 (Graduate School of Design, Records of the Office of the Dean, 1932–1935, courtesy of the Harvard University Archives).

75. "Haffner Resigns," *American Architect* 149 (December 1936), p. 106. On Hudnut's arrival at Harvard, Haftner's resignation, and Gropius's appointment, see Perlman, "Joseph Hudnut's Other Modernism at the 'Harvard Bauhaus,'" pp. 459–463. Walter Gropius became chairman of the Department of Architecture in 1938. See also Winfried Nerdinger, "From Bauhaus to Har-

vard: Walter Gropius and the Use of History," in Gwendolyn Wright and Janet Parks, eds., *The History of History in American Schools of Architecture, 1865–1975* (New York: Temple Hoyne Buell Center for the Study of American Architecture, 1990), pp. 89–98.

76. Anderson did not attend Le Corbusier's lecture because he was on a faculty exchange at the University of Minnesota (with Roy Childs Jones at MIT) during the fall of 1935. Lawrence B. Anderson, interview with author, Lincoln, MA, January 5, 1988 (hereafter cited as Anderson interview). See also Caroline Shillaber, *Massachusetts Institute of Technology School of Architecture and Planning 1861–1961: A Hundred Year Chronicle* (Cambridge: Massachusetts Institute of Technology, 1963), pp. 73, 78, 89.

77. "Ultramodern Cities on Stilts Pictured by French Architect," *Christian Science Monitor,* November 8, 1935, p. 6.

78. Gordon Bunshaft, interview with author, September 15, 1987. Bunshaft, who attended the school of architecture at MIT between 1928 and 1935, earned both bachelor's and master's degrees. See Carol Herselle Krinsky, *Gordon Bunshaft* (New York and Cambridge: Architectural History Foundation and MIT Press, 1988), pp. 3–4.

79. Emerson, who had studied at the Ecole des Beaux-Arts, led the school from 1919 to 1939. He was an unswerving Francophile. Under his deanship he appointed Jacques Carlu, a Grand Prix de Rome winner from the Ecole des Beaux-Arts, who taught at MIT from 1924 to 1933. Anderson interview, January 5, 1988. Shillaber, *Massachusetts Institute of Technology School of Architecture and Planning 1861–1961,* pp. 66–78; Lawrence B. Anderson, "Architectural Education M.I.T.: The 1930s and After," in Margaret Henderson Floyd, *Architectural Education and Boston* (Boston: Boston Architectural Center, 1989), pp. 87–90.

80. Anderson interview, January 5, 1988. See also Marvin E. Goody and Robert P. Walsh, eds., *Boston Society of Architects: The First Hundred Years 1867–1967* (Boston: Boston Society of Architects, 1967), pp. 63–66.

81. *Massachusetts Institute of Technology Bulletin, President's Report Issue* 72 (October 1936), p. 135.

82. Joseph Hudnut, "Memorandum, Reorganization of Instruction in Architecture at Harvard University," February 7, 1936 (Central Files, Columbia University).

83. *Massachusetts Institute of Technology Bulletin, President's Report Issue 1936–1937* 73 (1937), p. 127. Anderson interview, January 5, 1988.

84. *Cathedrals,* p. 142.

85. Ieoh Ming Pei (class of 1940) lecture, MIT, Cambridge, March 1, 1985. Ieoh Ming Pei, interview with author, New York City, August 6, 1985 (hereafter cited as Pei interview).

86. *Massachusetts Institute of Technology Bulletin, President's Report Issue* 72 (October 1936), p. 134. *Massachusetts Institute of Technol-*

ogy Bulletin, President's Report Issue 1936–1937 73 (1937), p. 128. Pei interview, August 6, 1985. Under the supervision of Professor Edward Bridge, first- and second-year students during the year 1936–1937 designed and constructed a colonial house. Emerson, believing that students should be in touch with the practical side of architecture, introduced the course. Anderson interview, January 5, 1988.

87. *Cathedrals,* p. 142.

88. "Monsieur Le Corbusier Speaks to Architects," *Tech* 55, November 1, 1935, p. 5.

89. Harry Weese (class of 1938), interview with author, December 8, 1987 (hereafter Weese interview).

90. Pei may also have attended Le Corbusier's lecture at Harvard. Pei interview, August 6, 1985. Ieoh Ming Pei lecture, MIT, Cambridge, March 1, 1985.

91. Pei interview, August 6, 1985. The volumes are *OC 1910–1929* and *OC 1929–1934*. A third volume, *OC 1934–1938,* was published in 1939 during Pei's final academic year at MIT.

92. Gordon Bunshaft, interview with author, September 15, 1987.

93. Weese interview, December 8, 1987.

94. Pei interview, August 6, 1985.

95. Weese interview, December 8, 1987. Harry Weese, "War Stories from the Educational Front," *Inland Architect* 31 (September–October 1987), p. 112.

96. Anderson was introduced to the French edition of *Vers une architecture* in the late 1920s after he graduated from the University of Minnesota (class of 1927). In 1930 he received a master's degree in architecture from MIT and won the Paris Prize that year. During his three years at the Ecole des Beaux-Arts he heard Le Corbusier give one of his controversial lectures at the Salle Pleyel in Paris. He joined the MIT faculty in 1933. Anderson interview, January 5, 1988. In 1944 the School of Architecture reorganized itself into the School of Architecture and Planning, with Anderson assuming direction of the Department of Architecture. Text accompanying exhibit, "Lawrence B. Anderson '30, Artist, Educator, Architect," MIT Museum, Compton Gallery, September 1990.

97. Pei interview, August 6, 1985.

98. Bunshaft interview, September 15, 1987. See also Krinsky, *Gordon Bunshaft,* p. 4.

99. Besides the Art Alliance and the Architecture Department, sponsors included the Philadelphia chapter of the AIA, T-Square Club, Moore Institute and School of Design for Women, Pennsylvania Museum of Art, and Pennsylvania Academy of Fine Arts. "Lecture by Le Corbusier," *Bulletin, Philadelphia Art Alliance* [November 1935], p. 3 (The Art Alliance, Philadelphia).

100. Paul Cret, a premiated student at the Ecole des Beaux-Arts, was appointed professor of design in 1903 and remained at the University of Pennsylvania until 1937. See E. Delaire, *Les Architectes élèves de l'Ecole des Beaux-Arts 1793–1907* (Paris: Librairie de la Construction Moderne, 1907), p. 224; Elizabeth Greenwell Grossman, *The Civic Architecture of Paul Cret* (New York: Cambridge University Press, 1996). Harry Sternfeld attended the Ecole des Beaux-Arts in 1914. See James Philip Noffsinger, *The Influence of the Ecole des Beaux-Arts on the Architects of the United States* (Washington, DC: Catholic University of America Press, 1955), p. 109. John Harbeson is the author of *The Study of Architectural Design* (New York: Pencil Points Press, 1926).

101. Joseph Esherick, "Architectural Education in the Thirties and Seventies: A Personal View," in Spiro Kostof, ed., *The Architect* (New York and Oxford: Oxford University Press, 1977), pp. 238–279.

102. The cost of the formal dinner was $1.50. Invitation, Philadelphia Art Alliance (FLC).

103. "French Visitor Here Urges 'Garden-cities' Up in Air," *Philadelphia Inquirer,* November 9, 1935, p. 2.

104. *VR,* pp. 188–189, 343–345. Le Corbusier, *Des canons, des munitions? Merci! Des logis . . . s.v.p. Pavillon des Temps Nouveaux* (Boulogne-sur-Seine: Editions de l'Architecture d'Aujourd'hui, 1938).

105. "Paul Philippe Cret," *Journal of the American Institute of Architects* 4 (December 1945), pp. 281–288. The Barnes Foundation was chartered as an educational institution in 1922. Henry-Russell Hitchcock, Jr., "Howe & Lescaze," in *Modern Architecture: International Exhibition* (New York: Museum of Modern Art, 1932), pp. 143–155.

106. Cret quoted Le Corbusier in "The Architect as Collaborator of the Engineer," written in 1927 and published in *Architectural Forum* 49 (July 1928), pp. 97–104; reprinted in Theo B. White, *Paul Philippe Cret* (Philadelphia: Art Alliance Press, 1973), pp. 61–65.

107. John Harbeson, who witnessed this incident, felt that it was an affront to Cret. John Harbeson, as told to Elizabeth Greenwell Grossman. I am grateful to Professor Grossman for sharing this episode with me. Letter, Elizabeth Greenwell Grossman to author, August 26, 1990. Norman Rice confirmed that when he met Cret, "Le Corbusier sort of brushed him off." Norman N. Rice, interview with author, August 8, 1985.

108. Jacobs interviews, November 21, 1984, June 7, 1987.

109. Howard Greenfeld, *The Devil and Dr. Barnes* (New York: Viking, 1987).

110. Aline B. Saarinen, *The Proud Possessors* (New York: Random House, 1958), p. 219. George and Mary Roberts, *Triumph on Fairmount, Fiske Kimball and the Philadelphia Museum of Art* (Philadelphia and New York: J. B. Lippincott, 1959), pp. 78–81, 246–253.

111. Barnes's quarrels with Cret and others are documented in Roberts, *Triumph on Fairmount,* p. 78; White, *Paul Philippe Cret,* p. 34; Greenfeld, *The Devil and Dr. Barnes,* p. 111. Draft of letter [not sent], Paul Cret to Albert Barnes, February 1, 1924 (Paul Cret Papers, Rare Book and Manuscript Library, University of Pennsylvania). See also Elizabeth G. Grossman, "Paul Philippe Cret: Rationalism and Imagery in American Architecture" (Ph.D. diss., Brown University, 1980).

112. Maurice Raynal, "La Fondation Barnes," *L'Esprit Nouveau* 18 (November 1923), unpaged.

113. *Cathédrales,* p. 155.

114. *L'Esprit Nouveau* was founded in 1919. Letter, Albert C. Barnes to Le Corbusier, November 12, 1935 (FLC).

115. Letter, Le Corbusier to Albert C. Barnes, November 13, 1935 (FLC).

116. Envelope, Le Corbusier to Albert C. Barnes (FLC).

117. "Mr. C. Albert Barnes de Philadelphie," *Cathédrales,* pp. 153–157.

118. *OC 1910–1929,* pp. 58–68; Tim Benton, *The Villas of Le Corbusier 1920–1930* (New Haven and London: Yale University Press, 1987), pp. 42–75. On the collection, see chapter 1.

119. *Cathédrales,* pp. 156–157.

120. Letter, R. Sturgis Ingersoll to Robert A. M. Stern, July 10, 1963, quoted in Stern, *George Howe,* p. 66.

121. Geoffrey T. Hellman, "Profiles: From Within to Without—II," *New Yorker* 23 (May 3, 1947), p. 38.

122. Letter, George Howe to Le Corbusier, undated (FLC).

123. Theo B. White, *The Philadelphia Art Alliance* (Philadelphia: University of Pennsylvania Press, 1965), p. 70.

124. S.[igfried] Giedion, "Vers un renouveau architectural de l'Amérique," *Cahiers d'Art* 8, no. 516 (1933), pp. 237–243. Le Corbusier owned this issue. On the French response to PSFS, see Isabelle Jeanne Gournay, "France Discovers America, 1917–1939 (French Writings on American Architecture)" (Ph.D. diss., Yale University, 1989), pp. 224–225.

125. Hellman, "Profiles: From Within to Without—II" (May 3, 1947), p. 38.

126. *Cathedrals,* p. 54.

127. Norman N. Rice, "I remember 35 Rue de Sèvres" (FLC); Norman N. Rice, "I Believe . . . ," *T-Square* 2 (January 1932), pp. 24–25, 34–35.

128. "Le Corbusier Favors Houses of Glass," *Brunswick Record,* November 14, 1935 (Special Collections, Bowdoin College Library).

129. "LeCorbusiere's [sic] Lecture on House at Bowdoin," *Lewiston Evening Journal,* November 13, 1935; "Le Corbusier Favors

Houses of Glass," *Brunswick Record,* November 14, 1935 (Special Collections, Bowdoin College Library).

130. Letter, Elbridge Sibley to author, December 14, 1984.

131. The celebrated tablecloth has not survived. Professor Harry Andrews, retired head of Bowdoin Art Department, as told to Elbridge Sibley. Letters, Elbridge Sibley to author, May 18, 1985, and February 7, 1990.

132. *Princeton University Weekly Bulletin* 25 (November 9, 1935). Le Corbusier credits himself with only two lectures and "a seminar with students in the form of criticism of plans for a villa," *Cathedrals,* p. 140. Agenda (FLC).

133. Letter, William L. Addkison (M.F.A. 1936) to author, August 9, 1987.

134. Letter, William L. Addkison to author, August 9, 1987.

135. Letter, Jean Labatut to Le Corbusier, November 12, 1935 (FLC). Jean Labatut outlines his "partnership" with Forestier, his education at the Ecole des Beaux-Arts, and his teaching at Princeton University where he was professor of design from 1928 to 1967 in "History of Architectural Education through People," *Journal of Architectural Education* 33 (November 1979), pp. 22–24.

136. Letter, G. E. Kidder Smith (class of 1936; M.F.A. 1938) to author, August 19, 1987.

137. Anderson interview, January 5, 1988.

138. *Cathedrals,* p. 140.

139. *Daily Princetonian,* November 14, 15, and 16, 1935; *Princeton University Weekly Bulletin,* 25 (November 9, 1935).

140. Letter, Melville C. Branch, Jr. (class of 1934; M.F.A. 1936) to author, August 24, 1987. Branch is a former president of the City Planning Commission in Los Angeles. See also Labatut, "History of Architectural Education through People," p. 24.

141. Letter, G. E. Kidder Smith to author, August 19, 1987.

142. Letter, William L. Addkison to author, August 9, 1987.

143. *Cathedrals,* p. 142. Le Corbusier's version of the story is uncorroborated.

144. Letter, Jean Labatut to Le Corbusier, November 12, 1935 (FLC).

145. Letters, Jean Labatut to Le Corbusier, November 12, 1935 (FLC); Melville C. Branch, Jr. to author, August 24, 1987; G. E. Kidder Smith to author, August 19, 1987. Borden's Milk Company displayed the rotolactor in its exhibit at the 1939 New York World's Fair.

146. "French Architect Guest in Princeton for Lecture Series," *New York Herald Tribune,* November 17, 1935, 4, p. 10. "Society," *Princeton Herald,* November 15, 1935, p. 3.

147. "Princeton Seeks Seventh Straight," *New York Times,* November 16, 1935, p. 8; "Football Scores," *New York Times,* November 17, 1935, p. 1.

148. *Cathedrals,* p. 134. Palmer Stadium had a seating capacity of 42,000; see Howard Dwight Smith, "Report on Trip to Princeton, College of City of New York, Yale and Harvard for the Purpose of Inspecting the Stadia at those Universities," part I, *American Architect* 118 (July 21, 1920), p. 95. During a weekend he was in New York City Le Corbusier may have read an article by Lewis Nichols, "Football—Cheers, Color, Coin," *New York Times Magazine,* November 3, 1935, pp. 11, 22.

149. See chapter 10 for Le Corbusier's stadium and national sports center project for 100,000 participants (1936–1937). *OC 1934–1938,* pp. 90–97. Le Corbusier, *Des canons, des munitions? Merci! Des logis . . . s.v.p. Pavillon des Temps Nouveaux,* pp. 98–103.

150. *Cathedrals,* pp. 134–144.

151. *Cathedrals,* p. 135. Photograph of football practice from University Archives, Department of Rare Books and Special Collections, Princeton University Library.

152. Telegrams, Robert Woods Bliss to Le Corbusier, October 24, 1935; Le Corbusier to Robert Woods Bliss, October 25, 1935 (FLC). Letter, Le Corbusier to Marguerite Harris, identified "Bowdoin—Brunswick" [November 12, 1935] (Frances Loeb Library, Harvard Design School). Agenda, November 6 and 17, 1935 (FLC).

153. "Noted Architect to Lecture," *News-Record of the Baltimore Museum of Art* 6 (November 1935).

154. "Modern Cities Waste Human Energy, Architect Asserts," *Sun, Baltimore,* November 19, 1935, pp. 5, 22.

155. Robert Judson Clark, "Cranbrook and the Search for Twentieth-Century Form," in *Design in America* (New York: Abrams, 1983), pp. 24–26.

156. "French Expert Sees Housing as the World's Next Industry," *Detroit Free Press,* November 22, 1935 (courtesy of Cranbrook Archives).

157. Florence Davies, "Thinks Home of the Future Will Be Evolved in Detroit," *Detroit News,* November 21, 1935. See also Florence Davies, "Le Corbusier's Buildings Designed for Sun and Air," *Detroit News,* November 21, 1935, and "French Architect to Tell of Match-Box Home Design," *Detroit News,* November 20, 1935 (courtesy of Cranbrook Archives).

158. Grant Hildebrand, *Designing for Industry: The Architecture of Albert Kahn* (Cambridge: MIT Press, 1974), pp. 91–123. The River Rouge plant was the newer of the two Ford plants.

159. *Cathedrals,* p. 167.

160. Letter, Le Corbusier to G. W. Buehrig, January 7, 1936 (FLC).

161. "French Expert Sees Housing as the World's Next Industry" (courtesy of Cranbrook Archives).

162. *Cathedrals,* p. 199; see also Le Corbusier, "What Is America's Problem?," *American Architect* 148 (March 1936), pp. 16–22.

The original French version appears as "Où est le problème américain?" in *Cathédrales,* pp. 173–191.

163. "French Expert Sees Housing as the World's Next Industry" (courtesy of Cranbrook Archives).

164. Agenda, November 22, 1935 (FLC); Le Corbusier, "Note p.[our] Wallace Harrison," December 6, 1935 (Wallace K. Harrison Papers, Avery Architectural and Fine Arts Library, Columbia University).

165. "French Expert Sees Housing as the World's Next Industry" (courtesy of Cranbrook Archives).

166. Saarinen was elected president of the Cranbrook Academy of Art in 1932. Davira S. Taragin, "The History of the Cranbrook Community," and David G. De Long, "Eliel Saarinen and the Cranbrook Tradition in Architecture and Urban Design," in *Design in America,* pp. 41, 61.

167. "French Expert Sees Housing as the World's Next Industry" (courtesy of Cranbrook Archives).

168. Kahn was chosen because of his long association with Cranbrook that began in 1907 when he designed a house on George Booth's farm estate (now Cranbrook House). See illustration in Taragin, "The History of the Cranbrook Community," p. 37, fig. 12.

169. Jacobs interview, November 21, 1984.

170. Hildebrand, *Designing for Industry: The Architecture of Albert Kahn,* p. 130. On the Centrosoyuz, see Jean-Louis Cohen, *Le Corbusier and the Mystique of the USSR* (Princeton: Princeton University Press, 1992), pp. 60–105.

171. Hildebrand notes that "Henry Ford introduced the powered moving assembly line at Highland Park in 1913. He did not invent it—it had previously been used for such operations as meatpacking—but he expanded it, refined it, and gave it an entirely new scale of application." See *Designing for Industry: The Architecture of Albert Kahn,* p. 91.

172. Le Corbusier, "The Atmosphere of Moscow," *Precisions,* p. 260. After the initial success of Kahn's design for a tractor plant at Stalingrad, his brother Moritz established a branch office in Moscow. The firm designed 521 factories in the USSR. Hildebrand, *Designing for Industry: The Architecture of Albert Kahn,* pp. 128–130; *The Legacy of Albert Kahn* (Detroit: Detroit Institute of Arts, 1970), p. 24.

173. *Cathedrals,* p. 169.

174. *Cathedrals,* pp. 143–144.

175. On the Taliesen Fellowship and its origins, see Edgar Tafel, *Apprentice to Genius* (New York: McGraw-Hill, 1979); Neil Levine, *The Architecture of Frank Lloyd Wright* (Princeton: Princeton University Press, 1996), pp. 218, 220, 221–222, 225–226.

176. *Cathedrals,* pp. 143–144. By October 1924 Saarinen had submitted to Booth a site plan and other drawings of his scheme for Cranbrook. On Saarinen in Chicago and Michigan and his early association with Booth, see De Long, "Eliel Saarinen and the Cranbrook Tradition in Architecture and Urban Design," pp. 48–50, 294nn23–26.

177. In addition to Alfred Barr, Philip Johnson, Henry-Russell Hitchcock, and Chick and Helen Austin, the circle included Kirk and Constance Askew whose brownstone at East 61st Street served in the words of Russell Lynes, as an "elegant Upper Bohemian salon." James Johnson Sweeney, John McAndrew (later director of architecture at the Modern), Julien and Joella Levy (whose Madison Avenue gallery specialized in modern and, more specifically, surrealist art), Agnes Rindge (head of the art department at Vassar), James Thrall Soby, as well as composers Virgil Thomson and Aaron Copland, artist Pavel Tchelitchew, and Lincoln Kirstein were early supporters of the museum. Russell Lynes, *Good Old Modern* (New York: Atheneum, 1973), pp. 108–109; Nicholas Fox Weber, *Patron Saints* (New York: Knopf, 1992). See also Julien Levy, *Memoir of an Art Gallery* (New York: G. P. Putnam's Sons, 1977), pp. 13–14, 104–110.

178. These editions include *The City of Tomorrow and Its Planning* (New York: Payson and Clarke, [1929]) and *Towards a New Architecture* (New York: Payson and Clarke, [1927]). Joseph Brewer was assistant editor at Payson and Clarke, New York (1926–1928) and later president as well as partner of the publishing house Brewer, Warren and Putnam Inc., New York (1928–1933), which produced the American edition of Amédée Ozenfant, *Foundations of Modern Art* in 1931. *A Biographical Directory of Librarians* (Chicago: American Library Association, 1970), p. 119.

179. Joseph Brewer, interview with author, New York City, December 12, 1984 (hereafter cited as Brewer interview). Henry Russel[l] Hitchcock, "Le Corbusier and the United States," *Zodiac* 16 (1966), p. 13.

180. Hitchcock, "Le Corbusier and the United States," p. 13. See also "Brewer Entertains French Architect," *Olivet College Echo* 46 (November 27, 1935), p. 1.

181. Brewer interview, December 12, 1984. Le Corbusier took the train from Kalamazoo to Chicago on November 23. He spent the entire next day in Chicago with no scheduled appointments. In early December Brewer thanked Le Corbusier for his "kind letter and the sketch for my house [*aimable lettre et le croquis pour ma maison*]." Letter, Joseph Brewer to Le Corbusier, December 7, 1935 (FLC). The present location of Le Corbusier's drawing and letter is unknown.

182. Letter, Le Corbusier to A. J. Raspetti, January 2, 1930 (FLC). Le Corbusier published drawings of the Brewer House in *L'Architecture Vivante,* series under the direction of Jean Badovici, 9, pl. 42. There it was identified as the "House of a president of a college in Michigan (U.S.A.)." Later when it was published in the *Oeuvre complète,* the project was identified inadequately as "plans for the residence of the president of a college near Chicago" *OC 1934–1938,* pp. 132–133.

183. Tim Benton makes this observation in his essay, "The Era of Great Projects," in *Century,* p. 181.

184. Letter, Le Corbusier to "Amie" [Marguerite Harris], [envelope postmarked November 23, 1935]; see chapter 1.

185. I am grateful to Charlotte Whitney, former member of the planning commission in Olivet, Michigan, for sharing with me her knowledge of the topography of Olivet as well as the site proposed for the Brewer House. Charlotte Whitney interview with author, September 16, 1991. See also Nancy Crawley, "Famed Architect's Visionary Work Never Saw Fruition in Olivet," *Enquirer and News,* Battle Creek, MI (August 3, 1977), p. A–14 (Archives, Olivet College Library).

186. Hitchcock, "Le Corbusier and the United States," p. 15.

187. Unlike for the Brewer House, Le Corbusier apparently did not visit proposed sites of either the Errázuriz House or the house at Mathes, where "the budget was so modest that it was impossible for the architect to travel to the site both before and during construction." See *Le Corbusier 1910–65,* p. 70, and *OC 1934–1938,* p. 185. See also Christiane Crasemann Collins, "Le Corbusier's Maison Errázuriz: A Conflict of Fictive Cultures," *Harvard Architecture Review* 6 (1987), pp. 38–53. Le Corbusier's attitude toward regionalism is complex and inconsistent. During his early years in Switzerland he had imbibed a peasant vernacular tradition associated with Jura regionalism. See Adolf Max Vogt, *Le Corbusier, the Noble Savage* (Cambridge: MIT Press, 1998). In *L'Art décoratif d'aujourd'hui* (1925), p. 198, Le Corbusier declared himself "a regionalist." By contrast, in *Vers une architecture* (1923) he repudiated vernacular elements ("Natural materials, which are infinitely variable in composition, must be replaced by fixed ones") in his chapter on mass-produced houses (*maisons en série; Towards a New Architecture,* p. 232. Le Corbusier's antiregionalist position is reflected in his position that architecture be the same "at the tropics and at the Poles"; unidentified quotation in Reyner Banham, *A Concrete Atlantis: U.S. Industrial Building and European Modern Architecture, 1900–1925* (Cambridge: MIT Press, 1986), p. 168. For discussions of his regionalist position during the 1930s, see Mary Caroline McLeod, "Urbanism and Utopia: Le Corbusier from Regional Syndicalism to Vichy" (Ph.D. diss., Princeton University, 1985); McLeod, "Le Rêve transi de Le Corbusier: L'Amérique 'catastrophe féerique,'" in J.[ean]-L.[ouis] Cohen and H.[ubert] Damisch, eds., *Américanisme et modernité* (Paris: EHESS and Flammarion, 1993), pp. 208–227; J.-C. V. [Jean-Claude Vigato], "Régionalisme," in *Encyclopédie,* pp. 342–343; and Curtis, "Regionalism and Reassessment in the 1930s," in *Le Corbusier: Ideas and Forms,* pp. 108–117. Recent scholarship by Francesco Passanti has defined the role of the vernacular in the construction of Le Corbusier's modernism (see chapter 2).

188. Many of Le Corbusier's villas of the 1920s and early 1930s indicated roof gardens and so-called outdoor living rooms, among them the Pavillon de l'Esprit Nouveau and Villa La Roche. By the mid-1930s he designed roof gardens less frequently.

189. *RC,* p. 7. "M. Le Corbusier Disclosed Plan for Cities on Stilts," *Kalamazoo Gazette,* November 23, 1935, p. 8.

190. See chapter 3.

191. *OC 1934–1938,* pp. 132–133.

192. On Le Corbusier's concept of *promenade architecturale,* see *OC 1910–1929,* p. 60.

193. The ramp became a principal element in many of Le Corbusier's early villas, notably Les Terrasses and the Villa Stein-de Monzie at Garches (1926–1928). A preliminary sketch of the Villa Savoye (September 1928) indicated the prominent role of a vehicular ramp as a precedent in Le Corbusier's oeuvre for circulation in the Carpenter Center for the Visual Arts. See Benton, *Century,* pp. 181–182; and William Curtis, "History of the Design," in Eduard F. Sekler and William Curtis, *Le Corbusier at Work* (Cambridge: Harvard University Press, 1978), pp. 67–68.

194. Le Corbusier, *Oeuvre complète 1957–1965,* ed. W. Boesiger (Zurich: Editions d'Architecture, 1965), p. 57. In his essay on the Carpenter Center for the Visual Arts, Tim Benton points out the linkages between both the Harris and Brewer houses and the Harvard building. *Century,* p. 181.

195. *OC 1934–1938,* p. 133.

196. Letters, Joseph Brewer to Le Corbusier, December 7, 1935; Le Corbusier to Joseph Brewer, January 30, 1936 (FLC).

197. Le Corbusier, "What Is America's Problem?," pp. 16–22. The article included no floor plans. *VR* and *RC,* p. 218. See also his Cartesian skyscraper project of 1938, *OC 1934–1938,* p. 76.

198. The lecture included a discussion of elevated highways. See "M. Le Corbusier Discloses Plan for Cities on Stilts," pp. 1, 8. In *La Ville radieuse* Le Corbusier included a photograph of a highway identified only by the caption: "1934, America, first appearance of the elevated street"; see *VR* and *RC,* p. 34. This is the Lincoln Express Highway that runs through the industrial sector of Newark, NJ; it was the subject of considerable interest in the French press. See "Urbanisme et architecture en U.S.A.: Notes de voyage de M. E. Beaudouin," *L'Architecture d'Aujourd'hui* 4 (November-December 1933), p. 59. Contrary to Le Corbusier's caption, it was not America's first "elevated street." José Luis Sert records that Chicago had constructed elevated streets (Michigan Avenue and South Water Street) as well as express highways to alleviate traffic congestion as early as 1922. See *Can Our Cities Survive?* (Cambridge: Harvard University Press, 1942), p. 160n12.

199. Le Corbusier noted in his Agenda the names and addresses of Blanche Hull and Virginia Pratt, two ardent supporters of the Kalamazoo Institute of Art. See Le Corbusier's annotation *"les dames de Kalamazoo"* to the letter he received from Joseph Brewer referring to the president's efforts to secure funds for construction of the house at Olivet. Letter, Joseph Brewer to Le Corbusier, February 27, 1936 (FLC).

200. Letters, Le Corbusier to Joseph Brewer, March 13, 1936; Joseph Brewer to Le Corbusier, February 27, 1936, April 14, 1936 (FLC).

201. In his article "Le Corbusier and the United States," p. 15, Hitchcock drew this conclusion: "Had this house been built the U.S. would have had a 'classic' example of Le Corbusier's early period, rivalling Les Terrasses if not the Villa Savoye. . . . I believe that actually, had it been erected, it would have had considerable influence on students, young architects, and even some already established practitioners."

202. Letter, Helen Sheridan (then assistant to the director for Collections and Exhibitions, Kalamazoo Institute of Arts) to author, November 27, 1984.

203. Mary Margaret McBride, "Houses on Stilts Win Favor as New Style of Building," "Man Who Builds on Stilts and Pylons to Speak Here" (newspaper clippings [identified October 1935], scrapbook, Kalamazoo Institute of Arts). See also "M. Le Corbusier Here This Evening," *Kalamazoo Gazette,* November 22, 1935, p. 13.

204. "M. Le Corbusier Discloses Plan for Cities on Stilts," p. 1. For Le Corbusier's explanation of the cell and its application to mass housing, see discussion of lectures in Princeton, Kalamazoo, Chicago (Renaissance Society), and Madison in chapter 3.

205. Designed by Marshall and Fox, the Drake Hotel (1920) is located on Lake Shore Drive at Michigan Avenue.

206. Penelope, "Le Corbusier Tells Chicagoans How to Beautify a City," *Chicago Daily News,* November 26, 1935, p. 12.

207. "Le Corbusier Lectures before Arts Club," *Chicago American,* November 26, 1935 (scrapbook 7, 1932–1936, Newberry Library); The Dowager, "Le Corbusier Here for Arts Club Talk Today," *Chicago Herald and Examiner,* November 25, 1935, p. 8. Elizabeth "Pussy" Paepcke was the wife of Walter Paepcke (1896–1960), a Chicago industrialist who organized the Container Corporation of America. He collected modern art and supported architecture including László Moholy-Nagy's School of Design (later Institute of Design). See Lloyd C. Engelbrecht, "Modernism and Design in Chicago," in Sue Ann Prince, ed., *The Old Guard and the Avant-Garde: Modernism in Chicago. 1910–1940* (Chicago: University of Chicago Press, 1990), pp. 121–122, 129. Elizabeth Paepcke recalled that she purchased through the Arts Club and John Becker her first painting by Le Corbusier in 1935 or 1936 and later a small painting. Letter, Elizabeth H. Paepcke to author, October 26, 1991. Elizabeth H. (Mrs. Walter) Paepcke, interview with author, November 12, 1991. See also Ted Conover, "Elizabeth Paepcke, Eve in the Garden of Aspen," *New York Times Magazine,* January 1, 1995, pp. 20–21. Katherine Kuh, Chicago dealer and curator, sold Elizabeth Paepcke her large Le Corbusier painting. Katherine Kuh, interview with author, September 26, 1991. On Bertha and Potter Palmer's taste in collecting, see Stefan Germer, "Traditions and Trends: Taste Patterns in Chicago," in Prince, ed., *The Old Guard and the Avant-Garde,* pp. 177, 181.

208. Lecture announcement, Renaissance Society of the University of Chicago (Exhibitions and Special Events Files, 1917–1965, Renaissance Society of the University of Chicago, Archives of American Art, Smithsonian Institution). See also letters, Ernestine M. Fantl to Inez Cunningham Stark (president of the Renaissance Society), September 12 and 17, October 29, and December 7, 1935, and related letters in "Correspondence, May-October 1935; November-December 1935" (Renaissance Society of the University of Chicago, Archives of American Art, Smithsonian Institution).

209. Museum of Modern Art traveling exhibition of Le Corbusier's work was displayed at the Wisconsin Union from November 26 to December 6, 1935. *Capital Times* [Madison], November 26, 1935, unpaged; "Le Corbusier Will Talk Here Nov. 26," November 19, 1935; "Corbusier Maps Vertical City of New Freedom," November 27, 1935; "Tall Cities on Stilts Predicted by French Architect in Lecture," November 27, 1935; "Corbusier Show Opens in Union Art Gallery Today," November 27, 1935; "Corbusier Idea Is Old—Jochen," November 28, 1935; all unidentified newspaper clippings (Wisconsin Union Historical Files, Archives, University of Wisconsin-Madison).

210. Other sponsoring organizations were the Chicago Architectural Exhibition league, Chicago Architectural club, Architects Club of Chicago, and Women's Architectural Club of Chicago. The dinner was at 6:30 P.M. and the lecture at 8:15 P.M. "Architects to Give Dinner Tonight for Le Corbusier," *Chicago Daily Tribune,* November 27, 1935, p. 19.

211. The Stevens Hotel, extending an entire block on Michigan Boulevard between Seventh and Eighth streets (1927; now the Conrad Hilton), was designed by Holabird and Roche. It contained an astonishing "3000 outside rooms," *The Stevens* (promotional brochure).

212. For a bibliography of French accounts of Chicago, see Isabelle Gournay, *Américanisme et modernité: Bibliographie raisonnée* (Paris: Institut Français d'architecture, 1985), 2 vols. See also Jean-Louis Cohen, *Scenes of the World to Come: European Architecture and the American Challenge, 1893–1960* (Paris and Montreal: Flammarion and Canadian Centre for Architecture, 1995), pp. 21–25.

213. Le Corbusier owned a copy of Upton Sinclair's *La Tête d'Holoferne* (Paris: Michel, 1931) (FLC). Sinclair was a contributor to *Plans;* see his "Le Martyre de Sacco et Vanzetti," 5 (July 1, 1932).

214. Sinclair Lewis, *Babbitt* (Paris: Librairie Stock, 1930). See also Theodore Dreiser, *La Couleur d'une grande cité* (Paris: Librairie Stock, 1930), traduction de Mme. P. Jeanneret; Theodore Dreiser, *L'Amérique tragique* (Paris: Rieder, 1933). See also Isabelle Gournay, "France Discovers America, 1917–1939 (French Writings on American Architecture)."

215. Albert Tissandier, an architect trained at the Ecole des Beaux-Arts in Paris, recorded his stark impressions of Chicago and the Midwest with a series of drawings, *Six mois aux Etats-Unis* (Paris: Masson, 1886). See also Louis-Ferdinand Céline, *Voyage au bout de la nuit* (Paris: Gallimard, 1932), pp. 285–301.

216. For accounts and analyses of them see Dudley Arnold, "A European Profile of American Architecture," *JSAH* 37 (December 1978), pp. 265–282; Gournay, *Américanisme et modernité: Bibliographie raisonnée;* Gournay, "France Discovers America 1917–1939 (French Writings on American Architecture)"; Cohen, *Scenes of the World to Come.*

217. Hegemann reproduces a number of images from the Burnham and Bennett plan in *Americanische Architektur und Stadtbaukunst,* (Berlin: Wasmuth, 1925), p. 36, figs. 99, 100. Hegemann also includes a rendering by Jules Guérin of the Chicago fair but the section on world's fairs in Le Corbusier's copy of Hegemann's book is uncut (FLC). Le Corbusier may also have known Hegemann's 1911 study *Der neue Bebauungsplan für Chicago* (Berlin: Wasmuth). See also Christiane Crasemann Collins, "A Visionary Discipline: Werner Hegemann and the Quest for the Pragmatic Ideal," issue devoted to "Modernist Visions and the Contemporary American City," *Center* 5 (1989), pp. 74–85. Le Corbusier may also have read Donat-Alfred Agache's publications on D. H. Burnham. For books, catalogues, and periodicals in Le Corbusier's library, see Paul Venable Turner, *The Education of Le Corbusier* (New York and London: Garland, 1977), pp. 232–238 and "Catalogue de la bibliothèque de Le Corbusier avant 1930," February 1970 (FLC).

218. *City of Tomorrow,* pp. 10–11. Le Corbusier had in his possession Bennett's presentation copy to the organization La Renaissance des Cités, signed and dated Chicago, December 20, 1919, from which he reproduced a plate of the "1917 General Plan, Minneapolis" in *Urbanisme,* p. 10. Edward H. Bennett, *Plan of Minneapolis* (Minneapolis: Civic Commission, 1917), fold-out map opp. p. 16 (FLC). On the reconstruction efforts of American planner George B. Ford and La Renaissance des Cités after World War I, see Cohen, *Scenes of the World to Come,* pp. 49–50.

219. Stanislaus von Moos and Simone Rümmele, "L'Amérique," in *L'Esprit nouveau: Le Corbusier et l'industrie 1920–1925* (Zurich: Ernst & Sohn, 1987), pp. 190–193.

220. Reyner Banham identified the locations—Montreal, Fort William, Buffalo, Buenos Aires and Bahia Blanca in Argentina, Minneapolis, and Baltimore—of such grain elevators in his chapter "Modernism and Americanism," *A Concrete Atlantis,* pp. 206–209.

221. In 1928 Gropius declared his admiration for such American models: "The most modern pieces of architecture I saw here are the River Rouge plant of Ford and the grain elevators of Chicago . . . the beauty of these is born out of the starkest utility and with no conscious attempt at decoration." "Gropius Praises Efficiency Here," *New York Times,* May 27, 1928, 2, p. 3.

222. *Vers une architecture,* pp. 25–28; *Towards a New Architecture,* pp. 37–41.

223. *Vers une architecture,* p. 226; *Towards a New Architecture,* p. 262.

224. *Urbanisme,* [p. 152]; *City of Tomorrow,* p. 157.

225. See news clipping, "Le Rêve d'un audacieux ingénieur: Le Projet Sullivan," *L'Illustré* (FLC). On a less visionary hotel project by Louis Sullivan, the Burnet House hotel in Cincinnati (1894), see Robert Twombly, *Louis Sullivan, His Life and Work* (New York: Viking, 1986), pp. 321, 505n35.

226. *Urbanisme,* p. 221; *City of Tomorrow,* p. 233.

227. Le Corbusier, "A Noted Architect Dissects Our Cities," *New York Times,* January 3, 1932, 5, p. 10.

228. *Almanach,* p. 187. Lönberg-Holm's entry was published in France; see "Projet de gratte-ciel pour la 'Chicago Tribune,'" *L'Architecture Vivante* (Fall and Winter 1924), pp. 24–25. Lönberg-Holm was born in Denmark. He taught in the School of Architecture at the University of Michigan in Ann Arbor. Later he was research editor of *Sweet's Catalogue.* As an American delegate to CIAM, he is best known for his contributions to the fourth congress in Athens (1933). K. Lönberg-Holm, *CIAM: Survey by American Group of CIAM IV (Athens 1933).* Marc Dessauce, "Contro lo Stile Internazionale: 'Shelter' e la stampa architettonica americana," *Casabella* 57 (September 1993), pp. 46–53, 70–71.

229. Letter, Le Corbusier to H. T. Wijdeveld, August 5, 1925, reproduced and analyzed in Paul Venable Turner, "Frank Lloyd Wright and the Young Le Corbusier," *JSAH* 42 (December 1983), pp. 350–359. This letter contradicts what Le Corbusier said to Wijdeveld, as told to Nikolaus Pevsner by Wijdeveld. When Wijdeveld invited Le Corbusier to contribute to an issue of the Dutch journal *Wendingen* on Wright, Le Corbusier replied, "I do not know this architect." Nikolaus Pevsner, "Frank Lloyd Wright's Peaceful Penetration of Europe," *Architects' Journal* 89 (May 4, 1939), p. 732. See also Thomas Doremus, *Frank Lloyd Wright and Le Corbusier, the Great Dialogue* (New York: Van Nostrand Reinhold, 1985).

230. Allen Brooks suggested that H. P. Berlage's lectures in Switzerland, after his visit to America and his encounter with the architecture of Sullivan and Wright, brought their work to Le Corbusier's attention. H. Allen Brooks, ed., *Writings on Wright* (Cambridge: MIT Press, 1981), p. 131.

231. Le Corbusier, "Introduction to the First Edition" (September 1929), *OC 1910–1929,* p. 13.

232. Sullivan's National Farmers Bank in Owatonna, Minnesota, was published in *Schweizerische Bauzeitung* 60 (September 14, 1912), p. 150; cited in H. Allen Brooks, *Le Corbusier's Formative Years* (Chicago: University of Chicago Press, 1997), pp. 423–424. See also H. Allen Brooks, "Le Corbusier's Formative Years in La

Chaux-de-Fonds," in H. Allen Brooks, ed., *Le Corbusier* (Princeton: Princeton University Press, 1987), p. 36.

233. Jacobs interviews, November 21, 1984, and June 7, 1987.

234. According to Taffel, Gropius met with a similar response when he visited the Midwest in 1928. Taffel, *Apprentice to Genius,* pp. 65–68.

235. Letter, Frank Lloyd Wright to Leo J. Weissenborn, November 8, 1935. Le Corbusier retained the original (FLC). "Leo J. Weissenborn," obituary, *New York Times,* August 14, 1967, p. 31.

236. Gertrude Stein, *Lectures in America* (New York: Random House, 1935). Stein traveled to many of the same institutions and venues as Wright and Le Corbusier.

237. Frank Lloyd Wright, *The Disappearing City* (New York: William Farquhar Payson, 1932). Other Wright publications include the Kahn lectures for 1930 at Princeton University, which appeared as *Modern Architecture,* and his first article on Broadacre City in the *New York Times Magazine* (March 20, 1932), which attempted to counter Le Corbusier's earlier *New York Times* article, "A Noted Architect Dissects Our Cities," promoting the Ville Radieuse as a solution to the American city. The first exhibit of a large model of Broadacre City in New York City at the Industrial Arts Exposition was held at Rockefeller Center (April 15–May 15, 1935) and received much critical attention. For these bibliographical references, see Robert L. Sweeney, *Frank Lloyd Wright: An Annotated Bibliography* (Los Angeles: Hennessey and Ingalls, 1978), pp. 43–53. Anthony Alofsin analyzed the debate between Wright and Le Corbusier from Wright's perspective in "Broadacre City: The Reception of a Modernist Vision, 1932–1988," *Center* 5 (1989), pp. 8–43.

238. Levine, *Frank Lloyd Wright,* pp. 218–253. Donald Leslie Johnson, *Frank Lloyd Wright versus America: The 1930s* (Cambridge: MIT Press, 1990).

239. Le Corbusier, "Article American Architect, 3 mars 1936" (FLC).

240. Cret considered Sullivan and Viollet-le-Duc as "individualists" who influenced the "Modernist movement." See Paul Cret, "The Architectural See-Saw," December 1930, reprinted in White, *Paul Philippe Cret,* p. 66.

241. In Le Corbusier's notes for his article "What Is America's Problem?" to appear in *American Architect,* he made the following notations for Chicago under the title "diverses impressions américains":

Chicago splendeur et horreur
grandeur du dessin//Style fort
et ample de Sullivan//Sullivan
grand architecte et vrai architecte//
les slums

"Article American Architect, 3 mars 1936" (FLC). Le Corbusier's opinion of Sullivan did not appear in his published article, probably because he did not want to dilute his criticism of Chicago.

242. *Cathedrals,* pp. 85–86.

243. On the effects of the South Side el, see Harold M. Mayer and Richard C. Wade, *Chicago: Growth of a Metropolis* (Chicago: University of Chicago Press, 1969), pp. 208–213.

244. Le Corbusier saw no contradiction in mocking Chicago's social register and attempting to get his own name on the S.S. *Normandie* list of notables.

245. *Cathedrals,* pp. 85–86.

246. Le Corbusier, "What Is America's Problem?," p. 19.

247. For a further exploration of these themes, see chapter 8.

248. *Cathédrales,* pp. 252–261; *Cathedrals,* pp. 171–178. Le Corbusier repeated the theme in his second lecture in Brazil during the summer of 1936. Entitled "La Dénaturalisation du phénomène urbain," it carried the subtitle "Le Grand Gaspillage" (The great waste). Elizabeth Davis Harris, "Le Corbusier and the Headquarters of the Brazilian Ministry of Education and Health 1936–1945" (Ph.D. diss., University of Chicago, 1984), p. 114.

249. Jacobs interviews, November 21, 1984, and June 7, 1987.

250. Nef wrote to Le Corbusier, "la ville que vous suggérez est une impossibilité." Letter, Elinor Castle Nef to Le Corbusier, December 9, 1935 (Elinor Castle Nef Papers, University of Chicago Library).

251. Le Corbusier notes "M. H. E. Bennet urbaniste . . . auteur d'un livre d'urb[anisme] sur Chicago," see entry for November 28, 1935, Agenda (FLC). This may refer to Daniel H. Burnham and Edward H. Bennett, *Plan of Chicago* (Chicago: Commercial Club, 1909), or to the later Edward H. Bennett and Harry T. Frost, *The Axis of Chicago* (Chicago: Bennett, Parsons and Frost, 1929).

252. Letter, Alfred Shaw to Le Corbusier, December 10, 1935 (FLC). Le Corbusier may also have met Irving Bowman and his brother Monroe before his Stevens Hotel lecture. Letter, Irving H. Bowman to Le Corbusier, November 26, 1935 (FLC).

253. Carl W. Condit, *Chicago 1930–1970* (Chicago: University of Chicago Press, 1974), pp. 3–4.

254. Condit, *Chicago 1930–1970,* p. 17.

255. Harvey Wiley Corbett, "The Significance of the Exposition," *Architectural Forum* 59 (July 1933), p. 1, quoted in Condit, *Chicago 1930–1970,* p. 17.

256. "Rush Outer Link on U.S. Aid," *Chicago Daily Tribune,* November 27, 1935, pp. 1–2, 34. "Plans to Extend Outer Drive to City Limits Told," *Chicago Daily Tribune,* November 28, 1935, p. 13.

257. On the completion of the Burnham and Bennett plan and the growth of Chicago after World War I, see chapter 5, "War and

Prosperity, 1917–45," in Mayer and Wade, *Chicago: Growth of a Metropolis*, pp. 283–373.

258. The Dowager, "Le Corbusier Here for Arts Club Talk Today," *Chicago Herald and Examiner*, p. 8.

259. A sheet with rough sketches of "la villa Hawaii ou Haïti" indicating a "galerie" is at the Fondation Le Corbusier.

260. Letter, Elizabeth Field to Le Corbusier, December 3, 1935 (FLC). For a sketch of the villa he proposed for Hawaii or Haiti, see document entitled "pour Vogue . . . réponse à une amie," A3–19 (191) (FLC).

261. Le Corbusier wrote in his Agenda, "Elis B Field//je fais villa// et acheter *La Ville*// de Léger je vous//donnerai 1 grande//fresque," December 1, 1935 (FLC). In the fall of 1935 Léger's *La Ville* was still owned by its painter, but had been lent by the Renaissance Society to the Museum of Modern Art for its Léger exhibition in October 1935. George L. K. Morris called "The City" "Léger's most important work": see "Fernand Léger versus Cubism," *Bulletin of the Museum of Modern Art* 3 (October 1935), p. 5. In December it would be on exhibit at the Art Institute of Chicago, *Bulletin of the Art Institute of Chicago* 29 (December 1935), p. 93.

262. Elizabeth H. (Mrs. Walter) Paepcke, interview with author, November 12, 1991.

263. Letters, Le Corbusier to Elizabeth Field, July 7 and October 9, 1936 (FLC). In *Cathédrales* his mention of "les îles, Tahiti avec de nouveaux divertissements" (the islands, Tahiti, and new amusements) may be a possible allusion to the villa in Hawaii or Haiti that he hoped to design for her, p. 120; *Cathedrals*, p. 84.

264. Le Corbusier enlisted the help of John and Elinor Castle Nef on a number of projects including architectural commissions, an exhibition of Louis Soutter drawings at the Arts Club of Chicago, and the purchase of sculpture by Henri Laurens. He even sent the Nefs, at their request, a note card (stationery from the Drake) with preparatory sketches for his Chicago lectures, which they used as their Christmas card for 1935. Letters, Elinor Castle Nef to Le Corbusier, December 9, 1935; Le Corbusier to Elinor Castle Nef, December 10, 1935. See also letters, Le Corbusier to John Nef, December 5, 1935; [John Nef] to Le Corbusier, December 9, 1935, and May 18, 1936 (Elinor Castle Nef Papers, University of Chicago Library).

265. John Becker lived at 179 Lake Shore Drive. See postcard, John Storrs and Fernand Léger to Le Corbusier, November 4 [postmarked 1931] (FLC). *John Storrs (1895–1956): A Retrospective Exhibition of Sculpture* (Chicago: Museum of Contemporary Art, 1976).

266. Letter, Le Corbusier to John Nef, March 6, 1936 (FLC).

267. Gordon McCormick tried to interest Le Corbusier in a new type of garage. Letter, Gordon McCormick to Le Corbusier, July 30, 1936 (FLC). There were preliminary inquiries from Richard

Lowenstein of Chicago for a town house with office and studio. Jacobs sent Le Corbusier a sketch of a plot plan for the Lowenstein property. Letter, Robert Allan Jacobs to Le Corbusier, December 6, 1935 (FLC).

268. Jacobs interview, July 5, 1989.

269. The photograph, incorrectly captioned "à Boston," appears in Jean Petit, *Le Corbusier lui-même* (Geneva: Editions Rousseau, 1970), p. 81. Jacobs interview, June 7, 1987. See also Hellman, "Profiles: From Within to Without—II," p. 38.

270. Jacobs interview, November 21, 1984. On his knowledge of aircraft and aviation, see Le Corbusier, *Aircraft* (London and New York: Studio Ltd., 1935).

271. In his moving review of the *Le Corbusier Sketchbooks*, William H. Jordy examined Le Corbusier's relationship to the airplane and the solitude he found in air travel, "'I Am Alone': Le Corbusier, Bathrooms, and Airplanes," *New Criterion* 1 (April 1983), pp. 41–49. *Le Corbusier Sketchbooks* (New York and Cambridge: Architectural History Foundation and MIT Press in collaboration with the Fondation Le Corbusier, Paris, 1981–1982), 4 vols.

272. *La loi du méandre* (the law of the meander) forms the theme of his sixth lecture in Brazil, October 14, 1929, published in *Précisions*, pp. 141–156. Harris, "Le Corbusier and the Brazilian Ministry of Education and Health." For an explanation of the "law of the meander," see Jordy, "'I Am Alone': Le Corbusier, Bathrooms, and Airplanes," p. 47. See also *Le Corbusier: Rio de Janeiro, 1929, 1936*, Yannis Tsiomis, organizer (Rio de Janeiro: Centro de Arquitetura e Urbanismo do Rio de Janeiro, 1998).

273. *Cathedrals*, p. 86.

5 The Enchanted Catastrophe

1. The quotation is a conflation of two versions of Le Corbusier's first image of America. See Le Corbusier, *Quand les cathédrales étaient blanches: Voyage aux pays des timides* (Paris: Librairie Plon, 1937), pp. 49, 273. A third version appears in *Cathédrales*, p. 163. During the late 1930s several chapters of the book, translated by Marguerite Tjader Harris, appeared in *American Architect* and an American avant-garde journal she published called *Direction*. Le Corbusier's considerable efforts to secure an American publisher for the book were not successful until after World War II. See *When the Cathedrals Were White: A Journey to the Country of Timid People*, trans. Francis E. Hyslop, Jr. (New York: Reynal and Hitchcock, 1947), pp. 34, 109, 186–187.

2. *Cathedrals*, pp. 40, 43. Marguerite Tjader, "Portrait of Le Corbusier," unpublished manuscript, 1984 (Harris family papers).

3. "La Catastrophe féerique," in *Cathédrales*, pp. 56, 119–129; *Cathedrals*, pp. 40, 83–91. I have translated *catastrophe féerique* and *splendeur féerique* as "enchanted catastrophe" and "enchanted splendor" instead of Francis Hyslop's "fairy catastrophe" and "fairy splendor." See Mardges Bacon, CASVA Colloquium 75, Washington, DC, May 1988. Figure 5.1 illustrates Le Corbusier's article "La Catastrophe féerique," *L'Architecture d'Aujourd'hui* 9 (January 1938), p. 12.

4. Stanislaus von Moos, *Le Corbusier: Elements of a Synthesis* (Cambridge: MIT Press, 1979), p. 303.

5. *Cathedrals*, p. 58.

6. *Almanach*, pp. 18, 19.

7. *Vers une architecture*, pp. 218–219.

8. *Almanach*, p. 186. Francesco Passanti analyzed the sources, particularly European, for the Ville Contemporaine. See his "Des gratte-ciel pour la Ville contemporaine," in *L'Esprit nouveau: Le Corbusier et l'industrie 1920–1925* (Zurich: Ernst & Sohn, 1987), pp. 54–65.

9. Werner Hegemann, *Der Städtebau nach den Ergebnissen der allgemeinen Städtebau-Ausstellung in Berlin nebst einem Anhang: Die Internationale Städtebau-Ausstellung in Düsseldorf* (Berlin: Wasmuth, 1911–1913), vol. 2, opp. p. 335; Hegemann used the same photograph in his *Amerikanische Architektur und Stadtbaukunst* (Berlin: Wasmuth, 1925), p. 53, pl. 179. See Le Corbusier, "Nos moyens," *EN*, no. 27 (November 1924), unpaged, and *Urbanisme*, p. 144.

10. Christiane C. Collins, "Hegemann, Werner," in Adolf K. Placzek, ed., *Macmillan Encyclopedia of Architects* (New York: Free Press, 1982), vol. 2, pp. 348–349.

11. *Urbanisme*, pp. 10–11; *City of Tomorrow*, p. 11.

12. *Almanach*, p. 186.

13. *City of Tomorrow*, p. 45.

14. *City of Tomorrow*, p. 96.

15. Le Corbusier, "Une ville contemporaine," *EN*, no. 28 (January 1925), pp. 2392–2409; *Urbanisme*, p. 164.

16. Le Corbusier published a photograph of the meeting of Broadway and Fifth Avenue at Madison Square with Burnham and Co.'s Fuller ("Flatiron") Building (1901–1903) to illustrate "the exact opposite" of his Plan Voisin for Paris, in *Urbanisme*, p. 273; *City of Tomorrow*, p. 288.

17. Walter Gropius, *Internationale Architektur* (Munich: Bauhausbücher, Albert Langen, 1925), p. 106.

18. Letter, Werner Hegemann to Le Corbusier, October 19, 1923 (FLC).

19. Hegemann, *Amerikanische Architektur und Stadtbaukunst*, p. 51. I thank Elizabeth Streicher for her generous assistance with a translation of text.

20. Perret's influence on Le Corbusier is discussed in chapter 1.

21. Hegemann, *Amerikanische Architektur und Stadtbaukunst*, pp. 44–55. Letters, Le Corbusier to Werner Hegemann, May 1, 1924; Werner Hegemann to Le Corbusier, November 13 and December 22, 1924; Le Corbusier to Werner Hegemann, February 26, 1925 (FLC). *Urbanisme*, pp. 172–175. By December 1925 Hegemann had received a copy of *Urbanisme* that Le Corbusier had sent to him. Letter, Werner Hegemann to Le Corbusier, December 11, 1925 (FLC).

22. Mary McLeod, "Perished Dreams of America: Le Corbusier's Reassessment of Industrial Utopia," symposium, "L'Américanisme et la modernité," Ecole des Hautes Etudes en Sciences Sociales and the Institut Français d'Architecture, Paris, October 24, 1985; Mary McLeod, "Le Rêve transi de Le Corbusier: L'Amérique 'catastrophe féerique,'" in J.-L. Cohen and H. Damisch, eds., *Américanisme et modernité* (Paris: Flammarion, 1993), pp. 208–227.

23. Mary McLeod elucidates the importance of Le Corbusier's associations with regional syndicalists and his contributions to its publications including *Plans, Prélude*, and *L'Homme réel*. Mary Caroline McLeod, "Urbanisme and Utopia: Le Corbusier from Regional Syndicalism to Vichy" (Ph.D. diss., Princeton University, 1985), including contents of these journals, pp. 458–497; Mary McLeod, "'Architecture or Revolution': Taylorism, Technocracy, and Social Change," *Art Journal* 43 (Summer 1983), pp. 132–147; Mary McLeod, "Le Corbusier and Algiers," *Oppositions* no. 19/20 (Winter/Spring 1980), pp. 55–85; in that same issue "Bibliography: *Plans*," *Oppositions*, pp. 184–201.

24. Le Corbusier, "Vivre! (habiter)," *Plans*, no. 4 (April 1931), pp. 49–[64]; reprinted in *VR* and *RC*, pp. 112–118.

25. Le Corbusier, "Vivre! (respirer)," *Plans*, no. 3 (March 1931), pp. 33–35; reprinted in *VR* and *RC*, pp. 104–108, 110–111.

26. Le Corbusier, "Invite à l'action," *Plans*, no. 1 (January 1931), p. 49; reprinted in *VR* [and *RC*], p. 92–97. Le Corbusier, "Mort de la rue," *Plans*, no. 5 (May 1931), p. 49; reprinted in *VR* [and *RC*], pp. 119–126.

27. For his definition of the Cartesian skyscraper, see Le Corbusier, "Descartes est-il américain?," *Plans*, no. 7 (July 1931), pp. 49–[64]; reprinted in *VR* and *RC*, pp. 127–134. See also *Cathédrales*, pp. 73–76; *Cathedrals*, pp. 51–54.

28. On the Ferriss and Corbett studies, see "Zoning and the Envelope of the Building," *Pencil Points* 4 (1923), pp. 15–18; Carol Willis, "Drawing toward Metropolis," in Hugh Ferriss, *Metropolis of Tomorrow* (New York: Princeton Architectural Press, 1986; orig. pub. Ives Washburn, 1929); Carol Willis, "Zoning and *Zeitgeist*: The Skyscraper City in the 1920s," *JSAH* 45 (March 1986), pp. 47–59.

29. *Précisions*, p. 203, and *Precisions*, p. 204; reprinted in *VR* and *RC*, p. 220.

30. Le Corbusier's drawing, entitled *Les Protecteurs de la patrie?—ce sont ceux qui la créent!* (Who are the protectors of the fatherland?—Those who create it!), illustrated a 1934 lecture in Algiers, *VR* and *RC*, p. 261.

31. Le Corbusier, "A Noted Architect Dissects Our Cities," *New York Times Magazine*, January 3, 1932, 5, pp. 10–11, 19.

32. In 1921 Nicola Sacco and Bartolomeo Vanzetti, two immigrant anarchists, were convicted of the murder of a paymaster and his guard during a robbery in South Braintree, MA. Although the evidence failed to prove their guilt, they were nonetheless con-

victed, and executed in 1927. Leftist political supporters in Europe used the case to denounce the methods and values of justice in America.

33. Paul Turner, *The Education of Le Corbusier* (New York: Garland, 1977); Paul V. Turner, "Catalogue de la bibliothèque de Le Corbusier avant 1930," Paris, 1970 (FLC).

34. Paul Morand (1888–1976) made four visits to New York from 1925 to 1929 in conjunction with diplomatic travels and as Paris correspondent to the *Dial,* an American journal of arts and letters. "Paul Morand, 88, Novelist, Is Dead," obituary, *New York Times,* July 24, 1976, p. 20. See also Bayrd Still, *Mirror for Gotham* (New York: New York University Press, 1956), p. 295. Le Corbusier made frequent annotations in his copy of Morand, *New-York* (Paris: Flammarion, 1930) (FLC). Within weeks of its publication in Paris, *New-York* had sold over 100,000 copies.

35. "Vivre à New York, c'est toucher le pouls du pays," in Morand, *New-York,* p. 268. See "Vivre à New-York suffisait: C'était toucher le pouls du pays," in Valéry Larbaud, *Walt Whitman poèmes et proses* (Paris: Gallimard, 1960), p. 36; Paul Morand, *New York* (New York: Henry Holt, 1930), p. 308. Below, the title *New-York* indicates the original French edition of Morand's book; *New York* the English translation.

36. Morand, *New York,* p. 305.

37. Morand, *New York,* pp. 3, 315–316, 320.

38. Among many literary references, see those to Edgar Allan Poe, Walt Whitman, Henry James, Edith Wharton, Theodore Dreiser, John Dos Passos, Upton Sinclair, Sinclair Lewis, W. E. B. Du Bois, Eugene O'Neill, Charles Dickens, Jean Jacques Rousseau, the Marquis de Lafayette, Paul Bourget, and Jules Verne in Morand, *New York,* pp. 20, 30–36, 80, 120, 124–126, 129, 134, 137, 168, 203, 275, 302–303, 308, 311, 319–320.

39. Morand, *New York,* pp. 20, 47, 88–127, 138, 170, 186, 196–197, 266–275, 277–279.

40. Morand, *New York,* p. 128.

41. Morand, *New-York,* p. 99; Morand, *New York,* p. 116.

42. Morand, *New York,* pp. 301, 307.

43. Morand, *New York,* pp. 168, 190–191, 222–226, 297.

44. Morand, *New York,* pp. 301, 307, 313.

45. André Maurois, *En Amérique* (Paris: Flammarion, 1933) (FLC).

46. In 1927 Maurois made his first trip to America, where he lectured at a number of colleges and universities. In 1931 he was visiting lecturer in French literature at Princeton University. "Andre Maurois Is Dead at 82; Prolific Biographer and Novelist," obituary, *New York Times,* October 10, 1967, pp. 1, 42.

47. Maurois, *En Amérique* (New York: American Book Company, 1933), pp. 21, 53.

48. See his chapter "Les Trois Fantômes de l'Amérique," in Maurois, *En Amérique* (Paris), pp. 71–94.

49. Georges Duhamel, *Scènes de la vie future* (Paris: Mercure de France, 1930) (FLC).

50. Duhamel and a group of young poets founded the phalanstery at Créteil on the Marne near Paris. In an effort to join manual labor and intellectual life, they established a typographic and publishing house there in 1906. *Who's Who in France, 1965–1966* (Paris: Editions Jacques Lafitte, 1965), p. 1058. "Georges Duhamel Is Dead at 81; Author of 'Pasquier Chronicles,'" obituary, *New York Times,* April 14, 1966, p. 35; "L'Ecrivain Georges Duhamel est mort hier, à 82 ans," obituary, *L'Humanité,* April 14, 1966, p. 8; "Georges Duhamel," obituary, *Times* (London), April 14, 1966, p. 14.

51. Georges Duhamel, *America the Menace,* trans. Charles Miner Thompson (Boston: Houghton Mifflin, 1931), p. 212.

52. *Cathedrals,* p. 121.

53. Christian Zervos, "Amérique," *Cahiers d'Art* 1 (1926), p. 60. Erich Mendelsohn, *Amerika* (Berlin: Rudolf Mosse, 1926), pl. 130. See also "M Christian Zervos," obituary, *Times* (London), September 15, 1970, p. 12.

54. Peter de Francia, *Fernand Léger* (New Haven: Yale University Press, 1983), p. 126. Léger's exhibition was held at the John Becker Gallery in New York City from October 1–23, 1931. Postcard, John Storrs and F. Léger to [Le Corbusier], November 5 [1931 postmark] (FLC).

55. Postcards, the Savoy Plaza (Hotel), [Fernand Léger] to [Le Corbusier], New York, September 29, 1931, nos. 1 and 3 of four cards (FLC).

56. F. Léger, "New-York vu par F. Léger," *Cahiers d'Art* 6 (1931), pp. 437–439; reprinted in French in Fernand Léger, *Fonctions de la peinture* (Paris: Gonthier-Seghers, 1965), pp. 186–193; reprinted in English in *Art Forum* 7 (May 1969), pp. 52–55, and in Fernand Léger, *Functions of Painting* (New York: Viking, 1973), pp. 84–90. A few years later Léger was even more sharply critical of America. In an unpublished essay of 1933 he identified the "catastrophe" and "colossal paradox" of New York, at once the most dynamic city in the world and, due to Wall Street speculation, the skyscraper, and traffic jams, "the *slowest* city in the world." Posthumously published in Fernand Léger, "Le Mur, l'architecture, le peintre," in *Fonctions de la peinture,* pp. 113–122; reprinted in English, "The Wall, the Architect, the Painter," *Functions of Painting,* pp. 91–99. Le Corbusier may not have read Léger's essay, but he was certainly aware of its substance (e.g., Léger's description that a "forty-story building must disgorge all its human content at the same time," p. 94).

57. On Le Corbusier's synthesis of the technical, the functional, and the biological in the Radiant City, see McLeod, "Urbanism and Utopia: Le Corbusier from Regional Syndicalism to Vichy," pp. 246–247. On Le Corbusier's social assumptions for the Radi-

ant City, see Robert Fishman, *Urban Utopias in the Twentieth Century* (New York: Basic Books, 1977), pp. 233–234.

58. Fishman, *Urban Utopias in the Twentieth Century*, p. 235.

59. *Cathedrals*, p. 91.

60. Le Corbusier wrote his article returning home on the *Lafayette*, December 18, 1935. "What Is America's Problem?," *American Architect* 148 (March 1936), pp. 17–22; reprinted in *Cathédrales*, pp. 273–291; *Cathedrals*, pp. 186–201.

61. On the uses of *techniques modernes*, see report by Paul Otlet, the Declaration at Congress at La Sarraz, CIAM I 1928, and the section "Techniques modernes," *VR*, and *RC*, pp. 18–62. See also *Cathédrales*, pp. 73, 89; *Cathedrals*, pp. 52, 63.

62. On the use of "les réflexes psycho-physiologiques" (psycho-physiological reflexes), see *Cathédrales*, p. 91; *Cathedrals*, p. 65. On the use of "conditions psycho-physiologiques admirable" (excellent psycho-physiological conditions), see *Cathédrales*, p. 76; *Cathedrals*, p. 54. For Winter's emphasis on human physiology, see "Le Corps nouveau," *EN* 15 (February 1922), pp. 1755–1758. See also Winter, "Sports," *EN* 14 (January 1922), pp. 1675–1677 and "Sports," *EN* 16 (May 1922), pp. 1951–1952. Earlier, as Reyner Banham observed, Le Corbusier was influenced by the research of Charles Blanc on human physiological responses to light, color, and form. See Banham, *The Architecture of the Well-Tempered Environment* (Chicago: University of Chicago Press, 1984), p. 145–146.

63. *Cathedrals*, p. 62. Harvey Wiley Corbett was project architect in charge of vertical circulation. Léger recounted a visit to Corbett's office: "He tells me: 'Accommodating 20,000 people living in one building, that is my current work' . . . it's a matter of the elevators. Maneuvering this army vertically!" Léger, "New-York vu par F. Léger," pp. 438–439; reprinted in Léger, *Functions of Painting*, p. 88.

64. Giedion noted that the slab of the RCA Building "is based on the principle of 27 feet of optimum light for working area around a core containing the elevators and service space." Sigfried Giedion, *Space, Time and Architecture*, 4th ed. (Cambridge: Harvard University Press, 1965), p. 749, fig. 454. *Cathedrals*, pp. 62–63.

65. *Cathedrals*, p. 64. A key technological component, elevators would determine the viability of the Radiant City apartment block. See Le Corbusier's report "Rational Division into Building Lots," CIAM III (Brussels 1930); *VR* and *RC*, pp. 38–39.

66. On Le Corbusier's intentions, see note opposite the entry for December 2, 1935, Agenda (FLC). See chapter 7.

67. Le Corbusier delivered a talk in French on the Women's Radio Review over the WEAF-NBC network on October 24 from 4:00 to 4:30 P.M. and published it in *Cathédrales*, pp. 46–50; *Cathedrals*, pp. 33–35. On sound and climate control in the RCA Building, see A. Warren Canney, "Sound Control and Air Conditioning," *Record* 75 (January 1934), pp. 77–88.

68. *Cathedrals*, pp. 61–62, 80–81.

69. Fernand Léger, "The New Realism," lecture at the Museum of Modern Art. *Art Front* (New York) 2 (December 1935), pp. 10–11; French text translated by Harold Rosenberg; reprinted in Léger, *Functions of Painting*, pp. 109–113.

70. *Cathedrals*, p. 33. Henry L. Logan, "Lighting National Broadcasting Studios," *Record* 75 (January 1934), pp. 89–92.

71. Earlier he had placed his confidence in a system of thermal control that relied on the *mur neutralisant*, in which hot or cold air would circulate between two panes of glass to achieve a constant room temperature of 18 degrees C no matter what the climate outside. Notwithstanding his own findings about the efficacy of this system of double glazing, the *mur neutralisant* proved to be relatively ineffective, impractical, and costly. As Reyner Banham pointed out, Le Corbusier used the term air conditioning only after his 1935 visit. Banham suggests that he was ignorant of the progress of the American Willis Carrier when he carried out his own research on the *mur neutralisant* with Gustave Lyon, acoustical expert and technician at the Saint-Gobain glass works. The architect had intended his Cité de Refuge, Paris (1929–1933), to use the system, but this was thwarted in favor of single glazing and operable windows, because budgetary constraints prohibited a cooling system. Banham, *The Architecture of the Well-Tempered Environment*, pp. 156–160.

72. "The Radio City Broadcasting Studios of the National Broadcasting Company," *Record* 75 (January 1934), p. 75.

73. Canney, "Sound Control and Air Conditioning," pp. 77–88; Logan, "Lighting National Broadcasting Studios," pp. 89–92.

74. *Cathedrals*, p. 61.

75. *Cathedrals*, pp. 33–34.

76. *Cathedrals*, p. 64.

77. For Le Corbusier's attitude on collaboration, see his "Méditation à propos de Ford" ("Thoughts about Ford"), section 5, "Nécessités des plans et entreprises communautaires" ("Necessity of Communal Plans and Enterprises") in *Cathédrales*, pp. 247–251; *Cathedrals*, pp. 167–170. On the collaborative process and the objectives of CIAM, see below, chapter 7, n.7.

78. On Le Corbusier's participation in both the site commission and an international team of architects to design a headquarters for the United Nations, see his *UN Headquarters* (New York: Reinhold, 1947) and chapter 10 below. Le Corbusier's *carnet de poche* from January to June 1947 confirms the central role of his contributions in the design process. George Dudley, "Le Corbusier Notebook Gives Clues to United Nations Design," *Architecture* 74 (September 1985), pp. 40, 44. On dissension within the ranks of CIAM, especially among the exponents of Team X, see Reyner Banham, "The End of an Old Urbanism," in *The New Brutalism* (New York: Reinhold, 1966), pp. 70–75.

79. For the use of *territoire-type,* see "La Catastrophe féerique" in section 2, "I Am an American," of *Cathédrales,* p. 124. Hyslop translates *territoire-type* as "type-area," *Cathedrals,* p. 87.

80. *Vers une architecture,* pp. 106–107; *Towards a New Architecture,* pp. 124–125; Von Moos, *Le Corbusier, Elements of a Synthesis,* pp. 48–49; Winfried Nerdinger, "Standard et type: Le Corbusier et l'Allemagne 1920–27," in *L'Esprit nouveau: Le Corbusier et l'industrie 1920–1925,* pp. 45–53; Stanislaus von Moos, "Standard et élite: Le Syndrome Citrohan" [Industrie], in *Encyclopédie,* pp. 190–199. Francesco Passanti has informed my understanding of Le Corbusier's notions of *standard* and *type.*

81. Von Moos, *Le Corbusier, Elements of a Synthesis,* pp. 43–51, 285–286; Alfred H. Barr, *Cubism and Abstract Art* (New York: Museum of Modern Art, 1936), pp. 163–166.

82. *Cathedrals,* p. 78.

83. That reading suggests that when he announces in the original French edition in English "I am an American," Le Corbusier identifies as the voice the city of skyscrapers with the businessmen who built them. It was not his own. He explains, "it was not they who said it. I thought it for them." *Cathédrales,* pp. 55, 59; *Cathedrals,* pp. 39, 42.

84. *Cathedrals,* pp. 41–42, 66, 188.

85. *Cathedrals,* p. 42.

86. "Et la poignée de main de fer de Nelson Rockefeller est une poignée de paysan," *Cathédrales,* p. 59. This reference to Rockefeller was excised from the American edition.

87. *Cathedrals,* p. 44.

88. The event was held on October 23 at the Rockefeller Center Luncheon Club on the 65th floor of 30 Rockefeller Plaza, changed from the original location at the Knickerbocker Club specified in Goodwin's invitation. Both Walker and Harmon were members of the executive committee of the New York chapter of the AIA and Brown was president of the Architectural League of New York. The guest list also included A. Everett Austin, Jr., Julian Clarence Levi, C. D. Jackson, Ely Jacques Kahn, Robert A. Jacobs, and Harold Sterner (undated press release, DAD, MoMA, NY). Letter, Philip Goodwin to Nelson Rockefeller, October 14, 1935 (Record Group 2, Cultural Interests, Museum of Modern Art 1934–1941, Box 20, Rockefeller Archive Center). Le Corbusier's Agenda confirms the Rockefeller Center venue. *Cathedrals,* p. 73; Agenda, October 23, 1935 (FLC).

89. In *Cathédrales* the text reads "Washington de Houdon." The statue was not the work of Jean Antoine Houdon, French sculptor celebrated for his statue of George Washington (1788), but of American sculptor John Quincy Adams Ward (1883). The American edition corrects the attribution. *Cathédrales,* pp. 103–104; *Cathedrals,* pp. 73–74. On Le Corbusier's encounter with the Subtreasury and skyscrapers of Wall Street, see H. I. Brock, "Le Corbusier Scans Gotham's Towers," *New York Times,* November 3,

1935, 7, pp. 10, 23.

90. Morand, *New York,* p. 61.

91. Brock, "Le Corbusier Scans Gotham's Towers," p. 23; *VR* and *RC,* p. 104.

92. The Subtreasury was built on the site of the first Federal Hall, constructed in 1699 and remodeled in 1788 by Pierre Charles L'Enfant, where George Washington took the oath of office as the first president. Hegemann, *Amerikanische Architektur und Stadtbaukunst,* pp. 22–24. *Urbanisme,* p. 11. See also John Reps, *The Making of Urban America* (Princeton: Princeton University Press, 1965), pp. 240–245.

93. *Cathedrals,* p. 75.

94. Le Corbusier, "What Is America's Problem?," p. 20.

95. On two occasions Le Corbusier viewed Manhattan from the air: first, when he flew to Baltimore to deliver his lecture at the Baltimore Museum of Art; second, when he returned from Chicago on Thanksgiving day. *Cathedrals,* pp. 47–48, 86.

96. *Cathedrals,* p. 50. For an illustration and analysis of the Commissioners' plan for New York City, see Reps, *The Making of Urban America,* pp. 296–299.

97. *Cathedrals,* pp. 80, 194.

98. Tjader, "Portrait of Le Corbusier" (Harris family papers). Le Corbusier, *Cathedrals,* p. 192; "What Is America's Problem?," p. 19.

99. Le Corbusier, "What Is America's Problem?," p. 21; *Cathedrals,* p. 197.

100. Le Corbusier, "What Is America's Problem?," pp. 16–22; reprinted in *Cathédrales,* pp. 273–291; *Cathedrals,* pp. 186–201.

101. Le Corbusier, "What Is America's Problem," p. 21; *Cathedrals,* pp. 197–198.

102. *Cathedrals,* pp. 40, 72, 86.

103. *Cathedrals,* p. 192; "What Is America's Problem?," p. 19.

104. On the evolution of the *à redents* type into the slab block, see Le Corbusier's illustrations for the Radiant City (1929–1930) exhibited at CIAM III in Brussels in 1930; *VR* and *RC,* pp. 156–173.

105. *VR* and *RC,* pp. 245, 250–261; *OC 1929–1934,* pp. 174–177. See "The Authorities Are Badly Informed," in *Cathedrals,* pp. 178–186. The project for the Rentenanstalt Insurance Building in Zurich (1933) employed a lozenge plan, *OC 1929–1934,* pp. 178–185.

106. After 1930 Le Corbusier proposed his reconfigured Cartesian skyscraper. *OC 1934–1938,* pp. 74–77; *Le Corbusier 1910–65,* pp. 122–123.

107. Le Corbusier published his plan in *OC 1929–1934,* p. 90; *VR* and *RC,* pp. 305–309. Eric Mumford discussed two versions of the plan and contribution of the Grup d'Arquitectes i Tècnics Catalans per al Progrés de l'Arquitectura contemporània (GATC-PAC) in "CIAM Urbanism after the Athens Charter," *Planning Perspectives* 7 (October 1992), pp. 394–396. In 1931 GATCPAC was changed to GATEPAC. On Sert's Barcelona type and on GATEPAC (Grupo de Arquitectos y Técnicos Españoles para el Progreso de la Arquitectura Contemporánea), see Knud Bastlund, *José Luis Sert* (New York and Washington, D.C.: Praeger, 1967), pp. 18–21, 34–37; David Mackay, *Modern Architecture in Barcelona 1854–1939* (New York: Rizzoli, 1989), pp. 94–112.

108. On Poelzig's skyscraper project, see *Der Schrei nach dem Turmhaus: Der Ideenwettbewerb Hochhaus am Bahnhof Friedrichstrasse Berlin 1921/22* (Berlin: Bauhaus-Archiv, 1998), pp. 114–119; see also Jean-Louis Cohen, *Scenes of the World to Come: European Architecture and the American Challenge, 1893–1960* (Paris and Montreal: Flammarion and Canadian Centre for Architecture, 1995), pp. 108–109. The Macià master plan for Barcelona may owe a debt to Poelzig's project through Fernando García Mercadal, a Catalan member of the GATCPAC group, who knew Poelzig. J. O. S. [Samitier], "Barcelone," in *Encyclopédie,* p. 59.

109. Le Corbusier used the Y-shaped model for housing blocks in his projects for a Rome suburb (1934) (*VR* and *RC,* p. 304) and Bat'a industries at Hellocourt in France (1935) (*OC 1934–1938,* pp. 36–37). He later used the *type Sert* housing blocks in his Bastion Kellermann project for the Exposition "Arts et Techniques" in Paris (1937), *VR* and *RC,* pp. 218–219; *OC 1934–1938,* pp. 148–151. Earlier he had employed the Y-shaped plan for offices in his project for Antwerp (1933), *VR* and *RC,* pp. 270–287; *OC 1929–1934,* pp. 156–159. Later he used it for the business towers in his project for Algiers (1938), *OC 1934–1938,* p. 103.

110. Amelia Thompson Vose, Vassar class of 1938, recorded in her own elegantly drawn and meticulously annotated lecture notes not only Le Corbusier's Y-shaped plan but also his preference for housing employing this typology. Vassar lecture notes, November 1, 1935 (courtesy of Amelia Thompson Vose).

111. *Cathedrals,* p. 185.

112. Le Corbusier, "What Is America's Problem?," p. 21; *Cathedrals,* pp. 39, 199.

113. "Une grand époque à commencé. Une époque nouvelle." *Prélude,* no. 13, September 27, 1934; *Cathédrales,* p. 10; *Cathedrals,* p. 9.

114. Le Corbusier and Pierre Jeanneret first made these observations in their report, "Analysis of the Fundamental Elements of the Problem of 'the Minimum House,'" presented at the CIAM II congress at Frankfurt-am-Main in 1929. *VR* and *RC,* pp. 29–34.

115. Le Corbusier, "What Is America's Problem?," pp. 21–22; *Cathédrales,* pp. 288–291; *Cathedrals,* pp. 199–201.

116. "Prosperity in U.S. Is Linked to Car Sales in Nation," *New York Herald Tribune,* November 3, 1935, 11, part 2, p. 2.

117. "6-Year Record Set at Closing of Motor Show," *New York Herald Tribune,* November 10, 1935, 1, p. 36.

118. Henry-Russell Hitchcock, translator's note to Le Corbusier, "What Is America's Problem?," p. 16. Marguerite Tjader Harris also translated and published an abridged version of this article as "New York—Glorious Catastrophe" in *Direction* 1 (June 1938), pp. 6–9.

119. Jane Jacobs, *The Death and Life of Great American Cities* (New York: Random House, 1961); Herbert Gans, *The Urban Villagers* (New York: Free Press, 1962).

6 Housing and the Public Sector

1. The dedication reads "Cet ouvrage est dédié à l'Autorité Paris, mai 1933," *VR,* title page.

2. Le Corbusier maintained, "My role has been a technical one. . . . I am an architect; no one is going to make a politician of me" (*Urbanisme,* pp. 281, 283; *City of Tomorrow,* pp. 298, 301). Similarly, he insisted, "I am only a city planner and an architect and perhaps an artist" (*Cathédrales,* p. 205, *Cathedrals,* p. 138); "I have never had anything to do with politics; I am an artisan. I make plans" (*Cathédrales,* p. 262; *Cathedrals,* p. 178).

3. Philip Goodwin, "Excerpt from lecture, delivered at the Museum of Modern Art, New York, by Le Corbusier, October 25 [sic], 1935. . . ." (see chapter 3) (DAD, MoMA, NY).

4. *New York Times* contributor H. I. Brock, editor Henry Humphrey, and others also provided Le Corbusier with introductions. See Agenda, (FLC).

5. Letters, Henry Humphrey to Le Corbusier, October 29 and November 8, 1935 (FLC).

6. See, for example, references to the "slums" of New York and Chicago in *Cathédrales,* pp. 122–123.

7. *Cathedrals,* p. 86. *Precisions,* p. 196.

8. *Precisions,* pp. 14, 235–236, figs. 200–208, 225, 226. On Agache's engagement in Rio de Janeiro, see David K. Underwood, "Alfred Agache, French Sociology, and Modern Urbanism in France and Brazil," *JSAH* 50 (June 1991), pp. 130–166.

9. *Cathédrales,* p. 122; *Cathedrals,* p. 86. For Le Corbusier's Plan Macià, see *OC 1929–1934,* p. 90; *VR* and *RC,* pp. 305–309; J. O. S. [Jordi Oliveras Samitier], "Barcelone," in *Encyclopédie,* pp. 59–62.

10. In *Urbanisme* Le Corbusier opposed the "depressing facades" of the slum dwellings that formed a "ragged" silhouette along the narrow corridor streets of American cities, especially Chicago and New York, pp. 220, 221; *City of Tomorrow,* pp. 232, 233, 236.

11. Letter, Henry Humphrey to Le Corbusier, October 29, 1935 (FLC). When the NYCHA was established on February 14, 1934,

Langdon W. Post became its chairman. James Ford, *Slums and Housing* (Cambridge: Harvard University Press, 1936), vol. 1, p. 239.

12. The 1934 act amended the State Housing Law of 1926. Unlike its predecessor, it placed no ceiling on rents other than to specify "low-cost housing," indicating the dubious assumption that low-cost construction would result in low rents. Ford, *Slums and Housing,* vol. 2, p. 640; Richard Plunz, *A History of Housing in New York City* (New York: Columbia University Press, 1990), p. 208.

13. *Toward the End to Be Achieved* (New York: New York City Housing Authority, 1937), pp. 5–6; *First Houses* (New York: New York City Housing Authority, 1935), pp. 13–15. For a history of the NYCHA, see Ford, *Slums and Housing;* Langdon W. Post, *The Challenge of Housing* (New York: Farrar and Rinehart, 1938); Richard Pommer, "The Architecture of Urban Housing in the United States during the Early 1930s," *JSAH* 37 (December 1978), pp. 235–264; Peter Marcuse, "The Beginnings of Public Housing in New York," *Journal of Urban History* 12 (August 1986), pp. 353–390; Plunz, *A History of Housing in New York City.*

14. *First Houses,* p. 9.

15. For a history of the social housing movement in New York City, see Robert W. De Forest and Lawrence Veiller, eds., *The Tenement House Problem* (New York: Macmillan, 1903), 2 vols.; I. N. Phelps Stokes, "Appendix: Historical Summary" and "Appendix: Notes on Plans," in Ford, *Slums and Housing,* vol. 2, pp. 867–905; Roy Lubove, *The Progressives and the Slums* (Pittsburgh: University of Pittsburgh Press, 1962); Roy Lubove, "I. N. Phelps Stokes: Tenement Architect, Economist, Planner," *JSAH* 23 (May 1964), pp. 75–87; Anthony Jackson, *A Place Called Home: A History of Low-Cost Housing in Manhattan* (Cambridge: MIT Press, 1976); Mardges Bacon, *Ernest Flagg: Beaux-Arts Architect and Urban Reformer* (New York and Cambridge: Architectural History Foundation and MIT Press, 1986), chapter 8, "Urban Housing Reform: An Incentive to Build," pp. 234–266; Plunz, *A History of Housing in New York City.*

16. "Les maisons de Post," Agenda, November 19 and December 3 [1935] (FLC). Letter, Mayor [La Guardia] to Governor Lehman, October 31, 1935 (La Guardia Records, Municipal Archives, New York City).

17. *New York City Housing Authority, Report of the Secretary, 1935* [second annual report], p. 5 (New York City Housing Authority papers, La Guardia and Wagner Archives, La Guardia Community College/The City University of New York, Box 11); *First Houses,* p. 15; *Toward the End to Be Achieved,* p. 7.

18. "La Guardia to Ask $150,000,000 Loan for Housing Here," *New York Times,* February 7, 1935, p. 1. "City Housing Plan Favored by Ickes," *New York Times,* February 8, 1935, p. 23.

19. *New York City Housing Authority, Report of the Secretary, 1935* [second annual report], p. 5 (New York City Housing Authority papers, La Guardia and Wagner Archives, La Guardia Community College/The City University of New York, Box 11).

20. *New York City Housing Authority, Fourth Annual Report, 1937,* p. 9.

21. In July 1935 the City officially condemned and took over four Manhattan blocks at Seventh Avenue between 151st and 153rd streets and between the Harlem River and Macombs Place. In February of that year architects were selected so that drawings could be completed and contracts executed by the following December. See *Toward the End to Be Achieved,* p. 11; *New York City Housing Authority, Report of the Secretary, 1935* [second annual report], pp. 23–24. In November 1935 a tentative site plan for Red Hook in Brooklyn had been developed but no demolition had yet begun. *New York City Housing Authority, Annual Report, 1936,* pp. 173–174 (New York City Housing Authority papers, La Guardia and Wagner Archives, La Guardia Community College/The City University of New York, Box 11). See also Rosalie Genevro, "Site Selection and the New York City Housing Authority, 1934–1939," *Journal of Urban History* 12 (August 1986), pp. 334–352.

22. For the housing competition program, see I. N. Phelps Stokes, "Appendix: Architectural Competitions," in Ford, *Slums and Housing,* vol. 2, pp. 921–923; Lubove, "I. N. Phelps Stokes: Tenement Architect, Economist, Planner," p. 84. See also Pommer, "The Architecture of Urban Housing in the United States during the Early 1930s," pp. 249–250. See "Names of Members and Associates of the Twenty-Two Architectural Firms Qualified by Competition for Work Under the New York City Housing Authority to Be Financed by Loans from the Public Works Administration," July 24, 1934; and memorandum, Frederick Ackerman to Langdon Post, January 24, 1935 (New York City Housing Authority papers, La Guardia and Wagner Archives, La Guardia Community College/The City University of New York, Box 11).

23. *New York City Housing Authority, Report of the Secretary, 1935* [second annual report], p. 23 (New York City Housing Authority papers, La Guardia and Wagner Archives, La Guardia Community College/The City University of New York, Box 11).

24. Richard Pommer makes this assumption in "The Architecture of Urban Housing in the United States during the Early 1930s," p. 250. Shreve was a principal in Shreve, Lamb and Harmon, the firm that designed the Empire State Building (1929–1931). Rather than selecting one of the architects on the approved list, the Authority chose instead to appoint Shreve and a team of architects including Matthew Del Gaudio, Arthur Holden, James F. Bly, and several associates. Plunz, *A History of Housing in New York City,* p. 216; Marcuse, "The Beginnings of Public Housing in New York," pp. 365–366.

25. In 1933 Lescaze worked on a case study of housing in the Astoria section of Queens with Carol Aronovici, Henry Wright, Henry Churchill, and Albert Mayer. The research was sponsored

by the Housing Study Guild, an organization founded that year by Wright, Mayer, and Lewis Mumford. Pommer, "The Architecture of Urban Housing in the United States during the Early 1930s," p. 253; "Realistic Replanning," *Architectural Forum* 61 (July 1934), pp. 49–55. Carol Aronovici was director of the Housing Orientation Study at Columbia University; Henry S. Churchill was a director of the Housing Study Guild.

26. Plunz, *A History of Housing in New York City,* p. 219.

27. Lescaze studied at the Eidgenössische Hochschule (ETH) in Zurich from 1915 to 1919. It is not known when he first met Le Corbusier, but his widow suggests that it was on one of his annual visits to Europe after he had immigrated to America in 1920. Lorraine Welling Lanmon, *William Lescaze, Architect* (Philadelphia: Art Alliance Press, 1987), pp. 28, 44n52. In 1927 Lescaze visited Le Corbusier in Paris, at which time he "mentioned to Le Corbusier that the only thing people wanted me for was interiors, and he replied: 'That's the way it always is. I didn't do anything else myself for years, besides writing articles and giving lectures. Keep it up.'" William Lescaze, *On Being an Architect* (New York: Putnam's Sons, 1942), p. 134; see also Robert A. M. Stern, "PSFS: Beaux-Arts Theory and Rational Expressionism," *JSAH* 21 (May 1962), pp. 90–91n35.

28. Lescaze was born in Geneva where his father was professor of languages at the College de Genève. At the ETH in 1915 Karl Moser taught a course in the principles of modern architecture, which Lescaze believed to be "the first . . . given in any school." So great was Moser's influence on Lescaze that he considered him the most important person in his professional life. Robert M. Coates, "Profiles [William Lescaze]," p. 29. See also Lanmon, *William Lescaze, Architect,* p. 16. In January 1927 Moser served on the jury for the League of Nations competition and supported Le Corbusier's cause. The next year he became a founding member of CIAM. R.Q. [Richard Quincerot], "Palais des Nations," in *Encyclopédie,* pp. 285–287. On Moser's contributions to the atelier, see Tim Benton, "Introduction, Le Corbusier l'atelier 35 rue de Sèvres," *Bulletin d'Informations architecturales,* supplement to no. 114 (Summer 1987); Marc Bédarida, "Rue de Sèvres, 35—L'envers du décor," in *Encyclopédie,* p. 357.

29. Lescaze may have seen Le Corbusier's Esprit Nouveau pavilion when he visited the 1925 Paris fair. On Lescaze's interest in the literature of art and architecture, see *On Being an Architect,* chapter 9, "Architectural Food for Mind and Taste," pp. 166–171. On Lescaze's work, see Robert M. Coates, "Profiles," *New Yorker* 12 (December 12, 1936), pp. 28–34; Gilles Barbey, "William Lescaze (1896–1969), sa carrière et son oeuvre de 1915 à 1939," *Werk* 58 (August 1971), pp. 559–563; Robert A. M. Stern, *George Howe* (New Haven: Yale University Press, 1975); Christian Hubert and Lindsay Stamm Shapiro, *William Lescaze,* Institute for Architecture and Urban Studies catalogue 16 (New York: Rizzoli, 1982); Lanmon, *William Lescaze, Architect.*

30. Letter, William Lescaze to William Jordy, January 25, 1962, quoted in Lanmon, *William Lescaze, Architect,* pp. 48, 61n4.

31. Curtis Patterson, review of Dorothy Todd and Raymond Mortimer, *New Interior Decoration,* in *International Studio* 94 (September 1929), p. 73. See also Pommer, "The Architecture of Urban Housing in the United States during the Early 1930s," p. 251.

32. These are well documented for PSFS (1929–1932); the Oak Lane Country School near Philadelphia (1929); the Hessian Hills School (1931–1932); the William Stix Wasserman House project, Whitemarsh, PA (1929–1930); the Frederick Vanderbilt Field House in New Hartford, CT (1931–1932); designs for the Museum of Modern Art project, New York (1929–1931) (with Albert Frey), and other work of this period. Henry-Russell Hitchcock, Jr., singled out the Oak Lane Country Day School as "a complete break with American traditions," in "Howe & Lescaze," *Modern Architecture: International Exhibition* (New York: Museum of Modern Art, 1932), p. 144. See also his *Modern Architecture: Romanticism and Reintegration* (New York: Payson and Clarke, 1929), p. 205, fig. 54. For a bibliography on these buildings, see Lanmon, *William Lescaze, Architect,* pp. 186–192. On the museum project, see "Plans for a Contemporary Museum, New York City," *Record* 80 (July 1936), pp. 43–50.

33. Lescaze's affinity for European modernism reached its early maturity in the late 1920s with the Capital Bus Terminal in New York (1927) and a series of New York interiors, both residential and commercial, as well as several projects for apartment houses and a country house. On Lescaze's early career and writings, see Lanmon, *William Lescaze, Architect,* pp. 23–47, 203.

34. Hitchcock, *Modern Architecture: International Exhibition,* p. 145.

35. However, Lescaze was not an American delegate to the first CIAM meeting in La Sarraz, Switzerland (1928), as has been suggested. See "Liste des participants," *Congrès préparatoire international d'architecture moderne au Château de la Sarraz les 26, 27 et 28 Juin 1928* (FLC).

36. Richard Pommer credited Frey. In a letter to Pommer, Frey indicated that he had executed most of the design, with Lescaze responsible for the program. Pommer, "The Architecture of Urban Housing in the United States during the Early 1930s," p. 251n39.

37. *VR,* pp. 156–173.

38. Lescaze and Frey may have responded to Le Corbusier's directive in *Urbanisme,* which juxtaposed images of a slum area in Chicago with his *à redents* model, p. 221. On design development, see also Lanmon, *William Lescaze, Architect,* p. 85.

39. On the financial structure of Chrystie-Forsyth, see Jackson, *A Place Called Home,* pp. 188–189, 193–195; Plunz, *A History of Housing in New York City,* pp. 208–209.

40. Hitchcock, *Modern Architecture: International Exhibition,* pp. 145–146, 154, 155. "Proposed Housing Development for Chrystie-Forsyth Sts. New York," *Shelter* 2 (April 1932), pp. 21–23; "Proposed Chrystie-Forsyth Housing Development for New York City," *Record* 71 (March 1932), pp. 194–195; "Proposed Housing Development, Chrystie and Forsyth Streets, New York," *Architectural Forum* 56 (March 1932), pp. 256–267.

41. Pommer, "The Architecture of Urban Housing in the United States during the Early 1930s," p. 252. Lanmon, *William Lescaze, Architect,* p. 85; Shapiro, *William Lescaze,* p. 75; Joseph Rosa, *Albert Frey, Architect* (New York: Rizzoli, 1930), p. 31.

42. *OC 1910–1929,* p. 117. That view appears in Le Corbusier's first article in an American journal, "Architecture, the Expression of the Materials and Methods of Our Times," *Record* 66 (August 1929), p. 125; Le Corbusier, "A Noted Architect Dissects Our Cities," *New York Times Magazine,* January 3, 1932, 5, p. 11. Reprinted as "We Are Entering upon a New Era," *T-Square* 2 (February 1932), p. 15. A similar aerial view of the Plan Voisin appears in *Urbanisme,* p. 274, and *City of Tomorrow,* p. 289.

43. Frey's concept was changed in the aerial view. Pommer, "The Architecture of Urban Housing in the United States during the Early 1930s," pp. 252–253n41.

44. Lanmon, *William Lescaze, Architect,* p. 85.

45. Pommer, "The Architecture of Urban Housing in the United States during the Early 1930s," p. 253.

46. Lewis Mumford contrasted the advantages of Sunnyside and Radburn with speculative housing and "fast-depreciating gridiron development" in his article "The Planned Community," *Architectural Forum* 58 (April 1933), pp. 263, 264.

47. Frederick Gutheim and John McAndrew endorsed the rotation as "a nice calculation of the direction of summer and winter sunlight and wind." See their "American Housing," in *Art in Our Time* (New York: Museum of Modern Art, 1939), p. 315.

48. Lewis Mumford, "The Sky Line," *New Yorker* 14 (February 26, 1938), p. 36.

49. Ackerman later published his critique of the *Zeilenbau* in his report with W. F. R. Ballard, *A Note on Site and Unit Planning* (New York: New York City Housing Authority, 1937). See also Plunz, *A History of Housing in New York City,* p. 221.

50. Mumford, "The Sky Line," p. 36.

51. Talbot Faulkner Hamlin, "New York Housing: Harlem River Homes and Williamsburg Houses," *Pencil Points* 19 (May 1938), p. 286. See also *Williamsburg Houses, a Case History of Housing* (Washington, D.C.: Federal Emergency Administration of Public Works, 1937); "Program of the Williamsburg Project, December 24, 1934" (New York City Housing Authority papers, La Guardia and Wagner Archives, La Guardia Community College/The City University of New York, Central W-399 and W-395-1). See also Pommer, "The Architecture of Urban Housing in

the United States during the Early 1930s," p. 255; Marcuse, "The Beginnings of Public Housing in New York," pp. 365–375; Plunz, *A History of Housing in New York City,* pp. 214–224.

52. Pommer, "The Architecture of Urban Housing in the United States during the Early 1930s," pp. 251, 255.

53. On Harlem River Houses, see Hamlin, "New York Housing: Harlem River Homes and Williamsburg Houses," pp. 281–292; James Sanders and Roy Strickland, "Harlem River Houses," *Harvard Architecture Review* 2 (Spring 1981), pp. 48–59; Plunz, *A History of Housing in New York City,* pp. 214–216; Marcuse, "The Beginnings of Public Housing in New York," pp. 369–375.

54. Agenda, December 9, 1935 (FLC).

55. Berle helped to draft the Bankruptcy Act of 1933. He served in the capacity of City Chamberlain from 1934 to 1937. Throughout his years in government service he maintained a law practice in New York City and a partnership in Berle & Berle since 1933. From 1927 to 1964 he was professor of corporation law at Columbia Law School. On Berle, see "Adolf A. Berle, 1895–1971, Biographical Sketch," and Biographical Information (General Correspondence, 1928–1940, Box 7, Adolf A. Berle papers, Franklin D. Roosevelt Library, Hyde Park, NY). Albin Krebs, "Adolf A. Berle Jr. Dies at Age of 76," obituary, *New York Times,* February 19, 1971, pp. 1, 40; Jordan A. Schwarz, *Liberal: Adolf A. Berle and the Vision of an American Era* (New York: Free Press, 1987).

56. *Cathédrales,* p. 262. Le Corbusier's depiction of Berle does not appear in the English and American editions.

57. Le Corbusier, "Liste des personnalités connues par M. Le Corbusier en Amérique" (FLC).

58. *Cathédrales,* pp. 262–266; *Cathedrals,* pp. 178–181. The American edition omits this passage from *Cathédrales* (p. 266): "M. Berlee a voulu m'envoyer à Washington parler à M. Roosevelt. Or la période électorale commençait en U.S.A. Une année de luttes formidables s'ouvre et l'incertitude est au bout de la partie. Il n'était pas séant d'aller déranger M. Roosevelt en un temps si agité. Le plan de rééquipement de la société machiniste réclame un examen minutieux, des méditations, des conclusions—si révolutionnaires soient-elles." Berle's appointment book gives no indication of the Harrison dinner or his discussions with Le Corbusier (Adolf A. Berle papers, Box 78, Franklin D. Roosevelt Library, Hyde Park, NY).

59. Tugwell studied economics and constitutional law, receiving his master's degree in 1915 from the University of Pennsylvania. In 1922 he completed the requirements for his Ph.D. from Columbia University. Bernard Sternsher, *Rexford Tugwell and the New Deal* (New Brunswick, NJ: Rutgers University Press, 1964), pp. 5–7.

60. The Resettlement Administration was an agency of the Department of Agriculture. Executive Order 7027, May 1, 1935, and Executive Order 7041, May 15, 1935, cited in Samuel I.

Rosenman, ed., *The Public Papers and Addresses of Franklin D. Roosevelt* (New York: Random House, 1938–1950), vol. 4, pp. 144–155, 180.

61. Lansill and Tugwell had been friends since the time they attended the Wharton School of Finance at the University of Pennsylvania. In 1933 Tugwell offered Lansill the job of directing the Land Utilization Division of the Federal Emergency Relief Agency, a position he held when they visited the Beltsville site together. See Joseph L. Arnold, *The New Deal in the Suburbs* (Columbus: Ohio State University Press, 1971), pp. 29–30, 36–37.

62. David Myhra, "Rexford Guy Tugwell: Initiator of America's Greenbelt New Towns, 1935 to 1936," *American Institute of Planners Journal* 40 (May 1974), p. 183. John Lansill, interview with David Myhra, 1972; David Myhra, interview with author, December 14, 1991. Grace (Mrs. Rexford G.) Tugwell, interview with author, August 26, 1992.

63. Joel Garreau, *Edge City: Life on the New Frontier* (New York: Doubleday, 1991).

64. Tugwell recorded that on May 17, 1935, he and Lansill "went to Rockefeller Center to see Frank Lloyd Wright's exhibition of his model city called 'Broadacres.' We found it very interesting." Rexford Guy Tugwell diary, May 19, 1935 (Rexford Guy Tugwell papers, Franklin D. Roosevelt Library, Hyde Park, NY). See also Arnold, *The New Deal in the Suburbs,* pp. 85–86. Lansill later corresponded extensively with Frank Lloyd Wright.

65. H. L. Mencken regarded Tugwell as a "kept idealist of the *New Republic,*" quoted in Richard Hofstadter, *Anti-intellectualism in American Life* (New York: Alfred A. Knopf, 1964), p. 264.

66. J. S. Lansill, "Suburban Resettlement Division" in *Interim Report of the Resettlement Administration* (Washington, D.C.: U.S. Resettlement Administration, April 1936), p. 17. Rexford G. Tugwell, "No More Frontiers," *Today* 4, part 1 (June 22, 1935), pp. 3–4, 21; part 2 (June 29, 1935), pp. 8–9, 22–23; Myhra, "Rexford Guy Tugwell," p. 179. See also "Summary Description of the Greenbelt Project," prepared by R. J. Wadsworth, February 1938, and "Summary Chronological History of Greenbelt Project, Greenbelt, Maryland," prepared by Wallace Richards, February 1938 (John Scott Lansill papers, University of Kentucky); Arnold, *The New Deal in the Suburbs,* pp. 36–37.

67. Rexford G. Tugwell, "The Meaning of the Greenbelt Towns," *New Republic* 90 (February 17, 1937), pp. 42–43.

68. FDR had long supported a "back to the land" movement in place of urban rehabilitation. Franklin D. Roosevelt, "Back to the Land," *Review of Reviews* (October 1931); Gertrude Almy Slichter, "Franklin D. Roosevelt's Farm Policy as Governor of New York State, 1928–1932," *Agricultural History* 33 (October 1959), pp. 167–176; Myhra, "Rexford Guy Tugwell," pp. 178ff. By March 1935, when Tugwell first conceptualized the new Resettlement Administration and assumed his responsibilities as head of the agency, he took a quasi-decentralist position because of the economic implications of federally financed housing in the inner city. With Secretary of the Interior Harold Ickes in charge of the Housing Division of the Public Works Administration, Tugwell felt that it was not logical for the Department of Agriculture to take on that task. Tugwell's diary records an early meeting with Roosevelt in which the president "let me off city housing, though he laughed at me for not wanting to do it. I talked to him about satellite cities as an alternative and interested him greatly. My idea is to go just outside centers of population, pick up cheap land, build a whole community and entice people into it. Then go back into cities and tear down slums and make parks of them. I could do this with good heart and he [FDR] now wants me to." Unresolved in this scheme was the issue of government compensation for urban land values. Rexford Guy Tugwell diary, March 3, 1935 (Rexford Guy Tugwell Papers, Franklin D. Roosevelt Library, Hyde Park, NY). After the collapse of the Greenbelt Town program in 1936 and an interlude in the private sector, Tugwell went on to head the New York City Planning Commission and direct inner-city public housing programs. He headed the Planning Commission between 1938 and 1941, but his efforts to implement a master plan were ultimately defeated by Robert Moses. See Rexford G. Tugwell, "Planning in New York City," *Planners Journal* 6 (April–June 1940), pp. 33–34; Mark I. Gelfand, "Rexford G. Tugwell and the Frustration of Planning in New York City," *Journal of the American Planning Association* 51 (Spring 1985), pp. 151–160.

69. *Cathédrales,* p. 268; Fowler is identified in the American edition as "the assistant police commissioner of New York," *Cathedrals,* p. 182. Also present at the lunch was A. Stuyvesant, whom Le Corbusier described as a "Real State [sic] ami harrison," Agenda, December 13 [1935] (FLC).

70. "Col. Fowler Dies, Ex-Police Aid, 70," obituary, *New York Times,* January 18, 1957, p. 21; "Aerial Study Made of Traffic Snarls," *New York Times,* June 24, 1935, p. 19; "Traffic Study in Blimp," *New York Times,* June 7, 1935, 1, p. 2.

71. VPR restaurant menu, "CB [*Cathédrales Blanches*] Conversation avec Déjeuner avec le Sous Prefect de Police N York 13 dec 1935" (FLC).

72. *Cathedrals,* pp. 182–186.

73. Robert Allan Jacobs, interviews with author, Pawling, NY, November 21, 1984, and June 7, 1987 (hereafter cited as Jacobs interview/s).

74. Among other government posts, he had served as treasurer of Franklin D. Roosevelt's election campaigns for governor. Albin Krebs, "Howard S. Cullman, 80, of Port Authority, Dies," obituary, *New York Times,* June 30, 1972, p. 38.

75. Le Corbusier, "Liste des personnalités connues par M. Le Corbusier en Amérique" (FLC).

76. *Cathedrals,* pp. 74–76.

77. Jacobs interview, November 21, 1984.

78. Letter, Le Corbusier to Robert Jacobs, November 28, 1936 (FLC).

79. *Cathedrals,* pp. 181, 186.

80. Ford, *Slums and Housing,* vol. 1, p. 80.

81. Encouraged by such philanthropic reformers as Jacob Riis and Elgin R. L. Gould, president of the City and Suburban Homes Company, the demolition of tenements and other buildings considered slums gave way to either parks or model housing projects. For example, to build its 373-unit model tenements, the Alfred Corning Clark Building (1896–1898), City and Suburban Homes demolished buildings on nineteen lots on West 68th and 69th streets between Amsterdam and West End avenues. Jackson, *A Place Called Home,* pp. 105–106; Ford, *Slums and Housing,* vol. 1, p. 198. *First Annual Report of the City and Suburban Homes Company* (New York, 1897); Bacon, *Ernest Flagg: Beaux-Arts Architect and Urban Reformer,* pp. 247–250.

82. The recommendations of the influential Tenement House Commission of 1894 called for "destruction of unsanitary buildings," replaced by new tenement houses, later endorsed by the Tenement House Act of 1901. Ford, *Slums and Housing,* vol. 1, pp. 193–197. On demolitions, see Real Estate Board of New York, *Apartment Building Construction, Manhattan, 1902–1953,* pp. 18–19, cited in Jackson, *A Place Called Home,* pp. 180, 330n39.

83. Werner Hegemann, *City Planning: Housing* (New York: Architectural Book Publishing Co., 1938), vol. 3, pp. 24–25; *City Planning: Housing* (New York: Architectural Publishing Co., 1936), vol. 1, 104–127, 131–140.

84. Post, *The Challenge of Housing,* p. 31; see James Ford's chapters, "Demolition: Existing Practices in New York City" and "Land Acquisition, Appraisal, and Condemnation," in *Slums and Housing,* vol. 2, pp. 511–540.

85. Post, *The Challenge of Housing,* pp. 28, 228–235; see also Jackson, *A Place Called Home,* p. 212.

86. Jane Jacobs, *The Death and Life of Great American Cities* (New York: Random House, 1961), pp. 21–25.

87. Ford, *Slums and Housing,* vol. 2, p. 922.

88. On the development of the perimeter block plan for tenements and garden apartments, and on the Amalgamated Dwellings, see Ford, *Slums and Housing,* vol. 2, p. 894, pl. 19A; Plunz, *A History of Housing in New York City,* pp. 124, 125, 127–128, 133, 135–137, 141–143, 164–169.

89. On Hillside Homes, see Henry Saylor, "Hillside Homes," *American Architect* 148 (February 1936), pp. 17–33; Pommer, "The Architecture of Urban Housing in the United States during the Early 1930s," pp. 236, 250n37, fig. 1; Plunz *A History of Housing in New York City,* pp. 212–213, 359n17; Mumford, "The Planned Community," p. 274.

90. S.[igfried] Giedion, "Vers un renouveau architectural de l'Amérique," *Cahiers d'Art* 8 (1933), p. 240.

91. On Le Corbusier's indebtedness to the Hénard model, see *Vers une architecture,* p. 46; Stanislaus von Moos, *Le Corbusier, Elements of a Synthesis* (Cambridge: MIT Press, 1979), pp. 150–151, 189, 225. Hénard's use of a *boulevard à redans* (boulevard with setback buildings), as Norma Evenson showed, sought to vary the monotony of Haussmann's Parisian blocks through indented facades creating U-shaped courtyards. Evenson, *Paris: A Century of Change, 1878–1978* (New Haven: Yale University Press, 1979), pp. 29, 31, fig. 15. On the *à redans* model, see Eugène Hénard, *Etudes sur les transformations de Paris,* reprint with introduction by Jean-Louis Cohen (Paris: Editions L'Equerre, 1982), pp. 45–46, pls. 5, 6; P. M. Wolf, *Eugène Hénard and the Beginning of Urbanism in Paris: 1900–1914* (Paris: Centre de recherche d'urbanisme, 1969). On the use of the meander plan by such German housing specialists as Paul Mebes, see Barbara Miller Lane, "Changing Attitudes to Monumentality and Urban Form 1880–1914," in *Growth and Transformation of the Modern City* (Stockholm: University of Stockholm and Swedish Council for Building Research, 1979, pp. 101–114; Alfons Leitl, "Bauten von Mebes und Emmerich," *Monatshefte für Baukunst und Städtebau* 22 (1938), pp. 177–184; "Dreissig Jahre neuer Wohnbau dargelegt an Bauten von Mebes und Emmerich," *Monatshefte für Baukunst und Städtebau* 22 (1938), pp. 233–240. For Mebes's influence on Le Corbusier, see Charles-Edouard Jeanneret, *Etude sur le mouvement d'art décoratif en Allemagne* (La Chaux-de-Fonds: Haefeli, 1912), p. 9.

92. On CIAM III, see Martin Steinmann, ed., *CIAM: Internationale Kongresse für Neues Bauen. Congrès Internationaux d'Architecture Moderne* (Basel and Stuttgart: Birkhäuser Verlag, 1979), pp. 74–109. Projects by Marcel Breuer, Walter Gropius, and Ludwig Hilberseimer as well as other *Zeilenbau* projects appeared in Lewis Mumford's housing section of the 1932 exhibition. See *Modern Architecture: International Exhibition,* pp. 179ff.

93. For Stonorov and Kastner's model of 1931–1932 for the Mackley Houses, see Pommer, "The Architecture of Urban Housing in the United States during the Early 1930s," p. 240, fig. 4. Stonorov served as editor (with Willy Boesiger) for a German edition of the first volume of Le Corbusier's collected works, *Le Corbusier und Pierre Jeanneret, ihr gesamtes Werk von 1910–1929* (Zurich: Girsberger, 1930). Stonorov was born in Frankfurt, Germany, studied at the ETH in Zurich (1925–1928; he claimed under Karl Moser), and emigrated to the United States in 1929. He was in partnership with Kastner from 1932 to 1936. On the Mackley Houses, see "The Carl Mackley Houses in Philadelphia," *Record* 78 (November 1935), pp. 289–298; Albert Mayer, "A Critique of the Hosiery Workers' Housing Development in Philadelphia," *Architecture* 71 (April 1935), pp. 189–194.

94. On the impact of the 1929 Multiple Dwellings Law on New York City housing, see Plunz, *A History of Housing in New York City,* pp. 194–198. Diana Agrest, "A Romance with the City: The Work of Irwin S. Chanin," in Diana Agrest, ed., *A Romance with the City: Irwin S. Chanin* (New York: Cooper Union Press, 1982), pp. 13–14, 76–85; Robert A. M. Stern, Gregory Gilmartin, and

Thomas Mellins, *New York 1930: Architecture and Urbanism between the World Wars* (New York: Rizzoli, 1987), pp. 403–416.

95. On St. Mark's, see "What Architects Are Talking About," *American Architect* 136 (December 1929), pp. 53–54; "St. Mark's Tower," *Record* 67 (January 1930), pp. 1–4.

96. Francesco Passanti, "Des gratte-ciel pour la 'Ville contemporaine,'" *L'Esprit nouveau: Le Corbusier et l'industrie 1920–1925* (Zurich: Ernst & Sohn, 1987), pp. 58–59; Passanti, "The Skyscrapers of the Ville Contemporaine," *Assemblage* 4 (October 1987), pp. 56–60.

97. Le Corbusier-Saugnier, "Trois Rappels à MM. les architectes," *EN* 4 (January 1921), pp. 465–466.

98. Each sixty-story tower was nearly as high (220 meters) and still located alongside parks, playing fields and roadways. See *Vers une architecture,* pp. 42–43; *Towards a New Architecture,* p. 54.

99. In French, Proposition de Lotissement carries two meanings: subdivision proposal (also development proposal) and proposal for a housing development. *Vers une architecture,* p. 42; *Towards a New Architecture,* p. 56.

100. Francisco Mujica, *The History of the Skyscraper* (Paris: Archaeology and Architecture Press, 1929), pp. 52, 54, pl. 20.

101. French and German housing reformers of the 1860s and 1870s popularized the cross plan based on a typology that Emile Muller employed in Mulhouse. See Nicholas Bullock and James Read, *The Movement for Housing Reform in Germany and France 1840–1914* (Cambridge: Cambridge University Press, 1985), pp. 110, 116–117, 148.

102. For example, in 1918 James B. Ford, then on the staff of the U.S. Department of Labor, employed the cross plan on a large scale (about forty rooms per floor) for his World War I urban housing study, which he published in his *Slums and Housing,* vol. 2, p. 890, pl. 14.

103. Henry Wright, "The Place of the Apartment in the Modern Community," *Record* 67 (March 1930), pp. 211–212. Hegemann, *City Planning Housing,* vol. 3, p. 153. *Alden Park Manor, Philadelphia* and *The Kenilworth at Alden Park, Philadelphia* (promotional brochures, c. 1926–1927). George E. Thomas, "Alden Park Manor," National Register of Historic Places Inventory Nomination Form, 1980. I wish to thank Dr. Thomas for sharing with me his knowledge of Alden Park. William Ballard, chief architect of the Queensbridge Housing project, would have been familiar with the project because he worked in the office of Henry Wright during the early 1930s when Wright published it. William F. R. Ballard, interview with author, London, October 26, 1987. Eric Mumford identified other cruciform-plan apartment buildings in America and reached similar conclusions about Le Corbusier's role in the development of the high-rise tower. See "The 'Tower in a Park' in America: Theory and Practice, 1920–1960," *Planning Perspectives* 10 (1995), pp. 17–41.

104. American models employing towers and advanced construction techniques included hotels, notably the Marlborough-Blenheim (1905–1906) and Traymore (1906 and 1914–1915), both in Atlantic City, NJ, by Price and McLanahan, as well as urban skyscraper apartment houses. See George E. Thomas, *William L. Price: Arts and Crafts to Modern Design* (New York: Princeton Architectural Press, 2000). Such German precedents as Hans Poelzig's project for a Y-shaped skyscraper in the Friedrichstrasse, Berlin (1921; see figure 5.30), which had been widely reported in American architectural journals, may also have been influential. See Dr. Ing. Walter Curt Behrendt, "Skyscrapers in Germany," *Journal of the American Institute of Architects* 11 (September 1923), p. 366; Hans Poelzig, "On Hans Poelzig," *American Architect* 128 (September 23, 1925), p. 258.

105. The high-rise versus low-rise debate in 1934 centered on the projected renewal site of Corlears Hook on the Lower East Side. "Higher Housing for Lower Rents," *Architectural Forum* 61 (December 1934), p. 421, quoted in Plunz, *A History of Housing in New York City,* pp. 224–225.

106. Unit plan HD–35, *Unit Plans,* Housing Division, U.S. Federal Emergency Administration of Public Works (Washington, DC: GPO, 1935).

107. Henry Wright, *Rehousing Urban America* (New York: Columbia University Press, 1935), pp. 72, 116–117.

108. Perret's Maison-Tour appeared in the journal *Science et Vie* (December 1, 1925). Le Corbusier published a plan and elevation of the project in *Almanach,* pp. 97, 187.

109. "Sunlight Towers," *Record* 65 (March 1929), pp. 307–310. Hitchcock admired Kocher and Ziegler's Sunlight Towers and used a drawing of it to illustrate the dust jacket of his early synthetic study, *Modern Architecture: Romanticism and Reintegration.* Kocher and Ziegler designed a second version of Sunlight Towers, a high-rise tower set in the hills of Westchester County that was probably inspired as much by suburban commercial development as by Le Corbusier's skyscraper projects of the 1920s. See "Sunlight Towers," *Record* 67 (March 1930), pp. 286–288.

110. Raymond Hood, "A City under a Single Roof," *Nation's Business* 17 (November 1929), pp. 18–20, 206–208); W. K. Harrison and C. E. Dobbin, *School Buildings of Today and Tomorrow* (New York: Architectural Book Publishing Co., 1931), p. 2.

111. "Higher Housing for Lower Rents," pp. 421–434.

112. Professor Walter Gropius, "Low Buildings, Medium-High or High Buildings?," Le Corbusier, "The Sub-division of Land in Cities," in Housing Study Guild, ed., *Abstract of Papers at the 3rd International Congress at Brussels of the International Committee for the Solution of the Problems in Modern Architecture,* trans. Werner Gottschalk (New York, 1935), pp. 3–11. Mumford, "The 'Tower in a Park' in America: Theory and Practice, 1920–1960," pp. 24–25.

113. *VR* and *RC,* pp. 38–39.

114. Terence Riley chronicles the history of the use of the terms "International Style" and "the Style" in his *The International Style: Exhibition 15 and the Museum of Modern Art* (New York: Rizzoli, 1992), pp. 14–15n13, 89–93.

115. Henry-Russell Hitchcock, Jr., "Frank Lloyd Wright," and "J. J. P. Oud," in *Modern Architecture: International Exhibition*, pp. 29–55, 91–109.

116. On the Dymaxion House (1927), see Martin Pawley, *Buckminster Fuller* (London: Trefoil, 1990), pp. 39–56.

117. Mumford demurred in his role as curator, giving credit to Hitchcock and Johnson.

118. Riley, *The International Style: Exhibition 15 and the Museum of Modern Art*, pp. 70–71.

119. But Hitchcock's suggestion that Oud's vision was "intellectually clear rather than emotionally stirred" offered a refined comparison with Le Corbusier. See his "J. J. P. Oud," in *Modern Architecture: International Exhibition*, p. 97.

120. See Marc Dessauce, "Contro lo Stile Internazionale: 'Shelter' e la stampa architettonica americana," *Casabella* 62 (September 1993), pp. 46–53, 70–71.

121. Alfred Fellheimer, "Planning American Standards for Low-Rent Housing," *American Architect* 146 (February 1935), p. 18, quoted in Ford, *Slums and Housing*, vol. 2, p. 898; see also Hackett, "Foreword," *Unit Plans.*

122. Ackerman and Ballard, *A Note on Site and Unit Planning*; Federal Emergency Administration of Public Works, *Urban Housing: The Story of the PWA Housing Division 1933–36* (Washington, DC: GPO, 1936), pp. 6ff. See also Plunz, *A History of Housing in New York City*, pp. 223–224.

123. The program also mandated that the PWA approve the selection of architects. Ford, *Slums and Housing*, vol. 2, p. 921.

124. The list included many New York firms specializing in housing: Horace Ginsbern, Ethan A. Dennison, Charles F. Fuller, Clarence Stein, Peabody, Wilson & Brown, John W. Ingle, Morris and O'Connor, Alfred E. Poor, and Electus D. Litchfield. "Names of Members and Associates of the Twenty-Two Architectural Firms Qualified by Competition for Work Under the New York City Housing Authority to Be Financed by Loans from the Public Works Administration," July 24, 1934 (New York City Housing Authority papers, La Guardia and Wagner Archives, La Guardia Community College/The City University of New York, Box 12).

125. Lescaze recorded that A. Conger Goodyear, chairman of the Modern's board of trustees, told him that one member of the board objected to giving him the commission because he was a foreigner. Lescaze, "Things which have hurt, should be filed away and forgotten," October 31, 1930, cited in Lanmon, *William Lescaze, Architect*, pp. 82, 96n101.

126. "City Selects Fifty as Its Architects on Large Projects," *New York Times*, December 23, 1935, p. 1. For criticism of methods used in the selection process favoring "insiders," especially those who had already received lucrative government commissions, see H. I. Feldman, "Architects for City Work," letter to the editor, *New York Times*, December 27, 1935, p. 18.

127. For some of their projects, see "New York of the Future," special issue of *Creative Art* 9 (August 1931), pp. 96–171; Thomas Adams, *The Regional Plan of New York and Its Environs*, vol. 2, *The Building of the City* (New York: Regional Plan of New York and Its Environs, 1931), pp. 189, 307, 314, 413.

128. Wright, "The Place of the Apartment in the Modern Community," p. 237.

129. Walter H. Kilham, Jr., *Raymond Hood, Architect* (New York: Architectural Publishing Co., 1973), pp. 13–14; Walter Kilham, interview with author, Cambridge, MA, January 16, 1992.

130. On Hood's project of 1929, see "A City under a Single Roof," pp. 18–20, 206–208; Rem Koolhaas, *Delirious New York* (New York: Oxford University Press, 1978), pp. 146–147; Manfredo Tafuri, "The Disenchanted Mountain: The Skyscraper and the City," in Giorgio Ciucci et al., eds., *The American City* (Cambridge: MIT Press, 1979), pp. 439–440; Robert Stern, *Raymond Hood* (New York: Institute for Architecture and Urban Studies and Rizzoli, 1982), p. 112.

In 1924 Hood proposed his project for a "City of Needles" that Hugh Ferriss illustrated. See Orrick Johns, "Architects Dream of a Pinnacle City," *New York Times Magazine*, December 28, 1924, p. 10; reprinted in *The American City* 39 (January 1926), p. 9; Carol Willis, "Drawing towards Metropolis," in Hugh Ferriss, *The Metropolis of Tomorrow* (Princeton, NJ: Princeton Architectural Press, 1986; orig. pub. Ives Washburn, 1929), pp. 162, 163, fig. 26; Carol Willis, "Zoning and *Zeitgeist*: The Skyscraper City in the 1920s," *JSAH* 45 (March 1986), pp. 57–58, fig. 10; Willis, "Towering Cities," review of Stern, *Raymond Hood* in *Skyline*, July 1982, pp. 10–11. In 1926 Hood published another visionary scheme, "forest of towers, each 500 feet apart." See Raymond M. Hood, "New York's Skyline Will Climb Much Higher," *Liberty* (April 10, 1926), p. 19, 21, 23. In 1927 Hood published "A City of Towers," intended to reduce traffic congestion. See Howard Robertson, "A City of Towers," *American Architect and Building News* 9 (October 21, 1927), pp. 639–643; Koolhaas, *Delirious New York*, pp. 137–138; on the model, see Kilham, *Raymond Hood*, pp. 90–91; see also "Tower Buildings and Wider Streets: A Suggested Relief for Traffic Congestion," *American Architect* 132 (July 5, 1927), pp. 67–68.

Hood's project of 1929, "Manhattan 1950" (aerial view showing cluster of skyscrapers), is illustrated in *Raymond M. Hood* (New York: McGraw-Hill, 1931), title page; "Three Visions of New York: Raymond Hood," *Creative Art* 9 (August 1931), p. 161; Koolhaas, *Delirious New York*, p. 147. For "Manhattan 1950" (proposed Manhattan bridge lined with apartment houses), see *Raymond M. Hood*, p. 87; *Architecture* 61 (May 1930), p. 276; "Three Visions of New York: Raymond Hood," p. 161; "Hood," *Architectural Forum* 62 (February 1935), p. 130; "A Manifesto of Manhattanism," *Progressive Architecture* 59 (December 1978), pp. 70–74; Tafuri, "The Disenchanted Mountain," in *The American City*, pp. 458, 460; Stern, *Raymond Hood*, p. 114. For "Manhattan 1950" (proposed bridges adjacent to business centers, December 26, 1929), see "Three Visions of New York: Raymond Hood," p. 160; *Raymond M. Hood*, p. 86; Koolhaas, *Delirious New York*, p. 148; Tafuri, "The Disenchanted Mountain," in *The American City*, pp. 458, 459.

131. Thomas S. Hines, *Richard Neutra and the Search for Modern Architecture* (New York: Oxford University Press, 1982), pp. 60–67. See also *Modern Architecture: International Exhibition*, pp. 159, 165; W[illy] Boesiger, ed., *Richard Neutra: Buildings and Projects* (Zurich: Girsberger, 1951), pp. 195–201.

132. Wright, "The Place of the Apartment in the Modern Community," p. 237.

133. Lawrence Veiller, "A Recent Proposal—Modernism Rampant," *Housing* 21 (March 1932), p. 13.

134. Post, *The Challenge of Housing*, p. 293.

135. Lewis Mumford, "Architecture as a Home for Man," *Architectural Record* 143 (February 1968), p. 114.

136. Charles C. Alexander, *Nationalism in American Thought, 1930–1945* (Chicago: Rand McNally, 1969), pp. 1–24, 60–84.

7 The Private Sector

1. In 1924 sugar manufacturer Henry Frugès commissioned Le Corbusier to design the Quartiers Modernes Frugès, a series of workers' houses at Pessac near Bordeaux. B. B. T. [Brian Brace Taylor], "Frugès (Henry)," in *Encyclopédie*, p. 161; Brian Brace Taylor, *Le Corbusier at Pessac* (Cambridge: MIT Press, 1972); B. B. Taylor, *Le Corbusier et Pessac, 1914–1928* (Paris: Fondation Le Corbusier, 1972); B. B. T. [Brian Brace Taylor], "Pessac," in *Encyclopédie*, pp. 306–307.

Gabriel Voisin, the automobile and airplane manufacturer, gave subvention to Le Corbusier's 1925 plan for Paris that was named in honor of him. The mobile Maisons Voisin inspired Le Corbusier. P. C. [Pascal Courteault], "Voisin (Gabriel)," in *Encyclopédie*, p. 470; Le Corbusier, "Les Maisons 'Voisin,'" *EN*, no. 2 (November 1920), pp. 211–215.

Czech shoe manufacturer Thomas Bat'a commissioned Le Corbusier in January 1935 to design the Bat'a works at Zlín as a quasi-linear city. J.-L. C. [Jean-Louis Cohen], "Bat'a (Tomás)," in *Encyclopédie*, pp. 62–67.

2. *Almanach*, pp. 102–103; *OC 1910–1929*, pp. 76–77; on Le Corbusier's *appel aux industriels* and Esprit Nouveau theory, see Mary Caroline McLeod, "Urbanism and Utopia: Le Corbusier from Regional Syndicalism to Vichy" (Ph.D. diss., Princeton University, 1985), pp. 65–67; Mary McLeod, "'Architecture or Revolution': Taylorism, Technocracy, and Social Change," *Art Journal* 43 (Summer 1983), pp. 141–142; M.McL. [Mary McLeod], "Taylorisme," in *Encyclopédie*, pp. 397–400; Stanislaus von Moos,

"Standard et élite: Le Syndrome Citrohan" [Industrie], in *Encyclopédie*, pp. 190–199; Thomas P. Hughes, "Appel aux industriels," in *L'Esprit nouveau: Le Corbusier et l'industrie 1920–1925* (Zurich: Ernst & Sohn, 1987), pp. 26–31.

3. On the Redressement Français, see McLeod, "'Architecture or Revolution': Taylorism, Technocracy, and Social Change," pp. 141–143; Robert Fishman, *Urban Utopias in the Twentieth Century: Ebenezer Howard, Frank Lloyd Wright and Le Corbusier* (New York: Basic Books, 1977), p. 218; Richard F. Kuisel, *Ernest Mercier, French Technocrat* (Berkeley: University of California Press, 1967).

4. Mary McLeod, "Bibliography: *Plans*," *Oppositions* 19–20 (Winter-Spring 1980), pp. 184–201; McLeod, "Urbanism and Utopia: Le Corbusier from Regional Syndicalism to Vichy," pp. 458–497.

5. *Vers une architecture*, pp. 213–230; *Towards a New Architecture*, pp. 267–289; McLeod, "'Architecture or Revolution': Taylorism, Technocracy, and Social Change," pp. 143–144; Mary McLeod, "Le Rêve transi de Le Corbusier: L'Amérique 'catastrophe féerique'," in J.-L. Cohen and H. Damisch, eds., *Américanisme et modernité* (Paris: EHESS and Flammarion, 1993), pp. 208–227.

6. In addition to Le Corbusier's writings in *Plans, Prélude*, and *L'Homme Réel*, see especially his articles "A Noted Architect Dissects Our Cities," *New York Times Magazine*, January 3, 1932, 5, pp. 10, 11, 19, reprinted as "We Are Entering upon a New Era," *T-Square* 2 (February 1932), pp. 14–17, 41–42; "Programme—denouement de crise—enthousiasme," *Journal Générale, Travaux Publics et Bâtiment* (January 28, 1933), p. 1, reprinted in *L'Architecture d'Aujourd'hui* 3 (October 1933), pp. 65–68; "Introduction" (July 1934), *OC 1929–1934*, pp. 11–18.

7. At CIAM II Frankfurt-am-Main (1929) the congress identified the importance of "working groups." The study of the "low-cost house" and the "functional city" required both the "collective study by many architects" and their "collaboration" with nonarchitectural specialists including economists, socialists, hygienists. The Athens Charter (1933) confirmed these objectives: "it is necessary to utilize the resources put at our disposal by *modern technics* and to procure the *collaboration of specialists*." José Luis Sert, *Can Our Cities Survive?* (Cambridge: Harvard University Press, 1942), pp. 242, 249.

8. *City of Tomorrow*, p. xxvi. Le Corbusier expressed a similar polarization in *Cathedrals*, pp. 214–216.

9. Letter, Le Corbusier to Irwin Chanin, January 27, 1930; Agenda, 1928–1929, p. 45 (FLC).

10. Diana Agrest, "A Romance with the City: The Work of Irwin S. Chanin," in Diana Agrest, ed., *A Romance with the City: Irwin S. Chanin* (New York: Cooper Union Press, 1982), pp. 10–15. Niven Busch, Jr., "Profiles: Skybinder," *New Yorker* 4 (January 26, 1929), pp. 20–24; reprinted in Agrest, ed., *A Romance with the City: Irwin S. Chanin*, pp. 16–18. See also Robert A. M. Stern, Gregory Gilmartin, and Thomas Mellins, *New York 1930: Archi-*

tecture and Urbanism between the World Wars (New York: Rizzoli, 1987), pp. 203–206, 403–416, 597–599, 604, 605.

11. "Green Acres, a Residential Park Community," *Record* 80 (October 1936), p. 285; Agrest, ed., *A Romance with the City: Irwin S. Chanin,* pp. 86–89.

12. Even after his trip Le Corbusier still hoped for a commission from Chanin, whose name and address he included in a list of potential American clients for his publicist, French photographer Thérèse Bonney. Le Corbusier, [list of names for] "Th Bonney" (FLC).

13. Agenda, November 8, 1935 (FLC). Jaoul was a member of the board of directors of the Société d'Electro-Chimie d'Electro-Métallurgie et des Aciéries Electriques d'Ugine in Saint-Priest-de-Gimel (Corrèze). In his efforts to market a steel-extrusion process he visited America frequently. In 1937 Le Corbusier designed a weekend house for Jaoul that was never built; the Maisons Jaouls at Neuilly-sur-Seine were under construction at the time of Jaoul's death (in New York City), "Andre Jaoul Dead; Paris Sales Aide, 60," obituary, *New York Times,* November 13, 1954, p. 15; *OC 1938–1946,* p. 12; Le Corbusier, *Oeuvre complète 1952–1957,* ed. W. Boesiger (Zurich: Editions d'Architecture, 1957), pp. 206–219; *Le Corbusier 1910–1965,* pp. 78–79; letter, André Jaoul to Le Corbusier, July 7, 1940 (FLC). Mardges Bacon, "The American Campaign of 1935," paper for symposium VIIes Rencontres de la Fondation Le Corbusier 1996–1997, "Le Corbusier, Travels and International Influence: Le Corbusier and North America," co-sponsored by the Fondation Le Corbusier and Harvard University, October 11, 1996.

14. Peter H. Spitz, *Petrochemicals: The Rise of an Industry* (New York: John Wiley, 1988), pp. 73, 77; "George W. Davison, Bank Executive, 81," obituary, *New York Times,* June 17, 1953, p. 27; Union Carbide and Carbon Corporation, *Annual Report for 1935* and *1936 Annual Report.*

15. *Cathedrals,* p. 104.

16. On the Union Carbide meetings and Le Corbusier's intentions, see Agenda, November 13, 27, 30, December 2, 1935 (FLC). "Union Carbide Elects High Officer to Board," *New York Times,* November 25, 1949, p. 40.

17. "'Synthetic Home' Shown," *New York Times,* July 16, 1933, 10 and 11, p. 2. The prefabricated kitchen-bathroom unit was developed by the housing research division of the John B. Pierce Foundation and reported by Robert L. Davison at the 1933 National Conference on Low-Cost Housing in Cleveland. See Robert L. Davison, "General Design Considerations in Low Cost Housing," *Proceedings of the National Conference on Low Cost Housing,* October 25–27, 1933, pp. 8–19.

18. "The Vinylite House," *Record* 75 (January 1934), frontispiece, p. 36; "Vinylite" (trade catalogue, Union Carbide and Carbon Corporation, 1934); Albert Farwell Bemis, *The Evolving House: Rational Design* (Cambridge: Technology Press, MIT, 1936), vol. 3, pp. 572–573.

19. Le Corbusier had at least two meetings with Huston. Agenda, December 9 and 10, 1935 (FLC). American Cyanamid Company, *Report of the Board of Directors for the Year Ended December 31, 1935,* no. 24, unpaged.

20. "Must Outlaw War Says League Agent," *New York Times,* July 24, 1928, p. 22; "Howard Huston, U.N. Consultant," obituary, *New York Times,* June 10, 1935, p. 25; Le Corbusier, *Une maison, un palais* (Paris: G. Crès, 1928).

21. Letters, Howard R. Huston to Le Corbusier, June 22, 1927; F. Lloyd to Pierre Jeanneret, June 8, 1927; Le Corbusier and Pierre Jeanneret to F. Lloyd, June 12, 1927 (FLC). Le Corbusier, "Note p. [our] Wallace Harrison," December 6, 1935 (Wallace K. Harrison Papers, Avery Architectural and Fine Arts Library, Columbia University).

22. "Liste des personnalités connues par M. Le Corbusier—en Amérique" (FLC). Among Cyanamid by-products were "gypsum products, including plaster, partition tile, precast roofs and ceilings, and fireproofing units; plastics for moldings for . . . radio cabinets . . . adhesives for the plywood industry and for laminated sheets, tiles, and architectural specialties; preparations for wood finishings and wall coverings; ingredients for oil-cloth and linoleum industries; materials for cork manufacturers. . . ." *After Thirty Years: 1907–1937* (New York: American Cyanamid Company, 1937). See also American Cyanamid Company, *Report of the Board of Directors for the Year Ended December 31st, 1939,* no. 28, unpaged.

23. Editor Richardson Wright captioned a photograph of the visitor, "Le Corbusier, prophet of modernism in France and influential throughout the entire architectural world, arrived in America too late to attend our symposium. He has read the findings, however, and pronounces them '*Très significatifs de l'incomparable force Américaine.*'" The discussants included John Ely Burchard (Bemis Industries), Robert L. Davison (Pierce Foundation), Howard T. Fisher (General Houses), J. André Fouilhoux, Harold D. Hynds (New York builder), Robert W. McLaughlin, Jr. (American Houses Inc.), and Raymond V. Parsons (Johns-Manville). "A Symposium on Prefabrication," *House and Garden* 68 (December 1935), pp. 68, 72.

24. Letters, Henry Humphrey to Le Corbusier, October 29 and November 8, 1935 (FLC).

25. The Pierce Foundation was established in 1924 according to the will of John B. Pierce, vice president of the American Radiator and Standard Sanitary Corporation. Alfred Bruce and Harold Sandbank, *A History of Prefabrication* (New York: John B. Pierce Foundation, 1944; Arno Press reprint, 1972), pp. 11–12.

26. Robert L. Davison, "Possibilities for Housing Research," *Record* 67 (March 1930), pp. 264–266. For American Radiator re-

search on air conditioning, see "Air-Conditioning Gains," *New York Times,* April 18, 1937, 13, p. 8.

27. "Steel Houses," *Architectural Forum* 58 (April 1933), p. 331; Bruce and Sandbank, *A History of Prefabrication,* p. 12.

28. Bemis, *The Evolving House: Rational Design,* vol. 3, pp. 467–468; "Microporite House," *Record* 78 (August 1935), p. 116.

29. Agenda, October 24, November 1 and 20, December 9, 1935 (FLC).

30. "Dr. Rufus E. Zimmerman Dies at 68; Headed U.S. Steel's Research Activity," obituary, *New York Times,* June 22, 1955, p. 29.

31. *Thirty-Fourth Annual Report of the United States Steel Corporation for the Fiscal Year Ended December 31, 1935,* pp. 6, 27.

32. *Thirty-Fifth Annual Report of the United States Steel Corporation for the Fiscal Year Ended December 31, 1936,* pp. 10, 30.

33. During the 1930s the company's founder Foster Gunnison pioneered methods of assembling houses on site from factory-made parts. Douglas A. Fisher, *Steel Serves the Nation, 1901–1951* (New York: United States Steel Corporation, 1951), p. 203; Bruce and Sandbank, *A History of Prefabrication,* p. 10.

34. Agenda, November 1, 1935 (FLC).

35. Le Corbusier learned about Bradley through a mutual friend from Vevey identified as B. C. Nuss. In a postcard to Le Corbusier Nuss referred to the "director of commercial aviation" as a person who "loves modern architecture and still dreams of building a house in the Vevey area." Postcard, B. C. Nuss to Le Corbusier, October 14, 1935; Agenda, October 24, 1935 (FLC). "S. S. Bradley Dies, Aviation Leader," obituary, *New York Times,* April 10, 1947, p. 25.

36. GM's new divisions included the Modern Housing Corporation, Modern Dwellings, Ltd., Argonaut Realty Division, Frigidaire Division, Delco-Frigidaire Conditioning Corporation, and Delco Appliance. *Annual Report of General Motors Corporation, Year Ended December 31, 1935,* pp. 24, 44.

37. "Dr. John O. Downey," obituary, *New York Times,* February 4, 1943, p. 23.

38. Le Corbusier confided to Wallace Harrison, "Je ne connais pas la valeur de ce monsieur." "Note p. [our] Wallace Harrison," December 6, 1935 (Wallace K. Harrison Papers, Avery Architectural and Fine Arts Library, Columbia University). The editors of *Architectural Forum* published Downey's commentary about prefabrication and integrated housing in "The Integrated House," *Architectural Forum* 66 (April 1937), 35 pp. See also "Standard Fittings Urged for Houses," *New York Times,* April 18, 1937, 13, p. 8.

39. In 1910 Le Corbusier entered the office of Peter Behrens in Berlin, just after Gropius resigned. Around that time he was introduced to Gropius's pioneering research in prefabricated hous-ing and later to Gropius's polemical images of mechanization in the *Werkbund Jahrbuch* (1913). In 1914 he visited the Deutscher Werkbund exhibition in Cologne and admired greatly the window wall of Gropius's pavilion. Gilbert Herbert, *The Dream of the Factory-Made House* (Cambridge: MIT Press, 1984), pp. 32–39; *Précisions,* p. 57; von Moos, *Le Corbusier, Elements of a Synthesis,* pp. 73–74, 340n14.

40. *OC 1910–1929,* pp. 23–26. In 1914–1915 Le Corbusier developed his Dom-ino house system that employed a standardized concrete frame and mass-produced windows. On his *maisons en série,* see Le Corbusier-Saugnier, "Maisons en série," *EN,* no. 13 (December 1921), pp. 1525–1542; *Vers une architecture,* pp. 185–211; "Mass-Production Houses," *Towards a New Architecture,* pp. 209–247; "Construite en série," *Almanach,* pp. 77–82. See also M. R. [Max Risselada], "Pages choisies: Maisons en série," in *L'Esprit nouveau: Le Corbusier et l'industrie 1920–1925,* pp. 170–173. In two publications of 1928 for the Redressment Français, "Pour bâtir: Standardiser et tayloriser" and "Vers le Paris de l'époque machiniste," Le Corbusier argued for the functional and economic justification of technology and its application to building. Le Corbusier, "Vers le Paris de l'époque machiniste," supplement to *Bulletin du Redressement Français* (February 15, 1928), 14 pp.; "Pour bâtir: Standardiser et tayloriser," supplement to *Bulletin du Redressement Français* (May 1, 1928), 8 pp.; *OC 1910–1929,* pp. 69, 78–86; McLeod, "'Architecture or Revolution': Taylorism, Technocracy, and Social Change," pp. 142–143.

41. See note 1.

42. On the Stuttgart houses, see *OC 1910–1929,* pp. 150–156; Richard Pommer and Christian F. Otto, *Weissenhof 1927 and the Modern Movement in Architecture* (Chicago: University of Chicago Press, 1991), pp. 77–79, 83–88.

43. On the Loucheur Houses, see Timothy Benton, "Le Corbusier and the Loi Loucheur," *AA Files* 7 (September 1984), pp. 54–60; T. B. [Tim Benton], "La Réponse de Le Corbusier à la loi Loucheur," in *Encyclopédie,* pp. 236–239.

44. *OC 1910–1929,* pp. 198–200.

45. Norman N. Rice, "The Minimal House: A Solution," *Record* 68 (August 1930), pp. 133–137. Le Corbusier, "Architecture, the Expression of the Materials and Methods of Our Times," *Record* 66 (August 1929), pp. 123–128.

46. *Towards a New Architecture,* pp. 227, 229, 264.

47. *Cathedrals,* p. 205.

48. Letter, Henry Sipos to Le Corbusier, October 28, 1935 (FLC).

49. See citation to letter, Henry Sipos to Mrs. John D. Rockefeller, Jr., March 23, 1934, entered in Index (Rockefeller Family archives, R.G. 2, Office of the Messieurs Rockefeller [hereafter cited as OMR], Housing Interests Series, Rockefeller Archive Center [hereafter cited as RAC]); letter, Joseph Hudnut to Frank D. Fackenthal, January 25, 1934 ("Joseph Hudnut," Central Files,

Columbia University). Sipos was later employed by American Houses, a company producing prefabricated units, led by housing specialists Robert W. McLaughlin, Jr., and Arthur C. Holden.

50. Carol Aronovici was born in Romania and came to the United States in 1901. He received his bachelor's and master's degrees in architecture from Cornell University in 1905 and 1906, respectively. In 1912 he earned a Ph.D. from Brown University. "Dr. Carol Aronovici Dies," obituary, *American Institute of Planners, News* (August–September 1957) p. 2; "Carol Aronovici (1881–1957)," *Planning and Civic Comment* 23 (December 1957), p. 54; "Dr. Carol Aronovici," *Journal of Housing* 14 (October 1957), p. 306.

51. Dr. Carol Aronovici founded the Housing Orientation Study group at Columbia University on December 18, 1933. The next year it became known as the Housing Research Bureau of New York City, located at 302 East 35th Street. The organization was started with 80 men and by November 1934 had increased to nearly 300. Their goal was "to present the authorities in charge of housing development with a correct and complete set of data on actual housing conditions in the City of New York, to show the necessity of slum clearance and improvement of the housing conditions, and to enable the government to choose most suitable locations for housing in New York City." *Report on Work of Housing Research Bureau,* November 20, 1934, p. 1; *Report on Work of Columbia University Housing Orientation Study,* June 30, 1934 (Avery Architectural and Fine Arts Library, Columbia University).

52. "America Can't Have Housing" (October 17–November 7, 1934) was jointly sponsored by the Modern, the NYCHA, Columbia University Housing Orientation Study, the Lavanburg Foundation, and the housing section of the Welfare Council. *Bulletin of the Museum of Modern Art* 1 (October 1934), p. 3.

53. Letter, Henry Sipos to Le Corbusier, October 28, 1935 (FLC). Georges Duhamel, *Scènes de la vie future* (Paris: Mercure de France, 1930), and *America the Menace,* trans. Charles Miner Thompson (Boston: Houghton Mifflin, 1931).

54. Letter, Henry Sipos to Le Corbusier, undated (FLC). Agenda, November 19, 1935 (FLC).

55. Henry-Russell Hitchcock, Jr., "Modern Architecture II. The New Pioneers," *Record* 63 (May 1928), pp. 452–460. On Le Corbusier as a "lost pioneer," see chapter 9.

56. Le Corbusier identified the representative from [American] Radiator as "Mr. Stubbs." See Agenda, p. 23 (FLC).

57. By his own account Le Corbusier's meeting with McGuire lasted ninety minutes. Le Corbusier, "Note p. [our] Wallace Harrison," December 6, 1935 (Wallace K. Harrison Papers, Avery Architectural and Fine Arts Library, Columbia University). "Realtors Decry Federal Inroads," *New York Times,* November 8, 1931, p. 30; "Daniel M'Guire, 82, Headed G.M. Units," obituary, *New York Times,* March 2, 1971, p. 38; "General Motors Realty Head," *New York Times,* December 2, 1935, p. 34; "Daniel C.

McGuire," Argonaut Realty Company press release, March 1940; "News Bulletin for GM Management," March 2, 1971 (Argonaut Realty, General Motors Corporation). McGuire was later instrumental in the construction of GM's Futurama Pavilion at the 1939 New York World's Fair.

58. Sipos met with Edgar I. Williams, chairman of the League's Committee on Annual Exhibition, who agreed to Le Corbusier's participation as long as he gave his personal consent when he returned to Manhattan. Letter, Henry Sipos to Le Corbusier, November 22, 1935 (FLC).

59. The translation of Le Corbusier's term *housing par grande industrie* as "housing by heavy industry" takes into account that a manufacturing-based economy prevailed in the United States during the 1930s, rather than the service-based or information-based economy of more recent decades.

60. In spite of his learning disability Nelson Rockefeller was elected to Phi Beta Kappa and graduated cum laude. Eileen B. Simpson, *Reversals: A Personal Account of Victory over Dyslexia* (Boston: Houghton Mifflin, 1979), p. viii; Joe Alex Morris, *Nelson Rockefeller: A Biography* (New York: Harper, 1960), pp. 3–4, 13, 29–31; John Ensor Harr and Peter J. Johnson, *The Rockefeller Century* (New York: Charles Scribner's Sons, 1988), pp. 267–268, 270, 303.

61. In 1929 while Nelson was still at Dartmouth College, Abby Aldrich Rockefeller wrote to her son, "My mind is also full of ideas for a new Museum of Modern Art for New York. I have great hopes for it. Wouldn't it be splendid if it would be ready for you to be interested in when you get back to New York to live." In his last year he was made a senior fellow, which allowed him to pursue studies independent of the classroom and revive a campus organization called The Arts. Morris, *Nelson Rockefeller: A Biography,* pp. 42–43, 53–55, 69, 73–75, 105–107. Harr and Johnson, *The Rockefeller Century,* pp. 217–220, 332. See also Russell Lynes, *Good Old Modern* (New York: Atheneum, 1973), pp. 3–18; Geoffrey T. Hellman, "Profile of a Museum," in *The Museum of Modern Art* (New York: Art in America, 1984), unpaged; Aline B. Saarinen, *The Proud Possessors* (New York: Random House, 1958), pp. 364–367. On the activities of the Rockefellers during the early years of the Modern, see "The Museum of Modern Art," *Fortune* 18 (December 1938), pp. 73–75, 127–128, 131–132, 134.

62. Letter, Nelson Rockefeller to John D. Rockefeller, Jr., quoted in Morris, *Nelson Rockefeller: A Biography,* pp. 92–93.

63. For Nelson Rockefeller's attitude toward business, see Morris, *Nelson Rockefeller: A Biography,* pp. 49–50.

64. Nelson Rockefeller joined with Fenton B. Turck, vice president of the American Radiator Co. and Standard Sanitary Company, and Webster Todd, son of John Todd, director of Rockefeller Center, to form Turck and Co. Later he bought out his partners to form Special Work, Inc. See Harr and Johnson, *The Rockefeller Century,* pp. 316, 334, 371; Morris, *Nelson Rockefeller: A Biography,*

pp. 92–94, 97–99; Samuel E. Bleecker, *The Politics of Architecture: A Perspective on Nelson A. Rockefeller* (New York: Rutledge Press, 1981), pp. 26–27.

65. By May 1933, when the RCA Building was opened, he served on seven of the sixteen committees established by the Center's board and its managing agents. Harr and Johnson, *The Rockefeller Century,* pp. 330, 332.

66. At Rockefeller Center, Nelson Rockefeller leased space at discounted rates. So effective was he that in 1934 August Heckscher, who owned a large office building, charged unfair competition and sued the Rockefeller Center board for $10 million. When Nelson Rockefeller, his brother John, and other directors of the Center were served papers, there was adverse publicity for all of them, but the suit was later dropped. See "Rockefeller Group Sued to $10,000,000," *New York Times,* January 11, 1934, pp. 1, 8; *Nation* 138 (January 24, 1934), p. 87; "Rockefeller Asks Dismissal of Suit," *New York Times,* February 6, 1934, p. 23.

67. As examples of Nelson Rockefeller's interest in labor relations and public relations, he participated in ceremonies to award certificates to the painters and decorators at Radio City Music Hall (1932), the British Empire Building (1933), and the International Building (1935). He raised the American flag at the ground-breaking ceremony for the Italian Building (1933). In the spring of 1935 he attended exercises at Rockefeller Center to honor mechanics for their "craftsmanship." See "31 Workers Honored for Craftsmanship," *New York Times,* April 24, 1935, p. 19. In 1934 he attended art openings, notably the "First Municipal Art Exhibition" held in the Forum of the RCA Building. See Harr and Johnson, *The Rockefeller Century,* p. 332.

68. Rivera departed from an approved sketch by incorporating a portrait of Lenin and other subjects. Speaking on behalf of the family, Nelson Rockefeller expressed his fear that the mural might "very seriously offend a great many people . . . in a public building." The Center's managers thought it entirely too "controversial." When Rivera refused to alter the mural, John D., Jr., was reported to have called the artist "off his scaffolding," paid him, and later ordered the unfinished mural destroyed. "Rockefellers Ban Lenin in RCA Mural and Dismiss Rivera," *New York Times,* May 10, 1933, pp. 1, 3. Rivera's account appears in his book (with an explanatory text by Bertram D. Wolfe) *Portrait of America* (New York: Covici, Fiede, 1934), pp. 21–32. See also Geoffrey T. Hellman, "Profiles, Enfant Terrible," *New Yorker* 9 (May 20, 1933), pp. 21–24; Bertram D. Wolfe, *The Fabulous Life of Diego Rivera* (New York: Stein and Day, 1963), pp. 317–334; Irene Herner de Larrea, *Diego Rivera: Paradise Lost at Rockefeller Center* (Mexico City: Edicupes, 1987); Morris, *Nelson Rockefeller: A Biography,* pp. 101–104; Harr and Johnson, *The Rockefeller Century,* pp. 333–334; Carol Herselle Krinsky, *Rockefeller Center* (New York: Oxford University Press, 1978), pp. 145–148; Cary Reich, *The Life of Nelson A. Rockefeller: Worlds to Conquer, 1908–1958* (New York: Doubleday, 1996), pp. 105–111.

69. From 1932 to 1935 Nelson Rockefeller held a series of minor posts in local government: budget committee for the town of Mt. Pleasant, NY (1932); member of the Westchester County Board of Health (1933); and member of the Chamber of Commerce of the State of New York (1935). A group of Young Republicans offered to support his run as the Independent Citizens Party candidate for "village trustee" of North Tarrytown, but Rockefeller declined. "Nelson Rockefeller to Aid Budget," *New York Times,* December 2, 1932, p. 23; "N. A. Rockefeller Gets Health Post," *New York Times,* January 5, 1933, p. 23; "Aided by John D. Rockefeller Sr. and Jr., Latter's Sons Join Chamber of Commerce," *New York Times,* March 8, 1935, p. 31; "Ask Rockefeller to Run," *New York Times,* March 3, 1935, p. 28; "N. A. Rockefeller Not Candidate," *New York Times,* March 10, 1935, p. 31.

70. Nelson Rockefeller proposed a new reorganization scheme. The Rockefeller board and committees would no longer serve in an advisory capacity. Instead, a new executive committee (consisting of himself, his brother John D., 3rd, and sympathetic senior board member Barton Turnbull) would have decision-making control over the managing agents. The takeover move was formally blocked by Thomas M. Debevoise, a respected lawyer and senior associate in the Rockefeller office, who supported the managing agents. John D., Jr., permitted the new executive committee to remain in place, but without the authority that Nelson Rockefeller had envisioned for it. Harr and Johnson, *The Rockefeller Century,* pp. 334, 371–375.

71. John D., Jr., established irrevocable trusts for his three eldest children in an attempt to transfer wealth to his heirs before new tax laws took effect. The deed for Nelson Rockefeller and John D. 3rd stipulated that neither the full income from the trust be paid nor the principal invaded until each reached the age of thirty. Harr and Johnson, *The Rockefeller Century,* pp. 357–362.

72. Reich, *The Life of Nelson A. Rockefeller: Worlds to Conquer, 1908–1958,* p. 122. Letter, Peter J. Johnson to author, May 20, 1992.

73. Reich, *The Life of Nelson A. Rockefeller: Worlds to Conquer, 1908–1958,* pp. 122–123.

74. Harr and Johnson, *The Rockefeller Century,* pp. 371–378.

75. As early as April 1931 Nelson Rockefeller became chair of the Museum of Modern Art's Junior Advisory Committee. Hellman, "Profile of a Museum," unpaged; Lynes, *Good Old Modern,* pp. 75–76. He became a trustee of the Metropolitan Museum of Art in 1932. Harr and Johnson, *The Rockefeller Century,* p. 332; Reich, *The Life of Nelson A. Rockefeller: Worlds to Conquer, 1908–1958,* p. 93.

76. Abby Aldrich Rockefeller (with Lillie P. Bliss and Cornelius J. Sullivan) was the guiding force in founding the organization in 1928. At his death in 1960 John D., Jr., together with his wife, had contributed more than $6 million. Harr and Johnson, *The Rockefeller Century,* pp. 217–219; Bernice Kert, *Abby Aldrich Rockefeller* (New York: Random House, 1993), pp. 267–426.

77. *Cathédrales,* p. 187. Le Corbusier omits the reference to Abby Aldrich Rockefeller in the American edition, *Cathedrals.*

78. Rona Roob, "1936: The Museum Selects an Architect," *Archives of American Art Journal* 23 (1983), pp. 22, 30n9. Harr and Johnson, *The Rockefeller Century,* pp. 363–364, 592n13; Lynes, *Good Old Modern,* pp. 95, 173–174.

79. Le Corbusier was incorrect in his assumption that "the Rockefeller Foundation *of* the Museum of Modern Art" had sponsored his American lecture tour. *Cathedrals,* p. 125.

80. Ellen Milton and Wallace Harrison were married on February 13, 1926. Victoria Newhouse, *Wallace K. Harrison, Architect* (New York: Rizzoli, 1989), p. 28; Harr and Johnson, *The Rockefeller Century,* p. 322.

81. Harrison was the youngest architect on the design team. In 1927 he joined Frank Helmle and Harvey Wiley Corbett, his former design teacher. Transcript of ten interviews with Wallace K. Harrison conducted by R. Daum between March 11 and November 4, 1978, pp. 47–48 (Oral History Research Office, Columbia University) (hereafter cited as Harrison interviews, Columbia Oral History). In 1929 William H. MacMurray became a partner. Herbert Warren Wind, "Profiles: Architect [Wallace Harrison]," *New Yorker* 30 (November 27, 1954), 2, p. 56; Newhouse, *Wallace K. Harrison, Architect,* pp. 30, 33, 45–46.

82. Wallace Harrison was born in 1895 in Worcester, MA. He was the only child of James and Rachel Kirkman Harrison, both descended from Yorkshire families. The Kirkmans were engravers by trade.

83. Harrison left school in Worcester to take a job with the contractor O. W. Norcross. James F. O'Gorman credits Norcross with the high level of craftsmanship in buildings by H. H. Richardson and McKim, Mead and White. See "O. W. Norcross, Richardson's 'Master Builder': A Preliminary Report," *JSAH* 32 (May 1973), pp. 104–113. Harrison learned drafting skills both at Norcross and at the Worcester firm of Frost and Chamberlin.

84. Newhouse, *Wallace K. Harrison, Architect,* pp. 15–16.

85. Herbert Warren Wind, "Profiles: Architect [Wallace Harrison]," *New Yorker* 30 (November 20, 1954), 1, pp. 72–73.

86. On Harrison's Beaux-Arts education, his early architectural career, and his eventual commitment to modernism, see Wind, "Profiles: Architect [Wallace Harrison]" (November 20, 1954), 1, pp. 59–73 and 2, pp. 52, 54, 56; Newhouse, *Wallace K. Harrison, Architect,* pp. 14–33.

87. W. K. Harrison, "The Design of the Modern School," in W. K. Harrison and C. E. Dobbin, *School Buildings of Today and Tomorrow* (New York: Architectural Book Publishing Co., 1931), p. 2; Harrison's conversion to modernism is discussed in chapter 4. On the publication of Le Corbusier's projects, see chapter 6.

88. For Perret's influence, see Harrison interviews, Columbia Oral History, p. 203.

89. See chapter 6.

90. *Modern Architecture: International Exhibition* (New York: Museum of Modern Art, 1932), p. 140.

91. "Country Home Development Proposed for Mass Production," *New York Times,* January 29, 1933, 10, 11, p. 1. See also "To Show Housing Trend," *New York Times,* January 18, 1933, p. 36; Edward Alden Jewell, "Art in Review," *New York Times,* January 21, 1933, p. 13; "Architects Show Modern Trends," *New York Times,* January 22, 1933, 10, 11, pp. 1, 2.

92. "Course in Architecture," *New York Times* (October 29, 1933), 10, 11, p. 1.

93. In June 1934 Nelson Rockefeller had to decline Harrison's request to lease office space at 19 West 53rd Street due to zoning restrictions. Letter, Nelson A. Rockefeller to Wallace K. Harrison, June 11, 1934 (Rockefeller Family archives, Friends and Relations, R.G. 2, Box 66, RAC).

94. At the end of 1935 Harrison and Fouilhoux moved their office to the eighth floor of the International Building at Rockefeller Center. By then ten of the Center's buildings were completed: RKO (opened October 1932), Radio City Music Hall (December 1932), Center Theater (December 1932), RCA (May 1933), RCA West (May 1933), British Empire (May 1933), La Maison Française (September 1933), Palazzo d'Italia (May 1935), International North (May 1935), and International (May 1935). Wind, "Profiles: Architect [Wallace Harrison]" (November 27, 1954), 2, pp. 61, 66.

95. Letter, Nelson A. Rockefeller to Harold R. Robinson, July 30, 1936 (Rockefeller Family archives, R.G. 2., Box 22; Cultural Interests, Museum of Modern Art, Box 22, RAC).

96. Wind, "Profiles: Architect [Wallace Harrison]" (November 27, 1954), 2, p. 68. See also Newhouse, *Wallace K. Harrison, Architect,* p. 46; Bleecker, *The Politics of Architecture: A Perspective on Nelson A. Rockefeller,* pp. 13–16.

97. Harrison interviews, Columbia Oral History, p. 145.

98. Max Abramovitz, interview with author, New York City, June 2, 1987.

99. Newhouse, *Wallace K. Harrison, Architect,* p. 49; Harrison interviews, Columbia Oral History, p. 37. In 1932 Rockefeller also consulted Harrison (and Raymond Hood) for a decision on Rivera's use of color for his mural. Letter, Nelson A. Rockefeller to Diego Rivera, quoted in Morris, *Nelson Rockefeller: A Biography,* p. 101.

100. Harrison interviews, Columbia Oral History, p. 93.

101. John D. Rockefeller, Jr., successfully blocked earlier efforts to transform the zoning of his own neighborhood from residential to commercial. Krinsky, *Rockefeller Center,* pp. 25, 84–87; Harr and Johnson, *The Rockefeller Century,* p. 318.

102. "Rockefeller Gives Apartment Plans," *New York Times,* November 20, 1935, p. 26; "Rockefeller Jr. to Build Suites in West 54th St.," *New York Herald Tribune,* November 20, 1935, p. 15. "John D. Rockefeller Jr. Reported Sponsoring Vast Apartment Colony," *New York Herald Tribune,* November 24, 1935, 10, pp. 1, 2; "Rockefeller Jr. Files Plans for 54th St. Suites," *New York Herald Tribune,* December 10, 1935, p. 19.

103. "Rockefeller Apartments," *Architectural Forum* 66 (January 1937), p. 5.

104. Lewis Mumford, "The Sky Line: Mr. Rockefeller's Center," *New Yorker* 9 (December 23, 1933), p. 30; "Modernity and Commerce," *New Yorker* 12 (October 3, 1936), p. 48; letter, Nelson [Rockefeller] to John D. Rockefeller, Jr., October 1, 1936 (Rockefeller Family archives, R.G. 2, OMR, John D. Rockefeller, Jr., Real Estate Interests, Box 36, RAC).

105. In 1928 John D., Jr., purchased a large parcel of land between Fifth and Sixth avenues from 48th to 51st streets on what became the site of Rockefeller Center, primarily to provide for a new Metropolitan Opera House. Earlier in 1927 Metropolitan Opera box holders selected Benjamin Wistar Morris as architect (with Joseph Urban as assistant architect). A rendering of Morris's Metropolitan Club Dinner scheme of April 1928 for the Metropolitan Opera House appears in Krinsky, *Rockefeller Center,* p. 27, fig. 17. For a history and analysis of the Metropolitan Opera House in the early designs for Rockefeller Center, see *Rockefeller Center,* pp. 22–43. Winston Weisman first studied the early development of the Center. A bibliography of his writings is contained in *Rockefeller Center,* p. 214. See also William H. Jordy's essay, "Rockefeller Center and Corporate Urbanism," in his *American Buildings and Their Architects: The Impact of European Modernism in the Mid-Twentieth Century* (New York: Doubleday, 1972) pp. 35–38. For the respective schemes of Morris and Urban, both of 1929, see Stern, Gilmartin, and Mellins, *New York 1930,* pp. 630, 631, 634, 635, 636, 637. For acquisitions in 1934–1935, see *Rockefeller Center,* pp. 82–85.

106. In the spring of 1934 agents for John D. Rockefeller, Jr., began to acquire several plots on West 51st Street just north of the Center's private street in anticipation of a possible northern extension. These plots increased his already extensive holdings north of 51st Street. Later his agents added a sizable number of land parcels in the area between Fifth and Sixth avenues from 51st to 55th Street. Harrison interviews, Columbia Oral History, p. 235.

107. The committee was chaired by Mrs. Henry Breckinridge. Letter, W. S. Richardson to Nelson Rockefeller, September 5, 1934 (Rockefeller Family archives, R.G. 2, OMR, Cultural Interests, Box 22, RAC). "Civic Art Centre Planned by Mayor," *New York Times,* January 7, 1935, pp. 1, 2; Edward Alden Jewell, "The Realm of Art," *New York Times,* January 13, 1935, 9, p. 9; "La Guardia Plans a City Orchestra," *New York Times,* January 16, 1935, p. 1

108. In the spring of 1935 Myron Taylor, chairman of the board of U.S. Steel Corporation and a member of the boards of both the Municipal Art Committee and the Metropolitan Opera Association, suggested to Rockefeller Center managers that the Center might be a desirable site for the mayor's proposed art complex. Letter, Myron C. Taylor to John R. Todd, April 18, 1935 (Rockefeller Family archives, R.G. 2 OMR, Cultural Interests, Box 22, RAC); *Thirty-Fourth Annual Report of the United States Steel Corporation for the Fiscal Year Ended December 31, 1935,* p. 2. "Myron Taylor Dies; Ex-Envoy to Vatican," obituary, *New York Times,* May 7, 1959, pp. 1, 33. Irving Kolodin, *The Metropolitan Opera 1883–1939* (New York: Oxford University Press, 1940), pp. 476–477.

109. In 1927 Morris was appointed architect of a proposed new Metropolitan Opera building then planned for Rockefeller Center. The Morris and O'Connor project is illustrated in Stern, Gilmartin, and Mellins, *New York 1930,* pp. 663 (top), 664.

110. Letter, Jay Downer to Thomas D. Mabry, Jr., August 2, 1935 (Rockefeller Family archives, R.G. 2 OMR, Cultural Interests, Box 22, RAC).

111. "Mayor Asks Opera in City Art Center Built by New Tax," *New York Times,* December 17, 1935, pp. 1, 20.

112. Jaoul may have intervened to assist Le Corbusier by speaking to U.S. Steel vice president Rufus Zimmerman and through him to the corporation's chairman of the board Myron Taylor who was an influential advocate of the Municipal Art Center. Agenda, December 9, 1935 (FLC).

113. On Harrison's redesign of the Rockefeller apartment at 810 Fifth Avenue, see Newhouse, *Wallace K. Harrison, Architect,* pp. 56–57. Le Corbusier documents at least three meetings with Nelson Rockefeller: the Goodwin lunch on October 23, the dinner at Rockefeller's apartment on October 31, and an appointment at Rockefeller's office on December 12. Rockefeller most likely also attended Le Corbusier's lecture and the opening of his exhibition on October 24 at the Museum of Modern Art. There may have been one or two other meetings or social gatherings. Agenda, pp. 8, 12, 33 (FLC). Rockefeller's appointment book for 1935 records the Goodwin luncheon on October 23 and the December 12 meeting but does not consistently show entries for evening events, including the October dinner (Rockefeller Family archives, R.G. 4, Nelson Rockefeller Papers—Personal, Activities series, Box 3, RAC).

114. "La Guardia to Ask $150,000,000 Loan for Housing Here," *New York Times,* February 7, 1935, pp. 1, 3.

115. Agenda, marginal notes, p. 15 (FLC); Le Corbusier, "Nelson Rockefeller" [notes on their meeting] (FLC).

116. Le Corbusier intended to propose to Rockefeller the creation of a children's orchestra for broadcasting from Radio City, and he hoped to have his brother Albert install the studio equipped with new sound. Agenda, marginal notes, pp. 13, 14 (FLC). Le Corbusier and Albert Jeanneret (1885–1973) shared an abiding in-

terest in music. See L.-M. C. [Luisa Martina Colli], "Musique," in *Encyclopédie*, pp. 268–271. From 1919 to 1933 Albert directed "L'Ecole française de rhythmique et d'éducation corporelle," which employed the method and theory of Emile Jaques-Dalcroze. See U. L. [Ute Lehrer], "La Rhythmique," in *L'Esprit nouveau: Le Corbusier et l'industrie 1920–1925* (Zurich: Ernst & Sohn, 1987), pp. 230–231. A list of Albert Jeanneret's articles on rhythm and music in *L'Esprit Nouveau* appears: *L'Esprit nouveau: Le Corbusier et l'industrie 1920–1925* p. 287.

117. C. Z. [Christian Zervos], "Qui bâtira le Palais des Nations?," *Cahiers d'Art* 3 (1928), 4, p. 87.

118. Agenda, p. 7 (FLC); *Cathédrales*, pp. 132–133, 161–162; *Cathedrals*, pp. 93, 108–109.

119. Agenda, marginal notes, pp. 13, 14, 15 (FLC); Le Corbusier, "Nelson Rockefeller" [notes on their meeting] (FLC). On the relationship between research and actual construction in the Loi Loucheur plans and the lodge for the Villa Savoye, see Tim Benton, *The Villas of Le Corbusier 1920–1930* (New Haven and London: Yale University Press, 1987), p. 203.

120. In his letter to Le Corbusier on December 2, 1935, Thomas Dabney Mabry, Jr., the Modern's executive director, informed the visitor: "According to our agreement our responsibility in connection with this tour ends with your return to Paris upon the date originally set by you, i.e., as near the first of December as possible. . . . We will therefore purchase passage for you on whatever boat you choose and pay your expenses up to and including November 30th. Extension of your visit to this country is beyond the terms of our original agreement." DAD, MoMA, NY; Agenda, December 2, 1935 (FLC).

121. Le Corbusier, "Note p. [our] Wallace Harrison," December 6, 1935 (Wallace K. Harrison Papers, Avery Architectural and Fine Arts Library, Columbia University).

122. Agenda, November 29, 1935 (FLC).

123. Le Corbusier intended to make a study of a proposed airport in New York that La Guardia advocated. Le Corbusier, "Concernant Mr Nelson Rockefeller pour Wallace Harrison," December 6, 1935 (Wallace K. Harrison Papers, Avery Architectural and Fine Arts Library, Columbia University).

124. Le Corbusier, "Concernant Mr Nelson Rockefeller pour Wallace Harrison" and "Edition de La Ville Radieuse Sous le patronnage du Musée d'Art Moderne," [December 6, 1935] (Wallace K. Harrison Papers, Avery Architectural and Fine Arts Library, Columbia University). Letters, Nelson A. Rockefeller to Le Corbusier, February 1, 1936; Le Corbusier to Nelson Rockefeller, March 13, 1936; Le Corbusier to Wallace Harrison, March 30, 1936; Le Corbusier to Nelson Rockefeller, May 15, 1936 (FLC).

125. Le Corbusier, "Nelson Rockefeller" [notes on Gotham Hotel stationary in preparation for their meeting on December 12, 1935] (FLC). For members elected to the fair's board of directors, see "M'Aneny Elected World's Fair Head," *New York Times,* November 21, 1935, p. 26.

126. Narciso G. Menocal, *Keck and Keck, Architects* (Madison: Elvehjem Museum of Art, University of Wisconsin-Madison, 1980), pp. 15, 34–37; Robert Boyce, *Keck and Keck* (New York: Princeton Architectural Press, 1993), pp. 43–53; Thomas M. Slade, "'The Crystal House' of 1934," *JSAH* 29 (December 1970), pp. 350–353.

127. Richard Neutra, *Wie baut Amerika?* (Stuttgart: Julius Hoffman, 1927). See Pauline Schindler's review in the Los Angeles *City Club Bulletin,* discussed in Thomas S. Hines, *Richard Neutra and the Search for Modern Architecture* (New York: Oxford University Press, 1982), pp. 65–66.

128. Le Corbusier, "Concernant Mr Nelson Rockefeller pour Wallace Harrison," December 6, 1935 (Wallace K. Harrison Papers, Avery Architectural and Fine Arts Library, Columbia University). In *Cathédrales* he elucidates his "Proposition de programme pour une exposition universelle à New-York 1939" and the purpose of the pavilion to keep "public authorities properly, radically, profoundly, and exactly informed about the possibilities of today (its techniques and needs), finally considering the necessity of undertaking the great work of reconstructing the cities," p. 291; *Cathedrals,* p. 201. Le Corbusier, "The Theme of a World's Fair" (Le Thème d'une exposition internationale ou universelle), June 30, 1936 (FLC). Letters, Le Corbusier to Richard de Rochemont [agent, the March of Time], February 18, April 7, July 6, October 23, 1936 (FLC).

129. Newhouse, *Wallace K. Harrison, Architect,* p. 81; Eugene A. Santomasso, "The Design of Reason: Architecture and Planning at the 1939/40 New York World's Fair," in *Dawn of a New Day: The New York World's Fair 1939/40* (New York: Queens Museum, 1980, pp. 29–30.

130. Letters, Le Corbusier to Alma Clayburgh, October 16 and 20, 1936; Le Corbusier to Thérèse Bonnet [sic], October 20, 22, 23, 1936 (FLC). See also [Le Corbusier,] "NOTE pour Mlle Thérèse Bonney" and "Envoyer à Thérèse Bonney" (FLC).

131. Marguerite was equally optimistic about an American edition of *Cathédrales,* announcing that it would "be published in the fall [1938] by the Architectural Book Publishing Co." Le Corbusier, "New York Glorious Catastrophe," *Direction* 1 (June 1938), p. 9.

132. Agenda, marginal notes, p. 17 (FLC); "Nelson Rockefeller," notes on Gotham Hotel stationery (FLC).

133. "Concernant Mr Nelson Rockefeller pour Wallace Harrison," December 6, 1935 (Wallace K. Harrison Papers, Avery Architectural and Fine Arts Library, Columbia University). Le Corbusier, *Des canons, des munitions? Merci! Des logis . . . s.v.p.* (Paris: Editions de l'Architecture d'Aujourd'hui, 1937), p. 78.

134. Project C was rejected in October 1936. Le Corbusier, *Des canons, des munitions? Merci! Des logis . . . s.v.p.,* p. 12. *OC 1934–1938,* pp. 152–155.

135. "Concernant Mr Nelson Rockefeller pour Wallace Harrison," December 6, 1935 (Wallace K. Harrison Papers, Avery Architectural and Fine Arts Library, Columbia University). On Le Corbusier's "synthesis of the arts," see Arnoldo Rivkin, "Synthèse des Arts: Un double paradoxe," in *Encyclopédie*, pp. 386–391.

136. Le Corbusier, *Des canons, des munitions? Merci! Des logis . . . s.v.p.*, p. 12. Rockefeller was in Washington, DC, on October 28 (Rockefeller Family archives, R.G. 4, Nelson Rockefeller Papers—Personal, Activities series, Box 3, RAC).

137. This typology is examined in chapter 3.

138. Roob, "1936: The Museum Selects an Architect," pp. 22–30.

139. Letter, Wallace K. Harrison to Le Corbusier, February 14, 1936 (FLC).

140. Letters, Nelson A. Rockefeller to Le Corbusier, February 1, 1936; Wallace K. Harrison to Le Corbusier, February 14, 1936; Le Corbusier to Nelson Rockefeller, March 13 and May 15, 1936 (FLC). Correspondence pertaining to Le Corbusier's request to Rockefeller that the Rockefeller Foundation grant funds to CIAM has been destroyed (Rockefeller Family archives, R.G. 2, OMR, Cultural Interests, Index "Le Corbusier," RAC).

141. Minutes of the 54th meeting of the Board of Trustees of the Museum of Modern Art, December 19, 1935, quoted in Roob, "1936: The Museum Selects an Architect," pp. 22, 30n4.

142. Given the competition for federal funds, La Guardia proposed that the new center be funded by a municipal tax set at 5 cents per $100 of assessed real estate. "Mayor Asks Opera in City Art Center Built by New Tax," pp. 1, 20. See also "Mayor to Tell Plan of City Art Center Today," *New York Herald Tribune*, December 15, 1935, p. 15.

143. Letter, Charles O. Heydt to John D. Rockefeller, Jr., July 1, 1935 (Rockefeller Family archives, R.G. 2, John D. Rockefeller, Jr., Real Estate Interests, Box 35, RAC).

144. Letter, president [A. Conger Goodyear] to Fiorello H. La Guardia, December 31, 1935 (Rockefeller Family archives, R.G. 2, OMR, Cultural Interests, Box 22, RAC).

145. Minutes of the 55th meeting of the Board of Trustees of the Museum of Modern Art, January 23, 1936, quoted in Roob, "1936: The Museum Selects an Architect," pp. 22, 30n6.

146. Letters, Jay Downer to A. Conger Goodyear, February 24, 1936; Fiorello H. La Guardia to Mrs. John D. Rockefeller, Jr., March 16, 1936; Nelson A. Rockefeller to Fiorello H. La Guardia, March 20, 1936 (Rockefeller Family archives, R.G. 2, OMR, Cultural Interests, Box 22, RAC).

147. Nelson Rockefeller arranged for the Modern's parcel on the south side (97 feet of frontage; nos. 6, 8, and 10) to be traded for land owned by John D., Jr., on the north side (129 feet of frontage; nos. 9, 11, and 13). This would provide a site for the museum at the north end of the proposed street. But to form an aggregate of lots sufficiently large, John D., Jr., also sold three contiguous lots adjacent to it (nos. 15, 17, and 19) on the north side for 60 percent of their book value. Abby Aldrich Rockefeller subsequently contributed funds to purchase the land. In 1939 John D., Jr. gave the Modern three lots on West 54th Street (nos. 12, 14, and 16) and further allowed lots 4 through 10 to be used as a sculpture garden. Minutes of the 59th meeting of the Board of Trustees of the Museum of Modern Art, September 28, 1936, pp. 1–5, quoted in Roob, "1936: The Museum Selects an Architect," pp. 22, 30n9. Harr and Johnson, *The Rockefeller Century*, pp. 363–364, 592n13; Lynes, *Good Old Modern*, pp. 95, 173–176.

148. Roob, "1936: The Museum Selects an Architect," p. 22.

149. Letters, Nelson A. Rockefeller to Fiorello H. La Guardia, April 9, 1936; Nelson A. Rockefeller to Harold R. Robinson, July 30, 1936; John M. Wallace to Nelson A. Rockefeller, September 4, 1936 (Rockefeller Family archives, R.G. 2, OMR, Cultural Interests, Box 22, RAC).

150. Letters, Nelson A. Rockefeller to Lewis F. Levy, October 5, 1936; Nelson A. Rockefeller to Solomon R. Guggenheim, October 5, 1936; Solomon R. Guggenheim to Nelson Rockefeller, October 8, 1936 (Rockefeller Family archives, R.G. 2, OMR, Cultural Interests, Box 22, RAC).

151. This plan indicates the Museum of Modern Art in relation to the "Proposed Municipal Center," *The Museum of Modern Art*, 66 pp. (undated report, submitted at the meeting of the Board of Trustees of the Museum of Modern Art on November 12, 1936), p. 34, chart 8 (Rockefeller Family archives, R.G. 2, OMR, Cultural Interests, Box 22, RAC). Roob, "1936: The Museum Selects an Architect," pp. 22–23.

152. Harrison and Foilhoux, in collaboration with Morris and O'Connor, subsequently developed a more ambitious scheme for a Municipal Art and Civic Center on the northern extension to Rockefeller Center. Although the Municipal Arts Committee endorsed the Rockefeller Center extension site and selected these two firms to collaborate on plans, the project slipped from their hands. In May 1938 La Guardia appointed Robert Moses, Parks Commissioner, to take charge of the plans, who then selected his own team (architect-engineer William Wilson and architect Aymar Embury II). Harrison interviews, Columbia Oral History, p. 235; Krinsky, *Rockefeller Center*, pp. 86, 87, figs. 43, 44.

153. "City Selects Fifty as Its Architects on Large Projects," *New York Times*, December 23, 1935, p. 1.

154. On Harrison and Abramovitz's early schemes for Lincoln Center, see Newhouse, *Wallace K. Harrison, Architect*, pp. 193–197, figs. 171–175; Krinsky, *Rockefeller Center*, p. 87.

155. *VR* and *RC*, p. 8.

156. Le Corbusier, "L'Autorité devant les tâches contemporaines," *L'Architecture d'Aujourd'hui* 5 (September 1935), pp.

22–23; reprinted in *L'Architecture d'Aujourd'hui* 43 (October–November 1971), p. 87.

157. "Le Plan dictateur," *VR* and *RC*, pp. 8–9; *Cathedrals*, p. 211.

158. Le Corbusier, "L'Autorité devant les tâches contemporaines," p. 22.

159. "What Is America's Problem?," *American Architect* 148 (March 1936), pp. 17–22.

160. For a classification and analysis of structural systems, see John Burchard 2nd, "Survey of Efforts to Modernize Housing Structure," in Bemis, *The Evolving House: Rational Design,* vol. 3, pp. 331–625.

161. On impediments to prefabricated housing, see Douglas Haskell, "Assembly Lines Reach Out," *Record* 93 (June 1943), pp. 62–69.

162. The Rockefeller Foundation, founded in 1910, had long been supporting projects in France. After World War I it contributed to reconstruction efforts in Reims, with which Le Corbusier was familiar through his work with the organization La Renaissance des Cités (see chapter 4). The Foundation also financed the Cité Universitaire in Paris where Le Corbusier's Pavilion Suisse is located. See William J. R. Curtis, "Ideas of Structure and the Structure of Ideas: Le Corbusier's Pavillon Suisse, 1930–1931," *JSAH* 40 (December 1981), pp. 295–310.

163. *Cathédrales,* pp. 186–187. The American edition is abridged; *Cathedrals,* pp. 126–127.

164. Le Corbusier, *Urbanisme,* p. 285; *City of Tomorrow,* p. 302.

165. *Cathedrals,* p. 181.

166. J. O. S. [Jordi Oliveras Samitier], "Barcelone," in *Encyclopédie,* pp. 59–62.

167. Max Abramovitz, interview with author, New York City, June 2, 1987.

168. Abramovitz, interview with author, New York City, June 2, 1987; Robert Jacobs, interview with author, Pawling, NY, November 21, 1984.

169. Le Corbusier, "Questions d'urbanisme," December 18, 1935 (FLC).

8 Le Corbusier's Reaction to the "Country of Timid People"

1. *Cathedrals,* pp. 167–170.

2. Le Corbusier, *Des canons, des munitions? Merci! Des logis . . . s.v.p. Pavillon des Temps Nouveaux* (Boulogne-sur-Seine: Editions de l'architecture d'Aujourd'hui, 1938). Danilo Udovicki-Selb, "The Elusive Faces of Modernity: The Invention of the 1937 Paris Exhibition and the Temps Nouveaux Pavilion" (Ph.D. diss., MIT, 1995); Danilo Udovicki-Selb, "Le Corbusier and the Paris Exhibition of 1937, the Temps Nouveaux Pavilion," *JSAH* 56 (March 1997), pp. 42–63.

3. *Cathedrals,* p. 215. Jean-Louis Cohen, *Le Corbusier and the Mystique of the USSR* (Princeton: Princeton University Press, 1992).

4. Colin Wilson, *The Outsider* (Los Angeles: Jeremy P. Tarcher, 1982).

5. "Quand les cathédrales étaient blanches," *Prélude,* no. 13 (September–October 1934), p. 1 (reprinted in *Chantiers* 8 [July 1935], pp. 513–515, and *Cathédrales,* pp. 3–11; *Cathedrals,* pp. 3–9). The "Preface" of *Cathédrales* first appeared in *Prélude,* which contained the announcement that "his next book on America . . . will appear in October (*chez Plon*)." *Prélude,* no. 16 (July–August 1936), p. 8 (reprinted in *Cathédrales,* pp. i, ii; *Cathedrals,* pp. xxi–xxii). Letter, Louis Carré to Le Corbusier, September 14, 1935 (FLC).

6. In anticipation of his forthcoming trip to the United States Le Corbusier framed this dichotomy of strong but timid in his lecture, "Brazilian Corollary" (December 8, 1929): "The USA is Hercules, whose heart, it seems to me, is still timid and hesitant," *Precisions,* p. 245.

7. Many of the themes that shaped Le Corbusier's critique of American culture in *Cathédrales*—advertising, publicity, waste, discordance within the family, and the state of women and blacks in the society—are thoughtfully explored by Mary McLeod in relation to his political activism. See "Perished Dreams of America: Le Corbusier's Reassessment of Industrial Utopia," symposium, "L'Américanisme et la modernité," Ecole des Hautes Etudes en Sciences Sociales and the Institut Français d'Architecture, Paris, October 24, 1985; "Le Rêve transi de Le Corbusier: L'Amérique 'catastrophe féerique,'" in J.-L. Cohen and H. Damisch, eds., *Américanisme et modernité* (Paris: Flammarion, 1993), pp. 208–227. See also Mary Caroline McLeod, "Urbanism and Utopia: Le Corbusier from Regional Syndicalism to Vichy" (Ph.D. diss., Princeton University, 1985), pp. 94–207, 458–497; "Bibliography: *Plans,*" *Oppositions,* no. 19–20 (Winter–Spring 1980), pp. 184–201.

8. Robert Aron and Arnaud Dandieu *Décadence de la nation française* (Paris: Editions Rieder, 1931); Le Corbusier's copy is extensively annotated (FLC).

9. Robert Aron and Arnaud Dandieu, "Le Cancer américain," *Plans,* no. 8 (October 1931), p. 37; see also Robert Aron and Arnaud Dandieu, *Le Cancer américain* (Paris: Rieder, 1931).

10. Le Corbusier owned a copy each of Georges Duhamel, *Scènes de la vie future* (Paris: Mercure de France, 1930), pages cut but no annotations; Louis-Ferdinand Céline, *Voyage au bout de la nuit* (Paris: Gallimard, 1931), pages cut but no annotations; Jean de Pierrefeu, *Contre la vie chère* (Paris: Magasins à prix uniques, 1933); pages cut and annotations (FLC).

11. See A. Alexandre, "U.S.A. 1932," *Plans,* no. 2 (May 15, 1932), pp. 12–16; P. Ch. Biver, "U.S.A. 1932: Quelques traits parmi des millions," *Plans,* no. 4 (June 15, 1932), pp. 27–31; Upton Sinclair, "Le Martyre de Sacco et Vanzetti," *Plans,* no. 5 (July 1, 1932), pp. 20–25; Sherwood Anderson and Magdeleine Paz,

"Crise aux U.S.A.: La terreur au Kentucky," *Plans,* no. 7 (August 1, 1932), pp. 21–25. Philippe Lamour, editor of *Plans,* was also a frequent contributor on American culture. See, for example, "Crise aux Etats-Unis," *Plans,* no. 2 (February 1931), pp. 129–135; "City Lights de Charlie Chaplin," *Plans,* no. 5 (May 1931), pp. 74–80; "Du voyage d'Amérique au plan européen," *Plans,* no. 9 (November 1931), pp. 6–15; "La Grande Peur de l'an 1932," *Plans,* no. 12 (February 1932), p. 7.

12. In 1929 Chicago gangsters disguised as policemen shot seven of their rivals. The killing has become known as the St. Valentine's Day Massacre. *Plans,* no. 3 (February 1931), pp. [108–109].

13. See Julian Jackson, *The Politics of Depression in France, 1932–1936* (New York: Cambridge University Press, 1985).

14. Le Corbusier may also have been influenced by Klee's use of diagrams and flow charts. See *Pädagogisches Skizzenbuch* (Munich: Albert Langen, 1925). The title appears in Paul V. Turner, "Catalogue de la bibliothèque de Le Corbusier avant 1930," February 1970 (FLC).

15. Le Corbusier, *L'Art décoratif d'aujourd'hui* (Paris: Editions Crès, 1925), pp. 1–12, 51–65; Le Corbusier, "Retours . . . ou l'enseignement du voyage," *Plans* no. 8 (October 1931), pp. 92–108, reprinted in *VR* and *RC,* pp. 10–11; Le Corbusier, "Décisions," *Plans* no. 10 (December 1931), pp. 93–108, reprinted in *VR* and *RC,* pp. 147–155.

16. *Cathedrals,* pp. 100, 194.

17. *Cathedrals,* pp. 81, 98–104, 106–107, 148.

18. *Cathedrals,* pp. 100–102, 108.

19. *Cathedrals,* pp. 46, 101; Geoffrey T. Hellman, "Profiles: From Within to Without—II," *New Yorker* 23 (May 3, 1947), p. 38; Robert Allan Jacobs, interview with the author, Pawling, NY, June 7, 1987 (hereafter cited as Jacobs interview).

20. *Cathedrals,* p. 46.

21. Hellman, "Profiles: From Within to Without—II," p. 38.

22. *Cathedrals,* p. 46.

23. *Cathedrals,* pp. 13, 81–82, 98, 124, 148.

24. *Cathedrals,* pp. 103–105.

25. *Cathedrals,* pp. 103–105.

26. *Cathedrals,* pp. 107, 110, 157, 165–166.

27. See, for example, images of the Tiller Girls as symbols of mechanization in American-influenced reviews of the Weimar years in Germany. Beeke Sell Tower, "Jungle Music and Song of Machines: Jazz and American Dance in Weimar Culture," in *Envisioning America* (Cambridge: Busch-Reisinger Museum, Harvard University, 1990), pp. 96–99.

28. See "The Family Divided," in *Cathedrals,* pp. 152–155.

29. *Cathedrals,* p. 138.

30. Alma Clayburgh Grew, interview with author, Boston, December 12, 1987.

31. *Cathedrals,* p. 145. Jacobs interview, November 21, 1984. In his letter congratulating the former Vassar student on her recent marriage to James Hooper Grew, a diplomat who would serve as ambassador to Japan in the 1940s, Le Corbusier described her as "la plus belle femme du monde," letter, Le Corbusier to Mrs. James Hooper Grew (Alma Clayburgh Grew), July 25, 1938 (FLC).

32. No. 4, *Head of a Young Boy,* attributed to Caravaggio (now identified as "follower of Caravaggio") was exhibited in "Italian Painting of the Sei- and Settecento" at the Wadsworth Atheneum from January 22–February 8, 1930. In 1943 Austin acquired Caravaggio's important work *The Ecstasy of St. Francis.* On Austin's history of collecting, see Eugene Gaddis, "'The New Athens': Moments from an Era," in Eugene Gaddis, ed., *Avery Memorial, Wadsworth Atheneum* (Hartford: Wadsworth Atheneum, 1985), pp. 32–58; Nicholas Fox Weber, *Patron Saints* (New York: Alfred A. Knopf, 1992), pp. 135–176; Julien Levy, *Memoir of an Art Gallery* (New York: G. P. Putnam's Sons, 1977), pp. 135–147.

33. *Cathedrals,* pp. 138, 145, 147, 149.

34. Sweeney lived at 120 East End Avenue near 86th Street. *Cathedrals,* pp. 42, 90.

35. For a list of René Allendy's articles in *L'Esprit Nouveau,* see Simone Rümmele, Index, *L'Esprit nouveau: Le Corbusier et l'industrie 1920–1925* (Zurich: Ernst & Sohn, 1987), pp. 285, 289, 290. See also Docteur Allendy, "Métastases et substitutions morbides," *Plans,* no. 3 (March 1931), pp. 49–53. René and Yvonne Allendy, *Capitalisme et sexualité* (Paris: Denoël et Steele, 1931); the authors inscribed Le Corbusier's copy (FLC).

36. Dolores Hayden's article "Skyscraper Seduction Skyscraper Rape" pioneered gender studies on the American skyscraper; *Heresies* 2 (May 1977), pp. 108–115. See also Elizabeth Lindquist Cock and Estelle Jussim, "Machismo in American Architecture," *Feminist Art Journal* (Spring 1974), pp. 8–10.

37. Louis Sullivan, "Growth and Decay," *Kindergarden Chats;* reprinted in Louis Sullivan, *Kindergarten Chats and Other Writings,* ed. Isabella Athey (New York: Wittenborn, 1947), p. 49.

38. Louis Sullivan, "The Tall Office Building Artistically Considered," originally published in *Inland Architect and News Record* 27 (May 1896) and reprinted in Sullivan, *Kindergarten Chats and Other Writings,* p. 206.

39. Montgomery Schuyler, *The Woolworth Building* (New York, 1913), the text of a brochure reproduced in Montgomery Schuyler, *American Architecture and Other Writings,* ed. William H. Jordy and Ralph Coe (Cambridge: Harvard University Press, 1961), vol. 2, p. 609.

40. *Cathedrals,* p. 41. On Le Corbusier and surrealism see, for example, Alexander Watt, "Fantasy on the Roofs of Paris; the Sur-

prising Apartment of M. Carlos de Beistegui," *Architectural Review* 79 (April 1936), pp. 155–159.

41. *Cathedrals,* pp. 145–146.

42. *Cathedrals,* p. 146.

43. On the economic forces in New York real estate, see Richard M. Hurd, *Principles of City Land Values* (New York: Record and Guide, orig. pub. 1903, 3rd ed. 1911). For a case study that examines the Singer Manufacturing Company's acquisition of land parcels by 1903 for its Singer Tower, see my chapter, "The Singer Tower and Skyscraper Reform," in *Ernest Flagg: Beaux-Arts Architect and Urban Reformer* (New York and Cambridge: Architectural History Foundation and MIT Press, 1986), pp. 209–233.

44. When Le Corbusier referred to African-Americans as *les nègres* (Negroes), he followed conventions of the 1930s. In reference to African-Americans and their culture during the 1930s, I follow that convention. *Cathédrales,* pp. 122–124; *Cathedrals,* pp. 85–87.

45. "Du salpêtre," *Cathédrales,* p. 220.

46. *Cathedrals,* pp. 155, 157, 158, 165.

47. Grand Central Palace was located at Lexington and 46th Street. "Local Road Growth Stresses Motor Transport Expansion," *New York Herald Tribune,* November 3, 1935, 11 p. 1; "6-Year Record Set at Closing of Motor Show," *New York Herald Tribune,* November 10, 1935, 1, p. 36; Le Corbusier attended the 36th annual National Automobile Show between November 2 and 10, but did not record the date of his visit. *Cathedrals,* p. 158. Gordon Buehrig, inventor of the Cord, probably saw the automobile show that fall. Letter, Le Corbusier to G. W. Buehrig, January 7, 1936 (FLC); see also Gordon M. Buehrig and William S. Jackson, *Rolling Sculpture* (Newfoundland, NJ: Haessner Publishing, 1975), p. 15.

48. *Quat'z Arts,* an elision of *Quatre Arts,* refers to the four arts taught at the Ecole des Beaux-Arts. "'Big Top' Circus to Be Seen at Beaux-Arts Ball," *New York Herald Tribune,* November 24, 1935, 4, p. 1. "Beaux-Arts Ball and Circus Tonight Will Be India Revel," *New York Herald Tribune,* December 6, 1935, p. 23. The ball received extensive press coverage. See also "17th Beaux-Arts Ball to Be Regal and Circus Fete," *New York Herald Tribune,* December 1, 1935, 4, p. 1; "Oriental Incense Marks Dinner Given for Subscribers to Ball," and "Brocades of East Adorn Gay Revel," *New York Times,* December 7, 1935, p. 21; "2,500 See Circus in Oriental Setting at Beaux-Arts Ball" and "Hindu, Chinese, Fanciful Costumes Mingle in Galaxy of Beaux-Arts Ball," *New York Herald Tribune,* December 7, 1935, p. 16. On Arthur Ware, see Henry F. Withey and Elsie Rathburn Withey, *Biographical Dictionary of American Architects* (Los Angeles: Hennessey and Ingalls, 1970), pp. 631–632. For an American experience of the Beaux-Arts ball in Paris, see T. Merrill Prentice, "Quatz Arts—My Experiences as a Student at the Ecole des Beaux-Arts in Paris 1924–1928," *JSAH* 44 (December 1985), pp. 384–387.

49. *Cathedrals,* p. 151.

50. Agenda, December 6, 1935 (FLC). Alma Clayburgh was among the celebrities and socialites who attended the ball. The guest list, widely reported in the New York press, did not mention Le Corbusier. See "2,500 See Circus in Oriental Setting at Beaux-Arts Ball," p. 16; "Beaux-Arts Ball Is Feast of Color," *New York Times,* December 7, p. 21.

51. Agenda, December 4, 1935 (FLC). Alma Clayburgh Grew, interviews with author, Boston, December 12, 1987, and June 10, 1994. Marguerite Tjader Harris called her a "warm, dark, exuberant dealer in personalities." Marguerite Tjader, *Theodore Dreiser: A New Dimension* (Norwalk, CT: Silvermine Publishers, 1965), p. 14. See also "Alma Clayburgh, Soprano, 76, Dead," obituary, *New York Times,* August 6, 1958, p. 25.

52. Le Corbusier may already have known Whitney Warren, who participated in post–World War I reconstruction efforts in France. See Marc Bédarida, "La Reconstruction de Reims (1918–1929)," in Cohen and Damisch, eds., *Américanisme et modernité,* pp. 262–263; Isabelle Jeanne Gournay, "France Discovers America, 1917–1939 (French Writings on American Architecture)" (Ph.D. diss., Yale University, 1989), p. 72.

53. *Cathedrals,* p. 150.

54. On the analogy with Astaire films, see John E. Mueller, *Astaire Dancing: The Musical Films* (New York: Alfred A. Knopf, 1985).

55. *Cathedrals,* pp. 150–151.

56. In 1933 Le Corbusier maintained that he did not frequent such events: "I don't like parties and it is years since I set foot in one." *VR* and *RC,* p. 6. Le Corbusier donned a military costume, as did Gabriel Guevrekian, Sigfried Giedion, and Pierre Jeanneret, at the first CIAM meeting at La Sarraz in 1928, *OC 1910–1965,* p. 13.

57. *Cathedrals,* pp. 150–151.

58. *Cathedrals,* pp. 149–151.

59. *Cathedrals,* pp. 110, 112, 123–124, 138, 140.

60. *Cathedrals,* pp. 98, 105, 109–110, 124, 140.

61. Alexis de Tocqueville, *Democracy in America,* ed. J. P. Mayer (Garden City, NY: Anchor Books, 1969), pp. 609, 629.

62. *Cathedrals,* p. 123. H. Allen Brooks, *Le Corbusier's Formative Years* (Chicago and London: University of Chicago Press, 1997), pp. 19–20.

63. *RC,* p. 91; *Cathedrals,* pp. 46–47, 166, 167–168.

64. Robert Benchley, "The Theatre," *New Yorker* 11 (November 23, 1935), pp. 26, 30.

65. *Cathédrales,* p. 308. Le Corbusier's analysis of *Jumbo* does not appear in the American edition.

66. *Cathedrals,* p. 157. Claude Autant-Lara, "Notes de voyage à Hollywood: La Première de 'City Lights,'" *Plans,* no. 3 (March 1931), pp. 142–144; Philippe Lamour, "'City Lights' de Charlie Chaplin," *Plans,* no. 5 (May 1931), pp. 74–80; Charles Chaplin, ". . . Humainement," *Plans,* no. 6 (June 1931), p. 57. Le Corbusier may also have been influenced by the image of Chaplin in Blaise Cendrars's *Hollywood, la mecque du cinéma* (Paris: Grasset, 1936). On Chaplin, see Richard H. Pells, *Radical Visions and American Dreams* (New York: Harper and Row, 1974), pp. 283–285, 286–287.

67. *Cathedrals,* p. 131.

68. As their manifesto of 1918 *Après le cubisme* makes clear, Le Corbusier and Amédée Ozenfant offered a corrective to cubism's preoccupation with what they considered to be its more decorative forms, which included those based on African art and the human form, through their engagement with purism based on machine age forms. Charles-Edouard Jeanneret and Amédée Ozenfant, *Après le cubisme* (Paris: Editions des Commentaires, 1918; reprint Turin: Bottega d'Erasmo, 1975). On purism, see Susan L. Ball, *Ozenfant and Purism: The Evolution of a Style 1915–1930* (Ann Arbor: UMI Research Press, 1981); Kenneth E. Silver, *Esprit de Corps: The Art of the Parisian Avant-Garde and the First World War, 1914–1925* (Princeton: Princeton University Press, 1989), pp. 227–234, 372–391. On the appropriation of forms derived from African art and culture by European and American modernists, see William Rubin, ed., *"Primitivism" in Modern Art: Affinity of the Tribal and the Modern,* 2 vols. (New York: Museum of Modern Art, 1984). On the interest of the Parisian avant-garde in *art nègre,* see Laura Rosenstock, "Léger, 'The Creation of the World,'" in William Rubin, ed., *"Primitivism" in 20th Century Art: Affinity of the Tribal and the Modern,* vol. 1 (New York: Museum of Modern Art, 1984), pp. 475–484; Patricia Leighten, "The White Peril and *L'Art nègre:* Picasso, Primitivism, and Anticolonialism," *Art Bulletin* 72 (December 1990), pp. 609–630; Marianna Torgovnick, *Gone Primitive: Savage Intellects, Modern Lives* (Chicago: University of Chicago Press, 1990). On the relationship between vernacular and modernism in Le Corbusier's theory and design, see Francesco Passanti, "The Vernacular, Modernism, and Le Corbusier," *JSAH* 56 (December 1997), pp. 438–451.

69. Reyner Banham argued that "works of engineering [especially American ones] were happily co-opted as manifestations of a kind of 'noble savagery' compatible with twentieth-century styles of life, and could be held up as models for emulation." *A Concrete Atlantis* (Cambridge: MIT Press), p. 15.

70. In his writings for *L'Esprit Nouveau* and elsewhere, Ozenfant confirmed that "for us Europeans a Negro mask is nothing more than a moving game of forms . . . " Julien Saint-Quentin [Ozenfant], "Nègres," *EN* 21 (March 1924), unpaged. See Vauvrecy [Ozenfant], "Ce mois passé . . . ," *EN* 9 (June 1921), pp. 1011–1015; and Vauvrecy [Ozenfant], "Ce mois passé . . . la music nègre," *EN* 10 (1921), p. 1087. See also F. D. [Françoise Ducros], "Pages choisies: La 'Mode nègre,'" in *L'Esprit nouveau: Le Corbusier et l'industrie 1920–1925,* p. 209.

71. The décor and costume designs for Léger's *Creation of the World* used "decorative" but "simple surfaces covered with flat colors." In collaboration with Darius Milhaud and Blaise Cendrars, Léger created an "African drama" using "African sculpture from the classical period . . . " in which "everything was transposed in it." Fernand Léger, "The Machine Aesthetic: Geometric Order and Truth," *Propos d'artistes* (Paris, 1925); reprinted in *Functions of Painting by Fernand Léger* (New York: Viking Press, 1973), p. 63. For an analysis of the ballet, see Rosenstock, "Léger, 'The Creation of the World.'"

72. James Clifford, *The Predicament of Culture: Twentieth-Century Ethnography, Literature, and Art* (Cambridge: Harvard University Press, 1988), pp. 122, 197.

73. Clifford, *The Predicament of Culture,* p. 136.

74. Ozenfant set out to show the "transcendental reality" between the culture of the Orient and that of the Occident. In his preface to the 1931 English edition of *Foundations of Modern Art,* he questioned rhetorically, "are we not ourselves Orientals long time emigrated?" This position also supported his broader agenda to seek a "universality of Great Art" through "common factors, physical and moral," but mostly formal. *Foundations of Modern Art* (New York: Brewer, Warren and Putnam, 1931), pp. viii, 241.

75. Clifford, *The Predicament of Culture,* p. 198n7.

76. Tower, "Jungle Music and Song of Machines: Jazz and American Dance in Weimar Culture," pp. 88, 95.

77. Léger intended them to show how "[modern] man becomes a mechanism like everything else; instead of being the end, as he formerly was, he becomes a means." In so doing he sought to transform the dancer into a mechanical object. Léger, "The Ballet-Spectacle, the Object-Spectacle," *Bulletin de l'Effort Moderne* (Paris, 1925); reprinted in *Functions of Painting by Fernand Léger,* p. 72, quoted in Rosenstock, "Léger, 'The Creation of the World,'" p. 482.

78. McLeod identified this transformation in "Le Rêve transi de Le Corbusier: L'Amérique 'catastrophe féerique,'" p. 211. Le Corbusier owned, for example, a copy of Carl Einstein's book *La Sculpture africaine* (Paris: Crès, 1922) (FLC).

79. On the political context of this synthesis, see McLeod, "Le Rêve transi de Le Corbusier: L'Amérique 'catastrophe féerique,'" pp. 219–221.

80. *Precisions,* p. 172.

81. On his return from America, Yvonne introduced him to a recording of "'Fifine,' a Parisian java," which she knew he would like. *Cathedrals,* p. 163. On the significance of jazz for Ozenfant, see Ball, *Ozenfant and Purism: The Evolution of a Style 1915–1930,* pp. 86–87.

82. *OC 1934–1938,* pp. 156–157.

83. Louis Carré, *Bronzes and Ivories from the Old Kingdom of Benin* (New York: M. Knoedler and Co., November 25–December 14, 1935) [FLC]. *Cathedrals*, p. 128. On Louis Carré's exhibition of Benin bronzes and ivories at Knoedler's, see Lewis Mumford, "The Art Galleries," *New Yorker* 11 (December 14, 1935), p. 96.

84. *Cathedrals*, p. 133.

85. Jean Petit, *Le Corbusier lui-même* (Geneva: Editions Rousseau, 1970), pp. 68–69. Elizabeth Davis Harris, "Le Corbusier and the Headquarters of the Brazilian Ministry of Education and Health 1936–1947" (Ph.D. diss., University of Chicago, 1984), p. 20. See also *Précisions*, pp. 12–13.

86. "Baker (Joséphine)," in *Encyclopédie*, p. 59; Petit, *Le Corbusier lui-même*, p. 69.

87. *Précisions*, p. 12; author's translation.

88. pour Josephine Baker
Ballet

cylindre ovale / on peut aussi // supprimer totalement // le cylindre // entrée // 2 / girls peintes tatouages Son // one step // ou sur *tam tam* pur nègre / sans musique 1 nègre sur // scène // 1 nègre porte 1 bananier // 3 L'homme et la femme modernes + N. York dansent exclusivement 1 one step // l'un contre l'autre // et lentement // 4 le cylindre descend // Joseph descend en singe // 5 elle met 1 robe moderne // s'assied // 6 s'avance sur socle, chante // 7 descend, chante // 8 dernier chant solennel: les dieux montent // fond mer méandres // de // Santos // et à la // fin 1 grand // transatlantique // Paroles traduites sur programme

for Josephine Baker
Ballet

oval cylinder // one could also eliminate the cylinder completely 1. entrance 2. showgirls made up with tattoos sound: one step or pure negro *tam tam* without music only one negro on stage // 1 negro wearing a banana tree // 3. a modern man and woman + New York dancing only 1 one step holding each other and slowly 4. the cylinder is lowered Joseph[ine] descends dressed as a monkey 5. she puts on a modern dress she sits down 6. goes forward on a podium, sings 7. steps off the podium, sings 8. last solemn song; the gods rise // background meandering sea of Santos and at the end a big ocean liner // Words translated on program

Le Corbusier Sketchbooks (New York and Cambridge: Architectural History Foundation and MIT Press), vol. 1, 1914–1948, B4, p. 14, no. 261.

89. No one will know the depth of their engagement. But it is not difficult to concur with her biographers that Baker and Le Corbusier probably had an affair, notwithstanding the presence in South America of her agent and husband, Pepito Abatino, whom some biographers have claimed was fabricated for publicity. See Phyllis Rose, *Jazz Cleopatra: Josephine Baker in Her Time* (New York: Vintage Books, 1991), pp. 114–117, 152; Jean-Claude Baker and Chris Chase, *Josephine: The Hungry Heart* (New York: Random House, 1993), pp. 164–165.

90. For a photograph of the party scene aboard the *Lutétia*, see Petit, *Le Corbusier lui-même*, p. 69; Charles Jencks, *Le Corbusier and the Tragic View of Architecture* (Cambridge: Harvard University Press, 1973), p. 108. Baker found his masquerade so amusing that she exclaimed, "What a pity you're an architect, Monsieur. You'd make a sensational partner." Baker and Chase, *Josephine: The Hungry Heart*, pp. 80–81.

91. Le Corbusier made the drawing on one of the ship's printed announcements, dated December 10, 1929. It is reproduced in *Le Corbusier Sketchbooks*, vol. 1, 1914–1948, B4, p. 13, no. 239.

92. Le Corbusier referred to "un village pour les petits enfants" and "Souvenez-vous du voyage en Amérique du Sud où j'étais en mission d'architecture et où vous m'aviez si gentiment demandé de vouloir collaborer avec vous à la rentrée en Europe, dans vos entreprises de construction." Letters, Le Corbusier to Joséphine Baker, February 4, 1935, and January 2, 1936 (FLC).

93. Josephine Baker arrived in New York in September 1935 to begin rehearsals for the Ziegfeld Follies engagement. Because of delays the show did not open until January 31, 1936. Rose, *Jazz Cleopatra: Josephine Baker in Her Time*, pp. 167–169. Back in Paris, Le Corbusier claimed he only then discovered that she had been living just five blocks from the Hotel Gotham where he stayed his last weeks. "Quel plaisir j'aurais eu à vous revoir, vous qui êtes si jolie, si gentille et nous aurions pu nous rappeler dans l'Amérique du Nord les bons souvenirs de l'Amérique du Sud. Je disais que je n'avais pas de chance avec vous. Parce que vous m'aviez fait promettre à Rio de Janeiro que je ne vous laisserais pas tomber; or c'est vous qui m'avez laissé tomber parfaitement et je ne vous pardonnerais pas si je ne savais que vous être (sic) une travailleuse acharnée." Letter, Le Corbusier to Joséphine Baker, January 2, 1936 (FLC).

94. Rose, *Jazz Cleopatra: Josephine Baker in Her Time*, p. 153.

95. The English translation is excerpted from the Le Corbusier text that appears in Jencks, *Le Corbusier and the Tragic View of Architecture*, p. 102. *Précisions*, p. 14.

96. On the Harlem Renaissance, see Nathan Irvin Huggins, *Harlem Renaissance* (New York: Oxford University Press, 1971; paperback edition, 1973). For a critique of Huggins's thesis that the Harlem Renaissance failed because it was too provincial, see David Levering Lewis, *When Harlem Was in Vogue* (New York: Alfred A. Knopf, 1981), p. 117; Houston A. Baker, Jr., *Modernism and the Harlem Renaissance* (Chicago: University of Chicago Press, 1987), pp. 9–14; Stephen Watson, *The Harlem Renaissance* (New York: Pantheon Books, 1995).

97. *Cathedrals*, p. 131.

98. Le Corbusier identified the first performance as simply *opéra nègre* and the second as *Porgy and Bess*. Agenda, November 17 and December 3, 1935 (FLC). The Alvin Theatre was located at 250 West 52nd Street, near Broadway. See George Gershwin, "Rhapsody in Catfish Row," *New York Times,* October 20, 1935, 10, pp. 1, 2. The other *opéra nègre* may have been *The Green Pastures,* which Olin Downes called a "Negro parable, or mystery play with popular music"; it may also have been *Emperor Jones,* which Downes referred to as Louis Gruenberg's "musical investiture of the celebrated play of Eugene O'Neill." Olin Downes, "The Week's News and Comment . . . ," *New York Times,* October 20, 1935, 10, p. 7.

99. On the significance of *Porgy and Bess,* see Huggins, *Harlem Renaissance,* pp. 295–296.

100. *Cathedrals,* p. 131. *Porgy and Bess* was a collaboration between Gershwin and DuBose Heyward, writer of the original play. Hollywood director Rouben Mamoulian staged the original play and directed the folk opera; Alexander Smallens (of the Philadelphia Orchestra) conducted the musical score. John W. Bubbles performed the role of Sportin' Life, and Todd Duncan and Anne Brown performed those of Porgy and Bess, respectively. Gershwin, "Rhapsody in Catfish Row," *New York Times,* p. 1.

101. Gertrude Stein wrote the libretto and Virgil Thomson the musical score for *Four Saints in Three Acts.* Sets were by New York artist Florine Stettheimer. On the significance of the opera (with a photograph of the production), see Gaddis, "'The New Athens': Moments from an Era," pp. 35–37.

102. Duhamel claimed, for example, that "the harsh, barbarous, and mysterious voice of Africa often wails" in the Negro spirituals sung at the Tuskegee Institute in Alabama. Duhamel, *America the Menace,* p. 145.

103. According to Nathan Huggins, Morand viewed Harlem Negroes to be "primitive men" and invested them with the ability to "shatter the mechanical rhythm of America." Paul Morand, *New York* (New York: Henry Holt, 1930), p. 270. For an analysis of Morand's view of Harlem, see Huggins, *Harlem Renaissance,* pp. 90–91.

104. Le Corbusier considered Negro hymns and folk songs comparable to "Gregorian chants, Dutch-English psalms, German and Tyrolean lieder." See *Cathedrals,* pp. 158–159.

105. McLeod, "Le Rêve transi de Le Corbusier: L'Amérique 'catastrophe féerique,'" pp. 208–227.

106. *Cathedrals,* pp. 158–161. From October 1935 to the spring of 1936 Armstrong, his band, and "an elaborate black-and-tan show" performed at a midtown Broadway club called the Great White Way. According to James Lincoln Collier that club was located on the "site of the old Connie's Inn which had died because of the Depression." In 1935 New Yorkers and the *New Yorker* still called it Connie's Inn. James Lincoln Collier, *Louis Armstrong, an American Genius* (New York: Oxford University Press, 1983), p. 276. "Goings On About Town," *New Yorker* 11 (November 30, 1935), p. 4.

107. Marguerite Tjader, "Portrait of Le Corbusier," unpublished manuscript, p. 40 (Harris family papers). The Savoy Ballroom, located at Lenox Avenue and 140th Street, opened in 1926. It was the largest dance hall in Harlem. On its history and significance during the Harlem Renaissance, see Jervis Anderson, *This Was Harlem: A Cultural Portrait, 1900–1950* (New York: Farrar Straus and Giroux, 1981), pp. 307–314.

108. *Cathedrals,* pp. 160–161.

109. Claude McKay, *Harlem: Negro Metropolis* (New York: Harcourt Brace Jovanovich, 1968; orig. pub. 1940), p. 119.

110. *Cathedrals,* pp. 131, 159.

111. Some European intellectuals, however, deplored jazz. Georges Duhamel, who heard jazz during his visit to the United States in 1928, believed that it was embraced by avant-gardists merely for the sake of being modern: "Jazz is a triumph of barbaric folly that has received praise, interpretation, and technical commentary from those educated musicians who, more than anything else, fear to be regarded as not in the last degree 'modern,' and thus to vex their clientèle, and who bow down to jazz as the painters of 1910 bowed down to cubism, for fear, as the phrase is, of missing the bus." Duhamel, *America the Menace,* p. 121.

112. *Cathedrals,* p. 161.

113. *Cathedrals,* p. 138.

114. *Cathedrals,* pp. 92, 110, 124, 128.

115. *Cathedrals,* p. 130. On Soby and Austin, see Weber, *Patron Saints.*

116. *Cathedrals,* pp. 127, 132.

117. *RC,* p. 177.

118. *Cathedrals,* pp. 3–6.

119. For commentary in the French popular and professional press on New York skyscrapers, see Francesco Passanti, "Le Corbusier and New York, before He Went There," paper for symposium "Le Corbusier, Travels and International Influence: Le Corbusier and North America," VIIes Rencontres de la Fondation Le Corbusier 1996–1997, co-sponsored by Harvard University. See also Gournay, "France Discovers America, 1917–1939 (French Writings on American Architecture)."

120. I owe this observation to Francesco Passanti. See Iain Boyd White, *Bruno Taut and the Architecture of Activism* (New York: Cambridge University Press, 1982), pp. 55–77.

121. Umberto Eco, "Dreaming the Middle Ages," in Umberto Eco, *Travels in Hyperreality* (New York: Harcourt Brace Jovanovich, 1986), pp. 64–65.

122. Le Corbusier's teacher Charles L'Eplattenier had introduced him to John Ruskin's writings. See Paul Venable Turner, *The Education of Le Corbusier* (New York: Garland Publishing), pp. 30–37. On the early impact of Ruskin, see Mary Patricia May Sekler, *The Early Drawings of Charles-Edouard Jeanneret (Le Cor-*

busier), 1902–1908 (New York: Garland, 1977). On the later impact of Ruskin on Le Corbusier, see Mary Patricia May Sekler, "Constancies and Changes in Le Corbusier's Urbanism: Part I. Attitudes Toward the Man-Made Environment," *Center* 5 (1989), pp. 44–59. Turner suggests that Auguste Perret was responsible for introducing Le Corbusier to the writings of Viollet-le-Duc. With his first paycheck from Perret in 1908, Le Corbusier purchased the full set of the *Dictionnaire raisonné de l'architecture française du XIe au XVIe siècle,* 10 vols. (Paris, 1854–1868); see Turner, *The Education of Le Corbusier,* p. 51.

123. Le Corbusier, *L'Art décoratif d'aujourd'hui,* p. 136.

124. On the "Lamp of Life," see John Ruskin, *The Seven Lamps of Architecture* (London: Smith, Elder, 1849), pp. 136–161.

125. On Viollet-le-Duc's rationalism, see John Summerson, "Viollet-le-Duc and the Rational Point of View," in *Heavenly Mansions* (New York: W. W. Norton, 1963), pp. 135–158.

126. Henry-Russell Hitchcock, "History," in Henry-Russell Hitchcock and Philip Johnson, *The International Style* (New York: W. W. Norton, 1932), p. 22. See also Henry-Russell Hitchcock, Jr., *Romanticism and Reintegration* (New York: Payson and Clarke, 1929). For Le Corbusier's understanding of "an international language" during the Middle Ages, see *Cathedrals,* p. 4.

127. *Cathédrales,* pp. 3, 26, 78.

128. *Cathédrales,* p. 175; *Cathedrals,* p. 119.

129. Referring to Duhamel, Le Corbusier complained, "I feel sorry for the visitor . . . who locks up . . . his understanding in advance." *Cathedrals,* p. 121.

130. *Cathedrals,* p. 42; for a similar statement, see p. 36.

131. Letter, Le Corbusier to [Richard] de Rochemont, April 7, 1936 (FLC).

132. *Cathedrals,* pp. 92, 93, 108–109, 212.

133. *Cathedrals,* pp. 29–30.

134. Letter, Le Corbusier to "Labatut," December 4, 1935 (Jean Labatut papers, Box 46, Manuscripts Division, Department of Rare Books and Special Collections, Princeton University Library).

135. *Cathedrals,* p. 112.

136. *Cathedrals,* p. 58; Le Corbusier made frequent annotations to his copy of Francis Delaisi, *Les Contradictions du monde moderne* (Paris: Payot, 1926) (FLC).

137. *Cathedrals,* p. 174.

138. Le Corbusier annotated and underlined his copy of Frédéric Nietzsche, *Ainsi parlait Zarathoustra* (Paris, 1908). See Turner, *The Education of Le Corbusier,* pp. 8–29, 55–69. Charles Jencks employs the Nietzschean analogy in *Le Corbusier and the Tragic View of Architecture.*

139. On Le Corbusier's use of these techniques, see Beatriz Colomina, *Privacy and Publicity: Modern Architecture as Mass Media* (Cambridge: MIT Press, 1994). For an analysis of the impact of Russian constructivist theory and design on *L'Esprit Nouveau,* Le Corbusier, and Ozenfant, see Jean-Louis Cohen, *Le Corbusier and the Mystique of the USSR* (Princeton: Princeton University Press, 1992), pp. 2–17. Le Corbusier employed a similar technique for the cover of his *Croisade, ou, le Crépuscule des académies* (Paris: G. Crès, 1933).

140. This analysis first appeared in my paper "The Trans-Atlantic Misunderstanding: Le Corbusier's First Visit to America in 1935," at the 1985 Paris symposium "L'Américanisme et la modernité." The illustration of the Manhattan plan was taken from a plate in Le Corbusier's well-perused book by Thomas Adams, *The Building of the City, Regional Plan of New York and Its Environs,* vol. 2 (New York: Regional Plan of New York and Its Environs, 1931), p. 300 (FLC).

141. *Cathedrals,* pp. 26, 68. On Le Corbusier's understanding of Manhattan's gridiron plan, see chapter 5.

142. *Cathedrals,* p. 9.

143. The dedication in *Cathédrales* reads "A MA MERE, femme de courage et de foi."

9 The "Country of Timid People" Responds

1. Letter, Wallace K. Harrison to Le Corbusier, February 14, 1936 (FLC). On the Mandel House designed by Edward Durell Stone, see chapter 10.

2. "Corbusierismus," *Time* 26 (November 4, 1935), p. 36.

3. For example, Abby Aldrich Rockefeller was not inclined to seek notice in newspaper society pages or to engage in "splashy events." John Ensor Harr and Peter J. Johnson, *The Rockefeller Century* (New York: Charles Scribner's Sons, 1988). Bernice Kert, *Abby Aldrich Rockefeller: The Woman in the Family* (New York: Random House, 1993), pp. 41, 80, 376.

4. Wallace Harrison designed for Nelson Rockefeller the Hawes Guest House at Pocantico in Tarrytown, NY, in 1939 and the Anchorage, a summer house at Seal Harbor, ME, in 1941. Victoria Newhouse, *Wallace K. Harrison, Architect* (New York: Rizzoli, 1989), pp. 68, 69, 99, 100, 101, figs. 45, 46, 80, 82, 83.

5. Richard Hofstadter, *Anti-intellectualism in American Life* (New York: Alfred A. Knopf, 1964), pp. 214–221.

6. Harold Stearns, "The Intellectual Life," in Harold Stearns, ed., *Civilization in the United States* (New York: Harcourt, Brace, 1922), as quoted in Richard H. Pells, *Radical Visions and American Dreams* (New York: Harper and Row, 1974), p. 24.

7. "Corbusierismus," *Time,* p. 36. The term "corbusierismus" previously appeared in a Museum of Modern Art press release suggesting that "in Germany and in Russia whole aspects of modern

architecture have crystallized around the word 'corbusierismus.'" Undated press release announcing Le Corbusier's speech, Woman's Radio Review, October 21, 1935, Museum of Modern Art (DAD, MoMA, NY). Articles on Wright appeared regularly in the Luce publications *Architectural Forum, Time,* and *Life.* See also Henry Russel [sic] Hitchcock, "Le Corbusier and the United States," *Zodiac* 16 (1966), p. 9.

8. [Henry Saylor], "The Editor's Diary," *Architecture* 72 (December 1935), p. 344.

9. Richard Pommer, "Lewis Mumford," lecture at the Institute of Fine Arts, New York University, May 1, 1989. I thank Francesco Passanti for generously sharing his lecture notes with me.

10. Henry-Russell Hitchcock, *Frank Lloyd Wright* (Paris: Editions "Cahiers d'art," [1928]); Henry-Russell Hitchcock, Jr., "Frank Lloyd Wright," in *Modern Architecture: International Exhibition* (New York: Museum of Modern Art, 1932), pp. 29–55.

11. "Corbusierismus," *Time,* p. 36.

12. Henry-Russell Hitchcock, Jr., *Le Corbusier* (New York: Museum of Modern Art, 1935), unpaged. For a discussion of Hitchcock's critical position with respect to American urban architecture, see my exhibition review of Janine A. Mileaf, *Constructing Modernism: Berenice Abbott and Henry-Russell Hitchcock* (Middletown, CT: Davison Art Center, Wesleyan University, 1993), in "Exhibitions," *JSAH* 53 (June 1994), pp. 232–234.

13. Lewis Mumford, "The Sky Line," *New Yorker* 11 (November 9, 1935), pp. 68–69.

14. ". . . le plus bon, je pense, qu'aucun à produit pour l'urbanisme contemporaine [sic]," letter, Lewis Mumford to Le Corbusier, September 18, 1937 (FLC). Lewis Mumford, *The Culture of Cities* (New York: Harcourt, Brace, 1938), p. [437], fig. 30. The plan of Nemours appears on the title page (and model on p. 5, fig. 22) of Werner Hegemann's *City Planning Housing,* vol. 3 (New York: Architectural Book Publishing Co., 1938).

15. See, for example, Camille Mauclair, "Toward a New Architecture," *Living Age* 344 (July 1933), pp. 441–433.

16. *VR* and *RC,* p. 340.

17. "Call to the Convention," *Bulletin [Technical America]* 2 (January 1935), p. 3.

18. Gerald Price, "Le Corbusier—Lost Pioneer," *Bulletin [Technical America]* 3 (January 1936), p. 5. I thank Marc Dessauce for drawing my attention to this article. See "Statement made by Mr. Le Corbusier, French Architect and City Planner on the Necessity and Possibility of Inaugurating Immediately a Rehousing Program on [a] National Scale in the United States" (FLC; see appendix C, below).

19. A photograph of Le Corbusier's Weissenhof housing appears in Simon Breines, "New Deal Housing—Successful Failure," *Bulletin [Technical America]* 2 (May 1935), p. 6.

20. Price, "Le Corbusier—Lost Pioneer," p. 5.

21. Price, "Le Corbusier—Lost Pioneer," p. 5; *Towards a New Architecture,* p. 269.

22. Price, "Le Corbusier—Lost Pioneer," p. 9.

23. *Cathédrales,* pp. 292–307; *Cathedrals,* pp. 202–212.

24. Percival Goodman, interview with author, New York City, February 20, 1986. Requests to the U.S. Department of Justice and other government agencies for information on Le Corbusier under the Freedom of Information-Privacy Act (FOIPA) were unproductive. To my inquiry, John H. Wright, Information and Privacy Coordinator for the Central Intelligence Agency, responded that the agency "can neither confirm nor deny the existence or nonexistence of any CIA records responsive to your request." Letter, John H. Wright to author, October 21, 1991.

25. Letters, Percival Goodman to Le Corbusier, January 14 and March 24, 1936; Le Corbusier to Percival Goodman, January 24, 1936 (FLC).

26. "Hearst Permits Le Corbusier to Envision Planned Future," *Bulletin [Technical America]* 3 (April 1936), p. 9. Perry's plans were included in a study on "The Neighborhood Unit" in *Regional Survey of New York: Neighborhood and Community Planning,* vol. 7 (New York: Regional Plan of New York and Its Environs, 1929), pp. 21–140; see also Thomas Adams, *The Regional Plan of New York and Its Environs,* vol. 2, *The Building of the City* (New York: Regional Plan of New York and Its Environs, 1931), p. 342; Clarence Arthur Perry, *Housing for the Machine Age* (New York: Russell Sage Foundation, 1939).

27. "Hearst Permits Le Corbusier to Envision Planned Future," p. 9.

28. Warren I. Susman, *Culture as History* (New York: Pantheon Books, 1984), pp. 172–173.

29. Percival Goodman, interview with author, New York City, February 20, 1986. On Le Corbusier's involvement with the Vichy government, see Rémi Baudoui, "Vichy: L'Attitude de Le Corbusier pendant la guerre," in *Encyclopédie,* pp. 455–459.

30. Charles C. Alexander, *Nationalism in American Thought 1930–1945* (Chicago: Rand McNally, 1969), pp. 165–169; Susman, *Culture as History,* p. 157.

31. Henry-Russell Hitchcock, interview with author, New York City, December 13, 1984 (hereafter cited as Hitchcock interview).

32. Lewis Mumford, *The Brown Decades: A Study of the Arts in America 1865–1895* (New York: Dover, 1955; orig. pub. 1931), p. 139. See also his article "Is the Skyscraper Tolerable?," *Architecture* 55 (February 1927), pp. 67–69.

33. "Répertoire des collaborateurs de Le Corbusier ayant travaillé à l'atelier 35 rue de Sèvres ainsi qu'aux travaux executés à l'étranger" (FLC). Reiner received his B.Arch. degree, later con-

verted to an M.Arch. degree, from Harvard's Graduate School of Design. Jan Reiner, interview with author, July 16, 1994.

34. "Introduction," *Cathedrals,* p. xvi.

35. Pells, *Radical Visions and American Dreams,* pp. 199–200; Susman, *Culture as History,* pp. 133–141. See also Morton and Lucia White, *The Intellectual versus the City* (Cambridge: Harvard University Press and MIT Press, 1962).

36. Alexander, *Nationalism in American Thought 1930–1945,* pp. 11–13; Lewis Mumford, "Mr. Rockefeller Must Lead," *Nation* 136 (February 8, 1933), p. 137, quoted in Pells, *Radical Visions and American Dreams,* p. 84.

37. George E. Sokolsky, quoted in Alexander, *Nationalism in American Thought 1930–1945,* p. 11.

38. Hitchcock interview, December 13, 1984.

39. Johnson's and Hitchcock's remarks are contained in Hitchcock, "Le Corbusier and the United States," p. 7.

40. Hitchcock interview, December 13, 1984.

41. Max Abramovitz, interview with author, New York City, June 7, 1987.

42. Max Abramovitz, interview with author, New York City, June 7, 1987.

43. Letter, Thomas Dabney Mabry to Le Corbusier, December 2, 1935 (DAD, MoMA, NY).

44. Letter, Carl Schniewind to Le Corbusier (fragment), May 5, 1935 (FLC).

45. "Le Corbusier Lecture Tour Statement of Receipts and Expenditures," Museum of Modern Art (FLC). Le Corbusier successfully challenged a line item of $70.37 in the account for the Pierre Chenal film *L'Architecture d'aujourd'hui,* which he himself supplied. Letter, Le Corbusier to Alfred Barr (fragment), December 11, 1935 (FLC). The museum later agreed to omit that expenditure. Letter, Thomas Dabney Mabry to Le Corbusier, December 13, 1935 (FLC).

46. "Expenditures for Publicity on Le Corbusier Lecture Tour . . . ," Museum of Modern Art (FLC). Letter, Thomas Dabney Mabry to Le Corbusier, December 13, 1935 (FLC).

47. Letter, Le Corbusier to Alfred Barr, December 11, 1935 (FLC).

48. Geoffrey T. Hellman, "Profiles: From Within to Without— II," *New Yorker* 23 (May 3, 1947), p. 38.

49. Letter, Philip Goodwin to Le Corbusier, January 25, 1936 (FLC).

50. Robert Jacobs, interview with author, Pawling, NY, November 21, 1984. Le Corbusier later thanked Papadaki for being "un bon compagnon à New York." Letter, Le Corbusier to Stamo Papadaki, c/o Wallace Harrison, April 7, 1936 (FLC).

51. Letter, Le Corbusier to Fernand Léger, February 20, 1936 (FLC).

52. Letter, Le Corbusier to Carl Schniewind, December 31, 1935 (FLC).

53. Letter, Le Corbusier to Philip Goodwin, December 31, 1935 (FLC).

54. *Cathedrals,* p. 97.

55. Genevieve Harlow Goodwin (Mrs. James Lippincott Goodwin), interview with author, Hartford, April 1, 1987.

56. Goodwin quoted the excerpt from Le Corbusier's letter to Carl Schniewind, April 8, 1935. Letters, Philip Goodwin to Le Corbusier, January 25, 1936 (FLC); Le Corbusier to Philip Goodwin, February 21, 1936 (FLC).

57. Letter, Philip Goodwin to Le Corbusier, January 25, 1936 (FLC).

58. Letter, Le Corbusier to Fernand Léger, February 20, 1936 (FLC).

59. Letter, Le Corbusier to Philip Goodwin, February 21, 1936 (FLC).

60. Letter, Philip Goodwin to Le Corbusier, March 9, 1936 (FLC).

61. *Cathédrales,* pp. 140–142; *Cathedrals,* pp. 97–99.

62. Letters, Le Corbusier to William Lescaze, May 7, 1936; Le Corbusier to Henry-Russell Hitchcock, March 30, 1936 (FLC).

63. The model of the Nemours project was not in New York because it had been included in the traveling version of Le Corbusier's exhibition (see appendix B).

64. Letters, Le Corbusier to Albert Frey, November 2, 1937; Le Corbusier to Wallace Harrison, October 15, 1938; Le Corbusier to "Madame Wallace K. Harrison," August 1, 1939; Le Corbusier to Stamo Papadaki, October 15, 1938; Le Corbusier to Fernand Léger, October 15, November 17, December 20, 1938, February 18, 1939 (FLC).

65. Letter, Le Corbusier to Wallace Harrison, October 15, 1938 (FLC). At Goodwin's own request Le Corbusier had sent over his model of the Palais des Soviets for the exhibition. Letter, Philip Goodwin to Le Corbusier, August 12, 1935 (FLC).

66. Letters, John McAndrew [to Mr. Garreau-Dombasle], April 23, 1940; M. Garreau-Dombasle to Le Corbusier, May 2, 1940 (FLC).

67. For example, in soliciting the work of Frank Lloyd Wright for the 1932 "Modern Architecture: International Exhibition," Johnson informed him that "the main part of the Exhibition will be composed of models by the most prominent architects of the world." Letter, Philip Johnson to Frank Lloyd Wright, April 1, 1931, cited in Anthony Alofsin, "Frank Lloyd Wright as a Man of Letters," in Anthony Alofsin, ed., *Frank Lloyd Wright: An Index*

to the Taliesin Correspondence, vol. 1 (New York: Garland, 1988), p. x.

68. Letter, Le Corbusier to Philip Johnson, December 6, 1950 (FLC).

69. Cathedrals, p. 186.

70. Cathedrals, pp. 9, 217. Compare, for example, his earlier statement, "Une grande époque vient de commencer" (a great epoch has begun) in Vers une architecture, pp. viii, 69; Towards a New Architecture, pp. 3, 89.

71. On the meaning of open works, see Umberto Eco, The Role of the Reader (Bloomington: Indiana University Press, 1984), pp. 33–34, 58–66.

72. Cathédrales, pp. 153–157.

73. Cathedrals, pp. 125–126.

74. Cathédrales, p. 187 (excised from Cathedrals).

75. Letter, Le Corbusier to Nelson Rockefeller, March 13, 1936 (FLC).

76. Letter, Le Corbusier to Nelson Rockefeller, May 15, 1936 (FLC).

77. Marguerite Tjader, "Portrait of Le Corbusier," unpublished manuscript, 1984 (Harris family papers).

78. Cathédrales, p. 56; I translate splendeur féerique as "enchanted splendor." Cathedrals, p. 40.

79. Letter, Le Corbusier to Marguerite Harris, December 14, 1935, written aboard the Lafayette (Frances Loeb Library, Harvard Design School). In her "Portrait of Le Corbusier," Tjader [Harris] reproduces excerpts of the letter in translation (Harris family papers).

80. Letter, M [Marguerite Harris] to Ah, cher Corbu, undated (FLC).

81. Inscription in Marguerite Tjader Harris's copy of When the Cathedrals Were White.

82. Marguerite Harris described Yvonne as "his beautiful, Mediterranean wife," who was his Gardien du Foyer [sic] (guardian of the hearth), as he had called her in his symbolic paintings, and of whom he said, "Yvonne, without whom I would not be what I am." Tjader, "Portrait of Le Corbusier" (Harris family papers).

83. Cathedrals, p. 214.

84. Cathedrals, p. 43.

85. Tjader, "Portrait of Le Corbusier" (Harris family papers).

10 The Consequences of Transatlantic Exchange

1. On the "second era of the machine age, the era of harmony," see VR and RC, pp. 340–341.

2. Giorgio Ciucci, "The Invention of the Modern Movement," Oppositions 24 (Spring 1981), pp. 68–91. In Cathedrals Le Corbusier alluded to discord at CIAM congresses and "resistance" from "our Continental associates" over the use of elevators, which he considered "the key to all the urban reforms," p. 64.

3. Jean-Louis Cohen, Le Corbusier and the Mystique of the USSR: Theories and Projects for Moscow 1928–1936 (Princeton: Princeton University Press, 1987), pp. 164–203.

4. For Le Corbusier's version of the Bastion Kellermann debacle, see Cathédrales, pp. 29–32; Cathedrals, pp. 21–24. On the League's rejection, see Cathédrales, p. 8; Cathedrals, p. 7. For his other accounts of these rejections, see OC 1910–1929, pp. 160–173; OC 1929–1934, pp. 13, 123–137; OC 1934–1938, pp. 148–151; Jean Petit, Le Corbusier lui-même (Geneva: Editions Rousseau, 1970), pp. 65–66, 74, 82–83. See also Le Corbusier, Croisade ou le Crépuscule des académies (Paris: G. Crès, 1933).

5. Cathedrals, pp. 60, 85, 142, 149.

6. Le Corbusier's Croisade ou le Crépuscule des académies supports defeat of the academy based on the ideology of the first machine age.

7. Cathedrals, p. 158.

8. Cathedrals, p. 133.

9. VR and RC, p. 133.

10. Cathedrals, p. 189.

11. Cathédrales, p. 306; Cathedrals, p. 211.

12. For an insightful comparison of the French and German texts, and the respective agendas of Le Corbusier and German participants of CIAM I, see Ciucci, "The Invention of the Modern Movement," pp. 75–79. For the French text of the CIAM I program, see Martin Steinmann, ed., CIAM, Dokumente 1928–1939 (Basel and Stuttgart: Birkhäuser, 1979), pp. 16–21.

13. Cathedrals, p. 207.

14. Ciucci, "The Invention of the Modern Movement," pp. 75, 78.

15. VR and RC, pp. 47–50, quoted in Ciucci, "The Invention of the Modern Movement," p. 88.

16. Philip Goodwin, "Excerpt from lecture, delivered at the Museum of Modern Art, New York, by Le Corbusier, October 25 [sic], 1935. . . ." (DAD, MoMA, NY); see chapter 3, text and note 21.

17. Ciucci, "The Invention of the Modern Movement," p. 88.

18. Cathedrals, p. 206.

19. Stanislaus von Moos, Le Corbusier: Elements of a Synthesis (Cambridge: MIT Press, 1979), p. 101.

20. Peter Serenyi, "Timeless but of Its Time: Le Corbusier's Architecture in India," in H. Allen Brooks, ed., Le Corbusier (Princeton: Princeton University Press, 1987), pp. 177–178.

21. *Cathedrals,* pp. 55, 66.

22. The Empire State Building, 350 Fifth Avenue (1928–1931), was designed by Shreve, Lamb and Harmon; the Chrysler Building, 405 Lexington Avenue (1929–1930), by William Van Alen; the Irving Trust Company Building, 1 Wall Street and Broadway (1929–1932), by Ralph Walker (Voorhees, Gmelin and Walker).

23. *Cathedrals,* pp. 59–60; see also H. I. Brock, "Le Corbusier Scans Gotham's Towers," *New York Times,* November 3, 1935, 7, pp. 10, 23.

24. For discussions of the tripartite division, see Winston Weisman, "A New View of Skyscraper History," in Edgar Kaufmann, Jr., ed., *The Rise of an American Skyscraper* (New York: Praeger, 1970), p. 136; Montgomery Schuyler, "The 'Skyscraper' Up to Date" *Record* 8 (January–March 1899), pp. 231–257, excerpted in Montgomery Schuyler, *American Architecture and Other Writings,* ed. William H. Jordy and Ralph Coe (Cambridge: Harvard University Press, 1961), vol. 2, pp. 437–441.

25. Louis Sullivan, "The Tall Office Building Artistically Considered," *Lippincott's Magazine* 57 (March 1896); revised version reprinted in Tim and Charlotte Benton, eds., *Architecture and Design: 1890–1939* (New York: Whitney Library of Design, 1975), pp. 11–14.

26. *City of Tomorrow,* pp. 45, 96.

27. The Gotham Hotel (1905; now Hotel Maxim's de Paris at Fifth Avenue and 55th Street) designed by Hiss and Weeks, is illustrated in Elliot Willensky and Norval White's *AIA Guide to New York City,* 3rd ed. (New York: Harcourt Brace Jovanovich, 1988), p. 271. The Ritz Tower apartment hotel at Park Avenue and 57th Street (1925) was designed by Emery Roth and Carrère and Hastings. *Cathedrals,* p. 60. On the Ritz Tower, see Robert A. M. Stern, Gregory Gilmartin, and Thomas Mellins, *New York 1930* (New York: Rizzoli, 1987), pp. 212–213.

28. *Cathedrals,* pp. 67, 89.

29. John Ruskin, *The Seven Lamps of Architecture* (London: Smith, Elder, 1849), p. 64.

30. John W. Cook and Heinrich Klotz, *Conversations with Architects* (New York: Praeger, 1973), p. 28.

31. *OC 1938–1946,* pp. 48–65.

32. Le Corbusier documents the early evolution of the *brise-soleil* in his design development in *OC 1938–1946,* pp. 108–113. See "Maison locative," in H. Allen Brooks, ed., *The Le Corbusier Archive* (New York, London, and Paris: Garland and Fondation Le Corbusier, 1982), vol. 11, *Immeuble, 24, rue Nungesser-et-Coli and Other Buildings and Projects, 1933,* pp. 485–497; *OC 1929–1934,* pp. 170–173. William Jordy called the *brise-soleil* the "most important architectural invention of the decade [1930s] to enlarge the grammar of the International Style." See "The International Style in the 1930s," *JSAH* 24 (March 1965), p. 14.

33. *OC 1938–1946,* pp. 61–62.

34. *EN* 19 (December 1923), unpaged; Le Corbusier, *L'Art décoratif d'aujourd'hui* (Paris: G. Crès, 1925), [p. 83].

35. Postcard, Blaise Cendrars to Le Corbusier, 5–26 [May 1926] (FLC).

36. *Urbanisme,* p. 273.

37. Serenyi, "Timeless but of Its Time: Le Corbusier's Architecture in India," p. 178.

38. *OC 1938–1946,* p. 50; *OC 1910–1965,* p. 124.

39. *Cathedrals,* pp. 61–63.

40. Agenda, December 2, 1935 (FLC). Otis elevators had been installed in some of the buildings at Rockefeller Center, but the contract for the RCA Building was awarded to Westinghouse because it rented nearly three floors at the Center. See Carol Herselle Krinsky, *Rockefeller Center* (New York: Oxford University Press, 1978), pp. 73, 76. In his proposal of December 6, 1935, to Wallace Harrison, Le Corbusier specified Otis elevators. See Le Corbusier, "Note p. [our] Wallace Harrison" (Wallace K. Harrison Papers, Avery Architectural and Fine Arts Library, Columbia University).

41. When Le Corbusier speaks of "Radio City" he is referring to the RCA Building with its National Broadcasting Company studios, rather than the theater adjacent to it. *Cathedrals,* p. 33, 62.

42. *Cathedrals,* pp. 54, 62–63. On the mechanical systems of the RCA Building, see Reyner Banham, *The Architecture of the Well-Tempered Environment,* 2nd ed. (Cambridge: MIT Press, 1984), pp. 162, 181.

43. *Cathedrals,* p. 43.

44. William H. Jordy, "Rockefeller Center," *American Buildings and Their Architects: The Impact of European Modernism in the Mid-Twentieth Century* (New York: Doubleday, 1972), p. 45.

45. *Cathedrals,* p. 74.

46. Von Moos, *Le Corbusier: Elements of a Synthesis,* p. 247; Cohen, *Le Corbusier and the Mystique of the USSR,* pp. 179–180, fig. 260.

47. On distinctions between the structural dynamics of suspension and concrete arch bridges, see Carl W. Condit, *American Building Art: The Twentieth Century* (New York: Oxford University Press, 1961), pp. 129–150, 195–207.

48. *Cathedrals,* pp. 75–77.

49. *Agenda,* November 27, 1935; Le Corbusier, "CCCC" [notes to Union Carbide executives Rafferty and Davison] (FLC). "Concernant Mr Nelson Rockefeller pour Wallace Harrison," December 6, 1935 (Wallace K. Harrison Papers, Avery Architectural and Fine Arts Library, Columbia University).

50. From 1932 to 1936 Le Corbusier submitted four proposals, the previous three (A, B, C) having been rejected. *OC 1934–1938,* pp. 140–155, 158–169. On the Temps Nouveaux pavilion, see Le Corbusier, *Des canons, des munitions? Merci! Des logis . . . s.v.p.*

Pavillon des Temps Nouveaux (Boulogne-sur-Seine: Editions de l'Architecture d'Aujourd'hui, 1938).

51. Danilo Udovicki-Selb, "The Elusive Faces of Modernity: The Invention of the 1937 Paris Exhibition and the Temps Nouveaux Pavilion" (Ph.D. diss., MIT, 1995), pp. 309–317; Danilo Udovicki-Selb, "Le Corbusier and the Paris Exhibition of 1937, the Temps Nouveaux Pavilion," *JSAH* 56 (March 1997), pp. 42–63.

52. Le Corbusier, *Des canons, des munitions? Merci! Des logis . . . s.v.p. Pavillon des Temps Nouveaux*, p. 13. On the use of open-truss pylons in France see, for example, the Pont Transbordeur in Marseilles (1905), illustrated in Sigfried Giedion, *Bauen in Frankreich, Eisen, Eisenbeton* (Leipzig: Klinkhardt & Biermann, 1928), pp. 62–63.

53. Le Corbusier, *Des canons, des munitions? Merci! Des logis . . . s.v.p. Pavillon des Temps Nouveaux,* p. 146; *Cathédrales,* p. 109; *Cathedrals,* p. 77.

54. *OC 1934–1938,* pp. 161, 166, 169.

55. *Cathédrales,* p. 112. This description is abridged in the American edition. *Cathedrals,* p. 79. For a section drawing of the ramps at Grand Central Terminal, see Condit, *American Building Art: The Twentieth Century,* p. 76, fig. 30.

56. For a discussion and section drawing of the underground levels at Rockefeller Center, see Krinsky, *Rockefeller Center,* pp. 74–75.

57. *OC 1934–1938,* p. 159.

58. Le Corbusier, "Construction du Pavillon des Temps Nouveaux . . . Contrat" and "1937 Construction du Pavillon des Temps Nouveaux . . . Manifestation de CIAM—Groupe France . . . divers pays" (FLC); Le Corbusier, "CCCC" [notes to Union Carbide executives Rafferty and Davison] (FLC); Agenda, November 27, 1935 (FLC). Le Corbusier may have been inspired by the tension structures of Buckminster Fuller, whom he may have met through Léger. Fuller signed a postcard sent by Léger to Le Corbusier, November 5, 1931 (FLC). Le Corbusier's knowledge of tension structures may have been informed by Sweet's Building Parts catalogue, which was then under the editorial direction of Knud Lönberg-Holm, whom Le Corbusier knew as an American delegate to CIAM and an "associate of Lawrence Kocher." Agenda, p. 3 (FLC).

59. The three bridges are the San Francisco–Oakland Bay, the Golden Gate, and Treasure Island. Like most foreign countries, France withdrew from the exhibition to devote its resources to a pavilion for the 1939 New York World's Fair. Kenneth W. Luckhurst, *The Story of Exhibitions* (London: Studio Publications, 1951), pp. 162–163.

60. *OC 1934–1938,* pp. 172–173. Von Moos, *Le Corbusier: Elements of a Synthesis,* pp. 97–98. For illustrations of the Nestlé pavilion, see *OC 1910–1929,* p. 174.

61. Mary Patricia May Sekler and Eduard F. Sekler, "Le Corbusier," in Adolf K. Placzek, ed., *Macmillan Encyclopedia of Architects* (New York: Free Press, 1982), vol. 2, p. 640.

62. *Le Corbusier 1910–1965,* p. 252. Marc Treib, *Space Calculated in Seconds: The Philips Pavilion, Le Corbusier, Edgard Varèse* (Princeton: Princeton University Press, 1996).

63. On Le Corbusier's synthesis, see Arnoldo Rivkin, "Synthèse des arts: Un double paradoxe," in *Encyclopédie,* pp. 386–391. Le Corbusier, *Oeuvre complète 1957–1965,* ed. W. Boesiger (Zurich: Editions d'Architecture), pp. 22–31; Le Corbusier, *Oeuvre complète 1965–1969,* ed. W. Boesiger (Zurich: Editions d'Architecture, 1970), pp. 142–157.

64. *OC 1938–1946,* pp. 100–101.

65. Warren I. Susman, *Culture as History* (New York: Pantheon Books, 1984), p. 172. Photograph of Palmer Stadium from University Archives, Department of Rare Books and Special Collections, Princeton University Library.

66. *Cathedrals,* pp. 12–13.

67. Le Corbusier would have seen an illustration of the impressive stadium in Philadelphia that appeared in *Plans,* no. 11 (January 1932), [p. 69].

68. On the formal and programmatic elements of the Palace of the Soviets, see Cohen, *Le Corbusier and the Mystique of the USSR,* pp. 176–188.

69. *OC 1929–1934,* p. 90; *VR,* p. 305; J. O. S. [Jordi Oliveras Samitier], "Barcelone," in *Encyclopédie,* p. 61.

70. *OC 1934–1938,* pp. 90–97. Le Corbusier, *Des canons, des munitions? Merci! Des logis . . . s.v.p. Pavillon des Temps Nouveaux,* pp. 98–103. Von Moos, *Le Corbusier: Elements of a Synthesis,* p. 101.

71. On earlier published excerpts, see chapter 8.

72. These arguments appear in chapter 8.

73. Like the Temps Nouveaux pavilion, *Canons* was dedicated to both direct action and promoting such projects as his Plan de Paris 37 and Ilot Insalubre no. 6. Le Corbusier, *Des canons, des munitions? Merci! Des logis . . . s.v.p. Pavillon des Temps Nouveaux.* Some of these themes appear in *VR,* pp. 189, 343–345.

74. "La Catastrophe féerique," *L'Architecture d'Aujourd'hui* 9 (January 1938), pp. 12–15; *Cathédrales,* pp. 83–87, 119–123. On French reports of American zoning policies, see [Eugène Beaudouin], "Urbanisme et Architecture en U.S.A. notes de voyage de M. E. Beaudouin," *L'Architecture d'Aujourd'hui* 4 (November–December 1933), pp. 54–68. On that journal's reception of the American setback skyscraper in France, see Isabelle Jeanne Gournay, "France Discovers America, 1917–1939 (French Writings on American Architecture)" (Ph.D. diss., Yale University, 1989), pp. 219–220, 383–387.

75. Lucien Métrich, "Quand les cathédrales étaient blanches," *Vendredi,* March 5, 1937, p. 6.

76. "Que sera la Cité de l'Avenir?," *Annales Politiques et Littéraires* 109 (January 10, 1937), pp. 24–26.

77. L. H. [Louis Hautecoeur], "Bibliographie," *L'Architecture* 51 (March 15, 1938), p. 40.

78. Jean Favier, in *La Construction Moderne* 52 (February 1937), p. xxvii.

79. For a comprehensive discussion of French literature associated with *américanisme*, see Gournay, "France Discovers America, 1917–1939 (French Writings on American Architecture)."

80. Theodore Zeldin, *France, 1848–1945,* vol. 1 (Oxford: Clarendon Press, 1977). On France's economic crisis, see Alfred Sauvy, *Histoire économique de la France entre les deux guerres,* vol. 1 (Paris: Economica, 1984).

81. Letters, Le Corbusier to Marguerite Harris, April 21, [1937], and undated [April 1937] (Frances Loeb Library, Harvard Design School). Marguerite Tjader, "Portrait of Le Corbusier," unpublished manuscript, 1984 (Harris family papers).

82. Le Corbusier, "When the Cathedrals Were White," *Direction* 1 (December 1937), pp. 4–7; 1 (January 1938), pp. 4–6; "New York—Glorious Catastrophe," 1 (June 1938), pp. 6–9; "Calendar of the World," *Direction* 2 (January–February 1939), pp. 4–5.

83. Carl O. Schniewind, "The Radiant City," review of *La Ville radieuse, Record* 79 (April 1936), pp. 27–28.

84. F. A. Gutheim, "Land of the Timid," review of *Quand les cathédrales étaient blanches, Magazine of Art* 31 (January 1938), p. 45.

85. "Le Corbusier Considers the New York Skyscraper," *Légion d'Honneur Magazine* 10 (October 1939), p. 284.

86. Reginald F. Trevett, "Cathedrals and Skyscrapers," *Catholic World* 147 (April 1938), pp. 80–81.

87. Gutheim, "Land of the Timid," p. 45. On his early support for Wright, see Jim Drought and Wortley Munroe [pseudonyms for Frederick L. Jochem and Frederick Gutheim], "Not without Honor," *Wisconsin Literary Magazine* 28 (February 1929), pp. 14–19; F. A. Gutheim, "An Autobiography: From Generation to Generation," *American Magazine of Art* 25 (July 1932), pp. 72–73.

88. George Howe, "Le Corbusier," *Légion d'Honneur Magazine* 10 (January 1940), pp. 380, 382.

89. On the roles of Mumford and Giedion in the historiography of the modern movement in America, see Robert Wojtowicz, *Lewis Mumford and American Modernism* (New York: Cambridge University Press, 1996); M. David Samson, "'Unser Newyorker Mitarbeiter': Lewis Mumford, Walter Curt Behrendt, and the Modern Movement in Germany," *JSAH* 55 (June 1996), pp. 126–139; M. David Samson "German-American Dialogues and the Modern Movement before the 'Design Migration,' 1910–1933" (Ph.D. diss., Harvard University, 1988), pp. 337–436; Eduard F. Sekler, "Sigfried Giedion at Harvard University," in Elizabeth

Blair MacDougall, ed., *The Architectural Historian in America, Studies in the History of Art 35* (Washington, DC, 1990), pp. 265–273; Gwendolyn Wright, "History for Architects," in Gwendolyn Wright and Janet Parks, eds., *The History of History in American Schools of Architecture, 1865–1975* (New York: Princeton Architectural Press, 1990), p. 32.

90. Gutheim, "Land of the Timid," p. 45.

91. On the impact of Gropius, Mies, and the Bauhaus on the curriculum in American schools of architecture, see Wright and Parks, eds., *The History of History in American Schools of Architecture, 1865–1975,* essays by Anthony Alofsin, "Tempering the Ecole: Nathan Ricker at the University of Illinois, Langford Warren at Harvard, and Their Followers," pp. 85–88; Winfried Nerdinger, "From Bauhaus to Harvard: Walter Gropius and the Use of History," pp. 89–98; Kevin Harrington, "Aphorisms, Axioms and Anonymous Heroes: The History of Architecture in Mies's Curriculum at the Illinois Institute of Technology," pp. 99–110; and see Bernard Michael Boyle, "Architectural Practice in America, 1865–1965—Ideal and Reality," in Spiro Kostof, ed., *The Architect* (New York: Oxford University Press, 1977), pp. 320–325.

92. Joseph Hudnut, "Le Corbusier and American Architecture," *Royal Architectural Institute of Canada Journal* 26 (April 1949), pp. 98–99.

93. Ieoh Ming Pei, interview with author, New York City, August 6, 1985.

94. Caroline Shillaber, *Massachusetts Institute of Technology School of Architecture and Planning 1861–1961: A Hundred-Year Chronicle* (Cambridge: MIT, 1963) pp. 92–93. I. M. Pei, "Standardized Propaganda Units for the Chinese Government," *Task* 1 (1942), pp. 13–16.

95. Ieoh Ming Pei, interview with author, New York City, August 6, 1985.

96. *VR,* pp. 332–337. *OC 1929–1934,* pp. 186–191. *OC 1934–1938,* pp. 104–115, 158–169.

97. Letter, Carl Koch to author, June 1, 1994. Daniel Kiley, interview with author, July 14, 1994. See Robert Woods Kennedy, *The House* (New York: Reinhold, 1953), pp. 96–97, 469–471.

98. Daniel Kiley, interview with author, July 14, 1994; letter, Daniel Kiley to author, June 6, 1994.

99. Letter, Carl Koch to author, June 1, 1994.

100. Reginald Isaacs, *Gropius: An Illustrated Biography of the Creator of the Bauhaus* (Boston: Little, Brown, 1991), pp. 227–228. On Joseph Hudnut's role in shaping the pedagogy of Harvard's program under Gropius, see Jill Perlman, "Joseph Hudnut's Other Modernism at the 'Harvard Bauhaus,'" *JSAH* 56 (December 1997), pp. 463–477.

101. On George Nelson (B.A. 1928, B.F.A. 1931), see Stanley Abercrombie, *George Nelson: The Design of Modern Design* (Cambridge: MIT Press, 1995), pp. 2–3; Carroll L. V. Meeks, "Yale and

the Ivy League Tradition," in "Modern Architecture Symposium (MAS 1964): The Decade 1929–1939," *JSAH* 24 (March 1965), p. 65.

102. Letter, Richard G. Creadick (Yale class of 1938, M.Arch. 1941) to author, September 12, 1991. On the meaning of "Craftsman," see H. Allen Brooks, *The Prairie School* (New York: W. W. Norton, 1976), pp. 21–23; on Craftsman tendencies at Yale, see Meeks, "Yale and the Ivy League Tradition," p. 65.

103. Victoria Newhouse, *Wallace K. Harrison, Architect* (New York: Rizzoli, 1989), p. 75; Meeks, "Yale and the Ivy League Tradition," p. 66.

104. Nelson used his own sketches to interpret Le Corbusier's unorthodox ideas. George Nelson, "Architects of Europe Today 5— Le Corbusier, France," *Pencil Points* 16 (July 1935), pp. 368–374.

105. Rosemarie Haag Bletter, "Modernism Rears Its Head—The Twenties and Thirties," in Richard Oliver, ed., *The Making of an Architect 1881–1981* (New York: Rizzoli, 1981), pp. 116–117.

106. Letters, Melville C. Branch to author, September 14, 1987; William L. Addkison (M.F.A. 1936) to author, August 9, 1987.

107. Joseph Esherick, "Architectural Education in the Thirties and Seventies: A Personal View," in Kostof, ed., *The Architect,* pp. 265, 267, 273.

108. Jordy, "The International Style in the 1930s," p. 11.

109. Henry-Russell Hitchcock, "The Architectural Future in America," *Architectural Review* 82 (July 1937), p. 2; Elizabeth Mock Kassler, "Sunday Session," transcript of discussion at Modern Architecture Symposium (MAS 1964): The Decade 1929–1939, *JSAH* 24 (March 1965), pp. 87, 92.

110. Hitchcock, "The Architectural Future in America," p. 2.

111. Elizabeth Mock, "Built in U.S.A.—Since 1932," in Elizabeth Mock, ed., *Built in USA: 1932–1944* (New York: Museum of Modern Art, 1944), p. 12.

112. Sheldon Cheney, *The New World of Architecture* (New York: Tudor Publishing Co., 1936), pp. 252–254.

113. John McAndrew, "Introduction," in John McAndrew, ed., *Guide to Modern Architecture, Northeast States* (New York: Museum of Modern Art, 1940), p. 9.

114. For illustrations of the Hood and Corbett projects, see *Forward House 1933* (Architectural Forum, 1933), unpaged.

115. Cheney, *The New World of Architecture,* pp. 255–256.

116. Caption to photograph of Le Corbusier by editor [Henry Humphrey] accompanying article "Le Corbusier's Home of Tomorrow," *House and Garden,* 78 (November 1938), p. 27. For references to the use by architects of such Corbusian aphorisms as *plan libre* and "machine for living," see James Ford and Katherine Morrow Ford, *The Modern House in America* (New York: Architectural Book Publishing Co., 1940), pp. 124–125.

117. Letter, Philip Johnson to Ernestine Fantl, August 15 [1935] (DAD, MoMA, NY). "Residence of Richard Mandel," *Architectural Forum* 60 (March 1934), pp. 185–186; "House of Richard H. Mandel," *Architectural Forum* 63 (August 1935), pp. 78–88. Richard Guy Wilson demonstrates the influence of Norman Bel Geddes's *Ladies Home Journal House* no. 3 (1931) on Stone and Desky's Richard Mandel House in "Architecture in the Machine Age," in Richard Guy Wilson, Dianne H. Pilgrim, and Dickran Tashjian, eds., *The Machine Age in America 1918–1941* (New York: Brooklyn Museum and Harry N. Abrams, 1986), p. 174.

118. Edward Durell Stone, *The Evolution of an Architect* (New York: Horizon Press, 1962), pp. 32–37, 42–47.

119. Mrs. Charles Liebman gave a dinner party for Le Corbusier at which he proposed designing a country house for her. He recorded the Liebman dinner with the notation "proposer villa" in his Agenda, November 4, 1935 (FLC). For an illustration of the Liebman project, see Stone, *The Evolution of an Architect,* p. 54. Robert Allan Jacobs, interview with author, Pawling, NY, June 7, 1987. For the A. Conger Goodyear House, see "Recent Work by Edward D. Stone," *Architectural Forum* 75 (July 1941), pp. 13–17; Mock, *Built in USA: 1932–1944,* pp. 42–43. On Stone's work with Harrison, see Newhouse, *Wallace K. Harrison, Architect,* pp. 53, 70.

120. Letters, Conger Goodyear to Alfred Barr, June 17, 1936; Thomas D. Mabry Jr. to Alfred Barr, June 18, 1936; Alfred Barr to Abby Aldrich Rockefeller, July 2, 1936; Alfred Barr to Philip Goodwin, July 6, 1936, quoted in Rona Roob, "1936: The Museum Selects an Architect," *Archives of American Art Journal* 23 (1983), pp. 22–27.

121. Margaret Scolari Barr, "Our Campaigns," *New Criterion* (Summer 1987), p. 46.

122. Letters, Joseph Hudnut to Alfred Barr, May 18, 1936; Thomas D. Mabry, Jr., to Alfred Barr, June 18, 1936; Alfred Barr to Abby Aldrich Rockefeller, July 2, 1936; Alfred Barr to A. Conger Goodyear, July 6, 1936; Alfred Barr to Philip Goodwin, July 6, 1936, quoted in Roob, "1936: The Museum Selects an Architect," pp. 22–27.

123. Letter, Alfred Barr to Philip Goodwin, July 6, 1936, quoted in Roob, "1936: The Museum Selects an Architect," p. 27.

124. Cables, A. Conger Goodyear to Alfred Barr, July 7, 1936; Nelson Rockefeller to Abby Aldrich Rockefeller, July 3, 1936 (postmarked August 6), quoted in Roob, "1936: The Museum Selects an Architect," pp. 27–28.

125. Letter, Alfred Barr to Joseph Hudnut, October 1, 1936, quoted in Roob, "1936: The Museum Selects an Architect," p. 29.

126. Letter, Joseph Hudnut to Alfred Barr, November 16, 1936, quoted in Roob, "1936: The Museum Selects an Architect," p. 29.

127. William Lescaze, "Things Which Have Hurt, Should Be Filed Away and Forgotten," October 31, 1930 (typescript),

quoted in Lorraine Welling Lanmon, *William Lescaze, Architect* (Philadelphia: Art Alliance Press, 1987), p. 82n101 (see chapter 6).

128. Hudnut wrote to Mies after his meetings with Harvard president James B. Conant and "members of the Governing Boards." Letters, Joseph Hudnut to Mies van der Rohe, November 16, 1936; Joseph Hudnut to Mies van der Rohe, October 26, 1936, and November 6, 1936 (Mies van der Rohe archive, Manuscript Division, Library of Congress). See also Franz Schultz, *Mies van der Rohe* (Chicago: University of Chicago Press, 1985), p. 208.

129. For front and rear elevations of the model, see "New Art Museum to Flout Custom," *New York Times,* January 12, 1938, p. 23. See also *L'Architecture d'Aujourd'hui* 1 (June 1938), pp. 77–78.

130. "The Museum of Modern Art, New York City," *Architectural Forum* 71 (August 1939), pp. 115–128. According to Margaret Scolari Barr, John McAndrew was responsible for the "round holes in the cantilevered canopy of the penthouse terrace of the Fifty-third Street side." See "Our Campaigns," p. 54.

131. Letter, Alfred Barr to Philip Goodwin, July 6, 1936, quoted in Roob, "1936: The Museum Selects an Architect," p. 27.

132. Jordy, "The International Style in the 1930s," p. 13.

133. Sigfried Giedion, "The State of Contemporary Architecture: The Regional Approach," *Record* 115 (January 1954), pp. 132–137; Sigfried Giedion, *Walter Gropius* (New York: Reinhold, 1954), p. 71.

134. William H. Jordy, "The Symbolic Essence of Modern Architecture and Its Continuing Influence," *JSAH* 22 (October 1963), pp. 177–187; Stanford Anderson, "The Fiction of Function," *Assemblage* 2 (February 1987), pp. 19–31; Reyner Banham, *Theory and Design in the First Machine Age* (New York: Praeger, 1960); Nicholas Bullock, "First the Kitchen—Then the Facade," *AA Files,* no. 6 (May 1984), pp. 58–67; Francesco Passanti, "The Vernacular, Modernism, and Le Corbusier," *JSAH* 56 (December 1997), pp. 438–451.

135. Le Corbusier, *Modulor* (Cambridge: Harvard University Press, 1954), p. 224. See Peter Serenyi, "Le Corbusier's Changing Attitude toward Form," *JSAH* 24 (March 1965), p. 16.

136. Henry-Russell Hitchcock, Jr., *Le Corbusier* ("Exhibition arranged by the Department of Architecture of the Museum of Modern Art") (New York: Museum of Modern Art, 1935) unpaged.

137. See illustrations of the Errázuriz House in *OC 1929–1934,* pp. 48–52.

138. On the Ferme Radieuse, see the cogent analysis in Mary Caroline McLeod, "Urbanism and Utopia: Le Corbusier from Regional Syndicalism to Vichy" (Ph.D. diss., Princeton University, 1985), vol. 1, pp. 273–332. *OC 1929–1934,* pp. 186–191.

139. On proposals to Elizabeth Field, see chapter 4. [Le Corbusier], "A Plan for Reconstructing Town and Country," pp. 27, 42.

140. On the Maisons Loucheur, see *OC 1910–1929,* pp. 198–200; Norman N. Rice, "The Minimal House: A Solution," *Record* 68 (August 1930), pp. 133–137; Albert Farwell Bemis, *The Evolving House,* vol. 3 (Cambridge: Technology Press, 1936), pp. 470–472. On the Maisons Monol, see *OC 1910–1929,* p. 30; *Towards a New Architecture,* pp. 242–243. On the villa for Madame de Mandrot, see *OC 1929–1934,* pp. 58–62; "La Ville Radieuse," *American Architect* 147 (November 1935), p. 17; Hitchcock, *Le Corbusier,* unpaged. On the Pavillon Suisse, see *OC 1929–1934,* pp. 74–89; Mock, "Le Corbusier's Swiss Pavilion," *American Magazine of Art* 27 (January 1934), pp. 18–19; Sigfried Giedion, "Swiss Pavilion, Cité Universitaire, Paris, Le Corbusier and P. Jeanneret, Architects," *Record* 75 (May 1934), pp. 400–403; Hitchcock, *Le Corbusier,* unpaged. On the Errázuriz House, see also Hitchcock, *Le Corbusier.* On the house at Mathes, see *OC 1934–1938,* pp. 134–139; "Two Villas by Le Corbusier and Jeanneret," *Architect and Building News* (December 13, 1935), pp. 319–323. On the Weekend House, see *OC 1934–1938,* pp. 124–130; "La Ville Radieuse," *American Architect* 147 (November 1935), p. 17; "Two Villas by Le Corbusier and Jeanneret," pp. 319–323. On the Brewer House, see *OC 1934–1938,* pp. 132–133. On the Ferme Radieuse, see "Le Village coopératif" (1934–1938), *OC 1929–1934,* pp. 186–191, and *OC 1934–1938,* pp. 104–115; "Le Corbusier's Home of Tomorrow," pp. 27, 42; *VR,* pp. 321–337.

141. Henry-Russell Hitchcock, "The International Style Twenty Years After," *Record* 110 (August 1951), p. 93.

142. Albert Frey, review of "The Work of Le Corbusier and P. Jeanneret from 1929 to 1934," *Record* 77 (June 1935), p. 28; Carl O. Schniewind, review of "The Radiant City," *Record* 79 (April 1936), pp. 27–28.

143. Sheldon Cheney and Martha Candler Cheney, *Art and the Machine* (New York: McGraw-Hill, 1936), pp. 173–174.

144. Mock, *Built in USA: 1932–1944,* pp. 13–14. On the architectural system and common principles that informed their respective work, see Richard A. Etlin, *Frank Lloyd Wright and Le Corbusier: The Romantic Legacy* (Manchester and New York: Manchester University Press, 1994).

145. Mumford's criticism is discussed in chapter 9. Lewis Mumford, "The Sky Line," *New Yorker* 11 (November 9, 1935), pp. 66, 68–70.

146. Walter Curt Behrendt, *Modern Building* (New York: Harcourt, Brace, 1937), p. 163.

147. McAndrew, ed., *Guide to Modern Architecture,* p. 13.

148. Ford and Ford, *The Modern House in America,* pp. 123–129.

149. See Vincent J. Scully, Jr., "Doldrums in the Suburbs," *JSAH* 24 (March 1965), pp. 36–47.

150. Mock, *Built in USA: 1932–1944,* pp. 18–19, 22.

151. Ford and Ford, *The Modern House in America,* pp. 13–14.

152. Ford and Ford, *The Modern House in America,* p. 129.

153. Mock, *Built in USA: 1932–1944,* p. 18.

154. Hitchcock makes his case for the Brewer House in "Le Corbusier and the United States," *Zodiac* 16 (1966), pp. 15, 23.

155. See also Lescaze's Garret A. Hobart III house and studio, Tuxedo Park, NY (1938). Lanmon, *William Lescaze, Architect,* pp. 112–117. Ford and Ford, *The Modern House in America,* pp. 72–73. Christian Hubert and Lindsay Stamm Shapiro, *William Lescaze,* Institute for Architecture and Urban Studies catalogue 16 (New York: Rizzoli, 1982), pp. 78, 92–93, 106. For an illustration of Le Corbusier's entrance canopy at the Cité de Refuge, see Brian Brace Taylor, *Le Corbusier, the City of Refuge, Paris 1929–33* (Chicago: University of Chicago Press, 1987), fig. 154.

156. Robert Allan Jacobs, interview with author, Pawling, NY, June 7, 1987. Newhouse, *Wallace K. Harrison, Architect,* pp. 66, 68.

157. Newhouse, *Wallace K. Harrison, Architect,* pp. 68–69, figs. 45, 46.

158. Breuer's Dexter M. Ferry Cooperative House at Vassar College (1948–1951) is a postwar demonstration of the residual impact of Le Corbusier's example. Jordy, "The Domestication of Modern: Marcel Breuer's Ferry Cooperative Dormitory at Vassar College," *American Buildings and Their Architects: The Impact of European Modernism in the Mid-Twentieth Century,* pp. 165–219. See also Henry-Russell Hitchcock, Jr., "Marcel Breuer and the American Tradition in Architecture," June 1938 (typescript, Frances Loeb Library, Harvard Design School).

159. These houses are illustrated in Ford and Ford, *The Modern House in America,* pp. 41–51.

160. Walter F. Bogner, "Why I Planned My House This Way," *House Beautiful* 83 (April 15, 1941), pp. 57–59, 102. Ford and Ford, *The Modern House in America,* pp. 22–23. F. R. S. Yorke, *The Modern House,* 5th ed. (London: Architectural Press, 1944), p. 132–133.

161. Paul Nelson provided a letter of introduction to Le Corbusier. Earlier West had worked for Nelson's father. Jane West Clauss, interview with author, April 23, 1994.

162. Although Jane West Clauss wrote to Le Corbusier with the intention of welcoming him to America, she did not see him. Letter, Jane West to Le Corbusier, October 22, [1935] (FLC).

163. "Two Houses at Knoxville, Tennessee," *Architectural Review* 96 (July 1944), p. 5. See also "In Knoxville, Tennessee," *Pencil Points* 26 (February 1945), pp. 60–62. For a discussion of the Clausses' Knoxville houses, see Lawrence Wodehouse, "Houses by Alfred and Jane Clauss in Knoxville, Tennessee," *ARRIS* 1 (1989), pp. 50–62.

164. Whereas Oued Ouchaïa called for duplexed apartment units linked by a *rue intérieure,* Yuba City employed blocks of row houses. *OC 1929–1934,* pp. 160–166. Mock, *Built in USA: 1932–1944,* pp. 60–63. On the Chandler community, see Alfred Roth, *The New Architecture* (Zurich: Girsberger, 1951), pp. 61–70. Roger Montgomery, "Mass Producing Bay Area Architecture," in Sally Woodbridge, ed., *Bay Area Houses* (New York: Oxford University Press, 1976), pp. 231–235. Yorke, *The Modern House,* p. 184. Philip Johnson, "Architecture in 1941," unpublished essay written in 1942, in *Philip Johnson Writings,* ed. Peter Eisenman and Robert A. M. Stern (New York: Oxford University Press, 1979), p. 57. *OC 1929–1934,* pp. 160–169. On both Yuba City and Chandler communities, see "Farm Security Administration," *Architectural Forum* 74 (January 1941), pp. 2–11. Neil Levine suggested parallels between Wright's San Marcos-in-the-Desert Hotel project and Le Corbusier's Durand housing project, Oued Ouchaïa in Algiers. Neil Levine, *The Architecture of Frank Lloyd Wright* (Princeton: Princeton University Press, 1996), p. 209.

165. Le Corbusier, "Concernant Mr Nelson Rockefeller pour Wallace Harrison," December 6, 1935 (Wallace K. Harrison Papers, Avery Architectural and Fine Arts Library, Columbia University). Le Corbusier defined his "Proposition de programme pour l'exposition universelle à New-York 1939" in *Cathédrales,* p. 291; *Cathedrals,* p. 201. Le Corbusier's proposal to Rockefeller as well as his efforts to secure a commission for the French pavilion are discussed in chapter 7. For a general overview of the fair's architecture and planning, see Stern, Gilmartin, and Mellins, *New York 1930,* pp. 726–755; Eugene A. Santomasso, "The Design of Reason: Architecture and Planning at the 1939/1940 World's Fair," in *Dawn of a New Day: The New York World's Fair, 1939/40* (New York: Queens Museum, 1980), pp. 29–41.

166. Lewis Mumford, "The Sky Line in Flushing: Genuine Bootleg," *New Yorker* 15 (July 29, 1939), p. 38.

167. It may have been in anticipation of his role as a member of the Shelter Advisory Committee supervising the housing section that Charles G. Meyer had two meetings with Le Corbusier in December. Agenda, December 6 and 9, 1935 (FLC).

168. Newhouse, *Wallace K. Harrison, Architect,* p. 81. Santomasso, "The Design of Reason: Architecture and Planning at the 1939/40 New York World's Fair," pp. 29–41.

169. See Lawrence Kocher's Demonstration Home No. 2, "The House of Plywood" (1939) and No. 7, "The Modern Home" (1940), in "The Town of Tomorrow," souvenir directory folder (private collection); *Going to the Fair* (New York: Sun Dial Press), p. 19. For Mumford's criticism, see "The Skyline in Flushing: Genuine Bootleg," pp. 40–41. "Home Building Center," *Architectural Forum* 68 (April 1938), pp. 281–283, 288–289.

170. *OC 1934–1938,* p. 75; *OC 1910–1965,* p. 122.

171. Affonso Reidy, Carlos Leão, Jorge Moreira, and Ernani Vasconcelos also collaborated in the design.

172. On the influence of Le Corbusier's visits to Brazil in 1929 and 1936 and his collaboration with Lúcio Costa, Oscar Niemeyer, and other young Brazilian architects (Ministry of Education and Health Building, 1936–1943, Rio de Janeiro), as well as the Brazilian Pavilion, see Stamo Papadaki, *Oscar Niemeyer* (New York: George Braziller, 1960), pp. 10–11; David Underwood, *Oscar Niemeyer and the Architecture of Brazil* (New York: Rizzoli, 1994), pp. 20–50.

173. Charles Downing Lay, "Playfield Space Requirements, High-Speed Trunk Highway," *Record* 73 (January 1933), p. 15; Lay used the image in Le Corbusier's *City of Tomorrow*, pp. 238–239. Richard Guy Wilson, "The Machine in the Landscape," in Wilson, Pilgrim, and Tashjian, eds., *The Machine Age in America 1918–1941*, pp. 98–101. See also Charles Downing Lay, "New Towns for High-Speed Roads," *Record* 78 (November 1935), pp. 352–354.

174. *Futurama* [guidebook] (General Motors Corp., 1940), unpaged.

175. *Futurama* [guidebook], unpaged.

176. Walter Dorwin Teague, *Design This Day* (New York: Harcourt Brace, 1940), figs. 120–121. In 1938 Shell Oil Company sponsored Bel Geddes's smaller urban model, *The City of Tomorrow*, to promote both the automobile and its fuel. Jennifer Davis Roberts, *Norman Bel Geddes: An Exhibition of Theatrical and Industrial Designs* (Austin: University of Texas at Austin, 1979), pp. 44–46.

177. Mumford, "The Sky Line in Flushing: Genuine Bootleg," pp. 40–41.

178. On the reaction of industrialists to Geddes's vision, see Arthur J. Pulos, "The Restless Genius of Norman Bel Geddes," *Architectural Forum* 133 (July–August 1970), p. 46.

179. Norman Bel Geddes, *Magic Motorways* (New York: Random House, 1940); Wilson, "The Machine in the Landscape," pp. 100–101.

180. Henry Wright, "The Place of the Apartment in the Modern Community," *Record* 67 (March 1930), p. 237. "Higher Housing for Lower Rents," *Architectural Forum* 61 (December 1934), pp. 421–434. Housing Study Guild, ed., *Abstract of Papers at the 3rd International Congress at Brussels of the International Committee for the Solution of the Problems in Modern Architecture* (New York: Housing Study Guild, 1935).

181. Professor Walter Gropius, "Low Buildings, Medium-High or High Buildings?," and Le Corbusier, "The Sub-Division of Land in Cities," in Housing Study Guild, ed., *Abstract of Papers at the 3rd International Congress at Brussels of the International Committee for the Solution of the Problems in Modern Architecture*, pp. 3–11.

182. Jane Jacobs, *The Death and Life of Great American Cities* (New York: Random House, 1961), pp. 21–25; Vincent Scully, *American Architecture and Urbanism* (New York: Praeger, 1969), pp. 165–171; Peter Hall, *Cities of Tomorrow* (London: Blackwell, 1990), pp. 204–212, 227–240. Oscar Newman is more measured in his criticism of Le Corbusier, *Defensible Space* (New York: Macmillan, 1972), p. 24.

183. Cost-cutting measures for Red Hook meant that elevator buildings were restricted to six stories, which Ackerman preferred, apartments were decreased in size, and building coverage was diminished. Richard Plunz, *A History of Housing in New York City* (New York: Columbia University Press, 1990), pp. 236–238.

184. New York City Housing Authority, *Fifth Annual Report*, 1938, p. 13. Frederick L. Ackerman and William F. R. Ballard, *A Note on Site and Unit Planning*, New York City Housing Authority, U.S. Works Progress Administration Project, 1937. Eliminating a central court and instead concentrating stairways and elevators in a service core, the Friedrichstrasse projects of Poelzig, Mies van der Rohe, and others were praised for their "wings projecting outward from the center of the block, permitting plenty of light and air to enter all rooms." Walter Curt Behrendt, "Skyscrapers in Germany," *Journal of the American Institute of Architects* 11 (September 1923), p. 367; Hans Poelzig, "On Hans Poelzig," *American Architect* 128 (September 23, 1925), p. 258.

185. For Ackerman's preliminary design and analysis of Queensbridge, see Plunz, *A History of Housing in New York City*, pp. 238–239. When asked whether the Y-shaped towers in Sert's Casa Bloc apartments for his Macià Plan for Barcelona and Le Corbusier's Radiant City project for Antwerp (1933) had any influence on Queensbridge, Ballard denied the connection, emphasizing their differences. William F. R. Ballard, interview with author, London, October 26, 1987.

186. Letter, Frederick G. Frost, Jr., to author, October 17, 1987. For unit and site plans, see *New York City Housing Authority 10th Annual Report 1944*, p. 41. See also Richard Pommer, "The Architecture of Urban Housing in the United States during the Early 1930s," *JSAH* 37 (December 1978), pp. 256–258.

187. William F. R. Ballard, interview with author, London, October 26, 1987.

188. Plunz, *A History of Housing in New York City*, p. 243; *East River Houses*, New York City Housing Authority Report, July 1941.

189. Plunz, *A History of Housing in New York City*, p. 245.

190. Eric Mumford, "The 'Tower in a Park' in America: Theory and Practice, 1920–1960," *Planning Perspectives* 10 (1995), p. 26.

191. Roberta M. Moudry, "Architecture as Cultural Design: The Architecture and Urbanism of the Metropolitan Life Insurance Company" (Ph.D. diss., Cornell University, 1995), pp. 360–361.

192. Moudry, "Architecture as Cultural Design: The Architecture and Urbanism of the Metropolitan Life Insurance Company," pp. 344–361.

193. Lewis Mumford criticized the high-rise towers of the Parkchester project for their "congested planning," where urban rebuilding had been "misconceived and frustrated." *City Development* (New York: Harcourt Brace, 1945), p. 171.

194. "Metropolitan's Parkchester," *Architectural Forum* 71 (December 1939), p. 413. See also Plunz, *A History of Housing in New York City,* pp. 253–254, 282, 284.

195. Letter, Frederick G. Frost, Jr., to author, October 17, 1987. William F. R. Ballard, interview with author, London, October 26, 1987.

196. For an analysis of the development of the high-rise tower in the park after World War II, see Mumford, "The 'Tower in a Park' in America: Theory and Practice, 1920–1960," pp. 29–41.

197. For a critique of these projects, see Scully, *American Architecture and Urbanism,* pp. 168–169; Newman, *Defensible Space,* pp. 82–83.

198. Hitchcock, "The Architectural Future in America," p. 1.

199. Mardges Bacon, *Ernest Flagg: Beaux-Arts Architect and Urban Reformer* (New York and Cambridge: Architectural History Foundation and MIT Press, 1986), pp. 179–180.

200. "Nelson Rockefeller Warns Real Estate to Check Business Decentralization," *New York Herald Tribune,* June 21, 1936, 10, p. 1.

201. Rockefeller's involvement in the planning of the United Nations Headquarters came about in December 1945 when William O'Dwyer, mayor-elect of New York City, appointed him to a committee of prominent businessmen and civic leaders under the direction of Robert Moses. The aim of the committee was initially to secure provisional headquarters for the organization and later to persuade it to be established permanently in New York City. The next April Harrison joined in the effort when Moses appointed him to a board of design for the proposal. Linda Sue Phipps, "'Constructing' the United Nations Headquarters: Modern Architecture as Public Diplomacy" (Ph.D. diss., Harvard University, 1998), pp. 48–49; George A. Dudley, *A Workshop for Peace: Designing the United Nations Headquarters* (New York and Cambridge: Architectural History Foundation and MIT Press, 1994), p. 9.

202. Le Corbusier began to follow U.N. activities when he arrived in New York on January 5, 1946, aboard the liberty ship *Vernon S. Hood.* He had been appointed by the French Ministry of Foreign Affairs to a visiting group of architects and urbanists for the purpose of studying American institutions and infrastructure as well as promoting French culture and technique. *Le Corbusier Sketchbooks* (New York and Cambridge: Architectural History Foundation and MIT Press, 1981), vol. 1, 1914–1948, D13, 802,

803, 804. There he gave a talk at the New School for Social Research on behalf of CIAM and attended an exhibition of his work at the International Building in Rockefeller Center, organized by the Walker Art Center in Minneapolis and sponsored by French ambassador Henri Bonnet. "Mission d'architectes et d'urbanistes français aux Etats-Unis organisée par la Direction Générale des Relations Culturelles au service du Ministère des Affaires Etrangères," documents dated August 30 and 31, 1945 (FLC). In 1946 the Museum of Modern Art organized what Linda Phipps has called a "polemical exhibition featuring images of the 1927 League competition entries and the completed buildings." See Phipps, "'Constructing' the United Nations Headquarters: Modern Architecture as Public Diplomacy," p. 20. See also "News," *Architecture–Pencil Points* 26 (October 1945), p. 1.

203. Of the nine countries that sent delegates to the Commission established by the Permanent Headquarters Committee (PHC) of the General Assembly, France appointed Le Corbusier, and the Soviet Union named engineer Nikolai D. Bassov, who later was a member of the U.N. Board of Design Consultants. Dudley, *A Workshop for Peace: Designing the United Nations Headquarters,* p. 12.

204. Le Corbusier lobbied the French Assistant Secretary General at the U.N. Henri Laugier, PHC president and commission member Eduardo Zuleta-Angel, and others. Le Corbusier's "Note à l'attention de Monsieur Henri Laugier" of May 11, 1946, instructed Laugier on the "great waste" and other conclusions he had drawn about American culture (FLC); Dudley, *A Workshop for Peace: Designing the United Nations Headquarters,* p. 16; Phipps, "'Constructing' the United Nations Headquarters: Modern Architecture as Public Diplomacy," p. 54. Le Corbusier's *Report* was later appended to the *Report of the Headquarters Commission* as Annex I. The next year it appeared in English translation. See Le Corbusier, *UN Headquarters* (New York: Reinhold, 1947).

205. For the United Nations's "permanent residents," he stressed the importance of establishing "'natural conditions,' sun, space, greenery" and to "do away with daily mechanical transportation of long distances between places of dwelling, places of work, places of recreation." He urged delegates to make "intellectual development available to all members of the community" through contact with "the immense resources of a nearby metropolis" and to "reduce . . . loss of time: conceive a city, collected in height, aired in vast spaces." Drawing on his experiences of both 1935 and 1946, Le Corbusier saw disadvantages (as well as advantages) to all five sites being considered in the environment of New York (among others in the United States): Rockefeller Center in the "terrifying city" of New York, the Palisades no more than a rocky crest, the Flushing Meadow Park site "inescapably a suburb of New York," and two remote Westchester-Fairfield regions too "desolate" and "deprived of the voltage always found at crossroads." Weighing the various sites, he concluded that there was only one option. "We (of the United Nations) . . . are not to take abode in the suburbs of New York but in "Manhattan . . . a fabulous fact." Le Corbusier, *UN Headquarters,* pp. 16–22, 47. That

fall the Commission was still seriously considering sites in New York City, Westchester and Fairfield counties, Boston, Philadelphia, and the San Francisco Bay area. In a report and exhibit (September 1946), Robert Moses vigorously promoted the Flushing Meadow Park site. Working in provisional quarters in Lake Success, New York, U.N. delegates eventually recognized the advantages of being in a metropolis. Dudley, *A Workshop for Peace: Designing the United Nations Headquarters,* pp. 12, 14–16.

206. On the X-City project and the Rockefeller offer, see Phipps, "'Constructing' the United Nations Headquarters: Modern Architecture as Public Diplomacy," pp. 76–113; Dudley, *A Workshop for Peace: Designing the United Nations Headquarters,* pp. 18–30; William Zeckendorf (with Edward McCreary), *The Autobiography of William Zeckendorf* (New York: Holt, Rinehart and Winston, 1970), pp. 63–78; Cary Reich, *The Life of Nelson A. Rockefeller: Worlds to Conquer, 1908–1958* (New York: Doubleday, 1996), pp. 383–387; John Ensor Harr and Peter J. Johnson, *The Rockefeller Century* (New York: Charles Scribner's Sons, 1988), pp. 432–433. Liberal critics such as Secretary of the Interior Harold Ickes objected to the Rockefellers' intervention on the grounds that the gift was contingent on the Manhattan site. See Harold Ickes, editorial, "Shot-gun Marriage: That Is What the U.N. Site Selection Looks Like," *Philadelphia Evening Bulletin,* February 27, 1947, cited in Phipps, "'Constructing' the United Nations Headquarters: Modern Architecture as Public Diplomacy," p. 124n19.

207. John C. Ross of the State Department prepared the text for Harrison's brochure. "From Mr. Lie's Personal File," U.N. Archive DAG 1/1.1.1.1—1, Office of the Secretary General; U.N. Archive, cited in Phipps, "'Constructing' the United Nations Headquarters: Modern Architecture as Public Diplomacy," p. 107n162. For an analysis of Le Corbusier's arguments in support of cultural renewal that appear in *Cathédrales,* see chapter 8.

208. Some in Harrison's camp were cautious about Le Corbusier's appointment, others opposed to it. But Harrison felt that Le Corbusier deserved the position "on his merits, not just because of the 'screwing he got from the League of Nations.'" Abel Sorenson (staff architect to the General Assembly responsible for drafting a list of space requirements), quoted in Dudley, *A Workshop for Peace: Designing the United Nations Headquarters,* p. 32. Trygve Lie made ten appointments to the Board of Design Consultants based on Harrison's recommendation. Bassov, Le Corbusier, Liang Ssu-Ch'eng from China, Niemeyer, and Howard Robertson from Great Britain were later joined by Gaston Brunfaut, Ernest Cormier, Sven Markelius, Gyle Soilleux, and Julio Vilamajo. In addition to engineers Bodiansky and Peter Noskov (to assist Le Corbusier and Bassov, respectively), Matthew Nowicki from Poland and Ernst Weissmann from Yugoslavia served as consultants on the Board. See Dudley, *A Workshop for Peace: Designing the United Nations Headquarters,* pp. 32–43; Phipps, "'Constructing' the United Nations Headquarters: Modern Architecture as Public Diplomacy," pp. 171–193. Bodiansky ac-

companied Le Corbusier on his mission for the Ministry of Foreign Affairs in January 1946. A founding member of the Atelier des Bâtisseurs (ATBAT), he worked in Le Corbusier's atelier from 1946 to 1950. P. S. [Pierre Saddy], "Bodiansky (Vladimir)," in *Encyclopédie,* pp. 76–77. Ernst Weissmann worked in the atelier from 1929 to 1930 on drawings for the Centrosoyuz in Moscow and immigrated to the United States in 1932. "Répertoire des collaborateurs de Le Corbusier ayant travaillé à l'atelier 35 rue de Sèvres ainsi qu'aux travaux exécutés à l'étranger" (FLC). Cohen, *Le Corbusier and the Mystique of the USSR,* pp. 93–94, fig. 131. Linda Phipps determined that Harrison appointed Le Corbusier to the Board of Design Consultants without a nomination from the French delegation and against the advice of Lie. Letter, Wallace Harrison to G. E. Kidder Smith, August 25, 1978, cited in Phipps, "'Constructing' the United Nations Headquarters: Modern Architecture as Public Diplomacy," p. 179n143.

209. Max Abramovitz, interview with author, New York City, June 2, 1987.

210. *Cathedrals,* p. 64. Phipps explained that Harrison "would abstain from personal involvement in the actual design process" but "maintain executive control over the project." See "'Constructing' the United Nations Headquarters: Modern Architecture as Public Diplomacy," pp. 146, 148.

211. Le Corbusier's "Declaration" affirmed: "We work as a team under the distinguished leadership of Wallace K. Harrison. . . . Today each is working for the clarification of an idea; each helps his neighbor. There are no competing plans. The overriding idea must never suffer such disfigurement . . . we are united, we are a team; the World Team of the United Nations laying down plans of a world architecture." For a text of the "Declaration" and reactions to it, see Dudley, *A Workshop for Peace: Designing the United Nations Headquarters,* pp. 210–213.

212. Le Corbusier met with Zuleta-Angel and Laugier (see above, note 204) on January 22 and with Angel again on January 24, 1947. Dudley, *A. Workshop for Peace: Designing the United Nations Headquarters,* p. 36.

213. Newhouse, *Wallace K. Harrison, Architect,* pp. 104–137. Dudley's *A Workshop for Peace: Designing the United Nations Headquarters* is based on forty-five meetings of the Board of Design Consultants. Phipps's emphasis is on the collaborative nature of the design process as well as on as its political and cultural significance. See Phipps, "'Constructing' the United Nations Headquarters: Modern Architecture as Public Diplomacy," pp. 194–298.

214. Le Corbusier's 1946 *Report* projected his personal agenda onto the design of the U.N. Headquarters, reviving many of the projects and typologies he had offered Rockefeller and other American authorities in 1935: the squared spiral form for the World Museum not only reconstituted his project of 1928 for a pyramidal World Museum for the Mundaneum in Geneva, but also proposals to Rockefeller for a center of urban studies and an

art museum in New York City; the lozenge form for the Secretariat; the high-rise tower, a tall slab lifted up on *pilotis,* for the World Library; the slab-block (vertical garden cities) for housing, the General Assembly, and World Law Faculty; and the slab-block/trapezoid for the International Association, recalling his designs for the League of Nations and Palace of the Soviets. See Le Corbusier, *UN Headquarters.*

215. Dudley, *A Workshop for Peace: Designing the United Nations Headquarters,* pp. 37–41, figs. 27–34.

216. Dudley showed that during the first month of meetings Le Corbusier dominated the discussions. His early drawings held to the concept of a large meeting hall block containing the General Assembly and a Secretariat lozenge. For these early drawings, see Dudley, *A Workshop for Peace: Designing the United Nations Headquarters,* pp. 65, 70, 83, 84, 87, 90, 91, 93, 95, figs. 49, 52, 57–59, 61–64.

217. When Niemeyer arrived from Rio de Janeiro to join the Board on March 10 and Harrison encouraged him to submit a design independent of his mentor (and only after Le Corbusier was absent on a two-week trip to Paris), an alternative scheme emerged. On March 21 Niemeyer and Nitzchke presented Scheme 17, which called for separation of the General Assembly and the Secretariat. Separation of the two functions had originated in Nitzchke's Scheme 6 presented at the meeting of March 4, 1947. For analysis and illustrations of Schemes 6 and 17, see Dudley, *A Workshop for Peace: Designing the United Nations Headquarters,* pp. 102–103, fig. 171, pp. 155–157, fig. 96.

218. Le Corbusier returned on March 22 to confront the first challenge to his authority. In response to Scheme 17, he presented (on April 3) Scheme 23. There he doggedly held to the idea of a monumental block for the meeting halls, evolving from a drawing of "an architectural concept" in his 1946 *Report* that called for a similar block containing wedge-shaped auditoria of varying dimensions for the General Assembly, Council, and Commission halls. Le Corbusier, *UN Headquarters,* pp. 28, 30, 32, 33, pl. 9. In addition, the meeting hall block of Scheme 23 engaged two volumes: a trapezoidal form for the General Assembly to the north and a tall slab for the Secretariat to the south. See *carnet* sketches dated March 28, 1947, and Hugh Ferriss's rendering of April 3, 1947, in Dudley, *A Workshop for Peace: Designing the United Nations Headquarters,* pp. 176–177, figs. 114–117.

219. On April 25 Niemeyer countered with Scheme 32, an evolution from Scheme 17, in which a tall slab lifted up on *pilotis* (Secretariat) towered over a small paraboloid form (General Assembly). What distinguished Scheme 32 was its separation of the two principal functions into discrete volumes, the Secretariat at midsite and the General Assembly to the south, with a public plaza approached from First Avenue. (Le Corbusier had previously employed both typologies, the paraboloid volume in his design for the Centrosoyuz in Moscow of 1928–1930. See Cohen, *Le Corbusier and the Mystique of the USSR,* pp. 60–105.) Scheme 32 is il-

lustrated in Dudley, *A Workshop for Peace: Designing the United Nations Headquarters,* pp. 235–237, figs. 156–158.

220. Scheme 23A, presented to the Board on April 28, adopted Niemeyer's separation of the Secretariat and General Assembly but reversed their positions. Moreover, Le Corbusier's representation of the General Assembly substituted a trapezoidal form (pulled apart and enlarged from the meeting hall block in Scheme 23) for Niemeyer's paraboloid. In one sense it could be regarded as an evolution of Niemeyer's Scheme 32. Team members still expressed their preference for Niemeyer's Scheme 32, but Le Corbusier obliged them to answer for it. Dudley, *A Workshop for Peace: Designing the United Nations Headquarters,* pp. 240–245, 258, figs. 162, 163.

221. Dudley, *A Workshop for Peace: Designing the United Nations Headquarters,* pp. 68, 70, 252, fig. 52.

222. Scheme 23/32 gave prominence to the General Assembly, trapezoidal in form and centered on the site, as in Le Corbusier's Scheme 23A. Niemeyer's separation of the Secretariat and General Assembly prevailed, but their respective locations reflected those in Le Corbusier's Scheme 23. Although Le Corbusier's meeting hall block disappeared, it was replaced by a public plaza, retaining an important element of Scheme 32. See Dudley, *A Workshop for Peace: Designing the United Nations Headquarters,* pp. 266–277, fig. 180.

223. On the final design Scheme 42G, see Dudley, *A Workshop for Peace: Designing the United Nations Headquarters,* pp. 309, 321, fig. 198.

224. Max Abramovitz, interview with author, New York City, June 2, 1987.

225. In the face of Harrison's decision on April 30 to favor Niemeyer's Scheme 32, Le Corbusier began at once to construct his own version of the record and claim credit for the final design. An allegorical drawing of May 4 in his *carnet* (fig. 49) and the caption to it give his interpretation: "May 1 Harrison decides that project 32, derived from 23, will be [the] definitive [one]." The drawing shows a split screen: on top, a reclining female nude identified as "No 23"; on bottom, a dismembered image of the same female nude marked "No 32." See George Dudley, "Le Corbusier Notebook Gives Clues to United Nations Design," *Architecture* 74 (September 1985), pp. 40, 44; Dudley, *A Workshop for Peace: Designing the United Nations Headquarters,* pp. 258, 266–267, fig. 175a. Later Le Corbusier made the inaccurate claim that the final design for the U.N. Headquarters based on Niemeyer's Scheme 32 was no more than a dismemberment of his Schemes 23 and 23A, which "from March 15, 1947 served as the pivot point in the discussions of the 10 experts." He also used a drawing of Scheme 23, signed and dated March 27, 1947, to claim proof of his authorship of the Headquarters, but this Harrison vigorously denied. Le Corbusier, *Oeuvre complète 1946–1952,* ed. W. Boesiger (Zurich: Editions d'Architecture, 1953), pp. 38–39; *OC 1910–1965,* pp. 130–131; Le Corbusier, *Creation Is a Patient*

Search (New York: Praeger, 1960, p. 151; Newhouse, *Wallace K. Harrison, Architect,* pp. 121–125. On the competing claims of authorship for the Headquarters, see Linda Phipps, "Rashomon in New York: Le Corbusier and the United Nations Headquarters," paper for symposium VIIes Rencontres de la Fondation Le Corbusier 1996–1997, "Le Corbusier, Travels and International Influence: Le Corbusier and North America," co-sponsored by Fondation Le Corbusier and Harvard University, October 12, 1996. On the contributions and claims of the designers, see Phipps, "'Constructing' the United Nations Headquarters: Modern Architecture as Public Diplomacy," pp. 194–292.

226. José Luis Sert, "U.N. Headquarters," *Progressive Architecture* 28 (October 1947), pp. 96, 98, 100, 102.

227. According to Hudnut, "Of all buildings projected in America those of the United Nations are most in tune with the ideas of Le Corbusier. His influence among the architects of that project was, if not dominant, at least determinate in the general issues." See "Le Corbusier and American Architecture," p. 99.

228. Lewis Mumford, "The Sky Line: Magic with Mirrors," *New Yorker* (September 15 and 22, 1951), reprinted in *From the Ground Up* (New York: Harcourt, Brace and World, 1956), p. 44.

229. Lewis Mumford, "UN Model and Model UN," in *From the Ground Up,* p. 21. Lawrence J. Vale, "Designing Global Harmony: Lewis Mumford and the United Nations Headquarters," in Thomas P. Hughes and Agatha C. Hughes, *Lewis Mumford: Public Intellectual* (New York: Oxford University Press, 1990), pp. 270–271.

230. *Cathedrals,* p. xiii.

231. William H. Jordy, "The Aftermath of the Bauhaus in America: Gropius, Mies, and Breuer," *Perspectives in American History* 2 (1968), pp. 485–543, reprinted in Donald Fleming and Bernard Bailyn, eds., *The Intellectual Migration, 1930–1960* (Cambridge: Harvard University Press, 1969).

Index

Church, Henry, 4
Churchill, Henry S.
  Queensbridge Houses, 299, **299**
Ciucci, Giorgio, 256, 258
Clarke, Gilmore D.
  Parkchester, 301–302, **301**
Clauss, Alfred, 6, 22, 165, 177, 292–293
  Hart House, 293, **293**
Clauss, Jane West, 5–6, 292–293
  Hart House, 293, **293**
Clavan, Irwin
  Parkchester, 301–302, **301**
Clayburgh Alma (daughter; later Mrs. James Grew), 95, **95**, 170, 211–212, 249
Clayburgh, Alma (mother), 95, **95**, 170, 197, 216, 238, 249, 261
Clifford, James, 221
Cohen, Jean-Louis, xv, xvi, 320n4, 349n212
Colbert, Jean-Baptiste, 201
Columbia University, 27–28, 29, 91–93, 192, 279, 281, 341n29
  Housing Orientation Study (*see* Housing Research Bureau)
  Le Corbusier lectures at, 59, 60, 67, 70, 74–81, **76–77**, 92–93, 155, 167, 198, 242, 265; **plates 2, 5, 6, 8**
Communism, 64, 79, 138, 242, 243
Commuting, 210, 214, 232
Cone, Claribel and Etta, 5
Congrès Internationaux d'Architecture Moderne (CIAM), xv, 63, 64, 84, 97, 105, 144, 146, 157, 160, 163, 169, 174, 183, 197, 198, 206, 250, 256–259, 269, 272, 287, 304
Considérant, Victor, 64
Construction Moderne, 277
Construction practices, U.S., 6
Constructivism, 232, 286
Consumerism, xvi, 13, 157, 176, 209–210, 214
Cook, William E., 4
Corbett, Harvey Wiley, 17, 22, 25, 59, 92, 118, 134, 178, 179, 192, 193, 279, 283
Corbett, Harrison and MacMurray, 191, 193
Corbusierismus, 380n7
Corn, Wanda, xvi
Cornell University, 29, 96
Costa, Lúcio

Brazilian Pavilion, New York World's Fair, 295–296, **295**
  Ministry of Education and Public Health, 296
Cranbrook Academy of Art, 102, 105–106, **107**, 110, 280
  Le Corbusier lecture at, 63, 73–74, **74**
Creative Art, 16
Cret, Paul Philippe, 16, 97–98, 118
Cubism, 146, 212, 289, 377n68
Cullman, Howard Stix, 38, 55, 165, 167

Dada, 232
Damisch, Hubert, xv
Dandieu, Arnaud, xiv, 207, 209
Darien (Connecticut), 52, 55, 57
Daub, George, 22, 177
Davison, George W., 185, 196, 272
Davison, Robert L., 19, 186, 269
Decentralization, urban, xvi, 64, 104, 118, 120, 132, 152, 157, 169, 178, 205, 234, 244, 278, 298, 302, 303, 310. *See also* Centralization, urban
Delaisi, Francis, 128, 232
Delamarre, Jacques, 170
  Century Apartments, 170, **171**
De Mars, Vernon, 294
  Woodville, 294
  Yuba City, 294, **294**
Demolition-based planning, xv, 120, 152, 156, 158, 160–161, 168, 170, 222, 232, 243, 297, 298, 302
De Monzie, Gabrielle, 4. *See also* Le Corbusier: Villa Stein-de Monzie
Descartes, René, 134. *See also* Cartesian skyscraper
Deskey, Donald, 333n30
  Mandel House, 283, **283**
Dessauce, Marc, 19, 381n18
De Stijl, 162
Detroit, 102–106, 264
Detroit News, 102, **103**
Deutscher Werkbund, xiv, 187
De Vos, Kenneth M., 173
Dial, Morse G., 185
Direction, ix, 197, 277
Dobbin, C. E., 192
Downey, John O., 186, 189, 196, 197
Dreiser, Theodore, ix, 53, 54, 56, 216, 227
Drew, Jane, 202
Dubreuil, Hyacinthe, 13

Dudley, George, 305, 307
Duhamel, Georges, xiv, 6, 13, 132, 137, 139, 140, 189, 207, 224, 230
Durante, Jimmy, 219

Easterday, Melville M., 27
Eco, Umberto, xvii, 229
Ecole des Beaux-Arts (Paris), 95, 192. *See also* Beaux-Arts principles
Edgell, George Harold, 28, 95
Eggers and Higgins
  Alfred E. Smith Houses, 302
Ehrlich, Matthew, 5
Eiffel, Gustave, 134
Elevators, 144, 196, 265
Emerson, William, 93, 95, 96, 97, 279
Engineering, U.S., 7, 54, 74, 265, 269. *See also* Bridges, U.S.; Skyscrapers, U.S.
Esherick, Joseph, 281
Esprit Nouveau, xiv, 3, 6, **7**, 10, **10**, 20, 98, 131, 132, 137, 170, 172, 192, 213, 264
Essential joys (basic pleasures), 61, 71
Etchells, Frederick, 16, 171–172
Exposition Internationale "Arts et Techniques" (Paris, 1937), 6, 30, 78, 197, 248, 257, 269. *See also* Le Corbusier: Pavillon des Temps Nouveaux
Exposition Internationale des Arts Décoratifs et Industriels Modernes (Paris, 1925), 14–15, **15**, 17, 91, 260, 286, 294. *See also* Le Corbusier: Pavillon de l'Esprit Nouveau
Exposition Universelle (Brussels, 1958), 274

Fantl, Ernestine, 41, 42, 47
Farm Security Administration, 293–294
Federation of Architects Engineers Chemists and Technicians (FAECT), 241–243, 258, 278
Ferriss, Hugh, 25, 134, 178, 179, 180, 257
  drawing of United Nations Headquarters, 305, **305**
Field, Elizabeth B., 120, 121, 288, 290
First machine age. *See* Machine age
Fishman, Robert, 141
Fisker, Kay, 14
Five points of a new architecture, 70, 75, 83, 162